Inshore Britain

Stuart Fisher

Imray Laurie Norie & Wilson

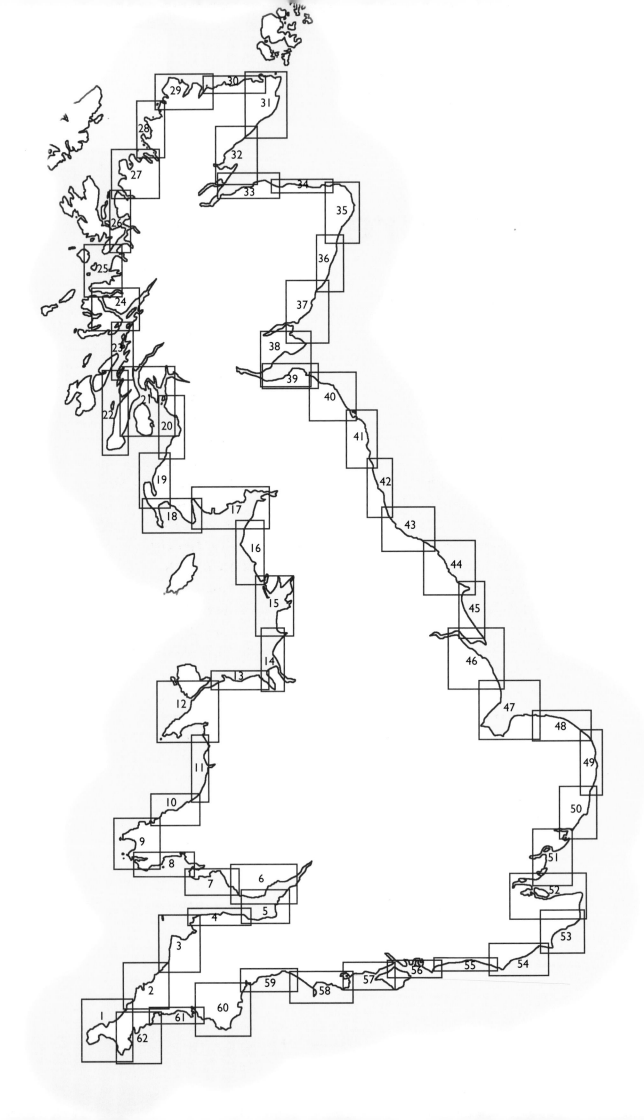

CONTENTS

Published by
Imray Laurie Norie & Wilson Ltd
Wych House The Broadway St Ives
Cambridgeshire PE27 5BT England
☎ +44 (0)1480 462114
Fax +44 (0) 1480 496109
Email ilnw@imray.com
www.imray.com

ISBN 978 085288 906 0

British Library Cataloguing in Publication Data.
A catalogue record for this title is available from
the British Library.

Printed in Singapore by Star Standard Industries

Updates

The coast is being changed endlessly by man and
nature. The author would be pleased to hear of
any text or pictures needing to be brought up to
date. Please email inshorebritain@canoeist.co.uk
or write c/o Imray Laurie Norie & Wilson Ltd,
Wych House, The Broadway, St Ives,
Cambridgeshire PE27 5BT.

FOREWORD

The coastline of the island of Great Britain is unrivalled in beauty, variety and history. Sitting in a battleground; the Atlantic Ocean to the west, continental Europe to the east, warm moist subtropical air to the south and cold dry polar air to the north, the weather at any time of year is unpredictable and often savage. With powerful tidal streams wrapping around the major headlands the island presents a formidable challenge to anyone contemplating a circumnavigation in a small boat. Yet many have felt compelled to take up the gauntlet in all manner of craft including yachts, powerboats, jet skis, sailing dinghies, windsurfers and kayaks. A few can legitimately claim a 'first' whilst overcoming the physical demands that such a journey entails.

But no-one has explored Great Britain's shoreline in such intimate detail as Stuart Fisher who selected the humble kayak as his mode of transport. Propelled by muscle and will power and driven by a desire to share his passion both for his sport and his island home, Stuart took 15 years to complete his circumnavigation. He chose to do it in stages, had land support from his wife most of the way, stayed in bed and breakfast accommodation most of the time and paddled in flat calm sunny conditions whenever he could manage it. But then he was not in a race to be first or to do it faster than anyone else. Stuart's mission was to describe and photograph the coastline, as seen from a kayak, and produce the first detailed guide to Britain's coast. Stuart published his first 'Coastal Guide' in Canoeist magazine in March 1989, and began with the coastline of west Cornwall, which I am now fortunate to consider as my home.

His meticulous research is such that he reveals details you are unaware of, even in your own 'backyard'. The content is always relevant and the photographs give you the sense of having been there before. Whilst planning my own circumnavigation of the UK and Ireland and all the inhabited islands I found the Coastal Guide articles an essential resource and they allowed me to prepare for the massive six month long journey that I was about to undertake.

Of course *Inshore Britain* is not just for circumnavigators; it is even more appropriate for those wishing to do day trips in small boats. By having a good idea of what you will see before you go out there you can be sure you will not miss a thing and be so much richer for the experience. Full of sound and practical advice, essential guidance on aspects of safety and an exhaustive directory of useful information, *Inshore Britain* is, at last, the one book that covers all that you need to know when planning a journey by small boat anywhere around Britain's coast.

There is always an untold story in a work such as this and *Inshore Britain* represents a lifetime's dedication to the sport of canoeing. Stuart Fisher began editing in 1975. It has always been a labour of love for Stuart and whilst there are those that do not necessarily share his outspoken views on the politics that surround all competitive sports, no-one can deny that he has made a hugely important and lasting contribution to our enjoyment and appreciation of all aspects of canoesport. Stuart deserves our gratitude for a lifetime's commitment to canoeing and for producing an invaluable resource for anyone venturing out onto Britain's coastal waters.

Sean Morley

In 2004 Sean set off from Falmouth and paddled solo to and round the outside of every inhabited island in Great Britain and Ireland in a single season (including Scilly, St Kilda and Shetland), a feat way beyond what has been achieved by anyone else. His own book on that phenomenal journey is eagerly awaited.

CLOSING OF THE CIRCLE

Unlike other sea kayak circuits of Great Britain, circumnavigation was not the main objective and it was completed in stages. The major purpose was to prepare coastal guides for the magazine *Canoeist*, which meant taking it slowly and staying close inshore rather than cutting corners. Solo crossings out of sight of land do not make for good photography or informative notes. The coast was divided into 62 sections and I kept with those original sections, taking four a year, unlike most people circumnavigating Britain who are working against the clock and the summer weather window, completing in a few months. For the record book, my fifteen year circuit is by far the slowest and I am probably the oldest to go round. At 4,810km, my route has certainly been the longest ever, including the 4,203km by those who went round Ireland on the way. You can accuse me of being a fair weather paddler. That is my aim, not only because it makes for better photography but also because it is more pleasant. I am out to enjoy my paddling, not to battle the elements and most nights have been in bed and breakfast accommodation. I can recommend being picked up from the water and driven for a bath or shower before going out for an evening meal.

My circuit has mostly been supported by my family on land but has covered every metre of the way, tides permitting, totally solo on the water.

At a Medway sea kayak symposium I shared a bunkroom with Simon Osborne who had just completed the circuit, supported and accompanied on the water on occasions. At only 23 years old with little previous experience of the sea and a compelling cause to support, I'd rather be selling his achievement!

A couple of dozen people have been round in total. You can count the solos or near solos on the digits of one hand. Add in Geoff Hunter, who took a short cut through the Caledonian Canal but did the rest of the circuit as long ago as 1970 in an unstable plywood Angmagssalik which had never previously been on the water, a remarkable trip. All have achieved in different ways. By coming back to it fresh each time I have not become punch drunk with paddling the sea and have not got fed up with having to get up each morning, put on damp gear and head out in less than ideal weather. I can't prove it but I believe I have had more enjoyment than anyone out of paddling round Britain. Posing the question of whether he would do it again, Medway trio author Bill Taylor said 'The answer from me would undoubtedly be in the negative.' With the benefit of hindsight, would I have set out on this journey fifteen years ago? You bet I would! Around our small island we have every kind of scenery and paddling condition from the remote and testing to the crowded and placid. I am sure there is no country in the world which offers such a variety for its size. If you cannot paddle all of our coast then do what you can. You will find it very easy to be drawn into keeping going further.

Stuart Fisher

Dedication

To Becky, without whose endless support this book and much more would never have come to fruition.

To Brendan and Ross for checking the play value of so many beaches.

Acknowledgements

I am particularly grateful to:

Ian Spanton for his invaluable advice on the book publishing industry.
Chris Bass and colleagues at the UK Hydrographic Office who sponsored most of the charts and pilots used in preparing this book.
Willie Wilson of Imrays not only for taking on a new author with a less impressive boat than is usually featured by Imrays but also for giving me a free hand with layout and cartography. The whole process has been made easier than I dared hope.
Readers of *Canoeist* who have repeatedly asked for this book.

Photo credits

Willie Wijdekop p. vii
Prof Dr Udo Beier p. 206
Becky Fisher p. 123, p. 135 top, p. 168 right, p. 171 bottom right, p. 311 left
Alan Hardwick p. 145 top
Andy Morton p. 206 bottom right
Sue Woodman p. 49 bottom

Maps copyright

THE LONG WAY ROUND

The highlights and lowlights of paddling around Britain

Paddling round Britain has allowed me to see the best and worst features of our coast, predominantly the former. I have tried to stay within a kilometre of the high water line as far as possible, as a result of which I have often gone far up estuaries. People paddling round Britain do not usually encounter the Severn, Forth and Humber bridges, for example. Even so, I have not seen all that I wanted. I was saddened to have passed the stacks at Bedruthan Steps on the Cornish coast without identifying them, lost in a grey drizzle. I was more alarmed to miss Mablethorpe on the Lincolnshire coast. I failed to appreciate that a couple of buildings were part of a large holiday camp and then saw nothing of the town, all 7km of it, hidden behind an embankment, and finally got my bearings from an offshore column.

I generally found the Lincolnshire coast the most lacking in features, not helped by having to stay well out because of lumpy conditions at times. The northeastern half of England gave me the most trying weather at the times I was able to go.

For stunning scenery there is no better view on the mainland than the panorama over the Firth of Lorn, seen from the northern end of Clachan Sound. For my best unexpected small find I nominate Lee Bay near Ilfracombe in Devon.

Pollution

For sewage pollution the worst place I found was off the beach at New Brighton. Hopefully, the Mersey sewerage scheme will now have taken care of that problem. The smelliest beach, with discoloured water, was at Skirza in the far northeast of Scotland. The EU require seaweed to be removed from beaches in order to get the desired clean beach awards but seaweed is a valuable animal habitat and provides the tang which is redolent of the seaside. Here it was piled deep and stank, such as I have only known it stink in France when being cleared in Finistère. Presumably it is driven in here by storms but its presence, accompanied by broken glass, did not make it a pleasant place to linger. Another unpleasant beach was at Bawdsey, north of Felixstowe, where I spent a night surrounded by broken glass and a sea of used polystyrene cups.

The noisiest place was near Lybster, again in the far northeast of Scotland. A bird colony, which included the largest mainland guillemot colony, made a row which was absolutely deafening, like being in the midst of a hive of very angry bees. It is possible to have too much of a good thing.

Low flying jets are met from time to time but the intrusion passes quickly. Near the end of the Lleyn peninsula we asked our landlady if she didn't find the noise of the jets from RAF Valley to be annoying but she said that it would be a more lonely place without these manifestations of civilization. It is people who live in noisy cities who seem to worry most about peace and quiet in the countryside.

Some of my most overexposed film was at Dounreay. This was where Brian Wilson had the only failed roll of film of his whole circumnavigation. Presumably this is just co–incidence.

Generally, the wildlife encounters have been fantastic. Many times I have passed complete cliff faces covered with birds. I have had a guillemot fly under the bow of the sea kayak, have had fulmars within a metre of my head as they checked me out for fish, have nearly collided with a sea otter in the Sound of Jura and photographed another eating a fish on a seaweed covered rock off Shuna. I have passed within two metres of a floating seal with its eyes closed, quietly chewing a fish off Great Cumbrae one morning, have been followed off the premises at close quarters by seals on numerous occasions and have had a dolphin hunting around me off Aberystwyth as an onlooker nearly wetted himself with envy.

Difficult conditions

The most difficult logistical problem was to paddle round three sides of the Wash rather than just cutting across, a line which takes more than one tide and where banks run out as much as 12km. I used the last two days of the school holidays, took a break overnight by turning up into the River Witham, followed porpoises through a field of ragwort at the top of a spring tide and ended up doing some walking on the east side of the Wash rather than waiting in King's Lynn for a further tide.

The Mull of Kintyre gave problems. I wanted neap tides and calm weather, conditions which just would not come together. One Wednesday in September, while I was waiting for the computer to print something out, I checked the forecast again and it gave the all clear. At that time the kids were in junior school and the teachers felt that these geography field trips were probably more beneficial than being in class, an attitude that sadly did not continue into secondary school. Two hours later we took the kids out of school at lunchtime and headed north. The following afternoon I went round the mull and the weather broke on Friday morning but the crux move was behind me. I only needed fine weather thereafter and that was easier to get on its own.

Cape Wrath had the same problems plus being even further away from Oxfordshire and having a bombing range with aircraft coming from as far away as Germany to download although they call a three week break for lambing. The conditions all came together a week into May. It was much too early in the year for a solo round Cape Wrath but the conditions might not come right again that year. On May 7th I went round without any problems.

The Pentland Firth can have very difficult water but I was lucky with perfect conditions although the tide race on the southeast side of Duncansby Head (which I had suspected despite little mention in the pilot) took me two attempts to ascend. I would not have wanted to leave it many more minutes before it got too powerful.

It did not always work. From Ullapool I got four hours on the water before my wife ordered me off in lumpy conditions and we drove back down south. Lossiemouth was worse. Having taken a break there, I returned on a weather forecast which proved to be overoptimistic and drove home again without unloading the boat. I finally got away on the third attempt after a lot of motoring. Another place which caused me problems was Withernsea on the Lincolnshire coast where I swam in the high tide dump both landing and setting off again.

Some of the strongest winds I met were the downdraughts from Troup Head on the Buchan coast. At the pleasanter end of the spectrum, a warm rockpool I found on the south Cornish coast in August was exceeded only by a depression in the sand on the north side of the Solway Firth. It was a hot day and with spring tides the water was able to flow across a great expanse of baking sand at maximum speed. I have had baths which were not as hot.

At times the weather could change quickly. Just as I was about to round Dunnet Head, the most northerly point on the mainland, the fog came in at considerable speed as a sloping sheet. It cleared again later and I timed sunset at 10.32pm a week off the solstice.

There could be long days on the water at this time of the year. I put in a 17 hour paddle from the Gower peninsula to beyond Pendine, taking in the estuaries. I pulled up half under a blackberry bush at the back of the beach in my sleeping bag, feeling I deserved a long night's sleep, only to be rudely awoken a few hours later by a young lady stripping off completely in front of me to go for an early morning swim in the otherwise deserted cove.

My start from Redpoint was even ruder as midges drove me out of my pit in the heather at a grey 4am at the start of what was to prove an 18 hour day on the water. All was peaceful until Stattic Point beyond Gruinard Island. Here, the wind was blasting out of Little Loch Broom and Loch Broom as it can out of sea lochs, the change from calm to at least force 5 coming in a few metres. My finish had to be Ullapool and I slogged into that headwind on Loch Broom for the last 15km. Somewhere beyond Rhue I lost the light and inched my way past something by the shore which looked like the tattered remnants of sails on a three master. I never did work out what it was but I had plenty of time to try to fathom it out. Perhaps I was hallucinating, having never had such a long day on the water with the last few hours of it working agonizingly hard after very limited sleep.

Officialdom

There have been several noticeable changes over the fifteen years. Naturists were rare when I started but now they are on every secluded or not so secluded beach as soon as the sun comes out. There has also been an explosion of sit–on–top kayaks for hire on beaches.

A welcome change has been the slight reduction in the many firing ranges around our coast in recent years. Most of them are well run with two notable exceptions. The Yantlet Demolition Range danger area on the Isle of Grain is supposed to be marked by a ring of orange buoys, of which I found three remaining, not where marked on the chart. Getting the range controller's number was difficult as it was not known by the coastguard, police, military switchboard, Port of London Authority, Sheerness port or local yacht club. On his instructions I waited out two hours of perfect paddling weather one evening, only to find that everyone had gone home. They don't bother taking down the red danger flag, even when not using the range, and the range is in use only when there is a sentry in the box (not visible from the water), meaning that he cannot see small boats, either.

The Chickerell range at Weymouth have been unhelpful on the two occasions I have approached them for advice on firing times. The only advice I could get this time was to see if their red flag was flying when I got there. Rounding Portland Bill, the most difficult piece of water on the south coast, is usually a one way trip and the shore dump on Chesil Beach usually prevents landing even when the nature reserve rules don't. 'Sorry if we are inconveniencing you,' said a sarcastic official as he put the phone down on me.

Without exception, the others all behaved responsibly and operated ranges safely, subject to tracking them down through a national military switchboard which seems to have little concept of the geography of even their own permanent sites. I found Luce Bay the most affable and was told of the paddlers who had sat on a yellow platform, eating their sandwiches and marvelling at the lack of other boats, perhaps because the RAF were using the next yellow platform or target at the time, less than 2km away.

Where I had anticipated problems was trying to cut through Dover harbour. Dover harbour police were reluctant to connect me to the port controller at first but the controller could not have been more helpful, even coming out of his office in person to wave me through. The only problem I had was from the wash of the over attentive vessel he sent to shepherd me.

Busy commercial estuaries such as the Tees and Stour generally proved easy to cross with care as the fairways are narrow and clearly marked. The most difficult ones I found were Portsmouth Harbour and Southampton Water. I crossed due west from Southsea, by which point craft were fanning out in all directions, although the closest encounter I had was with a yachtie flying a defaced blue ensign and giving no indication of noticing that I was close enough to put a dirty scrape down the side of his craft. Off Calshot the problem was simply the speed at which the Isle of Wight launches travel. Hopefully, they are used to looking out for small craft in these waters, the most crowded in the world.

The kit

As far as Lossiemouth most of the trip was done in a Green Resin Seamaster, a rare craft with a twin skeg at the rear which made it stable for taking photographs but not so clever for scooting between rocks as surges dropped, being quite wide at the stern. It suffered from the gel coat coming off in large pieces but, being taken as part payment (the only part) by a company about to go under, it did well enough to handle the greater part of the journey. Most of the rest of the trip was undertaken in two successive polyethylene P&H Capellas.

Is there anything I would have changed with the benefit of hindsight? I would very much like to have been able to pick the best weather, mark it up on my calendar and go when the time was right rather than going out in less than perfect conditions and having the weather improve once I went home, going home without going on the water at all because of an overoptimistic forecast or, more likely these days, staying at home and missing fine weather because of an overcautious forecast.

Putting things in context

It was a journey which has also brought home some of our history. I hadn't appreciated how many castles were built by Edward I, for example, often in places that were not for the defence of the residents. As a southerner, I think it lamentable that my school history taught me nothing about the Covenanters or about the Highland clearances which have had significant impact around the Scottish coast and still affect much of the Scottish coastal landscape today, two centuries later.

A journey of this kind and length holds a wealth of memories. The surprise which most sticks in my mind was paddling into the harbour at John o' Groats, to be presented with the Land's End–John o' Groats tie by my sons. Perhaps we should all have had them because it would not have happened without their shore support and few families have visited so many British beaches.

Glossary

Arête Sharp ridge where neighbouring corries have eroded towards each other.
Bombora Submerged reef producing breaking waves with appropriate conditions.
Bryophyte Moss or liverwort, found in damp places.
Caisson Watertight chamber to allow engineering work to be carried out below water level.
Chalybeate Water impregnated with iron salts.
Clapotis Peaks and troughs of waves reflecting from vertical surfaces pass through following approaching waves to give enhanced peaks and troughs, eggbox patterns or exploding peaks with appropriate conditions.
Discordant coast Where linear geological features are at right angles to the coast rather than being parallel to it, as in a concordant coast.
Doocot Dovecote, especially in Scotland.
Dun Fortified hill, especially in Scotland.
Freshet Discharge of spate water from a river.
Herring bus 15–18th-century slab-sided herring fishing boat which acted as a factory ship by salting herrings while at sea.
Porphyry Dyke equivalent of syenite with high alkali felspar content, especially carried by ice from Norway to East Anglia.
Rondavel Round hut with conical thatched roof, especially in South Africa.
Scend Wave impulse.
Seine–net Fishing net with floats at the top and weights at the bottom, used to encircle fish.
Sharpie or sharpy Long, narrow, shallow, flat-bottomed boat, usually with two masts each carrying a triangular sail.
Souterrain Underground chamber or passage.
Spilite Soda rich basalt, often in pillow form.
Tombolo Sand or gravel spit joining an island to the mainland.
Tuff Compressed volcanic ash.

1 WEST CORNWALL

The most colourful cliffs in England

Or whether thou, to our moist vows denied,
Sleep'st by the fable of Bellerus old,
Where the great Vision of the guarded mount
Looks towards Namancos and Bayona's hold,
 Look homeward, Angel, now, and melt with ruth:
 And, O ye dolphins, waft the hapless youth!

John Milton

The most southerly point on the British mainland is the nib of rock which separates Polpeor Cove from Polbrean Cove on Lizard Point and which carries a road down towards the former. Limited parking is available at the top in front of Polpeor Café, although parking and road access can be difficult everywhere in the summer. The nib is extended by the rocks of Vellan Drang.

The Lizard is an Area of Outstanding Natural Beauty, an upstanding mass of igneous serpentine, gabbro, granite and gneisses, probably Precambrian and offering the most colourful cliffs in England. It is the centre of the Serpentine turning industry which became fashionable in 1846, after Queen Victoria visited Cornwall and ordered a serpentine table. Beaches can produce such semi-precious stones as agate, citrine, carnelian, chalcedony, amethyst, serpentine and rock crystal.

Seas off the Lizard can be bad and Polpeor Cove's lifeboat station was in use from 1914 to 1959.

Polpeor Cove and the old lifeboat station. Note the wreck beyond

Mullion Island, residence of thousands of seabirds

Both geologists and climbers enjoy the 60m high cliffs in Kynance Cove beyond Lizard Point where there are signs of landslip. Caves begin to appear and there are prominent islands, Gull Rock, Asparagus Island and the Bellows which take their name from the Devil's Bellows fissure.

The high cliffs continue round the Rill (where there is a historic wreck on Rill Ledges) and Predannack Head into Mullion Cove. Mullion Island is covered with kittiwakes, guillemots, razorbills, shags and other seabirds which also throng the Lizard National Nature Reserve, an area of heathland and clifftop plants.

The underlying rock changes to Old Red Sandstone, but the harbour at Mullion Cove at the end of the B3296 was built of greenstone in 1895 after a storm two years earlier had wrecked most of the fishing fleet. A lifeboat was installed in 1909. A natural tunnel through the rocks is a feature here.

The waters of Mount's Bay have mackerel, pilchards, herrings, seals and plenty of the large but harmless rhizostoma jellyfish which are rare away from the southwest. Crabs and lobsters are caught in pots marked with flags, sometimes so frequent that the sea resembles a golf course.

Dollar Cove is where a Spanish galleon went down in 1785 with 2.5 tonnes of gold coins. Dubloons and other gold coins are still sometimes found on the beach. Both Pedngwinian and Gunwalloe have historic wrecks.

Porthleven Sands reach their maximum height at the Loe Bar which blocked the River Cober with chalk derived flint shingle in the 13th century and finished **Helston** as a busy port. The Loe, which has been formed behind it, is Cornwall's largest natural freshwater lake and had to be drained at intervals by digging through it although the flow is now controlled by a culvert. There can be a strong undertow and the sea can dump heavily. On one occasion a ship was thrown right over the bar in a storm. In 1807 Henry Trengrouse of Helston watched as a hundred men of the frigate *Anson*

Folded rocks at Pedngwinian with Porthleven Sands behind

Between Polurrian Cove (which can have good surfing) and Poldhu Cove is a monument where Guglielmo Marconi sent the first transatlantic wireless message, 'S' in Morse, to St John's, Newfoundland, on December 12th 1901. To the east and only visible from further out in the bay are the array of satellite dishes on Goonhilly Downs which do the job today.

Church Cove, another surfing venue, was chosen by St Winwalloe in the 6th century as the site for his church. The present building dates from the 15th century, has a Norman font, a wagon roof over the south aisle, some piers which are single stones and a quantity of wood from the *St Anthony*, a Portuguese treasure ship wrecked in the cove in 1526. The belltower is two centuries older and stands on the cliff edge 4m from the main building.

The Wheal Trewavas coppermine buildings and chimneys perch on the cliffs of Trewavas Head

The familiar silhouette of St Michael's Mount is usually seen from the landward side

were drowned within a stone's throw of the Loe Bar, after which he invented the rocket rescue line.

Royal Navy helicopters based at Culdrose Airfield come and go constantly.

Porthleven has a memorial cross to the 22 fishermen of the village drowned between 1871 and 1948. It also has a 50 tonne boulder of garnetiferous gneiss, not generally found in Britain so it could well have arrived on an iceberg. The harbour was built in 1811 to import mining machinery and export copper and tin. The village has toilets nearby and a pillbox overlooks the sands. The surf has a very hollow wave and is reckoned to be the wave to ride but it is not for beginners.

The granite face of Trewavas Head is dominated by the Wheal Trewavas copper mine, the cliffs streaked with blue on the far side of the head where mine water was emptied back down the cliffs into the sea, the blue contrasting with the pink of thrift and a column of weathered rock being as impressive as the tapering mine chimneys.

Beyond Rinsey Head the engine house of the Wheal Prosper copper mine, closed in 1860 after undersea workings began to let in water, has been restored.

Praa Sands is a fast break with a hollow wave. Prussia Cove, Bessey's Cove and Piskies Cove were smuggling centres, as was the King of Prussia inn. The King of Prussia was John Carter, the most famous of the Cornish smugglers, who mounted guns on the cliffs around the inn (a cover for his smuggling activities), officially to protect against French privateers but actually to intimidate revenue men. Today the hillside is covered with gorse and nothing more sinister than seals and ravens move around the coves.

Cudden Point has claimed more than its fair share of ships, including the 30,000t *Warspite* which was being towed to the breakers in 1947. Like most of the headlands, currents run rapidly around it.

The Greeb is a 400m long line of rocks only 20m wide and submerged at high tide. Also submerged at high tide is the causeway built in 1427 across to St Michael's Mount, one of the most romantic silhouettes in England, Milton's 'great Vision of the guarded mount'. A ferry with wheels operates when the causeway is closed. The story of Jack the Giant Killer is based around the giant Cormoran who is said to have stolen cows and sheep to eat.

One version of the story says that he was a common or garden giant who lived on the island and that Jack lured him into a pit which can still be seen. Another version has him as a super economy-sized giant whose wife at Marazion (little market) was so upset at his demise that she dropped the stone in her apron pocket and it rolled into the water to form the 90m high mount. Historical facts date from 320BC if this was the island of Ictis as the descriptions suggest, in which case tin was being shipped from here to the Mediterranean at that time. St Michael was said to have appeared to local fishermen here in 495 and there were subsequent pilgrimages by St Keane and St Cadoc in the 6th century. Edward the Confessor established it as a Benedictine chapel site in 1044, giving it to the monks of the similar Mont St Michel in Normandy. A priory was built in 1135. A church established in the 13th century was destroyed in an earthquake in 1275 and rebuilt in the following century, during which a castle was added. The Earl of Oxford captured it in 1473, surrendering to Edward IV after a 26 week siege. In 1497 Perkin Warbeck attempted to depose Henry VII from here, claiming to have been one of the princes supposedly murdered in the Tower of London before being shown to be an impostor and being executed in 1499. The beacon on top of the church was used to first signal the arrival of the Spanish Armada in 1588 and the island was subsequently sold by Elizabeth I to Secretary of State Robert Cecil to raise funds to pay off her soldiers and sailors. Charles II stayed here on his way to Jersey when his defeat in the Civil War seemed imminent and the island surrendered to the Roundheads in 1646. Colonel John St Aubyn became military governor the following year, later buying it for his family who have lived here since 1659 and continue to do so although its ownership has been handed to the National Trust. These days the invaders are tourists who swarm over it and gaze down on the sea of bluebells on its east side in the spring.

Here is some of the most prolific agricultural land in the country with the Golden Acres at Gulval growing early flowers for the London market. Gulval's church dates from the 15th century.

By the shore is the heliport for the Isles of Scilly and the terminus of the main west of England railway line from London.

Penzance (holy point) is also the terminus for the ferry to the Isles of Scilly. The town was sacked by the Spaniards in 1595 and a pier and fort were built in the 17th century to protect against pirates. Being involved in the tin trade, it was the main coinage town between 1663 and 1838 and smuggling was also rife. It was the first Cornish resort and is the only one with a promenade, claiming the mildest all year round climate in the British Isles. The Museum of Nautical Arts features a 1730 warship and recoveries from vessels while Penlee House has scale models of ships, a geology of the coast, local crafts and a history of fishing, the port catching coalfish, conger eels, ling and shark. The port is one of seven Trinity House depots for buoy servicing crews. Famous residents here have included the mother of Charlotte Brontë and Sir Humphrey Davey who was born in the town in 1778 and invented the miners' safety lamp.

Penzance Bay and Gwavas Lake have several fixed marks on submerged rock outcrops, Ryeman, Western Cressar and the Gear.

Large quarries overlook **Newlyn** which has a tidal observatory giving the Ordnance Survey's level datum and a base point in their trigonometrical mapping grid of the country. The firm Stevenson's have built the port up to the fourth largest fishing port in England with a canning factory. The militia were used in 1896 to settle riots after objections to east-coast trawlers fishing on Sundays. Breakwaters date mostly from 1866 to 1888 although a new fish quay was built in 1981 and a new fishmarket was opened in 1988. The new quay in the name was built in the 15th century. Shark fishing is also carried out. There is a Newlyn School of artists with the Passmore Edwards Art Gallery and local potteries.

Standing on Penlee Point is the lifeboat station which is remembered by the nation for the day in December 1981 when the 8 crew members of the *Solomon Browne* were lost while trying to rescue 8 crew members from the *Union Star*, the coxwain being awarded a posthumous Gold Medal, the RNLI's highest honour. Mousehole, sheltering behind St Clement's Isle, is an unspoilt fishing village clustered around the Ship Inn by the harbour and was Cornwall's main fishing port until Newlyn was developed in the 19th century.

Mousehole and Paul were both sacked and burned by 3 Spanish ships in 1595. It has a bird sanctuary which acts as a hospital for sea birds but perhaps its most unusual legacy to the nation is stargazy pie with pilchard's heads poking out through the crust. The name of the village is thought to come from one of several large caves in the cliff, most of which are formed in solid rock but have roofs in a stratum of loose boulders packed in soil, making them appear most unstable.

Beyond the dramatic headland at Carn-du is Lamorna Cove where Derek Tangye chose to base himself and some of his writing. Lamorna harbour was used for loading granite in the 19th century.

The first automatic lighthouse to be built in Britain was located at Tater-du in 1965, close by the water.

Penberth is possibly Cornwall's finest fishing cove with larger craft having been hauled out by a large horizontal capstan like a cartwheel.

Westward, the skyline becomes fantastic with the fortified Iron Age Treryn Dinas on Cribba Head and then Logan Rock, a 66t balanced rock on top of Horrace. In 1824 it was dislodged by Lieutenant Goldsmith, a nephew of Oliver

Carn Barges and, in the distance, Tater-du lighthouse

The irregular skyline which includes Logan Rock

Goldsmith. Such was the public outcry that the Admiralty were obliged to bring special lifting gear from Devonport to replace it. The outcomes were that it doesn't rock as well as it used to and the bill for replacing it nearly bankrupted Lieutenant Goldsmith, to whom it was presented.

arch of the Armed Knight standing offshore. Dr Syntax's Head is the most westerly point on the English mainland but it is possible to paddle right under the headland through a tall but narrow passage. On top are exhibitions, displays, craft workshops and a signpost which can be set to the

The white beach at Porth Curno and its open air Minack Theatre which has the sea as a backdrop

Porth Curno has a crushed shell beach, possibly the whitest in England although nothing like the white beach at Morar in western Scotland. The beach is the landing place for submarine cables including the one laid from India by the Great Eastern in 1870. West of the beach is the Minack Theatre, an open air amphitheatre cut into the hillside above the sea. Seating 600, it was opened in 1932. The village has an aerial and houses the Cable and Wireless training college.

St Levan, with its mediaeval church, fine carved pews and even older, tall, Celtic cross, takes its name from the saint who landed here in the 6th or 7th century after a voyage from Wales. There is a cleft rock where he rested, striking it with his staff and predicting that the world will end when a pannier-laden packhorse can walk through the gap.

Porthgwarra is approached through a ramp cut through the cliffs and is popular with climbers for such pitches as Seal Slab, Pendulum Chimney and Commando Crawl. It may also be the last landing point before Sennen.

The Hella Point skyline would not look out of place in Moscow's Red Square

The tunnel under Dr Syntax's Head

Land's End is protected by the Armed Knight standing just offshore

Gwennap Head has strong currents and is topped by a coastguard station and a mountain rescue post. The 130m high granite wavecut platform, which reaches from St Ives, arrives at its dramatic finale with the 60m high vertical cliffs of Land's End, great columns of rock guarded by the

mileage to the visitor's home town while being photographed standing in front of it. Land's End at the end of the A30 was bought by Peter De Savary in 1987 with new shopping, catering, interpretive facilities and an underground auditorium offering the 1,000,000 annual visitors the experience of standing on the deck of the Torrey Canyon. It is daunting to remember that schoolchildren have been swept off the cliffs by a wave.

The original Longships lighthouse (2km off) was built in Sennen Cove in the 18th century and moved out stone by stone. The current one was built in 1873 and the helipad added in 1974. The keeper was kidnapped by wreckers on one occasion, but the light was kept shining by his young daughter who reached it by standing on the family *Bible*.

Fifteen kilometres off is the Wolf Rock lighthouse, one of six that can be seen from the cliffs when conditions are good. The Isles of Scilly are also visible at times although there is no sign of the fabled land of Lyonesse which lies beneath the sea, possibly a folk memory of the drowning of Scilly at the end of the Ice Age.

The Sennen lifeboat station has a telegram from Margaret Thatcher paying tribute to the 9 hours the boat spent rescuing crews from the 1979 Fastnet Race. A plaque in the breakwater at Sennen Cove by Colonel H W Williams, MP for St Ives in 1908, thanks fishermen for their help in raising funds for its building. Fish brought in include mullet and mackerel. Facilities include parking, toilets, chip shop, café, Old Success Inn and Sennen Cove Hotel, the only easy landing place between Gwennap Head and St Ives and even here the dump can make it impossible to get out again. The ground swell is usually present, especially with northerly and westerly winds as waves can travel 6,000km uninterrupted.

The Brisons, seen from Sennen

The Isles of Scilly Skybus circles over Whitesand Bay to land at Land's End Aerodrome below Carn Brea hill, the hill which claims the widest sea view from the British mainland. A submarine powerline to Scilly was also landed on the beach in 1988.

The coast from Sennen to St Ives is very committing as it is often impossible to land at all between the two and there would be few places to swim ashore safely in an emergency. It is possible to land at Priest's Cove with difficulty and, indeed, it is so named as the point where St Just is said to have made his landing from Ireland in the 5th century. **St Just** is the last bastion of Old Cornwall

Looking across Whitesand Bay to Priest's Cove and Cape Cornwall

and was the Victorian centre of the tin mining industry. A 19th century tin mine stands at the back of Porth Nanven although older remains are the Bronze Age burial chamber, Ballowall Barrow at Carn Gloose. Cape Cornwall is surmounted by the chimney of the Cape Cornwall Mine, abandoned in 1870. Cape Cornwall, England's only cape, was presented to the National Trust in 1987 by H J Heinz. Offshore are the Brisons which have claimed many ships while the Vyneck lies submerged to the northwest of the cape, itself nearly as far west as Land's End. There are only razorbills here for company.

Porth Ledden, the next headland, is topped by Kenidjack Castle and a cairn circle. This pales into insignificance compared with the Botallack Mine which covers Botallack (dwelling on a brow) Head and overlooks Zawn a Bal. Closed in 1914, this was one of Cornwall's richest tin mines and peaked at 11 engine houses employing 500 men who could hear the sea moving the pebbles above their heads.

The last working tin mine, Géevor at Pendeen, has a museum. From Trewellard Zawn to Pendeen Watch the sea is stained red with the tin which does seem to have some calming influence on the waves.

The lighthouse at Pendeen Watch was built in 1900 and modernized in 1926 to prevent ships mistaking Gurnard's Head for Land's End and turning in behind it. The light is visible for 43km. This is some of England's finest coastal scenery, totally unrelenting, and is popular with rock climbers, having been used as a second world war commando training area. Off Pendeen Watch are the three rocks which form the Wra or 3 Stone Oar. The wreck in Portheras Cove is just one of the many this coastline has claimed over the centuries.

The coast is rich in history. Celtic fields above Whirl Pool may be the oldest human constructions still in use in England. The Iron Age Bosigran Castle, overlooking Halldrine Cove and Trereen Dinas on Gurnard's Head, is another cliff castle.

As recalled in *The Kangaroo*, D H Lawrence and his wife, Freida, were ordered to leave Cornwall in 1917 after he had worked on *Women in Love* in Zennor for two years. Freida was a cousin of Manfred von Richthofen, the Red Baron, and she was accused of being a spy, signalling from the cliffs. There have been other strange happenings in Zennor. The 15th century church has, carved on a bench end, a mermaid who came to hear the singing of chorister Matthew Trewella and then lured him back to the sea where their sweet singing can sometimes be heard at night.

The Carracks are a set of offshore rocks which protect a heavily shoaled area between Mussel Point and Carn Naun Point.

After countless headlands have been rounded, **St Ives** at the ends of the B3306, A3074 and railway to St Erth arrives suddenly. The Island (not an island) or St Ives Head has a coastguard lookout point although the view westward is only as far as Clodgy Point. Between the two is Porthmeor Beach where surfing is restricted during the holiday season. Floating wood is joined by cuttlefish shells.

Porthgribben Beach, with the Porthgribben Beach Café and toilets, is the haunt of a sand sculptor in a town renowned for the sculpting of Dame Barbara Hepworth. There is a museum of her work and the Barnes Museum of Photography while the artists' quarter drew in many who made up the St Ives school of painters and the producers of Leach pottery. Films come together with folk and chamber music, Cornish bands and choirs, theatre and poetry in the St Ives Festival.

St Leonard's on the landward end of John Smeaton's pier of 1770 is a fisherman's chapel on the site where St Ia arrived by coracle from Ireland in the 6th century, apparently making a better choice of landing place than most of his fellow saints of the time. The town was one of the most prosperous of the Cornish pilchard ports in the 19th century, exporting as far away as Italy. A shoal of 1905 was supposed to have been 160km long with the last great shoal of 3,000,000 fish in 1916 after which they declined quickly. An old pilchard cellar houses a museum of local maritime history including the Hain Steamship Company which began in the port with one boat in 1840 and grew to become one of the world's largest freight companies. **Carbis Bay**, overlooked by Knill's Monument, now produces mackerel, plaice and pollock.

The bar across the River Hayle resulted in the port of **Hayle** silting up in 1978 and the river mouth is now completely closed at lower stages of the tide and it has strong currents producing difficult conditions when it is covered. Beyond it, Lelant Saltings are one of the best birdwatching centres in Cornwall with cormorants, herons, kingfishers and terns breeding and unusual migrants often passing through. Peter De Savary purchased 240ha of land in Hayle, intending to spend £200,000,000 on an all-weather holiday resort under glass domes and also cut safe channels through the Hayle Bar.

Towans (dunes) form the coast for the next 5km around Upton Towans and these are backed by Atlantic Drive, the B3301, which runs from Hayle to Portreath. The towans are a location of holiday camps and St Ives Bay is used by surfers, windsurfers, water skiers and canoeists. Surfing is at its best at the mouth of the Red River, a fast beachbreak which picks up most small swells, the tin staining the water and often turning the sea red around the estuary and churning up a brown froth in turbulent conditions.

Godrevy Point is dominated by Godrevy Island and its lighthouse. The area has long been one of danger. In 1649 it claimed the ship carrying the wardrobe and possessions of Charles I, 60 people being drowned while only a boy, a dog and a few clothes were saved. It was the wreck of the *Nile* on 30th November 1854 which prompted the building of the lighthouse in 1859. This is the lighthouse featured in Virginia Woolf's *To the Lighthouse*. Unmanned since 1939, it is now the preserve of gulls, oystercatchers, pipits, primroses and thrift but landing is not allowed without a permit. The area used to be good for lobsters. Grey seals still use it and also breed at Navax Point where there are long caves which can only be reached from the sea. Fulmars, gannets, razorbills and shearwaters all frequent the coast.

The cliffs rise to 75m and the B3301 comes close occasionally but one cave that is no more is Ralph's Cupboard, now collapsed, which was used to store contraband. It was also the home of the giant Wrath who is said to have waded out to ships and eaten their crews, having the benefit of keeping the nosey public away.

The white daymark at Portreath avoids confusion with Gooden Heane Cove. The harbour was built in 1760 to serve tin mines and a horsedrawn tramway, the first railway in the county, was built to it in 1809. There was much trade with Swansea, the ore being traded for coal, harbour trade finally ceasing in the 1960s. It is now a surfing venue. Nancekuke Common's disused airfield has seen further life as a secret warfare research establishment and divers have reported hearing strange noises while exploring the seabed below the laboratories.

Porthtowan is another surfing venue with toilets, Commodore Inn, Nelson's bar and a café converted from a 19th-century copper mine engine house.

The Towanroath engine house ruin above Chapel Porth is that of the Charlotte United copper mine. Chapel Porth, too, is a surfing venue but there is a bad current off the beach and a bar 1km out can cause big seas. A nature trail features buzzards, jackdaws, ravens and wrens amongst the local bird population.

Godrevy Island with its lighthouse

Some of the best views in Cornwall are to be had from the 192m high **St Agnes** Beacon, set in an area rich in mining. Remains include the Wheal Coates tin and copper mine which closed in 1889 with shafts to depths of 180m. St Agnes Head stands 90m high with a large kittiwake colony and fulmars, guillemots and herring gulls breeding on its cliffs and grey seals beneath. Offshore are Bawden Rocks or Man and His Man.

Trevaunance Cove's cliffs are stained a deep red from tin mining and green from copper mining. It was the world's most productive source of copper from the 17th century until 1860 when copper was found in Michigan, to where some Cornish miners emigrated. Ore was sent down chutes and cargoes lowered by horse powered windlasses from the clifftops. There were many harbours, one lasting only six years, the last built in the 19th century and abandoned in 1920. Above is Trevellas Coombe, used as the setting for the TV filming of Winston Graham's *Poldark* novels.

Trevellas Porth is the home of the Blue Hills mine, operational from the 1830s to 1897.

Gliding and hang gliding take place from the airfield nearby while bass and harmless basking sharks glide beneath the sea.

St Piran, the patron saint of tin miners, was a Celtic monk who was said to have sailed from Ireland on a millstone, possibly a mistaken identity of a coracle. His white cross on a black field is now used as the Cornish flag. **Perranporth** (Pirran's port) on the B3285 was a tin and copper working centre in the Middle Ages. Today it is a surfing centre with sand yachting on Perran Beach in the winter and a carnival in July.

Perran Beach is backed by cave dotted cliffs covered in fulmars. Gear Sands and Penhale Sands are a sweep of dunes covered by caravan sites and holiday camps under which lies buried the supposed city of Langarroc, the inhabitants of which were said to have become greedy, immoral and lazy. Also buried was St Piran's 6th-century oratory, the oldest Christian building in the British Isles. Uncovered by a storm in 1831, it has now had a concrete shell built over it but has had to be buried again to keep it from the attentions of vandals. Parts of the dunes belong to the Penhale Camp military training area and bristle with aerials as the sound of shooting echoes from ranges.

Carter's or Gull Rocks off Penhale Point guard entry into Holywell Bay. Holywell is a silted up port with two sets of stepping stones across. More steps come in a flight of 15 cut into the rock at the northeast end of the bay and lead down to the well, a spring.

The sea can be difficult off Kelsey Head but this suits the seals which breed on the Chick.

Sand from Porth Joke has been used as fertilizer since the time of James II when approval was given for this use by Act of Parliament.

The River Gannel discharges down the northeast side of Crantock Beach between Pentire Point West and Pentire Point East, the latter guarded by the Goose.

Fistral Bay beach, possibly Britain's best surfing beach, is used for top contests and hosted Britain's first Wave Ski World Championships in 1989. Behind the beach is a golf course and a large red hotel.

A small beach on the west side of Towan Head at SW800627 has limited parking and gives a possible landing point if conditions permit.

Distance
From Lizard Point to Towan Head is 120km
Campsites
Lizard, Predannack Wollas, Cross Lanes, Carminowe, Porthleven, Praa Sands, Kenneggy, Marazion, Penzance, Trewoofe, Boskenna, Treen, Sennen, Carn Towan, Kelynack, Botallack, Trewellard, Trevalgan, Hellesveor, St Ives, Halsetown, Carbis Bay, Phillack, Gwithian, Coombe, Cambrose, Porthtowan, Goonvrea, Cross Coombe, Trevellas, Perranporth, Rose, Gear Sands, Holywell, West Pentire, Crantock
Youth Hostels
Lizard, Penzance, Land's End, Perranporth
OS 1:50,000 Sheets
200 Newquay and Bodmin
203 Land's End and Isles of Scilly
204 Truro and Falmouth
Imray Charts
C7 Falmouth to Isles of Scilly and Newquay (1:100,000)
2400 West Country
Stanfords Allweather Charts
23 West Country
Admiralty Charts
SC 154 Approaches to Falmouth (1:35,000)
SC 777 Land's End to Falmouth (1:75,000)
SC 1148 Isles of Scilly to Land's End (1:75,000)
SC 1149 Pendeen to Trevose Head (1:75,000)
SC 1168 Harbours on the North Coast of Cornwall. St Ives Bay (1:25,000). Newquay Bay (1:12,500)
SC 2345 Plans in Southwest Cornwall. Lizard Point (1:15,000). Mullion Cove (1:5,000). Porthleven (1:5,000). Penzance Bay (1:12,500). Penzance Harbour (1:5,000). Newlyn Harbour (1:5,000). Mousehole Harbour (1:5,000). Runnel Stone (1:15,000). Longships (1:15,000)
SC 5603 Falmouth to Padstow, including the Isles of Scilly
Tidal Constants
Lizard Point: HW Dover +0600, LW Dover −0620
Porthleven: HW Dover +0550, LW Dover −0610
Penzance: HW Dover +0550, LW Dover −0610
Newlyn: HW Dover +0550, LW Dover −0610
Mousehole: HW Dover +0550, LW Dover −0610
Land's End: HW Dover +0550, LW Dover −0610
Sennen Cove: HW Dover +0550, LW Dover −0620
Cape Cornwall: HW Dover +0550, LW Dover −0620
St Ives: HW Dover − 0600, LW Dover −0550
Portreath: Dover −0600
Perranporth: Dover −0600
Sea Areas
Plymouth, Lundy
Submarine Areas
Mounts Bay, B1
Rescue
Inshore lifeboats: Penlee, Sennen Cove, St Ives, St Agnes
All weather lifeboats: Lizard, Penlee, Sennen Cove, St Ives
Helicopter: Culdrose
Maritime Rescue Centre
Falmouth, 01326 317575

Legendary Australian wave ski surfer John Christensen at Fistral

Wheal Coates, St Agnes South-west England

Tin mine, St Agnes, Cornwall

2 NORTH CORNWALL

From King Arthur to 21st-century surfers

Does there even a place like Saint-Juliot exist?
  Or a Vallency Valley
  With stream and leafed alley,
Or Beeny, or Bos with its flounce flinging mist?

Thomas Hardy

Surf can occur on all beaches as far as the River Camel when the sea is up. Towan Head has a tide race off the end and a lookout manned in an emergency by local fishermen. Another lookout point is the whitewashed huer's house on the headland, in use until the late 19th century when pilchards became scarce. Using a 900mm long horn, the huer's job was to signal the arrival of the fish, of major importance to **Newquay**. One catch in the 1860s filled 1,000 carts and was worth £20,000. Today the fish are bass, mackerel, pollock and shark.

Building of the harbour was approved by the Bishop of Exeter in 1439. The sea breaks heavily off the entrance in onshore gales despite the apparently sheltered easterly facing position in Newquay Bay. Pilot gigs were raced for the prize of landing pilots on incoming cargo ships and a boat from 1812 and two others from last century are preserved and used for races in the summer. Newquay became a smuggling, fishing and trading centre, trading as far as North America.

In 1875 the railway arrived, bringing minerals and clay to the harbour and later, more importantly, tourists. Newquay is Cornwall's leading seaside resort and Britain's main surfing centre with 500 hotels and 75,000 tourists at the peak of the season. Surfing is restricted with boards over 1.5m long needing to be registered. The town has 11 beaches covering 11km of coast, semi-tropical gardens and a marine aquarium with local fish and shellfish. Unusually for a seaside town it is built on top of cliffs with the A3058. A colony of herring gulls nest on rooftops.

Trevelgue Head has an Iron Age fort on top and a blowhole in the headland. Porth limekiln imported limestone from south Wales for burning, to neutralize the acidic Cornish soil.

The B3276 follows Watergate Bay, used by surfers. In 1869 there was a riot when looters tried to prevent a steam tug relaunching a ship beached by the surf.

Griffin's Point has an Iron Age hill fort which is directly in line with one of the runways of St Mawgan Airfield, operated by the RAF.

The church at St Mawgan has a wooden memorial to nine men and a boy who died of hypothermia in a lifeboat in 1846 after their ship sank. Mawgan Porth is a surfing venue with a chip shop, toilets, Snug Bar, Merrydown public house, shop and dangerous currents. The settlement there may date from as early as the 5th century.

The former airfield above Trenance is now covered with aerials.

This is one of the most memorable stretches of coastline in Britain and includes Bedruthan Steps, a set of granite crags which were supposed to have been used as stepping stones by the giant Bedruthan. It is more likely that the steep cliff staircase, closed in the winter, was cut by wreckers. Most notable of the wrecks here was the *Samaritan* in October 1846, taking silks and cottons from Liverpool. Only two crew members survived but the ship was renamed the *Good Samaritan* by locals who dressed in its cargo for years. A memorial at the top of the steps commemorates a Derby man drowned in 1903, his friends being saved. Best known of the Steps is Queen Bess Rock which is said to resemble a full length figure of Elizabeth I. Other features are caves which cannot be reached by land except at low tide and the site of Redcliffe Castle at the north end of the steps.

Looking southwards from Treyarnon towards Park Head

Beyond Park Head with its Cow and Calf rocks and seabird breeding colonies is Porthcothan Bay backed by dunes.

Treyarnon beach with the Quies on the right

Treyarnon Bay has rock shelving on both sides of its entrance and a dangerous rip on the southern side. In the rocks is a natural swimming pool.

The backing of dunes fixed by marram grass returns behind the surfing beach of Constantine Bay, the dunes hiding the location of St

Sand dunes back the surfing beach at Constantine Bay

The Bull off Dinas Head with Trevose Head lighthouse
seen beyond

Constantine's church. The bay is extended
northwards by Booby's Bay towards the igneous
bulk of Trevose Head. This stands on the far side
of the tumulus topped Dinas Head and Stinking
Cove with the outliers of the Bull and the igneous
Quies. Trevose Head is dominated by its
lighthouse. Standing 62m above the sea, it was
established in 1847 and has a range of 43km. In
return, the beams of Hartland Point, Lundy,
Godrevy and Pendeen lights can be seen from the
top. Tidal flow either way is 4km/h on springs,
starting northeast at Dover HW and southwest at
Dover HW +0600.

Merope Rocks, a line of needles with the
occasional hole through, run east from Trevose
Head and protect the lifeboat station in Polventon
Bay where the Padstow lifeboat is based. The bay
is also known as Mother Ivey's Bay after a
formidable old lady who used to claim any
wreckage. Today the most conspicuous feature is a
large caravan site across the back of the bay.

Cataclews Point, with its blue Catacleuse stone
outcrop, divides the bay from Harlyn Bay,
overlooked by the houses of Harlyn. The village
has been in use for a long time and an Iron Age
cemetery has produced over a hundred cists of
local slate, each grave having a crouched skeleton.

There is a museum of discoveries although most
exhibits are now in Truro museum. The surf
dumps at high tide in Harlyn Bay.

There is also surfing in Trevone Bay, the Round
Hole of which resulted from the collapse of the
roof of a sea cave. A cliff collapse beyond Gunver
Head has left the Butter Hole.

Largest and furthest of the offshore rocks on
this section of coast is the igneous Gulland Rock
off Gunver Head. Onshore is the 12m daymark on
Stepper Point which also bears a coastguard
lookout built to view Padstow Bay and up the
estuary of the River Camel, the major inlet of
north Cornwall. Prominent are the houses of
Polzeath and New Polzeath on a cliff, part of
which slipped in the 1980s and had to be
stabilized. This is a popular surfing area as there
will be surf here if there is any in north Cornwall.
It is biggest at low tide, though not as fast as some
breaks, and 2–3m waves are common at the end of
the day. Amenities include a large carpark, toilets
with hot showers, supermarket, takeaway stores,
chip shop, Galleon Café and Cornish Chough
licensed restaurant.

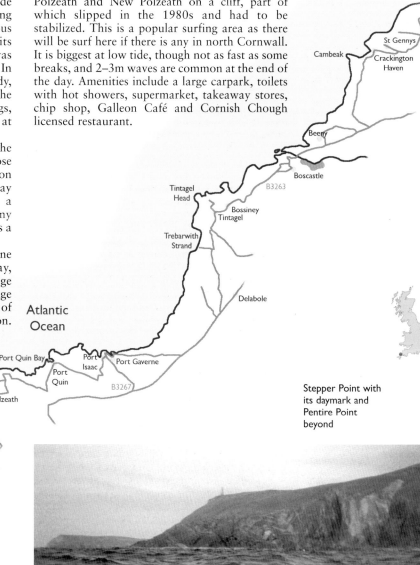

Stepper Point with
its daymark and
Pentire Point
beyond

The Mouls
standing off Rumps
Point

Pentire Point resembles a cock's comb from the west as outcrops of rock are divided by grassy slopes. The point consists of knobbly pillow lavas. Newland, too, is a 37m igneous pillar. A small tide race runs between Newland and the point with overfalls outside Newland.

Rumps Point bears an Iron Age cliff castle which is probably the finest on the Cornish coast. The point is igneous, as are the 50m high Mouls. The area can be turbulent although it was not on the day in the first world war when Lawrence Binyon landed on the Mouls from a small boat. He was moved by the solitude and tranquillity during those times of turmoil to write his Remembrance Day verse.

A natural arch has resulted from the collapse of a sea cave in Lundy Bay, part of Port Quin Bay. Another wreck is that of the Greek freighter *Skopalos Sky*.

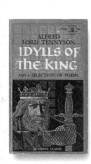

The little square tower of Doyden Castle is a folly. Built in 1839 by Samuel Symons of Wadebridge, it doubled as a marker for the narrow inlet to Portquin and as a drinking and gambling retreat. The port's entire male population was said to have drowned in the 18th century while trying to escape from a press gang, and it was again abandoned in the 19th century after all the people and fishing boats were said to have been lost in a storm. In the latter case it is more likely that they all emigrated to Canada after the antimony mines near Droyden Point were closed.

Varley Head leads into Port Isaac Bay. Port Isaac at the end of the B3267 appears to have a welcoming message laid out across the grass facing the sea, but closer inspection can show it to be the light reflecting off the windscreens of cars parked in three tiers. Deception is not new to the town and there are smugglers' caves here. The town also retains its character in such narrow old streets as Squeeze-Belly-Alley. Permission is needed in advance for launching in Port Isaac and a fee is charged. There are still some working fishing boats and mackerel frequent the area. From here to Boscastle is mostly slate and Port Isaac used to ship slate from the Delabole quarries.

Adjacent Portgaverne, with its cellars which were used for storing pilchards, also shipped slate. A tunnel through which slate was hauled has collapsed at Barrett's Zawn and there is evidence of an extensive slip on the cliffs. On top of the cliffs a tower with slots at the top resembles nothing more than a giant concrete litter bin.

Gull Rock and the cart road down to Trebarwith Strand

The prominent Gull Rock off Dennis Point marks Trebarwith Strand behind Port William. The sandy beach permits landing and is used by surfers.

Facilities include the Trebarwith Strand Hotel, Port William, House on the Strand bistro, Annie's Café and public toilets. In the 19th century a road was cut down through the rocks to allow access for carts to collect the shell sand for fertilizer. Carts also collected Welsh coal which had been tipped into the sea at high tide. Another high tide activity for ships was receiving slate lowered down from cliffside slate quarries on windlasses, the slate waste still being obvious on the cliffs to the north of the inlet. The same technique of loading slate was also used at Dunderhole Point.

Surely nowhere on the English coastline is more evocative than Tintagel Head with its castle remains, best seen through a thin drizzle outside the tourist season, the remains of dark, wet, stone walls clinging to the massive bulk of the Island which isn't really an island. Tennyson's *The Idylls of the King* and Sir Thomas Malory's *Le Morte d'Arthur* have done nothing to detract from this enchanted and forbidding spot. It was here that Gorlois, Duke of Cornwall, kept his wife, Ygraine. Uther, the invading King of the Britons, was changed by Merlin to resemble Gorlois and seduced Ygraine. Gorlois died on the birth of the resulting child, Arthur, who was to dwell here with his knights. Merlin's cave on the cliff face where Arthur first met Merlin seems to lack the basic mod cons which any self respecting magician should be capable of conjuring up. Historical fact is rather stronger on the Celtic settlement founded around 400 and abandoned three centuries later, St Juliot founding a monastery in about 500. The castle's great hall was built in 1145 by Earl Reginald while Richard, Earl of Cornwall and brother of Henry III, contributed the wall and iron gate from the 13th century. Edward, the Black Prince, the first Duke of Cornwall, made further additions in the 14th century, in the latter part of which it was used as a prison. The central portion had been washed away by sea erosion by the 16th century, repairs being carried out in 1852. The only other major development has been the building of a totally inappropriate large red-brick hotel right in the middle of this Area of Outstanding Natural Beauty.

A cliff face on Barras Nose has been eroded in such a way that it resembles the head of an elephant looking out to sea.

Bossiney Castle is a mound where the Round Table is said to be buried and from which it is claimed to rise on Mid-summer's Eve. Bossiney Haven has surfing, despite its inaccessibility. Lye Rock is a breeding ground for cormorants, fulmars, puffins and razorbills and seals frequent the area. Off Willapark are the Sisters, two large blocks of rock divided by a cleft through which it is easy to paddle if the sea is calm enough.

A more notable cleft is Rocky Valley through which a small stream falls, the haunt of the Cornish hermit St Nectan. Daphne du Maurier described it as 'superbly dissociated from humankind' and its appeal is certainly not new for the ruins of a mill have cup and ring markings from the Bronze Age on them. A caravan site on the hill above is not obvious from the valley although very conspicuous from the sea.

Meachard protects the approach to Boscastle

The harbour entrance is hard to find and can be missed totally

submerged and sometimes ready to damage the boats of the unwary. In 1894 seven people were lost here from the Swedish brigantine *William* and then another seven from the steamer *City of Vienna* and, six years later, the barque *Capricorna*. All are buried at St Gennys.

The folded strata of Samphire Rock, flowing out into a natural bridge

More towering rock islands follow and rock forms become more intriguing as the rock turns to sandstone and shale. Meachard and a nearby blowhole guard the totally inconspicuous entrance to the picturesque Boscastle harbour on the B3263. With a large swell or strong onshore winds it is unusable. The inner jetty was rebuilt in 1584 by Sir Richard Grenville. The seaport thrived until the mid-19th century and the outer breakwater dates from this time when slate was being shipped. In 1941 the outer breakwater was damaged by a drifting mine and it was repaired in 1962. The harbour drains at low tide to leave just the River Valency, a stream which drops steeply into the village and up the sides of which 14th-century cottages climb. People itching to blame a damaging flash flood in the valley in 2004 on global warming were thwarted by the fact that a very similar flood had taken place in Lynmouth 52 years earlier almost to the day. Land at the top is stitchmeal which has been used for over 1,000 years. Tenants grow crops on long thin stitches of land in summer and it is used as common grazing in winter. The nearby church has interesting monuments and there is a museum of witchcraft in the village, that includes the remains of Ursula Hemp, a witch executed in 1589.

At Pentargon another stream falls 36m to the sea.

It was while working on the local church that Thomas Hardy met his future wife. The area around Beeny was at the centre of his thoughts, his courting and his poetry. High Cliff, one of the highest in England at 223m, is the highest point on the Cornish coast and the setting for his crisis episode in *A Pair of Blue Eyes*. From the top it is possible to see Lundy. This section of coast was given to the nation in 1959 by Wing Commander A G Parnall to commemorate his brother and other airmen lost in the Battle of Britain. No other aerial display could be more fitting for this is some of Britain's most majestic coastal scenery. Not an area of safety, the Strangles having claimed over a score of ships in one year in the 1820s alone, it does possess magnificent cliff scenery and the rock folding becomes ever more dramatic until Samphire Rock, where the strata zigzag down the cliff face to burst forth at the bottom and emerge as a natural stone bridge, rather like a hand reaching out of a film screen.

Cambeak, itself a heavily folded structure being eaten back by the sea, is the last point before Crackington Haven, a small surfing beach overlooked by the Coombe Broughton Inn. Even this haven has a sting in the tail for a sharp ridge of rock runs out to Bray's Point on the southern side of the beach, sometimes obvious, sometimes

Crackington Haven has a line of sharp rocks, below the surface much of the time

Distance
From Towan Head to Crackington Haven is 55km
Campsites
Whipsiderry, Trevelgue, Tregurrian, Trevarrian, Mawgan Porth, Porthcothan, Treyarnon, Constantine Bay, Harlyn, Polzeath, New Polzeath, St Minver, Delabole, Tintagel, Bossiney, Trethevey, Beeny, Sweets
Youth Hostels
Treyarnon Bay, Tintagel, Boscastle Harbour
OS 1:50,000 Sheets
190 Bude and Clovelly
200 Newquay and Bodmin
Imray Charts
C7 Falmouth to Isles of Scilly and Newquay (1:100,000)
C58 Trevose Head to Bull Point (1:131,300)
Stanfords Allweather Charts
14 Bristol Channel and Approaches
Admiralty Charts
SC 1149 Pendeen to Trevose Head (1:75,000)
SC 1156 Trevose Head to Hartland Point (1:75,000)
SC 1168 Harbours on the North Coast of Cornwall. Newquay Bay (1:12,500) Approaches to Padstow (1:25,000)
SC 5603 Falmouth to Padstow, including the Isles of Scilly
Tidal Constants
Perranporth: Dover –0600
Newquay: Dover –0600
Padstow: HW Dover –0550, LW Dover –0540
Port Isaac: Dover –0600
Boscastle: HW Dover –0520, LW Dover √0600
Sea Area
Lundy
Rescue
Inshore lifeboats: Newquay, Rock, Port Isaac and Bude
All weather lifeboats: Padstow
Maritime Rescue Centre
Falmouth, 01326 317575

3 NORTHWEST DEVON

Literary giants and an eccentric vicar

Who hath desired the Sea? – the sight of salt water unbounded –
The heave and the halt and the hurl and the crash of the comber wind-hounded?

Rudyard Kipling

Leaving Crackington Haven beneath the 130m sheer cliffs on the north side results in turning towards Dizzard Point, a cliff which has seen plenty of slips and is covered by a scrub which is actually England's westernmost dwarf oak wood.

A break in the cliff reveals Millook which is probably the boundary of the traditional kingdom of Cornwall as the place names change suggests, despite the present jurisdiction continuing for some distance.

Black Rock, a remarkably striking finger of rock considering the amount of rock around, signals the southern end of Widemouth Bay. Coming ashore here are some transatlantic submarine cables, the 6,525km New Jersey cable of 1963, the 5,195km Nova Scotia cable of 1973 and the No 10/White House hotline.

Cliffs run up to Bude and passed on the way is Efford Beacon, a small grass mound.

A 6m high octagonal pointed stone tower marks Compass Point, the entrance to Bude Haven, an area of confused water resulting from the bar across it. Surf can be heavy and surfing may be restricted in summer, surfboards over 1.52m long need to be registered and a fee is charged for launching from the harbour. There is a saltwater swimming pool on the beach for those who want calmer conditions. Facing the harbour are the lock gates at the end of the Bude Canal, built in 1823 to carry beach sand to Launceston for use as fertilizer. Barges returning with oats and slate for shipment. A museum in the former barge horse blacksmith's shop at the Wharf covers the canal, shipwrecks and ecology of the surrounding area. Some of the latter can be seen on the nature trail at the 12th century Ebbingford

Manor. **Bude** remains the town described by John Betjeman as the 'least rowdy of British resorts' although it does rise to the occasion during the August carnival. Amongst those in Bude with a spirit of adventure was Sir Goldsworthy Gurney who, in 1830, built Bude Castle (now the council offices) on a raft of concrete on sand to prove that it was possible to build on shifting sand. The following year he began the world's first inter-town steam carriage service with 19km/h carriages of his own design.

The final beach is Crooklets at Flexbury where the Wrangle Point end of the beach is protected by a heavy concrete retaining wall. The beach is backed by beach huts, parking, a snack bar and the premises of Bude Surf Rescue Club, the first lifeguard club in the country. The beach was the site of the first kayak surfing contest in the mid-20th century when national coach Oliver Cock and friends were asked by harbourmaster Jack Dymond to develop their surfing get together into a competition to extend the Bude season by a fortnight at the end of September.

The unrelenting cliffs north of Flexbury

Now the cliffs begin in earnest. Although there are a few road access points it is not possible to remove a kayak safely from the water at most states of the tide in anything but light conditions as far as Clovelly. Boulders litter the shore and the cliff is frequently too steep to climb out, even if the kayak is abandoned. Cliffs are often exotically folded, a legacy of the Armorican period, especially at Sandy Mouth.

Badly stacked strata at Sandy Mouth

Crooklets Beach and the southern sweep of Bude Bay

At Duckpool the landing has the added complexity of strata up on edge with pieces chipped away to produce lines of saw teeth at intervals between the boulders, hardly the best things to meet on a landing in surf. To the north Steeple Point is massively landslipped, yet above this on Lower Sharpnose Point is a communications satellite tracking station with a battery of enormous white radar dish aerials which are conspicuous from the whole of Bude Bay.

A driftwood hut was built on the cliffs by the Rev R S Hawker, the eccentric vicar of Morwenstow

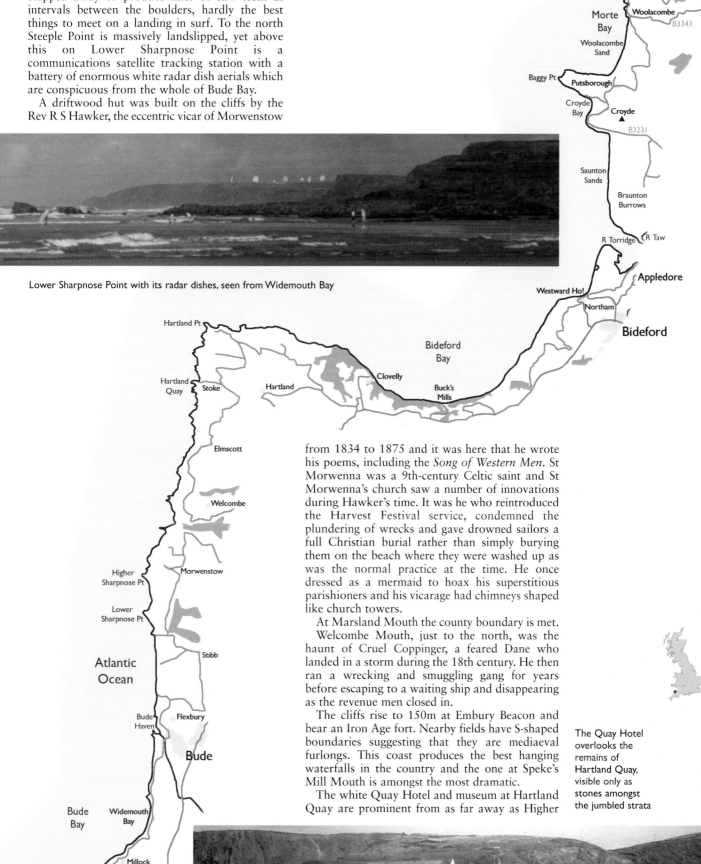

Lower Sharpnose Point with its radar dishes, seen from Widemouth Bay

from 1834 to 1875 and it was here that he wrote his poems, including the *Song of Western Men*. St Morwenna was a 9th-century Celtic saint and St Morwenna's church saw a number of innovations during Hawker's time. It was he who reintroduced the Harvest Festival service, condemned the plundering of wrecks and gave drowned sailors a full Christian burial rather than simply burying them on the beach where they were washed up as was the normal practice at the time. He once dressed as a mermaid to hoax his superstitious parishioners and his vicarage had chimneys shaped like church towers.

At Marsland Mouth the county boundary is met.

Welcombe Mouth, just to the north, was the haunt of Cruel Coppinger, a feared Dane who landed in a storm during the 18th century. He then ran a wrecking and smuggling gang for years before escaping to a waiting ship and disappearing as the revenue men closed in.

The cliffs rise to 150m at Embury Beacon and bear an Iron Age fort. Nearby fields have S-shaped boundaries suggesting that they are mediaeval furlongs. This coast produces the best hanging waterfalls in the country and the one at Speke's Mill Mouth is amongst the most dramatic.

The white Quay Hotel and museum at Hartland Quay are prominent from as far away as Higher

The Quay Hotel overlooks the remains of Hartland Quay, visible only as stones amongst the jumbled strata

Sharpnose Point. Building of the quay was authorized by Parliament in 1586 and financed by Sir Francis Drake, Sir John Hawkins and Sir Walter Raleigh. There were frequent cargoes here of coal, lime and timber as well as the lead needed to repair the roof of St Nectan's church at Stoke, the tower of which was built 39m high as a landmark for sailors. The quay broke up at the end of the 19th century and now little remains except the boulders on the shore, backed by strata which change from horizontal to vertical in a few metres. There is a seawater swimming pool amongst the rocks and a private slipway leads up to the hotel where a bar contains relics of the *Green Ranger*, a wreck in the rescue of which Hartland men played a gallant part. The hotel is the former harbourmaster's house, offices, stables, storerooms and workers' cottages. Opposite is the museum which covers four centuries of shipwreck at Morwenstow, Welcombe, Hartland and Clovelly, smuggling, coastal trades, geology and natural history.

Hartland Point. The two halves of the wrecked freighter lie right of centre, picked out in white corrosion

Two halves of a large freighter lie rusting on the rocks next to the lighthouse at Hartland Point, a reminder of the power of the sea. To the Romans it was the Promontory of Hercules. The lighthouse, low on the 110m high cliffs, has the strongest beam of any in Britain.

Here the coast is at its nearest to Lundy which can be seen lying 20km to the northwest.

Rounding the point into Barnstaple or Bideford Bay brings a change with the cliffs being nearly vertical until Clovelly and running parallel to the strike of the rocks rather than cutting across them as south of Hartland Point. There is a tide race off the point, but tidal flows are generally weak in Bideford Bay, flooding NE and ebbing SW except between Hartland Point and Clovelly where there is a significant westerly flow on the ebb.

Blackchurch Rock and Gallant Rock guard the northern approach to Clovelly

From Mill Mouth the woods of Gallantry Bower cover the 110m high cliffs which reach their best at Gallant Rock where they rise almost vertically and smoothly to their full height from the water.

Clovelly is a lobster fishing village which had huge catches of herring in the 18th and 19th centuries. The quay was lengthened in 1826 to give extra protection to the large fishing fleet, although it still suffers from a groundswell on a westerly or southwesterly wind and sometimes from a shallow bank of stones at the harbour entrance. The

The cottages of Clovelly set on their sheer and lofty cliff around the course of an old stream

colour-washed houses are 'built up the face of a sheer and lofty cliff' as Dickens described it in his *Message from the Sea* of 1860. It was also identified in *Westward Ho!* by Charles Kingsley, whose father was rector here. First settled in the Iron Age, it was mentioned in the *Domesday Book* and flourished in the 13th and 14th centuries. The village is best known for its main street which follows the bed of an old watercourse and is cobbled with beach pebbles set on edge, only being passable on foot or by donkey hauled sledge. There is a large carpark at the top and a narrow and very steep vehicle road to the bottom where there is very limited parking, use of which may be permitted to load and unload kayaks. Facilities at the bottom include the Red Lion Hotel and toilets. Lying amongst the lobster pots at the foot of the cliffs on the north of the village is a metal sectional kayak used in the making of the *Cockleshell Heroes* film about Blondie Hasler's Operation Frankton on the Gironde in 1942.

Cockleshell Heroes kayak at Clovelly

The woods continue to Peppercombe, initially with Holly Drive, described by Kingsley as 'a forest wall 500 feet high of almost semi-tropic luxuriance.' Made by Sir Charles Hamlyn, it may have been to provide employment during the slump which followed the Napoleonic wars.

The sweeping coastline is disrupted to the east of Lower Bight of Fernham by the Gore, an intertidal rocky ridge which runs out 1.2km northwards from the shore.

The bar causes problems at Buck's Mills, a tiny fishing village which imported limestone from south Wales in the 19th century to burn in the kiln by the shore to neutralize acidic soil. On the other hand, it has been used for the early experiments on tidal power, a reliable renewable source of power which does not involve ruining the countryside and which also gives refuges for fish stocks.

Below Peppercombe Castle the cliffs drop in height for a while and turn to the bright red so characteristic of Devon soils. Mermaid's Pool is more likely to produce bird life, particularly curlews, oystercatchers and shags.

Kipling's Tor is a gorse covered hill to the west of Westward Ho! reminding us that Rudyard Kipling was a pupil of the United Services College in Westward Ho! (now Kipling Terrace) from 1878 to 1882, as recalled in his *Stalkey and Co*. The town was started as a holiday resort speculation in 1863, the name coming from Kingsley's novel. Today it has beach huts, café, bars, hot dog and pasty stall, fast food takeaway, toilets and a giant yellow elephant outside the ice rink. Surfing is popular all along the foot of the Pebble Ridge, a natural phenomenon stretching 3km north from the town and sheltering Northam Burrows Country Park and the Royal North Devon Golf Club on low sandhills which form the burrows. A spit protects the Skern.

Tidal flows northwards from Westward Ho! to Baggy Point are significant on the flood. The major estuary of north Devon is that of the Torridge and Taw which discharge large tidal flows into Bideford Bay and can raise heavy seas over the Zulu Bank and Bideford Bar on the ebb with a westerly wind blowing.

The passenger ferry *Oldenburg* operates from **Bideford** to Lundy. The buildings of **Appledore** and Instow are seen on either side of the River Torridge and the hangers of RAF Chivenor on the River Taw.

Braunton Burrows on the north of the estuary is a nature reserve with marram grass, marsh orchids, roundheaded club rush, sand toadflax and sea stock. The public are kept away partly by ranges which are operational when red flags are flying with a danger area up to 6km offshore. It is one of the grandest sand dune areas in Britain with dunes up to 30m high, hiding Braunton, a former busy fishing port said to be Britain's largest village. It is here that US troops trained for the Normandy landings in 1944, recalled by the American Road.

Old Red Sandstone and tough Devonian slates now emerge from beneath the Carboniferous Culm Measures and there are three successive west-facing sand beaches terminated by rocky headlands.

Saunton Sands are popular for surfing and end below a large white hotel block, beach huts, a pillbox and what looks like the end of a tunnel emerging onto the beach.

Saunton Down, capped with two aerials and edged by the B3231, divides the beach from Croyde Bay. The bay is again backed by dunes, with aerials on Ora Hill and parking at the north end of the beach. Croyde has a coastguard station, the Gemrock and Shell Museum featuring semi-precious stones and shells, a village of thatched and colour washed cottages and the Ruda holiday camp.

Tide streams run N–S across the entrance to Morte Bay. While they are weak in the bay they can be 7km/h on springs at Baggy Leap where there may be a tide race or overfalls. One of the models in Bude museum is of the Salcombe smack *Ceres* which was built in 1811 and was the oldest

ship on Lloyd's Register for many years, coming to grief on Baggy Point in 1936.

The point has several caves including the enormous Baggy Hole which can be reached by kayak or by the climbers who frequent the near vertical slabs on the point.

Putsborough Sand at the southern end of Woolacombe Sand has surfing. Going north, dunes gradually build up, being sown with marram grass. Woolacombe faces the sea at the end of the B3343 with nearby parking, children's playground, donkey rides, beach café and toilets, a complete resort in miniature but without brashness.

The caves and slabs of Baggy Point, complete with climbers

Distance
From Crackington Haven to Woolacombe is 72km
Campsites
Treskinnick Cross, Widemouth Bay, Bude, Flexbury, Stibb, Welcombe Cross, Stoke, Hartland, Clovelly, Buck's Mills, Appledore, Braunton, Croyde, Woolacombe
Youth Hostels
Elmscott, Ilfracombe
OS 1:50,000 Sheets
180 Barnstaple and Ilfracombe
190 Bude and Clovelly
Imray Chart
C58 Trevose Head to Bull Point (1:131,300)
Stanfords Allweather Charts
14 Bristol Channel and Approaches
Admiralty Charts
SC 1156 Trevose Head to Hartland Point (1:75,000)
SC 1160 Plans on the Coast of Somerset and Devon. Barnstaple and Bideford (1:25,000)
SC 1164 Hartland Point to Ilfracombe including Lundy (1:75,000)
SC 1179 Bristol Channel (1:150,000)
Tidal Constants
Boscastle: HW Dover −0520, LW Dover −0600
Bude: Dover −0540
Clovelly: Dover −0530
Appledore: Dover −0520
Ilfracombe: HW Dover −0520, LW Dover −0540
Sea Area
Lundy
Range
Braunton Burrows
Rescue
Inshore lifeboats: Bude, Clovelly, Appledore and Ilfracombe
All weather lifeboats: Padstow, Appledore and Ilfracombe
Helicopter: Chivenor
Maritime Rescue Centres
Falmouth, 01326 317575
Swansea, 01792 366534

4 EXMOOR

England's highest sea cliffs

Porlock, thy verdant vale so fair to sight,
Thy lofty hills with fern and furze so brown,
Thy waters that so musical roll down
Thy wooded glens, the traveller with delight
Recalls to memory, and the channel grey
Circling it, surges in thy level bay.
Porlock, I also shall forget thee not.

Robert Southey

Ilfracombe is the largest town on this coast and has the largest harbour

The coast leading away from Woolacombe passes Mortehoe with its attractive church founded in the 13th century. A ridge of land covered with footpaths projects west from here to Morte Point which has been the death of many ships, assisted by wreckers in the 18th century and a tide race. Indeed, the Morte Stone alone claimed 5 ships in the winter of 1852. This might be said to be the starting point of the southern side of the Bristol Channel.

The tide stream between Morte Point and Ilfracombe is 6km/h on springs, starting eastwards at HW Dover +0400 and westwards at HW Dover –0520. A coastguard lookout covers the point and also Rockham Bay where there can be strong tides.

Bull Point. A race runs off the end of the rocks at some stages of the tide

Bull Point has had a lighthouse since 1879 but a cliff fall in 1972 caused so much damage that a new automatic one was built and opened in 1975, a white round tower above the overfalls off Bull Point.

Beyond Damage Cliff is Lee Bay, a delightful inlet backed by trees and surrounded by fuchsias and hydrangeas and with a slipway allowing access to the hotel in Lee.

An early wind generator is positioned at Higher Slade to take full benefit of the exposed position.

Passenger ferries from Lundy and south Wales operate into **Ilfracombe**. This was Alfred's valley from the West Saxon Ielfred and Old English cumb, a town with a long seafaring tradition. Once the fifth port in Britain, it sent six ships to the siege of Calais in 1346. St Nicholas' chapel on Lantern Hill was built as a landmark for sailors around 1300 and has been a seamen's chapel and lighthouse, still showing a light today. Now Ilfracombe has only fishing vessels in the harbour which is invisible from seaward, sheltering behind the promenade pier. Heavy swells and strong tides with a short confused sea in northerly winds are a feature of the area. Hotels and colourwashed cottages abound, the town having developed in the Victorian era with the coming of the former railway. A museum has models, paintings and photographs of ships, the harbour, the coast, minerals, natural history and archaeology. To the east of the town an aerial stands between a fort and the 1525 watermill at Hele. Now with its 5.5m wheel restored it produces wholemeal flour. Hele Bay itself, overlooked by a golf course on Widmouth Hill, has a tide filled paddling pool.

Rillage Point has a tide rip which develops over Buggy Pit with westerly winds.

Now begins one of the most impressive and remote stretches of cliff in England, reaching to beyond Porlock. The 300m high plateau of Exmoor with the A399 falls directly to the sea, possibly helped by Tertiary faulting. The view from Widmouth Head past Hangman Point and Highveer Point to Foreland Point with a virtually unbroken line of cliffs is breathtaking.

Water Mouth can be rough in NW winds. This inlet was used to test PLUTO, the pipeline under the ocean for supplying the Allies with fuel during

Lee Bay is a beautiful little inlet on a coast which is generally cliffbound

the Normandy landings in the second world war. Today it is overlooked by a small holiday camp while Watermouth Castle, dating from 1825, stands at its head with great hall, smugglers' dungeons, coloured fountain and waterfalls and various exhibitions.

Combe Martin is a linear village said to have the longest village street in England. It follows the River Umber down from the old London Inn past the oddly shaped Pack of Cards Inn. Other features include the castle, the old poor house, the church (included in *The Mighty Atom* by Marie Corelli who lived in the village), the motorcycle museum (which has T E Lawrence's Brough Superior) and the 13th-century silver lead mines which were worked until the 19th century. There is a carnival in August. There are the usual facilities such as a café near the beach, overlooked by caravans and chalets. Surf is a possibility.

From now on the coast is part of Exmoor National Park although this does not prevent the intrusion of jets. Wild Pear beach is overlooked by the Little Hangman which is followed by the Great Hangman, leading away onto Girt Down. Both peaks are of resistant sandstones, the Great Hangman being 318m, of deep red colour, from the top of which it is possible to see Wales on the far side of the Bristol Channel.

There is beach access at North Cleeve. Throughout most of this section of coast it is virtually impossible to scale the cliffs even if a landing can be made. An exception is at Heddon's Mouth where a footpath leads out beside the River Heddon past an 18th-century kiln used for burning Welsh limestone to neutralize the acidic Exmoor soil.

A tide race runs off Highveer Point but it is possible to avoid it by passing inside fallen rocks if conditions are not too rough.

On the cliffs above is Martinhoe Roman fortlet and signal station, built in 50 to 60 and abandoned in 75. It housed about 80 soldiers and had inner and outer enclosures with gates facing in opposite directions.

Woody Bay and Lee Bay are surrounded by oak woods, the cliffs being breeding grounds for auks, fulmars, guillemots, kittiwakes, razorbills, shags and gulls, mostly between March and July. Woody Bay has a slipway while Lee Bay has a beach landing. The latter is overlooked by Lee Abbey, built as a private house in 1850 and now used as a religious retreat centre. Onshore wildlife in this remote settlement includes dippers, herons, wagtails and mink.

A tower on Duty Point mirrors Castle Rock and other fantastic shapes along the cliffs. The outward extremity of the Valley of the Rocks has such formations as the Devil's Cheesewring, Rugged Jack and Mother Meldrum's Cave, Mother Meldrum being the character on whom R D Blackmore based the witch in *Lorna Doone*.

Lynmouth stands at the estuary of the East Lyn and West Lyn, 200m vertically below **Lynton**. The two are connected by a 263m working cliff railway built in 1890 at a gradient of 1:1.75. At that time it was the steepest railway in the world and the first of its kind in England, being powered by tanks each able to hold $3.2m^3$ of water. It was invented by local man Bob Jones and funded by Sir George Newnes and friends. Lynmouth has a lifeboat but the most famous rescue was that of the *Forest Hall* in a gale in 1899 when it was too rough to launch so the lifeboat was hauled overland to Porlock Bay, a journey which involved felling trees and other minor engineering works before the boat could be launched 10 hours later, saving 15 lives. There was a prosperous herring fishing and curing industry until 1607 but more recently it has been popular with tourists. Those coming for the scenery included the poets Coleridge, Southey and Wordsworth in the 19th century. Shelley and his 16-year old bride, Mary Wollstonecraft, hid here from her parents for 9 weeks, but Shelley got into further trouble for writing revolutionary pamphlets and floating them out to sea in bottles, resulting in his being reported to the Home Secretary.

It is for 15 August 1952 that Lynmouth is remembered. In one of the most violent British storms on record 130mm of rain fell in an hour with a further 100mm over the next 24 hours. Descending onto the sodden moorland and swept down into Lynmouth by the two rivers, it washed down an estimated 100,000 tonnes of debris in the process, sweeping away 34 people and gouging a swathe through the centre of the town. The subsequent appeal raised £1,336,425 from the stunned nation, a vast sum for over 50 years ago. Lynmouth has always been built on a delta of flood debris but the river bed has now been widened and the houses are not built quite so close to it. Many buildings did survive, including some old hotels near the harbour. A Rhenish tower on the harbour wall was rebuilt in 1954, replacing a 19th century one built by a colonel to supply salt water for his bath. For those wishing to bathe in salt today there is a tidefilled swimming pool.

Countisbury church to the east is a 19th-century DIY job by the parishioners.

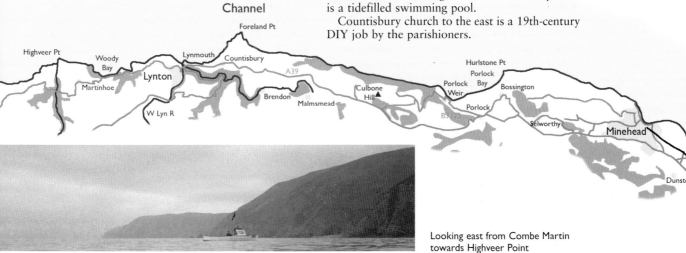

Looking east from Combe Martin towards Highveer Point

The cliff railway and rebuilt Rhenish tower at Lynmouth

Two withies mark the entrance to the harbour at Porlock Weir

century or even being Saxon in parts. It seats 30 including a family box pew and is still in regular use. The name derives from Kil Beun after St Beuno, a 6th-century Welsh saint, the church being founded by missionary Welshmen who crossed the Bristol Channel on rafts. Charcoal burners who worked in Culbone Woods were said to have been lepers who were not allowed to cross Culbone Water to approach Porlock.

Lynmouth to Porlock is very committing in anything above a force 3 with its long run of unbroken cliffs. Countisbury Hill offers the highest sea cliffs in England at 302m. Lynmouth Road runs east for 9¼ hours of each tide cycle at 3km/h on springs although the flow westwards on the ebb is barely perceptible.

Lynmouth Foreland lighthouse was established in 1900 with a range of 42km, a white round tower near the bottom of the cliff face. There are overfalls and heavy seas break over Foreland Ledge in bad weather and between the ledge and Sand Ridge in westerly gales. A channel through the rocks avoids the tide race.

Old Barrow Roman fortlet and signal station controlled Roman shipping in the Bristol Channel and watched out for trouble from the Silures in south Wales. It had the same opposite facing inner and outer gates as Martinhoe and was probably abandoned when the latter was built. The earthworks remain.

Between Foreland Point and Porlock Weir at the end of the B3225 only one house is passed, Glenthorne on the Devon/Somerset border. Landing is possible but difficult if the weather is bad. Woods run through to Porlock Weir except on the occasional spot where a slip has swept the cliffs bare of all vegetation bigger than grass.

Amongst the trees is the spire of Culbone church, the smallest complete church in England at 11m x 4m with a 6.5m x 3.9m nave, dating from the 12th

The small harbour at Porlock Weir

A low boulder promontory is striking because of its contrast with the incessant cliffs and gives notice of arrival at Porlock Bay, beneath which is a submarine forest. Porlock Weir was once a busy port trading pit-props for Welsh coal. Its colourwashed and thatched houses face a natural dry-dock, approached through a gap in the pebble bank marked with a pair of withies. The 11m tides here are used to drain the dock naturally. Pillboxes overlook the bay.

Dunkery Beacon is, at 519m, the highest hill adjoining the south side of the Bristol Channel. As it approaches the coast it includes the notorious Porlock Hill on the A39, first climbed by car in 1901 to win a bet.

Hanging waterfall on the cliffs to the east of Foreland Point

The long sweeping bank of pebbles at Porlock.

The eastern half of Porlock Bay is edged by a sweeping bank of pebbles with groynes at the Porlock Weir end but nothing to break the uniform wall of grey stones which curves round towards Hurlstone Point, hiding the thatched village of Bossington.

Selworthy Sand seen from Hurlstone Point

The remains of a futuristically profiled coastguard lookout on Hurlstone Point stand above the water to the west where there is a strong undertow.

From Hurlstone Point to Greenaleigh Point is another section of cliff with a landslip area in the Foreland sandstone. Selworthy Sand, between high and low tides, offers the first beach of golden sand since leaving Woolacombe. However, the cliffs have now returned, with sheep grazing precariously, and continue to Greenaleigh Point so it is not possible to climb off the beach. After the beach there are continuous boulders along the shoreline, making landing difficult.

The remains of Burgundy Chapel come as the land sweeps down from Bratton Ball to the shore for the first time with farmland and the Exmoor National Park and South West Coast Path come to an end with a nature trail.

Minehead is entered past a pair of beacon structures and a pillbox into a harbour which has a slipway, but which empties to leave an expanse of silt covered sand with surprisingly angular stones everywhere. The pier was built in 1488 by Sir Hugh Luttrell and extended two centuries later by another Luttrell as the sea level dropped. The sea breaks over the pier in northerly gales while SE winds and spring tides produce a swell for 3 hours around high tide. In addition, there can be 7–9m/h currents yet Daniel Defoe describes it as the safest harbour on the south side of the Bristol Channel. It was trading fish and woollen goods in the 15th century before problems with plague and raids by Welsh privateers. In the 17th century it was second only to Bristol of the Bristol Channel ports with ships going to the Mediterranean, Virginia and the West Indies. By 1716 coal was being imported from south Wales and cattle, hides and wool from Ireland with broadcloths, fish and grain being exported, herrings being a major part of the fishing activity. Trade slumped in the 19th century and it became a resort. Although most development has been since the 19th century there are colourwashed 17th-century cottages and records going back to Saxon times. On May Day the hobby horse dances through the streets, a custom dating from the mists of time; Mynheafdon meant the hill above two rivers, the E and W Myne. The 15th-century St Michael's church on North Hill had a lantern tower to guide mariners, not to mention a chest with the arms of the Tudor vicar Robert Fitzjames (who became a bishop and built Fulham Palace) and a sculpture on the east wall showing St Michael weighing a soul while the Devil clings on and the Madonna tries to restore the balance by prayer. A reminder that alabaster was once mined in Somerset comes with the alabaster statue of Queen Anne by Francis Bird, a protegé of Grinling Gibbons, which was moved from the church to Wellington Square. Much of the town's development was undertaken by the Luttrells of Dunster, although things have now changed on the seafront with holiday amusement centres flashing batteries of coloured lights along the back of the bay where there is roadside parking by the sea wall.

Moor Wood overlooks Minehead with its harbour wall

Distance
From Woolacombe to Minehead is 57km
Campsites
Woolacombe, Mortehoe, Borough Cross, Mullacott Cross, Ilfracombe, Watermouth, Combe Martin, Stony Corner, Dean, Lynton, Brendon, Malmsmead, Porlock, Minehead
Youth Hostels
Ifracombe, Lynton, Exford, Minehead
OS 1:50,000 Sheets
180 Barnstaple and Ilfracombe
181 Minehead and Brendon Hills
Imray Charts
C58 Trevose Head to Bull Point (1:131,300)
C59 Bristol Channel – Worms Head and Bull Point to Sharpness (1:115,000)
Stanfords Allweather Charts
14 Bristol Channel and Approaches
Admiralty Charts
SC 1152 Bristol Channel – Nash Point to Sand Point (1:50,000)
SC 1160 Plans on the Coast of Somerset and Devon. Ilfracombe (1:12,500). Lynmouth (1:20,000). Porlock (1:20,000). Minehead (1:20,000).
SC 1164 Hartland Point to Ilfracombe including Lundy (1:75,000)
SC 1165 Bristol Channel – Worms Head to Watchet (1 :75,000)
SC 1179 Bristol Channel (1:150,000)
Tidal Constants
Ilfracombe: HW Dover –0520, LW Dover –0540
Lynmouth: HW Dover –0500
Porlock Bay: HW Dover –0450, LW Dover –0530
Minehead: HW Dover –0440, LW Dover –0500
Sea Area
Lundy
Rescue
Inshore lifeboats: Ilfracombe and Minehead
All weather lifeboats: Ilfracombe and Barry Dock
Maritime Rescue Centre
Swansea, 01792 366534

5 BRIDGWATER BAY

Muddy waters beyond the Somerset Levels

The fair breeze blew, the white foam flew,
The furrow followed free;
We were the first that ever burst
Into that silent sea.

Samuel Taylor Coleridge

Smoke issues from chimneys on both sides of the bay at Minehead. Opposite is Aberthawe power station on the Welsh coast while behind the bay is the terminus of the West Somerset Railway, the longest privately owned railway in Britain, running steam and diesel trains 37km to Bishop's Lydeard.

Lying off the large holiday camp with its prominent waterslides are the Cables, a shingle reef which bears a submarine forest. Currents are swift, running at 7–9km/h close inshore on springs. Spring tides also cause a swell in the bay for 1½ hours and a half each side of high water, giving uncomfortable conditions with strong southeasterly wind.

A red pillbox fronts a golf course before lines of chalet huts stand between Dunster Beach and the Old Manor. At Dunster itself the Conyger Tower folly is prominent on a hilltop, but the much larger Norman Dunster Castle, Hardy's Stancy Castle (owned by the Luttrell family for 600 years), is also clearly visible. In 1645/6 the Royalists withstood a 6-month siege before surrendering to the Parliamentarians, one shot still being visible in the Yarn Market. The village also has a 13th-century Old Nunnery, tithe barn and dovecot, 17th-century watermill still operating, a mediaeval

The quaint Market House in Watchet, now the museum

Statue of the Ancient Mariner and albatross by the harbour at Watchet

Bristol Channel

Minehead

Dunster

packhorse bridge over the River Avill, a Holy Well and a Butter Cross.

A caravan site precedes Blue Anchor, a village which takes its name from Blue Anchor Bay, in turn reflecting the tenacious blue clay which comes up when vessels weigh anchor in Blue Anchor Road. The B3191 follows the shore for a while.

Reefs now form the shoreline and continue as far as Hinkley Point. At the same time, cliffs begin again, bright red at first but changing to grey with a sharp dividing line, the colours merging between red and grey as far as Stoke Bluff.

Warren Bay has fishing stakes in the form of scaffolding poles driven into the bed and also a swimming pool built in the rocks just before the harbour in **Watchet**. Clapotis occurs off the west wall of the harbour, especially during northerlies. Overlooked by a little red lighthouse on the end of the wall and by a coastguard lookout, the Clipper inn and public toilets, the harbour dries completely at low tide to leave an expanse of mud. This belies its importance as a port which handles timber, wood pulp, steel, fertilizers, animal fodder, cork, wine, cars, farm machinery and chemicals, trading with Portugal, Spain, the Azores and Pakistan. It has its own pilots. The present harbour was built after a storm and particularly high tide in 1900 destroyed the previous one. The port was used to load iron ore from the Brendon Hills to ship to south Wales during the Industrial Revolution. It was also the place where a Royalist ship was captured by a troop of mounted cavalry during the Civil War when caught on a falling tide and the place where Samuel Taylor Coleridge met an old sailor whose tales inspired him to write *The Rime of the Ancient Mariner*. A quaint little museum in the road by the top of the harbour slipway catalogues some of the port's history. It can be reached at low water by landing on the rocky shore to the west of the harbour when conditions permit.

There are more holiday camps both sides of St Audrie's Bay. Between them are the remains of the harbour built by Lord St Audrie in the 19th century to supply his private gasworks with coal from south Wales. Above the stonework is the end of a sunken track which was used by packhorses to carry the coal up from the harbour.

Blue Ben and Quantock's Head form the undramatic northerly extremity of the Quantock Hills as they slope down to the sea.

East Quantoxhead has a Court House owned by the Luttrell family who owned the hamlet since just after the Norman conquest. Less longlived was the Chantry at Kilve, burned down in the 19th century, a fire thought to have been fuelled by the smuggled liquor stored in it. Another old church is St Andrew's at Lilstock.

Two lookout positions top Stoke Bluff, the first being old and brick built while the second is a modern structure looking down over the practice bombing and air firing exercises area, marked by yellow buoys and a yellow target platform 2km off Stoke Bluff. At low tide the end of Stoke Spit dries so the safety margin is reduced for passing craft. A flag is displayed on Stoke Bluff when the range is in use.

Tide streams here run at 4km/h on springs, starting west–southwest at Dover HW –0400 and

east-northeast at Dover HW +0140. The boulder-lined bay beyond has groynes and a breakwater along the back.

The most prominent feature of this coast is the Hinkley Point nuclear power station. The cooling water intake stands offshore, surmounted by a large structure with a crane on top. By way of

Hinkley Point nuclear power station

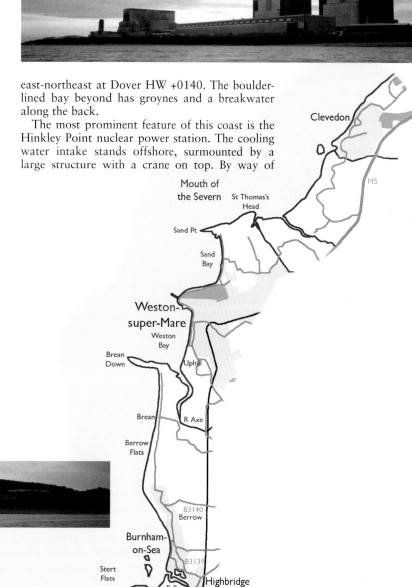

Sharp change in cliff colour from red to grey at the end of the Quantocks

contrast, the outlet water boils up from below the surface and it is easy to paddle through the warm water as it rises at the end of a reef having only a line of widely spaced minor obstacles marking the outfall route. Another submarine forest leads to Stert Flats, one of Europe's outstanding wetlands with 3km of mud at low tide and site of the Bridgwater Bay National Nature Reserve. The 24km² of mudflats, saltings and farmland provide a feeding and roosting ground in autumn and winter and a summer moulting ground for shelducks, wigeon, whitefronted geese and other wildfowl and waders.

Also present between April and December are fishermen from Stolford who use mud horses, load spreading wooden frames, to go out onto the Hinkley Point nuclear power station flats to collect shrimps, prawns and the occasional salmon from their nets.

Stert Flats are the seaward extension of the Somerset Levels, themselves formerly part of the sea with the Quantocks and Mendips as cliffs. Later they became an extensive area of fenland and raised mires although they have mostly been drained. Two of the draining rivers entering here are the Parrett and the Brue, streams running NE and SW at 6km/h on springs on the former with a small bore developing. The sea here becomes noticeably muddy with brown foam as waves break.

Other distinctive landmarks are a set of aerials at **Highbridge** while the silhouette of Glastonbury Tor is visible on the horizon.

Berrow has the ribs of a wrecked wooden ship on the foreshore at the top of the Berrow Flats. While there is a golf course above high water mark, lower down the activities range from horseriding to racing cars and scooters and it must be one of the few beaches with speed cops.

Beyond the holiday camp at Brean is the 13th century St Bridget's church which replaced a 6th-century building believed to have been founded by Irish monks.

The finger of Brean Down with the Welsh coastline visible beyond

The first of three headlands is the 97m high Brean Down, 64ha of limestone noted for the white rock rose and other rare lime-loving plants. It has a tropical bird garden and bird sanctuary established in 1912 with such birds as the skylark, jackdaw, rock pipit, peregrine falcon, gulls and autumn migrants. Such a distinctive outlier to the Mendips was bound to have attracted attention at different times. A field system is believed to be Iron

Brent Knoll overlooks Burnham-on-Sea, seen from Stert Island

Stert Island probably emerged as a sandbank in the 19th century and is now noted for its wildfowl and waders. Landing is only permitted between April and October and a permit is required. The surrounding waters have codling, conger eels, skate and whiting, not to mention waterskiers and sailors from the local sailing club at **Burnham-on-Sea** where the B3139 meets the B3140.

The town dates from Saxon times but didn't really make its name until spa wells of rather dubious quality were sunk. These days a holiday camp, a regatta in August and a carnival in November are greater attractions. In the 19th century the Revd David Davies was given permission by Parliament to build a lighthouse and levy tolls on passing Bridgwater ships. The wooden lighthouse, a square structure on stilts, is no longer used except that the red line down its front lines up with the red line on the present lighthouse behind to indicate the Bridgwater Bar across the Parrett.

Almost on the previously defined line is the flat topped 137m high grassy cone of Brent Knoll. It has an Iron Age fort on the summit and was used for refuge when the Vikings raided in the 8th century.

Age and a Roman temple site was excavated in 1957. A fort was built near the end in 1867 when there was fear of a French invasion, housing 50 men and 7 muzzle loaded cannon. In 1900 the magazine exploded and it was abandoned although it was used by an anti aircraft unit during the second world war.

Fortifications on the end of Brean Down

Overfalls run off to the west of Howe Rock in the direction of Steep Holm while bass, cod, conger eels and pollock inhabit the waters.

The River Axe at the foot of Bleadon Hill ends the Somerset Levels and is the Somerset/North

Somerset border as it enters Weston Bay with currents up to 13km/h. There is a sailing club at Uphill and also a windmill although the prominent building is a grey church.

Weston-super-Mare, on the other hand, has no shortage of prominent buildings, a great arc of elegant white hotels which are dazzling in the afternoon sun. The resort developed from a fishing village in the 18th century and grew rapidly after the railway arrived in 1841. The centrepiece is the 500m long Grand Pier which houses the National Penny in the Slot Machine Museum with an assortment of Victorian and Edwardian devices and a stock of old pennies to operate them. The town, however, is not dated and gliding from Weston Airport is accompanied by hang gliding and sand yachting at the south end of the bay and water skiing. There is a swimming pool on the front and a marine lake next to Knightstone harbour which dries out at low tide. In June there is a fair and a carnival in July.

Worlebury Hill is covered by Weston Woods but has the gash of a disused quarry on the south side and is topped by a red water tower, an aerial and Iron Age fortifications (4ha with ramparts, ditch, multiple defences and storage pits). The end slopes down to Anchor Head. Around the end are the Crescent Hotel, Dauncey's Hotel, Royal Pier Hotel, Ocean Bar, Tea Gardens and Cosa Nostra Restaurant. Crossing to Birnbeck Island is a pier on iron piles allowing access to a small pier used for boat trips in the summer and the lifeboat and inshore lifeboat station on the island, off which currents can exceed 7km/h on springs.

A large rope noose hangs from the pier and assorted scaffolding poles litter the seabed and extend round into Sand Bay. Whoever gave the bay its name had a strange sense of humour as it drains to leave an unbroken sea of deep mud, most of what little sand there is being on the road which runs past the convalescent home, Commodore Inn and holiday camp.

In the same way, Sand Point is of rock. It marks the official start of the Mouth of the River Severn and is the first point from which the Severn bridges can be seen.

Behind Middle Hope Cove at the break in Swallow Cliff are the tower remains of Woodspring Priory, used as a farmhouse for over 400 years. Now surrounded by apple trees, it was founded in 1210 by William de Courtenay, one of the descendants of Thomas Becket's assassins.

A field system is unseen on St Thomas's Head. Instead, buoys warn craft to stay away from MoD tests and a building on the cliffs is fronted by what appears to be an artillery piece facing out to sea.

The Rivers Banwell and Congresbury Yeo flow into Woodspring Bay as levées front the low marshy ground with the Blind Yeo coming in just before Clevedon. Beyond, the M5 can be seen climbing away steeply to the northeast.

Clevedon (Old English for cliff downland) is approached past the striking bulk of Wain's Hill with its fort on top, leading into Church Hill with St Andrew's church on top, to which Lord

Tennyson's *In Memoriam* refers. The town, with its many Georgian, Regency and Victorian buildings, also has links with William Thackeray and Samuel Coleridge. It was developed from a fishing village into a fashionable resort in the 19th century by the Elton family and its features include a marine lake where rowing boats are hired. The slipway used by Clevedon Sailing Club makes a convenient landing point with parking, Fortes' Ice Cream Parlour, Royal Oak, Express Café and Royal Pier Hotel close by.

Weston-super-Mare with the pier to Birnbeck Island on the left and the Grand Pier on the right

Wain's Hill obscures Clevedon as it is approached from the southwest

Distance
From Minehead to Clevedon is 63km
Campsites
Minehead, Watchet, West Quantoxhead, Fiddington, Burnham-on-Sea, Brean, Uphill, Kewstoke, Clevedon
Youth Hostels
Minehead, Quantock Hills, Cheddar
OS 1:50,000 Sheets
171 Cardiff and Newport
181 Minehead and Brendon Hills
182 Weston-super-Mare
Imray Chart
C59 Bristol Channel – Worms Head and Bull Point to Sharpness (1:115,000)
Stanfords Allweather Charts
14 Bristol Channel and Approaches
Admiralty Charts
SC 1152 Bristol Channel – Nash Point to Sand Point (1:50,000)
SC 1160 Plans on the Coast of Somerset and Devon. Minehead (1:20,000). Watchet (1:20,000).
SC 1165 Bristol Channel – Worms Head to Watchet (1:75,000)
SC 1176 Severn Estuary – Steep Holm to Avonmouth (1:40,000). Clevedon to Redcliffe Bay (1:25,000).
SC 1179 Bristol Channel (1:150,000)
Tidal Constants
Minehead: HW Dover –0440, LW Dover –0500
Watchet: HW Dover –0440, LW Dover –0510
Hinkley Point: HW Dover –0420, LW Dover –0450
Burnham: Dover –0420
Weston-super-Mare: HW Dover –0420, LW Dover –0500
Clevedon: Dover –0420
Sea Area
Lundy
Range
Stoke Bluff
Rescue
Inshore lifeboats: Minehead, Burnham-on-Sea, Weston-super-Mare
All weather lifeboats: Barry Dock
Maritime Rescue Centre
Swansea, 01792 366534

6 MOUTH OF THE SEVERN

Mudflats, docks and industry

'We'll cross the Tamar, land to land,
  The Severn is no stay, –
With 'one and all,' and hand in hand,
  And who shall bid us nay?

Robert Stephen Hawker

The Bristol Channel could be a relatively recent phenomenon following a period of trough faulting in Tertiary times and formerly flowed eastwards. The Severn is sometimes referred to as Britain's back door but that must be a matter of one's perspective.

The partially restored pier at Clevedon

Starting from the slipway at Clevedon, the paddler immediately passes under the graceful Victorian pier of 1869. Formerly 230m long, it partly collapsed but restoration was undertaken.

Houses on the B3124 come right to the edge of the cliffs which are well undercut in places with evidence of some repair work. Below the cliffs are rugged blocks of rock onto which it would be difficult to climb. By the secluded Ladye Bay the Lovers' Walk footpath has approached to follow the coast from Marine Parade to Portishead.

Once clear of the town, the blocks of rock gradually decline in size at the foot of Castle Hill which now has a golf course and, from earlier days, the remains of Walton Castle, enclosures, hut circles and field systems.

Farley is marked by the distinctive white tower of Walton Bay Signal Station and by a couple of caravan sites. On the other hand, the tank farm at **Redcliff Bay** is well camouflaged, everything grassed over and all concrete painted dark green. There were three pipelines here running out to offshore oil berths but these have now been abandoned.

The Nautical School overlooks the Black Nore lighthouse at Portishead

A small white lighthouse on stilts at Blacknore fronts **Portishead**'s grand Nautical School, set in a commanding position overlooking the Mouth of the Severn. Above are radio masts on Portishead Down. At the back of Kilkenny Bay a park with cricket ground and golf course sweeps down to the water. Battery Point or Portishead Point is dominated by a small lighthouse with a large bell. The headland was used for defence purposes in both world wars and in 1644 the fort was taken from the Royalists by General Fairfax.

Off the point lies the prominent Denny Island with a spoil dumping ground on the near side. Tides here are the second highest in the world, reaching 13.7m at the spring equinox.

A wooded shoreline leads below the Royal Hotel and past the carcase of a wooden ship to the steamer pier and the entrance to the dock with 1km of quays handling coal, wood pulp, timber and oil. The power station is now closed but there is a phosphorous factory.

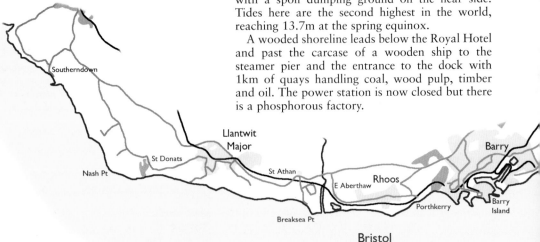

The tide sets towards the bank between Portishead and Avonmouth in a southwesterly direction on the ebb and in a northeasterly direction on the flood north of Avonmouth. The flood also gives a westerly eddy close inshore in Portishead Pool.

The low marshy ground behind King Road is now disappearing although some wildlife survives. A pair of shelduck were fitted with small telemetry boxes to their tails so that their movements around the estuary could be monitored by naturalists.

The Royal Portbury Dock, opened in 1977, has container cranes and an entrance lock which, at 367m long, is the longest in Britain. Beyond it are the silos of a molasses terminal.

Adjacent is the mouth of the River Avon, the North Somerset/Bristol border and the entrance for Bristol and the inland route to London, a route used by long lasting Severn trows with their distinctive D-shaped sterns which used to serve the Bristol Channel ports and go well inland on the canal system. From this seemingly insignificant rivermouth came Cabot in 1497 to explore Canada's east coast and in 1620 the *Mayflower* emerged with the first European settlers for the USA. The oldest ship plying these waters today is the *Waverley*, the world's last seagoing paddle steamer which makes trips to Penarth, Ilfracombe and Minehead in the summer. These days it is quicker by road and vehicles can be seen streaming over the Avonmouth Bridge on the M5 just upstream.

Avonmouth Docks, opened in 1877, have now replaced Bristol as one of Britain's busiest ports, despite the difficult 9km/h tidal flow across the entrance on springs. Royal Edward Dock was

added in 1908 and one of its more notable buildings is Number 1 Granary, built at the time and the first of five. Measuring 67m x 22m x 26m high, it contains 65 silos and was an early reinforced concrete structure designed to the Hennebique system.

For the first time since the Lizard the coastline is now heavily industrial with fuel depot, smelting works, fuel depot, chemical works, fuel depot, trading estate, fuel depot, chemical works, gas works and another chemical works strung out along the A403, in the midst of which is the Bristol/South Gloucestershire border.

Towards the northern end, Gravel Banks dry for up to 2km from the shoreline at low tide. These lead on to the English Stones and the most difficult part of the Severn for large vessels which have to negotiate the Shoots. The spring flow rate here is 15km/h and a southwesterly wind against the ebb can create great difficulties. The extensive area of boulders and weed which form the English Stones can be deceiving. In the Civil War a Royalist ferryman left a party of Roundheads there to drown after telling them they had reached the Welsh shore.

Beneath the northern end of the English Stones runs the Severn Tunnel, the longest in Britain at 7km. Built between 1873 and 1886, it used 76,000,000 bricks and was a notable engineering feat. The tunnel passes through gently dipping Triassic marls and sandstones for 2.4km and is then downthrown against Coal Measures before

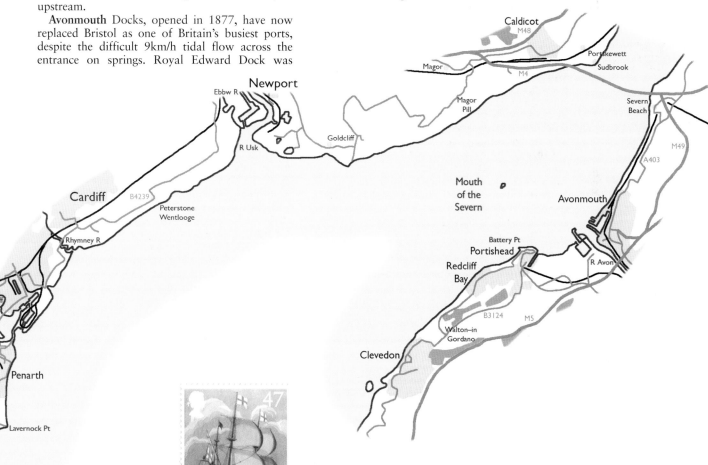

returning to the marls for the last 1.6km at the west end. There were many problems with inflow of water during construction and the flow broke through near the east portal, clay having to be tipped on the bed of the river at low tide to seal the leak. The Great Spring of Sudbrook proved the worst point of leakage. In 1929/30 the tunnel was grouted with 8,000 tonnes of cement, grout appearing on the surface and out of connecting fissures, many of which had obviously developed since the tunnel's construction. 6,000 tonnes of water is pumped from the tunnel each day by the largest pumping station to Whitbread's brewery at Magor and a papermill at Sudbrook, a town built as the tunnel work camp.

Because of the mud below the high water line, landing points are a problem before Penarth.

A sewage works marks Magor Pill, near which are Magor Fens, a wet meadow reserve. As the Gwent levels are drained there are progressively fewer wet areas and lapwings are being driven out as the ground becomes too hard for them to dig in to feed. Monmouthshire gives way to Newport.

The cable stayed Second Severn Crossing with the orginal suspension Severn Bridge beyond

Much the same line is used for the Second Severn Crossing, carrying the M4. This is 5.2km long with a central span of 456m, cable stayed from 148m high H frames, the total length including approach viaducts of 25 and 27 spans built from glued concrete segments.

A less obvious engineering achievement was the Binn Wall which runs northeast from Severn Beach. Dating from the early 17th century or even earlier, it was rebuilt in 1816–18 after storm damage as a 3m–5.2m high earth bank with 1.1m of stone pitching on the seaward side. Following overtopping, it was further widened and raised in 1979.

The railway originally ran to New Passage for the 3km steam ferry crossing to Black Rock. Opened in 1863 as a broad gauge line for passengers only, it reduced the journey between Bristol and Cardiff from 151km to 61km. In the distance are the first Severn Bridge, for which there was an urgent need to reduce the traffic loading, and the Wye Bridge.

Crossing the river from the English county of South Gloucestershire to the Welsh county of Monmouthshire is a difficult move, there being severe turbulence while the tide is running. There is no slack water at the turn of the tide, water running one way on one side while it is running the opposite way on the other side. Even millpond conditions elsewhere can reveal great swirls and areas of standing waves here. Such birds as pigeons are happy to commute across and even butterflies cross.

The railway emerges from its western portal at Sudbrook to meet the Gloucester to Newport line at Severn Tunnel Junction, the railway and two sets of powerlines being the major features on a shore which is generally flat.

From here the Welsh Grounds, sand and mud flats which dry up to 6km from the Welsh coast or most of the way to the English coast, widen out and continue until beyond Newport. Sand is firm on falling tides but can form quicksand on the flood.

The scale of the estuary is brought out by aircraft flying noiselessly down the middle. **Caldicot**, site of a Roman pottery kiln, is most noticeable for its shooting range. The coastguard suggest staying 500m offshore when the red flags are flying.

A levée begins and follows the coast all the way to Cardiff. Generally it is in good repair, faced in stone and topped with a low concrete wave wall.

On a totally different scale, the massive Llanwern steelworks cover an enormous area of ground further inland.

A battery of conical wire salmon traps reach out into the sea at Gold Cliff

Gold Cliff has two large batteries of conical wire salmon baskets reaching out into the current to collect a daily harvest. No longer in use is the other form of battery, a gun emplacement on top of the cliff. Goldcliff Pill leads down from the village of Goldcliff where a mark 700mm above the chancel floor in the church indicates the level of the 1606 flood which drowned 22 people.

A local form of fishing is by using rowing boats to lay out nets suspended from floats that are marked with flags at the free ends, but there is no problem in paddling over the top provided rudders and skegs are retracted.

The Usk and the Ebbw flow together into the Severn at **Newport**, a city marked by its transporter bridge (in the distance) and by the Uskmouth Generating Station (with its three chimneys, one reaching to 133m) by the confluence. Newport has 2 wet docks, several drying berths and a dry-dock. Timber, fruit and other foodstuffs and iron and steel goods including vehicles are imported while coal, vehicles, machinery, tinplate and other iron and steel goods are exported. At the entrance is the East Usk light structure, opposite the disused white West Usk light structure which resembles a large inverted water tower.

The 1606 flood left its mark 2m up the wall of the church at Peterstone Wentlooge on the B4239, typical of the flooding in the area, much of which is below sea level.

The Newport/Cardiff border is crossed. The Rhymney River marks the beginning of **Cardiff**, the Welsh capital, a city founded by the Romans which grew into a 19th-century coal and iron exporting port. The name comes from the Welsh caer, a fort, on the Taff, the dark river. In 1839 the 2nd Marquis of Bute expanded the docks and linked them by rail to the pitheads and ironworks.

The Taff and Ely flow into the Severn to the south of the city via the Cardiff Bay Barrage and a dredged entrance channel, which is an artificial cut through Cefn-y-Wrach, where tidal currents run at 4km/h parallel to the coast on springs. The Cardiff Bay Barrage was bitterly opposed by environmentalists who did not want to lose the mudflats. Butetown became the tough area of Tiger Bay on the east bank of the Taff, although it is now less forbidding and houses the Welsh Industrial and Maritime Museum. With a triple expansion steam engine, beam engine, turbo alternator, early Bristol Channel tug, pilot cutter, canal narrow boat, lifeboat, saddle tank locomotive and collection of wagons and dockside cranes it is worth a visit. The approach along the coast is past steelworks and a grain silo, with a helipad in front, cranes and a tank farm. The city is hidden. There are 3 wet docks, 6 dry-docks, 4 oil terminals and 8km of quays, importing steel products, timber, fruit, vegetables, petroleum and chemical products, refrigerated produce and scrap metal and

was damaged by fire in 1931 and by ship collision in 1947, but it remains a notable example of pier architecture. As often happens with pier towns, **Penarth** retains its gentility despite the new buildings being erected close by and the leisure centre built on columns over the beach, if such a term can be used for a rock pavement littered with debris ranging from car tyres to a water tank, all covered with barnacles. Facing the refurbished promenade and dinghy park are Rabaiottis, the Carlton, Tony's Sea Shore Grill and Pizzeria, the Caprice exclusive seafood restaurant, Chandlers Wine Bar with excellent food, toilets, Seacot Hotel and Il Piccolino. There is a busy sailing area towards the constantly changing Cardiff Grounds bank and the Monkstone Rock light tower. The name Penarth is from the Welsh penngarth, place at the end of the promontory.

A north–south eddy operates close inshore on the last two hours of the flood between Penarth Head and Lavernock Point with turbulence over Ranny Spit.

The Cardiff Bay Barrage and its symbol

exporting coal and coke. There is also equipment to handle bulk cargoes of crushed bones. Behind the Queen Alexandra Dock is the National Assembly of Wales building

Penarth Head beyond the Cardiff/Vale of Glamorgan border, is 65m high, almost vertical and veined with gypsum. Near it is the 200m long pier on cast-iron columns with the Captain's Bar, ice cream parlour and other facilities on concrete columns at the landward end. The century old pier

Lavernock Point with its 15m high cliffs of Sully Beds of green, grey and black Triassic marls is officially the end of the Estuary of the River Severn. On top is a church with a plaque in the wall recalling that the world's first radio message 'Are you ready?' was received here in 1897 from Marconi's transmitter positioned on Flat Holm some 5km away in the Bristol Channel.

Cliffs vary between 15 and 30m in height to Sully Bay with caravan park on top before and

Penarth pier dates from the 19th century

Brean Down, Flat Holm and Steep Holm as seen from Penarth

after Swanbridge. Swanbridge, with the Sully House restaurant and red cliffs topped by pine trees, is an attractive spot after all the low ground as far as Cardiff. Sully Island is connected to the mainland by a rocky ledge during the lower half of the tide, over which strong currents flow when the tide is up. A prehistoric fort on the end of the island was later taken over by the Romans and gold and silver Roman coins have been found here.

Sully Island, connected to the mainland by a causeway at low tide

The white Sully Hospital is prominent on the shore and hides a windmill but not the chemical works of Barry which provide an industrial backdrop.

Barry, reached by the A4055, was developed at the end of the 19th century to outstrip Cardiff with docks and railway being built in 1889. The idea was to cash in on the coal boom but the industry collapsed at the end of the first world war. The docks approach is overlooked by a cast-iron lighthouse with a lifeboat station inside the entrance. The 14m high dock walls were built in the dry with massive limestone blocks while away from the basins the excavation sides were battered back and left unfaced. Dewatering was with a surplus Cornish engine bought after construction of the Severn Tunnel and the cast-iron lock gates were the first ever to be operated with hydraulic rams rather than chains. In addition to the tidal basin there are three wet docks, a dry-dock, roll-on roll-off berths, a timber pond, a general cargo terminal, a bulk loading conveyor, 6km of quays and a helipad. Exports include coke, oil, resin and scrap metals but no longer coal while imports include timber, pit wood, grain, bananas and oil. The Marine Environment Research Council have a base here from which they operate the *Discovery*.

The harbourmouth at Barry Island, overlooked by the massive Butlin's holiday camp.

There is a large Butlin's holiday camp and Barry Island, now joined firmly to the mainland, is given over to holidaymaking from the holiday camp and the cable cars serving it to Caesar's Palace and the large funfair. Barry Harbour is now nearly silted up. The Welsh Barri means stream running from the hill.

Barry has large railway scrapyards which have proved a valuable source of engines for many of Britain's steam railways. A different kind of redundancy comes in the form of four submerged forest beds found at Barry.

Off Barry there is an explosives anchorage. Close inshore there can be small races off Nell's Point and Friar's Point and spring tidal flows of 7–9km/h across the mouth of Barry Harbour which continue to Breaksea Point.

The central feature of the Porthkerry Country Park with its golf course is the magnificent 19th-century viaduct carrying the Bridgend branch of the Barry Railway, just 600m from the end of the main runway of Cardiff Wales Airport. This is a freight railway which has recently been returned to passenger use.

Off **Rhoose** Point pilots for Barry, Cardiff, Avonmouth, Bristol and Gloucester are met. The point has 10m high limestone cliffs with a quarry on top and a cement works, flanked on each side by clifftop caravan sites.

Aberthaw Power Station dominates Breaksea Point

Breaksea Point is totally dominated by Aberthaw power Station, built in the 1960s. The River Thaw is crossed by a small castellated girder bridge which is painted in camouflage colours, a rather pointless exercise as the power station chimneys are clearly visible from the English coast 20km away. There may be overfalls or a race off the point and there is bound to be warm white water pouring from four cooling water discharge points, a dream find spoilt only by the amount of oil going into the sea with the water. A concrete tower off the point has a spherical top to it like a gas tank. Aberthaw Harbour itself has now silted up.

The coast is low until Summerhouse Point although the Breaksea Ledge of limestone boulders and gently shelving rock pavement continues at intervals for a considerable distance. 6km/h spring tides start west between Breaksea Point and Nash Point at HW Dover −0450 and east at HW Dover +0120. The 23km of coast to Porthcawl have become the Glamorgan Heritage Coast and the brown former coastguard lookout on Summerhouse Point has now become the Seawatch

The rock pavement at Llantwit Major.

Centre of the Friends of the Glamorgan Heritage Coast Association. The point also is the site of an old fort and there is an airfield behind at St Athan.

Over the next 8km to Nash Point the cliffs increase in height to 30m, usually with strata in a uniformly horizontal plane although one section behind Stout Bay has clearly dropped, exposing weaker strata to the waves and producing a section with rudimentary caves.

There never was a St Twit. **Llantwit Major** is a degeneration of the Welsh Llanilltud Fawr. St Illtyd came from Brittany in the 5th century and set up a monastery where St David and St Teilo were said to have studied. St Illtyd's church is over 1,000 years old with 8th-century crosses and fine painted wall frescoes.

After another section of cliff, with the beginnings of caves at the back of Tresilian Bay, St Donats is dominated by its Norman castle. It was built about 1300 by the Stradling family who occupied it until 1738 when they were on the wrong side of the political fence. In 1925 it was bought by American newspaper tycoon William Randolph Hearst who used a hammerbeam roof from a Wiltshire priory to repair the mediaeval monastery hall and also brought in a church roof from Lincolnshire for restoration purposes. The castle has a Tudor long gallery and cavalry barracks which were built in the 16th century when a Spanish invasion was feared. In 1962 it became the United World College of the Atlantic, the world's first international sixth form college, with 360 students taken from 60 countries in the interests of promoting international understanding and harmony. It has an inshore rescue boat which patrols 23km of coast.

The undercut cliff forms a jutting prow at Nash Point. To the right lies St Donat's Castle, home of Atlantic College

The undercutting of the cliffs at Nash Point draws attention to their unstable nature. There are two lighthouses on top, the current one built in 1830 and having an output of 144,000 candlepower which can be seen 32km away. There was once a settlement just by the point, an area where much wild cabbage is to be found.

Heavy overfalls occur off Nash Point on the eastgoing stream but the Nash Passage inside Nash Sand avoids the worst of the problem.

From Nash Point to Dunraven Bay the cliffs are bold, 30-60m high, and crumbling badly.

Traeth Mawr (large beach) has 60m cliffs of flat but crumbling rock and there is another old settlement site on the clifftops. Dunraven Castle is built on Trwyn y Witch.

Dunraven Bay at Southerndown has dangerous crumbly limestone cliffs on top of which a 17th-century wrecker family used to fix lanterns to the horns of grazing cattle, murdering crews and looting vessels when they were wrecked. One gang leader was said to have given up the business after recognizing the ring on a severed hand as that belonging to his son who had previously run away to sea.

Today Dunraven Bay is the first reliable landing point with vehicle access on this section of coast and has a pay carpark, toilets, ice cream kiosk and heritage centre.

Summer crowds enjoy Dunraven Bay below the ridge of Trwyn y Witch.

Distance
From Clevedon to Southerndown is 101km
Campsites
Clevedon, Portskewett, Duffryn, Llantwit Major, Porthcawl
Youth Hostels
Cheddar, Bristol, Cardiff
OS 1:50,000 Sheets
170 Vale of Glamorgan
171 Cardiff and Newport
172 Bristol and Bath
Imray Chart
C59 Bristol Channel – Worms Head and Bull Point to Sharpness (1:115,000)
Stanfords Allweather Charts
14 Bristol Channel and Approaches
Admiralty Charts
SC 1152 Bristol Channel – Nash Point to Sand Point (1:50,000)
SC 1165 Bristol Channel – Worms Head to Watchet (1 :75,000)
SC 1166 River Severn – Avonmouth to Sharpness (1:25,000)
SC 1176 Severn Estuary – Steep Holm to Avonmouth (1:40,000). Clevedon to Redcliffe Bay (1:25,000). Newport (1:20,000).
SC 1179 Bristol Channel (1:150,000)
SC 1182 Barry and Cardiff Roads with Approaches (1:25,000). Cardiff Docks (1:15,000). Barry Docks (1:12,500)
1859 Port of Bristol. King Road (1:10,000)
Tidal Constants
Clevedon: HW Dover –0420
Portishead: HW Dover –0400
English and Welsh Grounds: HW Dover –0410, LW Dover –0430
Avonmouth: Dover –0400
Sudbrook: HW Dover –0350, LW Dover –0340
Newport: HW Dover –0420, LW Dover –0410
Cardiff: HW Dover –0420, LW Dover –0440
Barry: HW Dover –0420, LW Dover –0500
Porthcawl: HW Dover –0500, LW Dover –0510
Sea Area
Lundy
Rescue
Inshore lifeboats: Weston-super-Mare, Penarth, Atlantic College, Porthcawl
All weather lifeboats: Barry Dock
Maritime Rescue Centre
Swansea, 01792 366534

7 SWANSEA BAY

Death by blast furnace and the first Area of Outstanding Natural Beauty

What seas did you sail
Old whaler when
On the blubbery waves
Between Frisco and Wales
You were my bosun?

Dylan Thomas

Hotels along the front at Porthcawl overlook the rocky shoreline

After Dunraven Bay, 30 to 60m high limestone cliffs, topped by the B4524, form the coast until the Ogmore River. Southerndown is largely hidden on top but Ogmore-by-Sea is much more conspicuous in front of Ogmore Down, an area of rounded grassland.

Tusker Rock with its tidal pond lies 2km off the coast, exposed at low tide. The spines have caught ships and there are wrecks on the inside of the rock.

The Ogmore River, on the Vale of Glamorgan/Bridgend border, also has hidden danger with difficult currents in the estuary. The Ogmore River leads down from Ogmore Castle, built by William de Londres. An oval ring with a rectangular bailey, it includes a 12th-century hall and chamber, a 13th-century limekiln and a 14th-century courthouse and guards the stepping stone crossing of the river leading to the more recent 15th-century Candleston Castle, a fortified manor house, the remains of which lie at the eastern end of the dunes of Merthyr-mawr Warren. These days the two are separated by a sewage works.

The lighthouse on Porthcawl Point. Coney Beach funfair lies beyond

The far end of the dunes is marked by Black Rocks after which there is an enormous holiday caravan park on the southeastern edge of **Porthcawl**. Porthcawl Point is marked by a white hexagonal lighthouse with a black base and a very strong race off the end of the breakwater which flows at 11km/h on springs. The harbour was built in the 1860s to export coal, but the development of Barry in the 1890s killed the trade and part of the old dock has been filled in and turned into a carpark. Instead, Porthcawl, which takes its name from sea kale, became a holiday resort with sailing and seven sandy beaches. Coney Beach funfair

behind the harbour is one of the largest and best equipped in the country and the town also has a miniature railway. The Pier Hotel is at one end of a front which stretches past a marine pool to the Seabank Hotel.

The low rocky coast continues to Sker Point with low ground inland for a couple of kilometres before the hills rise steeply. Heavy overfalls can develop off Hutchwns Point. In bad weather there are heavy seas breaking over Scarweather Sands, Hugo Bank and Kenfig Patches, all of which dry at low tide.

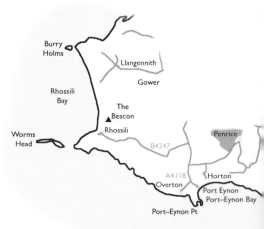

Rest Bay only produces surf with an onshore wind. The rocks are relatively soft, despite being deeply scoured into jagged points and being covered with barnacles. The softness is emphasized by the way a house brick has worn its way down into a deep hole at one point. The bay is overlooked by the Rest building and by a water tower 3km to the northeast.

Sker Point was used by R D Blackmore as the setting for his romantic novel *The Maid of Sker*. Beyond it, Kenfig Sands are only broken by the rocks of Gwely'r Misgl. Behind are Kenfig Burrows, the best dune system in south Wales with Kenfig Pool and a nature reserve which contains the rare fen orchid. In the 12th century a thriving community here was choked by advancing sand dunes. Only the castle ruins remain visible. It took Parliament another five centuries to get round to dissolving the Corporation of Kenfig.

The inconspicuous Afon Cynffig is the Bridgend/Neath Port Talbot border and flows down from an industrial estate and extensive railway yards. On the hillside beyond is Margam Country Park with its magnificent 18th-century orangery, 600 fallow deer, outdoor sculptures, adventure playground, abbey, castle ruins, museum of early Christian memorial stones, Iron Age fort, world's largest maze of 4,000m² and ponds, all in 3.2km² of grounds.

The Abbey Steelworks at Margam

Trees on the hillside to the northwest have been killed by pollution from the Abbey Steel Works with its blast furnaces and cooling tower which occupies Margam Moors at the back of what have now become Margam Burrows and Margam Sands. On the foreshore is a disused metal light tower.

Port Talbot was named in 1836 after the Talbot family who built the town's docks. The new docks handle only iron ore and coal for the British Steel Corporation with three iron ore grabs. Bulk carriers of 100,000 tonnes can be handled although a throughput of 2,500,000 tonnes/year requires the visits of some 120 ships. The walls of large riprap develop near the entrance into concrete sections with large rusting hooks and a coating of slippery green weed which makes it very hard even to swim ashore in an emergency. A groundswell causes a

Crymlyn Burrows are sand dunes which front Crymlyn Bog, Jersey Marine saltings, a golf course, the A483, the Tennant Canal, a tower, an oil refinery and a motor works, although it is oil tanks which are most prominent as the Neath Port Talbot/Swansea border is crossed.

Swansea is overlooked by the radio mast on Kilvey Hill, part of a Pennant sandstone ridge which rises to 200m and below which are the docks with their cranes. Three wet docks handle petroleum products, iron, steel, non-ferrous ores, coal and much general cargo, totalling some 5,000,000 tonnes/year with 6,000 ships visiting and a car ferry service to Ireland. There are also two drydocks. Swansea was a small harbour and fishing village at the mouth of the River Tawe before the Industrial Revolution, but plentiful coal and copper ore deposits led to a smelting works being built in the 18th century and the docks being expanded to handle 10,000 ships per year. Zinc and tinplate works were added in the 19th century and the industrial boom ended after the second world war with much dereliction. Rejuvenation has been taking place with a 30-berth marina with rapid action lock gates and waterfront village, art gallery, Dylan Thomas Theatre, stained glass studio and arts workshop. The Swansea Maritime and Industrial Museum in the Maritime Quarter features a Mumbles tram, fully working Abbey Woollen Mill, lightship *Helwick*, steam tug *Canning*, 500 tonne oak trawler *Katie Anne* and an old Mumbles lifeboat. An extensive leisure centre, opened in 1977, includes an 80m hydroslide and a wave machine.

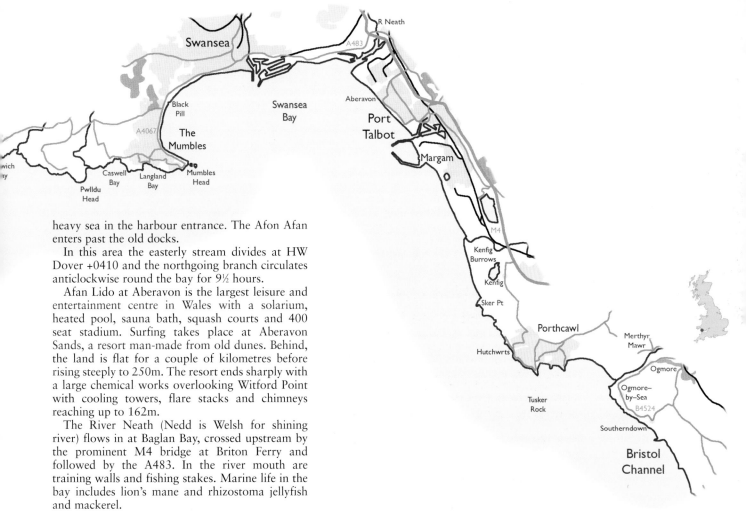

heavy sea in the harbour entrance. The Afon Afan enters past the old docks.

In this area the easterly stream divides at HW Dover +0410 and the northgoing branch circulates anticlockwise round the bay for 9½ hours.

Afan Lido at Aberavon is the largest leisure and entertainment centre in Wales with a solarium, heated pool, sauna bath, squash courts and 400 seat stadium. Surfing takes place at Aberavon Sands, a resort man-made from old dunes. Behind, the land is flat for a couple of kilometres before rising steeply to 250m. The resort ends sharply with a large chemical works overlooking Witford Point with cooling towers, flare stacks and chimneys reaching up to 162m.

The River Neath (Nedd is Welsh for shining river) flows in at Baglan Bay, crossed upstream by the prominent M4 bridge at Briton Ferry and followed by the A483. In the river mouth are training walls and fishing stakes. Marine life in the bay includes lion's mane and rhizostoma jellyfish and mackerel.

The Swansea Bike Path runs along the shore on the 10km line of the railway which used to run round the bay from 1807 to 1960 by the A4067. The first fare-paying passenger carrying railway in the world, it was the Oystermouth Railway until 1879 before becoming the Swansea and Mumbles Railway. Horses were replaced by steam in 1877. In 1889 it was extended to Mumbles Pier and electrified in 1928 with double deck tramcars, the largest in Britain.

The line passes the white tower of Swansea Guildhall and Singleton Park which houses the University College of Swansea with its Taliesin Arts Centre with theatre and Ceri Richards Gallery, miniature golf course and boating lake, all below the prominent hospital tower at Cockett.

The 2.8km² Clyne Valley Country Park includes Clyne Castle and a branch of the Swansea Bike Path on a disused railway line which leads down to Blackspill Station of the Swansea and Mumbles Railway. It also includes the remains of the electrical substation.

The remains of the Norman Oystermouth Castle stand 52m high while Oystermouth church has a stained glass window commemorating the 175th anniversary of the opening of the railway.

has silver bands and Morris dancing in the grounds in the summer. The bay was the site chosen for the first sea pollution health tests in 1988 with 400 swimmers taking part. It has, however, a strong undertow on the ebb and big surf on southerly winds.

Caswell Bay also has surfing and a strong undertow on the ebb. Amenities include beach kiosks, toilets and a telephone. A fort site tops the headland between Caswell Bay and Brandy Cove.

A stream flows down to Pwlldu Bay but then passes under the bank of boulders at the top of the beach. Pwlldu Head with its fort site on top is an overhanging bluff and then broken cliffs continue over 60m high. Breaks include the Bacon Hole and the Minchin Hole Cave which has produced one of the most important finds of southern Britain Ice Age warm fauna.

Penard Pill enters at Threecliff Bay where the Three Cliffs are a triple-pointed outcrop of rock with a natural arch underneath, much used by climbers despite the noise from overhead as it is directly in line with the main runway of Swansea Airport 4km away. In the vicinity are Pennard Burrows around which are to be found the remains of a church and a chapel, a motte, a burial

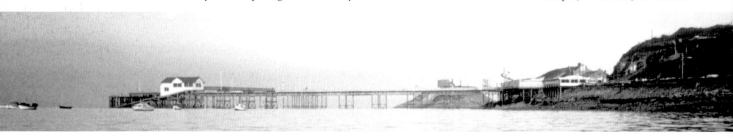

The pier at Mumbles

At the **Mumbles** the amenities include the George, Pilot, Seaview Tandoori Restaurant and Pier Hotel and café at the end of the 270m pier. The land rises to 60m on Mumbles Hill and the village, which was once famous for its oyster stalls, is now better known for its open-topped buses, its water skiing, boardsailing and yachting and as a setting for the TV series *Ennal's Point*.

There are slipways and small craft moorings. Wrecks lie north of Mumbles Head and there is a heavy groundswell with easterly winds, also with westerlies but this reduces with the falling tide. The spring flow northwards in Mumbles Road is only 2km/h, but off Mumbles Head it is up to 7km/h and there may be a race. Middle Head is topped by a 17m high octagonal lighthouse.

Beach House Hotel overlooks Bracelet Bay. The Mixom Sands are treacherous and Limeslade bell tolls when seas are rough, but there is an inside passage. Further out, pilots for Swansea and Neath are picked up from white, red and yellow pilot vessels 3km off.

From Mumbles Head to Pwlldu Head there are broken sloping cliffs 60m high with intermittent bays. Tides run up to 6km/h off the points as far as Port-Eynon Point on spring flows which are parallel to the coast.

This expanse of Carboniferous limestone, folded almost east-west as a plateau, is the Gower, the first Area of Outstanding Natural Beauty, a rural area within easy reach of an industrial area but pleasantly devoid of people. Extensive limestone cliffs provide a most attractive seascape as far as Worms Head and there are signs of three raised beaches.

The first inlet is Langland Bay, overlooked by a golf course and the Langland Castle Hotel which

Threecliffe Bay with the three peaks just visible on the east side of Penard Pill

chamber and Pennard Castle which, along with nearby cliffs, is the only British site of yellow whitlow-grass which flowers in March. Strata are vertical on the sea cliffs but the ridge of Cefn Bryn looks conical from the east end.

Oxwich Bay has an eddy operating and is used for surfing. Rhizostoma jellyfish can be washed up in large numbers. Oxwich Burrows are a dune system with a fort site at the east end and a salt marsh behind where they have dammed the natural drainage flow. Oxwich Ponds are an interesting freshwater site with water lilies and bulrushes. Built on the Millstone Grit behind is Penrice Castle which was deserted in the 16th century by the Mansel family who moved to the more comfortable, but less fortified, Oxwich Castle behind its impressive gateway with the Mansel crest.

The wooded cliffs running out to Oxwich Point are a nature reserve, below which are small craft moorings amongst which mackerel swim. The point has wrecks off it and overfalls at the height of the flow in either direction.

Port Eynon is at the end of the A4118. Port-Eynon Bay again has an eddy and a backing of Millstone Grit.

Port-Eynon Point rises abruptly to 43m with a small stone monument on the point. On its east

The sea serpent profile of Worms Head, seen from the north

side are the remains of the Salt House while the west side contains the Culver Hole, a natural cleft which has been filled in with a stone wall to a height of 18m. Several openings have been left and it is thought to have acted as a mediaeval dovecot.

Helwick Sands run out 11km to West Helwick as a line of shallows. Strong westerly winds against the tide cause heavy seas over the sands although the Helwick Pass gives a route through on the inside.

The 30–60m high limestone cliffs continue nearly vertical to Rhossili at the end of the B4247 and a coastal reef dries up to 200m from them at low water. Caves in the cliffs were used as prehistoric dwellings and Paviland Cave has

Rhossili Bay has land yachting, hang gliding and surfing. It is one of the most spectacular beaches on the Welsh coast and is backed at the south end by the rounded bulk of the Old Red Sandstone ridge of Rhossili Down, rising to 193m at the Beacon and 185m at High Barrow. At the south end there are 30m limestone cliffs while at the north end there are the dunes of Hillend Burrows with their caravan site. History of different ages shows in the ribs of the 19th-century wreck of the *Helvetia* at the south end of the bay, the lonely white house which used to be the rectory and the Sweyne's Howes burial chambers.

Landing is possible at Diles Lake (SS411911) at Llangennith Moors where a path leads through the dunes to a parking area beyond.

Rhossili Down sweeps down to the dunes of Hillend Burrows

The Culver Hole at Port-Eynon Point

produced the skeletons of the earliest prehistoric men discovered from the cold period. A series of forts and a settlement occupy the cliffs as far as Kitchen Corner.

A rather precarious small boat launching point exists immediately north of Tears Point.

Worms Head takes its name from wyrm, the Old English for sea serpent, because of its profile, helped, no doubt, by the blow hole at the nose end. It is two islands connected at low tide by the Devil's Bridge and by a causeway to Rhossili Point. The area is leased to the Countryside Council for Wales as a nature reserve with fine seabird colonies. The 400m wide Worms Sound lies below a further fort site which keeps lookout to the northeast near Rhossili.

Distance
From Southerndown to Llangennith is 66km
Campsites
Porthcawl, Penmaen, Oxwich, Horton, Overton, Rhossili, Hillend
Youth Hostels
Cardiff, Port Eynon
OS 1:50,000 Sheets
159 Swansea and Gower
170 Vale of Glamorgan
Imray Charts
C58 Trevose Head to Bull Point (1:131,300)
C59 Bristol Channel – Worms Head and Bull Point to Sharpness (1:115,000)
C60 Gower Peninsula to Cardigan (1:130,000)
Stanfords Allweather Charts
14 Bristol Channel and Approaches
28 SE Ireland to Wales & Lundy
Admiralty Charts
SC 1076 Linney Head to Oxwich Point (1:75,000)
SC 1161 Swansea Bay (1:25,000)
SC 1165 Bristol Channel – Worms Head to Watchet (1:75,000)
1167 Burry Inlet (1:25,000)
1169 Approaches to Porthcawl (1:25,000)
SC 1179 Bristol Channel (1:150,000)
Tidal Constants
Porthcawl: HW Dover –0500, LW Dover –0510
Port Talbot: HW Dover –0500, LW Dover –0520
Swansea: HW Dover –0450, LW Dover –0500
Mumbles: HW Dover –0450, LW Dover –0440
Burry Port: HW Dover –0500, LW Dover –0450
Sea Area
Lundy
Rescue
Inshore lifeboats: Porthcawl, Port Talbot, Mumbles, Horton and Port Eynon, Burry Port
All weather lifeboats: Barry Dock, Mumbles
Maritime Rescue Centre
Swansea, 01792 366534

8 CARMARTHEN BAY

Some of Britain's best limestone cliff scenery only visible from the water

By mountains where King Arthur dreams,
By Penmaenmawr defiant,
Llaregyb Hill a molehill seems,
A pygmy to a giant.

Dylan Thomas

Carmarthen Bay is subject to heavy seas on westerly winds but tidal flows are generally weak in the bay.

From Llangennith the coast is flanked by the dunes of Llangennith Burrows while the sandy beach contains the ribs of the 19th-century wreck of the *City of Bristol*.

For the top two hours of the tide cycle there is a channel inside Burry Holms, an island bearing the remains of an Iron Age fort and the 6th-century chapel of St Cenydd. Limekiln Point ends in Spaniard Rocks and the name may relate to the fact that 16th-century gold coins from a 17th-century Spanish wreck have been found at nearby Bluepool Corner. This is a magnificent little beach which the pedestrian can only reach with difficulty and which has some interesting lava flows at the back and an angular arch at the west end.

Broughton Burrows at the back of Broughton Bay and Whiteford Burrows at the back of Whiteford Sands are interrupted by Hills Tor which rises to 35m. Whiteford Burrows are a national nature reserve.

Burry Holms with the line of the inshore passage visible despite the fact that the tide has fallen

Bluepool Corner lies beyond this angular arch

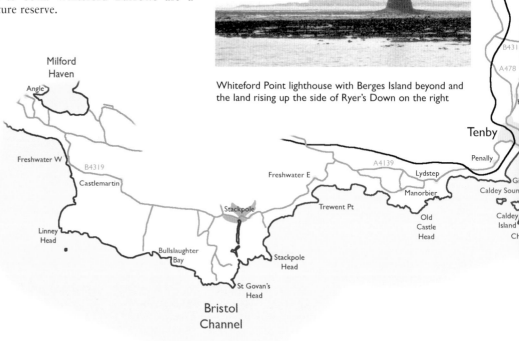

Whiteford Point lighthouse with Berges Island beyond and the land rising up the side of Ryer's Down on the right

The Wind Power
Museum and power
station at Burry
Point. The four
aerogenerators
include the
prototype vertical
axis model (left)

Ryer's Down has buzzard, cuckoo, linnet, meadow pipit, skylark, stonechat, willow warbler and yellowhammer.

A lighthouse on Whiteford Scar off Whiteford Point is the only wave swept cast-iron lighthouse in the British Isles. Built in 1865 to replace an earlier light on timber piles which had been shortlived, it was disused from 1921. Burry Port Yacht Club, however, felt the 19m high structure with its ornate wrought iron balcony could be used to help them and so they installed a solar powered light in 1982 (although this does not work when there is too much guano on the solar panels). Approach to the lighthouse is difficult because it is surrounded by stakes, mussel beds, quicksand and unexploded shells.

The Burry Inlet and Loughor estuary are popular with migratory birds and wildfowl. The River Loughor largely drains out and around the lower end of Burry Pill there are a series of pools formed by deep ribs of sand which are then used by fish waiting for the returning tide. The pill drains Great Pill which, in turn, drains Landimore Marsh below North Hill Tor with its fort. Further east, Llanrhidian Sands front Llanrhidian Marsh, a saltmarsh which protects Weobley Castle from the north. It appears to be in an ideal position but it was attacked, captured and partly destroyed by

which had its ups and downs is the Llanelli and Mynydd Mawr Railway which ran northwards from Llanelli on the line of the former Carmarthenshire Railway to limestone quarries near Castell-y-Graig. The second public railway to be authorized by Act of Parliament, it closed in 1844 as an economic failure, but as demand for anthracite increased it was rebuilt as far as Cross Hands in 1883 and now serves Cynheidre colliery.

Coming along the shore is the main line between Paddington and Fishguard, backed by the A484. Before Pwll is Stradey Park, the bastion of Welsh rugby.

Burry Port hoped to hold a pointer to the future for our energy requirements. To the southeast of the town is the Wind Energy Demonstration Centre with four different wind turbines including the prototype vertical axis turbine inaugurated in 1989. Behind it is a disused coal fired power station with three 91m chimneys.

The harbour is marked by a light in a cupola on the end of the pier. At the far end of the harbour is Pembrey and Burry Port station, one of the last two stations in Britain to stop using cardboard tickets in 1988.

This is an area where the currents flow shallow but very fast as the tide sweeps in and out. Boating

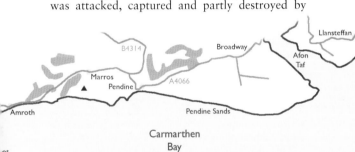

Carmarthen Bay

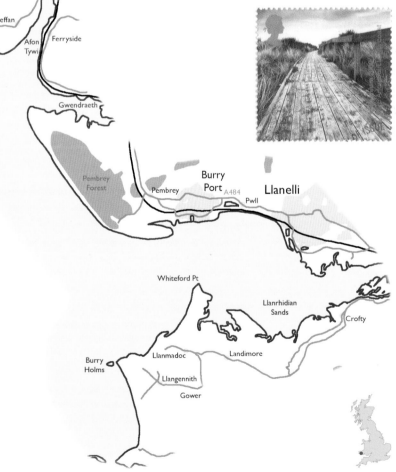

Owain Glyndwr in 1400, being rebuilt later in the century as a fortified manor house. There are the remains of another castle at Landimore, forts at Burry Green and Llanrhidian plus Sampson's Jack and other standing stones around Oldwalls.

Approaching Salthouse Point the River Loughor has a training wall but the flow switches from one side to the other of the wall at a point marked by beacons.

Crofty has a motorcycle trial park, but all is not peaceful on the mudflats either, where cockle fishermen go out with horsedrawn carts to rake up the cockles at low tide. There has been conflict between the fishermen and oystercatchers which have been taking increasing numbers of cockles.

The river forms the county boundary between Swansea and Carmarthenshire. On its north side is **Llanelli**, the gateway to west Wales. It developed on coal and steel and as the centre for the south Wales tinplate industry with the large Trostre tinplate works on the east side of the town. Today the docks are in disrepair and the town relies on automotive products, ophthalmic glass, petrochemicals and inflatable boats. One railway

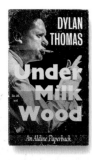

and parascending are local activities and the harbour is used mainly by recreational craft. It was a small fishing harbour before the Industrial Revolution but was developed to serve the coal industry up the Gwendraeth valley. The Burry Port and Gwendraeth Valley Railway was built in 1869 on the line of a former canal to bring high quality anthracite from Cwm-mawr. The construction method meant that there was insufficient headroom to use standard vehicles so special rolling stock and locomotives had to be employed. The pits were worked out after the second world war and the port closed down commercially. The town again came to the forefront of transport when the Burry Inlet was used as the landing site for one of the first transatlantic flying boat flights and was made famous by Emelia Earhart.

Pembrey harbour is no longer used and is silted up but there are plans to turn it into a marina. The church has the graves of several shipwrecked sailors.

The 11km long Cefn Sidan Sands are one of the best beaches in Wales. Backed by 2.2km² of country park, the dunes of Pembrey Burrows, Ashburton golf course, parkland, a visitor centre with natural history exhibition of the fauna and flora of the park, nature trails, picnic sites, hot food kiosk, Lion's Fortress adventure playground, narrow gauge and miniature railways, equestrian course, pitch and putt course, craft displays, sandcastle competitions, treasure hunts, land yachting and a very gently sloping beach, it is one of the most popular attractions in Wales except during bad weather when the sea breaks heavily onto the sands. Beyond Pembrey Forest with its Corsican pines is a disused Battle of Britain fighter airfield which has become the Welsh Motor Sports Centre, Wales' premier motor circuit with autograss, karting, rallycross, motorcycle racing and scrambling. There is a watchtower in the centre and another tower on the beach towards the north end where there are a number of stakes in the water at the edge of the Pembrey bombing range off Tywyn Point and also one or two wrecks around.

The Gwendraeth estuary is quieter with buzzards, curlews, herons, sparrowhawks, waders and wildfowl common, cranes and ospreys not being unknown.

At the head of the estuary is Kidwelly Castle. Built in 1274, it is one of the finest mediaeval castles in southwest Wales, using a walls within walls defensive system and positioned so that it could be supplied by sea if the land approach was cut off. It was begun in the 12th century with a square inner bailey and tall round curtain towers with the gatehouse being rebuilt in the 14th century. It is one of the best preserved castles in Wales and one of a line built right across south Wales which pushed the Welsh speakers northwards away from the fertile coastal area.

The main railway passes again briefly, skirting a caravan site and sweeping up beside the Afon Tywi through Ferryside.

Opposite is Llansteffan Castle, one of the finest ruins in Wales. 12th-century Norman, it had a masonry defence added in the 13th century at the time of the English conquests and the gatehouse came in the late 15th century. Nearby St Anthony's Well was once believed to have healing properties.

Laugharne Castle on the Afon Taf completes the trio of estuary fortifications. Founded in the 12th century by Rhys ap Gruffydd, it was mostly Tudor with a small polygonal bailey and 13th-century round towers. Frequently attacked in the 12th and 13th centuries, it became a mansion in 1782 and was painted by Turner. More famous these days is the boathouse in which Dylan Thomas wrote many of his plays. Laugharne forms much of the basis for Llaregyb in *Under Milk Wood* although he denied that its people became his characters, a matter hotly disputed and leading to much ill feeling. Perhaps it is ironic that Cefn Sidan Sands, within sight of the boathouse, should have nude bathing these days.

Beyond Ginst Point are Laugharne Burrows and Pendine Burrows, sand dunes which form Pendine artillery range which is in use when red flags are flying, usually on weekdays.

Pendine, at the ends of the A4066 and B4314, has a telephone kiosk, the Spring Well, Pendine Sands Restaurant and the Beach Hotel on the end of which is a notice reminding all that it was on Pendine Sands that Sir Malcolm Campbell and Thomas Parry made their attempts on the world land speed record. In 1924 Campbell set a record of 234.22km/h. Three years later Parry was killed when the drive chains of his Leyland Special, *Babs*, broke. The car was buried on the spot but in 1969 it was exhumed and taken to Capel Curig for restoration. The beach was subsequently abandoned when its 10km length became too short for further record attempts.

Antiquities include Castle Lloyd behind Llanmiloe, a settlement on Gilwen Point, chambered cairns on Ragwen Point and Top Castle at the far end of Marros Sands below Marros Beacon.

On the other hand, Amroth Castle is a relatively modern looking building by the Carmarthenshire/Pembrokeshire border. Amroth has a shingle beach where a submerged forest, fossilized acorns and deer antlers are sometimes seen after storms and over which waders wander when conditions are less onerous. There are no obvious signs that Amroth was formerly a mining village where the coalfield reached the coast.

This is the start of the Pembrokeshire Coast National Park, Britain's smallest and only coastal national park, 583km², designated in 1952. This is the sunniest part of Wales but gales blow at least 30 days in the average year. Beyond a line from Amroth to Newgale is sometimes referred to as Little England Beyond Wales, an area where place names, church styles, spoken language and layout of communities are more typically English than the part of Wales lying to the northeast of the line. The phenomenon dates from 1090 when Arnulph of Montgomery brought the Norman feudal system to the southwest extremity of Wales. Mainly an agricultural region, it repeats many of the geological features of the Gower with Mountain Limestone and Old Red Sandstone folded east–west and levelled in wave cut platforms at 60m and 120m. Following its perimeter is the Pembrokeshire Coast Path.

At Coppet Hall Point there is a tunnel for the footpath which used to take the 610mm gauge Saundersfoot Railway running to Wiseman's Bridge. Saundersfoot on the B4316 used to export anthracite around the world, the last of the mines closing in 1945. High up, St Issell's church has a 13th-century Norman tower and cast-iron tomb

Folded strata on the shore at Saundersfoot

monuments and is close to Hean Castle in the woods. The trees are stunted lichen covered oaks, larches, pines and spruces, amongst which are dotted the holes of coal mines. The village is one of the finest yachting centres in Wales. It also has windsurfing and waterskiing with a line of buoys right across the bay from April to October with a 9km/h speed limit inside. The harbour, marked by a stone cupola on the pierhead, has an impounding dock in the corner which holds water to release at low tide to scour out the harbour entrance. South of the village the rocks along the shore are heavily folded. Ivy covered cliffs lead to Monkstone Point which has a passage inside at higher levels of the tide. 50m cliffs continue to Tenby and on top are three masts. Now the Millstone Grit becomes limestone, seals frequent the rocks and razor shells are found on isolated beaches.

periods and remains of early frescoes on three interior walls. Daniel Defoe's *Tour Through Great Britain* of 1724 described Tenby as 'the most agreeable town on all the south coast of Wales, except Pembroke'. Sir William Paxton developed it as a refined watering place in the 18th century and bathing machines were used from 1860. The Georgian and Regency harbourside with its houses of pale grey Mountain Limestone includes the Fourcroft Hotel, Royal Lion Hotel and Belle Vue Hotel above the Burger Bar and Bretts Leisure Snack Bar of more recent vintage.

The harbour is a centre for sailing and windsurfing and is overlooked by TS Tenby. Easton House was built beside the harbour by Paxton in 1811 to house seawater baths and carries a motto in Greek to the effect that 'the sea washes away the ills of man.' More often quoted is

Georgian and Regency houses provide a genteel air around the harbour at Tenby

Tenby, a shortened form of Dinbych-y-Pysgod, Denbigh of the Fish, is at the end of the A478 and claims 4 beaches including North Beach which has the distinctive Goscar Rock on the waterline. Tenby was an important fish market in the Middle Ages and a strategic harbour, one of the most beautiful in Britain. The 700 year old town walls are the most complete in south Wales and took 50 years to build, the Five Arches being the old South Gate. St Mary's Norman church, marked by its spire, dates from the 13th and 15th centuries and is claimed to be the largest in Wales. In season it has music and choral singing. Plays are performed in the De Valence Pavilion. There is a 15th-century Tudor merchant's house with the original scarfed roof trusses surviving, furnishings in different

the = sign, invented by Tudor scientist Robert Recorde who was born in Tenby and who introduced algebra to Britain. There is a 120m pier with an assortment of stakes nearby.

The castle is Norman, hence the access to the sea, and has a museum built into it. Castle Hill also has a prominent monument. In 1644 Cromwell took Tenby under fire from both land and sea.

St Catherine's Island has a fortress built in 1868 to house 11 guns and 60 men to defend Milford Haven from French attack, another of Palmerston's Follies. Recently it has served as a zoo. St Catherine was the patron saint of spinners, spinning being an important industry in mediaeval Tenby.

The gap through to the Burrows is closed at low tide and partly occupied by portable jetties to serve boats taking trippers to Caldey Island and St Margaret's Island. The buildings end beyond the esplanade with Fountains Cafeteria. Behind the Burrows are the Whitland to Pembroke Dock railway and the A4139.

Carmarthen Bay ends at Giltar Point. On the top is an army rifle range which faces south and is frequently in use. Paddlers close in to the foot of the cliffs should suffer little risk of danger from stray bullets. The headland is where Virginia Woolf decided to devote her life to literature while walking in 1904, following the death of her father.

Caldey Sound is an eroded syncline with a 5km/h tide race running through on springs. Eel Spit runs 650m north from Caldey Island and the Fiddlers, a dangerous cross sea, breaks over it when the wind is against the tide.

St Margaret's Island is a nature reserve managed by the West Wales Naturalists' Trust and is connected to Caldey Island by a causeway which dries at low tide. Boats from Tenby and Saundersfoot bring trippers to see the cliffs and birdlife. There are over 300 pairs of cormorants, the largest colony in Wales. Limestone was quarried in the 19th century and an 11th-century watchtower is prominently positioned.

Holes and caves in the mainland cliff face continue towards Proud Giltar. Beyond is Lydstep Haven and its private beach, owned by a caravan site. The haven was the favourite place of Edmund Gosse and was also quite popular with Bishop Gower who was thought to have used the Palace overlooking the haven as a hunting lodge.

Shallows in the centre of Caldey Sound link back to Lydstep Point, a narrow 43m high ridge of vertically bedded limestone, steep to on the east

Caldey Island, St Margaret's Island and Giltar Point in the foreground

Caldey Island is the Old Norse keld ey (spring island), the former Welsh Ynys Pyr. It is an area of blowholes and caves, the largest being the Cathedral Cave with a nave 92m x 12m x 18m high, lit by daylight through hidden crevices. Another cave has produced the bones of mammoth and rhinoceros, showing that the island was formerly part of the mainland. Human occupation dates back to 10,000BC with mid-Stone Age tools from Nanna's Cave, Bronze Age implements and Roman pottery being found. The Ogham Stone is sandstone with a cross, inscription in Latin and Ogham script and possibly some defaced script from earlier times. It may have been from pre-Christian sun worshippers. The 6th-century Celtic missionary Pyro occupied a cell and was succeeded by Samson from Llantwit, later the first Bishop of Dol in Brittany. The inhabitants were probably killed in the 10th century by Danes. A Benedictine settlement was established in the 12th century and the ruins of the priory and the leaning spire of St Illtud's church were probably built in 1113 and occupied until the disillusion of the monasteries in 1534. The white round tower of the monastery with its red roof was built by Anglican Benedictines in 1912 and the island has been inhabited by Cistercian Trappist monks from Chimay in Belgium since 1928. In 1958 it became the Abbey of St Samson. Today they operate a perfumery based on the island's gorse, lavender and other herbs and also make chocolate, cream and yoghurt. All the island's buildings are whitewashed. Women are not allowed to visit the monastery and no-one is allowed to land on the island without the permission of the abbot. In 1983 the monks were disenfranchised because of an administrative error although this does not seem to have stopped their voting in elections. At the beginning of 1989 the local MP made great show of getting their voting rights restored formally.

The lighthouse at Chapel Point on the south side was built in 1828. The cliffs are said to be haunted by the ghost of the pirate Paul Jones although seals and sea birds are more tangible residents.

and south sides with a nature trail on top. There is also an old fort site on the top as the cliffs lead round into Skrinkle Haven and another on Old Castle Head. Tidal streams set towards the head and there can be overfalls and a short broken sea off it. The biggest danger, though, is the Manorbier range on top and lights may be shown when firing is taking place. Heat-seeking missiles have been fired, dropping down off the cliffs to fly some 3–5m above the water before rising to intercept a target released by a model aeroplane. These missiles can home on human body heat and occasionally go out of control. There is supposed to be a safety boat present to keep other craft out of the target area but it has been less than efficient at times, not stopping one group of paddlers until they were leaving the target area. Firing can take place at any time including weekends and public holidays with schedules not being released until the last minute and then being subject to change, the changes sometimes being notified after the firing has taken place. It has been postulated that rolling or capsizing might be the best course of action if one of these missiles is seen approaching but the theory has not been put to the test. There is a helicopter landing area on the west side of the headland.

The cliffs run out to Priest's Nose on top of which is King's Quoit, a 5,000 year old burial chamber, a communal Megalithic tomb with a 5m capstone supported by two upright stones at one end.

Manorbier Bay is backed by the massive bulk of Manorbier Castle, now a ruin. It was Norman, hence the access to the sea, and had an inner irregular bailey from about 1230 with round curtain towers, small square tower, hall and chapel and a gatehouse being added later in the century. Gerald of Wales was born in Manorbier in 1145 and was to call the castle 'the most delectable spot in all Wales'. Related to most of the Welsh princes, he was a brilliant scholar, witty and handsome. He wanted to be Bishop of St David's but Henry II prevented this for fear of a repeat of the Becket incident and a potential insurrection. Gerald debated his case three times with the Pope before resigning himself to studying and writing 17 books, notably *The Journey Through Wales*. He died in obscurity in Lincoln in 1223, never having held any high post.

The cliffs are now of Old Red Sandstone with their biggest break at Freshwater East with its shacks and chalets behind the dunes. Trewent Point provides protection although there is a rip tide at times off the point.

Greenala Point with its fort site is a much less obvious point. The sandstone changes back to limestone on the approach to Stackpole Quay. The harbour with its cluster of cottages was built to load limestone quarried from the cliffs and there is an abundance of fossils and the stump of a syncline on the rocks amongst the tumbling strata.

The expanse of sand backing Barafundle Bay is the last before the limestone assumes its full grandeur from Stackpole Head onwards. The head has a tide race off it but two tall arches through the head avoid the problem above low tide. Columns resemble subterranean cave structures, caves have collapsed into blowholes and scenery is now on a grand scale.

Church Rock, a spire of limestone, guards the entrance to Broad Haven with Stackpole Warren behind. The dunes hold back 30ha of the freshwater Fish Ponds which are crossed by many footbridges and are thick with water lilies in the summer and with wildfowl and waders in the winter. The ponds are one of the places where King Arthur is said to have disposed of Excalibur. In 1976 an 8km^2 estate was given to the nation by Lord Cawdor, a descendant of the 1797 hero. Home Farm, beyond the Fish Ponds, is an arts and adventure centre for the disabled with activities which include canoeing, abseiling, sand yachting and bivouacking.

The coast now becomes part of the Castlemartin artillery ranges, used mostly during office hours like the other ranges although night firing sometimes takes place. There is no safe landing point except at low tide between here and Frainslake Sands so this section of coastline is extremely committing.

St Govan's Head is 37m high, bare and perpendicular with a tide race at the foot. Tidal streams between St Govan's Head and Linney Head start SE one hour before high water at Dover for five hours until the flow reverses. The St Gowan lightvessel is moored 10km south–southwest.

A holy well on the southwest side of the head is now dry but until recently was thought to have eye-healing properties although the area is hardly

Stackpole Head Wales

20p

Arches through the cliffs at Stackpole Head, the start of the serious limestone scenery

St Gowan's chapel nestles halfway down the cliff face near St Govan's Head

ideal for those with poor eyesight. Perhaps only those with good eyesight returned safely. Nearby is St Govan's Chapel, a 13th-century building almost hidden halfway down the cliff face, probably replacing a 5th-century cell built by an early Christian missionary. Arthurian legend rears its head again with the suggestion that the missionary could have been Sir Gawain repenting of his licentiousness after the death of his king. The steps are said never to count the same going down to the

Distinctive stacks stand in Bullslaughter Bay at low water

put the legend to the test by colliding with the rocks.

Huntsman's Leap is a 200m long by 40m deep cleft in the cliffs with a gap variously measured between 2 and 6m. The huntsman concerned is said to have died of fright after looking back at what he had jumped over. Nearby is an armoured car in a delicate pale magenta colour.

Last of the more prominent crags is the Castle which must take its name from the old fort site on its top.

Bullslaughter Bay and Flimston Bay offer potential sandy landing sites at low water, the former with two prominent limestone pinnacles in the middle of the beach. The next kilometre contains some of the best limestone cliff scenery in Britain, an absolute feast of pillars, stacks and caves. Crickmail Down has a double cave like a crypt with a blowhole and the magnificent Green

Mount Sion Down with Linney Head visible in the distance

The true complexity of the Green Bridge of Wales is only seen from the water

chapel as going up but the official figure is 52. The bellcote is empty, the silver bell being claimed to have been stolen by pirates and returned by sea nymphs who hid it in a nearby rock which rings when struck, but this is rather too wild an area to

Bridge of Wales is flanked by the Elegug Stacks (a degeneration of the Welsh heligog, guillemot). There are bird sanctuaries in the area with nesting places for guillemots, fulmars, kittiwakes, razorbills and shags while blackheaded gulls search for eggs.

There was once a fort on top. Now there are the 24km² artillery and bombing ranges on land which once grew the best wheat in the county. There are observation towers, railways and tanks on top and firing covers a distance 20km out to sea. The army allow walkers access from the north to Elegug Stacks and then eastwards when the ranges are not in use but there has been considerable ill feeling that this fantastic coastline is not available at other times and west of Elegug Stacks may not be approached at all on land.

landscaped toilet block with a turf roof and a telephone on the end, the effort being somewhat wasted because of the Milford Haven oil refinery chimneys showing over the hill.

The one remaining seaweed collectors' hut at Freshwater West

Pen-y-Holt Stack breaks the Pen-y-Holt Bay skyline leading to Linney Head

In fact, the scenery is only seen at its best from the sea. However, because it can only be paddled when the army are not present and the public are excluded from the land, it means that the next 6km of cliff-lined coast must be undertaken without anyone else to spot paddlers in trouble if the elements get out of hand on this wild coastline.

The strata become mainly horizontal, the banding heavily marked and running for up to a kilometre at a time without any significant incursions by the sea. This is scenery on a grand scale running out as Pembrokeshire's solid rampart in almost a straight line to Linney Head. The only feature of an individual nature is Pen-y-holt Stack, looking like a slightly irregular column of giant millstones. Across Crow Sound lie the Toes and Crow Rock over which there are overfalls.

Linney Head is perpendicular, 37m high with a flat summit on top of which are a fort site, some rusting tank remains and a large fluorescent orange letter indicating the section of the range. Below is a tide race. The tide stream from Freshwater West is almost continuously SSE.

Wind Bay below Hanging Tar doubtless earns its name. Large waves bounce back off the cliffs and around several large rocks 100–200m away from their base, giving an unstable ride at the best of times. Beyond Blucks Pool the Pole runs out, a ridge of rock for the sea to break over before the sandy but often surf covered Frainslake Sands are reached, running up onto the dunes of Brownslade Burrows, an extension of Linney Burrows, around which tumuli are to be found.

A hut is the only survivor of a dozen built in the 1920s for boiling seaweed collected here. Once a week it was carried in baskets on women's heads to Pembroke station from where it was taken to Swansea for making into laver bread.

Freshwater West is reached after passing the extensive shelves of rock which form Great Furzenip and Little Furzenip, rock over which the sea breaks heavily, not that Freshwater West itself is known for its calmness, having strong offshore currents and undertows. There is a convenient carpark off the B4319 and an immaculately

Distance
From Llangennith to Freshwater West is 97km
Campsites
Hillend, Llangennith, Llanmadoc, Burry Green, Burry Port, Broadway, Llanmiloe, Pendine, Amroth, Pleasant Valley, Saundersfoot, Broadfield, New Hedges, Penally, Manorbier, Freshwater East, St Petrox
Youth Hostels
Port Eynon, Manorbier, Lawrenny, Marloes Sands
OS 1:50,000 Sheets
158 Tenby and Pembroke
159 Swansea and Gower
Imray Charts
C59 Bristol Channel – Worms Head and Bull Point to Sharpness (1:115,000)
C60 Gower Peninsula to Cardigan (1:130,000)
Stanfords Allweather Charts
14 Bristol Channel and Approaches
28 SE Ireland to Wales & Lundy
Admiralty Charts
SC 1076 Linney Head to Oxwich Point (1:75,000)
1167 Burry Inlet (1:25,000)
SC 1179 Bristol Channel (1:150,000)
SC 1478 Saint Govan's Head to Saint David's Head (1:75,000)
1482 Plans on the South and West Coasts of Dyfed. Tenby and Saundersfoot with Approaches (1:25,000)
2878 Approaches to Milford Haven (1:25,000)
Tidal Constants
Burry Port: HW Dover –0500, LW Dover –0450
Ferryside: HW Dover –0500, LW Dover –0350
Tenby: HW Dover –0510, LW Dover –0520
Stackpole Quay: HW Dover –0450, LW Dover –0510
Dale Roads: HW Dover –0500, LW Dover –0510
Sea Area
Lundy
Ranges
Pembury, Pendine, Giltar Point, Manorbier, Castlemartin
Rescue
Inshore lifeboats: Burry Port, Tenby, Angle
All weather lifeboats: Mumbles, Tenby, Angle
Maritime Rescue Centres
Swansea, 01792 366534
Milford Haven, 01646 690909

9 PEMBROKESHIRE

The southwest rampart of Wales

Rown i'n ishte dwe uwchben Pwllderi,
Hen gartre'r eryr a'r arth a'r bwci.
Sda'r dinion taliedd fan co'n y dre
Ddim un llefeleth mor wyllt yw'r lle.
All ffrwlyn y cownter a'r brethin ffansi
Ddim cadw'i drâd uwchben Pwllderi.

Dewi Emrys

Throughout this chapter there are considerable variations in tide stream times for small changes in position although at Freshwater West there is a nearly continuous south southeastgoing stream.

The air reverberates with the noise of tanks firing on Castlemartin artillery range, punctuated at times with machinegun fire or low flying jets. Yet, closer to hand, fulmars, oystercatchers and cormorants ignore the noise and rhizostoma jellyfish float peacefully in the water. Dunes behind the beach cover Stone and Bronze Age sites and the Devil's Quoit is an ancient burial chamber.

Lying between an ancient fort behind West Pickard Bay and a hilltop windmill is the site of the former Angle airfield, opened in 1941 for the RAF, used for a time by the Fleet Air Arm and finally closed in 1945, the buildings now having been mainly cleared.

Sheep Island, with its caves, has a low tide connection to the fort on Studdock Point but Rat Island is usually firmly connected to East Blockhouse Point with its masts. The final island on this corner is Thorn Island, topped by the most dramatic 19th-century fort in the area, now a hotel and restaurant in this commanding position overlooking the entrance to Milford Haven.

Milford Haven is Britain's best harbour and largest port. Founded in 1790, Nelson claimed it was matched only by Trincomalee in Sri Lanka. The name comes from the Norse, milfjord, suggesting its use may be somewhat older. The haven is the mouth of the Daugleddau and is a ria formed by a post-glacial rise in sea level.

There is a confused sea off the entrance. The flood begins HW Dover +0130 and the ebb HW Dover –0430, both at up to 4km/h. There are two deep water channels through the entrance, but

things are rather simpler to the north of Thorn Island where the channels have merged. The fairway lies between Chapel (starboard) and Stack (port) buoys but the dredged channel occupies only the southern half of the marked channel, passing to the south of South Hook south cardinal marker just up the channel. While this means that there is only a narrow channel to cross it is a busy one which allows tankers little room to manoeuvre. With vessels up to the 327,000 tonne *Kuwait Universe* which serves the Esso Marine Terminal, the potential for causing a very expensive accident is not insignificant. Even so, expenditure on developing the haven as an international maritime park has encouraged recreational boat use as the oil companies have withdrawn their involvement. It has hosted the start of the Cutty Sark Tall Ships Race with up to 80 sailing ships.

The juxtaposition of ancient and modern is fascinating. All around are long jetties, tank farms, flare stacks and tankers moored in Sandy Haven and Dale Shelf Anchorages. Five 31m high x 95m diameter concrete tanks, built at South Hook Point in 2005 for liquified natural gas from the Middle East, are probably the largest diameter tanks to have been slipformed in concrete in single operations. Defiantly in the midst of everything is the large 19th-century gun emplacement on Stack Rock and Sandyhaven Pill offers the delights described and painted by Graham Sutherland.

Little and Great Castle Heads both have leading light beacons and ancient fort sites, the beacon built on the fort site in the case of Great Castle Head.

St Ishmael's has a motte which was the site of a Norman castle. Serving the village is Monk Haven which was used in the Middle Ages by pilgrims heading for St David's who preferred to complete the journey on foot rather than risk the sea further west.

In Tudor times Dale at the end of the B4327 was well known as a smuggling centre. It was used by Nicolette Milnes-Walker when she set out from here to become the first woman to sail nonstop to America. Today it is one of the most photographed spots in Wales and is the third sunniest place in Britain, the early spring resulting in profuse flora. Between the white windmill ruins and the yacht moorings are Dale Flats, an area of mud and stones favoured by wildfowl and waders.

Everything from ornithology to diving is featured at Dale Fort Field Centre based on a defence fort of 1856 on Dale Point, near which is an Iron Age fort.

At the other extreme is the futuristic concrete pylon on Watwick Point, a leading light backmarker used in conjunction with more lights on West Blockhouse Point.

The sail training ship *Lord Nelson* is escorted into Milford Haven past Thorn Island

Because Mill Bay is out of sight of potentially hostile castles at Dale and Pembroke it was used as a landing place in 1485 by locally born Henry Tudor and 2,000 men. Henry rallied the loyal Welshmen and a fortnight later beat Richard III at Bosworth and placed himself on the throne as Henry VII, the first member of the present royal family.

The octagonal lighthouse he built on the site of a chapel to St Ann is the oldest one in Britain in continuous use. Today it is joined by a helipad, radio mast and coastguard Maritime Rescue Sub Centre on top of the 40m high red brown plateau of St Ann's Head which forms the end of what is generally a 60m platform.

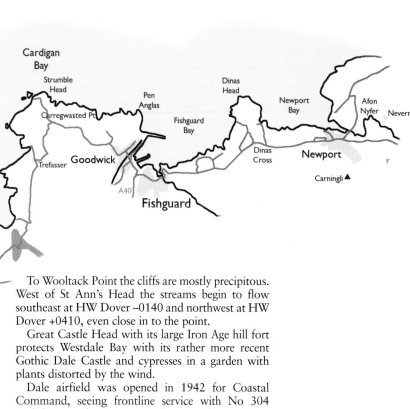

To Wooltack Point the cliffs are mostly precipitous. West of St Ann's Head the streams begin to flow southeast at HW Dover –0140 and northwest at HW Dover +0410, even close in to the point.

Great Castle Head with its large Iron Age hill fort protects Westdale Bay with its rather more recent Gothic Dale Castle and cypresses in a garden with plants distorted by the wind.

Dale airfield was opened in 1942 for Coastal Command, seeing frontline service with No 304 (Polish) Squadron using Wellingtons for maritime patrol until 1943, before being taken over by the Royal Navy until 1947. Many of the buildings were removed by the simple expedient of pushing them over the cliffs.

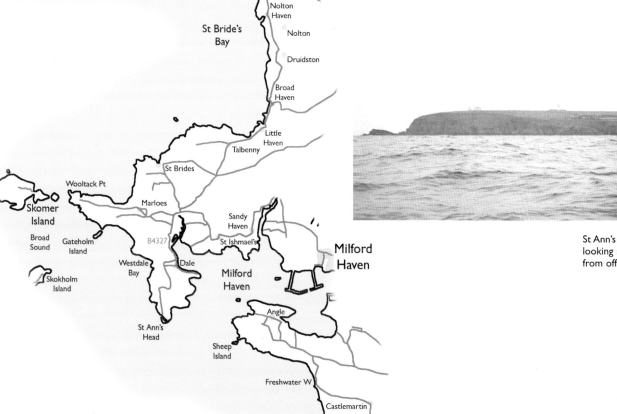

St Ann's Head, looking southwest from off Dale Point

Traeth Marloes, Cymru
Marloes Sands, Wales 68

The sweep of Marloes Sands was used as the setting for filming *The Lion in Winter*. Onshore winds bring good surfing. On top of the cliffs of volcanic Ordovician rocks is Lord Kensington's Deer Park which has never had deer because of the lack of suitable plant cover. The best known wildlife were the leeches in Marloes Mere, collected by villagers in the 18th century to supply London's Harley Street physicians.

Gateholm Island is attached at low water. It has the remains of rectangular huts, which may have been a monastic settlement, and 130 hut circles which date from Roman times. This is raven and chough country, in addition to all the wildlife which emanates from Skokholm.

colonies of guillemots, razorbills and kittiwakes and over 150 species recorded including cormorants, shags and the gannets which can be seen fishing as they spot their prey from on high, dive down and close their wings just before impact with the water, to emerge a few seconds later with their catches. Courses held on the island include bird watching, natural history and the history of the island.

East of Skokholm streams begin east and southeast at HW Dover –0030 and west and northwest at HW Dover –0530 at up to 6km/h.

More Iron Age forts lead along to Wooltack Point but the major feature is Renny Slip with a very large cave.

Jack Sound with Wooltack Point on the right and Midland Isle and Skomer Island on the left

Skokholm takes its name from the Norse, small island in the sound, but the Vikings were not the first here for there are many traces of early and mediaeval settlement. From the 12th century it was managed as a rabbit warren. When initial tests with myxamatosis were carried out on the island they proved unsuccessful because the rabbits here lacked the necessary fleas which are usually present on mainland rabbits. Dale Castle Estate became the owners in 1745 and built a farmhouse and limekiln in 1760. The lighthouse was built in 1916, now accompanied by a helicopter landing site. Resident from 1927 to 1933 was R M Lockley who wrote *I Know an Island*, popularized the seals and in 1928 recovered coal, fittings and the figurehead from the wrecked *Alice Williams*, the latter being attached by him to the rockface in South Haven.

The 97ha island has a flat top and 50m high cliffs of dark red sandstone. In 1939 it became the site of the first bird observatory in the British Isles and is now manned by the West Wales Naturalists' Trust. Permission to land needs to be arranged with the national park office. This nature reserve boasts 35,000 pairs of Manx shearwaters, 5,000 pairs of puffins, 5,000 pairs of storm petrels,

Jack Sound separates Midland Isle and Skomer Island from the mainland and runs at 13km/h on springs, starting south at HW Dover –0300 and north at HW Dover +0300. There can be overfalls from the Bench to Tusker Rock with a strong eddy round Tusker Rock and a considerable overfall. 27km of coastline around the island and the Marloes peninsula became Wales' first Maritime Nature Reserve, only the second in Britain.

Wooltack Point with its cliffs of volcanic Ordovician rocks separates Broad Sound from St Bride's Bay. In the bay there are weak currents with an eddy parallel to the main north–south stream.

Martin's Haven forms a useful inlet with a route up a steep path to a carpark. It is an embarkation point for boats going to Skomer. Rusting winding gear and an igneous intrusion of basalt lavas with quartzite and felspar overlook the little inlet which can be a favourite spot for divers. Nearby is a Celtic cross which was found in the base of a Victorian wall when it was being demolished.

On the Nab Head are a fort site and Kensington Hospital, the latter built in 1800 and formerly the stately home of Lord Kensington who owned St

Looking along the Gribin past the Solva inlet towards Black Scar, Green Scar and the Mare

Brides, a village which seems far too small to have given its name to the bay. The village was named after St Brigid of Kildare but there was also much influence from Brigid, the most important Celtic goddess, mistress of fire and patron of poets, whose father, Dagla, was Lord of Knowledge and greatest of the native Irish gods. The churchyard contains early Christian tombs set in the cliffs. The cleft of St Brides Haven has rusty iron mooring rings and ruined limekilns.

Stack Rocks form a conspicuous feature off Mill Haven

Inland from Stack Rocks was sited Talbenny airfield. No 311 (Czechoslovak) Squadron flew Wellingtons on maritime patrols in 1942/3, the station closing in 1946. For most of this period there was a substantial RAF radar site at Ripperston. Goultrop Roads flow west from HW Dover −0500 and east for a much shorter period from HW Dover +0200. Overlooking them are steep hazel and oak woods, covered with lichens and gnarled by the wind.

Little Haven is a fishing village with moorings and an inshore rescue boat in the summer. It was built in the 1850s as a coal port and the whole coastline from here to Newgale is the result of the sea having cut back into coal measures.

Broad Haven is a surfing venue with a café. The Sleek Stone area has great rolled sheets of lava lying right next to horizontal layers which have been cut away to form arches.

Surfing is also possible at Druidston Haven, named after a Norman, Drue. Traces of coal seams and workings are visible but nothing compared with Nolton Haven which only worked between April and October each year as Lloyds refused to insure boats using the quay in the winter. The anthracite, worked from the 15th century, was of high quality, burning without a flame, but was only to be found in thin, fractured beds. There is still believed to be 230,000,000 tonnes in unworked reserves. The chimneys and old shafts form the western end of the Pembrokeshire coalfield. The lane north used to be a tramway for coal tubs and the Counting House was used to check loads. The Trefân mine was closed in 1905.

Newgale Sands are another surfing beach. A parking area here has toilets and the Pebbles restaurant while the Duke of Edinburgh is an alternative source of sustenance nearer to Newgale itself. Newgale on the A487 was another coal exporting village. Its shingle storm beach is prominent and sometimes broken tree stumps from 7,000 years ago are revealed. The bay here is used for research and oceanographic instruments, along with sea bass, may be found off the beach.

Beyond the caravans Roch Castle may be seen which guarded the northwest end of the Landsker line, beyond which the native Welsh were left to their own devices. The line itself was marked by Brandy Brook but the castle was built on rock to reduce the risk of snakes, the Norman lord whose castle it was having been told by a soothsayer that he would be killed by a snake. In fact, he died after being bitten by an adder brought in with a bundle of firewood.

The next peninsula is formed of Precambrian and Cambrian igneous and sedimentary rocks in various colours, resulting in a range of pebble colours.

Brawdy Airfield to the north of Roch and Newgale is no longer used. A motte at Pointz Castle is followed westwards by a burial chamber and settlement, further signs of ancient settlement along the coast.

Solva is a magnificent spot, a little village hidden by the Gribin from passing pirates and raiders at the head of a ria drowned after the last Ice Age. Today there are yacht moorings but in the 19th

Contrasting geological features at the Sleek Stone, Broad Haven

Exploring caves at the entrance to Solva

An unusual mill tower is the central feature of Twr-y-Felin outdoor centre in St David's

century there were 30 boats supplying the village's four limekilns, one of which is still in perfect condition. Wrecking was an alternative form of employment but as recently as 1979 the villagers collected thousands of planks of Malaysian mahogany valued at £200 each from a wreck. A converted chapel in the village houses a butterfly farm which also has locusts, leafcutting ants and tarantulas. On the water, dolphin spotting is a popular local pastime.

Heading out of the sheltered natural harbour at Solva

Off the entrance are the Mare, Black Scar and 33m high Green Scar, a prominent group of islets which give an indication of conditions in the heavy southwesterly swell following westerly storms.

A fort on the coast has been sheared by a landslip. St David's airfield was opened in 1943 as a Coastal Command station and used by the Royal Navy until 1960, proposed as a high powered radar base with 35 masts up to 40m high.

St David's is the smallest city in Britain. St David was the son of St Non and Sant, Prince of

Amongst stacks along the northern edge of St Brides Bay

Ceredigion, and was born about 520, becoming the patron saint of Wales. His 6th-century monastery was hidden from the view of Norse pirates in the Vale of the Roses. Boia, the local chieftain, tried to get rid of the monastery by getting his wife and maids to go around undressed and use lewd language in front of the monks. All except David fell for this until Boia and his camp were destroyed by a thunderbolt. The monastery was sacked four times by the Vikings between 982 and 989 with Bishop Abraham being killed in 1080 and a further attack in 1091. It became the site of the cathedral, built of purple sandstone from Caerfai quarry in the 11th century. The tower collapsed in 1220 and the foundations were badly shaken in an earthquake of 1248. More recently the cathedral was wired up to study the sonic boom effects during Concorde's early test flights.

Inside, the nave slopes up steeply to the high altar, behind which is a casket said to hold the bones of St David and St Justinian. The choirstall misericords are noted for their witty carvings. In the Middle Ages two pilgrimages to St David's scored equal points to one to Rome and there were calls for the bishop to be made a full archbishop, independent of Canterbury. The Queen has a reserved seat in the cathedral and first distributed Maundy Money in Wales from here.

Other architectural highlights include the fine fan vaulting in the roof of Holy Trinity Chapel and the Bishop's Palace of 1340, dedicated to St Non, which included a tall arcaded parapet which served no purpose but gave an Italian style liked by the bishop, this feature being destroyed two centuries later by Bishop Barlow.

To sound a different note, St David's has a Bach Festival.

Below St David's are a series of bays. Caer Bwdy Bay has a notable 60m long cylinder of rolled Cambrian sandstone. Above Caerfai Bay is a park of caravans in tasteful environmental green. There is also a sea life centre. Between the two is a former windmill tower. By St Non's Bay is a well, said to have mystic powers, and a modern statue of St Non. This is the point where St David is believed to have been born in a great gale so it is to be hoped that there was rather more shelter then than now, just a rectangle of fencing on a bare hillside.

Caves and a cliff used by climbers lead to Porth Clais, used now for diving and moorings. Formerly a thriving coal importing harbour, it is protected by a wall probably dating from the Middle Ages. Limekilns have been restored. It was here that St David was said to have been baptized. Nobody had been organized to undertake the task but, right on cue, bishop of Munster, Elvis, landed in Preseli at this point.

Westgoing eddies on the ebb lead from Carreg Fran to the entrance to Ramsey Sound, one of the

most technical pieces of water in Wales. The west side of the sound is edged by Ramsey Island, Ynys Cantwr (Chanter's island), Ynys Bery (falcon's isle, formerly Margery Island) and others while the Bishops and Clerks form a line of smaller rocks much further out. Streams start south at HW Dover −0200 and north at HW Dover +0400 at 11km/h on springs. Eddies form on both sides of the sound and there are overfalls over the Horse rock. The major feature, though, is the Bitches on the west side, a ledge which produces heavy white water and which hosted the first kayak freestyle world championships. The St David's lifeboat was lost here in 1910 with 3 lifeboatmen drowned while saving 12 people from the ketch *Democrat*.

Ramsey Island is either Hrafn-ey (Hrafn's island) or Hranfsaa (raven's island) in old Norse or Ynys Dewi (St David's island) in Welsh. It covers 263ha and the higher of its two peaks, Carnllundain, rises to 136m. St Devynog or St Devanus is believed to have set up a monastery in the 2nd century and there are said to be 20,000 saints buried here, possibly monks from the monastery although the Celtic tradition desired people to be buried as far west as possible, making the island a prime cemetery. In the 6th century it became a holy place with pilgrimages being made by St David, St Patrick and St Justinian amongst others. St Justinian, a Breton saint, is said to have set up a cell and to have taken an axe to a land bridge across the Bitches to the mainland to gain solitude. The discipline proved too rigorous for his followers who cut off his head, a well with healing water forming at that place.

The island was owned by bishops of St David's from early times. Since the 12th century it has been let to farmers. Rabbits, considered a delicacy, were introduced in the 13th century but they ruined the pastures. A farmhouse was built in the 18th century and a cornmill with a 4.3m wheel added in the 1890s.

In 1961 the royal family came ashore from the Royal Yacht *Britannia* for a picnic, the first time the Prince of Wales had set foot on Welsh soil. Today it is a seabird sanctuary with thousands of razorbills, guillemots, kittiwakes and fulmars although puffin and shearwater colonies have been decimated by rats. Grey seals breed in the caves and at the foot of the cliffs. Deer and goats are kept.

Rocks on the mainland here are 600,000,000 years old, some of the oldest in Britain. Boat trips from Porthstinian go round Ramsey Island. There is a prominent lifeboat slipway and a conspicuous pink tower above the cliffs at St Justinian. There is also a roofless chapel to the saint who walked across from the island carrying his head in his hands after being executed.

St Patrick was from Whitesands Bay, had a vision of converting Ireland to Christianity and sailed from here to undertake his calling. A tablet marks the site of his chapel. The bay at the end of the B4583 has one of the finest surfing beaches in Wales. Also used for windsurfing, it has a storm

beach and a wreck. There is a northgoing eddy on the southgoing stream and small overfalls in the mouth of the bay.

A more significant tide-race runs off St David's Head, a 30m high igneous cliff topped with an Iron Age fort with earth banks, burial chamber, settlement and field system, described by Graham Sutherland. The cliffs are of particular interest for wildlife and the waters have bass, pollock and tope. This is one side of the narrowest point of St George's Channel.

From St David's Head to Penberry the cliffs are vertical. Streams in Cardigan Bay run parallel to the coast above 2km offshore, starting northeast at HW Dover −0530 and southwest at HW Dover +0100 at 4km/h although closer inshore local conditions may vary from this. All headlands are igneous intrusions with bays cut into the broken Ordovician shales between them. The conical hills of Penberry and 181m high Carn Llidi are residuals rising from the plateau. Beyond them, Dowrog and Tretio Commons are fine examples of lowland heath.

The paddler is never far from a fort or a castell coch but very much closer are the fulmars which glide past, just clearing the water, sweeping in close to the boat.

The southern end of Ramsey Sound with Meini Duon, Ynys Bery, Ynys Cantwr and part of Ramsey Island beyond Pen Dal-aderyn

Jumping into the Blue Lagoon

Abereiddy was a thriving slate centre. When it closed, fishermen blasted a channel from the sea to the slate quarry which was flooded to form the Blue Lagoon, a new harbour. The beach is of fine grey slate particles.

Porthgain, located with a small daymark after a series of caves, was another slate quarrying centre with a railway from the quarries to Porthgain, crushers, bins, chutes and buildings which were last used in 1931. Slates, bricks and crushed granite were produced for use throughout Britain. The sheltered harbour, slipway and moorings are still in use and facilities include the Sloop Inn, bar and restaurant and toilet. Again, the small beach is of black sand.

Trefin had an episcopal palace but it is the ruined mill overlooking the beach at Aberfelin, closed in 1918, which is remembered in the poem by William Crwys Williams. Here the sea is only 3km from the source of the Western Cleddau which flows into Milford Haven.

Carreg Sampson is the best of the area's cromlechau, a capstone lifted onto 7 uprights about 3000BC by, it is said, Sampson's little finger. The Grave of Sampson's Little Finger is on Ynys y Castell, the other side of the formerly busy slate port of Abercastle.

Aber Mawr was the site of a pioneer submarine telegraph office which was the first source to receive news of the Casement scandal. The castell coch is a spectacular fort and there are also the inevitable old quay and limekiln.

Dewi Emrys wrote a poem celebrating Pwll Deri and the compliment has been returned by a memorial at Pwll Deri to Dewi Emrys. Less well remembered is the farm at Trefasser which was said to have been the birthplace of Bishop Asser, friend and biographer of Alfred the Great.

invasion of Ireland by 15,000 troops and to take and burn Liverpool. It was a tactical disaster. They intended to live off the land but the French confiscated a cargo of wine from a wrecked Portuguese merchantman and got drunk. When the French saw Jemima Nicholas and the other local women approaching in their tall black hats and red petticoats they thought military reinforcements had arrived and forced Tate to surrender on Goodwick beach. Lord Cawdor, who had nearly walked into an ambush, became a hero and the Pembroke Yeomanry, now part of the Royal Corps of Transport (Volunteers), are the only remaining army unit to have won battle honours on British soil as a result. Eight Frenchmen were drowned, twelve were killed and one Welshwoman was shot accidentally while a pistol was being loaded in a public house.

There is an inconspicuous memorial on the point but this is confusing as the OS map marks this but not the much more obvious obelisk on Pen Anglas.

Carreg Onnen, Ynys Meicel with its light and the footbridge across to Strumble Head

Strumble Head is one of the most conspicuous headlands in Wales with a lighthouse on Ynys Meicel and accompanied by Carreg Onnen. Approach to the lighthouse is down steps on the cliff face and across a footbridge, not unlike that at South Stack. The steep cliffs include pillow lavas. It is a landmark on one of the transatlantic air routes, hence the frequent vapour trails on clear days. An old War Department lookout is now a bird watching post, one of the best British sites for watching migrating birds. Many rare species are spotted on their transatlantic flight path and it is also a convenient point to watch for dolphins, porpoises and basking sharks.

From Strumble Head to Pen Anglas there is a westerly eddy during part of the eastgoing stream. 2km north of Strumble Head there can be an 11km/h flow.

Carregwasted Point was the scene of the last invasion of mainland Britain. 1,400 French soldiers and released convicts landed in 1797 under the Irish American 'Colonel' Tate, planning to start a peasants' uprising to direct attention from an

400m off Pen Anglas the stream starts east at HW Dover +0530 at 4km/h and west at HW Dover −0340 at 5km/h, meaning east for 3¼ hours and west for 9¼ hours. A race runs 800m north from Pen Anglas. North northwesterly winds cause a bad swell in Fishguard Bay. Flows start east at HW Dover +0440 at 2km/h and west at HW Dover −0210 at 3km/h. On the south side outside the harbour there is little eastgoing stream but a very weak westgoing stream from HW Dover −0400 to HW Dover +0500.

Fishguard Harbour at **Goodwick** is overlooked by an aerial and guarded by north and east breakwaters with lighthouses. It was built as the terminus of the Great Western Railway line from London and as a transatlantic liner terminal with vast new port installations, opened in 1906. The Fishguard Bay Hotel was built to house America bound passengers and Cunard liners including the *Mauretania* docked here until 1914 when the war curtailed plans and the trade was switched to Southampton. Today it is the ferry terminus for Rosslare and the Cunard Café still sells fish and

chips. Foodstuffs and dairy produce are imported with machinery and general merchandise going to Rosslare and Wexford. There is also container traffic. There are yacht moorings.

The town of **Fishguard** where the A40 ends at the A487 is built on the Afon Gwaun. Castle Point has an old fort and three 18th-century cannons. In the 1960s the Lower Town was used for filming *Under Milk Wood*. Arts associations continue with the Fishguard Annual Music Festival and the town has hosted the Royal National Eisteddfod on occasions.

Behind Dinas Cross is 305m Garn Fawr with its distinctive rock on the summit but this is probably less striking than the wedge shape of Dinas Island, now connected to the mainland by a low swamp in a former glacial meltwater channel. Pwllgwaelod, at the end of the channel, has many smugglers' tales and has been used for many film settings.

Dinas Island has an earthwork near the bottom and a lookout hut on the summit of the folded Dinas Head, from where it is possible to see the Wicklow mountains on a clear day. There is a nature trail but perhaps nothing to match the guillemots, razorbills and greater blackbacked gulls of Needle Rock. Sea trout and bass are the local fish.

A strong race runs 400m north of Dinas Head. From here to the Afon Nyfer is a slate coast. The far end of the meltwater channel is at Cwm-yr-Eglwys, an attractive little hamlet of colourwashed cottages. The church in the name, St Brynach's, was reduced to a bellcote in a storm of 1859 which wrecked over 100 ships. This was another smugglers' cove.

Newport Bay has weak tidal streams but with onshore winds a considerable sea sets into the bay. Cat Rock has veins of white quartz through it but the prevailing colour is black on Newport Sands where there is parking near a golf course at Cesig duon and vehicles can be driven onto the beach for loading.

Newport was founded in 1195 after William de Turribus was driven out of Nevern by the Welsh. Court Leets still take place, as does the Beating the Bounds ceremony. The Norman lord gave burgesses the right to appoint the mayor in consultation with the Lord or Lady Marcher. Newport Castle has become a private house and riding school but the old quay and warehouses remain and Carreg Coetan, a Neolithic burial chamber, is to be found at the head of the estuary. Rising over all is 347m high Mynydd Carningli at the east end of the Carningli Common ridge.

Distance
From Freshwater West to Cerig duon is 100km
Campsites
St Petrox, Angle, Marloes, Little Haven, Broad Haven, Nolton Cross, Newgale, Solva, Caerfai, Porthclais, St Justinian, Porth-mawr, Abereiddy, Trefin, Fishguard, Penrhyn, Newport
Youth Hostels
Marloes Sands, Broad Haven, Penycwm, St David's, Trefin, Pwll Deri, Trefdraeth
OS 1:50,000 Sheets
145 Cardigan and Mynedd Preseli
157 St David's and Haverfordwest
158 Tenby and Pembroke
Imray Charts
C13 River Cleddau – Milford Haven to Haverfordwest. Approaches to Milford Haven (1:25,000)
C51 Cardigan Bay – Milford Haven to Tremadoc Bay (1:140,800)
C60 Gower Peninsula to Cardigan (1:130,000)
Stanfords Allweather Charts
28 SE Ireland to Wales & Lundy
Admiralty Charts
SC 1076 Linney Head to Oxwich Point (1:75,000)
SC 1478 Saint Govan's Head to Saint David's Head (1:75,000)
1482 Plans on the South and West Coasts of Dyfed. Jack Sound (1:12,500). Ramsey Sound with the Bishops and Clerks (1:25,000)
SC 1484 Plans in Cardigan Bay. Fishguard Bay (1:15,000). Newport Bay (1:37,500)
SC 1973 Cardigan Bay – Southern Part (1:75,000)
2878 Approaches to Milford Haven (1:25,000)
3273 Entrance to Milford Haven (1:12,500)
3274 Milford Haven – Saint Ann's Head to Newton Noyes Pier (1:12,500)
Tidal Constants
Dale Roads: HW Dover –0500, LW Dover –0510
Milford Haven: Dover –0500
Skomer Island: Dover –0500
Martin's Haven: HW Dover –0450, LW Dover –0440
Little Haven: HW Dover –0450, LW Dover –0440
Solva: HW Dover –0450, LW Dover –0440
Ramsey Sound: Dover –0430
Porthgain: Dover –0410
Fishguard: HW Dover –0350, LW Dover –0340
Sea Areas
Lundy, Irish Sea
Rescue
Inshore lifeboats: Angle, Little and Broad Haven, St David's, Fishguard
All weather lifeboats: Angle, St David's, Fishguard
Maritime Rescue Centre
Milford Haven, 01646 690909

The southern edge of Newport Bay running out to Dinas Head

10 SOUTH CARDIGAN BAY

Past remote slate cliffs

By Carreg Cennen, King of time,
Our Heron Head is only
A bit of stone with seaweed spread
Where gulls come to be lonely.

Dylan Thomas

Port **Cardigan** is the estuary of the Afon Teifi with the B4546 ending on one side and the B4548 on the other. High breaking seas may occur over the bar even in light winds, especially with the ebbing tide at full strength on springs. The southwest side of the estuary has a slip area between Penrhyn

Magnificent folding on the cliffs at Pen yr Afr

From Newport to Cemaes Head there are high slate cliffs with many slips, the haunt of every kind of seabird from oystercatcher through razorbill to cormorant. It is a rocky coast, not dramatic but off the beaten track as far as the general public are concerned. The first real inlet is Ceibwr Bay, site of an earlier settlement and a spot where coasters

Castle and the inshore rescue boat station. Beyond this are Poppit Sands, an area of dunes, gorse and drainage channels edged with mats of sea purslane. This is the end of the Pembrokeshire Coast National Park. The Pembrokeshire Coast Path also leaves, heading up the estuary to St Dogmaels and Pembrokeshire gives way to Ceredigion.

More folding leads to the cave at the end of Cemaes Head

used to land cargoes. The best of the rock formations are between Pen yr Afr and Cemaes Head where alternating Ordovician grits and shales have been subjected to geological pressures to produce some dramatic folding, finishing at Cemaes Head with a classic rounded cave roofed with thick rock strata. Cemaes Head rises steeply to 189m and has a covering of bracken.

Gwbert, on the east side of the estuary, takes its name from a wandering saint who probably landed here. There is a prominent white hotel near Craig y Gwbert.

Cardigan Island is 52m high, 16ha of Ordovician sedimentary rock, grassy and thick

with bluebells in the spring, with traces of field divisions and a small pond. In 1934 the *SS Hereford* was wrecked off the island and was thought to have introduced the colony of over a thousand brown rats which finished off the former puffin colony. The island became a nature reserve

in 1944 and has been owned by the West Wales Naturalists Trust since 1963. The rats were poisoned off in 1968 with 75kg of rat poison. To attract puffins, 200 concrete puffins were made and painted by schoolchildren to act as decoys and a number of starter homes for prospective puffins were dug in the ground. Attempts have also been made to attract Manx shearwaters by playing electronic voice noises. There are 900 pairs of nesting herring gulls, fulmars and many other seabirds. In addition, it is a seal breeding ground and the WWNT have introduced a semi-wild flock of Soay sheep. A permit is needed for landing.

Mwnt is located by the sharp pyramidal hill of Foel y Mwnt. Flemish raiders were defeated in battle here in 1155. This was celebrated in the festival of the Bloody Sunday of Mwnt every year until the 18th century. Ploughs still occasionally

turn up human bones and rusty weapons. Evasion was generally considered a better policy than confrontation and the Church of the Holy Cross of 1400, on the route from Bardsey Island to St David's, was built in a hollow on the site of an earlier church, hidden from the view of raiders. It is whitewashed and constructed with a herringbone pattern used in Cornwall and

Cardigan Island as it appears when seen across Port Cardigan, the estuary of the Teifi

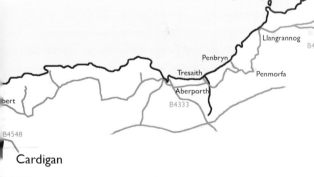

The plateau site of RAE Aberporth appears above the rocks of Pen-Peles

Tresaith nestles in a break in the cliffs

probably introduced from the Mediterranean. There is an old limekiln by the beach and modern facilities include parking on the clifftop, refreshment kiosk and toilets.

The Royal Aircraft Establishment's missile test and research centre is located on top of the 132m high Pencribach table headland amidst a plethora of chimneys, pylons and towers at Aberporth. There are buoys with scientific instruments within 1km of the headland and target buoys further out. Jets occasionally fly around to add atmosphere. Scientific instruments are also located on clifftops for some considerable distance on both sides of the centre. Buildings and a walkway with assorted

The aptly named Birds Rock rests at the foot of New Quay Head

Tresaith is also popular with holiday makers, as shown by the caravan park, and its clear waters encourage divers. It has caves and stacks but its most conspicuous feature is the waterfall on the Afon Saith which comes straight down the steep shale cliffs onto the beach.

A café and toilets are to be found beyond the low dunes at Penbryn. Caravans also back the resort of Llangranog at the end of the B4321 with the Ship inn in a small inlet behind dark shales in jumbled stacks.

When the tide and wave conditions are right there is a passage between the 4ha Ynys Lochtyn and the mainland although the gap is frequently

The harbour of New Quay backed by New Quay Head, seen from New Quay Bay

industrial apparatus are located near the water by Cribach Bay where there are moorings.

Aberporth on the B4333 is a fishing village which has become a resort surrounded by cliffs of silver grey slate.

narrow enough for anglers to jump across. Pendinaslochdyn has a prehistoric fort in the shape of an inverted pan, forming its top at a height of 165m, from where it is possible to see the Lleyn Peninsula and Snowdonia. Cwmtydu has yet more

caravans and the remains of another limekiln on the shore.

New Quay Head is a 92m high vertical cliff with a relatively small lump known as the Birds Rock lying in the sea at its base. The horizontal sedimentary layers which follow the folded rocks on the approach to New Quay Head form tier after tier of ledges which are coloured white from the guano of rows of guillemots and other seabirds which coat the cliff. The headland is only seen at its best from the water.

The effect is less attractive round the corner where a small factory built from concrete blocks on the rocks discharges dirty water down a slope into the sea.

incoming waves except when it gets washed away by freshets.

Perpendicular slate cliffs behind the beach return as far as Morfa Mawr, after which they pull back to 1km inland to leave a flat and low shore. The Afon Arth emerges from behind the groynes at **Aberarth**, formerly a busy coastal shipping port.

Llansantffraid's church has its stone tower and walls faced with purple slate. The centre of population has now shifted, however, to Llanon on the A487 at the foot of the cliffs.

A lane at Llanrhystud comes to SN525691 and gives parking for a few cars before getting involved with the large caravan site as the high land closes back on the shore.

New Quay, at the ends of the A486 and B4342, retains its traditional seafaring character from the days when it was a fishing port and shipbuilding and repairing centre. Despite having more of a Cornish atmosphere than a Welsh one, New Quay is believed to have been a model for Llaregyb in Dylan Thomas' *Under Milk Wood*. It was while living here in the 1940s that he wrote its precursor, *Quite Early One Morning*.

The quay itself was built in 1835 and on the noticeboard there is an old list of tolls for the landing of goods. There are pleasure craft moorings. Pollack are the local fish, but a much wider choice is available from the fish and chip takeaway while other sources of sustenance include the off licence, Harbour Club, Mariner Café, Wellington Inn, Reknown Cottage and Captain's Rendez Vous. There is an aquarium, parking and toilets before the quay.

Tide streams run across the mouth of New Quay Bay at up to 2km/h. From Ina Point to Aberaeron there are 40m high perpendicular slate cliffs with land rising behind. There are boulder beaches over the rest of this section of coast which make landing possible at any time but not without damage unless the sea is slight. At one point another waterfall cascades down the cliff.

Aberaeron, at the mouth of the Afon Aeron as the name suggests, was built by the Rev Alban Gwynne in the 18th century. A quarter of the houses are of special architectural or historical interest with a significant Georgian and Regency flavour. New quayside buildings include a sea aquarium and animal centre. The former shipbuilding industry used oak from local forests. There are still fishing boats present, joined by an assortment of yachts in this resort. Groynes protect the seafront and a harbour bar of shingle breaks up

Distance
From Cerig duon to Llanrhystud is 58km
Campsites
Newport, Allt-y-goed, Gwbert, Bigni, Aberporth, Penmorfa, Pontgarreg, Cwmtydu, New Quay, Cei-bach, Clogfryn, Aberaeron, Llanon, Llanrhystud
Youth Hostels
Trefdraeth, Poppit Sands, Borth
OS 1:50,000 Sheets
135 Aberystwyth and Mychynlleth
145 Cardigan and Mynedd Preseli
146 Lampeter and Llandovery
Imray Charts
C51 Cardigan Bay – Milford Haven to Tremadoc Bay (1:140,800)
C60 Gower Peninsula to Cardigan (1:130,000)
Stanfords Allweather Charts
28 SE Ireland to Wales and Lundy
Admiralty Charts
SC 1484 Plans in Cardigan Bay. Newport Bay (1:37,500). Approaches to Cardigan (1:37,500). Aberporth (1:30,000). New Quay (1:12,500). Aberaeron (1:18,000)
SC 1972 Cardigan Bay – Central Part (1:75,000)
SC 1973 Cardigan Bay – Southern Part (1:75,000)
Tidal Constants
Fishguard: HW Dover –0350, LW Dover –0340
Port Cardigan: HW Dover –0330, LW Dover –0300
Aberporth: HW Dover –0330, LW Dover –0300
New Quay: HW Dover –0320, LW Dover –0250
Aberaeron: HW Dover –0320, LW Dover –0240
Sea Area
Irish Sea
Rescue
Inshore lifeboats: Fishguard, Cardigan, New Quay
All weather lifeboats: Fishguard, New Quay
Maritime Rescue Centre
Milford Haven, 01646 690909

The Afon Aeron estuary at Aberaeron. The harbour is crossed by a recreation of the extraordinary 1885 aerial ferry

11 EAST CARDIGAN BAY

The great little trains of Wales

Pretty maidens come again
Join us in a merry strain,
To all who live on land or main
Say the Bells of Aberdovey.

Charles Dibden

A dolphin surfaces off the harbour at Aberystwyth

The unusual natural sculpting of the cliffs at Ffos-lâs near Blaenplwyf with the aerial behind

Aberystwyth at dusk with the war memorial and remains of the castle on the point

Leaving the beach at SN525691, a conspicuous caravan site is passed at Llanrhystud, together with the inconspicuous mouth of the Afon Wyre. After this the low shoreline is left at Carreg Ti-pw and cliffs are continuous until the mouth of the Ystwyth. In the vicinity of the 152m high transmission mast at Blaenplwyf the cliffs take on a rather unusual form, having been scoured by runs of water into shapes which resemble a line of bottles with ribs running down the outside. It is a lonely area with just a caravan site at Morfa Bychan and cormorants for company. Both tide-streams set towards the coast over this length with low shingle beaches in places as the tide drops.

Aberystwyth at dawn with the sweep of the bay from Constitution Hill on the left to the pier and Victorian Gothic building on the right

The Afon Ystwyth (Welsh for winding river) and Afon Rheidol meet in the harbour at **Aberystwyth**, flowing round opposite sides of the 124m high Pendinas, which has the Wellington Monument and one of the largest Celtic hill forts in Wales on the top. The harbour is almost derelict and no longer has shipping, just fishing and pleasure boats. It almost dries out and there is a bar off the mouth over which swells break near low water and often at high water. Tide-streams are weak with

2km/h outwards on the flood and 6km/h on the ebb. Dolphins frequent the area off the harbour mouth. They are not discouraged by the discolouration of the sea by the rivers and are possibly attracted by the discolouring material.

Aberystwyth Castle was begun in 1277 by Edward I although it was later captured and held by Owain Glydwr. Under Charles I it was used as a mint by Thomas Bushell who owned the concession on the Plynlimon lead mines and who discovered a new process for refining silver. It was reduced to ruins in the Civil War when Cromwell pounded it to rubble which was later used for housebuilding. The gatehouse remains close to the shore.

Beyond the point, on which the war memorial stands, is the building planned by Thomas Savin in 1860 as a Victorian Gothic hotel. He wished to popularize Aberystwyth by building his own railway line from Euston and offering a week's free board to each ticket holder. After spending £80,000 on the hotel the scheme failed and the building was bought for £10,000 by a patriotic committee for use as a college. The Prince of Wales (later Edward VII) was installed as chancellor and the building still serves as part of the campus of the University of Wales, along with a museum, and it was in the building that Gladstone made his last public appearance. Much of the campus is further inland, together with the National Library housed in an Edwardian building. The latter is one of Britain's six copyright libraries, containing 3,000,000 books. These include the largest collection of books in Welsh or relating to Wales, pictures, old deeds, maps, 30,000 manuscripts (including the 13th-century *Black Book of Carmarthen*, the oldest manuscript in Welsh) and the earliest complete text of the *Mabinogion* (the earliest Welsh prose, based on tales of the invading Irish from the 3rd to 7th centuries) founded on a collection begun by royal physician Sir John Williams who died in 1926. It contains some of the greatest Celtic treasures and is used for tracing ancestry.

Aberystwyth is the terminal for two railways. The Cambrian Coast Railway, opened in 1863–7, goes via Dovey Junction to Pwllheli, 113km, of which 48km is subject to coastal hazards. The Vale of Rheidol Railway was British Rail's only steam narrow gauge railway, running to Devil's Bridge at 597mm gauge. Built in 1902 to carry lead and zinc ore down to the harbour, it now has three locomotives which haul only passenger trains.

Once a walled town, Aberystwyth is now a resort with a summer festival in late July and early August. The largest town and shopping centre in mid-Wales, it was once described as the Brighton of Wales and retains its 19th-century dignity. The Coliseum, a restored music hall, contains the Ceredigion Museum which features the area since the Stone Age. The town has a 90m long pier plus a submerged damaged portion.

The town ends at the 148m high Constitution Hill up which runs the Aberystwyth Cliff Railway, the longest funicular railway in Europe, rising 120m in 240m. Of standard gauge with a static electric engine at the top, it was opened in 1896 and used a water balance system until 1921. The cars, each of which carries 30 people, are connected by a continuous wire rope. A modern Victorian type Camera Obscura at the top scans 26 peaks with a 360mm lens, the largest of its kind in the world.

From Aberystwyth to Craig yr Wylfa there are bold and rocky cliffs, varying between 6 and 37m in height, with the valley of Dyffryn Clarach and a deep ravine at Wallog.

At Garreg there is a folly built by Clough Williams-Ellis of the Welsh Guards in 1915 as a wedding gift to Annabel Strachey. Ellis subsequently went on to design Portmerion.

Charles Dibden's music hall song *The Bells of Aberdovey* relates to Wallog where the bells are sometimes said to be heard from the ancient kingdom of Gwyddno Garnhir, Lord of Ceredigion, when the sea is calm or danger threatens. The gates of the village of Cantref Gwaelod had to be closed every high tide, but one fateful night 1,400 years ago the drunken watchman, Seithenin, omitted to do so and the sea swept in through the 13km long sea wall. Sarn Wallog, Sarn Gynfelyn, Cynfelyn Patches and Outer Patch form an 11km ridge out to Patches buoy and are probably successive moraines of ice sheets emerging from Snowdonia during glaciation.

One quarrel between kings was settled here by the relatively civilized method of seeing who could stay seated for longest with the tide coming in. Maelgwyn was victorious. The contest is re-enacted each year with the winner being crowned King of Cors Fochno.

Spring tidal flows reach 2km/h. South of Gynfelyn they start northeast at HW Dover +0500 and southwest at HW Dover –0100. North of here they begin north at HW Dover +0430 and south at HW Dover –0130.

Company on this cliff lined section might take the form of jets overhead or jellyfish beneath. The rock strata are heavily folded on the approach to Upper Borth where there is a memorial before the cliffs come to an end as the B4572 meets the B4353.

Borth is a resort. The 3-week Borth Carnival offers Caribbean nights, donkey derbys, football, cricket and a barmen's race. There is a fortnight of water, beach and fun sports including a raft race. The fishermen's cottages are rather lost these days amongst the wave skis, windsurfers, water skis, jet skis, parascending, tennis, crazy golf and BMX

Upper Borth with Borth, Ynyslas, the Dovey estuary and Tywyn beyond

riding. Any camel seen on the sand dunes following overindulgence in the hotel should be treated seriously as such a sight is not unknown. Bass are not the only residents under the surface. At times the remains of a 7,000 year old sunken forest are seen in the sands, helping give further credence to the Cantref Gwaelod legend.

Groynes line the beach past the oldest golf course in Wales to Ynyslas (Welsh for blue-green island), behind which is Cors Fochno, 6m of semi-liquid peat, one of our finest lowland raised bogs. It is divided from the beach by the road, the Cambrian Coast Railway and the Afon Leri, the latter running dead straight for 4km parallel to the coast to the small harbour reached from inside the estuary of the River Dovey.

North of Ynyslas is the Dyfi National Nature Reserve which includes the Twyni Mawr and Twyni Bâch dune systems. This large windblown sand system has such plants as bee orchid, marsh marigold, marsh heleborine, restharrow, bird's foot trefoil, marram grass and sea spurge, making an ideal habitat for rabbit, polecat, weasel and such butterflies as the large skipper, grayling, wall brown and small heath. It is particularly good for birds in the winter and its birdlife includes skylark, meadow pipit, stonechat, reed bunting, linnet, ringed plover, oystercatcher, shelduck and various gulls. An information centre explains the natural history and there is a nature trail and guided tours. The distant views range from Strumble Head to the

Lleyn Peninsula and also to the Cambrian mountains and the peaks of Snowdonia.

Before the railway was built along the north side of the estuary there used to be a spur on the south side leading to a tower which is still present. Here passengers waited for the ferry to come across from Aberdovey to collect them.

Southwest winds raise a heavy sea over Aberdovey Bar off the estuary on the River Dovey, especially on the ebb when flow rates can reach 11km/h over the bar. At low tide the river channel meanders between expanses of sand.

Crossing the rivermouth brings the paddler from Ceredigion to Gwynedd, the Snowdonia National Park and the A493 with Aberdovey just up the estuary. Tidal streams from here to Sarn Badrig start northwards at HW Dover +0530 and southwards at HW Dover –0130 at up to 2km/h.

Looking up the Dovey estuary past Aberdovey at the southern edge of the Snowdonia National Park

Aberdovey was a busy fishing village in the 16th century and became a trading port in the 18th century but declined in the early 1800s when railways took away the coastal shipping trade. Plans to turn it into a serious rival to Fishguard and Holyhead for the Irish ferry trade never came to anything. In 1941 it was the site of the first Outward Bound course and the centre has an associated rescue post. In 1968 the old wharf buildings were renovated, the derelict coal wharf cleared and the seafront gardens created, resulting in an award from the Prince of Wales' Committee in 1972. These days it is a resort with sailing, windsurfing and water skiing. The maritime museum has model sailing ships, sailors' tools, ropework, photographs, drawings, navigation instruments and early RNLI equipment. The warm climate and few frosts allow early-flowering myrtle to grow here.

Dunes continue north of the estuary with a golf course immediately west of the estuary and pillboxes along the shore at intervals.

Tywyn (Welsh for sand dunes) is a resort protected by groynes and has plenty of parking with such facilities as toilets and an ice cream shop near the prominent aerial. It is used for surfing and has a carnival week early in August and a country fair with rural crafts and skills. It has two churches of historical importance. St Cadfan's was founded in 516, St Cadfan apparently being a French missionary who came to Christianize the region. It contains St Cadfan's stone, the 7th-century text which is thought to be the oldest writing in Welsh. One translation reads 'the body of Cingen lies beneath' but another arrives at the entirely different conclusion that it mourns the loss of three ladies carried off in the 6th century by Irish invaders, enough to leave one wondering if both translators read the same stone. Also to be seen are excellent effigies of a 14th-century knight in armour and a priest from Edward II's reign. Llanegryn Church has a lych gate and an interesting carved rood screen which reaches the full width of the church.

Just beyond is the terminus of the Talyllyn Railway which has been operated since 1865 to carry slate. It was built by James Swinton Spooner (whose family were involved with development of the Festiniog Railway) for Lancashire cotton baron William McConnell but never reached its intended destination of Bryn Eglwys quarry or Tal-y-llyn or Aberdovey. It was built to a 686mm gauge, the narrowest permitted by the enabling Act. In 1951 it was rescued from dereliction and restored, the first of many lines to be taken over by preservation societies. The Narrow Gauge Railway Museum is at Tywyn Wharf Station.

On the north side of Tywyn behind a caravan site is Morfa Camp, home of the Joint Services Mountain Training Centre (Wales), whose facilities include a helicopter landing site.

Broad Water lies to the right of Tal y Gareg with its quarry while the mountains run away to Cadair Idris in the distance

Inside the narrow mouth of the Afon Dysynni is a large tidal lake, Broad Water. This stores a significant quantity of water.

Behind Tonfanau, 178m high Tal y Gareg ends abruptly with Bwch Head Beacon, an 11m white pole on top and a quarry below. Stretching away into the distance are mountains leading up to Cader Idris. The other way, Sarn-y-Bwch runs out 6km from Pen Bwch Point as a subsea ridge.

Rhoslefain beach was once used by smugglers to land salt, but the activity these days is of a more innocent nature as climbers swarm over the cliffs, which run from here to Fairbourne. Oystercatchers are not the only wildlife on the rocks as seals like to clamber onto them to sunbathe.

Cliffs at Llangelynin. The sunbathing seal in the centre has lifted both head and tail in the typical sunbathing seal pose

Llangelynin church dates partly from the 12th century and is built on the site of an older church. An unusual item of equipment is a two-horse bier which was used to collect the dead from outlying farms.

The cliffs pull back to leave a low shoreline at Borthwen Point. Behind Llwyngwril (grove of green leaves) is an Iron Age hill fort, Castell y Gaer. There is a 17th-century burial ground on the way from the beach to Llwyn Du farmhouse which the Quakers used for meetings.

Various standing stones, cairns and homesteads dot the lower slopes of Pen y Garn as the coast arcs into Barmouth Bay. As it approaches Friog, the Cambrian Coast Railway is protected from rock

avalanches by a 60m x 300mm thick reinforced concrete roof slab.

Fairbourne is built on a low area of land which projects into the estuary of the Afon Mawddach. This resort has a beach which is said to be the finest and safest in north Wales. Behind it runs the Fairbourne and Barmouth Steam Railway of 1916, based on a former 381mm horse tramway of 1890 serving the estate of McDougall, the flour merchant. This is the smallest Welsh narrow gauge line but it is one of the few places where new engines are being built, replicas of famous narrow gauge engines. There are five steam engines, a diesel engine and a works shunter, twenty eight coaches and seventeen works vehicles and, during the centenary, it became the only line with a scheduled horsedrawn tram service. The line also carried the last narrow gauge boat train as it connects with the passenger ferry to Barmouth. Passengers have to hold out their tickets for the driver to see before he will stop the train at stations for them. Other features include a Victorian style station and a halt which now has the longest railway station name in the world, Gorsafawddachaidra'igddanheddogleddollônpenrhynareurdraethceredigion. The estuary is noted for its birdlife in the winter.

That station on the Fairbourne and Barmouth Steam Railway

Crossing the estuary behind Penrhyn Point is the timber Barmouth Bridge carrying the Cambrian Coast Railway. The viaduct is built on rocks, only at the northern end where there were two 12m spans, the navigable channel being crossed by a span which tilted and drew back over the track. These have been replaced by a 41m swinging span and a 36m fixed span, both hogback trusses on cylindrical piers instead of the original cast-iron screw piles. There are a further 113 spans of 5.5m which are encased in GRP reinforced concrete sleeves to resist attack by marine borer which threatened to close the viaduct and, hence, the northern end of the Cambrian Coast Railway.

Between 1750 and 1850 318 vessels were built along the banks of the Afon Mawddach, an estuary the approach to which is said to resemble that to Gibraltar.

The bar is dangerous with strong westerly winds. There is an RNLI museum by the causeway which connects Ynys y Brawd to the mainland. Above the A496 is Dinas Oleu, the first property acquired by the National Trust in 1895. Barmouth harbour is used for fishing and sailing boats and is the headquarters of Merioneth Yacht Club. Ty Crwn is a restored lockup for drunken sailors while Ty

Gwyn yn Bermo is a restored 15th-century building on the quay with an exhibition. This was chosen as the starting point of the yachting version of the 3 Peaks Race. Groynes protect one of the finest beaches in Britain and **Barmouth** sees surfing and water skiing. This resort has an art exhibition in August and an arts festival in September with the Dragon Theatre as an important venue.

Low sandhills continue to Llanenddwyn, overlooked by frequent large caravan sites.

Huge concrete blocks connected by chains protect the railway at Llanaber. The 13th-century church is one of the best examples of the Early English style in north Wales. In the 18th century its tombs not only contained the legitimate spirits but also the contraband kind, placed by the local smugglers.

An ancient homestead site is lost amongst the holiday caravans at Tal-y-bont but the Afon Ysgethin is not too obvious, either.

A historic wreck lies off Bennar beach but landmarks can be a little confusing. There is a carpark reached by a footpath through the dunes (and through a couple of difficult gates) but the footpath can be hard to spot from the water, being near a red and white-striped pole and one of several rescue rings.

Barmouth and the Barmouth Bridge across the mouth of the Afon Mawddach.

Pont Abermaw, Cymru
Barmouth Bridge, Wales

Distance
From Llanrhystud to Llanenddwyn is 57km
Campsites
Llanrhystud, Morfa Bychan, Aberystwyth, Glan y-môr, Upper Borth, Glanwern, Ynyslas, Tywyn, Rhoslefain, Fairbourne, Barmouth, Llanaber, Tal-y-Bont, Llanenddwyn
Youth Hostels
Borth, Kings, Llanbedr
OS 1:50,000 Sheets
124 Porthmadog and Dolgellau
135 Aberystwyth and Mychynlleth
Imray Charts
C51 Cardigan Bay – Milford Haven to Tremadoc Bay (1:140,800)
C52 Cardigan Bay to Liverpool (1:138,600)
Admiralty Charts
SC 1484 Plans in Cardigan Bay. Aberystwyth (1:18,000). Aberdovey (1:25,000). Barmouth (1:25,000)
SC 1971 Cardigan Bay – Northern Part (1:75,000)
SC 1972 Cardigan Bay – Central Part (1:75,000)
SC 5609 North West Wales
Tidal Constants
Aberaeron: HW Dover –0320, LW Dover –0240
Aberystwyth: HW Dover –0320, LW Dover –0230
Aberdovey: HW Dover –0250, LW Dover –0210
Barmouth: HW Dover –0250, LW Dover –0140
Sea Area
Irish Sea
Rescue
Inshore lifeboats: New Quay, Aberystwyth, Borth, Aberdovey, Barmouth
All weather lifeboats: New Quay, Barmouth
Maritime Rescue Centres
Milford Haven, 01646 690909
Holyhead, 01407 762051

12 LLEYN PENINSULA

An iron ring of castles and a backdrop of Snowdonia peaks

Men of Harlech in the hollow, do you hear like rushing billow
Wave on wave that surging follow battle's distant sound

'Tis the tramp of Saxon foemen, Saxon spearmen, Saxon bowmen
Be they knights or hinds or yeomen, they shall bite the ground.
Thomas Oliphant

Leaving Llanenddwyn, the coast runs past the dunes of Morfa Dyffryn with their unusual plants. Hidden beyond them is an RAE airfield from which fly some unusual aircraft including a pilotless plane, the Jindivik. There is also a mountain rescue post at Llanbedr while Maes Artro has memorabilia from RAF Llanbedr during the second world war, a Spitfire, an Avro Anson, an air raid shelter under simulated attack, a village of yesteryear, an old farm implements exhibition, an aquarium of local marine life, children's play area and giant draughts set. Canoeing, pony trekking, hill walking and orienteering are catered for with a watersports centre at the old wharf in Pen-sarn. There is a craft village in **Llanbedr**.

Shell Island is noted for over 200 varieties of shells, especially after stormy weather, and is good for lobsters which could be included as shellfish. Mochras Point was formerly an island of morainic deposits until the Earl of Winchelsea diverted the Afon Artro early in the 19th century to reclaim the land, creating a saltmarsh. The river now exits through a lagoon.

Sarn Badrig, St Patrick's Causeway, runs out for 22km from the point and dries for several kilometres at low water. It probably consists of moraine from the Snowdonia glaciation ice sheet. There can be overfalls when there is 3m of water over Sarn Badrig and at other states of the tide with strong winds, but these can be avoided by taking the East Passage on the inside. South of Sarn Badrig flows start north at HW Dover +0530 and south at HW Dover –0030. North of Sarn Badrig flows start northeast at HW Dover +0400 and southwest at HW Dover –0030. Maximum flow is only 2km/h except over shoals. Streams are weak in Tremadog Bay which is an area of accumulation of beach material because of the prevailing southwesterly winds. Shifting dunes have buried half of Llandanwg, including St Danwg's church.

From Llanfair with its slate caverns, homesteads and settlements dot the hillside across to Harlech.

Harlech is dominated by Harlech Castle, built in 1283–9 by Edward I, one of an iron ring of fortresses built to contain the Welsh in the mountains. The high point in mediaeval castle building, it was located on a cliff rising directly from the sea. It is unusual in that its twin-towered gatehouse is the strongest part rather than the keep, which would usually be the case. During the rebellion of Madoc ap Llywelyn in 1294 it was held by 37 men and supplied by sea from Ireland, the sea now having receded because of deposition. It was captured by Owain Glyndwr in 1404 and used for his court until it was retaken by the English in 1409. It was held by the Lancastrians in the Wars of the Roses in a siege ending in their surrender and commemorated in *Men of Harlech*. The castle now has jousting while the Royal St David's golf course is laid out where supply ships once sailed. Harlech is a resort and has a nature trail.

Morfa Harlech dunes have uncommon plants and edge a saltmarsh. There is now a reserve with a rabbit warren and numbers of wading birds. The winter proliferation of birds and the interesting

Harlech Castle, no longer next to the water

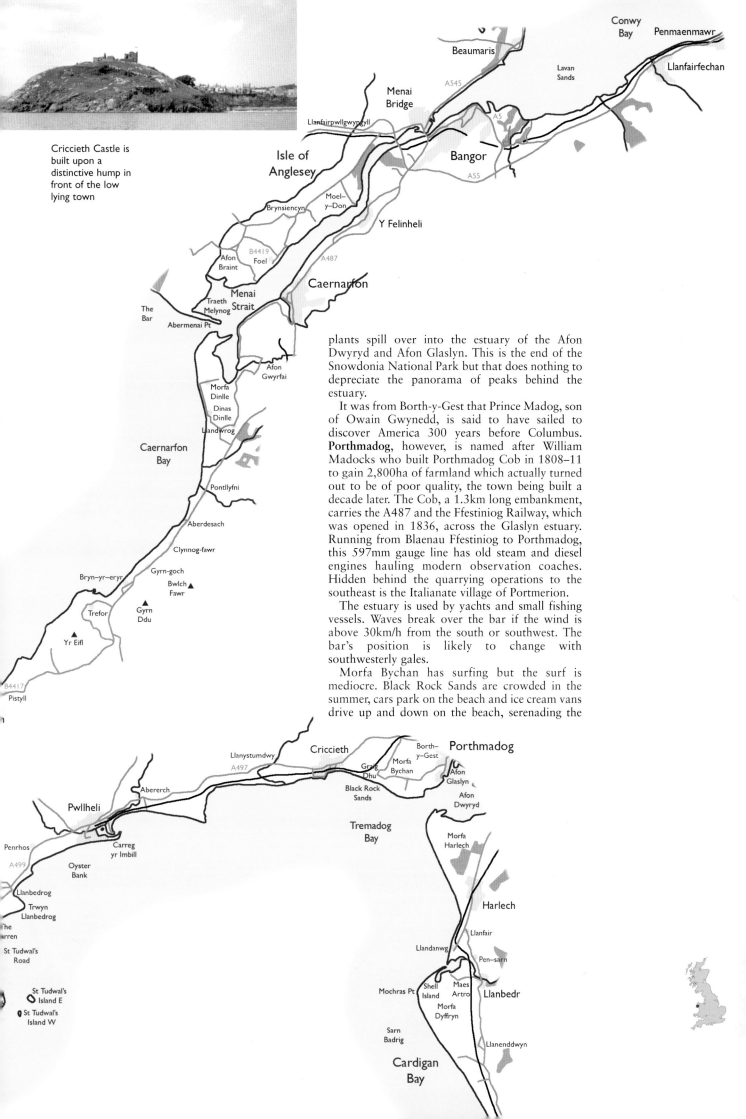

Criccieth Castle is built upon a distinctive hump in front of the low lying town

plants spill over into the estuary of the Afon Dwyryd and Afon Glaslyn. This is the end of the Snowdonia National Park but that does nothing to depreciate the panorama of peaks behind the estuary.

It was from Borth-y-Gest that Prince Madog, son of Owain Gwynedd, is said to have sailed to discover America 300 years before Columbus. **Porthmadog**, however, is named after William Madocks who built Porthmadog Cob in 1808–11 to gain 2,800ha of farmland which actually turned out to be of poor quality, the town being built a decade later. The Cob, a 1.3km long embankment, carries the A487 and the Ffestiniog Railway, which was opened in 1836, across the Glaslyn estuary. Running from Blaenau Ffestiniog to Porthmadog, this 597mm gauge line has old steam and diesel engines hauling modern observation coaches. Hidden behind the quarrying operations to the southeast is the Italianate village of Portmerion.

The estuary is used by yachts and small fishing vessels. Waves break over the bar if the wind is above 30km/h from the south or southwest. The bar's position is likely to change with southwesterly gales.

Morfa Bychan has surfing but the surf is mediocre. Black Rock Sands are crowded in the summer, cars park on the beach and ice cream vans drive up and down on the beach, serenading the boater for some distance out. At the west end are caves in Graig Dhu, beyond which is another beach with a burial chamber near the Criccieth end.

Prominent at **Criccieth** on the A497 is the mound which stands in front of the town, topped by the ruined Criccieth Castle. It was founded in 1230 by Llywelyn the Great and finished with a strong main tower and high outer wall in 1260. In 1282 it was captured by Edward I and incorporated into his defensive system, a lozenge shaped inner bailey being built between 1285 and 1292 with high twin-towered gatehouse and polygonal curtain wall without towers. The Engine Tower on the north side was built to house a seige engine to bombard attackers. It was captured, sacked and burned in 1404 by Owain Glyndwr and the scorch marks on the Leyburn Tower and heat cracks in the doorway stones probably date from this time. Inside the remains of the castle are exhibitions of castles of the native Welsh princes and of Gerald of Wales.

Dating from the 6th-century is St Cybi's Well. The resort of Criccieth is today protected by groynes. There is an annual festival of musical arts and in 1980 part of the *Life and Times of Lloyd George* was filmed here.

The Afon Dwyfor flows quietly down from Llanystumdwy, the village where David Lloyd George lived until 1890 and to which he retired in 1944, dying here a year later. The Liberal Prime Minister from 1916 to 1922 and one of the most colourful holders of the office, he was known as the Welsh Wizard for his oratory. There is a memorial here and a museum which has gold and silver caskets, deeds of freedom and other honours and gifts to him.

The ancient Tomen fawr site is unnoticed, unlike the Starcoast World from where the screams of those on the Boomerang rollercoasters can be heard from over a kilometre away although this does not seem to upset the seals and cormorants. It offers one of the longest cableways in Britain, one of the biggest subtropical waterworlds in Europe, a miniature railway and a whole range of other facilities which are claimed to make it the best theme park in Wales. Despite the obvious nature of the larger rides, the many buildings have been painted very effectively so that they are not visually obtrusive from the sea.

Pwllheli is the biggest and busiest town on the Lleyn Peninsula, given its charter in 1355 by the Black Prince. The port and market town have now become a resort at the terminus of the Cambrian Coast Railway. A prison museum was planned. The harbour is at the confluence of the Afon Erch and Afon Rhyd-hir but has suffered badly from silt brought down by them. The inner harbour formerly silted up and was no longer used while the outer harbour mostly dried. Part of the harbour has now been dredged to a reasonable depth for Hafan Pwllheli. There is an oddly shaped Carreg yr Imbill or Gimblet Rock off the harbour.

Behind the beach of Marian-y-de are toilets,

Ghost ships. Beyond are the St Tudwal's Islands

telephone, beach café and children's swings beside a stone circle.

From Pwllheli to Trwyn Llanbedrog the shoreline is mostly of low sandhills. Oyster Bank lies offshore. Streams up to 1km/h begin northeast at HW Dover +0340 and southwest at HW Dover –0400.

The coastline is interrupted at Llanbedrog by the 132m high bulk of Mynydd Tir-y-cwmwd with its conspicuous remains of quarrying operations.

The Warren with its caravans leads on to **Abersoch** at the end of the A499, a former fishing village around which bass are still to be found in the clear water. St Tudwal's Road forms a large mooring for this yachting, windsurfing and powerboating resort which is fronted by a prominent club building, but the waters can be subject to heavy seas in southerly and easterly winds and it can produce surf when other nearby beaches are not suitable. The lifeboat station at Penrhyn Du is no longer used. Between Abersoch and Machroes are beach huts and then a golf

Playing a sea kayak version of Chicken at St Tudwal's Island East

course based on dunes and protected at the front by groynes with a coastal marsh behind.

Off the coast lie the two St Tudwal's islands. St Tudwal's Island East has the remains of an 800-year old priory and chapel built by Tugdual, Bishop of Treguier, who fled from Brittany to avoid religious persecution following the collapse of the Roman Empire. Since then the island has been inhabited until a century ago. A chapel was built on the site of Tugdual's sanctuary in the 13th century and Edward I possibly visited it in 1284 when the island was inhabited by secular canons associated with Bardsey. A priory of Augustinian canons was present in 1410 but by the 16th century it was the haunt of pirates, including Morgan Irish. In the 18th century it was being farmed. Father Henry Bailie Hughes tried to revive the religious aspects in 1887 by founding a monastery in a converted barn, without success. It was last used, unofficially, during the second world war as a bombing target. There is a monument on the east side.

Puffins and rabbits are no longer harvested from the 11ha of the two islands and landing is not allowed. The islands, of Ordovician sedimentary rock, have grassy tops and low craggy cliffs with colonies of seabirds, particularly kittiwakes and fulmars, while the deep sea caves are inhabited by grey seals.

St Tudwal's Island West is similar to its neighbour but with a disused lighthouse redesigned as a private house.

Porth Ceiriad during a sea kayak symposium lunch stop

St Tudwal's Sound on the inside flows at up to 6km/h with HW slack 3 hours before Dover.

Porth Ceiriad can produce surf when Porth Neigwl is flat, being best in the northeast corner where the break is fast and steep. From here run 5km of cliffs with no landing point. This distance is extended if the surf is up. A settlement and burial chamber have been sited on the top in earlier times and the location suits cormorants and oystercatchers.

Trwyn Cilan is the point at which the northerly tide stream divides to circulate in Tremadog Bay or flow past the end of the Lleyn Peninsula and on northwards. There is a tide rip and the water ebbs at 6km/h. From Trwyn Cilan to Braich y Pwll streams are parallel to the coast, starting west towards the west shore of Porth Neigwl at HW Dover +0300 and east towards the west side of Trywn Cilan at HW Dover −0300, both sets being stronger with southerly winds.

Porth Neigwl's English name of Hell's Mouth comes from the threat it posed to sailing ships. The best known north Wales break, it produces the best surf after northwesterly winds, particularly at the southeast end where many boards will be found. During southwest winds the sea is heavy. Boulder clay cliffs at the back have been sculpted into peculiar shapes by the elements.

A conspicuous chimney is located by a former settlement in Llanengan. The church, not visible from the water, has twin naves and was founded 1,400 years ago by St Einion, King of Lleyn. A stone carved in the 5th century to 'Melus the doctor, son of Martinus' is the first to a doctor in Wales. It also has a beautiful carved rood screen, solid oak coffer and sacred vessel from the abbey on Bardsey Island.

Mynydd Rhiw forms 304m of mountain ending the beach, topped by two aerials and covered lower down by assorted artefacts, a holy well, long cairn, forts, standing stone and hut circle. Plas-yn-Rhiw is a small manor house, part Tudor with Georgian additions.

Rust coats the cliff face before Trywyn Talfarach, the start of Porth Ysgo which is backed by the gentler colours of ferns, gorse and foxgloves in season.

Offshore, Ynys Gwylan-fawr and Ynys Gwylan-bâch total 8ha with interesting plants, seals, cormorants and puffins breeding, hence their English name of Seagull Islands. They stand on one limb of a Y-shaped ridge which runs out from Ebolion and the boils, swirls and eddies caused by this are an indicator of what is to come.

Aberdaron Bay has heavy seas with a southerly wind and surf in southerly or southwesterly winds but it tends to dump at high water and there are rocks close in. Wave size decreases going westwards along the beach towards Aberdaron at

the end of the B4413. A strong eddy stream runs south southwest on the ebb. This fishing village is popular with divers. The church is mainly 12th century, built away from the sea but now with its own wall to check the advances of the water. It has a Norman doorway and some parts are 600 years older still. Y Gegin Fwr, the big kitchen, is a café and gift shop. Built in the 14th century, it was probably a resting house for pilgrims on their way

Ynys Gwlan-fawr and Ynys Gwlan-bâch off Pen y Cil with Bardsey Island beyond

to Bardsey Island. The climate here is mild. It is claimed that the sun shone on 316 days one year.

Pen y Cil tide race leads into Bardsey Sound, the most serious piece of water in north Wales, running at up to 11km/h. When there is wind against tide the whole sound can be a mass of confused and breaking seas and the island can be isolated for weeks when the boat cannot get out from Porth Meudwy. There is an almost continual tide race near Carreg Ddu with strong return eddies close to the mainland.

The violent turbulence around the island leads to a 2km long eddy at each end, the biggest breakouts in north Wales, perhaps an approriate place to find the storm petrel.

Bardsey Island is the Isle of 20,000 Saints. One of the white marble Celtic crosses in the churchyard commemorates 20,000 saints as this was the best place in north Wales for the Celtic tradition requiring burial to be in the west, hence the burial of so many saints here. Ynys Enlli (the Welsh name) means the island in the currents but other name derivations are from the Norse Bards Ey, the bards being drawn by the religious associations or named after the Norse warrior Bardr, or even Birdsey after the birds.

Hut circles show that there were inhabitants from very early times and the pasture still conforms to an old field system. St Cadfan founded an abbey in 516 and the Pope declared three pilgrimmages to Bardsey to be worth one to Rome. Dubricius died here in 612, just three years before the arrival of the ousted monks of Bangor-Is-Coed after the Battle of Chester. The present St Mary's abbey dates from the 13th century. Merlin was also listed amongst the inhabitants. In the 16th and 17th centuries it became a base for pirates. The lighthouse was built in 1821 with a helicopter landing site added more recently. The island had a farming community in the last century. At the beginning of this century there were 100 residents and Lord Newborough, one of the owners, proposed they appoint a king to settle disputes, having a crown of brass, a silver casket for his treasure and a painted wooden soldier as his army, a regime which continued until after the first world war. 400 Connemara ponies and sheep are raised here. The Bardsey Island Trust took over ownership in 1979. Today there are just three residents. Visitors are welcomed if numbers do not upset the farming or nature reserve purposes.

The schoolroom has been used as an observation post for bird migration since 1953. Mist nets and Heligoland traps are used for ringing, measuring and counting and species encountered range from

Porth Towyn, one of the small inlets on the north side of the Lleyn Peninsula

herring, lesser and greater blackbacked gulls, mallard, pigeon, blackbird, redwing, jackdaw, sand martin, swallow, wheatear, lanceolated warbler and hoopoe to the great white egret. Over 250 species have been recorded and 40 species breed here including chough, 300–400 pairs of razorbill, guillemot, shag, oystercatcher, kittiwake, fulmar, peregrine, 3,000 pairs of Manx shearwater, for which this is one of the major breeding sites, and the 500 puffins for which this is the main north Wales colony. The lighthouse is the worst in Britain for killing migrating birds and every morning the ground around is littered with up to a hundred migratory birds which have flown into the glass. There have been experiments with decoy lights, lighting up a patch of gorse to try to reduce the carnage.

Rat, rabbit, wood mouse, common shrew (but not, unusually, the pygmy shrew), slow worm, palmate newt, fox and hedgehog complete the land fauna while up to 150 grey seals breed in the sea caves and join the porpoises, dolphins, lobsters and mackerel which are present in the sea around the island. Even a fin whale has been seen offshore. Sallow willow shoots used to be cut for lobster pots and other plants include Wilson's filmy fern, sea pea, small-flowered buttercup, thrift, bracken, horsetail, 280 varieties of lichen, hops, herbs and European and miniature gorse which was originally grown for horse feed.

The 1.8km² rise, like half a pear with the stalk at the south end, to 167m on Mynydd Enlli and consist of large fault breccia in part of the Lleyn complex with gneiss, metamorphosed grits and shales, pillow lavas and tuffs all crushed into conglomerates and lenticular strips with gabbro and granite intrusions.

The 160m Mynydd Mawr marks Braich y Pwll from where a tide race runs north over the Tripods, a bank of sand and shells, at up to 6km/h. A considerable sea with overfalls forms with wind against tide although it is possible to pass inside. The cliffs are bold and steep with a coastguard lookout position and the concrete foundations of a wartime radar station. St Mary's Well is where pilgrims used to drink before embarking for Bardsey.

Streams start north northeast at HW Dover +0500 and south–southwest at HW Dover –0100 at up to 4km/h in Caernarfon Bay. The north Wales coast produces semi-precious pebbles of agate, jasper and serpentine but from here to Trywyn Porth Dinllaen it is mostly bold and rocky.

The first reliable landing site is Porth Oer where there is a beach café, but kayaks are not allowed on the beach from 10am to 6pm between June and August. It is also known as Whistling Sands Bay as the sand can squeak when walked on. Beyond the beach some of the rocks are bright purple in colour and there are stacks with sharp points at the top.

Porth Iago is a surfing inlet although earlier residents have left earthworks and the remains of St Merin's Church. Off the entrance Maen Mellt looks like a tugboat with light superstructure and dark hull when viewed from further down the coast. Far more real are the jets on training flights from RAF Valley, but some residents do not object to the sound intrusion, seeing them as a link with civilization which can seem a long way away at times.

The clear waters of Traeth Penllech are popular with divers, but not too far away at Porth Ysgaden there are still grains of coal dust in the sand from

when coastal colliers used to land coal for customers.

Porth Towyn has surf which works after northerly winds but some low tide rocks need to be watched. On top of the cliffs, caravans look across to Holyhead Mountain.

Inquisitive seals investigate at Carreg Ddu off Porth Dinllaen

The insignificant looking Aber Geirch is an inlet where many submarine cables were landed.

Trwyn Porth Dinllaen has the remains of a prominently positioned building on top, perhaps taking over the role of an earlier fort. Quiet approach to the rocks of Carreg Ddu and Careg y Chwislen with its cone shaped metal beacon may be rewarded by the sight of numbers of seals basking, not being in too much of a hurry to move provided there are no quick movements to worry them. There is a small tide race and an eddy in Dinllaen Bay, especially on the flood. A 15km/h speed limit is imposed within 100m of the coast in the summer and a flag indicates when firing is taking place in Caernarfon Bay. A quiet resort with silver sands, it is overlooked by **Morfa Nefyn** and **Nefyn** on the cliff tops. At one time Porth Dinllaen had a herring fleet. In 1800 there was an ambition to make this the ferry port for Ireland but Holyhead was chosen instead. Undeterred, the idea was launched again in 1837 with the coming of railways and a company was formed in 1844 to build a line, but it never happened and the bay remains unspoilt. Nefyn has moved on from fishing to surfing. In 1284 it was chosen by Edward I as the venue for a contest to celebrate the downfall of Llywelyn the Last and the conquest of north Wales. In 1355 it became one of the ten royal boroughs in north Wales.

From Trwyn Porth Dinllaen to the Menai Strait, streams start north at HW Dover +0500 and south at HW Dover –0100 at up to 3km/h. As far as Trwyn Maen Dylan the coast is at the foot of mountains, which slope down to the sea.

The church of St Beuno, possibly dating from the 6th or 7th century, at Pystyll on the B4417 was a stopping place for pilgrims going to Bardsey Island.

The remains of a disused quarry can be seen on Penrhyn Glas where cliffs rise 120m almost vertically. A further disused granite quarry follows at Porth y Nant with more workings on the 150m cliff at Trwyn y Gorlech. The workers' village at

Porth y Nant was abandoned in 1959 but has been restored as the European Centre for Lesser Used Languages. Nant Gwrtheyrn was named after Vortigern, who fled here after losing his kingdom to the Saxons. Above is Yr Eifl (the fork) with three peaks reaching up to 564m only 2km from the coast, a mountain with an aerial, cairns, hut circle and settlement along with choughs, puffins, guillemots and feral goats on the acid soils and a view to Ireland. Below are the remains of three piers.

At Trwyn y Tâl there are a marvellous collection of caves, including one which is horseshoe-shaped, and rhizstoma jellyfish float about at the foot of the vertical cliffs in which the caves are formed.

The wooden pier was built for loading granite and beyond it a short wall protects Trefor's tiny harbour. There is a toilet at the end of the carpark.

Gyrn Ddu, Gyrn Goch and Bwlch Mawr form another dramatic set of peaks with more evidence of quarrying on Gyrn Ddu.

A 4-legged cromlech burial chamber at Clynnog-fawr may be over 3,000 years old. Much more recently, in the 7th century, St Beuno built a wattle and daub church as a stopping place for pilgrims going to Bardsey Island. The site is now used for the present Perpendicular church which is one of the best known in Wales, an amazingly grand piece of architecture for this remote hamlet. Inside the church is St Beuno's chest, a wooden trunk made from a single log to hold money paid by the owners of lambs or calves born with the saint's mark, a notch in the ear. Also relating to the local animals are a pair of tongs for the removal of dogs during services.

St Beuno's holy well was believed to have curative powers but the treatment had to be completed by spending a night on the saint's tomb, hardly the ideal bed for anyone not in the best of health.

Bass live in the waters around Gored Beuno off Aberdesach. The Afon Llyfni enters and the Afon Llifon follows soon after below a prominent aerial.

Caer Arianrhod, a low tide rock, is the only visible sign of a village marked on a map of 1573 and described in the *Mabinogi* as a fortress with a causeway to the land. Here lived Arianrhod,

daughter of Don, one of the three most beautiful ladies in Britain. She had a son, Llew Llaw Gyffes, by her brother, the warrior wizard Gwdion. Llew received a strange wife, Blodeuedd, made of flowers. Unlikely though the story is, a mound of stones in 7m of water shows unnatural regularity, suggesting it may have been parts of buildings.

The 31m high Iron Age hill fort of Dinas Dinlle looks notably out of place on this low shore. The present community next to it is a holiday village which is a possible surfing venue, being best at mid-tide, dumping at high water.

The low-lying shingle shore of Morfa Dinlle is edged with large stones and a bank which protects against flooding. Sandhills run down the edge of the peninsula. The landing strip is now known as Caernarfon Airport. During the second world war it was RAF Llandwrog and it was here that the first RAF mountain rescue team was formed. In 1989 the Caernarfon Air Museum was opened with aircraft over which visitors may climb, the former RAF Varsity simulator, displays of the Dambusters Squadron, Welsh flying VCs, aviation history in Gwynedd and aviation stamp first-day covers, the Astra cinema with aviation films and an aviation adventure playground for children. Flights are available to Beaumaris, Caernarfon, Llanddwyn Island and Snowdon, one of the aircraft used being the last De Havilland Rapide in Europe still licensed to carry fare paying passengers.

The Bar has claimed its share of vessels over the years and a large mussel bank in the main channel presently gives problems for approaching boats, but an old breakwater runs along to Abermenai Point to protect against the worst ravages of the sea in Caernarfon Bay.

The Menai Strait was formerly three separate valleys with a watershed between the two bridges, prior to a postglacial sea level rise.

Tide movements in the Menai Strait are amongst the most complex anywhere on our coastline. At Menai Bridge the tidal flow reverses 1½ hours before the tide reverses its vertical movement. Surface flow may be in the opposite direction to the flow deeper down. The slack flow at Menai Bridge is over an hour before that at either Puffin Island or Caernarfon as tides flow into the strait from both ends, meet near the bridge and drain out again from this point. Here, the tidal range is some 2.7m larger than at the southwest end of the strait. The tide race at Menai Bridge can be 15km/h, the fastest on the Welsh coast, and so it is vital to work out timings correctly. To get the roughest water at the Swellies the mid-tide period should be used but there is no point in trying to travel too far in this case.

The southwest end of the Menai Strait is guarded by two arms of sand dunes enclosing two large sand bays. Traeth Melynog drains the Afon Braint and is crossed by footpaths to Abermenai Point. Until the 13th century there was a causeway across to the mainland. Foryd Bay, between a golf course

Penrhyn Glas with Yr Eifl beyond, both dropping steeply to the sea

DH Rapide landing at Caernarfon Airport.

£1.50

CAERNARFON CASTLE

and Fort Belan, drains the Afon Gwyrfai, teems with wildfowl and waders and conceals some treacherous quicksand. The large area of shallows is conducive to bass, tope and flatfish and there are clam, mussel and oyster fisheries.

Caernarfon is a strategic town. The Romans built their Segontium fort here in 78 but its current name comes from Edward I's fort opposite Anglesey, Y Gaer yn Arfon, Wales most famous fortress. With its single wall in banded stone modelled on Istanbul, it was begun in 1283 to emphasize English domination over the Welsh and has been owned continuously by the Crown ever since, a centre for English government over north Wales and Wales' nearest building to a royal palace. Edward II was born here in 1284 and introduced as a 'native-born prince who could speak no English', being made Prince of Wales in 1301. The tradition has continued. George V invested Prince Edward in 1911, when Winston Churchill read the Letters Patent. Prince Charles was invested Prince of Wales in the castle in 1969 by the Queen. Other royal visitors have included George VI and Queen Elizabeth the Queen Mother. The North East Tower has the Prince of Wales Exhibition, the Chamberlain Tower has an exhibition of castles of Edward I, the Queen's Tower is the home of the Royal Welch Fusiliers Regimental Museum and the Eagle Tower has a Prospect of Caernarfon exhibition. The King's Gate is said to be the mightiest in the land. The castle has been built on a peninsula between the now culverted Afon Cadnant and the Afon Seiont, crossed by a modern swing footbridge. Constable of the Castle at one time was Lloyd George, Member of Parliament for Caernarfon for 56 years. Part of the *Life and Times of Lloyd George* was filmed here in 1980.

The town has an open air market for Anglesey and the Lleyn Peninsula on Saturdays. It also has the church of Llanbeblig although St Peblig was probably no other than Publius, son of the Roman emporer Magnus Maximus, a throwback to the Segontium days.

Foel has a pier by the Mermaid Inn at the end of the B4419 but it was from Tal-y-Foel that a ferry crossed to Caernarfon from 1425 to 1849. The Anglesey Sea Zoo is now located nearby with masses of sealife, a walk through a shipwreck with conger eels, tanks where lobsters can be touched, tide and wave tanks, radio controlled model boats, a playboat in a sea of bark, an adventure playground and cooked or take away seafood, the zoo having won a British Tourist Authority Come to Britain Award of Merit. Ferodo's friction brake linings works is a little further along on the south bank.

Plas Menai is the Welsh Sports Council's National Watersports Centre. The complex of buildings is surprisingly large and modern with a concrete slipway running down from the boat storage area into the water. The centre has won both a Civic Trust Award and a European Community Award.

St Nidan's church tower is just visible over the trees at Brynsiencyn. Founded 1,300 years ago, it now has only one service each year. However, a stone in the rear porch still traps water which is supposed to have healing properties.

The muddy bottom of the strait appears to be covered with a carpet of dead leaves but closer examination shows that they are an unbroken coating of brittle-stars in assorted colours,

writhing about on the floor of the strait. Fish life includes bass and flounders and winkles are picked up at low tide. Herons fish and the curlew calls distinctively as it sweeps over the water.

Moel-y-Don was once a thriving shipbuilding port with a ferry across to **Y Felinheli**.

Y Felinheli was used by the Vikings in the 8th century but saw most of its development as the outlet for the Dinorwic slate quarries in the 19th century. There is much new housing and the Vaynol Dock marina contains berths for pleasure craft.

Gradually, the sides of the strait become steep and wooded and the channel steadily narrows.

Plas Newydd, built in the 18th century of Moelfre marble by James Watt, houses Rex Whistler's largest wall painting, a collection of military uniforms and relics of the first Marquess of Anglesey and Battle of Waterloo. Attached is the Nelson Centre, Cheshire County Council's outdoor centre. HMS Conway is also nearby. A 160m high Anglesey marble column built at the top of Craig-y-Dinas in 1816 carries a statue of the first Marquess of Anglesey, the second in command to Wellington at Waterloo, a battle in which he had his right leg hit by a cannon ball. It was replaced by a wood, metal and leather device known as the Anglesey Leg and for his remaining 39 years he joked about having one foot in the grave.

A statue of Nelson stands by the water with his 'England expects that every man will do his duty' speech inscribed on the front, not the most appropriate item for this distant part of Wales.

The village on the left is Llanfairpwllgwyngyllgogerychwrndrobwllllantysiliogogogoch, meaning the church of St Mary in the hollow of the white hazel over the rapid whirlpool and the church of St Tysilio by the red cave, two long names having been added together to produce a tourist pulling combination which the mere name of Swellies could not hope to emulate.

The Pont Britannia might have been the first box girder bridge. Built in 1850 by Robert Stephenson and William Fairburn, trains ran through the metal tubes. In 1970 a schoolboy set fire to it and it was rebuilt with metal arches and also an upper deck to take the A55. The great stone lions that used to guard the ends of the bridge now squint along steel girders running past their ears. The clearance of the bridge has been retained but craft using the Menai Strait now have to be smaller because of power transmission cables crossing the strait below bridge level.

The Swellies lie between the bridges and are sea rapids which reach grade 3 if the conditions are right. A standing wave over Swelly Rock sometimes breaks into a stopper, a bedrock rapid forms to the south of Ynys Gored Goch on the flood and a standing wave is located to the north of it on the ebb. Ynys Gored Goch, the island of the red weir, is actually two islands joined by a causeway. There was a commercial fishery there from the 13th century to 1915 which was owned by the bishop of Bangor until 1888 and supplied fish for the monasteries of Anglesey. The eastern island, Tern Island, has a herring smoking tower and a matey toilet with a double seat. The fish traps still exist with a number of dangerous projections which could trap paddlers playing on the rough water thrown up by the weir.

Bangor has built its importance on the Menai Bridge carrying the last public turnpike road in Britain. Thomas Telford built his bridge in 1826.

The remains of old fish traps on Lavan Sands

521m long with a 176m main span and a 161m high water clearance, it was the world's first iron suspension bridge and the longest suspension bridge in Britain for 150 years, being rebuilt in 1938 to 1940. The town has a Childhood Museum and the Tegfryn Art gallery. The Belgian Walk was built by refugees during the first world war. St Tysilio's church on Church Island is reached on a low tide causeway and was built in the 14th century on the site of the 7th-century original built by St Tysilio. Before the bridge was built, cattle were swum across the Menai Strait by drovers but bass, codling, conger eels, flatfish, pollack and whiting are the main swimmers now. **Menai Bridge** on the A545 has hosted Ffair y Borth, one of the largest local fairs in Wales, every October for four centuries. A more recent festival has been the Menai Strait regatta fortnight each August. The A5 leads towards Bangor pier which has been refurbished and a tractor pulls a train of carriages along it to carry members of the public. At the landward end is a building with a penny farthing on the gable and a helter-skelter next to it.

Port Penrhyn is the dock for **Bangor**. The town's cathedral, founded by St Deiniol in 548, is probably the oldest in the British Isles and the most abused. Gardd yr Esgob, the bishop's garden, has every plant mentioned in the *Bible* which will grow in Wales and also those associated with festivals and saints. As well as the Museum of Welsh Antiquities the town houses the Bangor campus of the University of Wales.

Streams rotate clockwise in Conwy Bay, which is dominated by Lavan Sands and Dutchman Sands. These are up to 5km wide in places and reach nearly to Puffin Island at low water. Before the bridges were built, travellers had to walk across the sands and try to attract the attention of boatmen in **Beaumaris** before the rising water made them retreat. Salmon weirs run out 1km over the sands with a black beacon at the north end of the west weir, but the fish traps are very delapidated and there are more bass than salmon in these waters now. There are also mussel banks and a good selection of birdlife from plovers to terns. The sands share (with the Conwy estuary) some 18,000 waders and wildfowl including 1,000 curlew of national importance and 6,000 oystercatchers, 5,000 dunlin and 1,500 redshank, all of international importance.

Behind Bangor Flats is the square shape of Penrhyn Castle. Neo Norman, dating from 1820 to 1845, it contains mock Norman furniture, panelling and plasterwork by Thomas Hopper, fine pictures and a Victorian walled garden. It was built for the Pennant family with the profits of the West Indies sugar trade and Bethesda slate quarries and includes a Grand Staircase, Great Hall floor, billiard table, some fireplaces and a bed all in slate, together with a display of industrial locomotives

including some from the slate quarries. A doll museum contains over a thousand dolls.

There is a sweep of 300m mountains to the Great Ormes Head from the northeastern part of Snowdonia. Tal y Fan, Llwtymor, Bera Mawr, Foel Grach and other peaks form a ridge with just a couple of clefts carved by the Afon Ogwen and Afon Rhaeadr-fawr. In the estuary of the former is a nature reserve. Beyond the latter Gwynedd gives way to Conwy.

The shoreline approaching **Llanfairfechan** past the Bryn-y-neuadd Hospital is well protected by a sea wall built in 1953, over which there is no obvious route from the resort to the beach. On the east side of the Afon Maes-y-bryn is a carpark with toilets, café and children's playground.

Distance
From Llanenddwyn to Llanfairfechan is 144km
Campsites
Llanenddwyn, Llanbedr, Llanfair, Harlech, Morfa Bychan, Llanstumdwy, Abererch, Penrhos, Llanbedrog, Mynytho, Llangian, Sarn Bach, Machroes, Llandegwning, Treheli, Aberdaron, Uwchmynydd, Rhidlios, Morfa, Tyddyn, Tudweiliog, Fron, Bryn-yr-eryr, Gyrn-goch, Pontllyfni, Dinas Dinlle, Morfa Dinlle, Caernarfon, Brynsiencyn, Cefn-bach, Bangor, Penmaenmawr
Youth Hostels
Llanbedr, Bryn Gwynant, Snowdon Ranger, Llanberis, Bangor, Rowen
OS 1:50,000 Sheets
115 Snowdon
123 Lleyn Peninsula
124 Porthmadog and Dolgellau
Imray Charts
C51 Cardigan Bay – Milford Haven to Tremadoc Bay (1:140,800)
C52 Cardigan Bay to Liverpool (1:138,600)
Admiralty Charts
SC 1464 Menai Strait (1:25,000). Swellies (1:10,000)
SC 1970 Caernarfon Bay (1:75,000)
SC 1971 Cardigan Bay – Northern Part (1:75,000)
SC 1977 Holyhead to Great Ormes Head (1:75,000)
SC 1978 Great Ormes Head to Liverpool (1:75,000)
SC 5609 North West Wales
Tidal Constants
Barmouth: HW Dover –0250, LW Dover –0140
Criccieth: HW Dover –0300, LW Dover –0150
Pwllheli: HW Dover –0300, LW Dover –0200
St Tudwal's Roads: HW Dover –0310, LW Dover –0200
Aberdaron: HW Dover –0300, LW Dover –0200
Bardsey Island: HW Dover –0320, LW Dover –0230
Porth Ysgaden: HW Dover –0210, LW Dover –0130
Porth Dinllaen: HW Dover –0200, LW Dover –0120
Trefor: HW Dover –0200, LW Dover –0120
Fort Belan: HW Dover –0120, LW Dover –0100
Caernarfon: HW Dover –0120, LW Dover –0040
Portdinorwic: HW Dover –0110, LW Dover –0040
Menai Bridge: HW Dover –0030, LW Dover
Beaumaris: HW Dover –0030, LW Dover
Sea Area
Irish Sea
Rescue
Inshore lifeboats: Barmouth, Criccieth, Pwllheli, Abersoch, Beaumaris
All weather lifeboats: Barmouth, Pwllheli, Porthdinllaen, Llandudno
Helicopter: Valley
Maritime Rescue Centre
Holyhead, 01407 762051

13 NORTH WALES

A coast of holiday resorts

They rowed her in across the rolling foam,
  The cruel crawling foam,
  The cruel hungry foam,
 To her grave beside the sea:
But still the boatmen hear her call the cattle home
 Across the sands of Dee.

Charles Kingsley

Llanfairfechan is a long established village with an ancient settlement although the most conspicuous feature is the one which is to dominate much of this coast, the A55 North Wales Expressway. It is a coast which throws up agate, jasper and serpentine along its length and is a popular holiday coast because of its proximity to Liverpool and Manchester. There is a small sailing club in the village.

The tunnels, viaducts and fences of Penmaen-Mawr Point

The eastgoing stream in Conwy Bay, populated by bass, runs southeast towards Penmaen-bach Point. First, however, comes Penmaen-Mawr Point, a high peak above a bold headland which pushes right to the sea and constricts communications, as shown by the headland's viaducts and tunnels. A major engineering success in 1850 was the opening of the Chester and Holyhead Railway, an important part of the connection between England and Ireland, which had to overcome many difficulties. Heavy coastal protection was needed for 70km of the route. This was the most exposed point and engineer-in-chief Robert Stevenson watched 12m waves destroy a section of the 500m solid masonry wall in 1846. He replaced it with the Penmaenmawr Sea Viaduct, a 170m open viaduct of 13 spans protected by an apron with large boulders set in concrete and protected by piles. Brick arches superseded the timber and cast-iron deck in 1908, but it still serves its purpose of dissipating energy as the sea surges through and around the piers. It feeds into the 230m Penmaenmawr tunnel which is extended at each end by avalanche shelters to protect against rockfalls. The danger remains and a series of unsightly fences have been strung across the slope to protect the new road.

There are disused quarries above, formerly served by a jetty for loading the stone, and the site

dates from the Stone Age when there was an axe factory with axes exported as far as Wiltshire and Ireland.

Penmaenmawr means large stone head. The village was the favourite holiday resort of Gladstone and attracts present day bathers, waterskiers and sailors.

Beyond Dwygyfylchi is Penmaen-bach Point, capped by a fort site on Alltwen, the northern extremity of the Snowdonia range and the end of the Snowdon National Park. Again, the cliffs forced the coaching road and railway builders to use cliff shelves and tunnels. There now three tunnels including a conspicuous new one carrying the westbound carriageway of the A55. The railway is protected by a 6m wall which was partly destroyed in 1945 and rebuilt in reinforced concrete.

The Conwy estuary seen from the Great Ormes Head with the West Shore in the foreground, Deganwy on the left overlooking Conwy Sands, Penmaen-bach Point in the centre and Penmaen-Mawr Point to the right with the nearest of the Snowdonia peaks rising behind

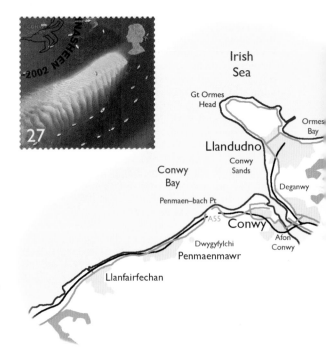

The Afon Conwy emerges between golf courses and discharges across the extensive Conwy Sands which has mussel banks in places. Behind the Conwy Morfa golf course is the town of **Conwy** and its castle of 1283, which replaced Deganwy Castle. Not visible is the A55 river crossing in Britain's first immersed tube tunnel, environmentally hidden by the estuary instead of using a bridge which would have been £15,000,000 cheaper.

Deganwy was Dinas Conwy, the fortress on the Conwy. The castle was built between 1244 and 1254 on a site which had been fortified since at least the 9th century. It was fought over and destroyed many times, once by lightning, abandoned in 1263 and reoccupied in 1277. The two hillocks formed natural mottes, the east one being defended by a large open backed U-plan tower while its counterpart formed an inner bailey with curtain wall, hall and large round tower. Between them was a large irregular oval bailey with curtain wall and gatehouse.

Tidal streams flow up to 9km/h in the channel, ingoing from HW Dover –0500 and outgoing from HW Dover –0030. A floating pontoon moored in the estuary is marked 'Rescue'.

Llandudno was built in the mid-19th century by Edward Mostyn and Owen Williams on a tombolo joining the former island of Great Orme to the mainland. They transformed the marshland into gracious terraces of Victorian elegance which still have some of the best shops in north Wales, the many large hotels proving popular for conferences.

On the West Shore are a putting green, children's playground, paddling pool and statue of the White Rabbit, unveiled in 1933 by Lloyd-George as a reminder that Henry Liddell's family had a holiday home here and that it was on this beach that Lewis Carroll used to stroll with Alice while composing *Alice in Wonderland*.

Running across the throat of the Great Ormes Head is a raised path which passes through an aviary and semi-tropical gardens, drawing attention to the mild climate, and past dozens of benches donated by or in memory of people who have enjoyed holidays in the town.

The final building on the West Shore is the Gogarth Abbey Hotel, the remains of the bishop's palace itself being a little further along at the hamlet of Gogarth where the most conspicuous feature now is a tower on the shore, approached by a walkway from on top of the cliffs.

Near the end of the Great Ormes Head are half a dozen gun emplacements, approached on the landward side down a long flight of steps.

Formerly the site of a Roman copper mine, the Great Ormes Head is now a country park with mountain limestone cliffs up to 120m high and a limestone pavement. The grass here is rich in unusual plants and is inhabited by feral goats and the dwarf grayling butterfly which is unique to this part of north Wales, flying in late June, earlier and less bright than the English species. The limestone is sculpted and on the north side of the head are several caves including Hornby Cave, a sanctuary for sealife of all kinds with grey seals here and common seals further east as far as the Dee estuary. Pigeon Cave has a way out to the cliffs above.

Rebuilding Marine Drive on Great Ormes Head after a landslip

There is a tide race off the head on springs with large waves in opposing winds and clapotis up to 100m offshore, but useful eddies close in to the cliffs if the flow is adverse. Marine Drive runs precariously round the cliff and new benching had to be cut in 1990 after a cliff fall.

Looking across Ormes Bay from Llandudno to the Little Ormes Head

Below the disused Great Ormes lighthouse are steep cliffs with row upon row of guillemots.

The ornate Llandudno Pier runs 900m out into Ormes Bay. Built in 1876 by John Dixon to a James Brunless and Alexander McKerrow design, it has an 18m T-shaped pierhead and 11 kiosks with an arm connecting along the shore with the pavilion. The following year the Great Orme Railway was built, climbing up to the 207m summit with a hotel on top. From here it is possible to see the Isle of Man and Cumbria on a clear day plus a lot of the Welsh coast nearby. Also running up it is the Cabin

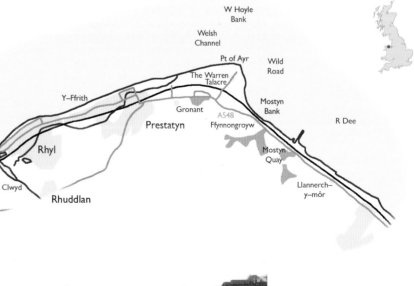

Llandudno Pier with Snowdonia beyond

Lift, Britain's longest cable-car railway at 1.6km. This small headland is dotted with many features of interest, a burial chamber, Stone Row, St Tudno's Well and an aerial to name but a few.

Water skiing and sailing take place in Ormes Bay or Llandudno Bay where tidal streams are negligible. From here to Point of Ayr streams generally run up to 6km/h, starting east at HW Dover −0610 and west from HW at Dover, protected from the north by the Constable Bank.

The bay ends with the Little Ormes Head, another limestone cliff and pavement block with rich grassland and unusual plants but this time with a conspicuous disused brown quarry. The vertical cliffs are actually higher than on the Great Orme and attract guillemots, razorbills, puffins, fulmars and climbers.

Penrhyn Bay was formerly the mouth of the Conwy until it was diverted by the Irish Sea ice sheet in the Ice Age, dredging up marine shells which can be seen in the subsequent boulder clay cliffs.

Off the shallow boulder-strewn beach there are bass, conger eels, flounders, mackerel, mullet, plaice, prawns and rays. At low tide the remains of triangular walls built as fish traps by monks can be seen at Rhôs-on-Sea. On the shore are the remains of the 16th-century chapel of St Trillo, a mere 3.6m x 1.8m, also associated with the monastery.

A wreck lies off Rhos Point while boats generally shelter behind a detached breakwater of stone which forms a makeshift harbour at this waterskiing and bathing venue. Just south of the harbour is the landing point for submarine cables from Heysham and the Isle of Man. The village is overlooked by the hilltop sites of an ancient settlement and Llys Euryn, but its most notable building is the Harlequin Puppet Theatre, built in 1958 by Eric Bramall and employing 1,000 puppets in a season of plays, operas, musical comedies and cabarets. Some 60 productions have ranged from the *Mikado* and the *Nutcracker Suite* to *Alice in Wonderland*.

Colwyn Bay has negligible tidal streams. Notable features are the 560m long Victoria Pier and an air dome building near the civic centre. Less obvious from the sea are the promenade miniature railway, Eirias Park's amusements, the indoor pool, the international folk dance festival or the fact that **Colwyn Bay** was the proud holder of the Royal Mail award for being the most successful twin town in the UK at improving world harmony (however that was assessed). Harmony cannot have been improved by the busy transport corridor which separates this resort from the beach with its bathing, waterskiing and sailing, the A55 running along the shore as far as Abergele and the railway following the coast to Flint.

An arc of footbridge rises, Le Mans style, over the road below the Seventy Degrees Hotel (presumably the temperature rather than the angle of lean) as the Denbigh Moors reach the coast at **Old Colwyn**. Mynydd Marian was formerly the site of Llysfaen Telegraph Station and remains the site of limestone quarrying operations from where stone is loaded onto ships up to 3,000 tonnes at 900 tonnes/hour from the 220m Raynes Jetty and 200m Llysfaen Jetty. There have been frequent landslips at Llysfaen and this section of A55 is protected by a slope of rock pieces up to 1 tonne each topped by 22,000 5 tonne dolosse units which make landing extremely difficult. The A547 on top of the cliff is supported by a great concrete arch which appears to be a bridge

which does not clear a gap, there being only solid rock visible below the arch.

There was a terrible railway accident in 1868 when a string of railway wagons loaded with paraffin rolled down from the quarry into the path of the Irish Mail. At that time the carriages were lit by gas and passengers were locked into the compartments for safety. 33 people died and were buried in St Michael's churchyard, Abergele. As a result, railway carriages were no longer locked until recently for the safety of passengers.

A green dinosaur and several brightly coloured fungi on the approach to Llanddulas advertise Dinosaur World.

The cliff pulls back behind Abergele Roads where it is topped by a prominent tower with more fortifications down below. Much larger, however, is the 1815 folly of Gwrych Castle with its 18 towers, now a facility with restaurant and bars but with jousting shows in the summer.

More conventional sports facilities are to be found in **Abergele**, together with a Monday livestock sale.

Seaside amusements and donkey rides are available at Pensarn, the beach where Captain Matthew Webb trained to become the first person to swim the English Channel in 1875.

Belgrano and Towyn seem to be one large static caravan site hiding behind the railway embankment, the Cob. 1.8km of shingle beach and groynes are followed by the 1.3km Rhuddlan Marsh wall, first embanked in 1800 by the trustees and improved in 1880 when the LNWR took over. In January 1990 the embankment was breached during a storm and Towyn flooded to a considerable depth. Eventually the water was mopped up and houses redecorated, only to discover subsidence setting in. Meanwhile, embankment protection work was undertaken and in technical circles there was hot debate as to whether such embankments (of which there are plenty in Wales) should remain the responsibility of British Rail or whether they should be managed by councils or the Environment Agency, the latter seeming to have drawn the greatest support.

In quieter times Towyn has harness racing, swimming and other seaside amusements. Swimming and donkey rides are also popular at Kinmel Bay, which has a funfair at each end.

The River Clwyd, which follows the strike faulting of the Vale of Clwyd and forms the Conwy/Denbighshire border, emerges inconspicuously past the Marine Lake in **Rhyl**. It discharges between a sewer running out to a buoy on the west side and revetment on the east side, producing dangerous currents as it leaves Foryd Harbour. The Marine Lake has waterskiing, windsurfing, pedaloes, sailing dinghies and a minature railway round the outside. Rhyl is made for holidaymakers. The Suncentre with tropical pools, silver surf and wavemakers, white water whizz down a green dragon and rooftop monorail claims to be Wales' premier tourist attraction. The Sports Centre has a heated pool, there is a paddling pool and the old pool has been stocked with sea trout for anglers to pull out. There is a roller skateboarding rink, Superbowl tenpin bowling, new Rhyl Theatre, a pylon overlooking the town, Butterfly Jungle, Botanical Gardens and Candyland children's theme park on the promenade and still they have to take shopping trolleys on the beach and abandon them in the intertidal zone. There is a helicopter landing site on the promenade near the hospital.

The disused Point of Ayr lighthouse with the North Hoyle windfarm on the horizon.

Behind the groynes of Ffrith beach is a golf course which produces a break in the buildings before further coastal protection work, the holiday camps of **Prestatyn** and a prominent hotel in a sorry state without its roof. Another holiday resort, Prestatyn has the Nova, developed from the old Royal Lido, Neptune's Fun Pools with waterslides and a large amusement park with vintage cars, motorboat pool and go-kart and motorcycle tracks.

The station is particularly interesting as one of the few remaining single-storey prefabricated station buildings produced at Crewe at the end of the 19th century. In 2m panels, the timber frame was faced with rusticated boarding, canopies with valences cantilevered out over the platform on timber beams and brickwork used for footings, fireplaces and chimneys. When it was rebuilt in 1979 the style was retained.

Prestatyn is located at the northern end of the Clwydian Hills (with their radio masts) and is at the end of Offa's Dyke and the Offa's Dyke Long Distance Path.

Behind the dunes to the east of the town is a river which eventually seeps away into the sand as it crosses the Denbighshire/Flintshire border and nears another holiday camp. The Warren continues to Point of Ayr where there is a conspicuous disused lighthouse on the beach at Talacre, a wreck, sandpipers and often a flock of cormorants drying their wings.

Unlike the days when sailing ships used to travel up the estuary of the River Dee to Chester, silting has resulted in the whole area largely drying at low tide, West Hoyle Bank drying up to 10km from the entrance. Pilots are picked up at Dee south cardinal lightbuoy, northeast of Point of Ayr on the far side of the Welsh Channel. At the east end of the Welsh Channel the flood runs northeast, becoming easterly at HW Dover –0530, reaching 5km/h at HW Dover –0240 and turning northerly at HW Dover –0015. Near springs it runs up to 7km/h between HW Dover –0330 and –0130. The ebb begins at HW Dover +0015, west–northwest, becoming northwest at up to 4km/h. Above Point of Ayr the streams run in the channels when the banks are exposed, otherwise running directly in and out. The navigation difficulties keep the estuary empty for the birds and it is mostly a SSSI.

To the south of Talacre is Point of Ayr Colliery, one of the last two pits in north Wales. Workings run out under the sea for 2km and it has been the scene of investigations for making oil from coal. A gas terminal has been proposed for Point of Ayr, causing consternation to the RSPB.

Wild Road runs past Mostyn Bank off Ffynnongroyw to Mostyn Quay, the last harbour in the estuary which can be reached by seagoing ships. Unexpectedly, the 650m training wall is on the east side of the port to protect against silt, rather than on the exposed seaward side. Ironworks have been replaced by small factories and workshops. The quay imports woodpulp, paper, timber, phosphate, sulphur, fertilizers and milk products and exports steel products, ferromanganese, coal, coke and building materials, together with a two way flow of general cargo. Several cranes surround the quay and it has pillbox defence arrangements on the training wall.

A coarse seawall leads to Llannerch-y-môr, a small creek dominated by the Fun Ship, the former cruise ship *Duke of Lancaster*, now beached high and dry. The dock has been considered for a yacht marina but nothing has come of it. On the west side of the stream is a craft centre with a large carparking area and parking may also be possible on the east side in an open air market site. Unless the tide is high enough to reach the railway bridge it would pay to disembark on the east side of the creek to avoid the security defences around the ship.

The *Duke of Lancaster* at Llanerch-y-môr

Distance
From Llanfairfechan to Llanerch-y-môr is 62km
Campsites
Penmaenmawr, Dwygfylchi, Conwy, Mynydd Marian, Abergele, Towyn, Rhuddlan, Prestatyn, Gronant, Caerwys
Youth Hostels
Rowen, Conwy, Maeshafn
OS 1:50,000 Sheets
115 Snowdon
116 Denbigh and Colwyn Bay
Imray Chart
C52 Cardigan Bay to Liverpool (1:138,600)
Admiralty Charts
1953 Approaches to the River Dee (1:25,000).
Mostyn Docks (1:12,500
SC 1977 Holyhead to Great Ormes Head (1:75,000)
SC 1978 Great Ormes Head to Liverpool (1:75,000)
SC 5609 North West Wales
Tidal Constants
Beaumaris: HW Dover –0030, LW Dover
Llandudno: Dover –0010
Colwyn Bay: HW Dover –0010, LW Dover +0010
Mostyn Quay: Dover
Sea Area
Irish Sea
Rescue
Inshore lifeboats: Beaumaris, Conwy, Llandudno, Rhyl, Flint
All weather lifeboats: Llandudno, Rhyl
Maritime Rescue Centre
Holyhead, 01407 762051
Liverpool, 0151 931 3341

14 MERSEYSIDE

Silted estuaries given over to the birds

Now no more the big cranes lie idle
the ships are fast turnin' round,
they're buildin' new docks up at Seaforth
all part of our own holy ground.
Now Liverpool is on the move
the sleepin' giant awakes,
the greatest port in all the world
and we've got what it takes.
So when I die, don't bury me
in Anfield or in Ford,
just lock me in a container
for the crane to lift on board,
for the crane to lift on board.

J B Jaques

From Llannerch-y-môr the main channel follows the southwest side of the estuary to Greenfield. Nearby Basingwerk Abbey was founded in the 12th century but acquired an unusual reputation for an abbey in the 15th century when there were many guests, fine wines and good food served in two sittings.

A textile works is protected by what must be one of the ugliest pieces of seawall anywhere, very broken reinforced concrete, the whole resembling a mass of giant, rusty wirewool. At Holywell Bank the flood starts at HW Dover –0445 and lasts for 5 hours. Conditions in the estuary should not be underestimated although the estuary is much used by small boats and an army of cockle collectors may be seen humping sacks of shells around on the Holywell Bank before returning to points such as Bagillt, where there are 3 disused wharves.

Flint Castle stands by large works. The first of Edward I's chain of castles in north Wales, it was built between 1277 and 1286 on the edge of the sea for replenishment. With a square inner bailey with curtain wall and three round towers, it was unusual in that the 3-storey round keep was detached from the rest of the fortifications and surrounded by its own moat, now dry. This is where Shakespeare claims Bolingbroke forced Richard II to surrender although Conwy Castle is more likely. The town's dock and approach channel have now silted up.

The River Dee proper emerges under a striking new cable stayed bridge between the power station at Connah's Quay and the former Shotton steelworks. To travel along the northeast shore of the estuary needs careful attention to tide levels as most of the estuary dries, leaving wastes with just curlews, terns and other birds.

A large area of marsh at the head of the estuary is a danger area because of a rifle range, but it should not be a problem anywhere deep enough to float a boat.

The shore crosses from the Welsh county of Flintshire briefly into the English county of Cheshire as it approaches **Neston**, the birthplace of Lady Hamilton, where the church has notable Edward Burne-Jones stained glass windows.

Perhaps nowhere illustrates the change in the estuary better than at Parkgate. When Chester

Flint Castle, the start of Edward I's chain, looks out over the waters of the Dee estuary

silted up in the 18th century this shrimping village became the embarkation point for Irish packet boats. Today it is fronted by up to 2km of marsh, even at high water, and water is not even visible across Gayton Sands for much of the time.

Dawpool Bank performs a similar function for **Heswall**, the next major place on the Wirral peninsula after crossing from Cheshire into Merseyside. Heswall Hill is red Keuper sandstone with gorse. Along its foot, behind the sewage works on the shore, is the 19km long Wirral Country Park on a former railway line.

Thurstaston Common is the same sandstone and gorse, acid heath rich in insect life, including Thor's Stone, a 7.6m pinnacle of weathered sandstone. The area is used for orienteering and the major building is Thurstaston Hall.

The sandstone and gorse continue to Caldy Hill with its two radio masts, off which lie Caldy Blacks sands, and the land finally drops away at **West Kirby** with Tell's Tower, the Grange Monument and the War Memorial all visible. Along the front is the 13ha Marine Lake, home of Dee Sailing Club, sailing dinghies, sailboards, rowing boats and canoes. The village at the end of the MerseyRail line and on the A540 was the setting of the film *Letter to Brezhnev* in 1984.

Offshore is a Bunter sandstone ridge which gets bigger as it runs out from Caldy Blacks through Seldom Seen Rocks, Lime Wharf, Tanskey Rocks, Little Eye and Little Hilbre Island to Hilbre Island itself, all of which are accessible on foot for half of the tide cycle and have many Ordovician, Silurian and Carboniferous fossils. Because of the ease of access, a permit is now required before visiting Hilbre Island but it proves rather hard to enforce once people arrive, especially by water. The last two islands have 17m cliffs on the southwest side. An idea of the rate of erosion is given by the fact that the islands were all linked and covered 3km^2 in the 17th century, having provided camping space for 4,000 soldiers and 200 cavalry on their way to Ireland a century before. Today Hilbre Island covers 4ha, Little Hilbre Island 1ha and Little Eye 2,000m^2 at high tide.

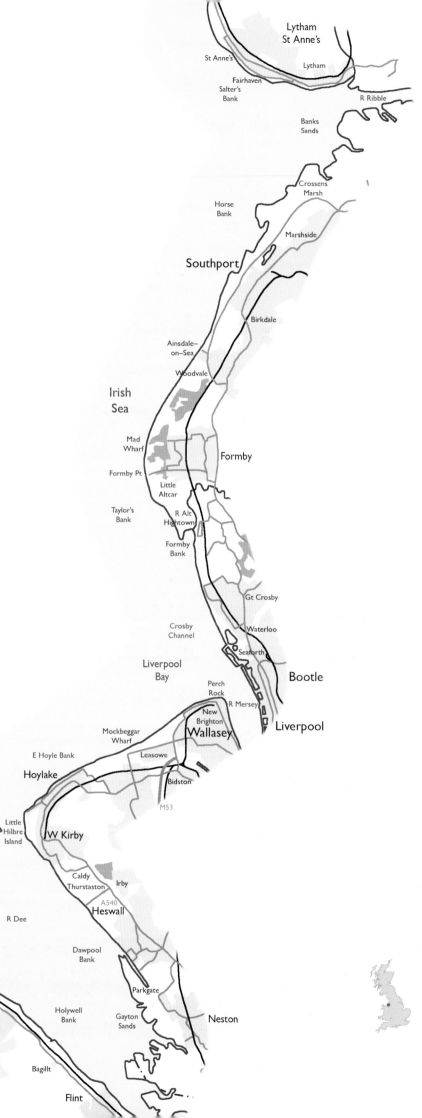

The Devil's Hole cave on Little Hilbre Island was used by smugglers while Lady's Cave on Hilbre Island takes its name from a shipwrecked woman fleeing her father, living here until she died. There was a small religious community before the arrival of the Norsemen in 905. After the Norman Conquest it was given to the Abbey of St Evroul, who maintained a small cell and shrine to St Hildenburgh, and there was a small order of Benedictine monks until 1541 when the parent abbey at Chester was suppressed. The buildings of a former telegraph station are now used by the keeper and staff of what is an important nature reserve. Most of the Dee estuary is a grade 1 SSSI and Special Protection Area under the EU Birds Directive. The RSPB claimed that the 100,000 wildfowl and waders, including 30,000 oystercatchers, 5,500 shelducks, 4,200 teal, 7,200 pintails, 1,800 grey plovers, 17,000 knots, 14,000 dunlin and 7,000 redshanks, were threatened with immediate and permanent damage because of waste tipping, port expansion, road development, pollution and recreation. The bird observatory is one of the finest sites in England for observing and photographing overwintering waders with over 1,000 birds ringed annually and 221 species recorded, including large flocks of curlews, ringtailed plovers, bar-tailed godwits and sanderlings. A number of hides include one in the stonework of the building which formerly acted as the lifeboat station at the top of its slipway.

Opposite the island on the West Hoyle Bank is a favourite spot for grey seals to sun themselves, often 100–200 at a time, their presence clearly audible as well as visible.

A golf course leads to Hilbre Point which ends with Red Rocks, the end of the Dee estuary and the start of Liverpool Bay. Beyond the disused lighthouse in **Hoylake** (lake by the hillock) is a seawater bathing pool. The East Hoyle Bank forms a 3km wide beach where sand filled Hoyle Lake as the Dee silted up.

Leasowe lighthouse is also disused. Initially, the shifting sand was not firm enough to support a tower but a wreck in 1760 deposited cotton bales on the beach. These were left to rot and the ensuing vegetation formed the sand into a base strong enough to support the tower.

Mockbeggar Wharf is sinking at 9mm/year and has caused concern that the Mersey might cut another exit, with all the problems that would cause for the port of Liverpool. To prevent this happening and to keep the sea from the low central part of the Wirral the Wallasey Embankment was started in 1794. The sand, clay, silt and peat structure was only partly successful so in 1829 2.7km of Old Embankment was built, 600mm of clay overlain with 200mm to 500mm sandstone blocks. In 1894 the 3.6km New Embankment extended it and a toe wall was added to prevent undercutting. In 1941 it was faced with

150mm of concrete in 4m squares which have since broken up, requiring a major rebuild to be started in 1973. The fight against the sea goes on.

Behind the wall is the North Wirral Country Park and four golf courses surrounding **Wallasey**, which takes its name from the Old English for island of the Welsh. Leasowe Castle, built four centuries ago by Ferdinand, the second heir to the throne, is now a hotel. The tree covered Bidston Hill, another outcrop of red Keuper sandstone, is 40ha of heathland with a windmill, a former lighthouse and an observatory famous for its tidal predictions and research. At the foot of the hill is Bidston Moss, on which is Bidston Moss Interchange at the northern end of the M53, its elevated structures built on the longest piles in Europe.

New Brighton has a breakwater of dolosse units, one of several breakwater structures scattered about this section of the coast. Groynes run out into the sea but that was clearly not all, the smell of sewage being particularly strong and all too clearly visible until the Mersey estuary sewerage scheme was undertaken. A bathing pool allowed visitors an alternative. As lifer is Old English for sludge, it seems that Liverpool had not benefitted from clean water for some while.

New Brighton grew in prosperity on the ferry connection to **Liverpool** from its former pier. Its most prominent features are tower blocks with a blackened church spire nestling between them but the New Brighton Tower of 1898 was even more notable, the tallest building in Britain until it fell into disuse and was demolished in 1921. Perch Rock bears the former Rock Lighthouse and Fort Perch from 1826, now the Museum of the Aircraft Wreck Recovery Group with associated tea rooms and nature trail. Indeed, wrecks seem to be the general feature of the area, the Brazil Bank and Great Burbo Bank being littered with them. Powerboat racers try to add more and there is a significant tide race past the end of Perch Rock.

The Crosby Channel of the River Mersey is edged by training banks. Streams flow in the channel when the banks are dry but take a direct line when they are covered. Flood flows in the channel set eastwards while the ebb set is northwest, both strong on springs. At Perch Rock the flow is up to 9km/h. The river is used by tankers up to 200,000 tonnes and the *Mersey Channel Collision Rules* need to be read as the penalties for causing an accident are heavy. There is least traffic in the river at low tide. Amongst the commercial traffic are passenger ferries for Dublin and Llandudno and vehicle ferries for Belfast, Douglas and Dublin.

The Mersey used to discharge via the Dee at Shotton but the present channel was possibly opened up by an ice sheet. Crossing the rivermouth from the Wirral to Sefton it is possible to see up to Birkenhead and Liverpool with the Royal Liver

Looking up the Mersey past the Royal Seaforth Docks and the Port Radar Station from the Crosby Channel

Building and the Cunard Tower. The tall ships have also left from here.

Ten kilometres of docks end at **Bootle**. Despite the loss of trade from Liverpool, this is still one of our busiest ports, not least because of the Royal Seaforth Docks with over 3km of quays, including the Seaforth Container Dock Terminal which handles ships to 75,000 tonnes. This revolutionized Liverpool as a port with the world's first computer-controlled container operations. There are roll-on roll-off facilities and berths for bulk liquids, meat and grain. The Port Radar Station is a striking mushroom shaped tower at the northwest end.

To the north is Great Crosby. In Norse days Crosby meant place of the crosses.

The present day settlement ends abruptly with a golf course and then the coast seems more rural, but this does not mean that it is time to relax. At Hightown on the River Alt are the Altcar ranges, firing at surface targets up to 2.4km from the coast. Notwithstanding, it seems an acceptable place for little gulls which are present all year round in the vicinity of Crosby Beacon.

Wrecks litter the shoreline from Formby Bank to Mad Wharf and out onto Taylor's Bank which reaches out to form the northern side of the

The remains of the very first lifeboat station on Formby Point. Rigs are visible on the skyline

Waterloo was the place wealthy Liverpool merchants chose to build their houses in the Regency and Victorian eras. Its largest feature is a 24ha marina with sailing and canoeing, a model boating lake, children's playground, heated indoor pool and bowling and putting greens.

Queen's Channel at low tide. Tides flood straight in and ebb straight out.

By Formby Point the coastline has become entirely sand dunes and 7km^2 of these, dotted with SSSIs, continue to Southport. Near another beacon can be found the remains of the first lifeboat

The very flat beach at Southport requires unusual safety cover in the form of a DUKW

station, in use from 1776 to 1916. The sea has been encroaching for 700 years and Mad Wharf sands dry up to 2km offshore, welcomed by many waders including oystercatchers and sanderlings. A line of tide poles run out from the point. A screen of trees, home of red squirrels, block out **Formby**, a commuter town for Liverpool after the railway arrived in the 19th century. The name is derived from the Norse man Forni.

Ainsdale Sands beyond Woodvale Airfield have blackheaded gulls on the beach and a National Nature Reserve behind the dunes with rich flora, sand lizards, natterjack toads and red squirrels. For all that, there is plenty of human activity, Pontin's holiday camp at Ainsdale-on-Sea, waterskiing and a 16km/h speed limit on the beach, dating from the time when the sands were used as a road, the speed limit not being applied when motor races take place on the sands. A little further along, the Birkdale Sands have an aircraft runway marked out below the high tide area and the sands are also used for training racehorses. The Birkdale Hills behind are the location of the Royal Birkdale golf course.

A length of road along the shore holds a lesson for road builders. This road was built across a former rubbish tip, was underdesigned and went into a switchback shape. At the legal speed limit its undulations give an interesting but not uncomfortable ride without damaging suspensions but, thereafter, the ride quickly becomes unpleasant, the ideal hump solution discovered by accident.

Southport is a mainly Victorian and Edwardian watering hole, the Parisian look of the main street being spoiled only by the many posters proclaiming that entertainers and groups last heard of several decades ago are alive and well and performing the summer season here. Behind the 35ha Marine Lake with powerboats, sailing, rowing and jet skis, is the heart of Southport's life. Pleasureland has over 50 attractions. There is a zoo, aquarium, Happiland with miniature railway, Floral Hall with one of the country's major flower festivals (the Southport Flower Show in August), botanical gardens, smallest public house in Britain next to Southport Theatre and golf courses. The pier was the first true pleasure pier and was the longest in the country at 1.097km when it opened in 1860, extended to 1.335km in the first decade of its life but subsequently shortened after repeated storm damage. The original tramway has been replaced with a miniature railway and there are modern amusement facilities, bar, café, shops and a Pier Festival in late July with 9 days of outdoor theatre, comedy, musical acts and sporting events. Now, back to its original length, it is still the second longest pier in Britain. Sadly, however, there is no approach channel and at low tide the sea is 3km away across Southport Sands.

The flat sands spawn a profusion of unlikely vehicles in addition to the hovercraft making trips to St Anne's. The lifeguards use a DUKW. Shrimpers use tractors in the sea or lorries with raised flat beds and large cabs with noticeably fewer windows than might be expected. These lorries seem almost sinister as they move slowly and quietly across the sand before driving into the sea and trailing their nets. Taken with diggers and dump trucks working to extract aggregate from the sands, the area can be more like a construction site on a wet day than the sea.

The Ribble estuary at high tide is a 10km long triangle penetrating inland, its southeast side edged by up to 3km of Banks Marsh with its many drainage channels and its northeast side edged by Lytham St Anne's. At low tide, however, it is totally different, an almost straight coastine, the river discharging and flooding in the Gut Channel between two irregular training walls at up to 3km/h. At this stage the estuary is an almost unbroken expanse of sandbanks which are a Special Protection Area under the EU Birds Directive. Crossens roost may have 150,000 waders present. The estuary is one of the top five European wildfowl areas and has the second largest British group of pinkfooted geese (10,000), the fourth largest concentration of common terns

Shrimping lorries off Southport

and the fifth largest blackheaded gullery. Numbers include 470 Bewick's swans, 290 whooper swans, 4,000 shelduck, 60,000 wigeon, 4,800 teal, 12,000 oystercatchers, 2,700 grey plovers, 12,000 bar-tailed godwits, 35,000 knots, 2,200 sanderlings and 1,600 redshanks. The RSPB claimed the estuary was in immediate danger of permanent damage to the bird colonies by marinas, land reclamation, waste disposal and recreation. Birds which sit unperturbed on the sands or continue squabbles already in progress as fighter aircraft thunder overhead on low level training flights up the estuary seem to suggest that it will take quite a lot to upset their present way of life.

It is an area with few features although there is a wreck off Horse Bank and numerous stakes on Marshside Sands. Over the course of Banks Sands the sand gives way to mud and Sefton gives way to Lancashire as the estuary tapers down to the river proper.

Warton Aerodrome's main runway is angled over the estuary at Warton Bank, just above the entry point of the Main Drain, the eastern limit of **Lytham St Anne's**. The most prominent feature on the north shore is a white windmill set amongst the churches of Lytham. Although it looks pristine its machinery was destroyed in 1929 when a gust of wind spun the sails the wrong way. Lytham takes its name from the Old English hlith, slope, although the whole area is notably flat.

The north shore is Lancashire but the refined nature of Lytham St Anne's is out of character for all of this part of the coast. There is a lack of brashness and the coastal entertainments are more conservative. Lowther Gardens and Fairhaven Lake between them offer flower beds, bowling greens, tennis courts, indoor pool, yachting, motor boating, rowing, canoeing, water skiing, launch trips, paddling and a model yacht pool.

The 140m St Anne's Pier of 1885 has a mock Tudor entrance, added last century, and has also suffered the loss of some of its structure. It faces onto Salter's Bank which leads out to Stanner Point, 5km away at low tide. The waters can be difficult. A monument close by relates to an incident in 1816 when the lifeboat and its 13 crew plus 14 of the 16 crew of the Southport lifeboat were lost while trying to reach the barque *Mexico*, and, as a result, improvements were made to lifeboat design.

St Anne's is the quieter and more reserved end of the town, predominantly Victorian and Edwardian villas. There is parking at North Hollow although this beach is used as a sand yachting centre with the national championships and other major events being held here. The beach runs the risk of being a racecourse at these times and it is not the ideal occasion to try to cross.

The windmill and churches of Lytham seen from the River Ribble at low tide

Distance
From Llanerch-y-môr to Lytham St Anne's is 79km
Campsites
Caerwys, Halkyn, Thursaston, Irby, Ainsdale, Banks, Peel Hill
Youth Hostels
Maeshafn, Liverpool, Slaidburn
OS 1:50,000 Sheets
102 Preston and Blackpool
108 Liverpool
116 Denbigh and Colwyn Bay
117 Chester and Wrexham
Imray Charts
C52 Cardigan Bay to Liverpool (1:138,600)
C62 Irish Sea (1:280,000)
Admiralty Charts
1951 Approaches to Liverpool (1:25,000)
1953 Approaches to the River Dee (1:25,000).
SC 1978 Great Ormes Head to Liverpool (1:75,000)
1981 Approaches to Preston (1:75,000)
3490 Port of Liverpool – Northern Part (1:12,500)
Tidal Constants
Mostyn Quay: Dover
Connah's Quay: HW Dover +0020, LW Dover +0400
Hilbre Island: Dover
New Brighton: Dover +0010
Formby: HW Dover, LW Dover –0010
Southport: Dover
Blackpool: Dover
Sea Area
Irish Sea
Range
Altcar
Rescue
Inshore lifeboats: Flint, West Kirby, New Brighton, Lytham St Anne's
All weather lifeboats: Rhyl, Hoylake, Lytham St Anne's
Maritime Rescue Centres
Liverpool, 0151 931 3341.

15 MORECAMBE BAY

Britain's favourite holiday destination

And this huge castle, standing here sublime,
 I love to see the look with which it braves,
– Cased in the unfeeling armour of old time –
 The lightning, the fierce wind, and trampling waves.

William Wordsworth

Weak tide streams are found between the Ribble and Morecambe Bay although the coast is affected by the wind. Lytham St Anne's ends suddenly with a golf course and Blackpool Airport at Squires Gate. Aircraft take off out to sea, flying fast and low over the holiday camp at the west end of the main runway.

Lancashire becomes Blackpool and the town of **Blackpool** lies entirely to the east of the A584 which runs along the top of cliffs with a seawall at their foot. The beach is 500m wide at low tide but disappears at high tide so the town has had to develop other more reliable attractions.

The cliff road is also the line of the Blackpool–Fleetwood tramway which runs from Starr Gate to Fleetwood Ferry Terminal. It opened in 1885 as the first electrical tramway in Britain with standard 1.435m gauge, taking power from an underground conduit. In 1899 overhead lines were introduced and other routes were added until 1920. Closures began in 1936 and now only this one remains. Two of the early vehicles can be seen in the Crich Tramway Museum in Derbyshire.

Despite its Old English name, Blackpool did not develop seriously until the railway came in 1846 but it has gone on developing ever since, the stress being on pure unashamed pleasure. The playground of the north of England and Britain's largest holiday resort, it attracts 16,000,000 visitors per year, equivalent to a quarter of the entire British population. Blackpool is synonymous with rock. It means illuminations which, with 375,000 bulbs, lasers, animated displays and tableaux, extend the season. It is also one of the small number of towns which benefit from being on the conference circuit. It has ice and roller skating rinks, a boating lake, a model village, donkey rides, boat trips, Punch and Judy shows and much more.

This rises to a peak at the Pleasure Beach on the South Shore, claimed to be Europe's greatest amusement park and Britain's number 1 tourist attraction. Here are the Revolution, Sir Hiram Maxim Flying Machine, Log Flume, Takaydo Express, Rainbow, Avalanche, Big Dipper, Grand National, first 360° loop the loop rollercoaster in Britain, shows and restaurant. Between the Swimming Bath and a rather unlikely windmill is the South Pier and its theatre, opened in 1893.

The 460m Central Pier with its theatre was opened in 1868 and has a big wheel on the pier itself.

The Golden Mile has amusement centres, discos, bars, restaurants, waxworks, dome and craft centre and a £6,000,000 Sea Life Centre with sharks swimming around viewers. Chiefly, though, it has the Blackpool Tower. 183m high and built 1891–4 with 2,500 tonnes of steel and 93 tonnes of cast-iron, it was modelled on the Eiffel Tower in Paris although only half the size. It has an aquarium, circus, zoo, ballroom, educational heritage exhibition, bars and restaurants.

The North Pier is the oldest of the three piers, being constructed in 1863, 326m long and again with a theatre. After four years a 144m steamer jetty was added and the pierhead enlarged to take a pavilion after a further decade. 12,000 tonnes of metal was used in its construction but it now has a damaged appearance.

Off the North Shore there is an isolated intertidal rock which seems out of character with the rest of this coast. Groynes begin at Norbreck and continue to the River Wyre. There are a couple of wrecks close inshore at Little Bispham.

Cleveleys began to grow after an architectural competition in 1906. It offers picnic sites, gardens, amusement centres, miniature railway and boating lake. Blackpool gives way again to Lancashire.

Fleetwood is a town designed by Decimus Burton for local squire Sir Peter Hesketh in 1836. The town is much less intrusive than those further south and initially the shoreline is more conspicuous with its groynes and the occasional deep pool between them, perhaps being dredged for fallout from the Rossall Oyster Grounds which lie off the coast. Rossall Point looks out across North Wharf which can be 3km wide at low tide with at least four wrecks dotted across it. The safe course into Fleetwood for ships is up the River Wyre past the disused Wyre light. The lighthouse, designed by Burton and Captain H M Denham, was built in 1840 and was the first structure to use Mitchell and Sons 910mm diameter malleable iron

Low Light, High Light and college building in Fleetwood

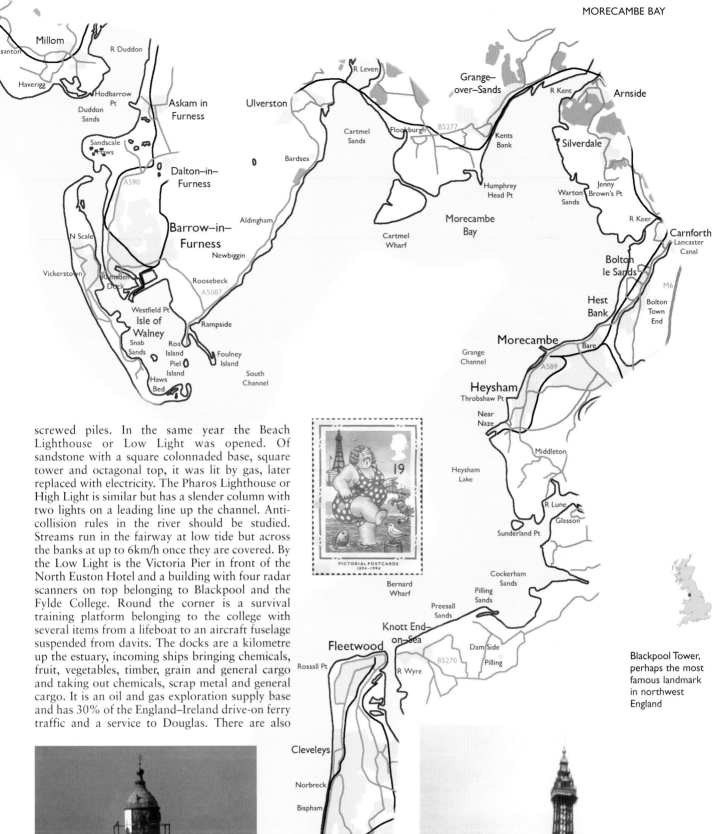

Millom
Kirksanton
R Duddon
Haverigg
Hodbarrow Pt
Duddon Sands
Askam in Furness
Ulverston
Sandscale Haws
Dalton–in–Furness
A590
Cartmel Sands
R Leven
Flookburgh
B5277
Grange–over–Sands
R Kent
Kents Bank
Arnside
Silverdale
Bardsea
Aldingham
Humphrey Head Pt
Jenny Brown's Pt
Warton Sands
R Keer
Carnforth
Lancaster Canal
N Scale
Barrow–in–Furness
Newbiggin
Cartmel Wharf
Morecambe Bay
Bolton le Sands
M6
Vickerstown
Ramsden Dock
A5087
Roosebeck
Hest Bank
Bolton Town End
Westfield Pt
Isle of Walney
Rampside
Grange Channel
Morecambe
Bare
A589
Snab Sands
Roa Island
Piel Island
Foulney Island
South Channel
Heysham
Throbshaw Pt
Haws Bed
Near Naze
Middleton
Heysham Lake
R Lune
Glasson
Sunderland Pt
Cockerham Sands
Pilling Sands
Preesall Sands
Knott End–on–Sea
Dam Side
Pilling
Fleetwood
Rossall Pt
R Wyre
B5270
Bernard Wharf
Cleveleys
Norbreck
Bispham
N Shore
Irish Sea
A584
Blackpool
S Shore
Squires Gate
Lytham St Anne's
R Ribble

screwed piles. In the same year the Beach Lighthouse or Low Light was opened. Of sandstone with a square colonnaded base, square tower and octagonal top, it was lit by gas, later replaced with electricity. The Pharos Lighthouse or High Light is similar but has a slender column with two lights on a leading line up the channel. Anti-collision rules in the river should be studied. Streams run in the fairway at low tide but across the banks at up to 6km/h once they are covered. By the Low Light is the Victoria Pier in front of the North Euston Hotel and a building with four radar scanners on top belonging to Blackpool and the Fylde College. Round the corner is a survival training platform belonging to the college with several items from a lifeboat to an aircraft fuselage suspended from davits. The docks are a kilometre up the estuary, incoming ships bringing chemicals, fruit, vegetables, timber, grain and general cargo and taking out chemicals, scrap metal and general cargo. It is an oil and gas exploration supply base and has 30% of the England–Ireland drive-on ferry traffic and a service to Douglas. There are also

19
PICTORIAL POSTCARDS
1894–1994

Blackpool Tower, perhaps the most famous landmark in northwest England

Plover Scar lighthouse on the River Lune

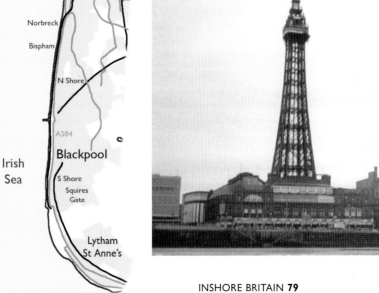

The River Wyre flows out from the pier across the sands to the Wyre Light at low water

The survival training rig on the River Wyre at Fleetwood

knots, 54,000 dunlins, 11,000 curlews, 6,700 redshanks and 1,900 turnstones. The RSPB also claimed the Wyre with 3,700 black-tailed godwits, 1,000 teal, 630 turnstones and 2,000 pinkfooted geese was in danger of permanent damage from marina development and construction of a barrage and that the Lune was in danger of permanent damage from recreation and cockling. The Wyre–Lune Sanctuary has been established between the two rivers.

Between **Knott End-on-Sea** at the end of the B5270 and Cockerham Sands are Bernard Wharf and Pilling Sands, drying up to 4km with a wreck at the seaward edge and backed by Pilling Marsh and Cockerham Marsh. Just to the east of Pilling's church spire is a windmill at Dam Side.

Sea defences behind Preesall Sands consist of tipped limestone from a quarry at Burton-in-Lonsdale. It is usual to specify materials with a grading curve which states the percentages of material passing successively smaller sieves. This doesn't work for large rocks so the consulting engineers specified the exact number of rocks of each size to be carried by each lorry from the quarry to get a suitable size distribution for the defences.

Cockersand Abbey, built in 1190, was one of the richest religious buildings in northwest England. The walls of a fish trap, constructed to catch salmon, still remain in the estuary.

At high tide the end of the River Lune is marked by the lighthouse at Plover Scar although tides do go out for a long way and there is a further 6km to Point of Lune at low tide. At Plover Scar there are mussel beds and a notice advising of the Wyre-Lune Sanctuary and that birds are not to be shot, adding in smaller letters, south of the lighthouse.

The hamlet of Sunderland gets cut off by the tide. Two centuries ago it was a port for the West Indies, which might help to explain Sambo's Grave.

Behind Heysham Lock, Sunderland Bank and Middleton Sands may be sprinkled with stakes or jellyfish depending on the state of the tide. Middleton's holiday camp and caravan parks have the unusual backdrop of an oil refinery and chemical works, an aerial and **Heysham** nuclear power station, a pair of Advanced Gas Cooled Reactors around which guided tours may be taken. Alongside the power station is a grey container with two slots in the side, presumably for use as an ornithological hide. The South Jetty runs out from the lighthouse. A section has disappeared at the shore end and is crossed by a bridging section which sags disconcertingly. Also disconcerting is the warm water, quite a respectable bath temperature as it leaves the power station cooling water outflow.

Another form of energy is based around Heysham's artificial harbour where British Gas have an office and use the harbour as a support base for the Morecambe Bay Gas Field. The 300m of quays also serve container traffic, a roll-on roll-off vehicle ferry to Douglas and passengers and freight to all parts of Ireland. Westerly winds cause a steep and awkward sea near the entrance and yachts are not permitted to enter except in an emergency. One person said to have landed here with difficulty was St Patrick when shipwrecked in Morecambe Bay. On the outside of the harbour at Near Naze is a disused lighthouse while submarine cables to Colwyn Bay and Roosebeck run from the apex of Half Moon Bay.

pleasure cruises, hovercraft and a passenger ferry across the estuary to add to the confusion. Most of all, however, Fleetwood is known for its fishing fleet. Until the Cod War with Iceland it was the third largest fishing port in the British Isles with middle and distant water trawlers, the premier west of England trawler port, but now it has mostly inshore vessels. A sobering monument made out of trawling hardware near the Low Light lists the many fishermen from the port who have been lost at sea over the years. There is a museum of local and fishing history.

Fleetwood has the largest model yacht lake in Europe, together with boating lake, sailboarding, swimming pool and model railway. Romans and Vikings came here and folk enthusiasts still come to the Fylde Folk Festival.

Morecambe Bay is unique for the way it drains to give 390km^2 of sand flats at low tide. The Triassic sandstone was denuded and then inundated by a post glacial sea level rise to result in an area which is now one of the five top wildfowl feeding areas in Europe. It is a Special Protection Area under the EU Birds Directive although the RSPB claimed it was in immediate danger of permanent damage from pollution. 200,000 waders and wildfowl include 6,300 eider duck, 2,200 pintails, 58,000 oystercatchers, 26,000

A tram waits at the Fleetwood terminus outside the North Euston Hotel

In Heysham Lake the streams run in the direction of the channel.

Throbshaw Point is unusual for the area in being rocky. St Patrick's Chapel to the east is one of the oldest churches in Lancashire. At 8.5m x 2.7m it is the only surviving Saxon church in England with a simple rectangular shape, not even a porch. Three 1,200 year old clifftop tombs are carved down into the rock itself. St Peter's is another ancient church, founded in the 7th or 8th centuries and rebuilt about 967, with a Saxon west doorway and window, early Norman chancel arch, 17th-century bellcote and 1864 north aisle. A carved stone inside shows a bear biting each side and Viking figures along the sides. The village developed from a 7th-century village and brews a notable non-alcoholic nettle beer.

Morecambe has developed from three fishing villages in Victorian times to become the resort it is today, but amongst the pleasure craft, yachts and waterskiers the fishing boats still go out for cockles, codling, shrimps and whitebait and fish weirs can still be found in the sands. Morecambe was actually the pioneer of seaside illuminations with 7km of candles in coloured glass jars in 1919. There are toilets just before the Grosvenor Hotel. Surprisingly, most of the hotels along the front are quite small while the Albert Café is an imposing building set back from the other buildings. There are two seawater pools but the modern amusements begin towards the Stone Pier. Frontierland Western Theme Park has rollercoaster, log flume, chairlift, bars, café and restaurants. The Marineland Oceanarium has performing dolphins, sealions, alligators, penguins and a well-stocked aquarium. The Bubbles Leisure Park has a swimming pool, band arenas, picnic areas, wave machine, cascade pool, 60m waterslide, water cannon, bubblers, children's play area, amusement arcade, bars and cafeteria. Happy

Mount Park offers Punch and Judy shows and marching band displays. An International Folklore Fiesta and a World of Music, Arts and Dance Festival also draw the crowds.

Heysham nuclear power station, a prominent landmark at the south end of Morecambe Bay

After the Stone Pier with its lighthouse is the dilapidated looking Central Promenade Pier with theatre, dance hall, bars and amusements, the latter including Moby Dick moored off the end.

Streams flow along the Grange Channel at up to 6km/h when the banks are dry but across the channel when they are covered. The Grange Channel becomes the Kent Channel and, when tides are suitable, the Kent bore can be met well out into Morecambe Bay.

The A589 gives way to the A5105 at Bare and the coastline now becomes peaceful again except for the inevitable low jets. There is a nature reserve at **Hest Bank** near where the Lancaster Canal comes close to the shore and at times, it is possible to see 50,000 birds from here. The most prominent feature of Bolton Town End and **Bolton-le-Sands** is the cliff which gives Red Bank Farm its name. Further back is an aerial and the green dome of the folly built in Williamson's Park by Lord Ashton, visible from the Lune estuary and coming back into view here.

Off the red bank is Priest Skear, an island of stones before the Keer Channel drains the River Keer. In the 19th century a sea wall was begun to reclaim land as far as Arnside but it was subsequently abandoned.

Jenny Brown's Point was named after an 18th-century resident. A stone chimney is a reminder of the local copper smelting industry but the environment is improved such that the local grass is sought after for gardens and bowling greens. Mrs Gaskell used to live in Lindeth Tower at Silverdale and Charlotte Brontë stayed in the village when she was young.

An indication of how the channels in the estuary can change, often overnight, is given by the fact that steamers from Morecambe used to call at **Silverdale** until the 1920s. The Arnside–Silverdale Area of Outstanding Natural Beauty remains attractive, the salt marshes being backed by low limestone cliffs with fossils, fields of daffodils in the spring and a nature trail in Arnside Park below Arnside Knott. Even a caravan site is quite well hidden.

This area is known as Cumbria's Riviera, the county boundary from Lancashire being crossed after Silverdale, and it was the scene of much smuggling.

A low tide footpath runs from Hest Bank across Warton Sands to Kents Bank but it is dangerous to use without local knowledge, especially as the tides sweep in. An official guide is still appointed for pedestrians but in Victorian days this was the stage coach route to the Lake District and his workload was more onerous. **Grange-over-Sands** was a watering place and at one time the residents used to cast lots for the belongings of people about to be engulfed, so frequent were the drownings. Named after the granaries or grange built by the monks of Cartmel Priory, it developed in the 16th and 17th centuries on the coastal coal trade and became a resort in 1857 with the arrival of the Furness Railway, now the Cumbrian Coast Railway which follows the B5277. It has an open air pool, tennis courts and bowling greens and is ideal for ornamental gardens because of its mild climate and shelter from westerly winds. Tractors still cross the estuary in the vicinity of one of the fish traps below Kent Bank and cockles, flukes, mussels and shrimps are still taken from here.

Humphrey Head is 53m high with such rare plants as spiked speedwell and goldilocks aster. Its other contribution towards rarity is that it is said to be the place where the last wolf in England was killed by John Harrington. The ridge also has a cave and St Agnes Holy Well which was supposed to cure ague, gout and worms, making it a place of pilgrimage and resulting in phials of its water being sold in the markets of Morecambe.

Wraysholme Tower behind the head is an 800-year old pele tower. It was used as a defence against sea raiders and belonged to the wolf exterminating John Harrington.

Whether the landward features are distinguishable will depend on the tide as Cartmel Wharf dries for 10km to Yeoman Wharf at low tide, probably the widest beach in Britain. At high tide a channel may just exist in front of the airfield at Flookburgh although care needs to be taken at the west end where a number of concrete posts stand in the sea, several having shed their concrete and bent over to leave just loops of reinforcing wire sticking up.

Behind Cartmel Sands is the 300-year old Holker Hall which takes its name from the Old Norse hol

kiarr, hollow fen. Built on land owned by Cartmel Priory, it has a newer wing following a fire in 1871 with a notable cantilevered staircase having each baluster carved with a different design. The former home of the Dukes of Devonshire for 300 years, it has paintings by Van Dyck and Sir Joshua Reynolds, a screen embroidered by Mary, Queen of Scots, distinctive furniture and one of the finest libraries in the north of England with over 3,500 books. Set in 10ha of gardens by Paxton, the designer of the Crystal Palace, it has a limestone cascade, formal, woodland and rose gardens, azaleas, rhododendrons, rare and unusual shrubs and trees and a fallow, sika and red deer park. The trees include the oldest monkey puzzle tree in the UK, dating from 1796. It blew down in a gale in the 19th century but with the assistance of 7 horses it was pulled back up again and now stands 24m high. The Lakeland Motor Museum has a 1914 Dennis fire engine, replica of Bluebird, 1920s garage, cars, motorcycles, bicycles, stationary engines, mascots, badges, toys and pottery. There are Victorian/Edwardian and Wartime Kitchen exhibitions, Craft and Countryside exhibition, quilting shop, baby animal farm, large model railway, car and boat shows, hot air ballooning and tethered balloon rides, Lakeland Rose Show, Ribble Dog Agility Show, various archery championships, model bus rides, parachute displays, model aircraft, horse driving trials, adventure playground, Punch and Judy, gift shop, cafeteria and restaurant, to name a few.

Roudsea Wood and Mosses are an oakwood ridge on Carboniferous limestone with raised and valley bogs and saltmarshes, acidic soil on Silurian Slate with peat and a fine selection of flora, some quite rare.

The River Leven has a bore and was formerly a slave trading route to Windermere. The railway crosses the River Leven estuary on the Leven Viaduct to **Ulverston** which is a delightful village with Tudor church and Quaker associations but is seen at its worst from the estuary, industrial chimneys and tipped waste to the fore. The tower on Hoad Hill is a memorial to Sir John Barrow, founder of the Royal Geographical Society, and is a copy of the Eddystone lighthouse. Further back, three aerials top the ridge to the north of **Dalton-in-Furness**.

Chapel Island takes its name from the old chapel located on it. Facing it on the west side of the estuary is Conishead Priory, founded in the 12th century by Gamel de Pennington. It was rebuilt in the 1820s in Gothic style but this bankrupted its owner who had to sell it to pay his debts. Had he but known that there were rich veins of iron ore under his estate which would have resolved his financial problems he would not have needed to sell it. It has been a convalescent home but is now a Tibetan Mahayena Buddhist college. It is noted for its fine decorative plaster ceilings, marble fireplaces and wood panelling, including an oak room with wood from Salmesbury Hall. It is set in 28ha of gardens and woods containing a 12th-century lake, grotto and hermitage, nature trail and craft shop.

Behind Ulverston Sands with its fish trap is Bardsea Country Park and some stone circles as the A5087 follows the shore.

At high tide there is a straight run down the coast to Rampside but at low water it is necessary to move into the South Channel to avoid Mort Bank or even Lancaster Sound which feeds out past Yeomans Wharf, some 9km from the coast. All this material has to come from somewhere and one source is the coast at Aldingham which has been progressively claimed by the sea, the 12th-century church of St Cuthbert now being just above the high water mark. Both a moat and a motte remain on this rural coast between here and Newbiggin.

The submarine cable from Heysham lands at Roosebeck. Another fish trap is located on Rampside Sands. Rampside Hall, built 300 years ago, has a row of chimneys known as the 12 Apostles. More prominent, however, is a brick navigation pillar which was used with another similar one at the end of Foulney Island. The island is connected to the causeway to Roa Island by a rubble embankment which is awash at high water springs, but may also appear to give a clear passage to Roa Island lifeboat station at other times because of mirage effects.

All around Foulney Island are mussel beds while further out are numerous structures littering the sea and related to the exploration activity.

Piel Island is connected to Walney at most times. Its large ruined castle was built in the 13th century as a defence for Piel Harbour and a warehouse for the monks of Furness Abbey. In 1487 Lambert Simnel landed and declared himself king. Henry VII did not agree and informed him in the manner of the times. However, the title King of Piel is still retained by the landlord of the Ship Inn which also had the formerly unique distinction of being open 24 hours every day. The inn stands at the top of a stairway up from the water, this acting as a landing point for the passenger ferry which operates from Roa Island in the summer.

Roa Island has a nesting colony of terns in the spring and summer. The island was fortified in the 12th century to guard the harbour. It is a popular sailing and windsurfing centre in the summer with moorings and a brick and flint former boathouse.

Piel Channel is relatively narrow, cutting between extensive sandflats, flanked by saltmarsh, particularly around Haws Bed. The northeast end of the channel has been edged by training walls in order to retain a deep channel suitable for use by large ships. Streams at up to 5km/h set northeast at the outside of the bend in Piel Harbour. The northwestgoing stream turns at high water. Westerly winds increase the duration and rate of the northwesterly stream and reduce the southeasterly stream, easterly winds having the opposite effect.

The Morecambe Bay Gas Field pipeline crosses from Snab Sands to Westfield Point.

In the 19th century the ships traded to Ulverston but silting up of the Leven estuary resulted in the loss of the trade to Barrow.

Off Ramsden Dock the stream flows at up to 3km/h, the northwesterly stream turning at HW +0130. Cormorants sit on posts on the training wall and watch the water flow past.

The main industry in **Barrow** is shipbuilding, especially naval ships, and the skyline is dominated by the hammerhead cranes in Vickers' yards. Ships have been built here since 1852. The expression 'Barrow-built' is used with pride in the town to refer to the shipbuilding tradition which has resulted in many fine craft sailing out down Piel Channel, including the Royal Navy's sixth *Invincible*, their first anti-submarine warfare carrier.

Barrow's involvement with submarines is over a century old. Swedish industrialist Thorsten Nordenfeld approached Barrow in 1884 to build an improved version of his first submarine. The *Nordenfeld* was launched two years later and led to the development for the Admiralty of the

Traditional sailing boat moored off the nuclear submarine assembly shop in Barrow

Hollands, of which *HM Submarine No 1* was launched in 1901. Improvement of this 'damned un-English weapon' followed through the D, H, L, T, K, A, 500, Dreadnought, Oberon, Valiant, Churchill, Swiftsure and Trafalgar classes. Trident nuclear submarines were launched from insignificant looking slipways on the mainland just before the bridge.

The docks themselves are entered via a large dock with double gates although some vessels do operate directly from the Walney Channel. Barrow is the deepest port between Liverpool and the Clyde. It has 3.4km of quays, handles roll-on roll-off traffic and exports limestone. It is used for building oil and gas industry structures in addition to ships.

The town grew up around Furness Abbey in 1127 with the monks smelting iron on Walney and having their own fleet of trading ships.

Local furnaces were built in the 18th century and the steelworks were the world's largest by 1870. The Furness name, however, comes from Fouldray Island promontory, a Norwegian island, the name being brought by Viking invaders from Barra in the 10th century, hence Barrow.

For such a narrow, flat island, believed to have been the inspiration for Thomas the Tank Engine's island of Sodor, Walney offers a remarkable variety of conditions. Situated adjacent to Barrow-in-Furness, Cumbria's main industrial town, it is reached on the A590 over the double-bascule Jubilee Bridge crossing Walney Channel to Vickerstown, a dormitory town built as a garden suburb by Vickers at the turn of the 20th century on an island which was then unoccupied except for a few farmers and fishermen.

Several navigation towers are located on the island. The channel around the northern end of the island dries out on the lower part of the tide. Setting off north from the bridge an hour before

Black Combe seen across the Duddon estuary at low water from the dunes of Sandscale Haws

high tide avoids the problem of shallows or worse. The northwesterly stream continues for nearly 2 hours after high water north of Jubilee Bridge with the maximum rate ½ hour after high water. The shallowness is emphasized by a public footpath and a public bridleway crossing Walney Channel from North Scale to the mainland.

The area around the Ferry acts as a small boat mooring and Barrow Sailing Club have their headquarters opposite.

The surroundings leave a little to be desired here. Cliffs on the east side of the channel are of slag, accumulated over many years. Beyond is the Dock Industrial and Maritime Heritage Museum, opened in the Victoria ship repair dock, giving the story of steel shipbuilding with displays, theatre, shop and café. New factories stand back from the bank.

As the built-up area is left behind the channel widens. Walney Airfield, home of the Lakes Gliding Club, is passed on the left and then the coastline becomes marshy, protecting the 6.5km² North Walney National Nature Reserve which has been leased to the Cumbria Wildlife Trust since 1984. Its sand dunes, dune slacks, grassland, vegetated shingle, saltmarsh and mudflats form an area which abounds with rabbits, foxes, shrews, weasels and stoats and is the major haunt of the rare natterjack toad, distinguished by the yellow stripe down its back.

Sand dunes gradually become the prominent feature although 600m high Black Combe on the far side of the Duddon estuary is a dramatic reminder of the proximity of the Lake District.

Lowsy Point is marked by a community of shacks. The area can be difficult and a hole forms in the water, having taken down 3 youths in a boat.

Duddon Mouth largely drains to leave Duddon Sands, drying up to 3km from the entrance. The flood begins at HW Dover –0600 and the ebb at

HW Dover. The estuary can have 31,000 waders and wildfowl including 1,300 pintails, 5,200 knots, 6,900 oystercatchers, 2,100 curlews and 1,500 redshanks in addition to gulls. The estuary has been proposed as an EU Birds Directive Special Protection Area which the RSPB claimed was threatened with immediate danger of permanent damage by tidal barrage and road developments. The barrage idea is not new. George Stevenson planned to build embankments across the Duddon, Leven and Kent estuaries as part of his railway scheme, to be paid for with the land reclaimed.

Sandscale Dunes and Roanhead Dunes are a fine complex of sandflats, dunes and saltmarsh with marram grass, sea holly and lizard tracks everywhere.

From **Askam in Furness**, Askam Pier points towards Millom which quarried red haematite iron ore under the sea bed until 1958. In the 19th-century the mine had 11 shafts and was the busiest in Britain. Now it is just the large Hodbarrow Hollow Lake behind Hodbarrow Point, marked with the remains of lighthouses. Tracks lead through the mine area to Millom where the folk museum has a full-scale drift of the Hodbarrow Iron Ore Mine as well as replicas of a miner's cottage kitchen and blacksmith's forge and a display of agricultural relics. A 2km bank, 12m high, 25m wide at the top and 64m wide at the bottom, runs from Hodbarrow Point and was built in 1900–5 to protect the mine.

The skeleton of a wooden ship is embedded in the sand at the point where one of Lakeland's most active rivers meets the energy of the Irish Sea while ships can be seen being broken up at Borwick Rails.

Overlooked by the spire of **Millom**'s church, Haverigg is a fishing harbour with more dunes which run westwards and reach 20m in height at Haverigg Point, hiding the open prison there.

A lane leading down to the beach at Kirksanton Haws next to a windfarm offers limited parking, located some 400m beyond a derelict building on the beach. The area has several signs of earlier use, the five Bronze Age stone circles on a hill at Lacra having been a religious centre, perhaps with two approaching avenues. The Giant's Grave is found south of Kirksanton village with two standing stones, one with cup marks.

Distance
From Lytham St Anne's to Kirksanton Haws is 113km
Campsites
Peel Hill, Little Singleton, Cold Row, Middleton, Morecambe, Bolton-le-Sands, Carnforth, Silverdale, Far Arnside, Flookburgh, Ulverston, Haverigg, Silecroft
Youth Hostels
Slaidburn, Arnside, Coniston, Eskdale
OS 1:50,000 Sheets
96 Barrow-in-Furness and South Lakeland
97 Kendal and Morecambe
102 Preston and Blackpool
Imray Chart
C62 Irish Sea (1:280,000)
Admiralty Charts
SC 1320 Fleetwood to Douglas (1:100,000)
1552 Ports in Morecambe Bay. Approaches to Fleetwood (1:25,000). Fleetwood (1:10,000). River Lune and Approaches to Heysham (1:25,000). Heysham (1:10,000)
SC 1826 Irish Sea – Eastern Part (1:200,000)
1981 Approaches to Preston (1:75,000)
2010 Morecambe Bay and Approaches (1:50,000)
3164 Barrow Harbour and Approaches (1:12,500). Deep Water Berth and Ramsden Dock Entrance (1:5,000)
Tidal Constants
Blackpool: Dover
Fleetwood: Dover +0020
Glasson Dock: HW Dover +0040, LW Dover +0240
Heysham: Dover +0020
Morecambe: HW Dover +0020, LW Dover +0040
Arnside: Dover +0130
Ulverston: Dover +0040
Haws Point: Dover +0020
Barrow (Ramsden Dock): HW Dover +0030, LW Dover +0040
Duddon Bar: Dover +0020
Sea Area
Irish Sea
Rescue
Inshore lifeboats: Lytham St Anne's, Blackpool, Fleetwood, Morecambe, Barrow
All weather lifeboats: Lytham St Anne's, Fleetwood, Barrow
Hovercraft: Morecambe
Maritime Rescue Centre
Liverpool, 0151 931 3341.

Windfarm behind the beach at Kirksanton Haws

16 LAKE DISTRICT

Scenic backdrop to nuclear and chemical industry

There was an old man of St Bees,
Who was stung in the arm by a wasp.
When asked, 'Does it hurt?'
He replied, 'No, it doesn't.
I'm so glad it wasn't a hornet.'

Sir William Schwenck Gilbert

From Kirksanton Haws, high red sand dunes and sandstone cliffs run northwest to Selker Head. Flows follow the coast to St Bees Head, but only at up to 2km/h although strong westerly winds produce heavy seas. The fells reduce and fall back going northwards but at this point the coast is only a kilometre from the foot of the magnificent Skiddaw slate bulk of 600m high Black Combe. Not surprisingly, the coast immediately becomes part of the Lake District National Park, here taking the form of a golf course surrounded by standing stones, all hidden behind the dunes.

Black Combe towers above the beach at Silecroft

A submarine cable from Douglas lands at Silecroft, a beach which has surfing except for the top 4 hours of the tidal cycle when it dumps.

Gutterby Spa never became a spa and now even the mineral spring is no more. In fact, there is more to see at Annaside where there are, at least, many rockpools.

High sand dunes to the north of Annaside

Selker Point with its mussel beds and perhaps a heron, signals the start of the 12km Eskmeals army gunnery range around the mouth of the River Esk. The coastline is marked by several towers, assorted

concrete block structures and two brilliant white geodesic domes. The beach is often covered with spent shells. There is a tide gauge at one point.

The River Esk gives access to Ravenglass and has been used by both Romans and smugglers in their turn. The flood in the estuary begins at HW Dover −0600 and the ebb at HW Dover.

The Ravenglass Nature Reserve and Gullery on Drigg Point contains one of the largest colonies of blackheaded gulls in Britain, 4 species of tern, many waders and shore birds plus natterjack toads, none of which seems to be unduly disturbed by the fact that they live in the middle of a firing range. A permit is required for entry.

The nature reserve is on a peninsula created by the River Irt which runs parallel to the coast for 2km from the far boundary of the national park. A site at Drigg used to discharge low level radioactive waste into a trench and thence into the river, but it now goes into an outfall directly into the sea. While the outfall was being installed, live shells from Eskmeals before 1940 were found all over the sea bed. Rizostoma jellyfish are now more likely to be found on the beach.

Seascale on the B5344 is separated by golf links from the complex which has also been known over the years as Calder Hall, Windscale and now Sellafield, one of the most important nuclear sites in the world, located at the mouths of Newmill Beck, the River Calder and the River Ehen, the latter following the coast closely for 2km. The nuclear fuel reprocessing plant was opened in 1951, to be followed in 1956 by the world's first commercial nuclear power station. In 1958 there was a serious nuclear leak and this is still recalled by those concerned with the high frequency of childhood leukaemia in the area. The site is one of the most controversial locations in the country for conservationists and Sellafield try hard to promote a better image for themselves. The Irish Sea is

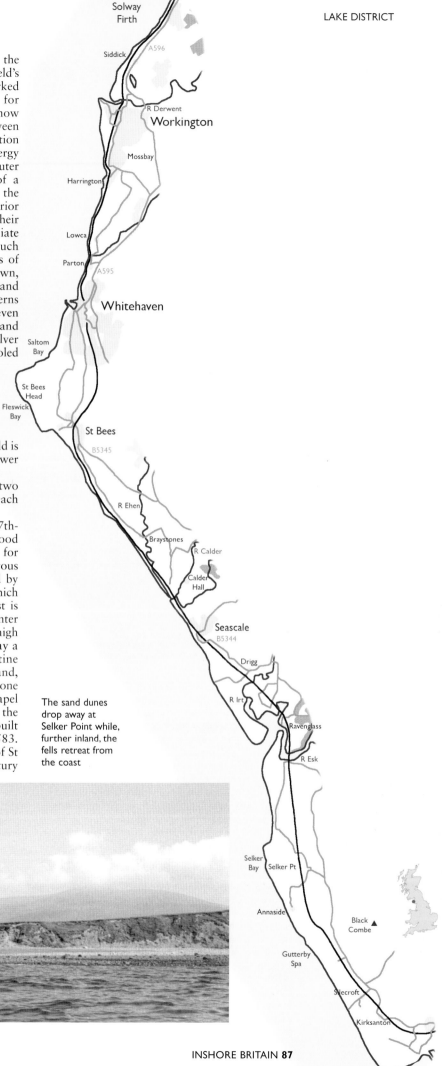

already the most radioactively polluted sea in the world, much of the blame being laid at Sellafield's door. The outfall from Sellafield used to be marked by a buoy but this made it too easy for environmentalists to find and block up and now there are two buoys, the outfall being between them, rather nearer No 2 buoy. An exhibition explains nuclear power, looks at world energy needs, radiation and safety and has computer games, a fission tunnel, a walk in model of a reactor core, a shop and guided tours with the possibility of seeing operations close up by prior arrangement. UK Nirex have declared this their preferred site for an underground low/intermediate level nuclear waste repository with as much excavation as in the Channel Tunnel. A series of 250m x 25m caverns would be dug 800m down, the radioactive waste mixed with concrete and stored in drums in the caverns and then the caverns backfilled with concrete. Research work has even considered the effect of a 70m drop in sea level and another Ice Age. The last item on the site is a silver sphere which holds an Advanced Gas Cooled

reactor, facing across to Starling Castle. Sellafield is also the site of a combined cycle gas turbine power station of just 170MW.

Sand dunes continue, amongst which are two caravan sites at Braystones and a line of beach shacks.

St Bees takes its name from St Bega, a 7th-century Irish princess who took a childhood religious vow. She asked the local lord here for land to build a convent and received the generous reply that she could have all the land covered by snow on mid-summer's day, an answer which needs to be seen in the context that this coast is normally free of snow even in the depths of winter because of the mild climate. Having friends in high places helps, however, and on the appointed day a snowstorm duly appeared. Her Benedictine convent was established in 650 and owned land, mines, salt-pans and quarries, including the one which was to supply stone for St George's Chapel at Windsor. The convent was destroyed by the Vikings and subject to many Scottish raids, rebuilt by the Normans in 1120 and dissolved in 1583. The church was restored as the parish church of St Mary and St Bega with the best 12th-century

The sand dunes drop away at Selker Point while, further inland, the fells retreat from the coast

The important nuclear power, fuel reprocessing and research plant at Sellafield

North Head at St Bees

deeply notched Norman arch doorway in the area although the church was much altered in the 19th century. The neighbouring stone buildings were Archbishop Grindal's school of 1583. Another notable item is the Dragon Stone, a door lintel carved with a sea monster.

The shore area now has caravan sites, playground, toilets, beach shop, café and Seacote Hotel. Off the beach is a wreck site. It is a popular place with walkers, not least because St Bees Head is one end of the Coast to Coast Walk. The head is the only significant set of cliffs in Cumbria, the red St Bees sandstone rising vertically to the 98m high flat summit with its white lighthouse, from where the Isle of Man can be seen. Access is forbidden to the RSPB reserve but the 10,000 cormorants, fulmars, razorbills, guillemots, puffins, kittiwakes and other gulls which breed on the cliffs can be viewed better from below.

Fleswick Bay between South and North Heads is a cove which was probably used by smugglers.

St Bees Head is, effectively, the start of the Solway Firth. Tide streams in the entrance to the firth are generally anticlockwise with E–W movement up to 3km/h and N–S movement up to 1km/h. The flood into the firth begins at HW Dover –0500 and the ebb starts at HW Dover +0100. In addition, there may be ripples and eddies from HW Dover –0540 for an hour as the eastgoing stream meets the ebb from the firth.

Despite the oyster grounds, Saltom Bay signals another change in the coastline, now high, composed largely of slag and topped with industrial complexes, often derelict. The plants include the large chemical works of Albright and Wilson, based on Triassic anhydrite, its conveyors silhouetted against the skyline. This firm is permitted to discharge 500 tonnes of zinc, chromium, copper and nickel per year into the Irish Sea, the largest such discharge around the British coastline.

Much of the industrial activity was founded on the now declined Cumberland Coalfield, such as the Duke Pit of 1747 with a shoreline building which looks like a ruined castle, the elaborate Wellington Pit of 1840 and the Haig Colliery running out under the sea.

Whitehaven is a derivative of the Old Norse for white headland haven. It consisted of 6 fishermen's cottages in 1566 but the Lowther family developed it as a shipbuilding and coal exporting port. It lies where the B5345 joins the A595 and was the first planned town since the Middle Ages. In its heyday it was the second port to London, only declining as Liverpool grew. The Brocklebank Line, now part of Cunard, was formed here and one of the better known trainee seamen from the port was John Paul Jones, the founder of the American navy. He put his knowledge to good use in 1778 during the American War of Independence when he raided the harbour, setting fire to some ships and capturing the fort but failing to capture the town, the last direct invasion of English soil by a foreign power. The artificial tidal harbour with its lighthouse and a column at the root of the harbour wall has 920m of quays, used for importing phosphates which have to be brought ashore in barges as silting restricts the harbour to ships of 1,500 tonnes. A heavy sea forms across the harbour entrance in westerly gales and the flood stream normally sets east across the entrance with eddies off it.

The *Clearway*, one of the world's last surviving steam dredgers, is kept at Whitehaven. Whitehaven Museum and Art Gallery covers local and social history, mining, maritime and industrial history, geology, archaeology, Whitehaven pottery and local paintings. Whitehaven Workshop produces earthenware and stoneware, screenprinting and batik and there are a sports centre and swimming

pool in the town. Another famous son was Jonathan Swift, author of *Gulliver's Travels*, perhaps the inspiration for the town's Biggest Liar in the World Competition.

A prominent church to the north of Parton is close to the site the Romans chose for their fort of Gabrosentum on the banks of a small river.

On top of the cliffs at Lowca are a disused mine and a brickworks, the derelict buildings clearly roofless against the skyline. Meanwhile, the railway snakes along the foot of the cliffs on an embankment which has been reinforced, none too beautifully, with a variety of tipped hardware. 3km off Cunning Point is a magnetic anomaly, probably resulting from the dumping of slag from Workington.

Heaps of white slag are prominent on the shoreline at Harrington where the small harbour is being developed as a yacht basin. The slag increases to form cliffs past the extensive works at Mossbay although the final kilometre to Workington has been landscaped.

Workington is located around the mouth of the Derwent but does not present its best face to the sea. The 460m South Pier ends in a line of rocks and a small race can form out to sea past these on the ebb with eddies at times.

The town developed on rich pockets of very pure haematite although the name is nothing to do with industry but is Old English for Weorc's farm. They used to ship coal to southern England and made railway tracks in the steelworks. Now the ironworks and steelworks are disused and even the chapel on the summit of Chapel Hill is in ruins. On the south side of the harbour is a disused shipyard, yet all is not dead. 1.6km of quays include a liquid sulphur terminal, the dock importing chemicals and petroleum products and exporting coal and railway track materials. A battery of small cranes are in use on the quay and fishing boats come and go, emulated by a flotilla of small boats taking out anglers.

It seems to have been a favourite destination for people making less than happy crossings from Scotland. Mary, Queen of Scots crossed to here with 30 others in an open boat after losing the Battle of Langside in 1568.

There is another mine to the south of Siddick. Between it and the Burrow Walls Roman fort is

Siddick Pond, a favourite spot for winter wildfowl. Beyond Siddick are two large Thames Board Mill factories and the only practical exit for some distance lies between them at NY001316, located by a small green cone beacon on the end of an outfall. The shore is of boulders, slag and pieces of brick but at least there is a right of way across the railway, if not actually a level crossing. Beyond a high flood embankment is a track with plenty of parking space, alongside a field used by microlights. They now have to make their final approaches over the A596 and turn sharply into the field to avoid the chimneys of the new factory which, inconsiderately, have been placed in the way.

Distance
From Kirksanton Hawes to Siddick is 59km
Campsites
Silecroft, Ravenglass, Braystones, Nethertown, St Bees, Sandwith, Gilcrux
Youth Hostels
Eskdale, Wastwater, Ennerdale, Cockermouth
OS 1:50,000 Sheets
89 West Cumbria
96 Barrow-in-Furness and South Lakeland
Imray Chart
C62 Irish Sea (1:280,000)
Admiralty Charts
SC 1320 Fleetwood to Douglas (1:100,000)
1346 Solway Firth and Approaches (1:100,000).
Ravenglass (1:15,000)
2013 St Bees Head to Silloth (1:50,000). Whitehaven Harbour (1:10,000). Harrington Harbour (1:10,000). Workington Harbour (1:7,500)
Tidal Constants
Duddon Bar: Dover +0020
Tarn Point: Dover +0020
Whitehaven: Dover +0020
Workington: HW Dover +0040, LW Dover +0030
Sea Area
Irish Sea
Range
Eskmeals
Rescue
Inshore lifeboats: Barrow, St Bees
All weather lifeboats: Barrow, Workington
Maritime Rescue Centre
Liverpool, 0151 931 3341.

17 SOLWAY FIRTH

White Steeds gallop past wooded Stewartry inlets

Now surf runs o'er the Solway sands,
Tweed runs to the ocean
To mark where England's province starts,
Such a parcel of rogues in the nation.

From Siddick the coast is low. This probably accounts for nearly 30 Roman forts and fortlets between here and the end of Hadrian's Wall at Bowness-on-Solway, intended to keep the Picts from landing behind the line of the wall.

A windsock just before **Flimby** indicates an airstrip. Off the coast there are frequent floats marking lobster pots.

Modern mine buildings precede **Maryport** with its lighthouse and hollow pier leading out from an area of excavation. Maryport harbour, sheltered by

The high ground beyond the town is topped by a house with a turret and by the Senhouse Roman Museum. Begun about 1550 and one of the most important collections of Roman antiquities in Europe, it is located at the Alavana Roman Fort, a naval base used to defend against attacks from across the Solway. The Roman road leading northeast from it is paralleled by the Allerdale Ramble which reaches the coast here and by the Cumbria Cycle Way which uses the B5300. The high ground ends with a golf course.

Allonby Bay has negligible current from HW +0200 to HW −0200 but the banks and shoals move frequently. There is a conspicuous triangular hill at Heatherbank, but the views inland to the mountains of the Lake District are largely unrestricted. There may be the odd jet ski about but conditions are generally quiet, appreciated by curlews, snipe, oystercatchers, blackbacked gulls and perhaps a sunstar floating on the surface.

Ponies graze freely on the green at Allonby, a whisky smuggling centre until two centuries ago

Carsluith

A75

Low
Auchenlarie

Ravenshall Pt

Sandgreen
Mossyard

Fleet
Bay

Wigtown
Bay

Murray's
Isles

Knockbrex

Ardwall
Isle

Kirkandrews

Islands
of Fleet

Barlocco
Isle

Meikle
Pinnacle

Dove
Cave

Borness Pt

Kirkcudbright
Bay

Gipsy Pt

Little
Ross

Port
Mary

Abbey
Head

Rascarrel
Bay

Castle
Muir Pt

Auche...
Ba...

a bar, is silted up but being redeveloped. Situated at the mouth of the River Ellen, it was named after Mary Senhouse, wife of Humphrey Senhouse who built the harbour and docks in the 18th century and whose eldest daughter gave her name to Elizabeth Dock. This dock now has the Clyde tug *Flying Buzzard* and the *VIC 96*, a second world war naval inshore supply ship based on the Clyde puffers, both steam vessels. Maryport Maritime Museum has displays on Christian Fletcher who was born locally in 1764 and who was to lead the *Bounty* mutineers, and on Thomas Ismay who founded the White Star Line whose best known ship was the *Titanic*. Captain W A Nelson's voyages under sail at the turn of the 20th century were made from here and the port also initiated the broadside launch, a procedure devised because of the limited space in the harbour. Senhouse Dock itself was used for loading railway lines made in Cumbria. The town has a carnival with procession and field events in July.

when it became a resort. The church at the south end of the village has a memorial to Joseph Huddart who was born here in 1741 and became a surveyor of unknown Far East coasts and harbours. After watching a cable snap at sea he invented a new method of making ropes and set up business in London to manufacture this vital commodity.

Stepped defences and cribwork lead to Dubmill Point. Sandhills follow from the point to Silloth and the coast is low-lying right round to Southerness Point. The first serious sandbanks come off Mawbray, the Beckfoot Flats drying up to 2.5km off Mawbray Bank at the high water line and then tapering in to the Lees Scar light structure off the golf course at Silloth.

Silloth's most conspicuous landmark is a bright green silo by the harbour, a harbour which imports grain, animal feed, molasses, cattle and minerals as well as handling general cargo. The

Silloth's green silo catches the sunlight as it stands by the harbour

Skinburness, with its whitewashed houses and occasional pine, has a Mediterranean air about it, a most attractive hamlet although not everyone thought so highly of it. Edward I chose it as his base for attacking Scotland, earning it special hatred. Large rocks placed around some of the houses come as a reminder that most of the village was swept away in a flood in 1303, resulting in a general exodus to set up **Newton Arlosh**.

Grune Point, with its pillbox, is notable for its birds and plants while sheep and cattle graze on the saltings of Skinburness Marsh and Newton

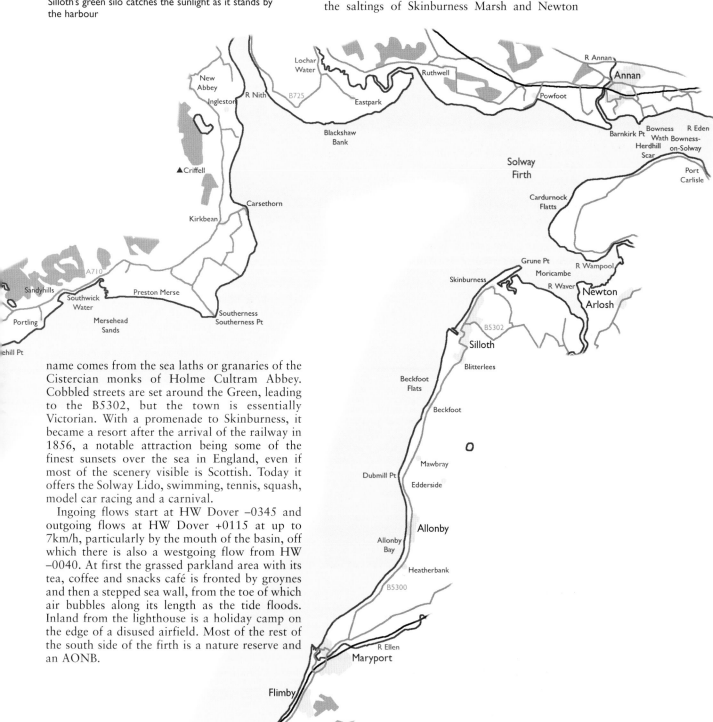

name comes from the sea laths or granaries of the Cistercian monks of Holme Cultram Abbey. Cobbled streets are set around the Green, leading to the B5302, but the town is essentially Victorian. With a promenade to Skinburness, it became a resort after the arrival of the railway in 1856, a notable attraction being some of the finest sunsets over the sea in England, even if most of the scenery visible is Scottish. Today it offers the Solway Lido, swimming, tennis, squash, model car racing and a carnival.

Ingoing flows start at HW Dover −0345 and outgoing flows at HW Dover +0115 at up to 7km/h, particularly by the mouth of the basin, off which there is also a westgoing flow from HW −0040. At first the grassed parkland area with its tea, coffee and snacks café is fronted by groynes and then a stepped sea wall, from the toe of which air bubbles along its length as the tide floods. Inland from the lighthouse is a holiday camp on the edge of a disused airfield. Most of the rest of the south side of the firth is a nature reserve and an AONB.

Cormorants nest on the former bombing target in Moricambe

Marsh. These surround Moricambe, the combined estuary of the rivers Waver and Wampool which largely drains at low tide to leave a large area of sandbanks. Three disused airfields surround the inlet which was used for bombing practice during the war. A structure in the middle used to carry a target but now supports a colony of nesting cormorants, alongside a bright blue canvas box which has apparently been provided for their use but which they ignore. Lying around on the sand are sections of aircraft wing and undercarriage.

A section of aircraft lying in the estuary. The aerials are just visible in the distance

Dominating all and the whole upper end of the Solway Firth are a forest of radio masts on a former airfield. These used to be part of the communication link with our submarine fleet but have been superseded by satellites. Even so, they have not been dismantled and are brightly lit at night. The 13 masts form a 6-pointed star, all linked with interconnecting wires. Around the perimeter at intervals are brick buildings.

Cardurnock Flatts widen as the Solway Firth narrows, pushing the entering River Eden's deep channel against the Scottish shore.

An embankment at Herdhill Scar faces its counterpart on the Scottish side of Bowness Wath. The Solway Viaduct was built across here in 1869 to carry a direct railway route from the iron ore mines of Cumbria to the smelting furnaces of the Clyde but never carried heavy traffic as it was

vulnerable to the weather. 1.8km long with 181 piers, it lacked an opening span, so forcing the closure of Port Carlisle. James Brunlees' design suffered from water freezing in the piers in 1875, cracking them, and in 1881 ice floes damaged 45 piers and 37 spans, making two breaks in the viaduct. Trains ceased in 1921 but then began its most popular period as it was used by Annan men to walk to English public houses on Sundays, those in Scotland being closed on the sabbath. It was dismantled in 1935.

It is possible to cross the estuary on foot or on horseback but the flows can be up to 15km/h and at times the White Steeds of Solway can be heard approaching 30km away with a bore on spring tides.

Crossing from the English county of Cumbria to the Scottish region of Dumfries and Galloway brings substantial fishing nets set in the fastest part of the flow on Gowkesk Rig.

Flows sweep through fish nets at Gowkesk up the River Eden. Beyond is the embankment to the former Solway Viaduct

Barnkirk Point, with its oil tanks amongst the gorse and light structure at the end, marks the mouth of the River Annan. Close by are the factories of Glaxo and boilermakers NEI Cochrane, both strangely isolated from **Annan** and their source of labour. The most conspicuous building for most of the upper estuary, however, is the nuclear power station to the northeast of the town. More fishing nets stretch out between Annan Waterfoot and Newbie Mains and terns are present in quantity.

From here to Southerness Point lie vast areas of sand and mud banks at low tide, reaching nearly to the English shore so tides need to be given serious consideration. At Powfoot, established in the 18th century as a bathing resort, sand yachting is popular. Powfoot Channel is ingoing from HW Dover −0245 and outgoing from HW Dover +0115 at up to 11km/h. Running out from the caravans at the edge of the golf course are more fishing nets.

Shelducks graze on the grass banks at the high water mark behind Priestside Bank. On a sunny summer's day when the extensive flats have had a chance to get hot before the tide floods, the water at the high tide line is pleasantly warm.

Another priestly bank was that begun by local vicar Dr Henry Duncan in 1810, the first branch of the Savings Bank (to become the TSB) which now houses the Duncan Savings Bank Museum at Ruthwell. The church houses the Ruthwell Cross, one of the most impressive stone carvings in Europe, inscribed with verses from the oldest-known English poem, Caedmon's *Dream of the Rood*.

Brow Well, sited by the mouth of Lochar Water, gives mineral water contaminated with iron. It was here that Scotland's most famous poet, Robert Burns, sought a cure during his final illness.

From here to the mouth of the Nith the coast is fringed by the marshes of the Wildfowl and

Wetlands Trust Caerlaverock National Nature Reserve. There is a refuge area with hides and towers at East Park Farm, used to view over 12,000 barnacle, pink-footed and greylag geese in autumn and winter plus other winter wildfowl and, in April, the start of the return migration.

Behind the trees is one of the finest examples of mediaeval architecture in Scotland, Caerlaverock Castle off the B725. Its triangular bailey with curtain and machiolated round towers and massive machiolated gatehouse in red sandstone are surrounded by a moat. Dating from 1270, it commanded a strategic landing point and was the seat of the Maxwell family, whose crest and motto appear over the gateway. Besieged by Edward I in 1330, it was taken by the Covenanters in 1638 after a 13-week siege and was ruined in 1640.

Blackshaw Bank with its mud, sand and even quicksand, dries up to 9km out, reaching almost to the English shore on spring low waters. The sands can cover faster than a horse can gallop, the water can recede from shallows with frustrating speed and the channel changes position very substantially. Northgoing flows in the River Nith start when sands cover and southgoing flows start at HW Dover +0030. The estuary is discordant, possibly eroded from overlying rocks by the river against the trend of the underlying rocks.

A motte stands near the shore at Ingleston and the Waterloo Monument is visible above New Abbey, but the scenery is dominated by Criffel, rising to 569m less than 3km from the coast. Carse Sands lie at its foot, tapering down to Southerness Point. Salmon nets are staked out in the sand and from February to September there is fishing with haaf-nets for salmon and sea trout, the men standing in the water with their nets.

The early lighthouse at Southerness

Preston Merse is a fine saltmarsh between the A710 and Mersehead Sands which dry up to 4km out nearly to Urr Waterfoot but which the RSPB said were threatened by mechanized cockling.

Criffel rises up on the west side of the Nith estuary

Houses in Carsethorn were built in the 19th century for the coastguard. Beyond them is the unusual Kirkbean church with a dome, a sundial giving the times in Calcutta, Gibraltar and Madras, (places where local men worked in Victorian days) and a font presented by the US Navy in memory of John Paul Jones. The latter is also remembered beyond McCulloch's Castle at Arbigland with its extensive woodlands and formal water gardens. Jones' father was the gardener and was living in a local cottage when his son was born in 1747. Jones junior joined the merchant navy when he was 13, subsequently founded the US Navy, returned to attack Whitehaven where he had been trained and later served under Catherine the Great.

Schooners bound for America benefited from a lighthouse at Southerness Point. Built in 1748 by Dumfries merchants, it is one of the oldest in Scotland although now disused. Mussel-covered rocks surround what was Salters' Ness from the 12th-century salt-panning industry but today it is a village of chalets, caravans and a golf course. Flows run at up to 9km/h here.

Southwick Water has both the Needle's Eye and Lot's Wife rocks. A bad place for camels, the golf course between Sandyhills and Portling overlooks another Needles Eye. The cliffs attract fulmars, razorbills and guillemots.

Castlehill Point marks arrival at Urr Waterfoot. A series of attractive inlets follow although the RSPB said that Rough Firth, which has 590 waders in winter, was in danger of irreversible damage from cockling and that Auchencairn Bay, with 2,000 winter waders, was in equal danger from port expansion.

In the mouth of the latter bay is Hestan Island, the causeway of Hestan Rack leading across the sands at low tide. A Neolithic midden of oyster shells shows it was occupied from earliest times although the most significant occupant was in the now ruined manor at the north end. From 1332 it was used by the puppet King Edward Balliol who issued decrees under the Great Seal of Scotland from Estholm. There are said to be underground caverns left by 17th and 18th-century smugglers. It was probably Isle Rathan in S R Crockett's *The Raiders*. In the 19th century it was occupied by an organ builder

Looking westwards to Hestan Island at the mouth of Auchencairn Bay

who liked the acoustics. On top is a lighthouse while Daft Ann's Steps on the south end of the island should not offer any hope of a landing point.

Balcary Fishery on the mainland catches salmon with nets staked out on the sand although bass are equally present. Balcary House hotel was built as a headquarters for smugglers to store wine and tobacco. Just before Balcary Point with its nesting seabirds is the Tower.

The coastline is now bold and rocky to Gipsy Point. Flows from Abbey Head are ingoing from HW Dover −0530 and outgoing from HW Dover +0030.

Bigamy creeps in with a second Lot's Wife. Below forts and a homestead the religious connotations continue with Adam's Chair.

Rascarrel Bay is backed by chalets and older huts grouped incongruously around roofless stone buildings. Thrift, bluebells, red campion and gorse enhance the attraction of the spot.

After Castle Muir Point the cliffs are festooned with greenery, particularly around the caves at Dropping Craig, and the Spouty Dennans hanging waterfall drops dramatically from the clifftop.

Port Mary is the point where Mary, Queen of Scots was thought to have left Scottish soil for the last time as she set sail for England, but it requires calm conditions to land a kayak amongst the boulders, let alone a larger boat.

From here to Gipsy Point are 8km of the Abbey Head tank and artillery range danger area, reaching up to 23km south. The army have handed over operation to civilians and it is in use 7 days a week although it closes some weekends. Boats may be escorted through in safe intervals by the range safety vessel. When the red flag is flying at Abbey Burn Foot the range is in use. Landing is not practical near the control cabin, but it is possible to paddle close enough to be recognized and be waved through if prior agreement has been obtained. Various military buildings are spread around Mullock Bay and gantries stand on the clifftops.

Kirkcudbright Bay is discordant and may have been eroded from a cover of newer rocks against the trend of general folding. It acts as the estuary of the River Dee. Flows start eastgoing and ingoing at HW Dover −0545 and westgoing and outgoing at HW Dover +0015 at up to 7km/h.

There are 720 waders and wildfowl in the winter, the RSPB having said the bay was in danger of permanent damage from port expansion. A good place to watch bird migrations is the island of Little Ross, separated from Meikle Ross by the Sound and topped by its conspicuous lighthouse of 1843. In 1960, lighthouse keeper Robert Dickson killed workmate Hugh Clark in what was described as the 'perfect murder'. The light was automated the following year.

Little Ross at the mouth of Kirkcudbright Bay has a much more prominent lighthouse than Hestan Island

The coast gradually curves round into Wigtown Bay where southerly winds rise with little warning and bring heavy seas. From Borness Point with the Borness Batteries the coast is bold and rocky, topped with an assortment of forts, settlements, homesteads and duns. By Dove Cave there is a curious formation which looks as though someone has tipped a load of waste concrete down the cliff to leave a rough concrete pillar, but this cannot be the case as there is an overhang to the cliff at this point. Sadly, at Meikle Pinnacle there is quite definitely a quantity of junk tipped down the cliffs.

Kirkandrews Bay has a selection of small inlets with mussel covered rocks and is surrounded by a range of artefacts, an old church, cup and ring marked rocks, motte, dun and a tower attached to what appears to be a rather unattractive church with a barrel roof, now reverted to being part of a farm.

The cliffs have already shown significant folding but they now become very complex with over 60 synclines and anticlines in the 2km to Knockbrex.

The Islands of Fleet lead up to Fleet Bay with wildfowl in winter. The Three Brethren are a group of rocks by Barlocco Isle, the grass top of which

Folded strata at Ravenshall Point result in some interesting rock sculptures

was once used for grazing and which is joined to the mainland by rocks at low water. Ardwall Isle or Larry's Isle was also used for grazing and is connected to land at low water by a sand ridge. It has the remains of a 9th-century chapel. Early stone crosses and a Northumbrian period inscription have been found. For 50 years it was occupied by the Higgins family who opened it to smugglers and honeycombed it with hiding places. Murray's Isles are also connected to the sand at low water.

There are cup and ring marked rocks and a burial chamber at Mossyard although it is two caravan sites which are prominent, a motte and a cross being found at Low Auchenlarie.

The coast now has a shoreline of boulders but then a level strip before the land rises steeply in a tree covered hillside alongside the East Channel, eventually climbing to 456m Cairnharrow. Ravenshall Point exhibits some interesting rock features and is quickly followed by Dirk Hatteraick's Cave, above which are a castle, the Neolithic horned-chambered cairn of Cairnholy of about 2000BC, Kirkdale church, another cairn and a cup and ring marked rock all on the west side of the Kirkdale Burn.

Carsluith Castle is much more easily seen from the water. More a fortified family house than a castle, it dates from the 1560s and is L-shaped in plan, now roofless. A much older fort site is to be found a little further up the hillside.

A limited amount of parking and a picnic bench are to be found beyond the disused quarry off the A75 at Carsluith (NX485546).

Distance
From Siddick to Carsluith is 131km
Campsites
Gilcrux, Allonby, Edderside, Beckfoot, Blitterlees, Silloth, Annan, Powfoot, Southerness, Sandyhills, Barnbarroch, Palnackie, Nun Mill, Pennymuir, Sandy Green, Mossyard, Low Auchenlarie, Creetown
Youth Hostels
Cockermouth, Carlisle, Kendoon, Minigaff
OS 1:50,000 Sheets
83 Newton Stewart and Kirkcudbright
84 Dumfries and Castle Douglas
85 Carlisle and Solway Firth
89 West Cumbria
Imray Chart
C62 Irish Sea (1:280,000)
Admiralty Charts
1344 Kirkcudbright Bay (1:15,000)
1346 Solway Firth and Approaches (1:100,000)
2013 St Bees Head to Silloth (1:50,000). Maryport Harbour (1:10,000). Silloth Docks and Approaches (1:10,000)
2094 Kirkcudbright to Mull of Galloway and Isle of Man (1:100,000)
Tidal Constants
Workington: HW Dover +0040, LW Dover +0030
Maryport: HW Dover +0040, LW Dover +0030
Silloth: HW Dover +0050, LW Dover +0100
Annan Waterfoot: HW Dover +0110, LW Dover +0300
Southerness Point: Dover +0040
Hesten Islet: Dover +0040
Kirkcudbright Bay: HW Dover +0030, LW Dover +0020
Garlieston: HW Dover +0040, LW Dover +0030
Sea Area
Irish Sea
Range
Abbey Head
Rescue
Inshore lifeboats: Silloth, Kippford, Kirkcudbright
All weather lifeboats: Workington, Ramsey, Portpatrick
Maritime Rescue Centres
Liverpool, 0151 931 3341.
Clyde, 01475 729988

Carsluith Castle dates from the 1560s on a hillside overlooking Wigtown Bay. It is roofless and lacks its intermediate floor but is otherwise in good condition with some beautiful stonework detailing

18 SOUTHWEST GALLOWAY

Avoiding Scotland's most southerly point

I'm going where the water's deep
And wrecks have sunk before,
And there I'll lay me down and sleep
And be reviled no more.

Gavin Maxwell

Nets stretch out from the coast at Carsluith and fish caught can be taken straight to the nearby Galloway Smokehouse for curing.

Around Kirkmabreck there are a cup and ring marked rock, standing stone, cairn and church from ancient times, items to be avoided by the extensive quarrying operations from which some rock is being levelled along the edge of the estuary.

The River Cree enters at the northern end of the estuary with flows ingoing from HW Dover –0515

Baldoon and Wigtown Sands with the tide out

The wooded shoreline at Jultock Point

and outgoing from HW Dover +0015 at up to 9km/h. The coast of the north and west of the estuary is low and the west side is largely occupied

by the Wigtown Sands and Baldoon Sands which attract 19,000 winter waterfowl including 1,800 curlews, 7,500 pinkfooted geese and numerous greylag geese. The RSPB said the area was in danger of irreversible damage from cockling, although the birds do not seem to be disturbed by jets flying low over the estuary. Fish like to sunbathe in the warm shallows.

Marsh separates the estuary from **Wigtown**, which takes its name from the Old English wic-tun, work or trading estate. On the edge of the marsh is the Martyrs' monument to two women of 18 and

63 who were staked out on the sand for their beliefs and left to drown by the rising tide in 1685 during the Killing Times persecution of the Covenanters. They are recorded, too, in Wigtown Museum which also has a display of 1707 weights and measures.

The River Bladnoch enters between a moat and castle ruin and an airfield and is guided across the sands by rock breakwaters.

Nets are laid out off Innerwell Fishery which deals with salmon. It is hard to believe that terns spaced out at one per post can make such a din, sounding nothing less than a mass fight.

After the exposed area to the north, Jultock Point is a magical spot, completely sheltered from the prevailing wind by a deciduous wood. The rocks are jagged but seaweed and thrift soften the view. The rocky shoreline and strip of woodland continue to Eggerness Point, sometimes with vertical strata. Beyond the fort site at Port Whapple there are a couple of concrete pontoons which have been sunk near the high water line.

Garlieston Bay largely drains at low water and suffers from heavy swells with southeasterly winds, yet the port is active and handles fodder and fertilizers and the bay has cod, flatfish and mackerel. The colourwashed houses were built in two lines, just giving room between them for one of the narrowest bowling greens in Scotland.

Rigg or Cruggleton Bay has a wreck and a large structure standing in the middle of the bay. Between the two bays is Galloway House, dating from 1740, the former seat of the Earls of Galloway, set in walled gardens with rhododendrons and fine trees.

From Sliddery Point to Cairn Head the cliffs are steep, popular with guillemots, with fort sites at intervals on the top. Most notable of these is the castle on Cruggleton Point, conspicuous with its stone arch above the skyline. Behind it lies the 12th-century Cruggleton Church, one of the first parish churches in the area.

From Cairn Head, where the B7063 runs along the back of Portyerrock Bay, the cliffs become bold and rocky as far as Port of Counan with races off the headlands.

Isle of Whithorn at the end of the B7004 was the port for **Whithorn**. The causeway making it a peninsula rather than an island is relatively recent. Before it was built, a smuggler's schooner escaped from a revenue cutter through an apparently dead end. At low water the keel mark could be seen in the sand. Heavy seas are generated by southerly winds, the harbour being used by fishing and pleasure craft. On the ebb the stream sets towards Screen Rocks.

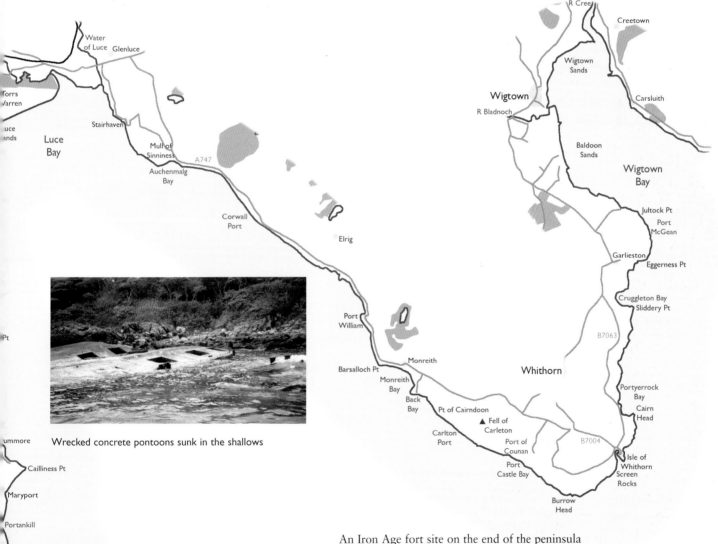

Wrecked concrete pontoons sunk in the shallows

An Iron Age fort site on the end of the peninsula fronts the white St Ninian's tower with its mast. Near the children's playground are the 13th-century ruins of St Ninian's Chapel. This was thought to have been built on the site of St Ninian's 5th century original but excavation work has failed to reveal any traces of it. On the north side of the village a castle was built and a cup and ring marked rock shows even older occupation of the location.

Folded strata on the shoreline at Port McGean.

Gulls crowd Cairn Head to the north of Isle of Whithorn.

The unusual shoreline below Fell of Carleton

Burrow Head marks the turning point from Wigtown Bay to Luce Bay, the latter having anticlockwise currents up to 2km/h in the main part of the bay and being subject to southerly winds at all times of year. The head has a race. It is home for many nesting seabirds, however, and a good watchpoint for bird migrations. A caravan site on top is served by conspicuous high sewerage pipes across gullies, not to be confused with the Devil's Bridge and nearby cave. The Burrow Head Iron Age promontory fort is the most notable of the clifftop forts and homesteads which follow from here to Port Castle Bay where St Ninian's Cave is to be found on the beach at the end of a well-established footpath. Here the first Scottish Christian missionary had his retreat in the 5th century. 8th-century Christian crosses have been carved into the rock and a service is still held here annually.

The coast from Port of Counan to Point of Cairndoon is rather unusual. There is a boulder beach, rising eventually to 146m high Fell of Carleton. Between these two extremes is a long level strip of land which slopes steeply down to the beach, covered with grass. It resembles a giant bench over which a sheet of green felt has been draped. The underlying soil looks like boulder clay but it is strange that it has not been eroded away in this relatively exposed position. Clifftop features include homesteads, a settlement, a cup and ring marked rock and the Laggan Camp fort.

Sections of a substantial metal ship lie wrecked on the boulders towards the southeast end of this section. The hillside drops away after Carleton Port. At this other end there is a conspicuous metal chute into an area resembling a silage clamp and a track down the hillside for access to the bottom of it on the beach.

Point of Lag between Back Bay and Monreith Bay has a carpark with toilets and children's wooden engine and boat. The road from it winds up across a golf course past Kirkmaiden, a sculptured rock, cup and ring marked rocks and an otter memorial to Gavin Maxwell. It was a favourite spot for the author of *Ring of Bright Water* who lived at House of Elrig as a boy (the title of another of his books) when his family owned the Monreith estate. The A747 now follows the coast and close by is Low Knock Open Farm with exotic ducks, peafowl, Shetland ponies and African pygmy goats.

Virtually the whole of Luce Bay is used as a bombing range and may be active at any time from 8am to 4.30pm on weekdays and sometimes at weekends although use is only intermittent. The work is experimental, such items as laser-guided bombs being dropped from considerable heights, not all of which detonate correctly. Thus, there is a lot of unexploded ordnance lying about on the seabed, some of which gets washed up onto beaches. Passage is permitted between the yellow buoys and the shoreline along each side of the bay at any time, but the head of the bay and the main body of the bay should only be entered when the range is not being used.

From Barsalloch Point to the Mull of Sinniness the coast is flat although the beach continues to be boulder-strewn. Barsalloch Point itself has an Iron Age hill fort on a raised beach, the rampart and ditch dating from 300BC.

There are bass, cod, rays and skate in the waters off the small resort of Port William. More significant, however, is the basking shark. Despite being quite harmless, the black triangular fins slicing through the water as the only visible signs of a large circling creature can get the adrenalin flowing very effectively.

Caravans behind the beach at Port William are followed by a caravan park at Barr Point. At Chippermore Point the residents are cormorants, favourite perch rocks being whitened with guano.

The coast is only sparsely inhabited now but is littered with homesteads, cairns and a hut circle from earlier times. Corwall Port was a landing place for Irish pilgrims going to St Ninian's church in Whithorn and Chapel Finian is a small oratory there from the 10th or 11th century, St Finian having studied at Whithorn.

Gannets fly over Auchenmalg Bay where they have a choice of bass, conger, dogfish, flatfish, mullet, rays and tope while another caravan site also overlooks all.

The Mull of Sinniness forms a prominent outcrop and has thus attracted attention over the years. Artefacts there include a standing stone, fort, the first of many brochs around the Scottish coastline, Castle Sinniness and Sinniness Barracks, the latter built in the 1820s to house 50 revenue men trying to stamp out smuggling in the Solway. The mull ends with Stair Haven, an 18th-century lobster fishing harbour which is almost deserted despite having a picnic area and toilets.

Behind a golf course at the northeast corner of Luce Bay is Castle of Park at Glenluce, a tall castellated mansion built by Thomas Hay of Park in 1590. Past it flows the Water of Luce and the Piltanton Burn also enters this corner of the bay. Raised beach material separates Luce Bay from Loch Ryan to the north, ending with the Torrs Warren dunes and their notable slacks, good for winter waders and wildfowl. Bareagle Forest of Sitka spruce and Corsican and Monterey pines has been planted to stabilize the shifting sands. The most obvious aspect of the beach material, however, is Luce Sands which stretch right across the head of the bay, 10km long by a kilometre wide at low tide yet closed to the public. Even when the bombing range is not in use there is a rifle range which is sometimes used at weekends, putting part of Luce Sands at risk.

The bombing aircraft operate from West Freugh Airfield behind a line of lookout towers, a large tower with an array of aerials and a white geodesic dome. Offshore there are two target platforms visible easily from the head of the bay and two groups of steel and concrete cones which look as though they have received direct hits, a giant version of the back lawn on November 6th.

The danger area comes to an end with a sand pit and a caravan site or two before the B7084 joins

The otter monument to Gavin Maxwell, overlooking Monreith Bay, a favourite spot for the author

Old and new bombing targets in Luce Bay

the A716 near Sandhead. At the southern end of the beach in Sandhead Bay, behind the children's playground, is Ginger Tom's, an inn with masses of character. The beach ends with a pipe which emerges vertically from the sand and curves over to dribble a liquid of unknown source into the water, not typical of other outfall pipes and an obstacle which occupies one of the obvious landing points on this coast.

Surprisingly, it is the east side of the Rhins of Galloway that is suffering erosion, the coast alternating between sandy sections and boulder-strewn areas. At Ardwell Mill there are fish nets staked out in the sea and swans also take to the salt water. Ringvinachan offers an array of domes and aerials to track the bombing movements out in the bay.

Ardwell House follows a caravan site. Dating from the 18th century, it has formal gardens with daffodils, rhododendrons, camellias, flowering shrubs, foliage, crazy paving and pond walks.

Another fish net is erected after Chapel Rossan in front of a prominent tower near the shore. More tracking aerials stand on Balgowan Point. Further caravans mark Drummore, a village that was once a smuggling centre.

From Cailiness Point to the Mull of Galloway there is an anticlockwise eddy on the eastgoing flow. There is one final caravan site overlooking Maryport Bay, but first there are eyes close at hand from seals resting up on the reef to the south of Cailiness Point. Kirkmaiden church at Portankill is followed by St Medan's Cave.

Until the last century fishermen portaged from East Tarbet over the ridge to West Tarbet to avoid having to round the Mull of Galloway and this option remains open today, the mull being one of the most dangerous points on the British coastline with a heavy and violent race off the point, especially with wind against tide, running at 9km/h with overfalls. The visible part of the mull is extended by an underwater ridge running a long way northeast from the mull. During the eastgoing stream the race extends north northeast towards the head of Luce Bay. During the westgoing stream it extends southwest and west. The optimum approach is from the north at HW Dover –0130 when it is fairly quiet and there is only about 100m of flow to be tackled by a paddler keeping close in against the rocks. This contrasts with a crossing of Luce Bay when the race must be crossed and arrival time is harder to predict. The northgoing stream begins just after Dover HW. An hour after the northerly flow reverses, an eastgoing eddy begins from Port Kemin to the mull. Tide stream directions close inshore begin much earlier than those further offshore that are documented on charts.

This most southerly point in Scotland is marked by a lighthouse dating from 1830. It is a bird migration watchpoint and a bird sanctuary with one of the best seabird colonies in Galloway, particularly kittiwakes. Several types of flora are on the northern or southern extremities of their ranges and there is plenty of thrift and carpets of heather.

View from the cliffs at the Mull of Galloway with the sea about as calm as it gets. The top left of the picture shows just a trace of the normal churning race

As Luce Bay gives way to the North Channel the coast becomes steep. The last two Picts were reputed to have been trapped here by Scots. Rather than reveal the secret of heather ale, which had a scent like honey, the father let them throw his son off the cliffs and then jumped to his own death. What cannot be disputed is the selection of earthworks, forts, cairns (including Kennedy's Cairn), homesteads and standing stones which cover the area.

Cormorants, gannets and seals occupy the cliff lined coast. Off Port Mona there are overfalls with more at Crammag Head and a race to 12km/h, overlooked by a tiny lighthouse, a lookout point and a dun. Guillemots, razorbills and jellyfish add to the wildlife in Clanyard Bay.

Slouchnamorroch Bay is backed by some fine folding in the cliffs with a dramatic syncline.

The first convenient landing point after the mull is at Port Logan on the B7065 where a ruined tower tops a breakwater protecting the abandoned 19th-century harbour. A sheltered sand beach and picnic tables in front of a community of whitewashed houses offers an oasis of tranquillity in a committing section of coast. On the north side of Port Nessock or Port Logan Bay a tidal fish pond was excavated in the rocks in 1800 to catch fish for Logan House, but the fish became family pets and tame cod now come to be fed when summoned by a bell. Up the hill from the pond are the Logan Botanic Gardens, an outstation of Edinburgh's Royal Botanic Gardens. The mildest weather conditions in Scotland allow cabbage palms, tree ferns and exotic species from the Southern Hemisphere, such as the Patagonian fire tree, to be grown.

A prominent pillar precedes the Mull of Logan, off which there may be overfalls. Forts and earthworks follow at regular intervals and Ardwell Point is topped by the broch of Doon Castle. The final set of major overfalls occur off Money Head but forts continue. The Dualdboys motte at Port of Spittal Bay has now been upstaged by Knockinaam Lodge, an exclusive hotel.

By far the most dramatic of all these fortifications is Dunskey Castle, an early 16th-century ruin on top of the cliffs. A wooden bridge forms part of a public walkway along the cliffs from Portpatrick which appears suddenly, firstly as a large hotel and then as a delightful cove with all the charms of a Cornish fishing village, inns and colourwashed houses jumbling up the steep slopes. Facing across to Belfast Lough 35km away and with the Northern Ireland coastline clearly visible across the North Channel, it used to be the Irish ferry terminal for Donaghadee until 1862, the

Victorian piers being destroyed by waves. The 17th-century church was much used for weddings by runaway Irish couples. Although the harbour, with black guillemots nesting in the wall, is used as a base for sailing and waterskiing, entry is still impractical in moderate southwesterly winds. The Lifeboat Week each year with raft racing and other activities is a major event, all being overlooked by an old lighthouse.

The village can be busy in season but when there is parking space the best place to land is on the small beach at the east side of the harbour.

Some visitors come here because it is the western end of the Southern Uplands Way long distance footpath. For the less energetic there is the Little Wheels exhibition with over 1,000 model cars and 100m of model railway, running 16 complete trains, over 100 engines and a variety of gauges, even the rare 009, plus an exhibition of dolls.

The village of Portpatrick, an isolated haven on the Rhins of Galloway. The low building on the left is the lifeboat station

Distance
From Carsluith to Portpatrick is 125km
Campsites
Creetown, Wigtown, Whithorn, Monreith, West Barr, Glen of Luce, Glenluce, Clayshant, Sandhead, Ardwell, Balgowan, Drummore, Portpatrick
Youth Hostel
Minigaff
OS 1:50,000 Sheets
82 Stranraer and Glenluce
83 Newton Stewart and Kirkcudbright
Imray Chart
C62 Irish Sea (1:280,000)
Admiralty Charts
2093 Southern Approach to North Channel (1:100,000)
2094 Kirkcudbright to Mull of Galloway and Isle of Man (1:100,000)
2198 North Channel – Southern Part (1:75,000). Portpatrick (1:4,000)
Tidal Constants
Garlieston: HW Dover +0040, LW Dover +0030
Isle of Whithorn: HW Dover +0040, LW Dover +0030
Port William: HW Dover +0020, LW Dover
Drummore: HW Dover +0050, LW Dover +0030
Portpatrick: HW Dover +0040, LW Dover
Sea Area
Irish Sea
Ranges
Luce Bay, Luce Sands
Submarine Areas
81 Peel, 79 Beaufort
Rescue
Inshore lifeboats: Kirkcudbright
All weather lifeboats: Ramsey, Portpatrick
Maritime Rescue Centre
Clyde, 01475 729988
Belfast, 028 9146 3933

Dunskey Castle stands on low cliffs to the south of Portpatrick

19 NORTHEAST NORTH CHANNEL

Dodging the fast Ulster ferries

Hearken, thou craggy ocean–pyramid!
Give answer from thy voice, the sea–fowl's screams!
When were thy shoulders mantled in huge streams?
When, from the sun, was thy broad forehead hid?
How long is't since the mighty power bid
Thee heave to airy sleep from fathom dreams?
Sleep in the lap of thunder or sunbeams,
Or when grey clouds are thy cold coverlid.
Thou answer'st not; for thou art dead asleep.
Thy life is but two dead eternities –
The last in air, the former in the deep;
First with the whales, last with the eagle–skies
Drown'd wast though till an earthquake made thee steep,
Another cannot wake thy giant size.

John Keats

From Portpatrick the northgoing flow starts at HW Dover –0130 and the southgoing flow starts at HW Dover +0430. Although the cliffs tend to be less forbidding than further south, the coast becomes more remote as there is an absence of public road access until Loch Ryan.

Leaving Portpatrick, the cliffs are lined with an array of aerials surrounding a golf course. The communications theme continues at Port Kale, a cleft which contains submarine cables from Donaghadee and Larne plus a further seven which are now disused.

The wreck of the *Craigantlet* at Portamaggie with Killantringan Lighthouse on Black Head

lighthouse above on Black Head had to be evacuated for 6 weeks.

As the Southern Upland Way turns eastwards and heads for Cockburnspath the peak tidal flows ease from 9km/h to 7km/h.

The coast is peppered with forts, a dun, a motte and two Salt Pan Bays. In Knock Bay another disused submarine cable lands.

The coast is largely left to gannets, cormorants, terns, oystercatchers, curlews, seals and jellyfish. There is some notable folding behind Strool Bay but none more so than Juniper Rock, a vertical slab which is roughly circular when viewed along the coast but banana shaped when looking in towards the shore. In complete contrast is Craig Laggan beacon which resembles a giant stone milk churn.

Heavily folded strata north of Portpatrick

Awash at Portamaggie are the remains of the coastal container ship *Craigantlet* which came to grief on a voyage from Belfast to Liverpool in 1982. Although lots of valuable clothes were washed ashore she was also carrying chemicals which were so dangerous that the keepers of Killantringan

Corswall Point lighthouse was built by Robert Stevenson in 1816 on low lichen-covered rocks which are characteristic of this shoreline for several kilometres. Up the hill from the lighthouse is St Columba's Well while a prominent aerial marks the hillside at Balscalloch.

Flows are to about 6km/h here but fall weak to Loch Ryan which provides shelter from westerly winds, the heaviest seas coming from northwesterly blows against the ebb. Currents in the entrance rotate clockwise, flowing south–southwest round Finnarts Point from HW Dover –0545 and north–northeast from HW Dover +0120.

The tranquillity after Milleur Point is usually pronounced and the greenery-clad cliffs of Clachan Heughs provide a marked contrast to the exposed rocks on the west side of the Rhins of Galloway.

danger from the wildfowl. The Scar pushes the fairway across to the east side of the channel. The fairway can be very busy at times, taking all the ferry traffic from Ulster. Ferries operate from Cairnryan to Larne and another 7km from Stranraer. Catamarans are smaller but much faster with aggressive looking forward swept outriggers. Although they drop their speed at the entrance to the loch and again before Cairn Point lighthouse they still move fast and so a crossing of the fairway needs to be undertaken with due respect. The pier at Cairnryan is used for shipbreaking but they don't need assistance from wandering paddlers. In

A catamaran passes Clachan Heughs as it arrives in Loch Ryan from Ulster

At Kirkcolm the Scar runs southeast into the wide part of Loch Ryan, an extensive area of shallow sand and stones which dries at low tide. Streams run straight in and out here and the Scar protects the Wig, a sheltered area used by seaplanes and flying boats during the two world wars. Now the Scar is used in the early summer by nesting terns and in the autumn and winter by hundreds of eiders, oystercatchers, dunlin and redshank, 2,200 wildfowl which the RSPB said were in danger of irreversible damage from port expansion, marina development, recreational pressure and pollution. Perhaps the tope are in

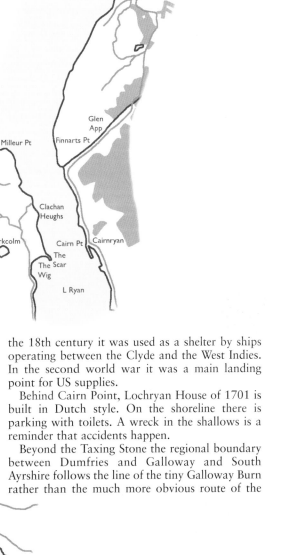

the 18th century it was used as a shelter by ships operating between the Clyde and the West Indies. In the second world war it was a main landing point for US supplies.

Behind Cairn Point, Lochryan House of 1701 is built in Dutch style. On the shoreline there is parking with toilets. A wreck in the shallows is a reminder that accidents happen.

Beyond the Taxing Stone the regional boundary between Dumfries and Galloway and South Ayrshire follows the line of the tiny Galloway Burn rather than the much more obvious route of the

From Finnarts Point the coast is isolated from roads until Ballantrae

The unmistakable silhouette of Ailsa Craig in the middle of the Firth of Clyde

Water of App which enters at Finnarts Bay. The A77, which has been following the east side of the loch, does take Glen App, however, disappearing behind relatively high peaks until Ballantrae. Situated on the clifftop at Finnart Bay is an observation post with gun sites overgrown in the scrub, providing cover for the mouth of Loch Ryan.

The coast is peaceful and secluded with only the company of disturbed cormorants diving into the sea for cover, leaving a fishy aroma in the air.

Flows to Bennane Head start north–northeast at HW Dover −0020 and south–southwest at HW Dover +0545 at up to 4km/h. A cairn, enclosures and standing stones are scattered over the top of

the steep Finnarts Hill. The cliffs are precipitous but there are occasional secluded landing points and the position of the house at Portandea is magnificent, all alone at the waterside with a small beach beside a tiny inlet.

Baile-an-Traigh means village on the shore, Ballantrae being located at the end of a long shingle spit which protects the mouth of the River Stinchar. Its major building is Ballantrae Castle, now a column and slab ruin but formerly owned by the Bargany branch of the Kennedys and visited by Mary, Queen of Scots in 1566. The church dates from the 17th century and the village was known for its smuggling in the 18th century. Terns nest on the cliffs in a reserve run by the Scottish Wildlife

Trust. Behind the village are an aerial and an old windmill.

The two conspicuous landmarks inland are Knockdolian, which rises steeply amidst what is otherwise relatively flat land, and the aerial on top of the less conspicuous Knockormal Hill. Between them lies Bennane Head and Bennane Lea with its cod and pollock. There is a race at Bennane Head where the stream from the west divides and flows both ways along the coast, reversing on the ebb. The effect for the coastal paddler is that the flow reverses at this point so that it would give most benefit to arrive at the bottom of the tide. From here it flows north–northeast from HW Dover +0545 and south–southwest from HW Dover –0020.

Sawny Bean's Cave at Balcreuchan Port was said to have housed a family of cannibals. Now there are caravan sites either side of Games Loup and a more refined eating venue in the form of a picnic area at Carleton Bay. Carleton Castle at Little Carleton was one of the line of watchtowers along the coast belonging to the local rulers, the Kennedys, who were somewhat above the law. This one was owned by baron Sir John Cathcart, whose memory has been recorded in song for pushing seven wives over the cliff at Games Loup but being disposed of in turn by the eighth, May Culean.

Lendalfoot is at the mouth of the Water of Lendal. A group of whitewashed cottages and a memorial mark the point where a couple of minor roads drop down from the higher ground to the A77 running along the shore.

Lying 14km offshore is Ailsa Craig, fairy rock in Gaelic or Paddy's Milestone as it lies halfway between Belfast and Glasgow. Only about 1km in diameter, it rises steeply on all sides to a 338m high peak, making it a distinctive landmark for the whole of the lower Clyde. A microgranite outcrop, it is the remains of an extinct volcano, the blue granite being used for kerbstones and the finest curling stones although the quarry served by a narrow gauge railway and a forge is now closed. The lighthouse dates from 1868 but the foghorns are now disused. There is a ruined castle and a tower which was used by the monks of Crossraguel Abbey and once held by the Catholics for Philip II of Spain. Former tenants used to pay their rents in gannet feathers and it has been one of Scotland's largest gannetries since at least 1526 with 10,000 pairs accounting for 5% of the world population. A bird sanctuary, it also has guillemots, razorbills, fulmars, kittiwakes and puffins nesting. Little Ailsa on the west side has hundreds of basalt pillars and there is Swine Cave at the north end.

North of Lendalfoot the higher land crowds the coast and the A77 squeezes through Kennedy's Pass as it heads towards Ardmillan Castle, another

Kennedy castle visited by Mary, Queen of Scots during her excursion of 1563.

Girvan is on the southern bank at the mouth of the Water of Girvan, formerly a temporary Roman camp, a town which has an air of gentility with its Rose Gardens, Orchard Gardens and Knockushan Gardens. It has a memorial on the front, golf course, putting greens, bowling greens, tennis courts, swimming pool and trampolines. There is the Girvan Folk Festival in May and Lowland Gathering, Civic Week and Gala Parade in June. Still building traditional wooden boats, it has pleasure craft, coasting vessels and a fishing fleet which catches cod, flounders, haddock, herring, mackerel, plaice, rock cod, salmon, trout, whiting and wrasse.

An industrial estate to the north of the town has a distillery and the mohair mill of Hugh Galt and Son.

A track beside Lady Burn at Dipple gives a convenient landing point past a large population of eiders and what is unusual beach pollution, a carpet of discarded potatoes, these being a notable crop on this coast.

Distance
From Portpatrick to Dipple is 69km
Campsites
Portpatrick, Bankhead, Heronsford, Maidens
Youth Hostels
Minigaff, Whiting Bay
OS 1:50,000 Sheets
76 Girvan
82 Stranraer and Glenluce
Imray Charts
C62 Irish Sea (1:280,000)
C63 Firth of Clyde (1:160,500)
Admiralty Charts
1403 Loch Ryan (1:25,000)
SC 1866 Ports in the Firth of Clyde. Girvan (1:6,250)
SC 2126 Approaches to the Firth of Clyde (1:75,000)
2198 North Channel – Southern Part (1:75,000). Portpatrick (1:4,000)
2199 North Channel – Northern Part (1:75,000)
Tidal Constants
Portpatrick: HW Dover +0040, LW Dover
Stranraer: Dover +0100
Ballantrae: HW Dover +0050, LW Dover +0100
Girvan: HW Dover +0040, LW Dover +0050
Sea Areas
Irish Sea, Malin
Rescue
Inshore lifeboat: Stranraer
All weather lifeboats: Portpatrick, Girvan
Maritime Rescue Centre
Belfast, 028 9146 3933
Clyde, 01475 729988

20 SOUTHEAST FIRTH OF CLYDE

Home to Scotland's national heroes

Scots, wha hae wi' Wallace bled,
Scots, wham Bruce has aften led,
Welcome to your gory bed,
Or to victory.

Robert Burns

From Dipple the coast is low and sandy with rocks scattered along the shoreline and dunes behind Turnberry Bay. Away from the alginate works there may be swans, eider ducks, cormorants, terns and oystercatchers on or beside the sea and seals around Brest Rocks which run out to a prominent beacon.

Turnberry is known for its golf course. It held its first open championships in 1979, already having the benefit of its own airstrip, one runway of which crosses the A719. There have been problems, however, the course being taken over by military command in both world wars.

The lighthouse on Turnberry Point terminates the golf course

Turnberry Point is the start of the Firth of Clyde where flows are weak and rotatory. It is a notable bird migration watchpoint. Behind the lighthouse is a memorial and a castle which was the home of the Countess of Carrick, mother of Robert the Bruce. This was reputed to have been his birthplace in 1274 and it may have been why he landed here in 1307 to begin his campaign.

There is a standing stone before Maidens but it is Maidenhead Rocks, the line of horizontal strata running across Maidenhead Bay, which are more striking. The fishing harbour wall was first built in the 1950s from rubble of wartime RAF buildings. Much earlier, Douglas Graham, smuggler and tenant of Shanter Farm to the south of Maidens, had kept his boat, *Tam o' Shanter*, here.

Beyond two caravan sites is Culzean Country Park, the first country park in Scotland in 1970 and still regarded as possibly the best in Britain, a park which looks interesting even from the sea. The centrepiece is Culzean Castle, a mansion built in 1777 by Robert Adam and thought to be his best, positioned around an ancient Kennedy tower for David, 10th Earl of Cassillis, hence its other name of Castle Cassillis. There is an Eisenhower

Barwhin Point, part of Culzean Country Park on the north side of Maidenhead Bay

Presentation which explains the general's part in European history and his involvement with Culzean. Guided walks take in the round drawing room, the fine plaster ceilings and the splendid oval staircase. There are tea rooms, restaurant, picnic sites, adventure playground and toilets. A walled garden of 1783, aviary, camellia house and orangery are set in the 2.3km² of park with its swan lake, wildfowl, red deer and red squirrels. There is always an extensive events programme and it remains the most visited property of the National Trust for Scotland. Around it are lava cliffs with agates, chalcedony and other forms of quartz, natural arches and a network of interconnected caves.

Two caravan sites surround an old well at Croy House. Above them on Croy Brae is a remarkable piece of road which seems to slope the wrong way. It is actually an optical illusion resulting from certain features of the landscape, but attempts to explain it in terms of electrical effects in the past have added the alternative name of Electric Brae. Those walking up to look at it should take something round to roll 'up' the hill.

Dunure Castle has a beautiful shoreline setting amongst rocks, caves and arches but has a less attractive history. The Kennedys of Cassillis were opposed to the Reformation and in 1570 they took Allan Stewart, the Commendator of Crossraguel, into the black vault and roasted him alive in an attempt to force him to give the abbey lands to the 4th Earl of Cassillis. Seven years earlier Mary, Queen of Scots had stayed here with the earl, one of her staunchest supporters, after her defeat at the Battle of Langside.

Dunure has toilets and neat whitewashed houses around a harbour which is used for yachting but was formerly a base for smuggling whisky from Arran.

Sometimes fields slope down to a shore dotted with rocks, providing sheltered pools for the heron, and sometimes there are cliffs, culminating in the vertical 79m high Heads of Ayr with low ground on each side and low ground surrounding Ayr Bay with its gannets.

The first buildings seen of **Ayr** are those of the Butlin's Holiday Camp. There is a railway (not to be confused with the dismantled public railway) and a cableway while horses plod steadily along the beach.

Greenan Castle is a 16th-century ruin with the remaining wall ready to topple down onto the beach. Mostly belonging to the Kennedys, it was in Davidson hands for a period. Thomas Kennedy of Culzean spent a night here in 1602 and was murdered at St Leonard's Road the next morning, his body being brought back here.

Doonfoot has mixed flocks of foraging waders. Ayr, one of the biggest resorts in Scotland, runs

Dunure Castle stands on the shoreline, a craggy silhouette with a disturbed past

The Heads of Ayr rise sharply above the surrounding land.

from the River Doon to the River Ayr and beyond. Ayr and Robert Burns are inseparable. Burns Cottage is where he was born in 1759 and where he lived until 1766. There is a Land o' Burns Centre with gardens and a tea room. Nearby is a Burnsiana museum and tea room. The haunted Alloway Kirk, a ruin in Burns' day, is where his father, William, is buried, inspiring Tam o' Shanter, who saw dancing witches and warlocks through its windows. The Auld Brig o' Doon, possibly 13th century, is a single arch where Tam's horse, Maggie, lost her tail to the witch Cutty Sark, accompanied by a Burns monument of 1823 and gardens with statues of his characters. The Tam o' Shanter Museum is in the former brewhouse supplied with malt by the aforementioned Douglas Graham of Shanter Farm, alias Tam o' Shanter. The Auld Kirk in Alloway, built in 1654 with notable lofts and its original canopied pulpit, is where Burns was baptized and sometimes attended. In June there is a week of Burns Festival with concerts, exhibitions, competitions, ceilidhs, Holy Fair with sideshows, bands, displays and a re-enactment of Tam's ride. This is only part of the calendar. April has the Ayrshire Agricultural Show, May is the Ayrshire Arts Festival with a week of plays, films and concerts, Ayr Golf Week is in June and August has Ayr Bowls Week and Scotland's leading flower festival, the Ayr Flower Show.

Bellisle Park to the south of Ayr centre is a deer park with wildfowl, formal gardens, golf course and cafeteria. Rozelle is an 18th-century mansion altered in the 1830s by David Bryce, the Maclaurin Gallery having Henry Moore and other sculpture, fine art, photographs, crafts, local military and other history, embroidery and civic relics in a converted stable block, not to mention a park with swan pond, nature trails and tea room.

The Gaiety Theatre claims to be Scotland's leading variety theatre and there is also a civic theatre. Another notable building is Loudoun Hall dating from around 1500, a town house for a rich merchant, one of the oldest surviving examples of Scottish Burgh architecture, belonging to the Campbells, earls of Loudoun and Moores, all prominent in the town. St John's Tower is the remains of the Burgh Kirk of St John the Baptist where the Scottish Parliament met in April 1315 after Bannockburn to confirm the succession of the Scottish crown. The Wallace Tower, a 34m high neo-Gothic structure, the second on the site, was designed by Thomas Hamilton and completed in 1834 by James Thom.

Burns' *Brigs of Ayr* describes two notable bridges over the River Ayr. The 13th-century Auld Brig, restored in 1910, was the scene of the 1601 battle between the Kennedys of Bargany and Cassillis. The New Bridge was built in 1788 and rebuilt in 1878.

The 38m high steeple on the Town Buildings was built in 1828 with an octagonal turret and tall, narrow windows. Miller's Folly is a sentinel port built on the wall of the Cromwellian Citadel by its Victorian owner.

Portencross Castle guarded the turning point into Fairlie Roads

Ayr is the major resort on Glasgow's seaside coast with golf courses, crazy golf, boating pond, paddling pool, miniature railway, children's playground, entertainers, fairground, swimming baths with Turkish and aerotone baths, tennis, riding, skating and curling. There is an esplanade and racehorses are exercised on the beach early in the morning.

Formerly the chief port of western Scotland, it still imports fertilizers, minerals and fish and exports coal and coke, as shown by the coaling plant by the harbour. There is sailing and sub-aqua and cod,

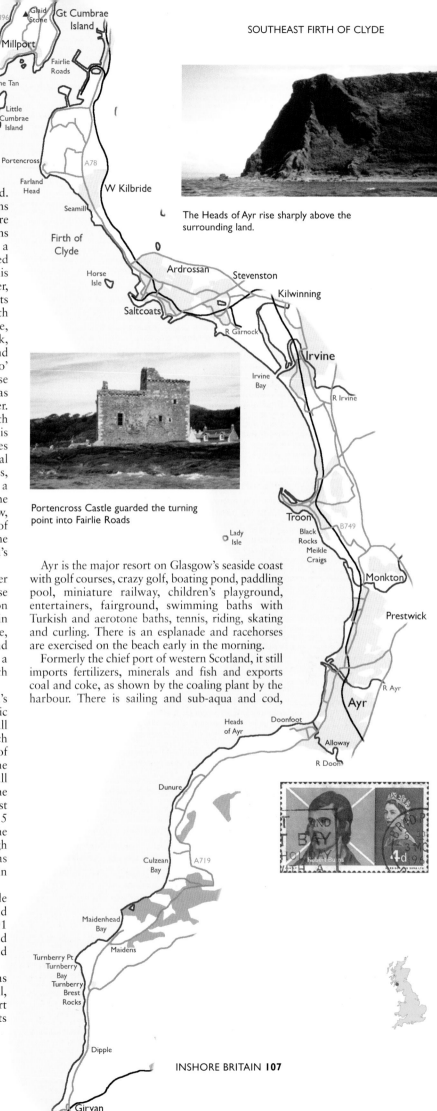

dabs, dogfish, flounders and mullet are caught locally. This is one of the harbours visited by the paddle steamer *Waverley*. The harbour is approached past beacons and a lighthouse and protected by a detached breakwater but westerly winds may still cause a swell in the entrance. Heavy rain causes freshets in the river and small vessels have been carried out to sea by ice breaking up after a hard frost. There is a coastguard station but a wreck shows they are not always successful.

Prestwick is one of the oldest burghs in Scotland, being referred to in 983, but is now contiguous to Ayr in one long sweep of housing. St Ninian's Episcopal church was built in the 12th century by Walter, High Steward of Scotland, and has the graves of knights templars, several provosts and many freemen with a mort safe to deter body snatchers. The Mercat Cross, although moved from its original site, is probably 13th century and one of the best preserved in southwest Scotland. Bruce's Well is where Robert the Bruce improved from a leprosy-like skin disease after drinking the water and there are also the ruins of the chapel of a royally founded leper hospital. More recent is the thyme-scented golf course built in 1867 on the site of the first British open championship in 1860. The club itself was founded in 1851 and members have included Eisenhower and the Duke of Windsor. Other activities include bowling, windsurfing and sailing and there is a heated swimming pool. A promenade ends with toilets and a leisure centre. Offshore there are coalfish, cod, dabs, dogfish, flounders, grey mullet, plaice, rays and tope.

On the north and east sides the town is bounded by Prestwick airport, the Tartan Gateway to Americans as it can take Jumbo jets and is the only fog-free airport in Europe, a better airport than Glasgow but not so well located for the major Scottish connurbation. The Pow Burn skirts the airport and emerges at the west end of the main runway.

Monkton church on the north side of the airport was dedicated to St Cuthbert in the 12th century and was where William Wallace was inspired by a dream of Caledonia urging him to fight for Scotland.

Golf courses continue with ten between Prestwick and Kilwinning. Despite the sandy beaches there are significant spreads of rock close inshore, particularly Meikle Craigs and Black Rocks with a beacon on the end.

Lady Isle lies 4km off **Troon**. With two towers and a light beacon, the ternery is a bird sanctuary with arctic, common and sandwich terns nesting and roseate terns present. The surrounding waters have cod, dogfish, flounders, haddock, plaice, pollack, rays, skate, thorn backs, tope, whiting and general flatfish, together with cormorants. The chief industry in Troon is shipbuilding and laying-up and repairing fishing vessels with the Ailsa Shipbuilding Yard shed and derrick cranes dominating the skyline. Two dry-docks, a marina with room for 340 yachts, lighthouse, gas holder and lifeboat station crowd onto the rocky promontory or trwyn in Old Welsh around the B749. Supports for a former double outfall pipeline provide an awkward obstruction off the southwest side. The houses are often Victorian, towered and turreted in red sandstone. There is a concert hall and other activities include saunas, squash, tennis, bowling, windsurfing and sub-aqua.

The coast of Irvine Bay is low with sand dunes and occasional rock platforms, particularly Stinking Rocks, just before the South Ayrshire/North Ayrshire border. Offshore are the lone Mill Rock and Lappock Rock with its beacons.

The Rivers Garnock and Irvine meet and flow into the sea at **Irvine** past the Irvine Bar. Between them is saltmarsh and the disused Bogside racecourse for horses. Until the Clyde was deepened in the 18th century it was the main port for Glasgow and is where Burns learned flax dressing. It still imports chemicals, clay, flints, sand and timber and exports coal, bricks, fireclay goods and chemicals although it is a resort. There are toilets by the Beach Park and major redevelopment work on the south side of the river. The Magnum Leisure Centre is one of the biggest and most comprehensive in the world with two swimming pools, twin flumes, solarium, indoor bowling green, table tennis, sports hall, ice rink, theatre/cinema, squash courts, fitness salon, soft play area, bars, restaurants, boating and rifle range near the old Tide Signal Station. It is easier to find by water than on Irvine's poorly signposted roads. Irvine Harbour Festival is popular and the Scottish Maritime Museum has been set up with an Irvine harbour tug, Edwardian shipyard worker's flat, wooden boat workshop and historical machinery.

There is sand yachting along Irvine Bay. For naturalists there are gannets, cormorants, eider ducks, oystercatchers, curlews and terns and for naturists there is a long expanse of sand to the north of the rivermouth.

Two chimneys mark the chemical works at **Stevenston**. Nearby **Saltcoats** takes part in the 3 Towns Festival with Ardrossan and Stevenston each May and is a resort with a fair. The North Ayrshire Museum in an 18th-century church has local and national exhibits and material from a former maritime museum. The harbour wall was built in 1686 but there is a heavy swell during winds from the south–southwest to west. Despite this pedaloes are still available for hire. At low water the remains of fossilized trees are visible. An indoor pool plus cafés, bars and amusements complete the attractions.

Ardrossan was built around an adjacent section of rock platform with Castle Craigs at the southern end although the castle is to the northwest of the town. The town was planned by the Earl of Eglinton in 1805 and has indoor bowling and a golf driving range. The harbour imports iron ore, limestone, oil, petrol, timber and scrap metal and exports oil, petrol, asphalt and steel. There is an ocean tanker terminal and a car ferry terminal for Brodick plus a lighthouse, all protected by a detached breakwater.

Beyond the breakwater is Horse Isle, 2ha of grass-topped nature reserve with a ternery, five species of gull and many varieties of butterfly. A slim pyramidal tower used to hold a barrel of water for the use of shipwrecked sailors.

The coast continues sandy in front of the A78 to Farland Head with low rocks at intervals. The railway, which has been following the coast, is very conspicuous as it runs along the hillside past motte, castle, dun and fort sites. There are caravans and a prominent bar food notice at the foot of the slope while black guillemots and jellyfish are to be found offshore.

Seamill is a village of baronial houses with red sandstone turrets, making a glass dome greenhouse by the shore seem as out of place as the aerial on Law Hill beyond **West Kilbride**.

At the end of the golf links there are submarine cables leaving for Arran before the steep Farland Head. The ruined 15th-century Portencross Castle stands right next to the water rather than using the higher site of the vitrified Iron Age fort and dun on the ridge on the north side of the village. This ridge runs north for 2km with a straight rock platform below it at water level.

Little Cumbrae Island has a disused lighthouse on top while there is a conspicuous ruined castle on the adjacent Castle Island.

Moving from the lower to the upper firth, neaps may have an almost continuous outward flow, especially at surface level, if there has been heavy rain or snowmelt. Northerly and easterly winds increase the outward flow and reduce the sea level, southerly and westerly winds having the opposite effect.

Piers project occasionally before Hunterston power station, a nuclear establishment. Its intake is 700m south of Little Brigurd while its outfall pipes extend seawards on the north side of the point to a beacon where a half-metre high mushroom of hot water rises from the depths of Fairlie Roads.

Hunterston House and castle are largely hidden behind the power station.

Hunterston construction yard was a £4,000,000 investment to build oil rigs, but it was never used until employed in the construction of the Coulport Trident submarine explosives handling jetty. At 200m x 80m x 47m high, it was the world's biggest floating dock and was towed from here to Loch Long. It was Europe's second most expensive civil engineering project to the Channel Tunnel at the time, delivered 2 years late and £539,000,000 over budget.

The construction yard fronts the Hunterston Ore and Coal Terminal, built to supply Ravenscraig steelworks. It can take the largest vessels afloat, delivering ore to the landward end on a 1.6km conveyor belt.

The buoyed deep water channel is near Great Cumbrae Island. Navigation regulations treat Great Cumbrae as a large traffic island and so there are fishing boats, bulk ore carriers, naval vessels and pleasure craft sailing in all directions. The Hunterston Channel is defined as a Narrow Channel under the 1972 International Regulations Preventing Collisions at Sea and in it a vessel less than 20m in length 'shall not impede the passage of a vessel which can safely navigate only within a narrow channel or fairway.'

Great Cumbrae is part of the Bute Estate. It consists largely of an old red sandstone plateau, rising to 127m at the Glaid Stone, old sea cliffs dropping to a new wavecut platform and a rocky ledge foreshore. Sheep and cattle farming predominate on the top and the road network is essentially an inner loop on the plateau and an outer B896 loop at the foot of the former cliffs. Great Cumbrae is a place where the Sinclair C5 caught on.

From the southern end of the island there are views through to Arran, perhaps Ailsa Craig and, of course, Little Cumbrae Island with the rugged drop of Craig Nabbin, separated from Great Cumbrae by the Tan at Portachur Point.

Significant eddies can form off Farland Point during some conditions.

Glasgow and London universities share the Marine Biological Station by Keppel Pier, containing the Robertson Museum and Aquarium. The buildings were the headquarters of the Scottish

Marine Biological Association from 1896 to 1970 when they moved to Dunstaffnage. Two vessels and diving facilities are maintained there. A blue and white flag will mean that biologists are diving in the often clear water which surrounds the island. Sea anemonies cling to the deeply pitted sandstone along the shoreline and all is quiet except for the occasional jet roaring overhead on a training flight.

Hunterston Ore and Coal Terminal, Little and Great Cumbrae and Arran

Approaching Keppel Pier on Great Cumbrae

Distance
From Dipple to Millport is 65km
Campsites
Maidens, Knoweside, Ayr, Prestwick, Bogend, Stevenston, Skelmorlie
Youth Hostels
Whiting Bay, Lochranza
OS 1:50,000 Sheets
63 Firth of Clyde
70 Ayr, Kilmarnock and Troon
76 Girvan
Imray Charts
2900.1 Upper Firth of Clyde and Loch Fyne (1:130,000)
2900.4 Firth of Clyde (1:50,000)
C63 Firth of Clyde (1:160,500)
Admiralty Charts
SC 1866 Ports in the Firth of Clyde. Ayr (1:10,000). Troon (1:6,250). Irvine (1:10,000). Ardrossan (1:7,500)
SC 1867 Firth of Clyde Hunterston Channel and Rothesay Sound. Hunterston Channel (1:12,500)
SC 1907 Little Cumbrae Island to Cloch Point (1:25,000)
SC 2126 Approaches to the Firth of Clyde (1:75,000)
SC 2131 Firth of Clyde and Loch Fyne (1:75,000)
2199 North Channel – Northern Part (1:75,000)
SC 2220 Firth of Clyde, Pladda to Inchmarnock – Southern Sheet (1:36,000)
2221 Firth of Clyde, Pladda to Inchmarnock – Northern Sheet (1:36,000)
SC 2491 Ardrossan to Largs (1:25,000)
SC 5610 Firth of Clyde
Tidal Constants
Girvan: HW Dover +0040, LW Dover +0050
Ayr: Dover +0050
Troon: HW Dover +0050, LW Dover +0010
Irvine: Dover +0010
Ardrossan: Dover +0010
Millport: Dover +0010
Sea Area
Malin
Submarine Areas
70 Turnberry, 63 Ayr, 47 Garroch, 46 Cumbrae
Rescue
Inshore lifeboats: Arran, Largs
All weather lifeboats: Girvan, Troon
Helicopter: Prestwick
Maritime Rescue Centre
Clyde, 01475 729988

21 UPPER FIRTH OF CLYDE

Wooded sounds forming Glasgow's playground

Imagine we've left Craigendorran behind,
And wind-happy yachts by Kilcreggan we find,
At Kirn and Dunoon and Innellan we stay,
Then Scotland's Madeira that's Rothesay they say.
Or maybe by Fairlie and Largs we will go,
Or over to Millport that thrills people so,
Maybe journey to Arran, it can't be denied,
These scenes all belong to the song of the Clyde.

From the Keppel Pier the B896 follows the coast of Great Cumbrae Island, also known as Big Cumbrae, an island with wildlife ranging from eider ducks to basking sharks.

The mainland, overshadowed by the hills of the Cunninghame District, is edged by a line of large installations on the far side of Fairlie Roads. The Hunterston ore terminal might be seen unloading iron ore from Japanese bulk carriers to send by conveyor to the rail terminal behind the construction yard. A NATO pier adjoins the Largs Yacht Haven.

table. There is also a Pencil memorial in **Largs** to record how Hakon was driven ashore on a stormy day and defeated bloodily by Alexander III to end the Viking domination. In September there is the burning of a replica Viking longboat, a Viking funeral procession, fireworks and a torchlight procession with Norwegians visiting to join in the celebrations.

Largs, dominated by two dark red sandstone church spires, has a promenade and is visited by the *Waverley*, the world's last seagoing paddle steamer, built on the Clyde in 1946. Smaller craft visit to take part in sailing regattas most weekends

The Lion, a distinctive igneous intrusion on Great Cumbrae

The island has a number of igneous intrusions of which by far the most spectacular is the Lion, a free-standing section which takes its name from its shape. Red sandstone ledges on the shoreline have been pitted and sculpted by the sea to provide extensive if less dramatic interest. Thrift adds a dash of pink to highlight the red of the rocks.

The Scottish National Water Sports Training Centre, with its purpose built chalets, is based near the north end of Great Cumbrae's east coast and includes canoeing, sailing, windurfing and sub-aqua in its repertoire. It is regularly used by national dinghy sailing squads from November to March.

The vehicle ferry terminal contains a telephone and toilets.

Toment End is the site of the graves of Norsemen killed at the Battle of Largs in 1263. A monument stands by the water's edge and next to it is a picnic

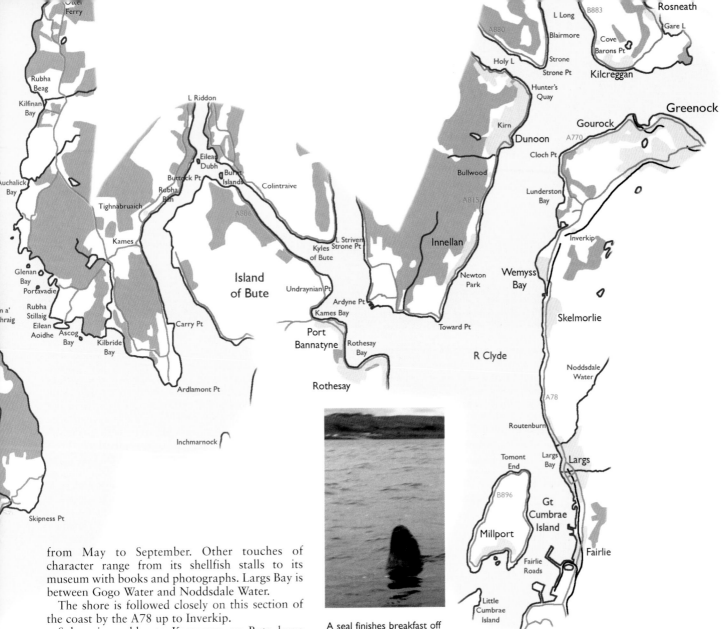

from May to September. Other touches of character range from its shellfish stalls to its museum with books and photographs. Largs Bay is between Gogo Water and Noddsdale Water.

The shore is followed closely on this section of the coast by the A78 up to Inverkip.

Submarine cables to Kerrycroy on Bute leave Routenburn near the golf course. Knock Castle and the restored Skelmorlie Castle are not obvious from the sea, unlike the Heywood Hotel and others which face the rocky beach at **Skelmorlie** where sea urchins may be found. A red building was a leading Clyde hydropathic from the 1860s to the 1930s, an early form of health farm.

A measured mile is a facility which allows ships to check their speeds.

From Skelmorlie to Cloch Point the flood begins at HW Dover −0500 and the ebb at HW Dover +0100 at up to 2km/h.

After North Ayrshire gives way to Inverclyde, **Wemyss Bay** is one of the main passenger ports of the Clyde with an Edwardian station and pier and a ferry service to Bute. A red stone shelter proves an interesting find on Wemyss Point. These older features are overshadowed by the massive chimney of the disused Inverkip power station and its jetty which can take 95,000 tonne tankers. Doubtless these new structures were not greeted with great enthusiasm, Inverkip having had nothing else there larger than a stone memorial in front of what is now Kip Marina and a tower on Ardgowan Point. The marina is one of the largest in Scotland in a village which was known in the 17th century for its witchcraft and in the 18th century for its smuggling.

Lunderston Bay has a picnic site and more submarine cables leaving it while guillemots sit out

A seal finishes breakfast off the Cumbrae ferry slip

on the water. A gun emplacement has been strategically located to cover the narrow entrance to the industry and naval installations of the Clyde and surrounding lochs. Shacks sit along the shoreline to Cloch Point where the lighthouse, built in 1797, has to be one of the most accessible on the British coastline, sandwiched between the water and the A770, which runs right alongside to the extent that lighthouse crews parked their cars on the footway.

Gourock is announced by the Stakis Gantock Hotel with its anchor, a modern building below Levan Castle. A ferry service connects with Hunter's Quay. Indeed, looking across the Clyde estuary it is a rare moment when there is not at least one ferry crossing somewhere. With all the shipping interest and lochs running away in different directions it is hardly surprising that Gourock should have become a resort. Even now,

Cloch Point lighthouse with Strone Point opposite

Hunter's Quay, Holy Loch, Strone Point, Loch Long, Ardentinny and Kilcreggan, seen across the Firth of Clyde from Gourock

it is a fascinating place just to spend time watching. Near the Anchor Hotel is an ornate wrought iron drinking fountain and some modern public toilets.

Monoliths have played an important role locally. One prehistoric stone used to be embraced by couples to ensure they had children and another was consulted by fishermen seeking fair winds. In 1662 a number of women were burned for trying to throw the Granny Kempock Stone into the sea to sink ships by witchcraft. As if to emphasize their failure, ferries operate from Kempock Point to Helensburgh, Kilcreggan and Dunoon and the only real oddity today is a giant yellow kettle near the pier.

The massive block of Fort Matilda was built to guard a narrow point of the Clyde estuary. Above it on Lyle Hill is a memorial in the form of an anchor and a Cross of Lorraine to the Free French sailors who died in the Battle of the Atlantic in the second world war. From here towards **Greenock** the coast is dominated by hammerhead cranes.

Crossing the Firth of Clyde from Inverclyde to Argyll and Bute needs to be done in consultation with the charts as no less than three recommended shipping channels pass through this gap.

The B833 joins the coast at **Kilcreggan** to the west of an aerial on Gallows Hill and continues around the coast, a shoreline of weathered rocks. From Baron's Point a skein of submarine cables cross Loch Long. Loch Long floods from HW Dover –0430 and ebbs from HW Dover +0130 at up to 1km/h. Because of the high mountains all around, it is subject to fickle winds. It is also one of the deepest sea lochs and is used by submarines, including nuclear craft, surfaced and submerged. It is subject to Narrow Channel regulations. North of Cove it is controlled by the Clyde Dockyard Port of Gareloch and subject to special regulations including restrictions on the use of whistles.

The pier at Dunoon, overlooked by the castle

Knockderry Castle guards a narrowing opposite Gairletter Point. This section of the Cowal Peninsula coast is part of the Argyll Forest Park as far as Strone Point and is followed by the A880. Despite the trees and the steep slopes, an area has been adopted as a golf course above Blairmore with its licensed grocer and Strone with its church right on Strone Point. In recent years, Holy Loch has seemed to have had a rather unsuitable name because of its association with US nuclear submarines. It took its name after a ship sank here while loaded with earth from the Holy Land which had been intended as a foundation for Glasgow cathedral. These days it is home for Lothian Region's Benmore Outdoor Education Centre.

The Hunter's Quay Hotel makes it clear that the pier receiving ferries from Gourock is, indeed, Hunter's Quay, named after the Hunter family who bought this section of coast speculatively when steamships started. It is not to be confused with the derelict Kirn pier by the Queen's Hotel a little further along the A815. A dark red church spire is one of the early features of **Dunoon** (named from the Gaelic dun obhainn, river fort), a resort with such venues as the Argyll Hotel, Rock Café and Cosy Corner Tearoom. The Esplanade Hotel name refers to the town's 6km front. The pier receives ferries from Kempock Point and is visited by the *Waverley*. This Gateway to the Western Highlands boasts tennis, bowling greens, squash, swimming pools, sauna and solarium, not to mention 150 pipe bands in the Cowal Highland Gathering at the end of August. The past has been more turbulent. In 1646 hundreds of Lamonts were butchered by the Campbells, a fact recorded by the Celtic stone cross erected by the Clan Lamont Society in 1906. In 1685 Atholl invaded the Cowal peninsula and burned the royal castle of 1371. The Castle Gardens were formerly the gardens of a villa

owned by the Lord Provost of Glasgow. Another memorial is the 1896 statue to Mary Campbell of Dunoon, better known as Highland Mary, the fiancée of Robert Burns before he married Jean Armour.

equally ruined pier, surrounded by the Osborne Hotel, Copper Kettle Tearoom and local shops. Close by in the woods is the church where blind George Mathieson wrote *O Love that will not let me go* in 1882.

The Gantocks are an outcrop of rocks marked by a light beacon. A Swedish ore carrier is one vessel which failed to benefit from the warning.

Flows flood from Toward Point from HW Dover −0500 and ebb from HW Dover +0100 at up to 2km/h. Cod and angler fish are amongst those in the flow.

The Berry Burn in Morag's Fairy Glen marks the end of Dunoon. Extensive wooded slopes are broken only by a quarry in the side of the Tom at Bullwood.

Innellan clings to the side of another Tom but still manages a golf course and bowling green. The ruined Knockamillie Castle was one of the most important in the area and now overlooks an

Innellan Beacon marks the Bridges shoal and is a perch for cormorants at Newton Park, a hamlet with a picnic area, overlooked by lattice tower TV masts. Another mast stands at Toward Point by the lighthouse. This low rocky area also houses a white heather farm.

The *Wallachia* sank here in 1895 with a cargo of whisky and beer. The wreck was rediscovered in 1976 and the whisky remained drinkable, much of it having been brought up by divers.

Rothesay Sound separates the Island of Bute from the mainland. Flows are weak at first.

Toward Castle was another Lamont building destroyed by the Campbells in 1646. It overlooks Toward Quay, as does Castle Toward outdoor

Toward Point lighthouse with Bute beyond and the peaks of Arran in the distance

Loch Striven has a NATO fuel jetty at the far end

The Burnt Islands at the head of East Kyle of Bute just short of Buttock Point

centre. Ardyne Burn runs in at Ardyne Point next to a series of basins which have been used as an oil platform construction area. Less obvious is that this is on the line of the Highland Boundary Fault. Submarine cables cross to **Port Bannatyne** on Bute. Across Kames Bay, a measured nautical mile between Undraynian Point and Ardmaleish Point takes craft past a small works.

Loch Striven is known as the Weatherglass of **Rothesay** as gathering clouds or mist on the shores give an indication of bad weather to come. The loch was used for testing Barnes Wallis' bouncing bomb before it was used for German dam destruction in the second world war.

Although it is now bare, Strone Point was remarkable for having been planted with trees to show the positions of the opposing armies at the Battle of Waterloo. Oaks and birches do follow the shoreline of East Kyle of Bute, but they give little shelter from the wind which manages to funnel straight down the channel even when the general wind direction is well away from the northwest. Flows increase from 2km/h to a maximum of 6km/h at the Southern Burnt Island Channel with inward flows meeting near Buttock Point, the exact position varying with the meteorological conditions.

West Kyle of Bute seen from Carry Point

A cairn at Colintraive precedes the shortest car ferry crossing to Bute, a route taken by the A886 and a series of submarine cables. The ferry is hard to see when it is on the mainland side and it takes little time to cross.

Despite their small size, the Burnt Islands are a haven for birds and one of them also has a fort site. A beacon near Eilean Buidhe helps shipping through the restricted channels to Buttock Point, opposite which is Loch Riddon or Ruel which has weak flows in and out. A disused lighthouse stands to the west of Eilean Dubh and a beacon to its north. Up on the wooded hillside above there is a picnic area and a forest trail which introduces blue hares, deer, herons and wild geese.

West Kyle of Bute is more picturesque than its partner. The first items of interest are the Maids of Bute, two rocks which resemble a pair of seated old ladies, easily missed were it not for the bright colours with which they have been painted. Another lattice radio mast stands above a marine farm.

Submarine cables cross to the south of Rubha Bàn.

Tighnabruaich, the house on the hill, is visited by the *Waverley*. It is the home of Kyles Athletic, one of the top shinty teams, and it also has tennis. It is the headquarters of the Kyles of Bute Sailing Club, as indicated by the moorings.

The most westerly point on Bute is Rubha Dubh. Opposite Kames is Kilmichael Chapel, destroyed by the Vikings, and Glenroidean chambered burial cairns.

Pines stand along the shore to Carry Point where there is another marine farm and a collection of caravans. Oystercatchers run along the shore of Blindman's Bay and gorse adds a splash of yellow.

A cup and ring marked rock shows that Ardlamont Point has long been of interest to man. The point provides dramatic views of the peaks of the Isle of Arran and is the best place on the west coast to see the harmless basking sharks.

Flow rates up into Loch Fyne are weak. Despite the relatively exposed position there are several sandy bays. Kilbride Bay or Bàgh Osde receives the Allt Osda while there are cairns at the back of Ascog Bay, flanked by Sgat Beag and Sgat Mór, the latter with a conspicuous white lighthouse. Sandy bays each side of Eilean Aoidhe do not quite meet up so that it is not a true island. The headland behind Rubha Stillaig has a range of antiquities, a cairn, standing stones and a chapel. This contrasts with Portavadie where an oil construction site was built at a cost of £14,000,000. It never won any orders and so the wall was breached and it has been converted to a rather expensive fish farm. Caledonian MacBrayne's newest ferry crossing is from Portavadie to Tarbert.

Coastal, woodland and moorland habitats with nightjars and bryophytes are attributes of Glenan Forest nature reserve facing onto Glenan Bay.

Rubha Preasach was chosen as a dun site while seals sun themselves on Eilean Buidhe.

Two spits almost meet at the back of Auchalick Bay, the River Auchalick just keeping the centre of the bay clear as the flow enters Loch Fyne past a set of standing stones. Kilfinan Burn echoes this as it flows past a cairn and standing stone and emerges from behind a spit to enter Kilfinan Bay.

A dun on Rubha Beag is followed by forts and a motte as the coast moves up to Otter Ferry. The oitir itself projects over halfway across Loch Fyne to a beacon, resulting in deposition of sand and silt in which large otter shells are to be found. Chalets are located along a private road which follows the shore. Here, the flood starts at HW Dover −0510 and the ebb starts at HW Dover +0140 at up to 4km/h.

There is always a passage to the north of Liath Eilean, but passage to the north of Eilean Mòr and past its wreck depends on the state of the tide. The southern end of the island has an example of a pillow lava. The outside route was chosen for the submarine cable from Port Ann to Loch Gilp rather than following a more direct overland route.

Duncuan Island with its beacon guards the entrance to Loch Gilp, much of which dries at low tide. Strong southerly winds can delay low water by half an hour and reduce its effect while a strong northerly can hasten it and increase the effect, the converse resulting at high water.

The Knapdale shore brings Ardrishaig and the end of the Crinan Canal. One of the village school's more notable former pupils is John Smith, former leader of the Labour Party, whose father was the headmaster.

Ardlamont Point with Arran beyond across the Sound of Bute

Looking down Loch Fyne from the mouth of Loch Gilp near Ardrishaig. Ardlamont Point is on the left, Skipness Point on the right and Arran beyond

Powerlines and the A83 follow the coast southwards.

Stronchullin Burn enters Bàgh Tigh-an-Droighinn after which the boulder-strewn shoreline is steep but uniform past the aerial topped Meall Mor to Barmore Island. Barmore Island is not an island, being connected to the mainland, but is a highly distinctive feature, its rounded shape contrasting with the rugged profile of the mainland, its outline being further softened by a covering of dark fir trees. 20ha of shrubs from South Africa and New Zealand and rare trees including Himlayan rhododendrons over a century old surround Stonefield Castle, the baronial house built by Sir William Playfair in 1837.

The beach of scallop shells on the south side of East Loch Tarbert is a reminder that **Tarbert** catches clams, prawns and fish and was formerly the chief port of the Loch Fyne herring industry. The fishermen are not giving up without a fight and blockaded in the contestants in a major sailing race in 1993 in protest at limitations on the number of days on which fishing boats may put to sea. The Bielding is a platform in the centre of the harbour which formerly held a capstan used for berthing sailing boats, while Cock Island has a miniature plantation of birches. The church at the head of the harbour has a fine crown. Tarbert Castle was built in the 13th century, was strengthened by Robert the Bruce and has a 15th-century keep. It was the last of a succession of castles which were mostly built as a defence against the Vikings. In the ongoing disputes between the Vikings and the Scots, King Edgar agreed with King Magnus Barefoot that the Scots would have the mainland and the Vikings the islands, islands being defined as anything which Magnus could sail round in his longboat. Magnus sailed round the Kintyre peninsula in 1098 and had his boat with him on board dragged 1.4km across the isthmus to complete the circumnavigation and claim Kintyre, something Edgar had certainly not intended, the Vikings retaining Kintyre until 1263.

Kintyre, cean tir, the head of land, is the longest peninsula in Britain. The coast is steep and remote as far as Skipness Point, but offers a number of small, secluded, sandy beaches once clear of the marine farm before Eilean a' Chomhraig.

The solitude comes to an end at Cnoc na Sgratha where there are radar domes, probably associated with the submarine exercises. The coastline levels down and thrift appears on the rocks towards Skipness Point, Norse for ship point. Skipness Point is the entrance to Kilbrannan Sound, named after Irish canoe navigator St Brendan. Tidal streams run strongly both ways round the point.

The remains of Kilbrannan Chapel date from about 1300 and are dedicated to St Brendan of Clonfert. Skipness Castle is large and roofless but under repair. It commanded Kilbrannan Sound, Loch Fyne and the Sound of Bute. Built early in the 13th century, possibly soon after 1222, it had a rectangular three-storey hall and chapel which were incorporated in an advanced later 13th-century quadrangular castle with crosslet arrow slits, to which a 16th-century three-storey tower house was added although its crenellations have been blocked in. It was owned by Dougald MacSween until 1261 and was then under MacDonald, Lord of the Isles, until given to the 2nd Earl of Argyll by the king. It held out against

Looking south from Carradale Point, a rocky headland frequented by wild goats

Colkitto and survived the 1685 firing of many of the castles in Argyll. It remained a Campbell stronghold until about 1700.

The post office at Skipness, overlooking the mouth of the Skipness River, acts as a general store with telephone and even serves hot drinks. A road now follows the coast again, the B8001 until Claonaig where the B842 takes over. Claonaig Water enters Claonaig Bay beyond the jetty where a car ferry service leaves for Lochranza on Arran.

Powerlines return at Port Fada and run down the coast to Grogport. Clyde Port Authority jurisdiction ends before Port nan Gamhna where the Crossaig Glen water enters.

To the south of Grogport, where the road leaves, there is another dun site.

Despite the replacing of its ornate cast-iron pier with a sheet piled sea wall, Carradale remains a good example of a small Scottish fishing port and is the second most important harbour on the Kintyre with herring boats present in the winter. To the north, submarine power cables cross to Arran. A beacon marks the harbour while palm trees show that it is sheltered not only at sea level. Despite the generally imperceptible currents, there are overfalls to the south on southgoing streams. To the south of Port Righ and the golf course there is a radio mast. Wild goats live on Carradale Point. Carradale Point Fort is one of the best examples of a vitrified fort, a 58m x 23m oval 21m above sea level.

A series of platform antiquity sites preceed Torrisdale Castle, an 18th-century castellated mansion which is not obvious from the sound.

A dun on Rubha nan Sgarbh and Pluck Point Fort lead down to Saddell Castle which is conspicuous beside Saddell Water as it enters Saddell Bay. The castle keep was built in 1508, almost surrounded by the river and sea, but this did not stop its being burned by the Earl of Sussex in 1559 when it passed to the Campbells. The roof was put back by William Ralston in 1680. The Argylls made additions in 1770 but it later fell into disrepair, being restored by the Landmark Trust.

Just up the glen from the castle are the remains of the Cistercian Saddell Abbey. Built in 1160 by Somerled, Lord of the Isles, who is said to be buried here, it was completed by his son, Reginald, who lived outside for 3 years to become hardy and was said to have scattered around some blessed soil from Rome. In the Middle Ages it was as important as Iona although it was later used as a quarry, including its gravestones. Tombstones from 1300 to 1560 show armed warriors, a priest with a chalice and a Cistercian monk, including Big Macdonald the Tyrant, one of whose less endearing actions was cutting off the hands of some unfortunate travellers in order to try out the blade of a new sword.

Saddell is Norse for saw dale and it is subject to heavy wind gusts down Saddell Glen although more noise is heard from low flying jets.

Ugadale Point has Bruce's Stone and a dun but Kildonan Dun is a notable example, a D-shaped structure with double stairs and cell within the walls. Built in the 1st or 2nd century, it may have been occupied to the 14th century. There is a further fort on Kildonald Point where there is also a stream of rubbish down the cliff.

Jagged slabs line Carrick Point. A chambered cairn overlooks Thorn Island while Seal Rock, overlooked by a standing stone, lives up to its name as a favourite hauling out place for seals.

Glen Lussa Water enters Ardnacross Bay before Peninver. Toilets, children's playground and parking accompany a caravan site while another submarine cable runs across to Blackwaterfoot on Arran.

Distance
From Millport to Peninver is 177km
Campsites
Skelmorlie, Rosneath, Gairletter, Invereck, Innellan, Carry, Ardacheranmor, Lochgilphead, Corranbuie, Lochranza, Bridgend, Machrihanish
Youth Hostels
Loch Lomond, Lochranza, Whiting Bay
OS 1:50,000 Sheets
55 Lochgilphead and Loch Awe
56 Loch Lomond and Inverary
62 North Kintyre and Tarbert
63 Firth of Clyde
69 Isle of Arran
Imray Charts
2900 Upper Clyde
C63 Firth of Clyde (1:160,500)
C64 North Channel – Belfast Lough to Lough Foyle and Crinan (1:160,000)
Admiralty Charts
SC 1867 Firth of Clyde Hunterston Channel and Rothesay Sound. Hunterston Channel (1:12,500)
SC 1906 Kyles of Bute (1:25,000). Burnt Islands (1:5,000)
SC 1907 Little Cumbrae Island to Cloch Point (1:25,000)
SC 1994 Approaches to the River Clyde (1:15,000)
SC 2000 Gareloch (1:12,500)
SC 2126 Approaches to the Firth of Clyde (1:75,000)
SC 2131 Firth of Clyde and Loch Fyne (1:75,000)
SC 2169 Approaches to the Firth of Lorne (1:75,000)
2199 North Channel – Northern Part (1:75,000)
2221 Firth of Clyde, Pladda to Inchmarnock – Northern Sheet (1:36,000)
2381 Lower Loch Fyne (1:25,000). Loch Gilp (1:10,000). East Loch Tarbert (1:6,250)
2383 Inchmarnock Water (1:25,000)
2477 West Loch Tarbert and Approaches (1:25,000)
SC 2491 Ardrossan to Largs (1:25,000)
3746 Loch Long and Loch Goil (1:25,000)
SC 5610 Firth of Clyde
Tidal Constants
Millport: Dover +0010
Wemyss Bay: Dover +0110
Helensburgh: Dover +0120
Coulport: Dover +0110
Rothesay Bay: HW Dover +0100, LW Dover +0110
Tighnabruaich: HW Dover +0110, LW Dover +0120
Lochgilphead: HW Dover +0120, LW Dover +0130
East Loch Tarbert: HW Dover +0120, LW Dover +0110
Loch Ranza: LW Dover +0100, LW Dover +0110
Carradale: HW Dover +0120, LW Dover +0130
Campbelltown: HW Dover +0120, LW Dover +0130
Sea Area
Malin
Submarine Areas
46 Cumbrae, 45 Rosneath, 43 Cove, 40 East Kyle, 38 West Kyle, 37 Skipness, 36 Tarbert, 35 Minard, 58 Lochranza, 59 Davaar
Rescue
Inshore lifeboats: Largs, Helensbrugh, Tighnabruaich, Arran, Campbelltown
All weather lifeboats: Troon, Campbelltown
Maritime Rescue Centre
Clyde, 01475 729988

22 WEST KINTYRE

Increasing races as the North Channel is squeezed

Mull of Kintyre, oh mist rolling in from the sea
My desire is always to be here
Oh Mull of Kintyre.

Paul McCartney

From Peninver the shore passes through a spread of wracks which must give Yellow Rock its name but rubbish strewn down the hillside beyond is less pretty. The remains of a castle and a church lead to Campbeltown Loch, overlooked by a prominent mast. At the head of the loch is **Campbeltown** itself.

punctured is a wrecked car which lies at the base of the cliffs before a cairn, cliffs now being the dominant feature to Polliwilline Bay.

Three radio masts and an aero radio beacon mark Ru Stafnish. North of here the flood begins at HW Dover at up to 6km/h while the ebb starts at HW Dover +0600 at up to 7km/h. To the south the coast is subject to the Black Tide, part of the main eastgoing tide which cuts close inshore before heading off towards the southern end of Arran.

There is a dun site on the Bastard, the lower levels of which reveal conglomerate rocks.

Island Davaar with Campbeltown Loch to the right and Ru Stafnish in the distance

Half of the mouth of the loch is blocked by Island Davaar which is connected to the southern shore by a low tide causeway. There is a lighthouse on the north side, goats grazing on the precipitous cliffs and seven caves on the south side, one of which contains a painting of the crucifixion by Alexander MacKinnon in 1887, later 'discovered' and repaired by him in 1934 and maintained since by a local artist. A race off the southeast corner of the island runs at 7km/h in both directions with overfalls on the ebb. Davaar House overlooks Kildalloig Bay to the south of the island, with its guillemots.

Caves in the southeast face of Island Davaar

Achinhoan Head is punctured by a series of caves, including St Kieran's Cave. Not just

At the end of Glen Hervie an excavator has expired on the beach, accompanied by more tipped rubbish.

The Castles are a series of dramatic rock formations on Gartnagerach Point, off which seals swim.

The places to which people have managed to get caravans are astonishing but the lower land behind Polliwilline Bay is an easy target for a mass of them. The headland before Macharioch Bay is a dramatic shape which has been chosen as a burial chamber site off which there is a small race, while the bay itself has a memorial cross. A long and attractive beach running to Cove Point has not

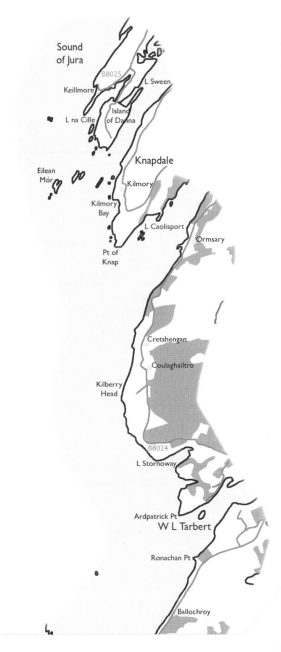

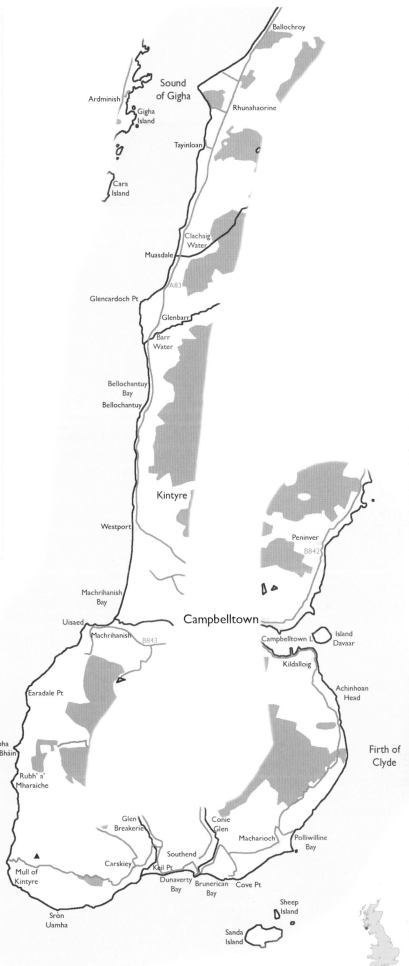

been improved by the dumping of farm implements and other scrap metal along the back. Cove Point, with another dun site, has sandwich terns and eider ducks.

There is a significant race through the Sound of Sanda, ebbing from HW Dover –0110 and flooding from HW Dover +0500 to 9km/h. Close inshore on the north side the activity begins 1 hour 10 minutes later and the effects are much reduced. Tum ba nach is a heavy race extending north from Sheep Island to mid-sound and race activity extends west and then south of Sanda Island. The old red sandstone Sanda and the other islands in the group were used for sheep grazing until 1946,

Sheep Island and Sanda seen across the Sound of Sanda from Ru Stafnish

the same year in which the Campbeltown reserve lifeboat picked up 54 people and a dog from the *Byron Darnton* in an 18-hour rescue in terrible conditions, pulling clear with engine trouble just as the ship broke in two. There is a rusty wreck near the lighthouse on Prince Edward's Rock or the Ship which is now served by a helicopter landing pad. There have been plenty of visitors prepared to risk the waters, though, particularly the Vikings. A burial ground contains a Norse grave. There are also ruins of the chapel of St Ninian and the Bloody Castle. A beacon is located on Paterson's Rock. Sheep and Glunimore Islands are the most important in the Clyde for puffin breeding and there are major colonies of guillemots and razorbills in the group which the RSPB said were at risk from oil exploration in the North Channel off Dumfries and Galloway.

Brunerican Bay has four of the typical signs of human habitation, a framework radio mast on Rubha MacShannuich, a standing stone, a golf course and the site of Dunaverty Castle. The latter was sited on Dunaverty Rock or Blood Rock and belonged to the Macdonalds, 300 of whom were put to death in 1647 by the Covenanters under General Leslie. Conieglen Water enters Brunerican Bay on the east side of the castle while an old slipway runs down from the west side into Dunaverty Bay, behind which more caravans are sited at Southend, the southern end of the B842. There is abundant oysterplant.

Dunaverty with, beyond, Borgadalemore Point, the start of the mull itself, in perfect weather conditions

churchyard. St Columba's Footsteps are two right footprints carved in the rock, perhaps 3,000 years old. They may actually be examples of Fealty Foot where a chief had to stand to promise allegiance and protection to his clan. Caves on Keil Point contain a slab which may have been an altar.

The next 25km is some of the most remote and difficult paddling around the entire British coastline. There is no road access except to the mull lighthouse. Beaches are virtually absent and any landing must be between large rocks with a steep hill climb of, typically, 300m and then several kilometres of walking to the nearest track or road. The mull is at the narrowest part of the North Channel, creating the fastest flows, and the west side is exposed to full Atlantic swells which funnel in, especially with northwesterly winds. Not surprisingly, there are a number of serious races.

Carskey Bay ends with Breakerie Water and there is one further sandy inlet with a wreck close by before the going gets serious. This corner of the Mull of Kintyre is high and rugged with an area of forest in the centre, forest with eagles and other raptors. The rugged hillsides have also provided suitable defensive positions in the past and occasional dun, enclosure and fort sites are present. At sea level the birds are cormorants and oystercatchers while the remoteness means that the rocks are frequently attractive places for seals to lie up.

From Sròn Uamha a race runs parallel to the coast round to the mull lighthouse. There is quieter water inside although eddies may operate. East of the point it may be calm for 1¼ hours of the race but as the race ceases at HW Dover +0610 there are heavy rollers for 5 to 10 minutes.

Rubha na Lice is the nearest point of Great Britain to Ulster, being only 21km from Torr Head, and is likely to be the most exposed point with the main race and whirlpools only a few hundred metres offshore and usually a large swell even in calm conditions, especially with the stream setting SE. The northgoing flow starts at HW Dover −0130 and the southgoing flow at HW Dover +0430 at up to 9km/h on springs. The view from the lookout point on top of this final extremity of the Mull of Kintyre must include some wicked conditions at times.

Dunaverty Bay is a surf beach with lefts off the beachbreak and rights off the rocks at the west end on the upper half of the tide. Southend Reef works at low tide with long runs left and the possibility of tubes on the right. Carskey Bay, which has little stream, produces rights off the rocks at the west end and lefts and rights off the steeply shelving beach at low tide.

St Columba is said to have first landed in Scotland here in 560 and there is a church dedicated to him with the holy well of St Columba behind the

The mull lighthouse is over 1km north. Below it is a rounded rock with two sharp pinnacles on top which appear in murky conditions like the silhouette of some giant animal.

After another 3km of the shoreline rising steeply to the peaks of Beinn na Lice and A'Chruach, the coast reaches a remote fort site. However, the remoteness is suddenly dispelled when a modern fence is spotted marching up the mountainside from the water and disappearing over the top, a major construction in this situation.

Distinctive strata on Rubha Dùin Bhàin mark it out from other headlands

Rubh' a' Mharaiche is overlooked by an inconspicuous dun but Rubha Dùin Bhàin is marked by its notable horizontal strata, a useful indicator for another point facing a race.

There are several caves at Uamh Ropa, the surroundings of one being white with cormorant guano, clearly a favourite spot for them.

Halfway between here and Earadale Point is a small beach, the first since Carskey Bay and a useful bolt hole although it is still a walk of several kilometres to the nearest track. The local residents are white goats with black heads and forelegs.

Seal on the rocks at Earadale Point

There is another race off Skerrinagal by Earadale Point.

Uisaed is marked by a prominent cairn. Off it lie the rocks of Skerrivore and a race which usually breaks. A bird hide watches guillemots, razorbills, herons and much more. A contra-eddy begins northwards at HW Dover –0300 and southwards at HW Dover at up to 1km/h. Machrihanish at the end of the B843 has toilets, telephone and post office and usually provides a safe landing regardless of conditions elsewhere. Across Machrihanish Water lie 5km of the best surf beach in southern Scotland, best at mid-tide on the flood. Machrihanish Bay catches the best of the Atlantic swells. The bay is backed by an extensive dune system which is topped by golf links. These are, in turn, overlooked by a line of watchtowers down the edge of the airfield. Used by NATO forces and with a significant American presence, the airfield is said to have been used by the secret American Aurora. Even the existence of the plane is denied but, were it to exist, it would be an ideal place to base it, away from roads, a long way from centres of population and with one of the longest runways in Europe at 3km. Standing stones mark the end of the airfield.

Westport is also a useful surfing venue as it has road access, the A83 now following the shore closely. This break has rights which are best on the upper half of the tide provided the swell is not over 2m. With larger swells the surf breaks on reefs further out.

Fort and dun sites start 6km of rocky shoreline with many sandy inlets which can be entered between the rocks in quieter conditions. Another group of duns and forts are grouped around Bellochantuy where the Argyll Hotel backs onto the beach with a telephone kiosk opposite.

Before the caravan site by Bellochantuy Bay is a burial ground which gives the Graveyard surfing break its name. It works best on a rising tide and breaks onto shifting sandbars. As the coast goes north there is progressively more shelter from Islay and Jura so the swells lessen in intensity.

A prominent arched stone bridge crosses the end of Barr Water which flows down past Glenbarr with its abbey, Clan Macalister Centre, shop and teas.

There are standing stones and duns both before and after the low rocky Glenacardoch Point. There

The Mull of Kintyre lighthouse with the monster silhouette below

Seals dotted about the rocks in Ronachan Bay. Ardpatrick Point lies on the far side of West Loch Tarbert

The MacCormaig Isles with Dubh Sgeir, Eilean Mór, Corr Eilean and Eilean Ghamhna laid out with the peaks of Jura in the background

is also a cave by a small beach as the A83 returns to the shore after a brief foray away, a point where submarine cables were previously landed. Flows start north from here at HW Dover –0100 and south from HW Dover +0500 at up to 5km/h. Predicted tide times vary by up to 2 hours 40 minutes with the time of day on this stretch of coast so an almanac should be consulted if accurate times are important. There is a shoal parallel to the shoreline with a passage inside. The coast is now low, ideal for curlews to pick over the beach debris.

Clachaig Water enters at Muasdale with yet more duns dotted about. At A'Chleit a church right by a line of rocks which run out into the sea shows a small belltower like a school bell. Progressively more shelter is gained from Cara Island with its distinctive Brownie's Chair and then Gigha Island itself as progress is made up the Sound of Gigha. The relics of dun, chambered cairn, standing stone and church ruin continue and seem totally in character, unlike the pair of swans swimming about self-consciously on the sea. Largie Castle was built at Tayinloan, but the village is more important today as the ferry terminal for Ardminish on Gigha. While the ferry only carries 12 cars, the terminal area has useful toilets. The submarine cable to Gigha, on the other hand, takes

the rather shorter route to Rhunahaorine Point, a low sandy elbow which sticks out into the sound with long narrow beaches to north and south, the southern beach fronting a caravan site and a wood.

Standing stones in a field at Ballochroy are easily seen from the water although a cist, cairn and dun over some 3km of coast are better hidden. Wildlife includes eider ducks and rhizostoma jellyfish but the most notable locals are the grey seals which haul out in bracken fringed Ronachan Bay, a popular viewpoint as there is a parking area where the A83 takes its leave of the west coast.

This is the mouth of West Loch Tarbert, the first of several sea lochs which make northeasterly cuts into the west coast. Down it come car ferries to Port Askaig and Port Ellen on Islay.

Ardpatrick Point is the southern extremity of Knapdale. Flows start north at HW Dover –0045 and south at HW Dover –0415 at 4km/h.

The coast becomes increasingly remote with Loch Stornoway issuing from between rugged hills terminated by a cliff known as the Coves. Gannets dive for fish and blackbacked gulls search for anything they can scavenge.

A series of rocky outcrops with intervening sandy bays and cud chewing cattle lead up to Kilberry Head. Behind Kilberry Point is Kilberry

Castle and a set of crosses which are fine late mediaeval sculptured stones.

To the north is a waterside caravan park while at the far end of Cretshengan Bay are a ruined church and standing stone. On the other hand, there is little to mark the site of Dun Cragach.

Somehow it seems right that knapweed should be growing here, but montbretia amongst the ragwort and brambles at Port Maluaig is a colourful intruder.

Ormsary Water discharges under the B8024 into the clear water of Loch Caolisport at Ormsary opposite the Point of Knap. Between the two are Eilean Traighe which is a beach but not an island and Liath Eilein which is a suitably grey rock island.

Point of Knap is high on the south side but drops away quickly on the north side. A beacon off the end marks Bow of Knap rocks. Flows north start at HW Dover −0040 and south at HW Dover −0545 at up to 3km/h to Rubha na Cille. The point breaks up into a series of rocky islands of various sizes from small rocks to the MacCormaig Isles for the next 7km, taking in the mouth of Loch Sween.

At the back of Kilmory Bay is Kilmory itself with a cairn, fort and, particularly, the Kilmory Knap Chapel ruin to St Maelrubha with 30 Celtic grave slabs depicting warriors, chiefs and hunters. Outside is a 3.5m high 15th-century MacMillan's Cross with mediaeval carving comparable with the best on Iona, showing Jesus Christ, St Mary, St John and sword and knotwork on the front and a hunter, dogs and stag on the back. It was constructed under the Loch Sween school of monumental architecture. Stone was supplied from a quarry here to Iona.

From Eilean na Leac the view up Loch Sween shows Castle Sween prominently. Its black bulk seen against the light can make it seem more dominating than when actually passing it on the loch.

Flows north from Eilean Ghamhna run up to 6km/h but only to 5km/h southwards. Strong streams run between all the islands with races and overfalls. Corr Eilean has a cairn but there is greater interest in Eilean Mór with a restored chapel, cell, cave and blue slate Celtic cross, possibly at the west end of St Cormac's tomb. The island is associated with John Paul Jones whose sloop, *Ranger*, is said to haunt the islands. This may be the galley with black sail which is said to pay an unexpected visit to the island every year and drive viewers mad. There was an illicit still for passing fishermen which may have contributed to the madness. These days the island is owned by the Scottish Nationalist Party.

The Island of Danna is no longer, being attached to the rest of Knapdale by a short embankment. Its calcareous rocks are the base for a rich flora.

Eilean nan Uan, Liath Eilean, Loch na Cille, Rubha na Cille and a number of other islets all follow the southwest–northeast trend in their orientations. Flows at Rubha na Cille reach 6km/h.

A possible landing point is over the rocks at Keillmore, avoiding the nonchalently swinging horns of a herd of highland cattle to reach the parking area at the head of the B8025. It is the route chosen for a submarine power cable which runs across the Sound of Jura to Jura which has been steadily closing on the mainland and is now only some 7km off, providing plenty of shelter from the west.

The locals at Keillmore with their view across the Sound of Jura to the northern end of Jura

Distance
From Peninver to Keillmore is 114km
Campsites
Southend, Machrihanish, Glenbarr, Muasdale, Low Dunashry, Clachan, Coulaghailtro
Youth Hostels
Whiting Bay, Islay, Lochranza, Inveraray
OS 1:50,000 Sheets
55 Lochgilphead and Loch Awe
62 North Kintyre and Tarbert
68 South Kintyre and Campbelltown
Imray Charts
C63 Firth of Clyde (1:160,500)
C64 North Channel – Belfast Lough to Lough Foyle and Crinan (1:160,000)
Admiralty Charts
SC 2126 Approaches to the Firth of Clyde (1:75,000)
2168 Approaches to the Sound of Jura (1:75,000)
SC 2169 Approaches to the Firth of Lorn (1:75,000)
2199 North Channel – Northern Part (1:75,000)
2396 Sound of Jura – Southern Part (1:25,000)
2397 Sound of Jura – Northern Part (1:25,000)
2475 Passages on the West Coast of Scotland. Sound of Gigha (1:25,000)
2477 West Loch Tarbert and Approaches (1:25,000)
SC 2724 North Channel to the Firth of Lorn (1:200,000)
2798 Lough Foyle to Sanda Island (1:75,000)
SC 5610 Firth of Clyde
SC 5611 West Coast of Scotland
Tidal Constants
Campbelltown: HW Dover +0120, LW Dover +0130
Sanda Island: HW Dover +0040
Southend: HW Dover +0040, LW Dover +0100
Machrihanish: Dover +0230
Sound of Gigha: HW Dover +0340, LW Dover +0420
Carsaig Bay: Dover −0610
Sea Area
Malin
Submarine Areas
59 Davaar, 68 Stafnish, 67 Sanda, 66 Kintyre, 57 Earadale, 56 Gigha, 33 Jura Sound
Rescue
Inshore lifeboat: Campbelltown
All weather lifeboats: Campbelltown, Islay
Maritime Rescue Centre
Clyde, 01475 729988

23 NORTHEAST SOUND OF JURA

The finest islandscape in Britain

Keillmore has a chapel with a 15th-century grave slab with sword and clasach, possibly for a father and son who were harpists to the MacNeills of Gigha. There are also other fine grave slabs. The chapel may have been visited by St Columba on his way to meet King Connal.

Streams start north at HW Dover –0100 and south at HW Dover +0500 at up to 7km/h but there can be eddies close inshore. South of Crinan most of the rise and fall takes place in the 3½ hours after the turn of the tide with a stand until the next turn.

Jura, seen across the Sound of Jura from Knapdale

Leth Sgeir, Eilean nan Coinean and Eilean Fraoich

Wildlife immediately makes its presence known with seals and sea otters. Oystercatchers and curlews operate along the shoreline and cattle graze the rough pasture. The shoreline is as interesting as the peaks up to 130m Barr Thormaid would suggest and the first few metres are sloping rock up to a wavecut platform, making it difficult to get out with a kayak.

The islets with their bracken and stunted bushes make a delightful trip. Inside Leth Sgeir a northgoing eddy works on the southgoing stream. There are passages inside Eilean nan Coinean and Eilean Fraoch. Inside Eilean Dubh with its herons a little more care is needed. The passage is outside Eilean Tràighe rather than the more obvious inside passage which is a dead end.

Carsaig Bay with its clear water is popular with holidaymakers, being well sheltered with a beach off which a power cable runs under the Sound of Jura to Jura. Contra-eddies run across the mouth in both directions.

Carsaig Island is not high, but the vertical rock strata have fallen away to produce an interesting rock sculpture.

A dun is lost in the forest between Sàilean na h-Earba and Sàilean Mór and red deer graze openly near the water's edge.

Flows start north at HW Dover −0130 and south at HW Dover +0450 at up to 7km/h. In the centre of the sound where a white lighthouse stands on Ruadh Sgeir the flows are up to 8km/h. Dolphins feed in schools, arcing over here and there as they surface for air with hydraulic hisses and disappear below the surface again.

As Jura closes in on the mainland there are two resulting effects. One is that the scenery becomes steadily more stunning with Jura, Scarba, Luing, Mull and a panorama of smaller islands of breathtaking beauty. Seen with evening or morning sunlight, it is a truly memorable area. The other is that the stream flowing up the Sound of Jura is steadily accelerated until it is off Crinan where it is forced to turn left through the Dorus Mór and out between Jura and Scarba through the Gulf of Corryvreckan with the world's second largest whirlpool, which can be heard roaring from Crinan when it is active.

There is a small race off Ardnoe Point to be faced by those making for the quieter waters of the Crinan Canal. Otherwise, flows at the mouth of Loch Crinan, overlooked by Ardifuir with its broch, are relatively weak. The main flow is not just making a sharp left turn but is doing so at a point where Loch Crinan, Loch Craignish and other passages are leading off from the outside of the bend and the main part of the flow is obstructed by a number of islands. The main feature is the Dorus Mór or great door between Garbh Rèisa and Craignish Point. The flow westwards begins at HW Dover −0200 and eastwards at HW Dover +0440 at up to 15km/h. There is an eddy next to Garbh Rèisa and another on the north side of the Dorus Mór, especially on the westgoing stream with heavy overfalls along the eddyline. There is a race up to Eilean nan Coinean, a race off Craignish Point, a race to the east of Rèisa Mhic Phaidean on the northgoing flow with a southgoing eddy along the mainland coast. During the southgoing flow there are overfalls across the north end of this channel, southwards along the mainland coast and across the entrance to the Dorus Mór. At full flow it can be a continuous area of turbulence from the south and east of the Dorus Mór to Coiresa on the westerly flow with races up to Luing and far beyond the Gulf of Corryvreckan. In 1820 it wrecked the *Comet*, the first steamship to go to sea. At slack neap tides there is barely a swirl on the surface.

Craignish Castle stands beyond the end of the B8002 at the head of the sheltered Loch Beag. Eilean Ona and its islets offer shelter to Achanarnich Bay, but even on the calmest of days the Atlantic swell finds its way through and fronds of kelp are pushed out of the water by the surges like the fins of a school of sharks. Cormorants watch, unimpressed.

A fort, dun and cairns sit at the base of a ridge which runs along the east side of the sound, broken only by Bàgh Bàn.

Beyond Eilean Arsa in Loch Shuna a forest of masts marks Craobh Haven, a yacht harbour which has been constructed by linking a ring of islands together with embankments to the mainland.

Although less than half the length of neighbouring Luing, Shuna is almost the same

The passage between Eilean Dubh and Eilean Tràighe is in the centre
of the picture with Eilean Fraich in the foreground on the left

The sheltered inside passage between Eilean Dubh and Eilean Tràighe

Carsaig Bay, the most heavily populated point on the Knapdale coast,
with hills rising to Torr Mór and Cruach Lusach in the background

Between Jura and Scarba lies the Gulf of Corryvreckan, deceptively
quiet at the turn of the tide on a still day

height, Druim na Dubh Glaic rising to 90m, and has considerably more woodland, the northern two-thirds being ringed with trees. Shuna provides excellent sheep grazing and the island's half dozen human residents are crofters.

round towers, the result of someone's flight of fancy.

A light on Sgeir Chregag is draped in debris and takes the shape of a person standing on the rocks. Eilean Gamhna is distinctively shaped like a large

The strata dip towards the east and so this side of the island has a low sloping rockface. At intervals the onshore waves have cut through to form small bays. Thrift takes a foothold on the rocks and there are long strands of seaweed.

Polle na Gile has a marine farm, there is another on the west side of Eilean Creagach and a third is located below Shuna House. Meanwhile, otters and herons catch their own fish. Shuna House is the most distinctive building on the island, castellated throughout and with

brimmed hat or a submarine. A float plane taking off from Loch Melfort, however, may not just be an illusion.

Beyond Shuna, Luing and then Torsa on the west side of Shuna Sound give protection from westerly winds. However, the prevailing wind blows up Shuna Sound and this can produce a significant chop on an ebb tide.

From Degnish Point the hillside climbs steadily past Dùn fadaidh to 273m high Dun Crutagain. Opposite, Ardinamar Bay divides Torsa from

Shuna Sound from Degnish Point with Scoul Eilean and Shuna on the left and Luing and, beyond, Jura on the right

Telford's Clachan Bridge over Clachan Sound

Looking west from the foot of Beinn Mhór with Eilean nam Beathach and Seil on the left and Eilean Dùin and Mull on the right

Luing. The channel is constricted and can produce a respectable sea rapid down into Ardinamir Bay when the tide conditions are right.

Birdlife is present in a constant stream, snipes, oystercatchers, cormorants and diverse divers.

Caistal nan Con near the northern end of Torsa guards where Cuan Sound joins Seil Sound. Seil is a slate island. An iron pillar marks the corner north of Pòrt Mór, before which Seil's only area of woodland rises up from the shore. While Seil is low and treeless, the mainland shore of Seil Sound is steep and wooded. Ardmaddy Castle stands back from the head of Ardmaddy Bay, but walls of extruded rock on the shoreline look like the remains of some former stronghold.

The west side of Seil Sound has marine farms and in front of a fort site an area of the centre of the sound is laid out with closely spaced floats. Balvicar Bay is a mooring for pleasure and lobster fishing boats. Balvicar had slate quarries, closed in 1965, and Winterton has boatyards. A wreck resembling an early car ferry rusts away on the mainland shore opposite Balvicar Bay. Research has shown that a colony of molluscs at Balvicar have marked genetic differences from a colony of

The rugged bulk of Meall Buidhe forms the southeastern side of the Sound of Kerrera

the same species 150m away at Winterton. Again, there are sea otters present.

Constructed by Thomas Telford in 1792, Clachan Bridge is also known as the Atlantic Bridge or the Bridge over the Atlantic as it spans part of the Atlantic, carrying the B844.

The matter of being overseas was important after the 45 Rebellion when the Scots could only legally wear kilts overseas. The nearby Tigh-an-Truish Hotel (house of trousers) at Clachan-Seil was used by returning men to change out of the hated trousers.

A biological rarity of the sound is the purple-flowered fairy foxglove which grows on Clachan Bridge. Clachan Sound is straight and narrow, almost like a large canal complete with swans, except for the swift currents through it and the many shells visible on the bed through the clear water.

In 1873 a school of 192 pilot whales, normally rare in British waters, were stranded in the sound by the tide. The sound dries at low water.

The north end of Clachan Sound opens out onto the Firth of Lorn and another panoramic view, perhaps seen at its best from the remains of the

quarry on the east side of the sound. The west side of the sound breaks up into a group of small islands, the largest and most northerly of which is Eilean Dùin. Then, in a much broader sweep are Scarba beyond Seil and Luing, Mull, Kerrera, the Kingairloch shore and a fair bit more. It is a place to spend some minutes or more absorbing the view before moving on to change the perspective of the kaleidoscope of islands.

The quarry is at the foot of 194m high Beinn Mhór which has a fort site near its summit at an excrescence known as the Toad of Lorn. The east side remains high as it leads into the Sound of Kerrera with Meall Buidhe at 207m. Between Beinn Mhór and Beinn Buidhe is the mouth of Loch Feochan, a tortuous affair which affords protection to the loch from the elements. Minard Point, on the north side of the loch entrance, is the location for An Dùnan while opposite it, to the east of Barrnacarry Bay, is Dùn Mhic Raonuill. Rising above all in the distance are the peaks of Cruachan.

Flows in Kerrera Sound start northeast at HW Dover −0100 and southwest at HW Dover +0500 at up to 3km/h with eddies on both sides.

Port na Tràigh-Linne and Aird na Cùile both have fish farms, the latter by a dun site at Gallanach, while three disused transatlantic submarine cables land at Port Lathaich.

Kerrera is formed of basalts, schists and old red sandstone. The Sound of Kerrera usually brings more sheltered water. The ivy-clad cliffs support trees where they can get a grip and the location is ideal for golden eagles which might be seen perched on rocks quite close to the water.

A white navigation light tower dominates Rubh'an Fheurain for ships using the sound, not least of which is the Colonsay to Oban car ferry.

The old slate quarriers' cottages behind the Little Horse Shoe and below Kerrera's highest point, 189m high Carn Breugach, were used as the base for a lobster trading business in 1910, becoming one of the largest on the west coast of Scotland, taking lobsters from Cullipool on Luing.

The mainland shore becomes extremely coarse conglomerate rock which can be used as a landing point at Gallanachmore to give access to the first road since Clachan Bridge.

Distance
From Keillmore to Gallanachmore is 51km
Campsites
Coulaghailtro, Carsaig, Gallanachmore
Youth Hostels
Inveraray, Oban
OS 1:50,000 Sheets
49 Oban and East Mull
55 Lochgilphead and Loch Awe
Imray Charts
2800 West Coast of Scotland
C64 North Channel – Belfast Lough to Lough Foyle and Crinan (1:160,000)
C65 Crinan to Mallaig and Barra (1:155,000)
Admiralty Charts
1790 Oban and Approaches (1:10,000)
2168 Approaches to the Sound of Jura (1:75,000)
SC 2169 Approaches to the Firth of Lorn (1:75,000)
SC 2171 Sound of Mull and Approaches (1:75,000)
2320 Loch Crinan (1:7,500)
SC2326 Loch Crinan to the Firth of Lorn (1:25,000)
2343 Gulf of Corryvreckan and Approaches (1:25,000)
2386 Firth of Lorn – Southern Part (1:25,000)
2387 Firth of Lorn – Northern Part (1:25,000)
2396 Sound of Jura – Southern Part (1:25,000)
2397 Sound of Jura – Northern Part (1:25,000)
SC 2724 North Channel to the Firth of Lorn (1:200,000)
SC 5611 West Coast of Scotland
Tidal Constants
Carsaig Bay: Dover −0610
Loch Melfort: Dover −0600
Seil Sound: HW Dover −0540, LW Dover −0550
Oban: Dover −0520
Sea Area
Malin
Submarine Areas
33 Jura Sound, 31 Mull, 32 Linnhe
Rescue
All weather lifeboats: Islay, Oban
Maritime Rescue Centre
Clyde, 01475 729988

Looking north across the Firth of Lorn from the northern end of Clachan Sound to Mull with Kerrera, Lismore and the Kingairloch to the right

24 SOUND OF MULL

The chain of castles of the MacDonalds and Macleans

The earth unto the Lord belongs,
and all that it contains;
All except the Western Islands,
they are all MacBrayne's.

From Gallanachmore flows start northeast at HW Dover –0100 and southwest at HW Dover +0500 at up to 5km/h with eddies on both sides.

Port nan Cuilc has a wreck which has only just missed a submarine power cable across to Kerrera and lies at the foot of a road reconstruction job at Gallanachbeg. A radio mast and fort site on Dùn Uabairtich look down on a crossing point to Kerrera which is used by a passenger ferry and two more submarine cables in Horse Shoe Bay.

The Horse Shoe has been the anchorage of fleets which have not been too successful in their activities. In 1249 Alexander II anchored here before attempting to win the Hebrides back from King Haakon of Norway but died suddenly, the land behind the bay now being called Dalrigh, field of the king. Haakon himself anchored here in 1263 on his way to the Battle of Largs where he was defeated. He used the anchorage on his way home but died, too, before he reached Norway.

A school and church dating from 1872 stand at the northeast end of the Horse Shoe. These days there is a population of about 50 on the island although it was 105 in 1861. Access is by the passenger ferry, summoned to the mainland by turning the white warning notice so that the ferryman can see it across the Sound of Kerrera.

There is a dry ski slope at Rubha Tolmach belonging to Lanarkshire Education Authority's Kildowie Outdoor Centre.

Heather Island stands in the centre of the sound on the approach to Oban Bay. There is a marine farm in Ardentrive Bay, guarded by cormorants. It also contains the rusting wreck of a small boat. At one time cattle were brought across to Kerrera from Mull and were then swum from here to Oban.

A contributory factor to the position of **Oban** (Gaelic for little bay), at the end of the A85, as one of the best natural ports on the west coast of Scotland and its title of the Gateway to the Isles is the island of Kerrera which acts as a substantial weatherbreak. The piers are bases for fishing vessels and the occasional diving support vessel

but, most importantly, they include the terminal for the Caledonian MacBrayne ferries, paddle steamers having operated from here from 1851. The ferries to Mull, Coll, Tiree, Barra, South Uist, Lismore, Fort William and Morvern operate through the narrow northern entrance to Oban Bay, passing the monument to founder David Hutcheson on the northeast end of the island. The company successfully fought off Government attempts at privatization, to the widespread relief of islanders worried about their future ferry services which are currently heavily subsidized.

An unlikely item on the Oban skyline is McCaig's Folly of 1897–1900, built with Bonawe granite by local labour to counter unemployment. Its 9–14m high walls 600mm thick are based on the Colosseum. Local banker and gasworks owner John McCaig wanted to make it a museum to his family, but he died before adding the huge lookout tower which was to have graced the centre. The next hill has another folly, the remains of what was to have been a hydropathic centre where people would come to take the waters but the project ran out of money. An observation platform was added in 1983 and the courtyard landscaped. Floodlit at night, it is used for drama productions in the summer and the Gaelic Mod, a fortnight's festival of song, music and poetry. On each side is a transmission mast.

Caves in Oban were occupied in Stone Age times. Boswell House is on the site of a 'tolerable inn' used by James Boswell and Dr Johnson. The Oban distillery was founded in 1794 and produces a 12-year old malt whisky. More recent arrivals include the railway in 1880, a vital transport link with the islands. The Roman Catholic cathedral is

Oban with the cathedral on the left, McCaig's Folly on the skyline in the centre and the Caledonian MacBrayne ferry terminal on the right

as recent as 1952. Other features include the Heritage Wharf centre, Oban glassworks making Caithness Glass paperweights, the Highland Discovery Centre with theatre, cinema and exhibition, Scotland in Colour Photo-gallery showing the work of Dennis Hardley and World in Miniature with ½th scale rooms, furniture, dioramas and holograms. There is a swimming pool. This used to be the yachting centre of the west.

Heading out towards the red and white light tower at the mouth of the bay, three items of local interest are passed on the right, the diminutive

entrance in the north wall. Mary, wife of 19th chief Iain Ciar, held out against the Argyll militia during the 1715 uprising until he returned. The present chief's mansion of 1746 stands below the castle.

Maiden Island is in the middle of the exit from Kerrera Sound but Camas Bàn is well studded with rocks so larger craft all stay west of the island. Going out beyond Maiden Island into the less sheltered waters of the Firth of Lorn brings the full majesty of the scenery into perspective. Here, in one panoramic sweep, are the Island of Mull with Duart Castle, the Sound of Mull, Eilean Musdile with its lighthouse, Lismore and the mountains of Morvern right up Loch Linnhe to Ben Nevis, Britain's highest mountain. There are few indications that man has ever been here, at least,

Dunollie Castle on its rock has guarded the entrance to Oban Bay for many centuries

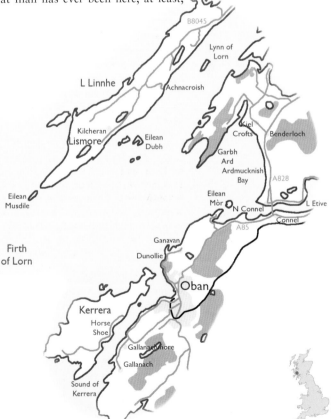

lighthouse, the Dog Stone and Dunollie Castle. The Dog Stone is an isolated finger of rock where the Gaelic hero Fingal is reputed to have tethered the great dog Bran, the tether wearing the neck at the base of the pillar or perhaps it was just near the castle kennels. In fact, the neck was probably produced by wave action at the time of the forming of raised beaches, widespread in the area. Dunollie Castle was the principal seat of the MacDougalls, the Lords of Lorn, who once owned a third of Scotland and have owned Kerrera since the clan was formed in the 12th century. The ivy covered ruin occupies a long used site, the Irish having burned a wooden fort on it in 698. The present structure was started in the 13th century and developed into a four-storey stronghold in the 15th century. It has a barrel-vaulted cellar and zigzag

when the yachtsmen are not out. Nature rules supreme in breathtaking surroundings.

Ganavan Bay is the local resort with a caravan site, leisure centre, bar, restaurant, shop, children's play area, donkey rides and watersports yet still the eider ducks are not put off. There is a submarine cable to Mull and a couple of others, now disused.

A marine farm is sited in Camas Rubha na Liathaig. Just across the ridge on the Dunstaffnage Bay side is the Dunstaffnage Marine Laboratory which was moved up from Millport in 1970.

Two notable buildings stand in the woods, Dunstaffnage Castle and its chapel. The castle was built here to control entry to Loch Etive and the approach to Ardchattan Priory. The site was close to the capital of the old Scots kingdom of Dalriada and a previous castle was home of the Stone of Destiny until 843 after it was brought from Tara. The present castle is a 13th-century quadrangle on a rock with two round towers, one of three storeys acting as a keep, with a 3m thick curtain wall, built for the MacDougalls. The chapel was built with beautiful architectural detail in wood to St Maelrubha in about 1250. It is now roofless but has been used as a burial place for many of the Captains of Dunstaffnage, the Campbell hereditary constables since the 14th century. The castle was taken by Bruce in 1300. In 1470 it passed to Colin, 1st Earl of Argyll, who married one of the three daughters of Sir John Stewart, 3rd Lord of Lorn after the Stewarts took over the lordship. Sir John also had an illegitimate son, Dugald, and to ensure the succession did not pass to Argyll he planned in 1483 to marry Dugald's mother, a MacLaren of Ardveich. In a plot involving Argyll and Sir John's brother, Walter, Allan Macdougall stabbed Sir John during the service but the priest managed to complete the ceremony before Sir John died, securing the succession although Argyll did eventually receive the castle, leaving the Stewarts with Appin. In the 17th century a tower house was added over the 13th-century entrance. Close by, Old Colkitto was hung from the mast of his own galley. During the risings the castle was garrisoned and the last notable visitor was Flora MacDonald who was brought by Captain Fergussone in the sloop *Furnace* and held for 10 days in 1746 on her way to the Tower of London.

There is a quiet passage inside Eilean Mòr, but a race runs both sides of Eilean Beag and the water is very interesting all the way down from the Falls of Lora which are crossed by a distinctive steel bridge which used to take a railway line northwards but now carries the A828.

Flows at the entrance to Ardmucknish Bay start northeast at HW Dover −0100 and southwest at HW Dover +0500 at up to 3km/h. In addition, there may be a weak clockwise stream round the bay.

Lednaig Point forms a significant shingle spit running out from North Connel. Connel Airfield is squeezed in along the shore next to the road and is used by gliders which ridge soar around 308m high

Beinn Lora. The final section of shoreline before the mountain is given over to a caravan site.

Benderloch has forest walks on the flanks of the mountain and has been a popular point for some time, judging by the standing stones and forts including the ruins of Beregonium vitrified fort. These days the attraction is the sandy beach, both for leisure and for a sand pit.

Lady Margaret's Tower rises above the trees on Garbh Ard. Between the thrift flanked Rubha Garbh-àird and Rubha Fion-àird is the secluded but relatively weather exposed inlet of Camas Nathais. Birdlife proliferates with cormorants, oystercatchers, sandpipers, blackbacked gulls and guillemots.

Flows into the Lynn of Lorn begin at HW Dover −0045 and out again at HW Dover +0515 at up to 2km/h.

Eilean Dubh in the centre of the channel must take its name from its dark covering of brown heather.

Lismore, Ieis Mor, the great garden from its early Christian settlement, takes its fertility from the Dalradian limestone grassland on which it is based.

A concrete cross at the water's edge gives warning of arrival at the village of Achnacroish with its wreck. The pier is visited by the car ferry from Oban. A telephone box looks remarkably conspicuous for being unvandalized and two large curved pillars just up the hill look quite grand until it is realized that they are, in fact, only the remains of the end of a Nissen hut.

Bluebells and thrift on Eilean nan Gamhna

Looking up into Loch Etive with Connel Bridge over the Falls of Lora and Ben Cruachan behind

There is a marine farm at Sean Dùn. Cairns and duns dot the hillside around Dùn Mòr although they are far from conspicuous.

What appears to be a broch on Eilean nan Gamhna turns out to be a block of rock although there is a broch by Loch Fiart, not visible from a water near the island. The islets are covered with heather and Eilean nan Gamhna has a fine display of bluebells in the spring. The B8045 runs along the island above Port Kilcheran.

From here conditions become more exposed with views across to Oban, Kerrera and Mull if the weather is fine. An eddy runs southwest along the southeast shore of Lismore from here during the flood tide.

More duns follow in profusion including the broch at An Dùn and Dùn Chruban. Meanwhile, off the coast are moored large conical fish farms which appear to owe some of their design to offshore oil platform technology while repeating the lines of the bridge at Connel.

Appearance of the lighthouse on Eilean Musdile gives warning of the end of the island. Eilean Musdile is really two linked islands, frequented by shelducks. It is possible to paddle through the gap between Rubha Fiart and the islands if the flow is appropriate as there are races through the gaps. Slack water is needed for the crossing to Mull.

This constriction where Loch Linnhe meets the Firth of Lorn has a race most of the way across, even in fine weather. This runs at up to 11km/h to Lady's Rock and then to 7km/h to Mull. Notwithstanding, ferries pass through here from Oban to Craignure, Lochaline, Lochboisdale on South Uist, Castlebay on Barra, Arinagour on Coll and Scarinish on Tiree.

Lady's Rock has a light beacon. The lady in question was Lady Elizabeth, a Campbell and daughter of Archibald, 2nd Earl of Argyll. She had failed to provide an heir for her husband, Lachlan MacLean of Duart, and had twice tried to poison him so in 1523 he decided to drown her by chaining her to a covering section of the rock. This would have left him free to marry the daughter of MacLean of Treshnish, but Lady Elizabeth was rescued by Tayvallich men who were rewarded by Argyll with a mill on Loch Sween. MacLean was said to have seen her at a subsequent funeral and escaped, to be caught and murdered by her brother in law, Sir John Campbell of Calder.

The Island of Mull, meaning mass of hill, is the third largest of the Hebrides and is a lava plateau or trap which saw extensive Tertiary volcanic activity. The Sound of Mull was probably a tributary of a former Firth of Lorn/North Channel/Irish Sea river. It floods and ebbs from the northwest end. From here to Scallastle Point the stream runs northwest from HW Dover +0100 at up to 5km/h and southeast from HW Dover −0600 at up to 4km/h.

On the shore is the William Black Memorial tower with proportions like a castle. There is, however, no mistaking Duart Castle which stands prominently on Duart Point, overlooking Duart

Bay. The keep was built about 1250 by the MacDonalds who were ousted by the Macleans as Lords of the Isles. The Macleans received their charter in 1390. The castle, with its walls up to 3.7m thick, was extended in 1633 to 100 rooms by Sir Lachlan Maclean and it was acquired by the 10th Earl and 1st Duke of Argyll in 1647. The Jacobite Sir Hector Maclean was imprisoned in the Tower of London during the 1745 rebellion, during which the castle was garrisoned, after which it fell into ruin. The estate was restored in 1912 by Sir Fitzroy Maclean and is still the home of the clan chief. There are exhibitions of Scottish relics, the Macleans and Scouting, Lord Maclean of Duart having been a Chief Scout. In the dungeon is a tableau of two Spanish officers from the Armada galleon *San Juan de Sicilia* which was blown up in 1588 while her crew were helping Maclean of Duart lay siege to Mingary Castle. Duart Castle was one of a defensive chain which could relay a message from Mingary Castle to Dunollie in half an hour.

Duart Bay has a historic wreck. Torosay Castle on the other side of the bay is rather different from Duart, a Victorian baronial sandstone building completed in 1858. It has exhibition rooms, good furniture, pictures and photographs of life at the turn of the century, 5ha of Italian terraced gardens by Lorimer, a statue walk with 19 figures by Antonio Bonazza, woodland and water gardens and rockery, Japanese garden and eucalyptus as well as many rare plants. Running from the castle for 2km past a monument, lattice radio mast and, in the springtime, primroses and rhododendrons, is the 260mm gauge Isle of Mull Railway with steam and diesel engines pulling their loads of passengers along the shore.

The railway ends by a beacon at the end of Craignure Bay by the A849. Craignure is served by ferries from Oban although the setting of oil tanks does not frighten away the red deer. There is a campsite at Rubha na Sròine while the other side of the bay also caters for visitors at Java.

The rocky shoreline to Sgeir Mhic Chomhain is well festooned with wracks. The low point ends in a series of rocks and it is possible to thread between these, missing the overfalls around Sgeir nan Gobhar. Glas Eileanan, in the centre of the Sound of Mull, is marked by a round white light tower, standing out against the dark headland of Rubha an Ridire which forms the southern extremity of the Morvern.

Large fish farm units moored off Lismore. The lighthouse on the right is on Eilean Musdile while Mull stands in the distance

Duart Castle has long controlled the southern entrance to the Sound of Mull

Sgeir Mhic Chomain has low water slack at HW Dover –0100 and high water slack from HW Dover +0600 to –0600. The rocks are at the end of Scallastle Point, which is topped by a golf course. At the back of Scallastle or Scallasdale Bay is a standing stone.

Submarine power cables cross the sound from Rubha Leth Thorcaill to Lochaline and a vehicle ferry follows a similar A884 line from Sgeir Mhór, where a small trailer offers hot food at the ferry terminal.

A marine farm is located along the edge of Fishnish Bay and at Rubha na Leitreach a boat is loaded with pit-prop sized lengths of timber produced by the island's forestry operations.

Pennygown Chapel ruin has the shaft of a Celtic cross with the Virgin and Child, probably from Iona. There used to be benevolent fairies who would complete any items of work left here, but when someone left a short piece of wood to be made into a ship's mast the service was brought to an end and no more favours were done.

Glenforsa Airstrip at the mouth of the River Forsa was built in 54 days in 1966 as an exercise by the 38th Engineer Regiment. It is the airfield for Mull and can be very busy with light aircraft active low over the sound.

Little now remains of Casteal nan Con at Killundine

paddler from Argyll and Bute to the Highland region.

Marine farms along the northeast shore are accompanied by many antiquities, notably the ruin of Caisteal nan Con, dog's castle, the hunting lodge of the Macleans of Duart. Around the Killundine River are a stone circle, cairns, chapel and Càrn na Caillich. The mountainside is forested with gorse on lower slopes and wracks along the rocky shore, even swans at the rivermouth. Low water slack is at HW Dover –0030. There is a local magnetic anomaly which can increase compass variation by up to $5\frac{1}{2}°$.

The B489 coast road ends beyond the burial ground at Bonnavoulin. Across the sound, **Tobermory** remains largely hidden behind Calve Island. Nearer at hand, sea urchins may be seen perched on the rocks. There is something

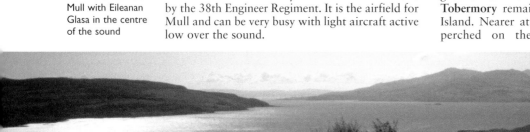

Looking south down the Sound of Mull with Eileanan Glasa in the centre of the sound

Looking up the Sound of Mull past Auliston Point to the mouth of Loch Sunart and the bulk of Ben Hiant

Eileanan Glasa, the green islands, are grass covered. Dearg Sgeir has the Eileanan Glasa light beacon which replaces a lighthouse demolished in 1935 by the cargo ship *Rondo*. Low water slack here is half at HW Dover +0030. Using the islands as a stepping stone to cross the Sound of Mull to the Morvern shore, avoiding the ferries, brings the

endearing about watching a pair of normally quarrelsome gulls sharing an urchin, taking it in turns to pick daintily at the contents of their packaged meal.

Low water slack at Auliston Point is at HW Dover –0130 and there is a weak clockwise current to 2km/h in the entrance to Loch Sunart. Most of

Maclean's Nose, a nose or a face?

the loch is sheltered by Oronsay which makes a sheltered haven out of Loch na Droma Buidhe. The upper end of the Sound of Mull north of Tobermory is susceptible to the weather, particularly with southerly and westerly winds, and this area can be rough even when millpond conditions exist through the rest of the sound.

Beyond Rubha Aird Shlignich is Camas nan Geall, bay of the cells or churches. Either meaning could apply as there is a chambered cairn and Cladh Chiarain which was dedicated by St Columba to his friend St Ciaran who is buried here, having died in 548 after funding the monastery at Clonmacnoise on the Shannon. Contrasting with the silver sand is a red granite monolith with carvings of hunting dogs and a cross.

There is a weak eddy in Port a Chamais on the flood. At Maclean's Nose the flows start out at HW Dover +0130 and in at HW Dover −0415.

The scenery is of gabbro. The large protrusion on the lower flanks of Ben Hiant would appear not to have been given the name Maclean's Nose by one of his friends, being flattened rather than flattering. If the nose is viewed from the front, however, and looked at as a head it takes on the striking form of a bearded face with grey eyes and well proportioned nose.

Another marine farm is located in Camas nan Clacha' Mora.

Mingary looks exactly right for a mediaeval castle, apparently cube-shaped with no more than a hint of a taper and no features to break up the bottom three quarters of the plain walls. It was the seat of the MacIans of Ardnamurchan with a commanding view down the Sound of Mull. It had a 13th-century high hexagonal curtain wall with sea gate and land gate, receiving small turrets in the 17th century and internal barracks in the 18th century. It was besieged unsuccessfully with great loss of life by Lachlan Maclean of Duart with the help of the crew of the *San Juan de Sicilia* in 1588, hence the name Port nan Spainteach for the adjacent inlet. In 1644 Young Colkitto captured three Covenanting ministers as hostages for release of his father, placed wood against the outside of the castle and smoked and baked those inside until

they surrendered. He then put the ministers inside and left to join Montrose. Argyll laid siege for seven weeks to the castle, which lacked a well, until it was relieved by Clanranald. Two of the minsters died and one was exchanged. During the 1745 uprising it was garrisoned by Campbell of Ardnamurchan. It was inhabited until the early 19th century and the ruins still belong to the Campbells.

There is a convenient slip at the back of Kilchoan Bay, off the B8007, surrounded by such antiquities as a chambered cairn, stone aisle and two churches, in one of which is buried Macbeth, together with modern facilities such as a shop and a telephone kiosk.

Ardmore Point and Rubha nan Gall on Mull, seen from Kilchoan Bay

Distance
From Gallanachmore to Kilchoan is 82km
Campsites
Gallanachmore, Ganavan, Kiel Crofts, Craignure, Corrynachenchy, Pennygown, Fiunary, Tobermory
Youth Hostels
Oban, Tobermory
OS 1:50,000 Sheets
47 Tobermory and North Mull
49 Oban and East Mull
Imray Charts
2800 West Coast of Scotland
C65 Crinan to Mallaig and Barra (1:155,000)
Admiralty Charts
1790 Oban and Approaches (1:10,000)
SC 2171 Sound of Mull and Approaches (1:75,000)
2378 Loch Linne – Southern Part (1:25,000)
2379 Loch Linne – Central Part (1:25,000)
2387 Firth of Lorn – Northern Part (1:25,000)
SC 2390 Sound of Mull (1:25,000)
2392 Sound of Mull – Western Entrance (1:25,000)
2394 Loch Sunart (1:25,000)
SC 2724 North Channel to the Firth of Lorn
(1:200,000)
SC 5611 West Coast of Scotland
Tidal Constants
Oban: Dover −0520
Dunstaffnage Bay: Dover −0520
Port Appin: HW Dover −0520, LW Dover −0540
Craignure: HW Dover −0500, LW Dover −0510
Loch Aline: Dover −0510
Salen: HW Dover −0450, LW Dover −0500
Tobermory: Dover −0500
Sea Area
Malin
Submarine Areas
32 Linnhe, 29 Staffa
Rescue
All weather lifeboats: Oban, Tobermory
Maritime Rescue Centres
Clyde, 01475 729988

25 SOUND OF ARISAIG

The most beautiful area of sea in Britain

Sound the pibroch loud on high
Frae John o' Groats, the Isle of Skye,
Let every clan their slogan cry,
Rise and follow Charlie.

Other than the road which runs along the hillside a little further to Ormsaigmore and Ormsaigbeg, Kilchoan is the last point of civilization before tackling the final part of the Ardnamurchan peninsula, the most sparsely populated area in Britain.

The water is clear and the birdlife active with redthroated divers, guillemots, black guillemots, cormorants, blackbacked gulls and fulmars amongst the species present.

Streams are weak to the Point of Ardnamurchan but the coast is steep and rocky, turning to cliffs. Sròn Bheag rises to 342m high Beinn na Seilg. The cliff section becomes better defined after Eilean nan Secachd Seisrichean. Occasionally the cliffs are white with cormorant guano at favoured points.

Point of Ardnamurchan, Gaelic for point of great waves or sea nymphs, is not as dramatic as its location would suggest. It is much lower than the coast which precedes it and has bays on both sides. Although it is the most westerly point on the British mainland, it is surrounded by islands, notably Mull, Coll, Muck, Eigg, Rùm, Canna and Skye, a dramatic panorama.

The lighthouse, designed by Alan Stevenson and built by Robert Hume in 1849 of pink granite from the Ross of Mull, stands 36m high, the light 55m above the sea with a range of 32km, reached by 140 spiral steps, all of which is protected by a high white wall on this wave-battered headland with its interesting volcanic rocks. On a clear day the view from the light includes Barra and South Uist.

Streams start north and northeast HW Dover +0130 and south and southwest HW Dover −0430 at up to 3km/h, flows generally being weak to Rubh' Arisaig. The shoreline is rocky to Sanna Point, but interspersed with those rocks are several beaches of white shell sand which now become a feature of the coast.

Eilean Carrach is the island of the uneven surface, which does not seem to be overstating the case. Port ne Cairidh is the port of the fish weir while the beach of Port Macneil was named after Macneil of Barra, who landed cattle here for driving along the drove roads to the Falkirk fairs.

Sanna Bay has the best beach on the Ardnamurchan peninsula, backed by dunes and spoiled only by an old water tower. There are seals, oystercatchers, sandpipers, eider ducks, mergansers, razorbills, meadow pipits, skylarks and even the cuckoo to be heard inland in the spring. Arnamurchan is home to the belted beauty moth, of which the female is flightless. Many tenants were moved here from Swordle, further

Looking past the Ardnamurchan light towards Muck, Eigg, Rùm and Skye

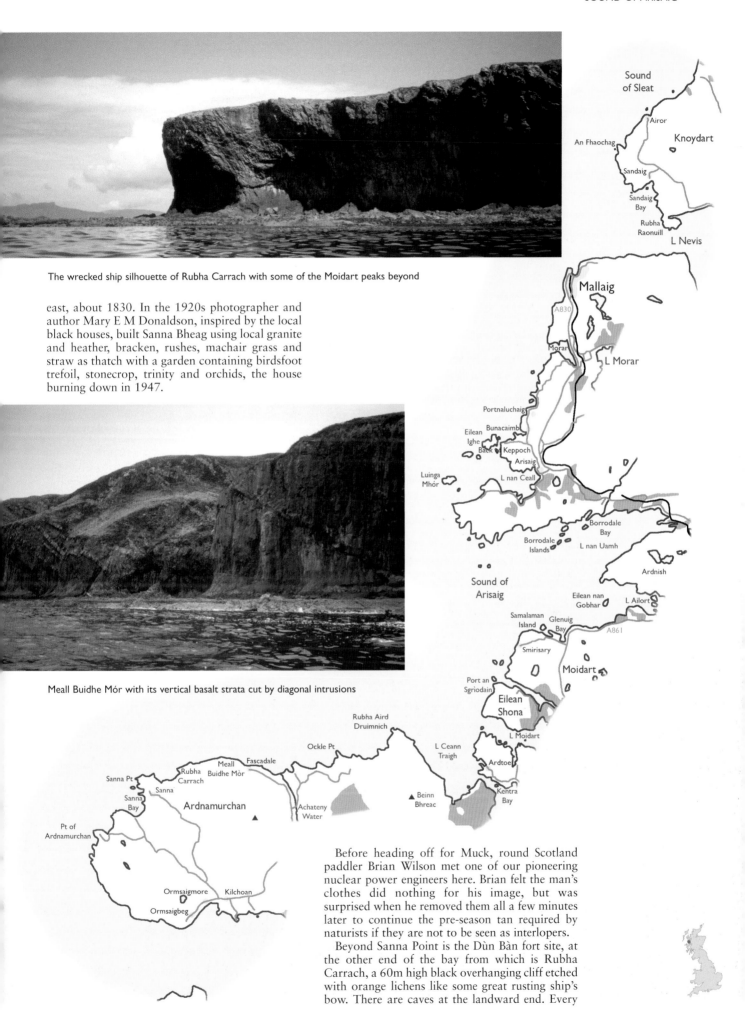

The wrecked ship silhouette of Rubha Carrach with some of the Moidart peaks beyond

east, about 1830. In the 1920s photographer and author Mary E M Donaldson, inspired by the local black houses, built Sanna Bheag using local granite and heather, bracken, rushes, machair grass and straw as thatch with a garden containing birdsfoot trefoil, stonecrop, trinity and orchids, the house burning down in 1947.

Meall Buidhe Mór with its vertical basalt strata cut by diagonal intrusions

Before heading off for Muck, round Scotland paddler Brian Wilson met one of our pioneering nuclear power engineers here. Brian felt the man's clothes did nothing for his image, but was surprised when he removed them all a few minutes later to continue the pre-season tan required by naturists if they are not to be seen as interlopers.

Beyond Sanna Point is the Dùn Bàn fort site, at the other end of the bay from which is Rubha Carrach, a 60m high black overhanging cliff etched with orange lichens like some great rusting ship's bow. There are caves at the landward end. Every inlet seems to have an inflatable full of sub-aqua enthusiasts. Further along the coast towards Meall Buidhe Mór is another cliff with the crump of waves resounding from deep inside the rocks. The 90m high cliffs have close vertical fissures but long intrusions run diagonally across them.

The cliffs come to an end at Fascadale Bay although 437m high Meall nan Con and 401m Beinn an Leathaid still push up the skyline inland. The skyline at Fascadale includes a well camouflaged hut.

Achateny Water discharges at Port Bàn, a bay with rare shells on the beach. Assorted caves, duns and a chambered cairn continue from here to Port an Eilean Mhóir from where the tenants of Swordle were displaced to Sanna.

The northeast side of Ockle Point has columnar basaltic cliffs with another dun and more caves following before Rubha Aird Druimnich.

Dunes surround much of Loch Ceann Traigh, together with a couple of fish farms, but they are totally overshadowed by 357m Beinn Bhreac to the south and 888m Beinn Resipol and the other peaks of Moidart, Sunart and the Morvern to the southeast, a magnificent skyline.

A channel leads in past Ardtoe to Kentra Bay. The islets at the north side of the entrance to the South Channel of Loch Moidart bring azure green water as sunlight reflects off the white sandy bottom.

The west coast of Eilean Shona, rugged grey rock with just sheep grazing on the grassy crags and low cliffs by the sea, is devoid of features. The peaks of Aonach, Cruach a' Choire, Cruach Bhuide and Sgurr an Teintein all merge into each other above Port an Sgrìodain.

Strong flows into Loch Moidart start at HW Dover +0110 and the ebb starts at HW Dover −0510. Rocks and islands around the entrance to the North Channel dampen out swells. The Atlantic swell makes its presence felt beyond the bar a kilometre inside the entrance. Breakers may

crash across the jagged water level rocks of Rubh' Aird an Fheidh. The white barnacled bottom of the North Channel can be seen through clear water amongst the floating seaweed. Both entrances to Loch Moidart are tortuous, narrow and rock studded, making passage for larger craft quite risky unless they are well acquainted with the waters.

Smirisary brings a selection of holiday chalets. Rubha Ghead a' Leighe leads into the Sound of Arisaig, the south side of which is mostly steep and rocky and catches a heavy sea with onshore winds.

Sixteen metre high Samalaman Island is connected to the shore at low water and is an attractive spot with picnic area and the return of trees, together with yellow irises and birds from the hooded crow to the heron. Fish farms are located in Glenuig Bay, facing onto which is the A861 and Glenuig Inn, which has rooms for divers and other watersports enthusiasts. Flows inward start at HW Dover +0110 and the ebb starts at HW Dover −0510 although flows are barely perceptible.

Forty metre high Eilean nan Gobhar or goat island is the site of a vitrified fort. It stands in the mouth of Loch Ailort which winds away inland and is separated by Rubha Chaolais on the end of the Ardnish Peninsula from Loch nan Uamh. It is an area frequented by shags, blackbacked gulls, black guillemots, seals and jellyfish and surrounded by birch, larch and oak woods festooned with healthy lichens. It is overlooked by 601m high Sidhean Mór. Very weak streams are ingoing from at HW Dover +0110 and outgoing from at HW Dover −0510.

Loch nan Uamh, the loch of the caves, is central to the movements of Prince Charlie. He landed in Borrodale Bay on July 25th 1745 from the *Du Teillay*. He met the chiefs in Borrodale House, subsequently fired by Captain Fergussone of the sloop *Furnace* and the people maimed and murdered by his crew as part of the Duke of Cumberland's retribution. On April 26th 1746 at 8pm Prince Charlie sailed from here to Rossinish

The Borrodale shore seen across the Sound of Arisaig from Glenuig

The South Channel from the skerries off Loch nan Ceall with seals hauled out amongst the weed

on Benbecula with a dozen others in an eight oared boat. Conditions were gale force and the boat lost its bowsprit as it rounded Rubh' Arisaig. A day later the French privateers *Bellona* and *Mars*

landed 35,000 gold Louis and six casks to help fund the cause, some of the money becoming the Loch Arkaig Treasure. The ships had to fight a six hour battle in the loch before making their escape.

The busy fish pier at Mallaig with the Armadale car ferry loading beyond

Prince Charlie made several further visits here and it was from here that he made his final departure for France in *L'Heureux* on 20th September with a reward of £30,000 on his head. Prince Charlie's Cave is 30m long by 3.5m high and is where he lived for at least a week with his followers on the floor lined with heather.

Rubh' Aird Ghamhsgail has a fort site. Further up the valley of the Borrodale Burn is Arisaig House, used as the field training headquarters of the Special Operations Executive under General Sir Colin McVean Gubbins during the second world war.

Offshore are dotted the Borrodale Islands, the 17m high block of rock on Eilean an Sgùrra looking like a castle. Further along the coast lies Eilean an t-Snidhe with a 10m high basaltic pillar. Closer inshore is Eilean a' Ghaill, 21m high, its cliffy top looking like a ruin from the northwest although there is a real fort site on the east side. Terns and oystercatchers live on the rocks and in the sandy bays. These latter are also occupied by diverse humans, it being possible to find nude sunbathers in one bay and hikers in boots and rollneck sweaters in the next on the same day, reflecting the varied aspirations of holidaymakers.

It is possible to use routes inside islets at the mouth of Port a' Bhathaich and Eilean Port nam Murrach amongst drifting moon jellyfish.

A white painted mark locates Rubh' Arisaig and the start of what is arguably the most beautiful area of sea in Britain. Arisaig lies at the head of Loch nan Ceall, the loch of the hermit's cell. A passenger ferry operates through the South Channel to Eigg, Muck and Rùm which all lie offshore. Inshore, however, are 3km of skerries between which lies clear water through which the clean shell sand bottom can be seen. Largest of the islands is 17m high Luinga Mhór while innumerable rocks are used by a particularly large seal colony and the smell of fish lingers on the air. In the shallower water waders go about their business. Streams into the North Channel begin at HW Dover +0120 and the ebb starts at HW Dover −0510, strongly in the lower half of the tide when sandbanks are uncovered. Meanwhile, streams along the coast are northgoing from HW Dover −0100 for seven and a half hours and southgoing for five hours from HW Dover −0400.

From Eilean Ighe to Mallaig the streams are northgoing from HW Dover +0115 until HW Dover −0445, weak but sometimes with eddies on a shore which is rocky, but with sandy beaches as far as the River Morar.

Back of Keppoch has a selection of masts and towers plus a caravan site, more caravans and a golf course following at Portnaluchaig with an aerial and yet more caravans at Glenancross. The attraction of this coastline for the campers is not hard to see.

When the River Morar is at low tide it reveals expanses of the whitest sand in Britain, the location used for filming *Local Hero* in 1983. Twenty years earlier the Mosquitos of *633 Squadron* had droned in over the same estuary to be filmed in action over an imaginary section of the Norwegian landscape near Loch Morar.

The West Highland and Marine hotels are amongst the cluster of buildings which lead up to the mark on Rubha na h-Acairseid. **Mallaig** harbour is entered from the north past the breakwater of caissons built in 1986. The northern end of the port loads 20,000 cars and 100,000 passengers each year to Armadale with a passenger ferry also to Kyle of Lochalsh. The southern end of the harbour is well used by fishing boats, this being the premier fishing port of the west coast although overfishing in the Minch has caused a decline in catches. There can be over 80 boats per day handling fish, prawns and lobsters with exports to Europe, Canada and the USA. Mallaig Marine World has live sea creatures, all caught by local fishing boats. The town is at the end of the A830, the Road to the Isles, and expanded after the arrival of the West Highland Line in 1901. This is one of the most scenic railway lines in the world, as shown by the running of observation cars and the popularity of the present steam train service, boosted by its Harry Potter associations.

Off the harbour stands a 6m metal framework with a light. Flows are northeast from HW Dover +0130 and southwest from HW Dover −0430 at up to 2km/h although flows can be stronger off points.

A submarine cable crosses from Mallaigvaig to the north side of Loch Nevis, the deepest sea loch in Europe. Flows into the loch start at HW Dover

The entrance to Loch Nevis with Rubha Raonuill guarding its northern side

−0110 and out again from HW Dover −0510. They are only up to 1km/h but winds, especially from the southwest or southeast, can bring violent squalls of confusing direction in Loch Nevis. This is porpoise territory. The north entrance to the loch is guarded by 104m high Rubha Raonuill with a golden statue of the Virgin Mary, Bogha Don beacon and, hidden on the east side, a cave. The coast is rugged to Loch Hourn.

The Sleat Peninsula on Skye is also rugged and makes dramatic viewing across the Sound of Sleat as it gradually reduces in distance.

Sandaig Bay seems to collect an undue number of fish crates and floats, perhaps something to do with the fact that it is normally downwind of Mallaig. Scant shelter to the bay is given by Glas Eilean and Eilean Dearg. The latter is 20m high and covered with heather, Eilean nan Gàmhna being as high but covered with long grass. Sandaig itself is now little more than a couple of ruins, one being a chapel.

An Fhaochag is steep and 6m high, the western extremity of Knoydart. Despite its present remoteness, it has a memorial, ruins and Dun Ban to add to the interest of its caves.

Airor is a small harbour sheltered by 8m high Airor Island and a harbour wall. Its facilities are even less comprehensive than they seem, however. The road goes only as far as Inverie on Loch Nevis and is not connected with the rest of the road system. For the locals this does mean that they do not have to be so fastidious with the normal driving laws. After all, they are hardly likely to be stopped by a passing police car.

In *Quest by Canoe*, describing a 1930s paddle from Bowling to Kyleakin, Alastair M Dunnett describes Airor as offering the best view from the mainland in all his journey

Distance
From Kilchoan to Airor is 83km
Campsites
Tobermory, Back of Keppoch, Bunacaimb, Glenacross
Youth Hostels
Tobermory, Armadale
OS 1:50,000 Sheets
33 Loch Alsh, Glen Shiel and Loch Hourn
40 Mallaig and Glenfinnan
47 Tobermory and North Mull
Imray Charts
2800 West Coast of Scotland
C65 Crinan to Mallaig and Barra (1:155,000)
C66 Mallaig to Rudha Reidh and Outer Hebrides (1:150,000)
Admiralty Charts
SC 2171 Sound of Mull and Approaches (1:75,000)
2207 Point of Ardnamurchan to the Sound of Sleat (1:50,000)
2208 Mallaig to Canna Harbour (1:50,000)
2392 Sound of Mull – Western Entrance (1:25,000)
2541 Lochs on the West Coast of Scotland. Mallaig Harbour (1:7,500). Loch Nevis (1:25,000)
SC 5611 West Coast of Scotland
Tidal Constants
Tobermory: Dover −0500
Loch Moidart: Dover −0500
Mallaig: Dover −0450
Inverie Bay: HW Dover −0500, LW Dover −0450
Sea Area
Malin
Submarine Areas
29 Staffa, 25 Eigg, 21 Sleat
Rescue
Inshore lifeboat: Kyle of Lochalsh
All weather lifeboats: Tobermory, Mallaig
Maritime Rescue Centre
Clyde, 01475 729988
Stornoway, 01851 702013/4

Looking across the Sound of Sleat to Skye from the moorings at Airor, sheltered by Airor Island

26 EAST INNER SOUND

A saucy princess with a chain

Speed, bonny boat, like a bird on the wing;
'Onward!' the sailors cry;
Carry the lad that's born to be king
Over the sea to Skye.

Sir Harold Edwin Boulton

something which will not have escaped the attentions of foxes and golden eagles in the vicinity.

Rubha Ard Slisneach marks the end of the south side of Loch Hourn, a loch which always seems to be referred to with the prefix 'dark'. The

Skye with the Cuillin Hills, seen across the Sound of Sleat

Loch Hourn with Beinn Sgritheall bathed in sunlight

From Airor the coast continues to be inaccessible by land while beaches are of rounded tennis ball sized stones, uncomfortable to walk on. Opposite Eilean Shamadalain is a chapel ruin and a sheep shelter built from nailed fish crates. The Sound of Sleat can be stormy.

A gravel spit has been formed by the Abhainn Inbhir Ghuiserein. Inverguseran is a sheep station,

surrounding high peaks block out the light and encourage precipitation. Notable on the south side of the loch are Beinn na Caillich at 785m and Ladhar Bheinn at 1,020m, while 974m Beinn Sgritheall presents an uncompromising slope on the north side. Loch Hourn is one of the most remote and spectacular of the western sea lochs and has one of the heaviest rainfalls in the British Isles.

At Croulin on the south shore there is an area of silt brought down from Beinn na Caillich by the Croulin Burn while a tripod on Sgeir Ulibhe, on the other side of the loch, marks another shallow area. Streams are very weak, the flood starting at HW Dover +0155 and the ebb at HW Dover −0415.

From Loch Hourn to Kyle Rhea the coast becomes increasingly high, steep and rocky.

Sandaig Island lighthouse stands on 19m high Eilean Mór, the outer of the Sandaig Islands, a 7m structure with a white octagonal tower. Most of the Sandaig Islands are connected together and to the mainland at low tide, exposing banks of mussels around which oystercatchers and herons pick. This was Camusfeàrna in Gavin Maxwell's *Ring of Bright Water* and there is a memorial cairn near the Allt Mór Shantaig at Sandaig to Edal, the last of the otters here, killed when the house burned down in 1968.

Northeastgoing flows in the Sound of Sleat begin at HW Dover +0130 and they start southwest at HW Dover −0430, initially at up to 4km/h although the figure increases greatly further north.

Eilanreach stands at the mouth of the Abhainn a' Ghlinne Bhig, up the valley of which are several broch sites. One of the finest Pictish brochs is Dun Telve, still 10m high despite having been used as a source of stone for the building of Bernera Barracks.

The Island of Skye takes its name from the Norse Skuyo, the isle of clouds. In Gaelic it is Eilean à Cheo, the isle of mist, and to the Celts it was the winged isle. It became popular in Victorian times when the railway was opened to Kyle of Lochalsh and has long had a romantic air about it. The sabbath is still kept in the face of changed priorities elsewhere.

Sandaig, setting for Gavin Maxwell's otter story

It was part of the mainland until separated by denudation and coastal movement. The Sleat peninsula forms the northwest side of the Sound of Sleat and it is frequently steep, rising to 610m Ben Aslak.

Dùnan Ruadh is a 25m high headland. Seals hang around near the fish farms and submarine cables cross the sound.

The northeastgoing flow begins to pick up. On the southwesterly stream there are northgoing eddies on both sides and there can be heavy overfalls, dangerous to small boats on the

Looking up the Sound of Sleat. Kyle Rhea cuts through the cleft on the left

southwesterly stream if southwesterly winds are blowing across Bàgh Dùnan Ruadh. From between Ben Aslak and 739m Sgurr na Coinnich flows the Kylerhea River to discharge below circling blackbacked gulls at Kylerhea.

Kyle Rhea during a summer evening slack, looking northwards towards Loch Alsh

The Sound of Sleat seems to end promptly at Glenelg Bay but Kyle Rhea leaves in the north corner between steep mountainsides. The passenger ferry from Kyle of Lochalsh to Mallaig takes this route and it is crossed by a vehicle ferry to Skye's oldest ferry terminal. Until 1906 cattle were swum across here, up to 8,000 per year in strings of six to eight tied behind boats. Streams through the kyle are fierce although there are eddies on both sides. The northgoing stream begins at HW Dover +0140 at up to 13km/h, although it has been measured at 22km/h, while the southgoing stream begins at HW Dover −0420 at up to 15km/h, the latter increased in strength and duration by strong and long lasting northeasterly winds, snowmelt and rainfall while converse factors increase the northerly flow. Powered craft being washed through out of control are not unusual.

Kylerhea forest nature reserve has ancient birch, ash and oak woodland with golden eagles and seals. Otters are observed from a hide near the Kyle Rhea light beacon on the west side and so this area should be avoided so that the watchers are not disturbed. Powerlines pass high over the kyle before it opens out into Loch Alsh.

Sgeir na Caillich light beacon is a 2m concrete pillar below 753m Beinn na Caillich. From this area it is possible to see the distinctive Eilean Donnan castle 8km to the east at the head of the loch.

Flows are weak in the loch, up to 2km/h but affected by wind, heavy rain and snowmelt.

The far side of the loch is dominated by 452m Auchtertyre Hill, on the flanks of which is Sgurr Mór which has large red earthmarks amongst the dark heather. At water level Donald Murchison's Monument stands 8m high in white granite. 26km² of the locality are accounted for by the Balmacara Estate.

Black guillemots fly over the water and moon jellyfish drift in the currents. Fish farms are located near where the wreck of *HMS Port Napier* lies submerged.

Rubha Ard Treisnis stands 13m high in the middle of Loch Alsh, dividing Loch na Béiste from Kyle Akin. The latter probably took its name from King Haakon of Norway, who took his fleet through in 1263 prior to his defeat at the Battle of Largs.

Times of tidal flows in the kyle vary considerably not only with wind, heavy rain and snowmelt but also with the day of the tidal cycle. Several islands stand in the centre of the kyle, the largest of which is Eileanan Dubha, 15m high and heather covered. A light beacon is located on an islet at its east end.

Caisteal Maol, roofless castle, is a 29m high square tower used as a lookout post and defence against Norse raids, the stronghold of the MacKinnons of Strath from the 12th to 15th centuries. Its original owner had been a Norwegian princess with the unlikely name of Saucy Mary who ran a chain across the loch to sink any ship not paying a toll.

A monument stands beside what was the main ferry terminal for Skye. The Sunday service did not start until 1965 and, even then, it was in spite of strong protest from the kirk locally. To watch an ambulance drive off the ferry at high speed at the Kyle of Lochalsh end, its light flashing as it headed for Inverness, was a reminder of how remote the island was.

Kyle of Lochalsh is at the end of the railway from Dingwall. Submarine cables cross the kyle here.

Kyle House has 1.2ha of gardens planted in the 60s by Colin Mackenzie with a notable kitchen garden and tender plants attaining large size because of the warmth of the Gulf Stream.

Eilean Bàn, the white island, has the 21m white tower of Kyle Akin lighthouse and white sands surrounding its 5ha, as described in John Buchan's *Prince of Captivity*. Another author involved was Gavin Maxwell who bought the island in 1963 to turn it into a zoo for west Highland birds and mammals. He moved there in 1968. After his early death the following year his partner, John Lister-Kaye, wrote a book about the island and the project. Teko, the last otter, is buried here.

Over the Sea to Skye took on a new meaning with the construction of the Skye bridge to carry the A87 from next to the golf course at Plock of Kyle via Eilean Bàn to the Skye shore. Stone for the project was taken from a quarry at the Kyle of Lochalsh end. The 2.4km bridge was Scotland's first finance, design, build and operate bridge, a concept badly soured by the highest bridge toll in Europe until rescinded in December 2004. It is the world's longest span balanced cantilever concrete box girder bridge. Embellishments are supposed to make it appear like a couple of giant seagulls in flight. It is also Scotland's most exposed bridge site

with severe weather during the construction resulting in significant delays. An imposing backdrop comes in the form of 775m Glamaig and other peaks in the Cuillin Hills.

Kyle Akin leads out into Inner Sound. Streams start at HW Dover +0100 and south at HW Dover –0500, later in the south and earlier in the north, to 2km/h at salient points. Rafts of fish farms are watched by seals inside Eilean a' Mhal and other islets leading up to the Black Islands in Erbusaig Bay.

After Portnacloich Point there are more islets dotted along the rocky shore, Eilean na Crèadha, Eilean nan Gobhar Mór, 6m high Eilean Dubh Dhurinish and An Dubh-aird, which is almost an island, 35m high and covered with steeply rising heath, fronting Plockton Aerodrome as it lies between Camas Dubh-aird and Camas Deannd. There are several hamlets including Drumbuie at the head of Port Cam and Port-an-eorna before Bagh an t-Srathaidh. Cormorants, blackbacked gulls and herons frequent the islands.

Streams are weak at the mouth of Loch Carron, but there are several navigation marks including a disused 13m light tower on Eilean a' Chait in the Cat Islands and a spar buoy by Hawk Rock. The warm climate around Plockton encourages the growth of palm trees and there is a rare breeds farm.

There is an ancient prophesy that a monster would come from Loch Kishorn. It would rise to the surface three times then sink beneath the waves for ever. The Garra Islands stand at the mouth of the loch. Garbh-eilean is forested while Kishorn

Island stands 19m high, the largest of the group. Precast bridge units for the Skye bridge were made near the head of the loch. Because of the depth of the loch it was used in the 1980s by Howard-Doris as their North Sea oil platform construction site although it is now no longer used for that purpose. Their biggest project was the Ninian Central Platform. It stood 237m high, had a 136m diameter base and weighed 320,000 tonnes. At the time it was the largest moveable object ever made by man and was towed to its present location 177km off the coast of Scotland where it sits on the bottom in 134m of water. It puts a spine-chilling twist on the old prophesy.

The Skye Bridge and old lighthouse during a sea kayak symposium weekend

Loch Carron with Loch Kishorn beyond, seen along the coast from Erbusaig Bay

The northwest side of Loch Kishorn reaches up in a wall to 896m Beinn Bhàn and 776m Sgurr a Ghaorachain and continues with a steep coast of weathered red sandstone all the way to Rubha na

h-Uamha where it is overhanging. At the northern end the Allt a' Chumhaing and Allt a' Chois both have waterfalls over 70m high. There are occasional small stone beaches backed by heather, bracken, foxgloves and trefoils amongst the flotsam. Fulmars sweep low over the water in their distinctive manner.

There was a settlement above Rubha na Guailne but the only signs of man's activity are more rusting cars and a motorbike at the foot of the cliffs. Either the roads around Applecross Bay are extremely dangerous or the locals have a disappointingly limited level of environmental responsibility.

Caolas Mór with the Crowlin Islands on the left and Sgeir Shalach at the end of Loch Toscaig on the right. In the distance is Raasay

Streams in Caolas Mór begin southeast at HW Dover +0145 and northwest at HW Dover −0415 at up to 2km/h.

On the far side, the Crowlin Islands are a volcanic outcrop in three islands, the two longer of which join up at low tide although mostly separated by a narrow cleft, the Harbour. The largest, Eilean Mór, rises to 114m at Meall a' Chòis. It has a cave and the ruins of a chapel said to be dedicated to St Cormac. Eilean Meadhonach lies along its west side while at the north end is Eilean Beag with a lighthouse and caves occupied by common and Atlantic seals. To the west there is, again, a dramatic skyline with a truncated cone

Sand is the descriptively blunt name for an inlet with a bay of sand and a virtual cliff of sand flowing down to the beach.

Inner Sound has the deepest continental shelf water around the British Isles, possibly a former river course. For this reason it is used as a submarine exercise area and for carrying out torpedo tests. The British Underwater Test and Evaluation Centre with helipad is located in a modern building on the low cliffs and its presence prevented Inner Sound being used for oil platform construction. When a red flag or lights are showing it is necessary to pass through the area without stopping.

Ardban is marked out by its dazzling white beach

rising high above the general trend of the mountains on Raasay.

Loch Toscaig with Toscaig at its head has clear water through which the sandy bottom can be seen. Eilean na Bà stands 22m high while An Ruadh-eilean disappears at high tide in an area used for fish farms.

Ardban, a couple of houses on a peninsula, would hardly be noticed but for the glistening white beaches on each side, shell sand but with a texture like coral sand. Otters might also be seen in the area.

Eilean nan Naomh has a wreck on the inside despite a beacon on each end. It was the Holy Island where St Maelrubha landed in 671. It offers some shelter to Poll Creadha which lies between Culduie and Camusterrach.

A couple of aerials have been erected at Camusteel, but steel is also found where the road comes between the shore and Loch a' Mhuilinn to the south of Milton where cars have dropped over the cliff and lie rusting at the bottom.

Applecross looks out over Applecross Bay and a deep cleft between the peaks of Applecross Forest, a gouge obviously made by something much larger than the River Applecross which currently discharges here. Applecross House is used by the Fairbridge Drake Society to help youths who have not managed to get the best out of life. Close by is a chapel which has fragments of a stone cross from a monastery built in 672 by St Maelrubha for fugitives, one of the oldest seats of Christianity in Scotland, destroyed by the Vikings.

The view south from Ardban includes Scalpay with the Cuillins beyond

Weathered rocks at Ardban. Beyond are Camusteel and Meall na Fhuaid above Applecross

The cliffs seem fairly remote for several kilometres. Occasionally there are caves and Callakille has a natural arch. Waders and otters are likely to be the only life close inshore. Across the sound, Raasay gives way to Rona.

Passing Rubha Chuaig brings an inlet in the form of Ob Chuaig. It is fed by the Abhainn Chuaig, beside which a track runs up to the road at Cuaig.

Waterfall at Rubha na Guailne... and a less pretty picture of wrecked cars and a motorbike

Balanced section of rock strata provides an interesting shoreline sculpture

Distance
From Airor to Cuaig is 84km
Campsites
Glenacross Balmacara Square, Applecross, Shieldaig
Youth Hostels
Armadale, Kyleakin, Broadford, Raasay, Torridon
OS 1:50,000 Sheets
24 Raasay and Applecross
33 Loch Alsh, Glen Shiel and Loch Hourn
Imray Charts
C66 Mallaig to Rudha Reidh and Outer Hebrides (1:150,000)
Admiralty Charts
2208 Mallaig to Canna Harbour (1:50,000)
2209 Inner Sound (1:50,000)
2210 Approaches to Inner Sound (1:50,000)
2479 Inner Sound – Northern Part (1:18,000)
2480 Inner Sound – Central Part (1:25,000)
2498 Inner Sound – Southern Part (1:25,000)
2528 Loch Gairloch and Loch Kishorn to Strome Narrows. Loch Kishorn to Strome Narrows (1:15,000)
2540 Loch Alsh and Approaches (1:20,000). Kyle Rhea (1:12,500). Kyle Akin (1:12,500)
2541 Lochs on the West Coast of Scotland. Loch Hourn (1:25,000)
Tidal Constants
Inverie Bay: HW Dover –0500, LW Dover –0450
Loch Hourn: HW Dover –0510, LW Dover –0500
Glenelg Bay: HW Dover –0500, LW Dover –0450
Kyle of Lochalsh: HW Dover –0440, LW Dover –0420
Plockton: Dover –0420
Applecross: HW Dover –0430, LW Dover –0420
Loch a' Bhràige: Dover –0420
Sea Areas
Malin, Hebrides
Submarine Areas
21 Sleat, 14 Raasay, 13 Rona South
Rescue
Inshore lifeboat: Kyle of Lochalsh
All weather lifeboats: Mallaig, Portree
Maritime Rescue Centre
Stornoway, 01851 702013/4

Across Inner Sound Raasay gives way to Rona

27 SOUTHEAST MINCH

Dramatic forests without trees

The entrance to Ob Chuaig is occupied by Eilean Chuaig which offers a notably ship-shaped silhouette to the bay. Along the cliffs there are caves. Jellyfish and fulmars are present with cormorants and waders in Ob na h-Uamha. Each side of this latter bay are the low Rubha na Fearna and the Rubha na Fearn.

From here to Red Point, 10km away, the buildings can be counted on the fingers of one hand. One is the fishing station near Red Point where more fish farms are located.

37m high Red Point is where Loch Torridon is left for the Minch. A large sandy bay backed by dunes is found at Redpoint, a village of a dozen

Beinn Eighe, Beinn Alligin, Liathach and other peaks at the head of Loch Torridon, seen beyond Ob na h-Uamha and Rubha na Fearn

This second point brings a turn into Loch Torridon which has steep shores on the northwest side but weak streams. It is one of the wildest and least spoilt stretches of Highland coastline.

In Britain it would be difficult to match the mountainscape around the head of the loch. The peaks of Applecross Forest, Glenshieldaig Forest, Ben-Damph Forest, Torridon Forest, Shieldaig Forest and Flowerdale Forest crowd round with an array of peaks which are not high by world standards but which have dramatic shapes, mountains with character. Here are Beinn Bhàn at 896m, Beinn Damh at 902m, Tom na Grugaich at 922m, Sgurr Mhor at 985m and Baos Damh at 875m to name a few. Rising behind them are the higher peaks of Beinn Eighe. Paddling for an hour while looking at these is an uplifting experience.

The southwest side of the loch is less dramatic. The rocky shoreline is lower although still able to produce the odd arch and there are fish farms at intervals at Fearnbeg, in Camas an Eilean and in Loch a' Chracaich.

Loch a' Chracaich and Loch Beag are tucked in behind the Aird peninsula on the southwest side of Loch Torridon. On the other side of Loch Torridon, 142m high Rubha na h-Airde produces a mirror image with Loch Diabeg. Between the two peninsulas is a gap which leads to Loch Shieldag and Upper Loch Torridon. It is a remote area with guillemots and porpoises for company and still that backdrop.

Loch Diabeg has fish farms. Above the grey cliffs are the whitewashed croft houses of Lower Diabeg.

crofts scattered around a viewpoint and the B8056. The dunes hold back a steep marshy area with bog cotton and orchids. The birdlife is rather more common with blackheaded gulls and oystercatchers.

Low cliffs hide much of South Erradale and Port Henderson. Between them is Sròn na Carra, the entrance to Loch Gairloch. Peaks around the head of the loch rise to 420m Meall an Doirein but in the distance are the much higher peaks of Letterewe Forest, Fisherfield Forest and Strathsheallag' Forest with Slioch at 980m, Mullach Coire Mhic Fhearchair at 1,019m and An Teallach at 1,059m.

The low shoreline of the loch is used by black guillemots and otters and there are brown trout, sea trout and salmon in the loch. Badantionail has a fish farm while there are mackerel in Caolas Bad a' Chrotha where there is a fish curing station.

36m high Eilean Horrisdale takes its name from the Norse god Thor and was used by the Vikings to lay up their longships for the winter.

A 2m metal light pedestal stands on 7m high Glas Eilean, to the southeast of which lie Loch Shieldaig and Loch Kerry, entrance to which is past a peninsula with An Dùn, a golf course and Flowerdale House.

Formerly a fishing port where the B8021 leaves the A832, **Gairloch**, is now a place for waterskiing, paragliding, canoeing, windsurfing and sailing. It has the Gairloch Heritage Museum which covers from the prehistory of the area to the present day, including the 17th-century Loch Maree ironworks,

Gairloch and Charlestown at the head of Loch Gairloch.

Inner Sound

Ob Chuaig

fishing and illicit whisky distilling. The coast is particularly rich in mosses and liverworts.

Beyond Carn Dearg is Caolas Beag, frequented by shags, guillemots, cormorants, blackbacked gulls, fulmars and porpoises. Streams in the loch are ingoing from HW Dover +0200 and outgoing from

Caves in the cliffs at Port Erradale

Natural arch to the south of Rubha Réidh

HW Dover –0420, reaching a maximum of 2km/h in Caolas Beag. The River Sand enters between the dunes at Big Sand and there is another fishing station beyond the dunes.

Longa Island is 145ha of grass and heather-covered sandstone, reaching a height of 70m at

which has been cut into a series of vertical ribs by water runoff. There are two aerials, each at a Maol Breac, in the middle of the moor. The rest of the coast to Rubha Réidh is much harder with a number of natural arches, those around Sròn na Cléite being particularly fine with an accompaniment of seals.

The lighthouse at Rubha Réidh

The hidden jetty serving the lighthouse at Rubha Réidh

Druim an Eilein. The island is uninhabited but takes its name from the fact that it was also used by the Vikings to lay up their longships for the winter.

Beyond Rubha Bàn is Port Erradale with North Erradale. Between Peterburn and Melvaig there are heather moors .with peat cutting and a soft cliffline

The ridge of land which peaks at 296m high An Cuaidh finishes steeply at Rubha Réidh with its 25m white tower lighthouse. A small jetty serves an otherwise inaccessible length of coast. The cleft in which the jetty is located also contains a significant cave which is working back towards the sea from the landward end. Assuming it is natural, it must be doing all its erosion on the backwash from each wave. Rua Reidh, an exploration centre with canoeing and abseiling, is located here. From the top of the sandstone cliffs there are views to the Hebrides.

Streams start northeast at HW Dover +0430 and south at HW Dover –0115 at up to 6km/h at Camas Mór. Camas Mór is a pristine sand beach, inaccessible by land because of the cliffs. It has arches and a prominent red sandstone stack, well covered with greenery at its top end.

The ringed plover might be seen around Sròn a' Gheodha Dhuibh. A block which resembles a fortification, but is completely natural, guards the entrance to Caolas an Fhuraidh which runs inside 20m Eilean Furadh Mór. Sgeir Maol Mhoraidh at its far end links up to the shore at low tide.

In the centre of Loch Ewe is the Isle of Ewe. The loch was where north Atlantic convoys were assembled during the second world war when there was an anti-submarine boom across the mouth of the loch. It is still used for refuelling NATO ships and the remains of gun emplacements and pillboxes can be seen near a hydrographic survey pillar on the west side of the mouth of the loch. The loch floods from HW Dover +0210 and ebbs from HW Dover –0415 at up to 2km/h. In the open sea, streams begin north–northeast from HW Dover +0430 and south–southwest from HW Dover –0115 at up to 5km/h.

The cliffs at Gob a' Gheoda seem to offer doorways into the unknown

Slaggan Bay is conspicuous for its golden sandy cliffs, Slaggan village at its head having a nature trail. At Gob a' Gheodha there is a return to rocky cliffs. These are deeply fractured and in one place a block has dropped out to leave what looks like a shadowy doorway in the rock.

Greenstone Point is low and flat, marked with a 3m iron pole. A wreck lies 200m north of the point and other vessels are misled by a magnetic anomaly in the area. Porpoises are to be found all around Rubha Mór. There a couple of arches, the second near Leac Mhór. Beyond Rubha Beag is Mellon Udrigle, near where a kelpie or water spirit was once said to have lived, while to the south of Meall nam Meallan is Loch na Béiste, loch of the beast.

Tidal streams are weak in Gruinard Bay which takes its name from the Norse grunna fjord, shallow ford. At its southwest corner is Laide where a line of rocks protect moorings and there are the remains of a chapel next to a caravan site, located where St Columba is said to have founded a church. There is also a salmon fishing station and a fish farm. A cave precedes the hamlets of First Coast and Second Coast. Suddenly several rivers carve deep channels into the bay, the Little Gruinard River, the Inverianvie River and the Gruinard River, the latter with Gruinard House and its sawmill by the loch.

The most important feature in the bay is Gruinard Island, over 2km long with a steep gravel spit in the southeast corner and rising to 106m at An Eilid. Formerly inhabited, today it stands as a monument to the follies of biological warfare. During the second world war it was used for an experiment in which sheep were infected with anthrax. Half a century later it was still infected and landing strictly prohibited although this has now been terminated. Rabbits, seals and seabirds are unaffected and sheep are once again grazing on the island, but protesters sent soil samples from the island through the post several years ago to the authorities and they were found to contain viable anthrax spores. If such an experiment was necessary why was such a large and accessible island used rather than one which was small and remote?

Little Loch Broom is crossed between Stattic Point and Cailleach Head, a loch subject to heavy squalls. Southwesterly winds bring whirlwinds and anything static is appreciated. Even so, the remote village of Scoraig, which had been abandoned, has been repopulated and there are fish farms. The flood in the loch begins at HW Dover +0210 and the ebb at HW Dover −0415 at up to 2km/h.

Cnoc Sgoraig, at 147m high, runs down as a ridge which ends with 45m rock and earth cliffs, topped by the 6m white tower of Cailleach Head light beacon. At the southern edge of the headland the red rock dips steeply at Sròn a' Gheodha Dhuibh while the intervening earth layers support vegetation so that the cliff is coloured in striking red and green diagonal stripes.

Camas na Ruthaig gives some shelter to terns and paddlers from prevailing southwesterly winds while rounding Carn Dearg into the long mountain edged sweep of Annat Bay which provides further shelter as 635m Beinn Ghobhlach towers overhead and even the ruin at Badacrain is a significant landmark.

Loch Broom ebbs from HW Dover −0415 and floods from HW Dover +0200. Flows are very weak but the loch is subject to squalls. Vessels

Storm clouds gather around Beinn Ghoblach but leave Annat Bay bathed in afternoon sunlight

passing in and out include the car ferry between Stornoway and Ullapool.

Landing can be made on a beach of rounded stones to the east of the lighthouse at Rhue, from where a track leads up the hillside to the parking area at the end of the road.

Rubha Cadail light is low on the shoreline at Rhue. Beyond are Carn Dearg and the Summer Isles

Distance
From Cuaig to Rhue is 100km
Campsites
Shieldaig, Gairloch, Big Sand, Laide, Badcaul, Ardmair
Youth Hostels
Torridon, Carn Dearg, Ullapool
OS 1:50,000 Sheets
19 Gairloch and Ullapool
24 Raasay and Applecross
Imray Charts
C66 Mallaig to Rudha Reidh and Outer Hebrides (1:150,000)
C67 North Minch and Isle of Lewis (1:155,000)
Admiralty Charts
1794 North Minch – Southern Part (1:100,000)
2210 Approaches to Inner Sound (1:50,000)
2479 Inner Sound – Northern Part (1:18,000)
2500 Approaches to Ullapool (1:25,000)
2509 Rubha Réidh to Cailleach Head (1:25,000)
2528 Loch Gairloch and Loch Kishorn to Strome Narrows. Loch Gairloch (1:15,000)
3146 Loch Ewe (1:12,500)
Tidal Constants
Loch a' Bhràige: Dover −0420
Shieldaig: Dover −0430
Gairloch: HW Dover −0430, LW Dover −0420
Tanera Mór: Dover −0420
Sea Area
Hebrides
Submarine Areas
13 Rona South, 5 Minch South, 6 Ewe
Rescue
All weather lifeboats: Portree, Lochinver
Maritime Rescue Centre
Stornoway, 01851 702013/4

28 NORTHEAST MINCH

Some of the world's oldest rock

A rainbow crosses Camas Mór while low cloud blanks out Ben Mòr Coigach beyond

The low rocks at Rhue have a series of inlets which collect large numbers of moon jellyfish with a summer westerly wind. Further off, killer whales attempt to catch seals, fulmars sweep past paddlers and shags move to safer distances.

The Rubha Cadail light is a 9m white tower down at sea level although its position makes it a conspicuous and important navigation mark.

Protecting the mouth of Loch Kanaird is Isle Martin, 1.6km² and 120m high. A stone cross is to be found at its south end but its houses are on the sheltered east side. There was a herring curing factory in the late 18th century and there has also been a salmon curing house, 33 people being resident at the start of the 20th century although they had all gone by the start of the second world war. One of the more spectacular travellers was a cooper who was miraculously transported to South Rona by the fairies to cut brooms and was then transported back again. The west side of the island includes cliffs of red Torridonian sandstone.

Sound is sheltered by Horse Island and Meall nan Gabhar, although there is no protection for feeding gulls from the attacks of the great skuas trying to take possession of their food. Blackbacked gulls also search for food items to steal. Other notable birdlife is to be found on 60m high Horse Island which is no longer inhabited but has a fish farm. There have been wild goats since 1937. Armada gold was said to have been hidden here in 1588.

The wall of a Pictish tower is to be found to the east of the low red sandstone cliffs of Rubha Dùnan. Another tower is found round the point near Achiltibuie in Badentarbat Bay. The village has a hydroponicum which grows bananas and other exotic fruit and vegetables, a salmon fishing station and a smokehouse for seafood and meat and even used to have a buffalo farm. A ferry service runs across the bay to Tanera Mór, the cabbage patch, and boats also visit the rest of the Summer Isles which number about twenty in total. These consist of Torridonian sandstone covered in

Horse Island and Meall nan Gabhar merge together across Horse Sound

These pale into insignificance against the mainland coast rising steeply up to 743m Ben Mòr Coigach, some of the oldest rocks in the world. To see the mountain full height with a menacing dark blue storm sky behind and just a wisp of white

peat, blooming with flowers in the summer and many are grazed by sheep. Their caves, cliffs and lochans are also home for breeding seabirds, greylag geese, herons, shelducks, fulmars, eider ducks and otters.

Tanera Mór with Eilean Dubh to its southwest

cloud peeling off its pointed peak like cigarette smoke is a magnificent sight.

Culnacraig is the start of the road again and the Coigach mountains gradually withdraw. Beyond the 25m high cliffs of Rubha Dubh Ard, Horse

Most interest, however, relates to the largest of the islands at 3.3km², Tanera Mór rising up to 122m at Meall Mor. The Anchorage is one of the best natural harbours in the northwest. A fishing station was founded in 1783 at Tigh-an-Quay, thriving on the plentiful herring in the sea with up to 200 ships in the bay at a time and exports going as far as the West Indies. A century later there were 119 people resident, just enough for an illicit whisky distilling business, but the last tenants left in 1931. From 1934 to 1944 its most important resident lived here, farmer and pioneer ecologist Dr Fraser Darling who wrote his *Natural History in the Highlands and Islands* and the *Island Years* about his time here, recording 43 bird species. Human life returned to the island again in the 1960s when the schoolhouse and some cottages were restored, there now being permanent residents again and 250 sheep. The Summer Isles Post Office issues legal stamps for carriage to the mainland and the Offshore Islands Philatelic Society is run from here. There are marine farms and the rich plant life continues to the thrift and luxuriant lichens on the rocks. Sailing is another local activity.

Streams start north–northeast past the Summer Isles from HW Dover +0500 and south–southwest from HW Dover –0100 at up to 3km/h.

Across Dorney Sound an aerial is located on 203m Meall an Fheadain.

Caolas Eilean Ristol cuts inside 71m high Isle Ristol and is frequented by cormorants and curlews. There are moorings for fishing boats in the channel while smaller craft can get into the natural harbour at Old Dornie and land at the jetty or moor in the shallows. A drying reef from the island to the mainland allows passage for paddlers at most times into Loch an Alltain Duibh. The island's 18th-century herring curing factory did not survive, but there is a smokehouse at Altandhu on the mainland and a marine farm close by although there is also a less attractive slide of rubbish down into the sea, a car included in the debris.

The road ends at Reiff where Reiff Bay is exposed to the prevailing wind. On a clear day the peaks of Lewis in the Outer Hebrides can be seen 60km to the west.

The coast to Rubha Coigeach is rugged and broken up by the inlets of Camas Eilean Ghlais and Faochag Bay, frequented by black guillemots, cormorants and oystercatchers. The cliffs are not particularly high, being 18m at the point, but the area is remote. At the point the streams flow north–northeast from HW Dover –0515 and south–southwest from HW Dover at up to 5km/h. Once into Enard Bay, the prevailing wind will produce a swell which may be surfable.

Looking from Altandhu over Isle Ristol and the Summer Isles with Strathnasheallag, Fisherfield, Letterewe and Flowerdale Forests and the coast to Rubha Reidh

The entrance to Loch Inver is sheltered by Soyea Island which has a number of islets at its east end. Bo Caolas is the most dangerous to shipping and is marked with a green post and cage structure. Seals use this as a popular area for hauling out.

Loch Roe forms another sheltered inlet before Achmelvich Bay with its white sand. Much more conspicuous is the approach to Bay of Clachtoll. A large wedge of red rock has slid some distance down its sloping strata, leaving an imposing vertical sided doorway or so it seems from the distance. Razorbills swim about, unimpressed.

Between the houses of Clachtoll and Stoer on the B869 is a broch overlooking the Bay of Stoer with its white sand and caves. Wildlife seen here could be anything from falcons to whales. The hamlet of Balchladich overlooks Balchladich Bay off which is an area with a local magnetic anomaly of up to 15°.

Achnahaird Bay is a marine farm site despite most of the bay being subject to dune conditions or drying sand.

Enard Bay has a backdrop of peaks which few others can approach, not just the number and height but also the distinctive shapes. At the southern end is Ben Mór Coigach while other notable peaks include Stac Pollaidh at 613m, 769m Cùl Beag, 849m Cùl Mor, 731m Suilven and 846m Canisp. These are salient features of the Inverpolly

The dramatic skyline of peaks to the east of Enard Bay, including Quinag, Suilven, Canisp and Cùl Mor, rising up to Ben More Assynt

National Nature Reserve, Britain's second largest, covering 109km². Many of the summits are of white quartzite covering red Torridonian sandstone on a base of Lewisian gneiss, the oldest British rock at 1,400,000,000 to 2,800,000,000 years. As well as the summits, cliffs and features of geological interest at a high level there is woodland, moorland and bog, almost uninhabited and attractive to a range of wildlife including golden eagles. A network of lochs are drained into Garvie Bay by the Abhainn Osgaig and Polly Bay by the River Polly.

Beyond Green Island there is a dun on Rubha Pollaidh. Eilean Mór, Fraochlan, Eilean Mòineseach and what is virtually another island, Rubh' a' Bhrocaire, shelter Loch an Eisg-brachaidh, giving a calm landing where the road meets the shore. Stunted birches and pines also derive enough shelter to take a foothold here.

Soyea Island and assorted reefs make entry to Loch Inver more hazardous for fishing boats

Snipe might be seen near Cluas Deas. From here to Point of Stoer the flows start north–northeast from HW Dover –0515 and south–southwest from HW Dover at up to 5km/h.

Stoer Head lighthouse is set on the cliffs, a 14m white tower above an assortment of rock slabs ditched in the sea. Geodh' nan Uan tumbles down from the cliffs between assorted caves, but the primary feature of interest is the Old Man of Stoer, a 60m detached column of rock, first climbed in 1966. It takes its name from the Norse staurr, stake. Puffins might be seen on the water and skate below the surface. A race runs off Point of Stoer.

Although the Lewisian gneiss, which forms the shore of Eddrachillis Bay, is some of the oldest rock it has managed to resist the elements remarkably well. Geodha an Leth-roinn is another place where a stream has failed to carve itself a valley in the rock before dropping to the sea.

Rubh'an Dùnain has a cave, a natural arch and a dun but approach needs to be made with care as it also has a reefbreak where the larger swells rise and break quickly without warning. It may be safer to land behind the jetty in Bay of Culkein and walk along from Culkein.

Eilean Chrona, at 22m high, is a miniature of 100m high Oldany Island. Both have fish farms and lobster pots set around them. Oldany is used for grazing and is separated from the mainland by a narrow sheltered channel in an archipelago of islets and drying channels. Small fishing boats are pulled up on rocks covered with a thick layer of seaweed like green moss and lobster pots are piled up. Seals and herons wait about and would probably not turn down any reject fish morsels. The only trees around are, inevitably, stunted.

Stoer Head lighthouse atop wave-battered cliffs 3km south of Point of Stoer

Loch Kirkaig is the mouth of the River Kirkaig which drains another network of lochs and forms the southern boundary of Sutherland. The name sounds odd for the most northerly part of the country but it was the south land for the Vikings.

The hamlet of Culkein Drumbeg overlooks Loch Dhrombaig, the first of several inlets along the shore, Loch Nedd, Camas nan Bad and Loch na Droighniche. It is not the shoreline which is impressive, however, but what stands above. This section of coast is dominated by the peaks of Quinag, Sàil Garbh being the highest at 808m but 776m Sàil Gorm being closer to the water and only

The stark needle of the Old man of Stoer

Looking north through the archipelago towards Handa with Oldany Island on the left

2km from Loch a' Chàirn Bhàin which runs inland from the southeast corner of Eddrachilis Bay.

The eastern side of Eddrachillis Bay is littered with islands with heather slopes and stunted trees and bushes in places. 41m high Calbha Beag has grassy slopes and caves at its south end, being overlooked by the slightly larger and higher Calbha Mór.

The Badcall Islands are in two groups. The southwest group comprise Meall Mór and Meall Beag. The larger northeast group are bunched in the mouth of Badcall Bay. Seals haul out on the northeast corner of Eilean na Rainich, facing Eilean na Bearachd and Ceannamhór, the highest island at 48m. 31m high Eilean Garbh divides into two at high tide, giving a passage through in suitable conditions.

A hut circle site is located behind the next bay, but the coast is too rugged and rocky to permit landing under most conditions.

Eilean a' Bhuic is distinguished from the islet off Rubh' Aird an t-Sionnaich by its 17m height and larger size although both have clear passages inside and similar layouts, especially at high tide. After Eilean a' Bhuic, passage across the mouth of Scourie Bay, at the back of which the A894 runs, leads into the Sound of Handa. Although sheltered from most winds, there are flows through the sound at up to 6km/h, starting northwards at HW Dover +0400 and southwards at HW Dover −0200. There are heavy overfalls over Bodha Morair and over Bodha Iasg through the Dorus Mór. Flows are a couple of hours earlier than the main coastal flows. It may be possible to find eddies on the downstream side of Handa on the second half of the flow.

A midden of limpet shells between Port an Eilein and Traigh an Teampaill shows that there has long been human occupation of Handa. The island was used extensively as a graveyard for people on the mainland to prevent corpses being disturbed by wolves. Until the middle of the 19th century there were seven families with the oldest woman as queen and the men having a daily parliament to discuss the work to be done. They lived on potatoes, fish and birds' eggs until the 1848 potato famine, when they emigrated to America.

In 1962 the 3km² island became a nature reserve and RSPB seafowl sanctuary with the only inhabitable building being refurbished as an ornithological base with a warden in the summer.

The island rises steadily from the sound to 123m high Sithean Mór almost on the far side of the island, the north and west coasts having red and brown Torridonian sandstone cliffs up to 110m high on a Lewisian gneiss base. These include Great Stack, three pillars with 12,000 breeding birds, horizontal white lines of guillemots, kittiwakes, razorbills, fulmars, puffins, gulls, shags and other seabirds, especially during the breeding season. 141 species have been recorded, 35 breeding. The last white-tailed sea eagles nested here in 1864. The Arctic skuas have been resident from 1968, the year after the death of an albino oystercatcher, now in the Royal Scottish Museum in Edinburgh. Other species present include meadow pipits, wheatears, skylarks and curlews. The rough pasture has been used for grazing sheep and for rabbits and there is plenty of peat bog. 216 species of plant have been recorded including heather, deer grass, purple moor grass, lodgepole pine, alders, heath spotted orchid, bog asphodel, northern marsh orchid, lovage, pale butterwort, pyramidal bugle, eyebright, devils bit, ragged robin, biting stonecrop and over a hundred varieties of moss. There are lobsters offshore. White sand faces the sound. RSPB members may stay in the bothy if booked in advance through the Edinburgh office.

In the prologue to her book, *Something Amazing!*, Rebecca Ridgway opens with the description of a capsize off Handa Island. She also notes that no house in Tarbet has failed to lose at least one of its menfolk to the local waters.

Port of Tarbet is relatively sheltered, offering a small jetty, a limited parking area and a telephone kiosk.

Distance
From Rhue to Tarbet is 86km
Campsites
Ardmair, Brae of Achnahaird, Achmelvich, Clachtoll, Scourie
Youth Hostels
Ullapool, Achininver, Achmelvich Beach
OS 1:50,000 Sheets
9 Cape Wrath
15 Loch Assynt
19 Gairloch and Ullapool
Imray Chart
C67 North Minch and Isle of Lewis (1:155,000)
Admiralty Charts
1785 North Minch – Northern Part (1:100,000)
1794 North Minch – Southern Part (1:100,000)
2500 Approaches to Ullapool (1:25,000)
2501 Summer Isles (1:25,000)
2502 Eddrachilis Bay (1:25,000)
2503 Approaches to Kinlochbervie (1:25,000)
2504 Approaches to Lochinver (1:25,000). Lochinver (1:12,500)
Tidal Constants
Tanera Mór: Dover −0420
Loch Inver: Dover −0420
Badcall Bay: Dover −04 00
Loch Laxford: Dover −0400
Sea Area
Hebrides
Submarine Areas
6 Ewe, 3 Stoer
Rescue
All weather lifeboat: Lochinver
Helicopter: Stornoway
Maritime Rescue Centre
Stornoway, 01851 702013/4

29 SUTHERLAND

The British mainland's highest vertical cliffs and best linked caves

The shelter of Handa Island, Eilean an Aigeich and the Sgeirean Glasa is gradually lost on moving north from Tarbet. Fulmars are the commonest of the circling gulls, but to the southwest the vertical cliffs of Handa can be seen wheeling with flocks of assorted birds.

The coast of dark and rugged rocks is brightened by the red rocks of low Rubha Ruadh. Behind, darker and frequently with heads in the clouds are the summits of 721m Ben Stack, 757m Arkle and 908m Ganu Mór, the highest peak of Foinaven. Cutting in towards them is Loch Laxford. Lax is Norse for salmon and local accents retain a Norse whirr.

Adjacent is Loch Dùghaill. Cormorants and gannets fish off the mouth of the two lochs.

The coast continues steep and rocky to Lochan nam Meallan with hills up to 120m high, while the offshore area is littered with islets, Eilean na Saille the largest at 36m high. The Dubh Sgeirean include 17m high Whale Islet with the Whale Back drying 4m.

Bàgh Loch an Ròin has a narrow exit at the back from Loch an Ròin while Loch Ceann na Saile is almost as tortuous, located to the south of 17m high Glas Leac and Eilean Dubh. Between these two and the bold red Rubha na Leacaig is the mouth of the rather larger Loch Inchard which gives access to Loch Bervie, the main fishing harbour for Kinlochbervie. This stands on the isthmus created by Loch Bervie and Loch Clash, the latter less well sheltered but also used by a few fishing boats. The most northerly port on the west coast, Kinlochbervie is important for the white fish it sends to Aberdeen, Hull, Grimsby and Europe. The port has a rescue-line throwing apparatus.

Eilean an Ròin Mór and Eliean na h-Aiteig seen across the dunes from Oldshoremore

Loch Clash with Eilean a' Chonnaidh beyond. The leading light is for Loch Bervie, across the isthmus to the left of the picture and approached from the opposite direction

The mouth of Loch Clash is protected from the northwest by 52m high Eilean a' Chonnaidh and 5m high Na Cluasnadh.

Oldshoremore is where Hakon began his invasion of Scotland in 1263, providing the first sheltered landing on the west coast. Nevertheless, it produces surf on westerly or northerly swells,

A race forms between Eilean an Ròin Mór and the mainland

best at the higher end of the tide. As ever, it has plenty of midges and fish boxes.

37m high Eilean na h-Aiteig has vertical cliffs on its southeast side, providing a divider from the bay at Oldshore Beg with its dune system. On a rather larger scale, 63m high Eilean an Ròin Mór and Eilean an Ròin Beag run out from the shore to give more shelter, a race running through inside the former. Birdlife includes razorbills, guillemots, black guillemots, puffins, oystercatchers, eider ducks and blackbacked gulls.

Port Chaligaig has a pier which provides scant shelter, as evidenced by the mush of rotting weed lying amongst the rocks. The picnic tables and hamlet of Droman are little reason for landing, but this inlet is important as the last road access point before the Kyle of Durness, a serious and committing section of coast.

There are now continuous cliffs to Rubh' a Bhuachaille. Flows start north to Cape Wrath at HW Dover –0530 and south at HW Dover +0045 at up to 3km/h, but an eddy on the southgoing tide means that the flow inshore is almost continuously northwards.

The final offshore rocks here are 10m high Dubh Sgeir and 19m high Seanna Sgeir protecting Bàgh Sheigra.

The distinctive feature of Rubh' a Bhuachaille is Am Buachaille, the guardian, a 76m high stack which looks like a rigged sailing ship when seen from the southwest. Offshore is 45m high Am Balg where puffins and guillemots breed, a rock which is reminiscent of the Armed Knight off Land's End at the other extremity of this coast.

Birds are usually the only residents at Sandwood Bay, one of the finest beaches in Britain. It is 6km from the nearest road, part of the track being driveable but the remainder having to be walked. Some surfers are prepared to make the effort as the bay receives more swell than any other Scottish beach and it has nine bars and reefs which work at all stages of the tide. Lón Mòr drains Sandwood Loch through the pale pink sand and marram grass

Droman is the last road access point on the west coast but there is little protection from westerly winds which drive straight onto the boulders

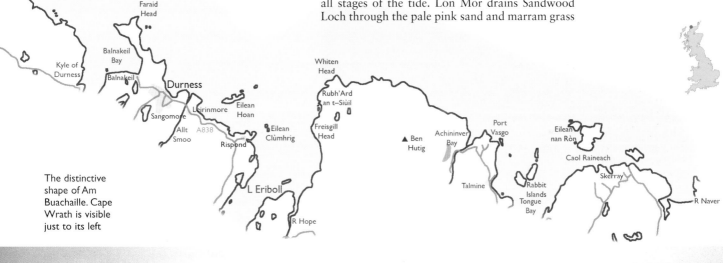

The distinctive shape of Am Buachaille. Cape Wrath is visible just to its left

Sandwood Bay, one of the finest beaches and best surf breaks in Britain with Foinaven beyond

of this fine dune system. The currents are strong and the waters chilly. The ghost of a bearded sailor might be seen and it is the haunt of mermaids. Indeed, local shepherd Sandy Gunn met a mermaid here on 5th January 1900. Although this is not the most obvious place in the world for mermaids and the beginning of January not the usual season, the meeting surely had nothing to do with this being the sobering up period after Hogmanay.

The coast continues with red vertical sandstone cliffs and rugged coves. Inland is one of the largest areas of uninhabited land in Britain. Like tundra, the Parbh is 260km² of peat bog, heather, scrub and oak.

Cape Wrath, seen from the race in calm conditions and at neap tides

Cape Wrath takes its name from the Norse hvarf, turning point, where the west coast of Britain meets the north coast. Nevertheless, the usually assumed meaning of the name is not inappropriate. This is the windiest corner of Britain and catches all winds except those between southwest and southeast. It is almost always turbulent, dangerously so with strong winds. For the last kilometre to the cape there is a race inshore and usually clapotis from the swells to foil any attempt to paddle inside the race. Any inshore passage should be made in settled conditions with neap tides. The 110m high red headland is topped by the 20m white lighthouse tower built by Robert Stevenson in 1828, from where there are views to the Hebrides and Orkney. Those wishing to experience the view usually have to cross the Kyle of Durness by ferry in the summer and then travel in a minibus for 18km along a section of road which is not connected to the rest of the road system.

Immediately after the corner there are arches at the start of a coast which is well endowed with cliffs all the way to Dunnet Head, albeit frequently indented. The easterly stream starts at HW Dover +0415 and the westerly stream at HW Dover −0145 at up to 6km/h, although there are eddies locally and sometimes there are temporary local flows up to 1km/h from northeasterly to southeasterly. Their cause is not known.

The first landing place is a jetty at Clais Chàrnach. The first beach is where the Kearvaig River enters.

Clò Mór, the highest cliffs in mainland Britain. The white is mostly guano

Flows begin east from Stack Clò Kearvaig at HW Dover +0545 and west at HW Dover −0030. The stack is two pillars with a fallen block wedged between them. They would look more impressive were it not for the cliffs behind them, the highest vertical cliffs in mainland Britain, rising 260m directly from the water. There are interesting plants such as the Scots primrose which has pink or purple flowers and is not found south of here. There are birds of prey and huge colonies of nesting seabirds which create a deafening din. Even at some distance there is a dizzying wheel of fulmars and guillemots with collisions not unknown. Seals keep a much quieter presence.

Off Cléit Dubh, the black cliff, is An Garbh-eilean, 33m high but being reduced in size by bombing. A target buoy is moored off it and live rounds are fired from ships and from aircraft which fly in from as far away as Germany and the army also fire on the 34km² range. The danger area stretches from Cape Wrath to Faraid Head and the range is the largest of its kind in Europe. When in use there are red flags or vertical pairs of red lights. Navigation is permitted but not cruising. A flag at half mast warns of being in the exercise area. The pattern of use is irregular but usually quiet during the lambing season, April to mid-May, although guillemots and razorbills have been deserting their nesting sites because of the bombing and have been found with blast concussion.

The coast then becomes white marble with red veins.

The Kyle of Durness drains for 7km, barely perceptible currents flooding from HW Dover +0300 and ebbing from HW Dover −0315. There are weak streams across the entrance. The east side

Faraid Head, seen across the moorland from Leirinmore

of the entrance opens into Balnakeil Bay, edged with dunes which cross the neck of Faraid Head.

Balnakeil church was built in 1619 and the churchyard contains a monument to the Gaelic bard Rob Donn. A skull and crossbones in the church wall are a rather different monument for highwayman Donald MacLeod who was said to have killed at least eighteen people, and to have paid at least a thousand pounds for this special position to prevent desecration of his grave.

Only twice this sum was paid for the buildings which form Balnakeil craft village. Built as an early warning station, they were never used as such and since 1984 they have housed sixteen businesses with horn work, paintings, jewellery, knitwear, pottery, winemaking, candles, leatherwork, woodwork, bookbinding, metalwork, printing, picture framing, photography, stonework, weaving, sculpting in bronze and aluminium, fish box furniture and driftwood sculptures.

100m high Faraid Head has a nesting puffin colony. Strong streams sweep round the head and indented cliffs follow to An t-Aigeach. Puffins and other seabirds occupy the 51m pinnacle of Clach Mhòr na Faraid at the end of a line of rocks which run out from the shore like jagged canine teeth. A less conspicuous second line follows at Aodann Mhór, including the dun site at Seanachaisteal, old castle.

Durness, on the A838, comes from the Norse dyrnes or dyra ness, deer, beast or wolf promontory. These days the area has crofting and sheep farming while a visitor centre has displays on the landscape and people of the northwest. There is a highland gathering in July and surfers gather when the swells into Sango Bay are from the north.

Geodha Smoo takes its name from the Norse smjuga, a cleft or creek. The Allt Smoo has cut a straight channel through the limestone rocks. More importantly, it has produced the three magnificent caverns of Smoo Cave. The first chamber is 60m x 34m where the river drops 24m down a shaft. The second cavern is flooded and may only be explored in a rubber raft. The final 37m chamber is dry again and has a large opening at the high tide mark. The caves are floodlit and have been made accessible to the public. In the past they have been associated with both smugglers and the supernatural. There is a helicopter landing site nearby.

Eilean Hoan, at 24m high, was used as a local burial site to avoid disturbance by wolves. In 1840 there were four families living here but now it is only used for grazing. In 1980 it was bought by the RSPB, without whose permission landing is not permitted. There are great northern divers and up to 400 barnacle geese in winter. The reserve is a nesting site for eider ducks, oystercatchers, ringed plovers, lapwings, arctic terns, lesser blackbacked gulls, black guillemots, storm petrels and many other species.

Currents to 1km/h begin southeast at HW Dover +0420 and northwest at HW Dover −0150. The corresponding times for weak flows in and out of Loch Eriboll at An t-Aigeach are HW Dover +0300 and −0315, respectively. The two halves of 13m high Eilean Clùimhrig stand off the point at the entrance to the loch.

Despite its sheltered position, Rispond Bay is a surf break. It needs to be approached from the calm waters of the hidden harbour, but parking is difficult without causing obstructions for the residents.

Loch Eriboll's name comes from the Norse for a home on a gravelly beach. During the Highland Clearances the population were moved from the fertile east side to the rocky west side, where they remain today. It is one of the deepest sea lochs, to 110m, and sheltered by steep hills. This is where Atlantic convoys gathered in the second world war, to whose crews it was Loch 'Orrible. At the end of the war it was where the German U boat fleet surrendered. These days it is the gathering point for nothing more disturbing than great northern divers prior to their spring passage to Iceland.

Beyond the head of the loch are Foinaven, Arkle and Meall Horn while 927m Ben Hope lies due south beyond Loch Hope, from which flows the River Hope.

Whitewashed cottages around the small east facing harbour at Rispond

Caves and arches don't come much better than at Rubh'Ard an t-Siùil. Eilean Hoan is visible through the centre arch

Geodha an t-Srathain is one of several waterfalls down the pink cliffs. There are caves in 43m high Freisgill Head, but they are totally eclipsed by those on Rubh'Ard an t-Siùil which are possibly the best linked caves and arches on the British mainland. A large cave leads into a smaller one which turns a corner and disappears into the darkness. A cloistered exit leads through arches to a deep round cave with three large exits. Seabirds nest on ledges. There is something disturbing about watching a brown shape on a ledge gradually unroll to reveal an alligator shape of head with amber eyes glowing in the darkness as the slapping of waves echoes around, the very stuff of horror stories even if it is only a cormorant.

Flows are weak across the mouth of Loch Eriboll but increase to 6km/h around Whiten Head, flows starting east to Strathy Point at HW Dover +0545 and west at HW Dover −0030.

There are confused seas off the head. Cliffs reach up to 160m high, white crumbled quartz and dark slate coloured with red veins. In reasonable conditions there are passages inside a series of rocks off the coast, of which the most notable are the white stratified quartz pillars of the Stacan Bána rising 54m and 46m from the sea.

6km of cliffs to 240m height follow to Achininver but there are now plenty of lobster pots and small boats out checking them, so the coast is not as deserted as might otherwise be the case. Inland, the ground rises to 408m Ben Hutig.

Achininver Bay is at the mouth of the Strath Melness Burn where the *MV Sealagair* is stranded on the beach.

Port Vasgo provides a sheltered landing point with road access. Inland is an aerial, but it is not as conspicuous as the one on Ben Tongue on the

Stacan Bána, add a further dash of character to Whiten Head

east side of the Kyle of Tongue, another Norse name. The kyle opens out into Tongue Bay at the north end and is littered with islands. Sgeir an Oir rises to 43m with a natural arch in the centre. The Rabbit Islands were Eilean na Gaeil, the island of strangers, used by the Norsemen. In 1745 a French sloop went aground on them with gold for Prince Charlie. These days the islands are a surf break with a dune system and numerous breeding birds.

The largest island is Eilean nan Ròn or Roan, seal island, red sandstone rising to 75m and extended westward by Eilean Iosal and Meall Thailm. There are several caves and arches and a secret entrance to an inner sanctuary. Ruins remain from when the island was abandoned in 1938. A century earlier the residents made their living by drying fish in the salty wind. Mackerel are to be found in the local waters now.

Caol Raineach, between Eilean nan Ròn and the mainland, flows at up to 4km/h. At HW Dover +0545 the southgoing stream west of Eilean nan Ròn divides to flow east through Coal Raineach and south into the Kyle of Tongue. At HW Dover −0310 this southgoing flow meets the flow ebbing from the Kyle of Tongue to produce turbulence between Eilean nan Ròn and the Rabbit Islands. At HW Dover +0030 the ebb stream from the Kyle of Tongue meets the westgoing stream through Caol Raineach to produce dangerous turbulence off Sleiteil Rocks. At HW Dover +0300 the westgoing stream through Caol Raineach divides to flood south into the Kyle of Tongue and west northwest to the sea when the turbulence subsides.

The first road access after Tongue Bay is Skerray Bay, sheltered on the west by land and on the northeast by a rock platform.

Distance
From Tarbet to Clashbuie is 77km
Campsites
Scourie, Durness, Talmine, Bettyhill
Youth Hostels
Achmelvich Beach, Durness, Tongue
OS 1:50,000 Sheets
9 Cape Wrath
10 Strath Naver
Imray Charts
C67 North Minch and Isle of Lewis (1:155,000)
C68 Cape Wrath to Wick and the Orkney Islands (1:160,000)
Admiralty Charts
1785 North Minch – Northern Part (1:100,000)
1954 Cape Wrath to Pentland Firth Including the Orkney Islands (1:200,000)
2076 Loch Eriboll (1:17,500)
2503 Approaches to Kinlochbervie (1:25,000).
Kinlochbervie (1:10,000)
Tidal Constants
Loch Laxford: Dover −0400
Loch Bervie: HW Dover −0350, LW Dover −0400
Kyle of Durness: HW Dover −0340, LW Dover −0320
Portnancon: Dover −0310
Sea Areas
Hebrides, Fair Isle
Range
Cape Wrath
Submarine Area
3 Stoer
Rescue
All weather lifeboats: Lochinver, Thurso
Maritime Rescue Centre
Stornoway, 01851 702013/4
Shetland, 01595 692976

Dramatic coastline to the east of Whiten Head

30 NORTH HIGHLAND

Prime Scottish surfing venues

We stood wi' heads bowed in prayer
While factors burned our cottages fair.
The flames licked the clear mountain air
And many were dead by the morning.

Jim McLean

A gap in the rock shelf on the northeast side of Skerray Bay allows an exit to Caol Beag which runs inside Neave or Coomb Island, a 70m high structure with pink quartz and mica slate in nearly vertical stripes. It was the site of the earliest Christian settlement in the area and St Cormaic is said to have been heard preaching by the congregation on the mainland across Caol Beag.

The cliffy coast is indented as far as Strathy Point with weak streams inshore.

Torrisdale Bay seen from Bettyhill

A distinctive stack pierced by a large round hole in Port a' Chinn

Torrisdale Bay is fed by the River Borgie and the River Naver with its salmon. Between the two rivers is the Invernaver Nature Reserve with fine dunes and many interesting plants. Birdlife includes eider ducks, oystercatchers, fulmars, guillemots, black guillemots and cormorants. In bad weather the sea breaks well out. There is a beachbreak with a good right on rivermouth bars,

best on the lower half of the tide although quicksand is a danger.

Between Torrisdale and Bettyhill there are a number of antiquities, a dun, a chambered cairn, a broch and a settlement.

Bettyhill was set up as a fishing and agricultural centre during the Highland Clearances and named after Elizabeth, Countess of Sutherland, wife of the Duke of Sutherland who was responsible for many of the evictions. Some of the worst atrocities were committed in the Strathnaver clearances of 1814 and 1819, recorded in the Strathnaver museum in Farr's 18th-century former church. Another room is dedicated to Clan MacKay and the churchyard contains the Pictish Farr Stone, a fine example of early Christian Celtic art.

Semiprecious stones can be found in Farr Bay where the surf works to produce lefts on the top half of the tide and rights at low tide.

Farr Point is steep with caves, rising to 110m Ard Farr. A natural arch under an isthmus marks the position of the remains of Borve Castle, a mediaeval stronghold of Clan MacKay.

An aerial on Cnoc Mór faces out over Kirtomy Bay to 140m high Kirtomy Point, the first of several such points.

Port Mór after Ardmore Point has some caves and a large flying buttress. It also has fish nets staked out, as has Port a' Chinn. The latter has quite an unusual appearance with an assortment of net drying poles on top of the cliff and an aerial ropeway to get the catch up to Armadale. The bay is studded with rocks and pointed stacks, including one with large holes, one of which can be paddled through, the structure being more hole than stack.

Round the corner is Armadale Bay with its best surf at high tide when it gives lefts and rights.

Strathy Point projects 4km out from the coast. The most conspicuous feature on its west side is Boursa Island, covered with grass like a pitched roof.

Strathy Point is often subject to local windy conditions. The lighthouse on the point, opened in 1958, stands as a 14m white tower on a 35m high headland yet its windows have been hit by waves during gales. During better weather it is possible to see Cape Wrath, Dunnet Head, Orkney, a natural

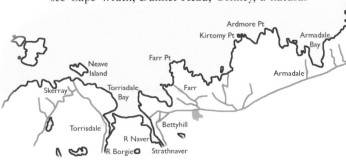

arch and a pile of rubbish tipped down the side of the cliff to fall into the sea. It is on a migratory bird route, best in May and September. Gannets and skuas nest on the cliffs and puffins, storm petrels and blackbacked gulls might be seen. In June and July it has rare flowering plants, not to mention insect-eating specimens. Whales, dolphins and basking sharks may be seen, especially after August. A sheltered route passes between Garbh-eilean and the point itself, but there are flows up to 6km/h off the point and a tide race and overfalls where the nearly continuous northgoing flow, resulting from the eddy on the east side of the promontory, meets the main longshore flow. Out to sea, the eastgoing flow begins at HW Dover –0610 and the westgoing flow at Dover HW at up to 4km/h.

Caves dot the cliffs at intervals down the east side of the point and there is a jetty halfway along although the climb up to the road is long and steep. The sea is sheltered from the prevailing wind and is inhabited by razorbills, rizostoma jellyfish and porpoises, to name a few species.

The River Strathy enters Strathy Bay past sandhills up to 60m high. Although protected from westerly swells, surfers may find good rights off the rocks at the east end. Strathy has some of its buildings thatched, now rare in the Highlands.

The 90m cliffs of Baligill Head are topped by Baligill and a couple of fort sites, one Iron Age, while there is another beyond the 80m cliffs of Rubha na Cloiche.

Portskerra at low tide

are found in the bay, together with the inevitable midges. On the southeast side of the bay is Bighouse, ancestral home of the Clan MacKay, overlooked by 96m Rubha an Tuir. Low hills with coarse grass and heather occupy the coast to Sandside Head where there is a 44m overhanging cliff guarded by the Stags, a pair of offshore rocks. There are holes in the cliff strata and incipient caves. Even when Sandside Bay is turbulent, there

Rubha na Cloiche

Portskerra was a fishing village created at the time of the Clearances, well sheltered from the prevailing wind by Rubha Bhrá, the red rock, but with boats having to be negotiated through the rocks and pulled up the steep grassy cliff.

Melvich Bay is the mouth of the Halladale River. Melvich stands behind orange sandhills up to 35m high and has rescue apparatus and pony trekking. The surf gives a good right off the rocks at the east end of the bay, but is protected by Strathy Point from westerly swells. Crabs, lobsters and mackerel

Sandside Head leans out over the foam carpet at its base

is a calm jetty landing at Fresgoe. The bay is the mouth of the Sandside Burn and has a good dune system. It catches surf from northerly or large westerly swells. Because of low tide rocks it is better to surf at the higher end of the tide where

there are lefts off a reefbreak and both lefts and rights on bars at the beach.

Reay was rebuilt in 1740 when the village was inundated by dunes. The buildings from that date include the whitewashed church which has the pulpit facing the raised laird's loft where there is a gallery for the laird's family.

In 1797 the schoolmaster in Reay watched a mermaid combing her hair, but the report did not appear in the *Times* for another dozen years as it would not have been good for his professional reputation.

There is a lobster fishery in the bay, but a point of concern with the water and the beach is the fact that radioactive particles are being washed up and deposited from a leaking 60m shaft at the nuclear power station. The shaft is used for dumping waste radioactive material and resolving the problem was estimated at £500,000,000.

From Isauld to Brims Ness there are low, dark, vertical cliffs. As with so much of Caithness, they have a sloping rock chamfer at the bottom, making landing very difficult. Flows along the coast run at up to 1km/h.

oystercatchers and seals might be seen in the bay while gannets and possibly the blow of a whale might appear further out to sea. Less attractive is the rubbish being tipped down the side of Ushat Head. The head is 35m high but the cliffs reduce towards Brims Ness.

Brims Ness, Norse for surf point, is aptly named, offering surf when all other breaks are flat. There is tidal disturbance where the Atlantic flow runs over the Whale's Back at up to 6km/h. Like Thurso East, the break has the strata in a sawtooth formation, rising gently then dropping vertically a number of times in an irregular pattern moving shorewards. The Bowl gives fast rights to more than 2m, best towards the top of a tide. The Cove is a slightly slower version while the Left is a left point break with rides to 100m on the lower half

The nuclear site at Dounreay with the original reactor sphere on the left

It was on the low cliffs between the castle and chambered cairn at Lower Dounreay that the Dounreay Nuclear Power Development Establishment was set up, Britain's only prototype and the world's first fast reactor power station, closed in 1977 after 18 years of use, having been superseded by a bigger prototype fast reactor in 1974. The site is marked by the distinctive 58m diameter pale blue reactor sphere on the cliffs and seven orange flashing lights along the shore. Its purpose was to develop technology and the establishment has become the area's major employer. It has been proposed as a burial site for nuclear waste, a strategy which must be enhanced by the fact that it is so remote from protesters, but the area already suffers from a cluster of childhood cancer and leukaemia. In 1995 there was a brief foray into wavepower when Osprey 1, the first commercial sized wave-power generator, was installed off the coast. It broke up and sank only a few days later.

The nuclear establishment has its own airfield then the cliffs have nothing of note other than the occasional cairn or broch site until a heavily fenced establishment at Crosskirk with two aerials, one of which is 220m high. Forss Water flows into Crosskirk Bay past another broch site, St Mary's Well and St Mary's chapel. This may be 12th century and has doors which are low and taper at the top in the Irish style. Black guillemots,

of the tide. Approach to the breaks is through the yard of a longsuffering farmer. The adjacent Brims Castle is still occupied by the Sinclair family and there is a chapel site by the point.

The cliffs gradually increase in height and become steeper again with a couple of fort sites. Ness of Litter has caves and disused quarries on the side of 115m Brims Hill and there are more caves beyond Spear Head. Blowholes are present in the cliffs. Holborn Head has a viewpoint but needs to be treated with care. In 1842 Commander Michael Slater fell to his death while setting up a survey theodolite station for the Hydrographic Office.

The successive headlands of Ness of Litter, Spear Head and Holborn Head

Forss Water empties over the stones into Crosskirk Bay. The ducks are eiders

Streams start east–northeast from Holborn Head at HW Dover –0600 and west–southwest from HW Dover at up to 4km/h although they only reach half this rate across Thurso Bay and Dunnet Bay. Eddy streams start north at HW Dover +0530. In the northern part of Scrabster Road there is an outgoing undertow with easterly weather.

A 17m white light tower stands on what is confusingly called Holbornhead but more clearly understood as Little Head. Scrabster was a 19th-century port for exporting flagstones and is now a vehicle ferry terminal at the end of the A9 for Stromness (Orkney) and summer services to Thorshavn (Faeroes), Bergen (Norway), Hanstholm (Denmark) and Seydisfjörder (Iceland). Port facilities range from oil storage tanks and a lifeboat to a fishmarket and icehouse, lobster creels and salmon nets, fish landed including coalfish, cod, conger eels, pollack, skate and halibut to over 100kg.

Thurso is the most northerly town on the British mainland, taking its name from Thorsa, Norse Gaelic for the mouth of Thor's river, the River Thurso entering here. Although dating from Viking times with the remains of Scrabster Castle from 1328 or earlier to the west of the new town, it was not laid out in its grid pattern until the early 19th century by Sir John Sinclair, whose statue stands in Sir John Square. It was then that Thurso became a flagstone exporting town. The town tripled in size in the 1950s with the development of Dounreay. St Peter's church, used until 1832, was built in the 13th century with much rebuilt in the 17th century. Many former aspects of the vicinity, the Ulbster Stone, the Pictish relic with carved symbols, agricultural and domestic life, local trades, crafts and the room of an old Caithness cottage are to be found in the Thurso Heritage Museum and the Royal Hotel has a whisky museum. The town also boasts the only indoor heated swimming pool on the north coast. There are also glass workshops.

Thurso is a world championships surfing venue. Thurso Reef or Sewer Pipeline gives lefts and rights in small swells but only rights with big swells. Seabirds gather around the outfall pipe to feed. Thurso East, Castle Reef or the Mecca Break is the classic, a flat paddle out then rights with long tubes onto the reef, working at all states but best at the top of the flood. It has been surfed above 4m. Maximum northerly swells cause the two reefbreaks to close out. In this situation a bombora forms in the middle of Thurso Bay but it has never been ridden. The River Thurso brings in a strata of brown peaty water. Only the big waves suck up water from the bottom so there is the novelty of waves colour coded for size, the biggest waves being a suitable brown.

A disused canon overlooks Thurso East in front of Thurso East Castle, a substantial ruin built in the 17th century for the 6th Earl Sinclair and largely rebuilt in 1872. A little further on, Harold's Tower marks the grave of Earl Harold, the 12th-century ruler of part of Caithness, Orkney and Shetland.

Caves and clear water are to be found at the foot of Clardon Hill, marked by a range of radio and radar masts and a sphere. Tank traps are placed beyond Methow Hillock around Murkle Bay and the area is difficult to access, of concern to surfers who wish to try the lefts which run at Nothing Left, Silos and the Pole in northerly or westerly

Thurso East on a day when no exaggeration of wave size was required

swells and off the Spur when there are large swells from those directions. A wreck remains on the Spur from a boat which didn't pick the right wave and the cries of curlews set a forlorn mood. A beacon in Murkle Bay marks the launching point of a submarine power cable to Hoy.

The rock platform continues for 3km until Castlehill where there is a small harbour, used for salmon netting and pleasure craft, fish nets being staked out in Dunnet Bay in several places. Castletown was developed on a grid in the 19th century when the now disused quarry was opened. Flagstones were exported south and even to India, Australia and New Zealand although, square flags still edge many of the local fields as walls. There have been few trees on the north coast but the woods here were planted in 1824 by James Traill who founded the quarries. There is a Castlehill Flagstone Industry interpretive trail, including a small conical tower amongst the local brochs.

Distance
From Clashbuie to Castlehill is 60km
Campsites
Bettyhill, Melvich, Reay, Thurso, Dunnet
Youth Hostels
Tongue, John o' Groats
OS 1:50,000 Sheets
10 Strath Naver
11 Thurso and Dunbeath
12 Thurso and Wick
Imray Charts
C23 Firth of Forth to Moray Firth (1:250,000)
C68 Cape Wrath to Wick and the Orkney Islands (1:160,000)
Admiralty Charts
1462 Harbours on the North and East Coasts of Scotland. Scrabster Harbour (1:10,000)
1954 Cape Wrath to Pentland Firth Including the Orkney Islands (1:200,000)
2162 Pentland Firth and Approaches (1:50,000)
Tidal Constants
Portnancon: Dover –0310
Scrabster: HW Dover –0240, LW Dover –0230
Sea Area
Fair Isle
Rescue
All weather lifeboat: Thurso
Maritime Rescue Centre
Shetland, 01595 692976

31 CAITHNESS

Britain's most ferocious sea currents

Hear, Land o' Cakes, and brither Scots,
Frae Maidenkirk to Johhny Groat's; –
If there's a hole in a' your coats,
I rede you tent it;
A chiel's amang you takin' notes,
And, faith, he'll prent it!

Robert Burns

From Castlehill a magnificent 3km sweep of sandy beach runs up the east side of Dunnet Bay, backed by an extensive dune system. The bay catches westerly and northerly swells, giving surf breaks along the bars on the beach with lefts at the south end and rights at the north. There is a disused airfield behind the dunes at the end. The public tend to use the north end with its carpark and natural history displays but there is plenty of room for all, including horses from the pony trekking centre at Dunnet, where there is also a furniture manufacturer, Wooden Ewe. Mary Ann's Cottage is a traditional Caithness croft house with assorted relics and vintage farm machinery on show.

In the bay and around to Dunnet Head there are numerous seabirds, terns, black guillemots, fulmars, cormorants, razorbills, guillemots, skuas, blackbacked gulls and puffins while wildlife in the sea includes rhizostoma jellyfish and seals.

Picnic tables are sited beside a slipway at Point of Ness while Dwarwick Head is the landing point of several disused submarine cables.

From Briga Head to Dunnet Head there is an almost continuous north to northeast going eddy. The cliffs are over 60m high, a warm honeycomb colour but heavily weathered and not infrequently subject to falls. Older sections of cliff are highlighted with ledges of pink thrift.

Hoy seen across the Pentland Firth from Tang Head

Large waves may be met at Briga Head. A northwesterly swell produces confused seas off Dunnet Head which is 102m high with vertical cliffs, the lighthouse on top being a white stone tower a further 20m high, yet its windows have been broken by stones thrown up in winter gales.

This is the most northerly point on the British mainland. 12km away across the Pentland Firth are the cliffs of Orkney, the highest cliffs in Britain, changing colour with the light and still

Dunnet Head, mainland Britain's most northerly point. Note the sleeping seal

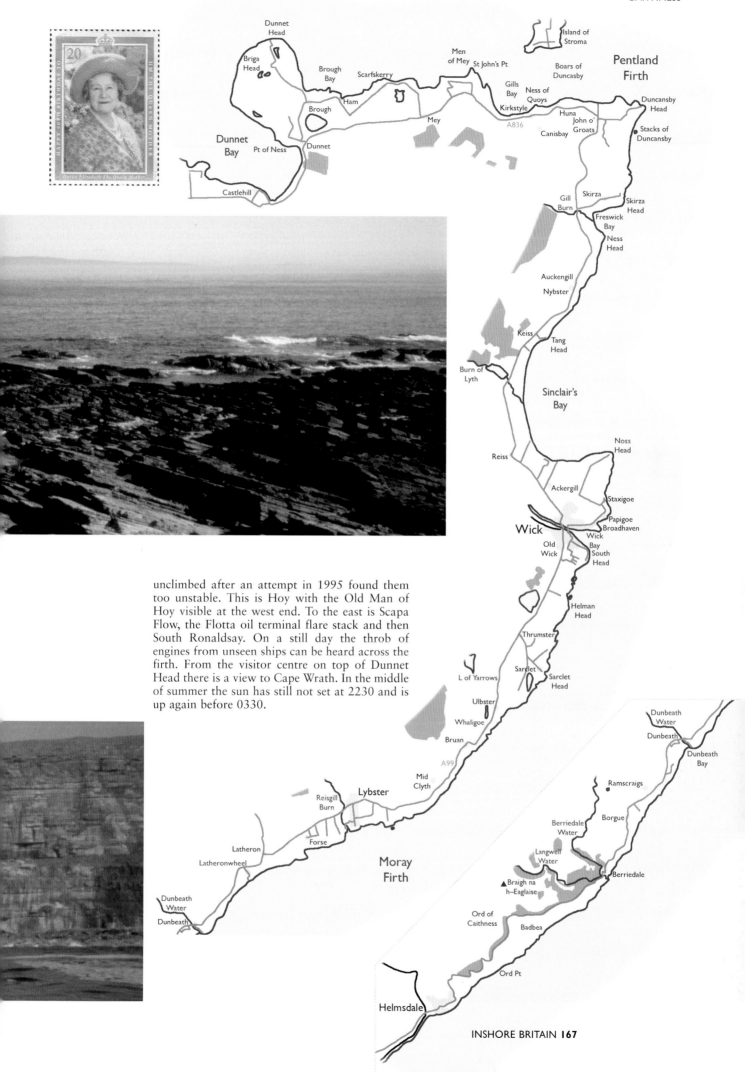

Dunnet Head
Briga Head
Brough Bay
Scarfskerry
Men of Mey
St John's Pt
Island of Stroma
Boars of Duncasby
Pentland Firth
Gills Bay
Ness of Quoys
Kirkstyle
Duncansby Head
Ham
Brough
Huna
John o' Groats
Canisbay
A836
Stacks of Duncansby
Dunnet Bay
Pt of Ness
Dunnet
Mey
Castlehill
Gill Burn
Skirza
Skirza Head
Freswick Bay
Ness Head
Auckengill
Nybster
Keiss
Tang Head
Burn of Lyth
Sinclair's Bay
Reiss
Noss Head
Ackergill
Staxigoe
Papigoe
Broadhaven
Wick
Old Wick
Wick Bay
South Head
Helman Head
Thrumster
L of Yarrows
Sarclet
Sarclet Head
Ulbster
Whaligoe
Bruan
Mid Clyth
A99
Lybster
Reisgill Burn
Forse
Latheron
Latheronwheel
Moray Firth
Dunbeath Water
Dunbeath
Dunbeath Water
Dunbeath
Dunbeath Bay
Ramscraigs
Borgue
Berriedale Water
Langwell Water
▲ Braigh na h–Eaglaise
Berriedale
Ord of Caithness
Badbea
Ord Pt
Helmsdale

unclimbed after an attempt in 1995 found them too unstable. This is Hoy with the Old Man of Hoy visible at the west end. To the east is Scapa Flow, the Flotta oil terminal flare stack and then South Ronaldsay. On a still day the throb of engines from unseen ships can be heard across the firth. From the visitor centre on top of Dunnet Head there is a view to Cape Wrath. In the middle of summer the sun has still not set at 2230 and is up again before 0330.

Formerly an east flowing river tributary valley to a north flowing river, the Pentland Firth is the fastest, most treacherous and most feared tideway in Europe. On springs it usually runs to 22km/h although 30km/h has been recorded. Streams start east at HW Dover +0500 and west from HW Dover –0100 at 6km/h off Dunnet Head although streams begin earlier near the coast. There is heavy turbulence in the races even in calm conditions and it is dangerous when streams are opposed by strong winds or swell. To add interest, patchy fog is common and can arrive with astonishing rapidity.

The east side of Dunnet Head is a nesting site for line after line of seabirds. Indeed, various cliff nesting sites between here and Helmsdale must provide the nesting requirements of a significant proportion of Britain's guillemots.

In Brough Bay a northgoing eddy runs for twelve hours from HW Dover +0500. Little Clett stack in the corner of the bay has a grass top and is white with seabirds. The pier was built in the 19th century to be able to supply Dunnet Head and other lighthouses by sea.

Brough has knitwear and handwoven tweed workshops. By the Stacks is a souterrain. Skylarks and curlews add their own distinctive contributions to the environment.

The pier at Ham is built of flagstones and served a now derelict watermill above the beach which was used to grind corn shipped with oatmeal to Scottish, English and European ports. A reefbreak gives lefts so the narrow entry to the pier would not have been easy to negotiate with a sailing ship.

A flagstone-cutting factory was built in 1871 and there is an overgrown light railway near the harbour. Local lobster fishermen complain that large boats are laying long lines of pots in deeper water and taking immature lobsters so that the breeding stocks are diminishing rapidly.

Overlooking Cairn of Mey is Castle of Mey, built between 1566 and 1572 by the 4th Earl of Caithness, a Z plan castle. In 1952 it was restored as the home of Queen Elizabeth the Queen Mother.

St John's Point has the distinction of being one of the two most distant points on the British mainland as the crow flies, being 977km from Lizard Point in Cornwall although Dunnet Head and Duncansby Head are each just over 100m short of its distance. Off the point, the Men of Mey rocks stand 11–18m high, always with enough swell causing turbulence to prevent paddling between them. On a westgoing flow the Merry Men of Mey stretch out all the way to Hoy, a race which might be treated as a 14km long stopper for practical purposes. The eastgoing stream starts at HW Dover –0545 at up to 10km/h. The most violent part of the race is 6km west of Stroma on a westerly flow. This is just clear of the Swelkie, a 5km eddy which forms on the downstream side of the 4km long island on the westerly flow, that on the easterly flow being a mere 2km long. If all else fails, St John's Point is only 15m high and the portage is not as hard as some. The cost of getting it wrong can be high. A large ship parked on the rocks at the southwest end of Stroma makes the point.

Flows at the edges of Inner Sound start eastwards at HW Dover +0340 and west from HW Dover –0230 at up to 2km/h. However, in mid-channel they start at HW Dover –0530 and west from HW Dover +0030 at up to 9km/h with a violent race off Ness of Huna on the eastgoing stream. On the west side of Gills Bay there is a northgoing eddy for nine hours from HW Dover –0230.

Gills Bay, backed by the A836, has more surfing opportunities, lefts at the west end and rights at Ness of Quoys. The water itself is clear and porpoises might be seen in the bay.

The Haven at Scarfskerry with Dunnet Head visible away to the left

John o' Groats harbour with Stroma across Inner Sound

St John's Point in exceptionally calm conditions. Above the breaking wave in the centre is the ship stranded on Stroma

Sir John's Castle and a chambered cairn follow before further reefbreaks at Kirk o' Tang and the Haven, the latter with a steep slipway up to Scarfskerry. Scarfskerry still builds wooden fishing boats. It also has a reefbreak and another at Tang Head works on the upper half of the tide.

The harbour at Harrow serves lobster boats, but was built in the 19th century to export flagstones.

At Kirkstyle is a church with an unusual pitched roof to its tower, seeming more Norman than traditional Scottish. Canisbay church dates from the 15th century although there was an earlier one there from 1222.

After winning Orkney back from Norway, James IV instructed Jan de Groot to start a ferry service to Orkney in 1496. That most Scottish of names

Duncansby Head with its lighthouse

Ledges of guillemots at Duncansby Head

was actually Dutch, the site of the man's house marked by a mound and flagstaff. In the summer a passenger ferry still operates to Bur Wick on South Ronaldsay. Why John o' Groats should have become such a legendary place is hard to see, apart from being at the end of the A99 and the terminal for a minor ferry. Its sole claim to fame is as the village most distant from the most westerly point on the English mainland. Even Sennen to John o' Groats or Land's End to Duncansby Head would be more logical for long distance walkers, cyclists and the rest who want a long distance route. At least John o' Groats offers a harbour and slipway rather than the high cliffs at Land's End, allowing visits to be made to Caithness Candles, John o' Groats Pottery, a satin craft studio, the Last House in Scotland Museum which includes shipwrecks. Flows here are up to 7km/h.

Ness of Duncansby is an innocuous low grassy point from where the Duncansby Race runs out into the Boars of Duncansby. It is only significant and to be avoided on the southeast going stream which starts at HW Dover −0500 at up to 17km/h. The race extends northwards from the ness at HW Dover −0220 and begins to subside at HW Dover +0040. The northwest going stream begins at HW Dover +0115 at up to 15km/h with a temporary cease in the race. From HW Dover +0500 the race forms again until HW Dover −0530 when there is another cease.

In the distance Muckle Skerray presents a silhouette which resembles a submarine.

The 60m vertical cliffs of Duncansby Head are topped by the 11m white lighthouse tower. There are superb spring flowers and a packed cliff of extremely noisy and odorous nesting guillemots which watch what is happening on the water right in front of them. For most boats, Duncansby Head's race is less significant as it is at the foot of the cliffs and, so, easily avoided. Not so the paddler, who faces turbulence throughout on the southeastgoing stream or a northgoing stream against which it is usually too fast to paddle.

On the south southeastgoing stream there may be a northgoing eddy round the corner. The Moray Firth has a weak clockwise circulation and colder water but the problems generally subside once clear of the Pentland Firth. The whole Pentland Firth needs to be studied thoroughly in advance. Neap tides, calm conditions and slack water all help reduce the difficulties.

South of Duncansby Head the scenery is spectacular with the 60m arch of Thirle Door, the Knee stack, the twin-pointed Stacks of Duncansby and numerous caves and clefts in the cliffs which are still 30m high at Skirza Head, along with an assortment of geos, Wife Geo with two entrances and another with a natural arch across it. There are oystercatchers around the Stacks of Duncansby.

There is a large seabird colony below the broch at Skirza Head and seals haul out on the rocks. There is a reefbreak with long heavy lefts. The surf drives weed in beside the pier at Skirza where it collects and rots to produce a putrid smell and a polluted white colour to the water, not enhanced by pieces of broken glass lying around. Beaches from here to the Forth may throw up semiprecious stones such as smoky quartz, serpentine, jasper, amethyst and agate.

The mouth of the Gill Burn has a sand and boulder reefbreak, backed by a good dune system. In the centre of Freswick Bay is a wreck. The bay

The Knee and Thirle Door. The northgoing race is already running quite strongly through the gaps

has a northgoing eddy from HW Dover −0545 to HW Dover +0315.

Beyond Ness Head, with its broch site, is Bucholly Castle, just one wall remaining of the 12th-century stronghold of the Norse pirate Sweyn Asleifson. The Vikings of the late Norse are

Seals sunbathing on rocks below Skirza Head

The Stacks of Duncansby, the only major rock features here e asily visible from on land

featured in the Northlands Viking Centre at Auckengill, together with Picts, chambered cairns and brochs, there being dun and broch sites near the shore at Nybster.

The 18th-century Keiss Castle is inhabited, unlike its 16th-century predecessor which is now

just a tower on the shoreline. Brochs overlook the fierce race around Tang Head but Keiss has a small crab fishing harbour with a warehouse and icehouse from the herring fishing days.

A pillbox and tank traps line the shore at Rough of Stain where there is a reefbreak producing lefts. A 5km sweep of beach backed by dunes and golf links edges Sinclair's Bay. The best beachbreak is at the mouth of the Burn of Lyth, just south of another broch site.

Old submarine cables landed at Reiss, near which there are shallow reefbreaks with rights.

Noss Head with the contrasting silhouettes of Castle Sinclair and Castle Girnoe along the southern edge of Sinclair's Bay

The island at the Brough

Ackergill Tower, five storeys high, is one of the oldest inhabited dwellings in the north of Scotland. In 1699 it passed into the hands of the Dunbars who still live there. Ackergill has a small fishing harbour backed by Wick Airport.

Castle Girnoe was built in 1476 to 1486 and neighbouring Castle Sinclair in 1606/7, strongholds of the Sinclairs, the Earls of Caithness. Both were deserted about 1679 and in ruins by the end of the century.

There is a continuous easterly flow around the southern edge of Sinclair's Bay, ending at Noss Head which is vertical and 43m high, a major seabird colony. There is a fierce race around the head, on which is the 18m white lighthouse tower. Streams start south–southwest from Noss Head to Wick at HW Dover –0430 and north–northeast at HW Dover –0140 at up to 3km/h. The coast is low and rocky but contains caves. A broch site is located between Staxigoe and Broadhaven at Papigoe with another beyond Broadhaven.

Wick Bay has no currents, but heavy seas build up with onshore winds and moon jellyfish collect in calmer conditions. North Head is 14m high with low cliffs and a battlemented memorial tower. There may also be unexploded ordnance on the north side of the bay.

Wick was a Viking anchorage, vik being Norse and inbhir uige Gaelic for creek or rivermouth. It became a Royal Burgh in 1589 and has 18th-century housing on a mediaeval street plan, much enlarged, in the 19th century. In its heyday the port had 1,000 herring boats and the large fishmarket remains. The Main Harbour imports lime, coal, cement, fertilizers and road salt, exporting barley, while the River Harbour has six fuel tanks used by the oil and gas industry. Caithness Glass was set up in 1960 by Lord Thurso, especially known for its paperweights and there is a ceramics factory nearby. Wick Heritage Centre covers domestic life, cooperage, a blacksmith's shop, kippering kilns, herring fishing, a fishing boat and a lighthouse while Wick Harbour Gallery features pictures.

A refreshing geo at the Brough

Yet another stack, this time the Stack of Ulbster. The Caithness hills are becoming clearer in the background

The south side of the bay out to South Head has a white octagonal tower and a 3.7m iron beacon which marks the end of a former breakwater on a spit. Blackbacked gulls watch near a swimming pool set in the rocks.

Invershore was once Scotland's third largest fishing station

The coast has dark indented cliffs to Helman Head, often pierced by caves. The square tower ruins of Castle of Old Wick or the Old Man of Wick, one of the oldest in Scotland, with 2.1m thick walls, date back to the Norse occupation in the 12th century. These days they come under fire from a rifle range, a flag and lookout seated alongside indicating firing.

A steep island in the Brough deserves closer investigation. A high passage runs through it from end to end and the centre of the roof has fallen in, added to which is all the noise from a seabird colony.

Four aerials follow the A99 and the former Wick-Lybster railway from Wick to Thrumster, the highest 99m tall. From Helman Head with its cairn the cliffs are more broken to Sarclet Head, where eider ducks might be seen. Ires Geo has a major seabird colony. The Haven at Sarclet is a

fishing harbour with ruined breakwaters on each side.

From Sarclet Head to Clyth Ness the cliffs begin to rise again, up to 46m high with the hills behind rising to over 160m, the site of a large number of antiquities, stone rows, settlements, standing stones, cairns, chambered cairns, forts and brochs between Loch of Yarrows and Bruan.

Beyond Stack of Ulbster there is a major seabird colony at Ulbster. Whaligoe claims to be a fishing village, but is a minute beach with two rusty boat mooring chains attached to the overhanging cliff, approached down 365 steps which are slippery when wet. Round the corner, Wester Whale Geo was a herring station. A natural bridge across the mouth of a cave is an interesting variation on the cliff scenery. More major seabird colonies follow at Bruan and Halberry Head. Above Stack of Mid Clyth are the monument and stone rows of Mid Clyth. Ousbacky is a notably insignificant point, barely a bend in the coast but marked by the Clythness lighthouse, a 13m tower low down on the cliffs.

Seals rest up near the Stacks, perhaps looking up past the broch site to Kyleburn Confectionery where lettered rock and boiled sweets are handmade.

The **Lybster** lobster and crab fishing port of Invershore at the mouth of the Reisgill Burn is easy to miss, the lighthouse in Lybster Bay being well hidden by the cliff on the east side. In fact, at the height of the herring fishing boom it was the third largest fishing station in Scotland. Most of the boats have gone but the oystercatchers, gulls and midges remain. The golf course on top of the hill is possibly the shortest in Britain, but it makes up for it with its views.

The cliffs increase in height to over 50m at Forse Cove and then drop away again to Latheronwheel. Forse Castle, dating from Norse times, retains some of its walling including a 9m tower.

At Latheron there is a belltower, two Bronze Age standing stones and the Clan Gunn Heritage Centre in a 1735 church, charting Scotland's oldest clan from Norse origins. Along the road,

The Needle, the air filled with flying guillemots and a quite deafening sound from the tens of thousands lining the ledges

Kenn and the Salmon at Dunbeath. Wave defences are tetrapods, unpleasant to negotiate

Latheronwheel with its broch and two chambered cairns stands above the tiny fishing harbour and stack, arch and caves although ropes leading out to fishing nets in the sea are more important features to notice.

The cliffs are low to Dunbeath, rarely exceeding 20m but with frequent offshore rocks. Knockinnon has the Laidhay Croft Museum, a cruck constructed barn and a stable dwelling and byre in a longhouse of 1842. The Dunbeath Heritage Centre records the natural and social history of the area from the Vikings and early settlers to more recent crofting and fishing. It was an important herring fishing centre but suffers from the activity of Dunbeath Water which regularly brings down boulders, needing to be removed from Dunbeath Bay, the rivermouth frequently changing position. There are wrecks in the centre of the bay and on the west side. Through all the debris a power cable runs out for 18km to the production platforms on the Beatrice oilfield. A picnic table is conveniently placed near the pier and a statue of Kenn and the Salmon recalls Highland writer Neil Gunn, born here in 1891.

There is another cave at the end of Dunbeath Bay and then a striking castle. Dunbeath Castle is painted white and is imposing in its 20m clifftop setting. Built in 1428 or earlier for the Sutherlands, it was enlarged in the 19th century. It has changed hands several times and is still inhabited. The surrounding waters have hundreds of seals and thousands of shags.

Flows start southwest to Berriedale at HW Dover −0400 and northeast at HW Dover +0200 at up to 2km/h, past cliffs up to nearly 50m high.

Another chambered cairn, broch and standing stone follow at Ramscraigs while, down at Borgue, An Dùn is another major seabird colony.

Berriedale Water is joined by Langwell Water at Berriedale to discharge at a rivermouth which is frequently choked with boulders. The village has weaving and the Kingspark llama farm with rare breeds and guided llama walks. The hamlet also has two towers, Berriedale Castle ruins and graveyard near the rivermouth, Achastle's 14 to 15th-century ruins and Langwell House, the Caithness estate of the Duke of Portland, containing white deer and a windmill.

Flows south begin at HW Dover +0200 and north at HW Dover −0330 at up to 1km/h, setting towards and away from the coast as implied. Cliffs run up to 150m high, red sandstone with white streaks. Over the next 6km the seabird colonies reach their zenith with Inver Hill, Badbea and the 61m Needle. The colonies are enormous, including the largest guillemot colony on the mainland with 130,000 birds. As well as the thousands of birds in flight and calling at any time there are countless ledges of birds creating a loud and urgent background buzz which resembles a very large and angry beehive. The whole experience is totally deafening and dazzling, accompanied by regular wafts of stale fish odour.

There are occasional brochs and a monument at Badbea. The high cliffs rise to the Paps of Caithness, 626m, Scaraben with East Scaraben and Sròn Garbh about the same height while Morven rises higher to 706m behind with white quartz at the top which looks like snow.

The Ord of Caithness rises to 230m, from where there are spectacular views of the scenery, possibly including herds of red deer. Braigh na h-Eaglaise rises to 422m and Creag Thoraraidh to 405m with

a radio mast. The great fault at Dùn Glas separates Mesozoic from older rocks.

A rather specific piece of folklore states that it is unlucky for a Sinclair to cross the Ord on a Monday dressed in green. This derives from the fact that William, Earl of Caithness, led 300 troops in green tartan this way to support James IV at the Battle of Flodden, all but one perishing amongst 10,000 Scotsmen.

Helmsdale has cliffs with granite outcrops, a wide area of reefs forming for a kilometre to the east of the town. In calm conditions it is possible to weave a route between them but normally it is necessary to remain outside. Landing at the east end of the harbour gives a slipway to parking on the quiet road alongside the harbour.

The harbour at Helmsdale. Entry is in the far corner and exit is easiest in the foreground

Distance
From Castlehill to Helmsdale is 110km
Campsites
Dunnet, Huna, John o' Groats, Wick, Dunbeath, Lothbeg
Youth Hostels
John o' Groats, Helmsdale
OS 1:50,000 Sheets
11 Thurso and Dunbeath
12 Thurso and Wick
17 Helmsdale and Strath of Kildonan
Imray Charts
C23 Firth of Forth to Moray Firth (1:250,000)
C68 Cape Wrath to Wick and the Orkney Islands (1:160,000)
Admiralty Charts
115 Moray Firth (1:200,000)
1462 Harbours on the North and East Coasts of Scotland. Wick and Approaches (1:7,500). Helmsdale (1:6,250)
1942 Fair Isle to Wick (1:200,000)
1954 Cape Wrath to Pentland Firth Including the Orkney Islands (1:200,000)
2162 Pentland Firth and Approaches (1:50,000)
2581 Southern Approaches to Scapa Flow (1:26,000)
Tidal Constants
Scrabster: HW Dover −0240, LW Dover −0230
Stroma: Dover −0100
Duncansby Head: Dover −0100
Wick: HW Dover +0010, LW Dover
Lybster: HW Dover +0020, LW Dover +0010
Helmsdale: HW Dover +0030, LW Dover +0040
Sea Areas
Fair Isle, Cromarty
Range
Old Wick
Rescue
All weather lifeboats: Thurso, Longhope, Wick
Maritime Rescue Centres
Shetland, 01595 692976
Aberdeen, 01224 592334

32 DORNOCH FIRTH

Some of the most beautiful sunsets on the east coast

Island earth for folk no longer
Grace the sheaf of tyrant lords.
Waits the boat to sail the landless.
Island earth for folk no more.

Joe Corrie

Helmsdale is from the Norse Hjalmundalr, Hjalmund's dale. The Timespan visitor centre covers the area from the Picts to North Sea Oil and has a riverside garden. The fishing port is at the mouth of the River Helmsdale, from which freshets side and, on the other, the Wolf Stone which records the shooting in about 1700 of the last wild wolf in Scotland. Other than occasional sections of rock platform, the shore is sandy beach all the way to Brora. Kintradwell Broch is Iron Age, measuring 9.4m across inside its double walls. Excavation in 1880 unearthed two headless skeletons.

Rhizostoma jellyfish float about on one side of the beach while golfers do likewise on the other.

A bar of gravel and rock can make entry to the estuary of the River Brora difficult. **Brora** has yarn and tweed mills and a curling rink.

The bar at the mouth of the River Brora

flow well out to sea and a bar of stones and boulders collect off the harbour. In addition, the breakwater is damaged, convenient for easy departure from the harbour for paddlers. The A9 bridge crosses next to the harbour, its construction requiring the ruins of the castle to be cleared and the entrance of the Old Harbour to be blocked. An 18m white memorial clocktower is located near the bridge. Pottery is made in the town and gold prospecting takes place in the hills.

Long distance paddlers tend to cut the corner here, not least to avoid the Tain bombing range.

The cliffs are very low to Brora and this was a suitable place to land submarine cables, now disused. The A9 is joined by the North Highland railway line between Thurso and Inverness, both now following the coastal strip.

The water is fairly clear with moon jellyfish, cormorants, terns, oystercatchers, fulmars, blackbacked gulls, shelducks and razorbills. This stretch of coast is very mild so palm trees can thrive at Portgower, while the hillside behind is a blaze of yellow broom flowers. Skylarks twitter by the shore and many seals lie up on the sandy beach at Kilmote. Caravans behind the beach to Lothbeg Point show how much more benign the conditions are than further north.

Lothbeg, on the river which flows from Glen Loth, has the Long Cairn chambered cairn on one

Flows begin southwest at HW Dover −0600 and northeast at HW Dover −0100 at up to 1km/h. The coast is low although there is a 15m cliff terrace inland, rising eventually to 521m Ben Horn. It is a good area for wildfowl at sea.

After a memorial the well preserved lower walls of Carn Liath Broch stand near the entrance to the Dornoch Firth.

Dunrobin Castle is one of the most distinctive in Scotland with its spires and 160 year old gardens based on Versailles. It was constructed around a 1275 square keep by Robert, Earl of Sutherland, on a natural rock terrace, as the home of the Countess of Sutherland, making it one of the oldest inhabited houses in Scotland despite its appearance. Most of it dates from 1845–50, based by Sir Charles Barry on Balmoral, as the seat of the Dukes and Earls of Sutherland. The interior is mostly by Sir Robert Lorimer following a fire in 1915 and contains French furniture, paintings which include Canaletto views of Venice and family portraits by Reynolds and Landseer, silver Wemyss Ware, ceramics, tapestries, a 10,000 volume library, a horsedrawn steam-powered fire engine, a Victorian museum, hunting spoils, local archaeology, Pictish stones, natural history, geology and Clan Sutherland exhibits including robes, uniforms and medals. A private station was built for the 3rd Duke who also had

The distinctive Dunrobin Castle with the monument to callous greed beyond

his own carriages and engine. A couple of other buildings close by are circular with conical roofs, mimicking the style. 394m high Beinn a' Bhragaidh is topped by the massive Ben Bhraggie Statute by Sir Francis Chanter of the 1st Duke of Sutherland, the Leviathan of Wealth. Such a man needs no monument. Between 1810 and 1820 he evicted 15,000 tenants, often violently, to make way for sheep and the damage he did to the Highland population lasts to this day.

Golspie is a Norse farm name. The town is on the Golspie Burn where Golspie Mill is claimed to be Scotland's only organic water-powered flourmill. Orcadian Stoneware have a geological exhibition with natural stone products, cutting, grinding, polishing, tumbling and jewellery sales. The 17th-century church has a fine Sutherland loft of 1737.

Off the town is the Bridge bank but there is no tidal stream to cause problems.

Golspie Links offer one of the country's longer bunkers as golfers play shots back off the sandy beach. Beyond the golf course and a caravan site the dunes take on a more natural form.

The River Fleet enters Loch Fleet and then discharges to the sea past Littleferry. Shallow water results in a race out to sea on the ebb. There is a sand bar across the entrance and sand spits on each side at the mouth. The ferry ceased in 1815 when Thomas Telford built the Mound causeway across the head of Loch Fleet to carry what would become the A9. The loch is flanked by pinewoods with rare creeping lady's tresses orchid and twinflower in Ferry Links woods. Ducks (especially eiders), waders and other birds are attracted by the loch and there are seals and migratory salmon. Jackdaws are seen around the 14th-century Skelbo Castle.

The coast continues low and sandy to Dornoch Point. Embo is fairly conspicuous, including Embo House with its high white front. There is a burial chamber before the caravan site which continues as far as the pier. A cairn is sited in front of another less conspicuous caravan site at Embo Street.

Dornoch at the end of the A949 has two golf courses of which Royal Dornoch is the third oldest golf course known. The town is built of local stone and has a Mercat Cross and 16th-century Bishop's Palace. The cathedral was formerly the cathedral

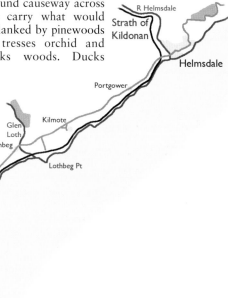

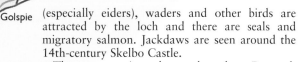

Britain's second tallest lighthouse on Tarbat Ness

Sunset seen across the Dornoch Firth from Portmahomack

of the Bishops of Caithness, founded in 1224 by Gilbert, Archdeacon of Moray and Bishop of Caithness. Except for the central tower it was mostly destroyed by fire in 1570, but was restored in the 17th century, 1835–7 and 1924, retaining fine 13th-century stonework and outstanding stained glass. Dornoch Old Post Office Visitor Centre covers southeast Sutherland with its wildlife and there is a craft centre with jewellery, tartan weaving and exhibits in the former jail cells. The Sutherland County Show is held in July. Earl's Cross stands to the north of the town while the Witches Stone in Littletown marks the burning at the stake in 1722 of witch Janet Horn for turning her daughter into a small horse and taking her to the devil to be shod. There is also a landing strip to the south of the town.

Dornoch Point is a spit which is continually changing shape, 4m high with marram grass on top.

Stretching out for 3km into the firth is Gizzen Briggs, a bank of drying quicksand with a Norse name, eventually meeting up with Whiteness Sands to form the Tain Bar. The flood tide begins at HW Dover –0530 and the ebb at HW Dover +0120 at up to 1km/h but increasing to 2km/h on the flood and 3km/h on the ebb off Dornoch Point, increasing with snowmelt or after heavy rain, although it can feel faster in the shallow water. The shifting banks of Dornoch Sands are over 1km wide at low tide and lead on to Cuthill Sands. Other than a few eider ducks, swans and herons, the area is the preserve of large numbers of seals which rest up out of the water which can be very warm in the summer.

Seals sunbathe on Cuthill Sands as traffic on the A9 crosses the Dornoch Bridge

undertaken here since at least 1703 and the older buildings date from 1843. It is one of the smallest distilleries in Scotland with a staff of 16 and is unusual in having a coastal location. The kilns are small and lightly peated but have the tallest still columns in Scotland at 5.2m, using hard barley from the Black Isle. The whisky matures in bourbon-soaked oak casks from Missouri.

Tain takes its name from the Viking for thing or council. It is Scotland's oldest Royal Burgh, receiving its charter in 1066. The 900 Roses Garden was planted to celebrate the 900th anniversary. It was the birthplace of St Duthus about 1000. St Duthus' Chapel was built between 1065 and 1256 but destroyed by fire in 1427. The saint is buried in St Duthus Church, built in Decorated style about 1360 by William, Earl and Bishop of Ross, which became a centre of Christian pilgrimage. James IV came every year for twenty years and James V came on foot from Edinburgh. Robert the Bruce's wife was dragged from sanctuary here and taken to England. The town was the administration centre for the Highland Clearances. There is a Victorian Gothic town hall and the Tolbooth is a square tower overlooking the Mercat Cross. Museum exhibits include the Clan Ross centre. Pottery, weaving, tartan manufacture and Highland Fine Cheese manufacture are amongst local industries. St Mary's Well is just below high tide level while the River Tain winds around the town and then flows across Whiteness Sands to Mussel Scalps between the various sandbanks.

It is the sandbanks and shallows, making navigation for larger boats difficult, which permits

A jet makes a low level bombing run towards Tain

The 780m long Dornoch Bridge carries the rerouted A9 across the end of the Kyle of Sutherland, draining the rivers Oykel and Shin. The flood at the bridge begins at HW Dover –0330 at up to 4km/h and the ebb at HW Dover +0215 at up to 5km/h.

The most conspicuous buildings in Morangie are those of the Glenmorangie distillery, producing a 10-year old malt whisky. Distilling has been

nearly 100km² of the Dornoch Firth and the metre high Morrich More marshes to be used as the Tain firing and bombing range. Jets racing in low and banking away are frequent visitors. There are occasional lights on the firing range and lookout towers amongst the marram grass and dunes on Innis Mhór and its neighbouring island, but large herds of seals still lie up on Whiteness Sands off Rubh'na h-Innse Moire.

Seafront houses at Portmahomack

Inver is a fishing village and fishing boats are just able to slip out of Inver Bay and up the east coast of the firth. Portmahomack, at the end of the B9165, is one of the few places on Scotland's east coast to enjoy beautiful sunsets, perhaps the reason why caravans are lined up in front of the drying sandbanks and rocks along the shore. There is a golf course above the village. A Reformation church has an unusual domed tower and there is a Victorian iron drinking fountain by the beach. The Oystercatcher and the Castle Hotel are both by the beach. It is a lobster fishing village with a sheltered position and lack of tidal flows.

The yellow target float seems very close to this coast. From Portmahomack to Tarbat Ness there are pebble ridges fringed with rocks through which there are a number of narrow inlets, accessible in calm conditions. Salmon nets are strung out in the sea at several points.

The lighthouse on Tarbat Ness stands 41m high, the second highest in Britain, its white tower striped with red bands. The peninsula itself is less than 60m high with relatively gentle slopes up from the water so it is less severe than many such points.

Gentle flows start northeast at HW Dover +0120 and southwest at HW Dover –0450 although the eastgoing flow can pick up close to Tarbat Ness. Strong westerly to southwesterly winds with heavy rain inland and snowmelt can all make the east northeasterly stream run longer and more strongly. Once round the point, flows start a little earlier and more strongly, going southwest from HW Dover –0530 and northeast from HW Dover +0100 at up to 1km/h.

The line of red sandstone cliffs start out as gentle slopes of grass and gorse, gradually steepening and becoming higher with seabirds. Salmon nets are staked out from mid-February to late August.

Wilkhaven is a fishing village with a jetty conveniently close to the point. The cliffs here are only 12m high but they increase to twice that height further south, topped by a framework radio tower at Bindal.

Ballone Castle on low cliffs

The roofless remains of Ballone Castle, built for the Earl of Ross, later owned by the Mackenzies and abandoned in the 19th century, stand on the cliffs near Rockfield.

Rockfield has a jetty which can be valuable as the shoreline is mostly studded with rocks which make landing difficult although there is a flat strip of land all the way along the coast between the cliffs and the shoreline, easy to traverse once ashore.

The red sandstone cliffs increase towards 50m at Cadboll Point with just a token cave. A grassy shore at Cadboll has the remains of Cadboll Castle. Cadboll Mount was said to have been built by the Laird of Cadboll who had a feud with Macleod of Geanies and who wished to look down on his neighbour.

On the other hand, Hilton of Cadboll is on the shore, a former fishing village with the remains of a chapel and an adventure playground.

Near Geanies House, the Moray shore beyond

Higher cliffs approaching Cadboll

Balintore was also a fishing village at the end of the B9166, its harbour overlooked by the Commercial Inn.

There are frequently rollers in Shandwick Bay but it is the landing point for the pipeline from the Beatrice oilfield and in quiet conditions it can also be a convenient landing point for paddlers, a limited amount of parking being available next to the sandy beach. There is an airfield just beyond the village.

Distance
From Helmsdale to Shandwick is 82km
Campsites
Lothbeg, Dalchalm, Embo, Embo Street, Dornoch, Tarlogie
Youth Hostels
Helmsdale, Carbisdale Castle, Inverness
OS 1:50,000 Sheets
17 Helmsdale and Strath of Kildonan
21 Dornoch and Alness
Imray Chart
C23 Firth of Forth to Moray Firth (1:250,000)
Admiralty Charts
115 Moray Firth (1:200,000)
SC 223 Dunrobin Point to Buckie (1:75,000)
1462 Harbours on the North and East Coasts of Scotland. Helmsdale (1:6,250)
Tidal Constants
Helmsdale: HW Dover +0030, LW Dover +0040
Golspie: HW Dover +0030, LW Dover +0040
Meikle Ferry: HW Dover +0100, LW Dover +0110
Portmahomack: HW Dover +0040, LW Dover +0100
Balintore: HW Dover +0040, LW Dover +0050
Sea Area
Cromarty
Range
Tain
Rescue
All weather lifeboats: Wick, Invergordon
Maritime Rescue Centre
Aberdeen, 01224 592334

33 MORAY

Britain's biggest dune system and most extensively forested coast

Leave the fishing trade lads, there's money to be made,
The handline and the Shetland yawl are from a bygone day,
Come to Aberdeen lads, there's sights ye've never seen,
Be a mudman on a pipeline or a fitter at Nigg Brae.

Archie Fisher

Flows from Shandwick begin at HW Dover –0530 and northeast from HW Dover +0100 at up to 1km/h.

At the southern end of Shandwick Bay the submarine pipeline from the Beatrice oilfield lands and is taken between Clach a' Charridh and an airfield for the final land leg to the oil terminal at Nigg Bay.

Salmon fishing nets run out from the coast between mid-February and late August. Beds of kelp will also be met in the clear water. Blackbacked gulls, razorbills, guillemots, oystercatchers, cormorants and eider ducks all frequent this coast with its steep red cliffs which can usually be climbed, although landing through the rocks on the shoreline cannot be attempted except in the calmest of conditions. Forts and a homestead remain hidden on the top at Port an Righ, but there is the occasional clump of trees and gorse spills down the hillside. Several waterfalls also drop down, including the burn fed by Bayfield Loch on Kraken Hill.

The largest of the caves is King's Cave which looks out over the Three Kings spoil dumping ground and there are some arches at the approach to the mouth of the Cromarty Firth. There are

Beds of kelp below the cliffs at Port an Righ

Waterfall down the cliff near King's Cave

South of the firth lies the Black Isle which is neither an isle nor black, although it does remain free of snow when the surrounding hills are covered. Indeed, at the foot of 156m high Gallow Hill, the end of a ridge to Rosemarkie, are Blue Head and Red Nose, the green vegetation gashed by new slips to reveal red rock beneath. A marine farm is moored off the cliffs.

The symmetry about the firth continues with McFarquhar's Cave and St Bennet's Well by a cliff stream.

Eathie fishing station has fossils on the foreshore. These were new to science in the days when stonemason and geologist Hugh Miller learned his craft here.

Caves continue and there are small stacks which mock the TV masts on the ridge above. From time to time there are beaches which can only be reached from the water or by air, as indicated by curlews which pace sedately across the sand.

Sutors Stacks on the south side of the entrance. The firth is the best deep water harbour in northeast Scotland and one of the largest natural harbours in Europe. In the distance the Invergordon aluminium smelter and a distillery can be seen, but these are much less conspicuous than massive oil rigs being constructed in the Nigg Bay fabrication yard and numbers of them anchored in the firth. Dunskeath Castle and an

At the back of Rosemarkie Bay is Rosemarkie on the A832 with its red stone houses and its red sandstone exposed by landslides around the Fairy Glen with its two waterfalls. This resort includes the Groam House Museum which has the Rosemarkie Stone, an intricately carved Pictish slab, and other stone carvings from the

The entrance to the Cromarty Firth with Cromarty beyond South Sutor on the left and an oil rig at the Nigg Bay fabrication yard

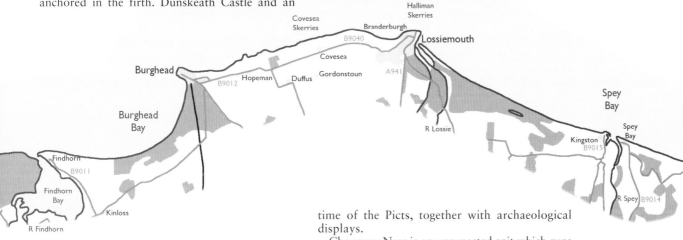

earthwork are not likely to be noticed on 150m high North Sutor, but the village of **Cromarty** is clear enough beyond the 140m high South Sutor.

The gap can act as a wind funnel. Tidal flows are ingoing from HW Dover −0400 and outgoing from HW Dover +0115 at up to 3km/h while the flow across the mouth starts west–southwest at HW Dover −0600 at up to 1km/h and east–northeast from HW Dover +0030 at up to 2km/h.

time of the Picts, together with archaeological displays.

Chanonry Ness is an unexpected spit which runs out into the Moray Firth, ending at the 13m white light tower at Chanonry Point. The ness also has a golf course, a cross and a memorial to the 17th-century prophet Brahan Seer who made portents of doom for the Mackenzie family. For his pains he was burned in a barrel of tar on the point, presumably an outcome he did not foresee.

Crossing the Moray Firth and the line of the Great Glen Fault at this point, after the North Channel and South Channel have merged, is simpler in terms of shipping movements but there can be considerable turbulence between Chanonry Point and Fort George at peak flows. Streams run southwest from HW Dover –0400 at up to 5km/h with a slack at Dover HW and then northeast from at HW Dover +0115 at up to 6km/h with another slack at HW Dover +0530.

The largest population of dolphins around our coast live in the Moray Firth, probably over a hundred of them. In addition there are white beaked dolphins and common porpoises. 49,000 waterfowl winter in the inner Moray Firth including 2,800 redshanks, 2,100 bar tailed godwits, 1,400 red throated divers, 1,400 red breasted mergansers and long tailed ducks and common and velvet scoters. The RSPB claim that they are at risk of permanent damage from pollution and land claim.

Aerial activity also results from Inverness Airport 5km to the southeast beyond Ardersier.

the waves but not leaning against anything. A pipe drum on the point is in scale with the main fabrication shed, but the spindly cranes bring home the enormous size of these items as if models of differing scales have been used in the same scene. There is a steady noise of machinery but terns are undisturbed by it.

The low shingle ridge develops into sand dunes and rough grassland up to 24m high, forming the Carse of Delnies, used for a golf course at the east end.

The Golf View Hotel, Invernairne Hotel, children's playground, ornamental iron bandstand and even swans on the sea are clues along the front that **Nairn** on the A96 is a refined resort. Indeed, it was the favourite resort of Charlie Chaplin. Granted a charter in the 12th century by Alexander I, it was to become a spa. It has a mild climate and low rainfall. It also has highland games in mid-August while local features include ornamental

The 18th-century Fort George was sited to control entry to Inverness and beyond from the Moray Firth

The far side of the Moray Firth from Chanonry Point is dominated by Fort George at the end of the B9006. Built from 1748 to 1769 for George II following the Jacobite rebellion and the Battle of Culloden, it never saw action and remains one of the finest late artillery fortifications in Europe. Land approach is through two tunnels and over a timber bridge across a ditch, all covered by at least two walls of cannons. The 17ha site is protected by 1.6km of ramparts. It contains the museums of the Queen's Own Highlanders with the Seaforth Highlanders, the Queen's Own Cameron Highlanders and the Lovat Scouts, medals and uniforms, the Seafield Collection of arms gathered by Sir James Grant in the 18th century for a regiment of foot and militia, an Armstrong gun of 1865 with early rifling and typical barrack rooms of 1868, 1813 and 1780, the oldest featuring Private James Anderson of the 42nd Royal Highlanders. The fort is still in use as a barracks and military depot, including the chapel of 1763–7. More recent features are a helicopter landing site and a water tower. Firing on the ranges normally stops while boats are passing.

Whiteness Head is at the end of a narrow shingle ridge alongside a lagoon and saltings, the greater part of which dry. The area is dominated by McDermott's oil platform construction yard. The surrealism begins with a metal ladder rising from

Nairn harbour, looking inland, the entrance on the left

gardens, a clocktower with a spire, a swimming pool and Nairn Pottery. The Duke of Cumberland spent his 25th birthday here in 1747 before going on to beat Prince Charlie at Culloden, a battle which is featured with other local history in the Viewfield Museum. Nairn Fishertown Museum covers herring fishing in the steam drifter era, model boats, the Moray Firth and domestic life.

The harbour is off the oily River Nairn, a pre-Celtic name for penetrating river, the mouth of which is obstructed by a drying sand bar at low tide. Indeed, the river also drains and even a kayak

McDermott Base with the Cairngorms rising behind, seen from Whiteness Head

The Gut at low water divides the Bar from Culbin Forest

would have difficulty ascending the gravel rapid to gain entry.

To the south stands the Ord, a 214m high summit. Beyond another golf course begins a dune coast with drying sandbanks to Findhorn. Ridges of shingle stand 3–8m high with 10km of spits, the Bar and the Old Bar with the Gut inside being islands at high tide until recent years. They are subject to continual change. There is a wreck offshore. The area is a nature reserve with a thousand greylags roosting on the Bar in the winter, skylarks in the summer and seabirds and waders all year. The Highland region gives way to Moray in the midst of the forest. Culbin Sands are the largest dune system in Britain following a series of storms which overwhelmed a village and rich farmland in the 17th century. The formerly bare sandhills up to 30m high now support 15km of the Culbin Forest, its conifers forming one of the most thickly-wooded coasts in Britain. It has many rare dune and pinewood plants and wildlife includes roe deer, badgers, red squirrels and crested tits. Capercaillies became extinct in Britain in the mid-18th century but were reintroduced to Scotland in the 1830s. They have been in decline again since the 1970s and are probably below 2,500 in number now so those who shoot them for pleasure have proposed a voluntary ban on killing them.

Beyond the Bar the Highland region gives way to Moray. The resort of Findhorn, at the end of the B9011 and at the mouth of the River Findhorn and Muckle Burn and of Findhorn Bay, is the third village of this name. The first was buried beneath sand in fierce storms in the 17th century and the second destroyed by floods in 1701. A spit runs out from the entrance to the bay, the sand having razor and mussel shells and dozens of sunbathing seals in settled conditions. With even moderate northerly weather a confused sea breaks over the bar. Huge numbers of longtailed ducks and common scoters winter offshore and ospreys might be seen. This is the main yachting centre for northeast Scotland. In 1962 the Findhorn Foundation religious retreat was set up 2km to the south with interests in ecology, organic gardening, weaving, pottery and candlemaking. The Findhorn

Village Heritage Centre has the story of the village, a salmon fisherman's bothy and some models.

Two picnic areas are surrounded by tank traps in the dunes. Along the southern shoreline of Burghead Bay are a line of pillboxes in various states of capsize. They were to protect the airfield at Kinloss. An aircraft might be seen through the pines on the 3–15m high sandhills at the back of the beach, as will be aerials and an aerogenerator, but military aircraft will also be seen and heard taking off and landing.

Formerly Moray's main grain port, **Burghead** is a busy fishing harbour at the end of the B9089 with a prominent white mark and 300m of quays handling barley and Scandinavian timber. There is a considerable sea off the port in strong winds but it is protected from easterly winds. The 20m high promontory is of heavily-weathered honey coloured sandstone strata, heavily disfigured with spray-paint graffiti. The old coastguard station occupies an Iron Age fort with a high chamber well cut into the rock, possibly an early Christian baptistery. Another old ceremony is the burning of the Clavie at the Clavie Stone, the breaking up of a blazing tar barrel which has been carried round the village on January 11th, the old New Year's Eve, possibly a ceremony of Norse origin. The village has a museum and a maltings in a large concrete building. At St Æthans a set of radio masts dominate the skyline behind the B9012 and B9040.

The rocky shoreline with grassy slopes gradually increases in height to 70m at Hopeman, the freight railway from the south of Burghead formerly running along the coast to beyond Hopeman.

The 19th-century fishing harbour of Hopeman mostly dries and entry is impractical in heavy weather. It has a watersports centre which was well known to the Duke of Edinburgh and Prince Charles in their respective years as pupils at Gordonstoun.

After a disordered collection of beach huts, 50m sandstone cliffs continue to Covesea,

Listing pillboxes around Burghead Bay which protected RAF Kinloss

Seals on the beach at Findhorn. Findhorn Bay entrance is to the right of the picture

A masterpiece of sculpting by the sea, a freestanding arch at Covesea

Covesea Skerries light faces out towards Halliman Skerries with their daymark

initially topped by a golf course and later by a quarry with a scree slope of tailings, four radio masts and a 10m white coastguard lookout tower. From Clashach Cove there are an assortment of caves, including Sculptor's Cave, and arches, including a superb freestanding arch which looks as if it has been made by balancing sandstone slabs precariously on each other. Neil and Jane are a ridge of drying rocks off the coast.

Covesea was formerly the estuary from Loch Spynie, now 7km away and only 1km long but once occupying a substantial area inland. St Peter's church at Duffus, now a ruin, was built on an island in the loch.

Streams as far as Portknockie start at HW Dover +0200 and west at HW Dover −0420 at up to 1km/h.

Covesea Skerries lighthouse is a 36m white tower standing amongst the dunes by the beach.

Covesea Skerries themselves are not marked but there is a 15m iron pyramid framework on the Halliman Skerries, which are closer to potential shipping routes. The Little Skerries and Ooze Rocks lie off Lossiemouth's west beach, on which there is a charge for landing. Aircraft fly low over the beach and the adjacent golf course to land beyond at Lossiemouth Airfield. Tank traps and a pillbox also provided defences for this airfield.

Lossiemouth was developed as the port for Elgin after the former port of Spynie silted up. The Spynie Canal drains Loch Spynie into the River Lossie, the river of herbs, which discharges on the east side of the town over a drying bar. The streams run northwest from HW Dover –0300 at up to 3km/h with a southerly wind, more if heavy rain has put the river in spate. The east facing harbour at the end of the A941 was hewn from solid rock as a seine-net fishing harbour in Branderburgh which was founded in 1830. It suffers considerable scend with easterly winds. Its 600m of quays import coal and export oats. There is also a covered fishmarket. The Lossiemouth Fisheries and Community Museum includes a reconstruction of the study of local Prime Minister Ramsay MacDonald. Also of note in this resort is the belfry of St James' church.

Beyond the River Lossie, crossed by a footbridge, the beach of concrete boulders gives way to a long sandy beach backed by sandhills up to 15m high with forest behind all the way to Spey Bay. There is a beachbreak which works best at high water with a big swell. Fulmars fly over the sea but the airfield behind the trees is now disused and the flights of former days are finished. Having Leuchars House at the end of the main runway could cause confusion with RAF Leuchars in Fife.

Binn Hill rises to 68m towards the far end of the beach, helping to locate an active rifle range with a danger area extending offshore.

Kingston, at the end of the B9015, was named after Kingston upon Hull, home of timber merchants who began floating logs down the Spey from the Rothiemurchus and Glenmore pine forests to build ships for international use. These operations proved the Spey a public navigation in the access case which Clive Freshwater won in the House of Lords. The village declined after steel ships began to be made.

Spey Bay has huge numbers of longtailed ducks and common scoters wintering offshore despite the fact that the sea breaks a long way out with northeasterly winds. The spit changes position at the mouth of the river with overfalls and tidal swirls off the end. The head of the bay is silted up by sand and gravel brought down by the Spey, the most rapid river in Scotland. Near the end of the Speyside Walk footpath in the village of Spey Bay, at the end of the B9104, is the Tugnet Ice House museum, Scotland's largest ice house, dating from 1830 and restored with an exhibition on the Spey, salmon fishing, ice packing for salmon and a display on wildlife.

The beach has a beachbreak which works best at high water with a big swell. In quieter conditions a landing may be made onto the track where a campsite is located to the east of the hotel which fronts one of the village's two golf courses.

The mouth of the Lossie with the harbour on the right and dunes backing the surfing beach

Distance
From Shandwick to Spey Bay is 88km
Campsites
Tarlogie, Fortrose, Moss-side, Nairn, Dyke, Findhorn, Burghead, Hopeman, Lossiemouth, Spey Bay
Youth Hostels
Inverness, Tomintoul
OS 1:50,000 Sheets
21 Dornoch and Alness
27 Nairn and Forres
28 Elgin and Dufftown
Imray Chart
C23 Firth of Forth to Moray Firth (1:250,000)
Admiralty Charts
SC 222 Buckie to Fraserburgh (1:75,000)
SC 223 Dunrobin Point to Buckie (1:75,000)
1077 Approaches to Cromarty Firth and Inverness (1:20,000)
1462 Harbours on the North and East Coasts of Scotland. Nairn (1:6,250). Burghead (1:6,250). Hopeman (1:6,250). Lossiemouth (1:6,250)
1889 Cromarty Firth. Cromarty Bank to Invergordon (1:15,000)
Tidal Constants
Balintore: HW Dover +0040, LW Dover +0050
Cromarty: Dover +0020
Fortrose: Dover +0100
McDermott Base: Dover +0100
Nairn: HW Dover +0040, LW Dover +0050
Findhorn: HW Dover +0040, LW Dover +0050
Burghead: HW Dover +0040, LW Dover +0050
Lossiemouth: HW Dover +0040, LW Dover +0050
Buckie: HW Dover +0040, LW Dover +0050
Sea Area
Cromarty
Ranges
Fort George, Binn Hill
Rescue
Inshore lifeboat: Kessock
All weather lifeboats: Invergordon, Buckie
Helicopter: Lossiemouth
Maritime Rescue Centre
Aberdeen, 01224 592334

34 NORTH ABERDEENSHIRE

Fishing villages on a rugged coast

From Spey Bay the coast continues low, flat and sandy to Portgordon. Once again there is forest hiding a landing strip and there is also the line of a disused railway, which formerly reached the coast at Portgordon where gorse now covers the slopes as the A990 joins the coast. To the south is 264m Whiteash Hill with a 99m aerial on its east side.

Portgordon is an 18th-century village of old red sandstone houses. The salmon caught with net and line were stored in Gollachy Ice House. The drying harbour was closed in 1947 and a spoil ground to the north might not be helping its depth.

the first Roman Catholic church built in Scotland after the Reformation, a church which was the secret headquarters of the Roman Catholic church in the north of Scotland during a period of persecution. St Ninian's Chapel is the oldest post-Reformation church in Scotland which is still in use. St Peter's is a more recent Roman Catholic church, dating from 1857, while the North church of 1879 has a crowned tower.

In 1814 two Buckie fishermen of integrity were 400m offshore in calm conditions when they saw a merman near them, close enough to see no scales

The West Muck mark stands off Buckie

Beyond the next golf course Buckpool harbour has been filled in. Instead, Cluny harbour is a fishing port with boatbuilding and importing and exporting timber and grain. With 400m of quays, it is one of the largest commercial harbours in the Moray Firth, serving **Buckie**. It receives a dangerous swell in northerly winds. There is a light tripod on West Muck and the leading lights are to avoid this outcrop rather than to lead into the harbour, the end of which is marked by a lighthouse. By 1913 the town had the largest steam drifter fleet in Scotland and was the major fishing port of the Moray Firth, with its net makers and fish processors remembered in the Buckie Drifter museum with a 1920s quayside and *The Doctors* lifeboat which served at Anstruther until 1990. Buckie had a new lifeboat station in 1995. These days the fishing has changed from herrings to scampi, although the guillemots and cormorants find plenty of lobster pots marked by flags off the harbour. The Buckie Maritime Museum and Peter Anson Gallery has exhibits and paintings relating to the coastal fishing communities, while the Buckie Studio has a craft shop and makes pottery. The town boasts a distillery. The 6.4m first world war memorial is one of the finest in Scotland. The twin spires of St Gregory's church of 1788/9 mark

Findochty's reef strewn harbour overlooked by brightly painted houses

on his tail. He dived and came up some distance away, accompanied by a mermaid, while the men rowed for the shore and safety as quickly as they could.

The coastal road is now the A942, passing Portessie, a much more simple fishing village where boats are beached on the gravel.

Craig Head rises to 60m with an obelisk on the summit, the coast now being cliffy to Scar Nose. Behind a golf course is the ruin of a castle built by the Ord family. Thomas Ord also had workmen's cottages built in 1716 in Findochty. A measured mile leads past caves and a former smugglers' route.

Surrounded by reefs and with a drying bar across the outer harbour, entry to **Findochty** may be dangerous in a strong northerly. In quieter conditions, eider ducks swim placidly in front of caves and a memorial. For once the caravans parked in this former fishing and smuggling village are upstaged by the colours of the houses, particularly the stepped window surrounds. Originally painted for weatherproofing, they now

present a colourful and cheerful background to the harbour. To the south the bald headed Bin of Cullen rises above the surrounding forest to 320m.

The former fishing and pleasure craft harbour at **Portknockie** has silted and partly dries but is the best naturally-sheltered harbour on the south side of the Moray Firth, although it suffers from considerable scend in the harbour with fresh northerly winds. The village, sited on top of the cliffs, dates from the Iron Age and has a 7th-century Pictish fort. It also has a church with a belfry but during the 19th-century religious revival the villagers used Preacher's Cave, the largest of three caves in the cliffs where the rocks are covered with mussels and blackbacked and other gulls, fulmars and dolphins are found offshore.

Vertical strata at Logie Head

Bow Fiddle Rock is one of the most spectacular formations on this coast

kittiwakes, razorbills, guillemots, puffins and the Moray/Aberdeenshire border.

Logie Head has 60m high vertical strata. Somebody singlehandedly built a flight of steps down to the head so that walkers could reach the water but then everyone rallied round to build a monument to record his efforts. Thrift and orange lichen coats the rocks, the haunt of tiny orange butterflies.

Scar Nose ends with Bow Fiddle Rock, a flying buttress where granite beds dipping steeply to the southeast have been eroded by the sea.

Streams to Knock Head start at HW Dover +0430 and begin eastwards at HW Dover −0150.

A golf course backs Cullen Bay with its fast breaking lefts and rights, but **Cullen**'s most conspicuous feature is the disused 19th-century viaduct, designed to look like an ancient gateway. Old Cullen, 1km up the Burn of Deskford, has the 17th-century Cullen House with the 14th-century Auld Kirk in use in its grounds. The 14th-century Cullen church with 16th and 17th century additions was the burial place of Robert the Bruce's queen. In 1823 the Earl of Seafield and Findlater moved Cullen to its present site in order to give his house greater privacy. A domed and pillared pavilion complements the railway structures. The entrance of the drying fishing harbour with its entrance mark is dangerous in strong northerly winds. The town is known for Cullen skink, a haddock, onion and potato soup.

Along the coast are the 3 Kings and Boar's Craig rock formations and Black Lady's Cave. The caravans on the cliffs look down onto gulls, shags,

A large white dovecote on the hillside precedes the cliffs where the 15th–century Findlater Castle ruin is to be found, built as an Ogilvie stronghold.

Sandend Bay surfing is best at low to mid-tide. There is a disused distillery and a windmill behind the bay. Much further south the land rises to 430m high Knock Hill.

Rock strata dominate the landscape at Logie Head

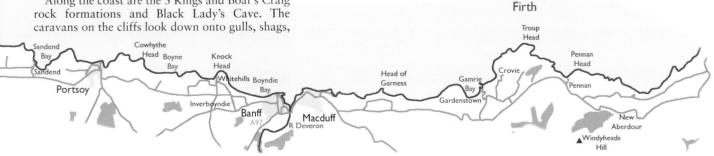

Looking east from Logie Head past West, East, Knock, More and Troup Heads

Entry to **Portsoy** is difficult with a swell. In 1550 it was declared a Burgh of Barony by Mary, Queen of Scots and a charter was granted to the Ogilvies of Boyne. The drying old harbour was built in 1692 with stones laid vertically by Patrick Ogilvie, Lord Boyne, for fishing and for marble export, the latter including cargoes to France, not least two of the chimneys for the Palace de Versailles. The Star Inn of 1727 has an arch which led to a previously cobbled courtyard which was a smuggling centre. The new harbour was built in 1825 by Lord Seafield and rebuilt in 1839 after it was damaged in a storm. It imported coal, seed grain, iron and salt, exporting grain, herring, salmon and timber, and is still used by crab and lobster boats. In the 1880s the steep railway line serving the harbour was closed. A Saltire Award was received for the restoration work on the 17th and 18th-century harbour warehouses and tenement houses refurbished for accommodation, a precursor for subsequent docklands projects elsewhere. A prominent local business is Portsoy Marble and Pottery, based in the late 18th-century Corf House, polishing local red and green marble, the green serpentine coming from the Breeks. A recent development has been the Small Boats Festival which includes a race to Sandend where each boat picks up a creel of smoked fish, returning to Portsoy where it is cooked on the pier. There are 50 traditional sailing boats, models, vintage commercial vehicles, boatbuilding, creel and net, lace, clootie rug, quilt and basket making, coopering, knot tying, fish filleting, knitting, wood turning, weaving, crochet and embroidery, music, dancing, drama, street theatre and jugglers.

Cowhythe Head is composed of crystallized limestone which has been used in nearby limekilns. By Boyne Bay is the ruin of Boyne Castle, an Ogilvie stronghold of about 1580. To the south lies a disused airfield.

Whitehills developed around a sheltered fishing harbour which has 300m of quays and a mark. It is the smallest northeast village to retain its own fishing fleet and daily fishmarket, dealing in cod, haddock, sole, plaice and whiting. Red Well was built by the Romans and in the 19th century it became fashionable to take the waters from the chalybeate spring.

Streams flow east from HW Dover −0130 and west from HW Dover +0430 at up to 1km/h.

Boyndie Bay has an ancient church behind the cemetery in the centre. Reefs at the west end of the bay break in deep water on bigger swells and there is a long right reefbreak at the east end of the bay which works best at mid-tides in low to medium surf, but through to high water on bigger swells. There are two caravan sites behind the bay and a children's playground at the west end.

Banff at the end of the A97 takes its name from the Gaelic banbha, a sucking pig. It was a 12th-century Hanseatic trading port but silted up in the 19th century and now dries. It has 500m of quays but is exposed to northeasterly winds, the sea breaking a long way out with a moderate breeze. Banff Bay is shallow and exposed to the north with a groundswell even during an offshore wind, setting to the east, especially with a northerly wind. The eastgoing stream starts at HW Dover −0130, changing slowly from northeast to east–southeast. The westgoing stream starts at HW Dover +0430, changing slowly from southwest to west–northwest at up to 1km/h. The River Deveron results in shifting sands and undercurrents with lefts breaking over a sandy rock reef onto the rivermouth on all tides. The river is crossed by the A98 on a seven-arched bridge by John Smeaton. Beyond it are a golf course, woodland walk and Duff House, built in Italianate Georgian baroque by William

More steeply dipping rock strata to the east of Macduff

More Head with Troup Head in the distance

Adam for Lord Braco between 1725 and 1740 and now part of the National Gallery of Scotland. Following a refit with decorations in period style, it has 17 to 19th-century works of art including Baekhuysen's *Shipping in a Choppy Sea*. The Temple of Venus is a fantastically designed building and there is no shortage of Greek columns, crowstepped gables, Venetian windows and delicate steeples around. Georgian buildings result from when this was a fashionable winter resort. The town's museum features Banff silver, arms and armour, local history, natural history, geology and 18th-century astronomer James Ferguson. The Harbour Workshop has painted silk goods. Bowls, tennis and a distillery add to the entertainments.

range. A target float is moored offshore and 1.6km north of the target is considered safe.

Between Lion's Head and Cullykhan Bay are Hell's Lum chasm, Fiddes Fort and a cave.

Pennan is a fishing village and was formerly used for smuggling. Uniquely, the telephone box on the front is a listed historical monument, having played a central role in *Local Hero*, much of which was filmed here.

Pennan Head is 110m high, subject to violent downdraughts with offshore winds but plenty of seabird colonies. The purple cliffs continue 120m high to Strahangles Point, hiding the radio masts on Windyheads Hill. The red sandstone cliffs run on to New Aberdour with holes through the base and a very large arch. At one point there is a bird hide but it would be equally suitable for watching the seals.

There is parking by the beach nearest New Aberdour in an area where there are many spring flowers. The 10th-century church of St Drostan was founded at the centre of the original village, one of the oldest in the north of Scotland although the modern village is further inland.

Across the river is **Macduff**, noted for its sunsets. The fishing harbour with 400m of quays, fishmarket and 11m white lighthouse is partly protected, even from the west, and is also engaged in some coastal trade. Fishing nets are made for deep sea trawlers and others. The port is the start or finish each year for the Mobil North Sea Yacht Race to or from Stavanger. Landmarks include a war memorial and a church with a domed tower. In front of the golf course to the east of the town is a break in the cliffs which leads in to a group of four paddling and swimming pools, a playground and a rock arch in the form of an inverted V.

Thirty metre cliffs of indented slate with limestone bands are to be found to Head of Garness, after which the cliffs increase in height to More Head, which is 140m high.

At the southern corner of Gamrie Bay St John's church was built above a ravine in 1513 to commemorate a victory over the invading Danes in 1004. It faces Gardenstown where the drying fishing harbour has 500m of quays, exposed to swell from northeasterly winds but protected from the northwest by the 7m high Craig Dagerty ridge.

Beyond a picnic area is Crovie with its pier and a slip. Much of the beach is inaccessible from the road as the houses hug the slope, built ends towards the sea for protection from the weather.

110m cliffs continue to the 112m vertical Troup Head with guillemots, gulls and gannets nesting on the cliffs around Collis Head in their thousands and black guillemots, puffins, kittiwakes, shags and cormorants all present, not to mention sea urchins.

From Troup Head to Fraserburgh the coast is all considered to be part of the Rosehearty bombing

Distance
From Spey Bay to New Aberdour is 54km
Campsites
Spey Bay, Portessie, Findochty, Portknockie, Cullen, Sandend, Portsoy, Inverboyndie, Macduff, Bonnyton, Fraserburgh
Youth Hostels
Tomintoul, Aberdeen
OS 1:50,000 Sheets
28 Elgin and Dufftown
29 Banff and Huntly
30 Fraserburgh
Imray Chart
C23 Firth of Forth to Moray Firth (1:250,000)
Admiralty Charts
SC 222 Buckie to Fraserburgh (1:75,000)
SC 223 Dunrobin Point to Buckie (1:75,000)
1462 Harbours on the North and East Coasts of Scotland. Buckie (1:10,000). Banff and Macduff (1:20,000).
Tidal Constants
Buckie: HW Dover +0040, LW Dover +0050
Cullen: Dover +0050
Whitehills: HW Dover +0050, LW Dover +0100
Banff: Dover +0010
Gardenstown: HW Dover +0100, LW Dover +0110
Sea Area
Cromarty
Range
Rosehearty
Rescue
Inshore lifeboats: Kessock, Macduff
All weather lifeboats: Buckie, Fraserburgh
Maritime Rescue Centre
Aberdeen, 01224 592334

Crovie has its houses built end on to the sea for protection against the worst excesses of the weather

35 NORTHEAST ABERDEENSHIRE

Landing fish, gas and oil

So fare ye weel, ye Mormond Braes,
For often I've been cheery;
Fair ye weel ye Mormond Braes,
For it's there I lost my dearie.

There's as good fish into the sea
As ever hae been taken
I'll cast my line and try again
For I'm only ainst forsaken.

There are several large caves and arches in the red sandstone at New Aberdour, with channels into them through the rock shelf as the tide rises. East of here there are cliffs of blue mica, decreasing in height towards Rosehearty, with oystercatchers, eider ducks, black guillemots, blackheaded gulls, cormorants, fulmars, gannets, seals and starfish.

Dundarg Castle ruin and a fort are located at the end of the rock shelf. There is a dovecote tower at Quarry Head and a control tower near the picnic tables by **Rosehearty**, looking out towards the bombing range target floats.

Rosehearty was founded in the 14th century by shipwrecked Danes and is one of the oldest fishing villages in Scotland and is accessed by the B9031. Entry is difficult with onshore winds and there is a shorebreak. A museum features fishing gear and local history and other features of the village are a seawater swimming pool, golf course and 19th-century Mounthooley Doocot.

To the south of the village are a radio mast, the ruin of Pittulie Castle and, almost between them, the ruin of Pitsligo Castle. This castle was built in 1424 by the Frasers of Philorth, the 4th and last Earl Pitsligo being generous to the poor and successfully evading arrest after the 1745 rebellion. It became a stronghold of the Forbes family.

The coast beyond Rosehearty begins low and sandy, backed by dunes, but becomes more rocky towards Sandhaven.

Sandhaven was a fishing village but the harbour is disused, having been badly battered in 1953. Sandhaven Meal Mill survived longer, working for two centuries until 1981.

From Sandhaven to Fraserburgh, at the end of the A90, the coast is rocky with drying ledges frequented by seals, blackheaded gulls and other birds.

Scotland's oldest lighthouse on Kinnaird Head

Kinnaird Head is 20m high, topped by a 10m white lighthouse tower on top of a 1570 castle by Sir Alexander Fraser, after whom **Fraserburgh** was named in 1592. The lighthouse was added in 1787, Scotland's first, and attached to it is Scotland's Lighthouse Museum. Also close by is the three-storey Wine Tower which has no floors and the purpose of which is unknown despite the name.

A 21m lighthouse is built on Balaclava Pier, part of the major fishing harbour and fishmarket at Fraserburgh. 3km of quays service the large fishing fleet, import coal, lime, iron, salt and timber and export oats, potatoes, preserves and pickled herrings. Surfers enjoy a left break at the harbour wall but, inside, there is a tight left turn for fishing boats, particularly difficult with a southerly wind.

Fishing boats back at base in Fraserburgh Harbour

A room in the library is devoted to Thomas Blake Glover who spent his childhood here and then founded the Japanese navy and the Mitsubishi car company. A 17th-century Mercat Cross is unique in having pre and post union royal arms of Scotland. A further place of interest is the Craft Shop which has woodturning and pyrograph demonstrations.

Dunes up to 30m high along the back of Fraserburgh Bay shelter a golf course and the B9033 while a good beachbreak may be found in front with jellyfish for added interest. At the east end of the bay the Water of Philorth enters from the direction of the restored Cairnbulg Castle or, in the distance, Mormond Hill with its array of NATO aerials.

Cairnbulg Briggs is a drying rock ledge, marked by an 8m light on Cairnbulg Point which resembles an oil rig from the distance. Cairnbulg is a fishing village with a harbour built in 1987.

Rock ledges and shoals continue to Inzie Head. **Inverallochy** is a fishing village which still lacks a harbour at the end of the B9107.

Whitelinks Bay has a wreck offshore and a golf course and aerial on land. St Combs is another harbourless fishing village with 18th-century cottages and a church dedicated to St Columba, hence the village name. The Tufted Duck hotel has

Moray
Firth

Kinnaird
Head

Quarry
Head

Sandhaven
Rosehearty
B9031

Fraserburgh
Bay

Cairnbulg Pt
Inverallochy

Fraserburgh

B9033   B9107

St Combs

Inzie
Head

New
Aberdour

L of Strathbeg

Rattray
Head

North
Sea

St Fergus

Scotstown
Head

Kirkton
Head

R Ugie
Inverugie

Buchanhaven

A982

Peterhead

Peterhead
Bay

Sandford
Bay

Boddam
Buchan
Ness

A90

Dundonnie

Longhaven

A975

Bullers
of Buchan

Cruden
Bay

Port
Erroll

Bay of
Cruden

Whinnyfold

Kirktown
of Slains

Collieston

St Catherine's
Dub

Sands of
Forvie
R Ythan

Hackley
Head

Newburgh

Foveran

Newburgh
Bar

Belhelvie   Balmedie

Blackdog

Aberdeen

a name to appeal to all of its customers, mostly birdlovers and bird shooters. Inland is Inverallochy Castle ruin.

A ridge runs 2km east from Inzie Head then dunes begin which continue all the way to Peterhead with a beachbreak as far as Rattray Head. Halfway down the beach a stream discharges from the Loch of Strathbeg, a 2km^2 loch in a 9km^2 RSPB nature reserve. On the migration routes to Iceland and Scandinavia, hides look onto fresh and saltwater marshes and dune slack pools in one of the most important wildfowl havens in Britain, especially in the spring and autumn. It is a major breeding centre for geese and otters and a roost for large numbers of wildfowl in winter including whooper swans, greylag geese, mallards, wigeon, pochard, tufted ducks, goldeneyes, goosanders and pinkfooted geese. In summer there are great crested grebes, eider ducks and breeding terns. 2,000 greylag and pinkfooted geese and 600 whooper swans roost in autumn and birds on passage include mute swans, marsh harriers and green sandpipers. In all there are 40,000 birds per year present. Around the loch are a windpump and windmill, disused airfield, radio masts, ruins of St Mary's chapel and Castle Earthworks built by the Comyn Earls of Buchan. There was a harbour but it silted up.

Just before Rattray Head there is an arrangement of pipes rising up in the intertidal range on a line likely to be taken by paddlers, its location not marked.

For a major headland Rattray Head is unusual in being low-lying and backed by dunes. However, there is fast flow around the head with northeasterly winds, a small race forming while oystercatchers stand nearby and appear to express surprise. 8km off the head, streams begin southeast at HW Dover –0220 at up to 4km/h and northwest at HW Dover +0400 at up to 3km/h. Dunes have engulfed the community. Before the lighthouse was built in 1893 many ships were wrecked on Rattray Briggs. Now the 34m white brick tower stands offcentre on a granite base built in the shallows.

St Fergus was an 8th-century bishop and, while it is not unusual for a village to have been named after a bishop, the giving of his name to the gas terminal for the Brent and Frigg oilfields is a little more incongruous. To many paddlers the distinctive call of the great northern diver is the definitive sound of the North American backwoods. To hear it repeatedly to a backdrop of flare stacks, accompanied by the wailing siren of the St Fergus terminal and the foghorn at Rattray Head calls for a rethink.

Terns may also be present here. A pillbox where a stream discharges through the dunes is to be followed by more before Peterhead. Scotstown, marked by aerials, has a surf break near the rocks of Scotstown Head which is popular with seals. It

is followed by the Kirkton Head break, approached past an old church and cemetery.

Inverugie's motte had a Norman castle on it at one time. The remains of a later castle, built for the Keith family, are on the other side of the village. The River Ugie winds round a golf course to

Rattray Head
lighthouse

Flare stacks and other columns are part of the St Fergus gas terminal behind the dunes

discharge in front of the fishing harbour of Buchanhaven. The river contains brown and sea trout and the Ugie salmon smokehouse is the oldest salmon and trout house in Scotland and the oldest building in **Peterhead**, built in 1585 and still smoking.

the mainland by a bridge, but at most states of the tide there is solid rock beneath the bridge and no passage for boats.

Red granite cliffs up to 73m high run down the coast as far as Bay of Cruden with Cave o' Meakie

Seals crowd onto skerries at Scotstown Head

A race forms off the rocks and tidal streams run to 3km/h, reducing southwards.

Peterhead Bay, on the A982, is almost enclosed by two breakwaters which were begun in 1886 and finished in 1958 by prisoners from Peterhead prison that lies at the end of the southern breakwater. Peterhead Harbour is Britain's principal fishing port with one of Europe's busiest fishmarkets, up to 400 boats and 14,000 boxes of fish per day, and was the principal whaling port. The port also deals in grain, fertilizers, coal and limestone with a total of 2km of quays. Peterhead Bay Harbour is a North Sea oilfield supply base and has a tanker jetty to import fuel. The bay seems to be a vast empty area when viewed from outside the breakwaters.

The entrance to the large Peterhead Bay with oil industry supply vessels and Europe's largest fish market

and other caves, arches, stacks and blowholes. There is a castle site just south of Boddam. Seals and moon jellyfish frequent Dundonnie and Long Haven is an important seabird colony. There are also innumerable seabirds at the Bullers of Buchan (the name coming from boil), a cauldron hollowed out by the sea to a depth of 60m and visited by Boswell and Dr Johnson during their Scottish tour in 1773.

This pair also visited Slains Castle. Built in 1597, it was extended and rebuilt by the 9th Earl of Erroll in the 17th century and became the centre of a tourist boom in Edwardian times when the railway arrived, being partly demolished in 1925 when interest waned. Perhaps the most important visitor was Port Erroll holidaymaker Bram Stoker

The town itself is built of pink granite from Boddam. The Arbuthnot Museum and Art Gallery has herring and whaling, Arctic and Inuit, local history, photographic and coin displays. The Peterhead Maritime Heritage museum tells about the region's whalers, fishermen, sailors and navigators. In front of the Town House is a statue of Field Marshal James Keith, a favourite general of Frederick the Great, the statute being presented by William I of Prussia. Other notable buildings include the pre-Reformation church of St Peter and Kirkburn Mills which made wool and woollen cloth.

Beside Sandford Bay is a large modern power station, its high chimney a prominent landmark but not enough of a landmark to prevent a wreck being deposited on the Skerry directly in front of it.

The pink granite fishing village of **Boddam** is surrounded by rocks on which seals haul out and around which eider ducks swim. Buchan Ness, with its lighthouse, is the most easterly point on the Scottish mainland. The lighthouse was built in 1827 by Robert Stevenson and the ness is linked to

Sheltered channels amongst rocky islets at Dundonnie

Buchan Ness, the most easterly point on the Scottish mainland, together with its lighthouse and bridge over the dry channel

who saw the castle and was inspired to use it as the setting for *Dracula*.

Fish nets are staked out at various points on this part of the coast. Bay of Cruden is surrounded by dunes and the inevitable golf course. There is a powerful break which works best in the winter. In 1997 a school of seven sperm whales were washed up. Port Erroll is the harbour for **Cruden Bay** on

Slains Castle, the ruin which inspired Bram Stoker to write his story, Dracula

the A975, located at the mouth of the Water of Cruden and home to lobster fishing boats.

The skerries of the Skares signal the start of another run of rocky cliffs as far as Hackley Head. Whinnyfold, the landing point for oil pipelines from the Forties field, has an important seabird colony. Cave Arthur lies to the south of the village.

Off Mains of Slains is Broad Haven (which lies to the north of North Broad Haven), on the south side of which is the ruin of the old Slains Castle, destroyed by James VI when he discovered the Earl of Erroll was involved in a plot to land Spanish troops. The castle has been further ruined by the construction of a three-storey chalet in front of it.

Caves to the north of Colliston were used by smugglers from the fishing village. St Catherine's Dub was named after the Spanish galleon *Santa Catherina* which was wrecked in 1594. This was the holiday destination for T E Lawrence, perhaps attracted by the area to the south, one of the largest dune systems in Britain, undisturbed but shifting, a miniature Arabia. A continuous sweep of 20km of beach runs down to Aberdeen, mostly backed by dunes up to 60m high. The dunes, which have overwhelmed Iron Age and mediaeval settlements in the last two millennia, now form the Forvie National Nature Reserve. Forvie church ruin is all that remains of the village of Forvie which was probably overwhelmed during a 9-day gale in 1688. The Forvie Centre near Sand Loch has information on the wide range of fauna and flora. This is an important feeding ground for wildfowl and waders and the 2,000 pairs of eiders form the largest breeding colony in Britain for the species. Common, Arctic, little and Sandwich terns all breed and there are 50 species of bird and 60 species of plant in the area. The beach has many shells and the nets suggest that the sea provides stocks of salmon.

Newburgh is near the mouth of the River Ythan with a harbour, Udney Links golf course, windsurfing and an annual raft race. The channel position is constantly changing over the Newburgh Bar.

Tank traps line Foveran Links to the south of the river and pillboxes are seen at intervals.

Hackley Bay, the last outcrops before the long sweep of beach down to Aberdeen

A coastal vessel was wrecked off Menie Links and surf breaks continue from here to the River Don, north of Aberdeen.

Balmedie has a country park with picnic site, barbecue stands and visitor displays on the shipwrecks, wildlife and dunes and their conservation. Behind are a range of Pleistocene hills of water-rounded gravel, sand and clay.

A military range creates a danger area out to sea at Blackdog, marked by yellow buoys 2km off the coast.

In 1871 the Ordnance Survey set out a baseline from Belhelvie to Blue Hill, south of Aberdeen. The length was computed from a baseline at Hounslow. When the 8km line was measured it was found to be in error by about 80mm. By coincidence, the two baselines are near to what have become Britain's two busiest airports, Heathrow and Dyce, the latter being unusual in having mostly helicopter traffic heading for the rigs, as is only too obvious to anyone on this coast.

As the only rock for 20km, Blackdog Rock is small but distinctive. Just to the north is the mouth of the Blackdog Burn, fished by a heron. A track comes down to the shore where submarine cables land and it might also be a place for paddlers to land.

Blackdog range and the dunes reaching into the distance

Distance
From New Aberdour to Blackdog is 76km
Campsites
Fraserburgh, Peterhead, Newburgh
Youth Hostel
Aberdeen
OS 1:50,000 Sheets
30 Fraserburgh
38 Aberdeen
Imray Chart
C23 Firth of Forth to Moray Firth (1:250,000)
Admiralty Charts
SC 210 Newburgh to Montrose (1:75,000)
SC 213 Fraserburgh to Newburgh (1:75,000)
SC 222 Buckie to Fraserburgh (1:75,000)
1438 Harbours on the East Coast of Scotland. Approaches to Peterhead (1:20,000). Peterhead Bay and Harbour (1:6,250)
1462 Harbours on the North and East Coasts of Scotland. Fraserburgh Approaches(1:20,000). Fraserburgh (1:6,250)
Tidal Constants
Gardenstown: HW Dover +0100, LW Dover +0110
Fraserburgh: HW Dover +0110, LW Dover +0100
Peterhead: Dover +0140
Aberdeen: Dover +0220
Sea Area
Cromarty
Ranges
Rosehearty, Blackdog
Rescue
Inshore lifeboats: Macduff, Aberdeen
All weather lifeboats: Fraserburgh, Peterhead, Aberdeen
Maritime Rescue Centre
Aberdeen, 01224 592334

36 SOUTHEAST ABERDEENSHIRE

The oil capital starting a geological jumble of cliffs

As the waves lash the platform and soak us with spray,
The rig seems to twist in the teeth of the gale.
Our fumbling fingers just get in the way
But the drill never stops as we cling to the rail.
When we flew out this morning with three weeks to go
Even Aberdeen's granite seemed warm to our eyes,
Each thinking how bitter these northern winds blow,
Unwilling recruits only trying to get by.
It's hard working away, working away.

Alistair Russell

17 PENCE · INDUSTRY YEAR 1986

From Blackdog the beach crosses from Aberdeenshire into Aberdeen and continues south past golf courses at Balgownie and **Bridge of Don**, the latter carrying the A956 in front of an exhibition centre.

The River Don or Deen, in dialect, may formerly have entered the sea east of Seaton Park or been a tributary of the River Dee, joining it near the harbour. A sharp demarcation line can be seen in the fickle currents at the mouth of the Don where the brown river water meets the blue-green of the sea. Just occasionally the surf can be worthwhile here but the rivermouth can be dangerous.

The Donmouth nature reserve has a hide and the waters contain flounders, eels and mackerel. Seals, dolphins, eider ducks, guillemots and cormorants might be seen in the area.

The city is Scotland's largest resort and frequent winner of the Britain in Bloom competition with roses, crocuses, daffodils and other spring flowers in profusion despite the latitude. Along the front are the King's Links golf course and several amusement centres. The Beach Leisure Centre has a sports hall, climbing wall, pool, flumes, Linx ice area, skating, ice hockey, disco and curling. Codona's Amusement Centre and Park claims to be Scotland's largest funfair. Sunset Boulevard has tenpin bowling, Rambo's children's adventureland and virtual reality. Times have changed since Byron was resident as a youth.

Aberdeen harbour, off the estuary of the River Dee, is one of the largest fishing ports in Britain with a large fishmarket and is the main base for the North Sea oil industry. Fortunately, the city seems to have lost much of its 1970s oil town Americanism. There is also vehicle ferry traffic to Lerwick, Stromness, the Faeroes and Bergen. Footdee is the fishing village designed in 1808/9 with input from the fisherfolk.

One of the ships built here was the tall ship *Malcolm Miller* in the late 1960s. The Tall Ships Race has since visited the harbour.

Flow in the Dee may reach 11km/h and there can be an outward flow even on a flood tide. Entry between the two breakwaters can be difficult over the bar, especially with easterly winds which can also produce significant clapotis off the southern breakwater.

A rig supply vessel leaves the mouth of the Dee past Girdle Ness lighthouse

Aberdeen is Scotland's third largest city, its high rise skyline fronted by a 3km promenade and a beach of groynes. The Granite City takes its nickname from the by-law which has required all buildings to have granite fronts, supporting local quarrying interests. Most buildings are built completely of the grey granite with mica flecks. These include Marischal College, the world's second largest granite building, formerly part of Aberdeen University but possibly to become a hotel on the university's exodus to the Old Aberdeen campus. The quadrangle of 1836–44 buildings includes the newer Mitchell Tower. Despite the size of the building and its 1km distance from the open sea, its tower has been measured to rise and fall 20mm with the tide. The building also houses the Marischal Museum of Human History which includes an Inuit who paddled his kayak to the Scottish coast, apparently lost, and then died.

The lighthouse on Girdle Ness was built in 1832 by Robert Stevenson as a round tower 40m high, now visible for 36km. There is a race off the point on the southgoing stream. Streams flow southeast from HW Dover −0230 and northwest from HW Dover +0330 at up to 6km/h, staying strong close inshore.

Nigg Bay is the possible former mouth of the River Dee. At the head of the bay boulder clay at the northern end is covered with glacial sands and gravels, while morainic material further south includes erratics in drift from Belhelvie, Boddam, Strathmore, Deeside and Oslo. On the north side of the bay St Fittick's church was granted by William the Lion to the abbey of Arbroath. The bay was used for saltmaking and lay below the gaze of the Torry Battery. Oil rigs have been anchored in the bay and to the southeast of Greg Ness, above which aerials are prominent.

From here to Inverbervie the cliffs are almost continuous with Stonehaven the only major break. To Garron Point they are almost vertical with mica slate over granite. Running along the edge of the cliffs is the Aberdeen to King's Cross railway line as far as Stonehaven, seen several times in the form of viaducts over clefts. Behind the railway the A90 is close for much of the way, but remains hidden from the sea.

At Bridge of One Hair there is a layer of red Strathmore boulder clay with quartzite and lava to add to the geographical jumble.

Above Doonies Yawns is Crab's Cairn, a picnic site and a model farm with rare breeds, Clydesdales, cattle, sheep, pigs and Shetland ponies.

Caves are found in the cliffs, on top of which is Altens industrial estate where many of the oil industry support companies have their premises.

Fishing ropes drying by the harbour at Cove Bay

Cove Bay has a well-sheltered harbour with fishing boats pulled up on the beach and hanks of rope hanging up to dry. There is moraine material to the northwest and more Strathmore drift from the south with signs of glacial polish on the rocks.

There are quarries at Hare Ness and Blowup Nose, the latter name suggesting blasting operations. Between them the coast returns from Aberdeen to Aberdeenshire.

Findon recalls Finnan haddies, haddock which were lightly smoked over cottage fires until the 19th century when legislation was used to stop the industry and allowed it to be moved to Aberdeen smokehouses while the village nearly died. Portlethen village, separate from the much larger modern community of **Portlethen**, was formerly a fishing village working off the beach.

Stones set on a hillside at **Newtonhill** were from a former breakwater when this was a busy fishing port. The boats sitting on the beach at the mouth of the Burn of Elsick suggest that the steep hillside would have made access to the harbour somewhat inconvenient on a regular basis.

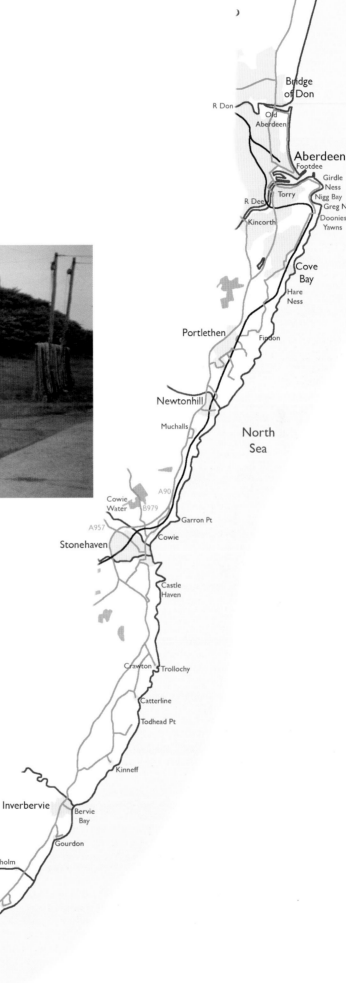

Muchalls castle has fine 17th-century architecture, notable plasterwork in the Great Hall with the Burnett coat of arms and fine fireplaces. There was a tunnel to the Gin Shore, used by smugglers until it was blocked in the 19th century.

Garron Point is the distinctive end of the Highland Boundary Fault which runs right across Scotland to Bute. Brown dolomitic rock can be seen dividing the Highland Border from the Precambrian rocks. Below the golf course

hanging round the necks of policemen while trying to force flasks between their lips.

From Downie Point to Craig David the cliffs are of coarse conglomerate which birds find no problem gripping, although they leave it in a much more soiled state than would be the case with fine grained rocks.

A war memorial above Strathleven Bay consists of a deliberately unfinished circle of pillars and pediments to represent the unfinished lives.

Dunnotar Castle, steeped in history on the cliffs to the south of Stonehaven

Craigeven Bay has cut into the older rocks, exposing spilities, red jaspers and black shales with Cambrian fossils, dipping steeply north but leaving the Highland Border rocks at each end. St Mary's church was built by the shore.

Cowie is a fishing village based around a weathered quartz porphyry dyke through sandstone. The village replaces a previous royal burgh created by David I but burned down in 1645 on the orders of the Duke of Montrose, a Royalist supporter in the Civil War.

Stonehaven Bay has streams to 2km/h where lion's mane and moon jellyfish swim. At the northern end of **Stonehaven**, Cowie Water descends under Glenury Viaduct as the railway heads away inland.

Stonehaven, where the B979 meets the A957, comes from the Old English Stanehythe, stone wharf. Stonehaven's harbour is at the mouth of the Carron Water although the town occupies the space between the two rivers. Few fishing boats remain in the harbour but the resort does have some yachts. The Stonehaven Tolbooth Museum is located in a 16th-century storehouse belonging to the Earls Marishal but later used as a prison. Three Episcopal ministers were incarcerated in 1748 for breaking post Culloden laws which banned them from holding services for more than 5 people, but they were still able to baptize babies passed in through the windows to them. The museum also has displays of fishing, local history and archaeology. Other buildings of interest include the Arcadia stained glass studio.

A notable annual event is the fireball, a festival with origins lost in time but undoubtedly relating to the Vikings. As the church clock strikes midnight to announce the New Year, about a score of fireballs are lit. These are wire cages each about

The site above Castle Haven was fortified for St Ninian in the 5th-century. Dunnotar Castle was built in the 14th century and visited by Mary, Queen of Scots in 1562, when it was like a fortified village. In 1645 the 7th Earl Marischal, a Covenanter, retreated inside at the approach of the Royalists under the Duke of Montrose who could not get in and so burned the earl's lands instead. When Cromwell attacked in 1651 the Scottish crown jewels were lowered to a fishwife who carried them past the Roundheads to safety in Kinneff church. During Monmouth's rebellion of 1685 122 men and 45 women were locked in the Whigs Vault, a 5m x 16m room, for several months, during which many of them died. The original ridge of land from the shore was cut through by the defenders for extra security. These days it is in a ruined state but was used by Zeffirelli for his filming of *Hamlet*.

There are aerials on the top of the cliffs. The occasional blackbacked gull gives way to increasing numbers of gulls nesting on the cliffs, cliffs with caves in the conglomerate. At Trollochy a blowhole has diverted the Crawton Burn eastwards to form a fall over the cliff. Fowlsheugh (birds cliff) is an RSPB seabird colony, one of the largest mainland seabird colonies with 30,000 kittiwakes, 30,000 guillemots and hundreds of razorbills, fulmars, herring gulls, shags, puffins and eiders breeding between April and July.

Crawton is a largely abandoned village where the cliffs change from grey to deep red brown. Three basalt lava fingers containing quartz and agates, the lower central flow with angular columns, run into the sea between Lower Old Red Sandstone and there are eroded conglomerates in the bays, dipping gently west. Rock platforms and stacks add to the geological interest.

Rocks impersonate a submarine below the village at Catterline

the size of a pillow on a wire handle, stuffed with pitch and other inflammable materials. The bearers walk up and down the main street, swinging the fireballs around their heads until they burn out after about 20 minutes. By this time the crowds are melting away and the more sociable have given up

Catterline has a pier and is frequented by seals, terns and artists. A maroon outcrop in front of the village has the oversize silhouette of a submarine.

Todhead Point has 15m cliffs topped by a 13m white lighthouse tower with many nesting birds. It seems to be another of these places which is not

significant enough to justify a lighthouse even though the following red cliffs, the Slainges, are quite impressive. Whistleberry Castle remains are close to the cliffs while at Shieldhill the cliffs overhang the sea. 137m high Bervie Brow with a radio tower on top brings the cliffs to an end. King's Step is where David II and his wife, Johanna, were driven ashore in a storm after escaping the English while returning from a nine-year exile in France.

At the back of Bervie Bay is **Inverbervie** where Bervie Water enters. The village has a seafood factory and a jute mill. Hallgreen Castle is by the shore.

From here to Milton Ness there are grassy slopes leading to a foreshore which was wide enough to take a railway from Montrose, now dismantled. There is stiff black shelly clay and a fairly continuous rock platform with reefs running out into the sea at right angles with inconvenient regularity.

Gourdon has a fishing harbour which can only be entered in moderate weather, but is a village which looks better from the land than from the sea, the latter vista being of a rather rundown and industrial community. It has a spinning mill and, on the hill behind, a long cairn and fort.

Mill of Benholm, set on a stream, is a working mill with waterwheel and a selection of farm animals. The stream leads down to Haughs Bay where there are Damside Garden Herbs and Arboretum with seven herb gardens ranging from Celtic to the present day.

The most notable building seen from the water is Lathallen School, set in trees at Johnshaven, a lobster fishing village with lobster processing plant. The village has a drying harbour.

Ruined cottages, new chalets and a shoreline caravan park mark Milton of Mathers. A stream flows down to the water through Den Finella, named after a 10th-century queen who killed her

husband, King Kenneth, and then threw herself down a 12m waterfall.

The rock platform comes to an end at Milton Ness. Tangleha is a small harbour, at low tide reached through a narrow break in a reef, when the route up to the beach is silty at first.

A lighthouse marks Todhead Point which is quite insignificant on a map

The small harbour approached through the rocks at Tangleha. On the horizon is a three masted sail training ship involved in the Tall Ships Race

Distance
From Blackdog to Tangleha is 55km
Campsites
Newburgh, Kincorth, Inverbervie, Johnshaven, Milton of Mathers
Youth Hostel
Aberdeen
OS 1:50,000 Sheets
38 Aberdeen
45 Stonehaven and Banchory
Imray Chart
C23 Firth of Forth to Moray Firth (1:250,000)
Admiralty Charts
SC 190 Montrose to Fife Ness (1:75,000)
SC 210 Newburgh to Montrose (1:75,000)
1438 Harbours on the East Coast of Scotland.
Stonehaven Harbour (1:12,250)
1446 Aberdeen Harbour (1:7,500). Approaches to Aberdeen (1:15,000)
Tidal Constants
Aberdeen: Dover +0220
Stonehaven: Dover +0230
Inverbervie: Dover +0300
Montrose: HW Dover +0320
Sea Areas
Cromarty, Forth
Rescue
Inshore lifeboats: Aberdeen, Montrose
All weather lifeboats: Aberdeen, Montrose
Maritime Rescue Centres
Aberdeen, 01224 592334
Forth, 01333 450666

Reefs run out into the sea at Milton of Mathers

37 ANGUS

A surfeit of sand

The Abbot of Aberbrothok
Had placed that bell on the Inchcape Rock;
On a buoy in the storm it floated and swung,
And over the waves its warning rung.

Robert Southey

Fish nets at the mouth of the River North Esk

The lighthouse on Scurdie Ness at the mouth of the River South Esk, Montrose

Tangleha is left past Milton Ness, the end of the rock platform for the time being. Montrose Bay eats into the hillside with a castle site at the end of the bay, the 70m high cliffs below the Heughs of St Cyrus, the spire of one of St Cyrus' two churches prominent on the top and fish nets below.

The River North Esk acts as the boundary between Aberdeenshire and Angus, but first comes a marsh lagoon and the St Cyrus National Nature

An 8km sweep of dunes run to Montrose. Behind the dunes are a distillery and then two golf links before cranes take over at Montrose. **Montrose** is a commercial and fishing port which has become an oilfield supply base and now includes the Montrose Fire and Emergency Simulator Centre for training offshore workers. From the 13th century it was a seaport, exporting skins and hides and importing timber and flax. Montrose Museum covers local maritime and natural history, local art, Pictish stones, Montrose silver and pottery, whaling artefacts and Napoleonic items including a copy of the emperor's death mask. For heads of the Royal Family and sculptures the William Lamb Memorial Studio is the place to go.

The shoreline changes abruptly with the River South Esk which discharges through the large Montrose Basin and out through the dredged channel which can have breakers to the end of the dredged section even in calm weather. Streams run in the channel when the Annat Bank is dry, but spread out over the bank as the tide floods, weakening at the outer end. The ebb sets south across the harbour entrance from HW Dover −0300 and sets north from HW Dover +0320 at up to 13km/h, heavy rain and snowmelt decreasing the flood and increasing the ebb. The drift direction reversed in 1991, the beach having

The limekiln and drying salmon nets on Boddin Point with Red Head in the distance

Reserve with a marine life tank and over 300 plant species including clustered bellflower and wild liquorice. Birdlife ranges from herons, cormorants, oystercatchers and eider ducks to fulmars, terns and gannets at this end of the bay.

now scoured back to its 1940 line, exposing anti-tank blocks and barbed wire.

A tall lighthouse is located on Scurdie Ness and daymarks edge the southern side of the channel. The Gaelic monadh ros means moor on the

promontory. The rock platform now begins again, the haunt of blackheaded gull and curlew. The lifeboat used to be housed in a tower at Mains of Usan.

Those who suffer pink elephants need to be warned about a red one. Elephant Rock is an extrusion which has been sculpted to give a trunk and legs.

What appears to be a castle on Boddin Point is a massive limekiln which was used to prepare fertilizer for the farmland. These days it is surrounded by drying salmon fishing nets in the midst of waters with cod and lobsters. Agates may be found on the rocks. A real castle is Dunninald Castle, up the hill and hidden beyond the Aberdeen to King's Cross railway which runs along the cliffs for 3km, crossing Black Jack and another chasm on high viaducts.

A fort and monument begin the dune backed curve of Lunan Bay, but the distinctive feature is the tottering ruin of Red Castle which stands on the bank of Lunan Water in the middle of the bay. The current structure has been a ruin since 1770

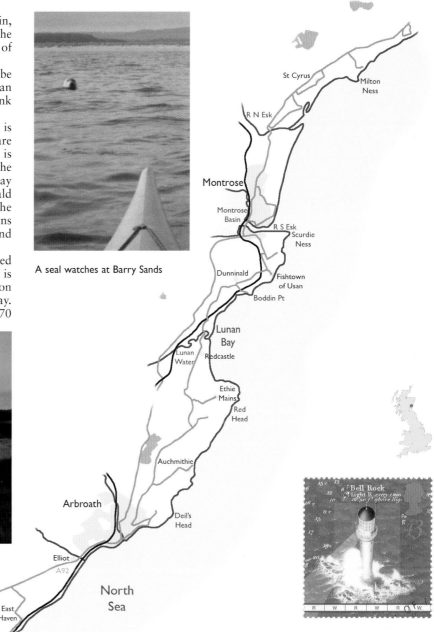

A seal watches at Barry Sands

Red Castle breaks the skyline of dunes above Lunan Bay

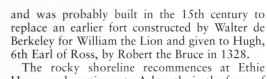

and was probably built in the 15th century to replace an earlier fort constructed by Walter de Berkeley for William the Lion and given to Hugh, 6th Earl of Ross, by Robert the Bruce in 1328.

The rocky shoreline recommences at Ethie Haven and continues to Arbroath, in the form of red sandstone cliffs from 80m high Red Head to Whiting Ness. On top are the site of a chapel and

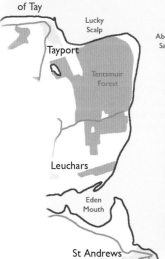

Puffins swimming off Red Head

The Needle E'e with the Deil's Head beyond

The entrance to Arbroath harbour with the disused Bell Rock signal tower on the far side

along the lines of Canterbury Cathedral, the remains include one of the best examples of an abbot's residence. In 1320 the *Declaration of Arbroath* was sent from here to Rome, declaring Scotland independent. The abbey was dissolved in 1608 but independence came up again when the Stone of Scone was stolen from Westminster in 1951 and left on the high altar. There was also regal interest with a visit from Queen Mary in 1562.

Between the fishing harbour at the mouth of the Brothock Burn (from the Gaelic brothaig, little boiler) and the football stadium is the disused signal tower of 1813, used to signal to the Bell Rock. Robert Southey's *Inchcape Rock* tells of a feud between the abbot and the wrecker, Ralph the Rover, who cut the warning bell's rope on the rock. The tower is now a museum for the history of the town, fishing, the sea, the flax industry, Shanks lawnmowers, folk life, wildlife, archaeology and the Arbroath lifeboat. Arbroath Art Gallery features local artists.

The Bell or Inchcape Rock has a lighthouse built by Robert Stevenson.

Dunes replace the rocks, being followed by the A92 for 2km, the Aberdeen to King's Cross railway to Carnoustie and Kerr's Miniature Railway of 1935, a 260mm gauge line with steam and petrol engines hauling passengers. Beyond Elliot Water is a golf course and tank traps along the dunes.

The last section of rocky shoreline before St Andrews continues to Carnoustie with a gap at East Haven, with its picnic area, after a disused airfield and a pillbox add to the fortifications.

a number of forts, including Praile Castle, while guillemots, razorbills, puffins, blackheaded gulls and moon jellyfish frequent the lower levels.

Red caves in the cliffs were used for smuggling in the 18th century at Auchmithie, the harbour not being built until the 1890s. At the height of its prosperity the harbour had a fleet of 33 fishing boats, but it was damaged by a loose German mine in the second world war. Until recently the men were carried to the boats on the women's backs to avoid getting their feet wet, a wonderful precedent for chauvinists. The beach was where Arbroath smokies originated, the local method of preparing haddock.

Forts and caves continue from Lud Castle (with its cave through the head) to Maiden Castle. The Deil's Head, Pint Stoup and Poll Stack are assorted

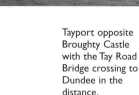

The Old High lighthouse breaks the low sweep of land which forms Buddon Ness

names for a vertical finger of rock near the Needle E'e, a block with a suitably shaped hole through it. This section of coast has a nature reserve with a nature trail visiting sea plantain, scurvy grass, red campion and wood vetch.

In calm conditions there are routes through the rock platform and past the remains of a walkway

Sailing, windsurfing, swimming and angling all take place at **Carnoustie** on the A930, although it is probably best known for its golf course.

Barry Links are a problem area with rifle ranges along the sides firing east and west over the sea and heavy gunnery in the centre. Lookout huts are located along the 6–9m high dunes which back

Tayport opposite Broughty Castle with the Tay Road Bridge crossing to Dundee in the distance.

to reach the parking area with toilets, ice cream van and old well at the approach to **Arbroath**.

Arbroath Abbey, now a set of red sandstone ruins, was founded in 1178 by William the Lion, whose tomb is inside, and was dedicated to St Thomas of Canterbury. Built in towering Gothic

Barry Sands along two sides of the triangular peninsula. In places there are conspicuous areas of tipped rock to resist where the sea has been on the attack. On the other hand, Gaa Sand runs out from Buddon Ness for a considerable distance and usually has breaking waves over it. It is extending and passage over it is dangerous for most boats, but large numbers of seals congregate here.

There are two disused lighthouses, the Old Low and the Old High, the latter with a 32m white tower. In addition there are isolated piles in the sea. The dunes increase to 9–12m high.

Barry Buddon camp and the golf course at **Monifieth** are on an 8m beach, across which the Aberdeen to King's Cross railway runs to follow the shore and across which the Angus/Dundee border also runs. Dunes are covered in marram grass but caravans detract from the shoreline.

Dighty Water separates Monifieth from Barnhill which merges into Broughty Ferry, the town where the wealthy **Dundee** jute barons built their mansions. The dominant building on the point, though, is the 15th-century Broughty Castle, controlling the estuary with a square tower and now a museum on local history, the growth of the town, fishing, the lifeboat, ferries, Dundee whaling industry relics including harpoons, knives and scrimshaw, seashore wildlife, arms, armour and the military history of the castle. There is turbulence off the point, especially on the ebb with westerly winds. Rain and snowmelt decrease the flood (which has a northwest set) and increase the ebb. There are plenty of yachts while small coasters are restricted to the fairway. Upstream are the Tay road and rail bridges.

The Firth of Tay separates Dundee from Fife. **Tayport** used to be the ferry port to cross to Dundee before the Tay Road Bridge was built. Off the drying harbour and Larick Scalp is a disused timber pile lighthouse, threatening to collapse under the weight of guano. The church at Ferry-Port-an-Craig has a 17th-century tower with a list, but a more substantial building is a spinning mill.

Northeast Fife has some of the finest weather in Britain with low rainfall and long hours of sunshine, especially in the spring and in September and October. The Fife shoreline can throw up an interesting selection of semiprecious stones including agate, amethyst and smoky quartz.

Tents Muir woods follow the coast for 8km, mostly pines behind a line of tank traps growing on an 8m beach. Flows are strong north of Lucky Scalp, which does not cover, the flood setting towards Tayport and the ebb towards Green Scalp where a wire fence runs out into the estuary.

Running out into the North Sea is the spit of Abertay Sands, uncovered for 6km at low water and frequented by large numbers of seals. The sands are unstable, increasing in length, the Elbow and Bar moving northeast, and considered dangerous for boats to cross.

Tentsmuir Sands consist of acid dunes forming the Tentsmuir Point National Nature Reserve with curlews, chaffinches and yellowhammers plus gannets off the coast, a nature trail and a picnic site.

Leuchars Airfield is one of the most active military airfields in Scotland with jets descending over the sea at Eden Mouth onto the main runway, even more active during the Leuchars Air Show.

The estuary of the River Eden almost dries up to the papermill at Guardbridge and is a nature reserve, the birds being undisturbed by the jets. The extensive mudflats are good for winter birds. A count put the curlew as the most prolific summer species at 200 birds, ahead of oystercatchers at 187, but the excitement was reserved for the single Chilean flamingo which had lost its way.

Landing can be made at Out Head where there is plenty of public carparking beyond a beach littered with razor and other shells.

Larick lighthouse, a derelict timber piled structure off Tayport

Distance
From Tangleha to Out Head is 64km
Campsites
Milton of Mathers, West Mathers, St Cyrus, Brechin, Arbroath, Carnoustie, Monifieth, Clayton, St Andrews
Youth Hostels
Aberdeen, St Andrews
OS 1:50,000 Sheets
45 Stonehaven and Banchory
54 Dundee and Montrose
59 St Andrews
Imray Charts
C23 Firth of Forth to Moray Firth (1:250,000)
C24 Flamborough Head to Fife Ness (1:250,000)
Admiralty Charts
SC 190 Montrose to Fife Ness (1:75,000)
SC 210 Newburgh to Montrose (1:75,000)
1438 Harbours on the East Coast of Scotland. Montrose Harbour (1:7,500). Arbroath (1:12,500)
1481 River Tay (1:25,000)
Tidal Constants
Montrose: HW Dover +0320
Arbroath: HW Dover +0310, LW Dover +03 00
R Tay Bar: Dover +0320
Monifieth: Dover +0340
Sea Area
Forth
Range
Barry Buddon
Rescue
Inshore lifeboats: Montrose, Arbroath, Broughty Ferry
All weather lifeboats: Montrose, Arbroath, Broughty Ferry
Maritime Rescue Centre
Forth, 01333 450666

38 FIFE

A coast of saints and kings

Half owre, half owre to Aberdour
'Tis fifty fathoms deep,
And there lies gude Sir Patrick Spens,
Wi' the Scots lords at his feet.

West Sands run south from Out Head to St Andrews. They are popular as the city's main beach but are best known as one of the settings for *Chariots of Fire*. Behind the beach are the Links, including interesting dune plants. **St Andrews** has seven golf courses including the Royal and Ancient, the home of golf since at least 1547 and a place of pilgrimage for golfers from around the world. The rules were first set down in 1754 and the clubhouse built exactly a century later, acting as the headquarters of the game. The name may come from the Dutch kolf, a club. The rest of the game's history, together with memorabilia, documents, clubs and balls, appears in the British Golf Museum. There is a Golf Week in April or May and, for those who miss it, every second shop in the city seems to be golf related.

St Regulus or St Rule was shipwrecked off the coast in 347 and founded a church here, bringing the bones of St Andrew which attracted pilgrims in the days of the Celtic church. It had become an ecclesiastical establishment by 747 and the country's most important bishopric was founded in 908 with an Augustinian priory following in 1126. St Andrews cathedral was the biggest in Scotland. Founded in 1160, it included the 33m 12th-century St Rule's Tower, the cathedral itself being mostly 12th and 13th-century Celtic with mediaeval carved stones including an 8th or 10th-century sarcophagus, perhaps built to hold the relics of St Andrew. It was the ecclesiastical capital of Scotland. Here James V married Mary of Guise, the daughter of Mary, Queen of Scots who visited the cathedral in 1563 and 1564. The foundation above the harbour is that of the Celtic church of St Mary of the Rock. Holy Trinity Church was founded in the 12th century, moved to its present

Protestants, was murdered here in 1546 and John Knox was condemned as a galley slave when he and other Protestants were besieged in the castle, the start of the Reformation struggle.

The university is the oldest in Scotland, founded in 1410. At its heart is St Salvator's Chapel with John Knox's pulpit. The initials in the cobbles are those of Lutheran preacher Patrick Hamilton, burned at the stake in 1528, the face which appears to be etched high on an arch said to be his since the time he was martyred. The Old University Library was founded in 1612 and the Scottish Parliament met here in 1645/6. The royal presence has also kept the university in the public eye.

Other notable works in this small city are the Pends, a magnificent vaulted gatehouse to the Priory Precinct, due to collapse when the wisest man in Christendom walks under the arch. So far he has had the sense not to do so. There is also a remarkable 16th-century Precinct Wall. The A91 meets the A917 and many of the streets are Victorian and Edwardian. There is an Archaeology Museum with local and Near East artefacts, the St Andrews Museum with local history and the St Andrews Preservation Trust Museum with fishermen's houses, grocer's shop contents, chemist's, fishing equipment, photographs, weights and measures, furniture and paintings. The Byre Theatre has been set up in an old cowshed, there is a Kate Kennedy Pageant in April and a biannual St Andrews Festival with revue, opera, film, jazz, dance, folk, exhibitions and theatre. The Lammas Fair in early August is the oldest mediaeval market. Not forgetting the sea is the Gatty Marine Laboratory and the Sea Life Centre.

The shoreline becomes rocky now with agate, amethyst and smoky quartz sometimes being

The St Andrews skyline with the cathedral on the left and castle centre right

site in 1410 and restored in 1909 with notable stained glass.

The castle was founded in 1200 with a palace, fortress and prison, including a bottle dungeon with no exit, carved out of the rock. Also on show are rare mine and counter-mine mediaeval siege techniques. Cardinal Beaton, the scourge of the

found. The harbour, rebuilt in the 17th century with stones from the abbey and some not already reused from the castle in the 16th century, is used by fishing and pleasure craft but dries despite being fed by the Kinness Burn. A caravan site overlooks the east end of the city.

Cliffs run 20–30m high. Birdlife includes blackheaded gulls, fulmars, oystercatchers, sanderlings, cormorants, curlews, herons, blackbacked gulls and eider ducks, while both moon and compass jellyfish are found in the water.

An interesting geological feature is the Rock and Spindle, like a rectangular chimney with a large bevel gear wheel leaning against it. A little further along is Buddo Rock, a large rectangular block with an Islamic arch shape in the centre.

Kenly Water flows down through Boarhills. Below Kingsbarns is the popular white beach of Cambo Sands. Close by are Cambo Gardens with walled gardens, blossoms, bulbs, lilacs, over 200 varieties of rose, a notable Chinese bridge, Cambo Woodland Walk and Nature Trail, 18th-century farm, farm machinery display, Living Land display, rare breeds, traditional poultry, Scottish farm animals, pets corner, fossils, BMX track and

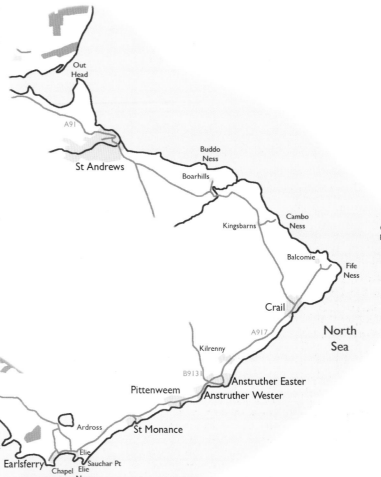

The Rock and Spindle to the south of St Andrews

adventure playground, not to mention more caravans.

Above a golf course is the square tower of Balcomie Castle while, offshore, Carr Brigs are marked by the North Carr Beacon, a red column on a stone base. The final kilometre to Fife Ness is well littered with rocks which have claimed many ships. The ness has 10m high dark cliffs with a 5m white lighthouse building.

There was a Danish settlement here, recalled by Danes Dike (where an aerial is located) and by King Constantine's Cave, named after the Scottish monarch murdered by the Danes in 874.

Low cliffs, grassy banks and a rocky foreshore are typical to Elie Ness, good for birdlife, while further offshore is a submarine and minesweeper exercise area. Flows run at up to 3km/h off points.

The rocky shoreline normally acts as a barrier to the nature reserve at Danes Dike and to the picnic area by the disused airfield above Kilminning Castle.

A collection of chalets and caravans give a less attractive welcome to the very attractive East Neuk or corner of Fife, a line of villages which grew affluent on trade with France, the Low Countries and Scandinavia in mediaeval times, exchanging wool, coal, leather and fish for timber and manufactured goods, also importing Flemish crowstepped gables. In the 19th century there was a big herring fleet instead and now tourists make a contribution to the local economy.

The first village south of Fife Ness is **Crail** with a harbour which cannot be entered with strong southeasterly winds although stoplogs can be

Crail, one of the jewels of the East Neuk coast

Fife harling

Lobster pots piled up on the quayside at Crail Harbour

Pittenweem shelters behind its harbour wall

Dutch tower was also a town hall with a Dutch bell of 1520, the oldest in Fife. A Mercat Cross has a unicorn which is now rather worn. Crail Museum and Heritage Centre in an 18th-century cottage features local history, people and archaeology, the Isle of May, golf, miniature dolls, lace, *HMS Jackdaw* and fishing. There is a 17th-century customs house. Indeed, it was a prosperous town in the 17th century but never recovered from an attack of the plague.

Viewed from here, the Isle of May has a distinctive profile, rising steadily from the east and ending abruptly with vertical cliffs on the west, a lighthouse centred on the flat top, magh being Celtic for plain. The 51ha island is of greenstone and basalt. David I founded a chapel, dedicated to St Aidan, murdered by the Danes in 870, and gave it to his sister, Queen Maude of England, for the monks of Reading Abbey to found a priory. The 12th-century monastery is built on the grave of St Aidan. There is good sheep grazing. 15 fishing families lived on the island in the 18th century with an annual party to celebrate the end of the herring fishing season. Fishermen from Crail and Pittenweem used to join in but in 1837 a boat capsized, drowning 13, mostly women, and the festivities were discontinued. From 1815 the island was owned by the Northern Lighthouse Commissioners, when and for whom Stevenson built the square lighthouse on a house. There has been a lighthouse on the island since 1635. The island has been a National Nature Reserve since 1956 with large breeding seabird colonies and a seal rookery. Fife Council permission is needed to land. The bird observatory was furnished from shipwrecks. The island has been the site of naval battles involving the Picts, Norse, Danes, English and pirates and wreckage includes two steam driven submarines.

The A917 follows the coast from Crail to Kirkton of Largo. Located on the rocky shoreline are the ruins of the Pans and, near a cave, the Hermit's Well. More caravans grace the coast at Kilrenny.

Anstruther Easter, at the end of the B9131, allows use to be made of some sheltered waters behind the reefs. There is a small harbour near the Haven Restaurant but the main harbour has two parts and 1.2km of quays. It is a fishing harbour, of which the inner basin dries, and can be rough with strong winds from the south or east. It was the home of the East Neuk herring trade until the 1940s. The Scottish Fisheries Museum is housed in 16th to 19th-century buildings with an aquarium, fishing and ship's gear, a Fifie fishing boat and models, fisher home interiors, Anstruther lifeboats, the 1900 herring drifter *Reaper* and, since 1976, the North Carr lightship.

Anstruther Wester has a golf course behind a small but distinctive tower, the course reaching to **Pittenweem**, Pictish for place of the cave. St Fillan's Cave is a shrine, having been a 6th-century

positioned to close off the harbour entrance. There is a beach of shell sand which adheres tenaciously to everything. Above the red boulder harbour are crowstepped houses with red-tiled roofs, some with fishing motif decorations, some with outside staircases so that fishermen can live above their workshops and net storage. There are lobsters, crabs and sea urchins around, a building beside the harbour offering to cook lobsters to order. Toilets are an adjacent service. The village was an important ecclesiastical centre from the 12th century, important enough for the Devil to have thrown the Blue Stane at the church, currently lying in the churchyard, having missed its target. The 13th-century collegiate church has fine woodwork and an early Pictish cross. The 16th-century Tolbooth was both library and town hall with a 1602 coat of arms and a gilded salmon weathervane on which gulls can comfortably perch and aspire to higher things. The

missionary hermitage, although later used by smugglers. It is under a yellow sandstone overhang below the priory where witches were put to death, the Great House and prior's lodging being built by Augustinian monks from the Isle of May in the 12th century. The parish church of 1588 is noted for its tower and spire with a Swedish bell of 1663. Also imported was the Flemish architecture. The small fishing port is busy, the inner basin drying. It is the home of the Fife fishing fleet and has a fishmarket with codlings, flatfish, crabs and lobsters.

At Pans Goat there is an unusual windmill on the cliffs. In good condition, it has a cylindrical body, a flattened conical roof and flimsy looking sails, seemingly a disguise for something else. In fact, it was built to pump sea water up to nine salt-drying pans located on the cliffs.

St Monans or **St Monance** takes its name from an Irish missionary who had a cave or shrine near the church. St Monans Auld Kirk may have been a Ninianic foundation of about 400. David I was cured of an arrow wound here. Alexander III started new building work in 1265 and David II renovated it in 1362 in thanks for delivery from a

marked by a 12m pyramidal cage, while West Vows are more likely to have singing seals on top and be surrounded by diving gannets and terns.

The 63m Grangehill ridge rises steeply in what is otherwise rather flat terrain, topped by a radio mast. Kincraig is a volcanic plug, hollowed out and undercut by the sea. One cave is said to have sheltered Macduff from Macbeth. Some strata run vertically and there is a lookout point on the hillside.

Vertical strata at the foot of Grangehill

storm at sea. About 1460 James III gave it to the Dominicans and it became a parish church in 1646. Inside the transept hangs a fully rigged model of 1804 of a 100 gun sailing ship donated by a local naval officer (who made money out of the Napoleonic wars) as a memorial to 37 fishermen who lost their lives in a storm in 1875.

A boatyard of 1747 builds wooden and steel fishing boats. Although it is only a small fishing port, it was one of the four biggest in Scotland in the 1790s with 14 boats. The harbour dries but is not easily approached in strong southeasterly winds or with a northeasterly swell.

On the rocks is the block of Newark Castle, the 17th-century home of the Covenanter General Leslie, defeated at Dunbar by Cromwell. A little further along the coast is another castle ruin at Ardross, near which is a souterrain. On the other hand, the round stone tower on Saucher Point is Lady's Folly, the private bathing box of 18th-century beauty Lady Janet Anstruther who used to bathe unrobed after a bellringer had been sent through the streets of Elie to warn away onlookers.

Elie Ness, topped by an 11m white light tower, has flows to 2km/h and is the outer end of the Firth of Forth. At the head of Wood Haven or Ruby Bay are toilets and parking, together with banks of thrift and other flowers. The royal burgh of Elie and Earlsferry has a larger bay with windsurfing and a golf course.

Chapel Ness at **Earlsferry** takes its name from a chapel built in 1093 by the Earl of Fife for pilgrims visiting St Andrews. Off the ness is East Vows,

After Shell Bay and the low Ruddons Point comes the sandy sweep of Largo Bay, the Scottish Riviera, backed by a former railway line and a 4-arched viaduct and with fish nets on the beach. 290m Largo Law is a distinctive volcanic peak against the generally higher ground of the Lomond Hills. There are reefs and mussel banks along the beach near Lower Largo. Up the hill is Scotland's Larder, a restaurant in an old farm barn offering high class local produce. Down from it is the Temple area of Lower Largo, named from its association with the Knights Templar, now with parking and toilets and very crowded when used for sailing regattas. The village was a haddock fishing hamlet and still lands lobsters and crabs although it is subject to scend with southerly winds. Guillemots and little gulls live in the bay. It was the birthplace in 1676 of Alexander Selkirk who, as a castaway for over 4 years on Juan Fernandez off the Chile coast, inspired Daniel Defoe's *Robinson Crusoe*, of whom there is a statue outside Selkirk's house, now a museum on his marooning.

Kirkton of Largo or Upper Largo has a unique church in that the 16th-century spire is supported only on the chancel roof. It has a Pictish stone in the churchyard with designs including a hunting scene. Graves include that of Sir Andrew Wood, Scotland's greatest admiral, whose *Yellow Caravel* led the Scottish fleet to victory against the English in the Forth in 1489. Sir Andrew owned Largo House, of which only one tower remains and which was designed by Robert

Lower Largo's beach is mostly behind a reef but there are breaks to land

Adam for the Durhams, the lairds of Largo. When Sir Andrew became too ill to travel to church he had a canal dug to it so that he could be rowed to services.

Lundin Links has golf courses on both sides of the A915, two of them 18th century, leading to a caravan park. On one of them are the Standing Stones of Lundin, sandstone blocks which may have been memorials to the Druids or to a battle with the Danes. There is a tower near them. This is considered to be the gateway to the East Neuk and from here there is some industry and deep water moorings to Burntisland.

Leven was the entry point for the Scottish court when travelling to Falkland Palace. It later became a coal port although it is no longer commercial, having become blocked by shifting sands and being subject to a considerable sea with a southwesterly wind. In winter, scaup collect around the sewage outfall near the River Leven. The A955 crosses the river and follows the coast to Kirkcaldy.

gypsies and contains a Viking picture of Thor with his hammer and earlier Pictish designs. Doocot cave has square niches which may have been for dove nesting boxes or for funeral urns.

Coaltown of Wemyss is not what it was, the Michael Mine having closed in 1967 but estate houses are well kept. Wemyss Castle stands at the top of wooded cliffs.

Wemyss Castle, less well fortified than many

Kvaener's fabrication site at Methil

Methil is dominated by its power station chimney, off which there is a wreck. The docks have 840m of quays, trading with Copenhagen, Hamburg and Spain. It is a town of tower blocks and towering cranes on the fabrication site of Kvaener Oil and Gas. A 1930s post office contains smaller items of the town's history in the Lower Methil Heritage Centre.

Methil and **Buckhaven** run together on the B931 and were made a single burgh in 1891. Buckhaven harbour is silted up and disused, but a museum features the region's fisherfolk in better days. The church hall was the Church of St Andrew, a Gothic pre-Reformation church which had stood in St Andrews for four centuries before being rebuilt here.

Macduff's Castle at **East Wemyss** is a ruin of two towers and a red block sited in a cemetery, possibly the stronghold of the Macduff thanes of Fife. Close by are two caves or weems, after which the village is named, with Bronze Age to mediaeval inscriptions and with a risk of rockfalls. Court Cave is where James V is believed to have received

Interesting architecture at West Wemyss

An interesting progression of housing is found at West Wemyss, firstly flats, then a whole street where houses have been boarded up and windows painted on the boards and, finally, around the harbour, a marvellous selection of houses in a style which would not look out of place on a Mediterranean coast. There is rather too much rubble lying around and the stench of rotting seaweed, but there are indications that improvements are in hand.

Black spoil from Blair colliery spills down to the beach, to contrast with the whitewashed, crowstepped gabled houses at Dysart, grouped in

Grass covered spoil from Blair colliery is black on the beach

front of St Serf's church tower which was built as a refuge against pirates, although visiting boaters to the harbour these days mostly come in yachts. The John McDougall Stuart Museum is in a 17th century building which was the birthplace of the first explorer to cross the heart of Australia from south to north in 1861. The Tolbooth was used as a powder magazine in the Civil War until a drunken Cromwellian soldier wandered in with a lighted torch. The roof has since been put back. An ornithologists' hide stands by the beach.

The Aberdeen to King's Cross railway now follows the coast, as does a nature trail running through the woods to **Kirkcaldy**, the Lang Toun, Fife's largest town.

Ravenscraig Castle, now with a surreal backdrop of three tower blocks, was one of the first constructed to withstand artillery. It was built in 1460–3 by James II in octagonal shape, later passing to the Sinclair Earls of Orkney. On a promontory, it has two D-shaped towers for cannon, a four-storey one serving as a keep and an artillery platform added to a raised curtain wall in the early 16th century. Kirkcaldy has a small commercial port handling cut timber and with a ship breaker. The town's prosperity was built on linoleum and this is featured in the Kirkcaldy Museum and Art Gallery, together with linen, mining, industrial heritage, local history, craft and art including Scottish paintings, notably Scottish Colourists, especially Samuel Peploe. The Adam Smith Theatre recalls the economist and author of *The Wealth of Nations*, born here in 1723. Georgian architects Robert and James Adam were also born here, as was Michael Scott, the mediaeval wizard and astrologer to the Holy Roman Empire. Historian Thomas Carlyle taught here as a schoolmaster from 1816 to 1819.

Fine 17th-century houses in Sailor's Walk are now occupied by HM Customs, while coal dust on the beach remains from the past and the Spring Links Market on the Esplanade is one of the oldest fairs in Britain. The A921 runs along the Esplanade past a large stadium and follows the coast.

Part of the sea wall has collapsed near Seafield Colliery. The Seafield Tower remains to look out over the Vows and their seals, the East Vows actually being west of the West Vows.

Kinghorn, with its grey sandstone buildings, has been a royal burgh since the 12th century. A monument records how Alexander III met his death here in 1286 when his horse stumbled in the

dark and threw him over the cliff. The village has a railway station high above the beach.

Pettycur harbour on Kinghorn Ness dries. The hillside behind is steep, but not too steep for a golf course or hundreds of chalets, although the A921 is squeezed in next to the railway.

Inchkeith in the middle of the firth is a 55m high island of igneous rock on which landing is forbidden without Fife Council permission. It was given to Robert de Keith of Keithness (Caithness), chief of the warlike German clan Catti, together with the hereditary title of Grand Marischal of Scotland, for his help in resisting the Danish invasion of 1010. It was later used as a plague island with an asylum built in 1497. A castle was added for Mary, Queen of Scots in 1564 and the island garrisoned by French soldiers, a 19m stone tower subsequently being built on the site of the castle and acting as a battlemented lighthouse. The island was fortified in the Napoleonic and both world wars with triple fortifications and batteries in 1881 able to cover the whole of the firth at this point. James IV carried out the experiment of leaving two babies on the island with a deaf and dumb nurse to see what language they would speak, the result being passable Hebrew. Dr Samuel Johnson visited in 1773 although the commonest visitors these days are birds, this being an RSPB reserve.

A prominent landmark for this part of the coast is the radio mast on the Binn, a high ridge to the north of Burntisland. The sandy shore, used for staking out salmon nets, dries for a kilometre.

Entertainment in **Burntisland** includes a museum with an Edwardian fairground, a summer regatta, highland games in July and a prominent waterslide next to the bay. The octagonal towered church was the first post-Reformation church in Scotland and here the James I Assembly of the Church of Scotland suggested the Authorized Version of the *Bible*. Somerville Street and Square were referred to as Quality Street because of the nature of the residents and the fine 17th-century town houses. Lammerlaws Point has former fortifications. The military involvement goes back a long way, Agricola having landed his legions here in the 1st century and second world war convoys having been mustered here more recently. These days the small commercial docks are journey's end for bauxite for the aluminium works. To their east are Royal Navy degaussing ranges, marked by four yellow buoys, and no approach should be made

St Serf's church tower and houses at Dysart

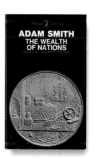

Inchcolm with the Forth railway and road bridges in the background

The view from St Colm's Abbey tower

St Colme's Abbey

when Navy vessels are there. The firth is now controlled by the Dockyard Port of Rosyth. Beyond Ross Point is another aerial.

Silversands Bay has children's playgrounds, trampolines, putting green and toilets. Beyond Hawkcraig Point is Aberdour with its small harbour used for sailing and water skiing. The castle ruin is part 14th century, built by the Douglas family with a walled garden started in the 16th century and a fine circular doocot. St Fillan's parish church is part Norman, part 16th century.

A series of stepping stones cross the firth, those to the north of the Oxcars Lighthouse forming part of Fife while those to the south are part of Edinburgh. Between them are two deep water channels for large vessels. The first is Mortimer's Deep with tidal streams up to 5km/h, running north of Car Craig, a fairly narrow channel marked by red and green lateral buoys. It primarily caters for tankers up to 60,000m^3 serving the Braefoot terminal for Mossmorran petrochemical complex which exports ethylene, propane, butane and natural gasoline. An amber flashing light on the jetty shows from 2 hours before a tanker movement is due until the movement is completed.

The largest of the islands is Inchcolm, 27m high and mostly greensand, named after St Colme or Columba who was resident in the 6th century. St Colme's Abbey was founded in 1192 by Alexander I after being saved from shipwreck by the resident hermit who shared his own meagre supply of milk and shellfish. It has a square tower with a grey spire, 13th-century octagonal chapter house and monastic buildings which are the best preserved early mediaeval architecture in Scotland. Known as the Iona of the East, it was the place to be buried to be close to heaven. It was abandoned in 1560 after the Reformation and was mentioned in *Macbeth*. More recent buildings are fortifications from the two world wars. There used to be many stones with the arms of Norsemen but only one remains. Wildlife includes grey seals and puffins. Fife Council permission is needed to land and there

The Maid of the Forth at Inchcolm's jetty

is a charge, but responsible groups of canoeists are sometimes allowed to camp here. The *Maid of the Forth* trip boat operates from Queensferry with several loads of tourists per day.

Between Inchcolm and the Oxcars Lighthouse is the Forth Deep Water Channel, the main route down the firth. It ebbs to 2km/h and floods to 1km/h, the flow reversing rapidly and being affected by melting snow and rainfall. Traffic includes tankers and vessels of the Royal Navy from Rosyth. 7km upstream are the Forth Bridge and the Forth Road Bridge, the former with probably the world's most distinctive bridge silhouette.

Cramond at the mouth of the River Almond

Oxcars lighthouse with the Cow and Calves and Inchmickery beyond but Edinburgh blotted out in poor visibility

Oxcars lighthouse is a 22m white tower with a red band, built on rocks which cover. A spoil dumping ground separates it from the Cow and Calves which all but cover and yet still need council permission before landing.

RSPB permission is needed to land on Inchmickery, which is a bird sanctuary with a roseate ternery and other breeding birds. It covers only 1ha and rises to 15m. The name means isle of the vicar and it may have been the dwelling place of the priest from Inchcolm. It is nearly covered with second world war fortifications but the Mickery Stone, a standing stone, survives. The Forth has 72,000 winter wildfowl including 8,900 knots, 2,800 bar-tailed godwits, 4,100 redshanks and 8,900 pinkfooted geese, which the RSPB claimed were at risk from marina development and land reclaim.

Cramond Island is uninhabited and needs council permission to land. The 8ha island is connected to the mainland by a causeway running across Drum Sands. Cramond is a corruption of caer Almond, the Romans having built a fort at the mouth of the River Almond which housed the 2nd and 10th legions under Lollius Urbicus as a supply base for the Antonine Wall. These days the rivermouth forms a pleasant harbour area with parking, but sewage pollution discourages swimming and the local mussels are no longer safe to eat.

Distance
From Out Head to Cramond is 80km
Campsites
St Andrews, Crail, Pittenweem, St Monance, Kincraig, Kirkton of Largo, Leven, Kirkcaldy, Kinghorn, Muirhouse
Youth Hostels
St Andrews, Edinburgh Eglinton
OS 1:50,000 Sheets
59 St Andrews
66 Edinburgh
Imray Charts
C23 Firth of Forth to Moray Firth (1:250,000)
C24 Flamborough Head to Fife Ness (1:250,000)
C27 Firth of Forth (1:75,000)
Admiralty Charts
SC 175 Fife Ness to St Abb's Head (1:75,000)
SC 190 Montrose to Fife Ness including the Isle of May (1:75,000)
733 Firth of Forth – Burntisland to Dalgety Bay (1:7,500)
SC 734 Firth of Forth – Isle of May to Inchkeith (1:50,000)
735 Firth of Forth – Approaches to Leith and Burntisland (1:10,000). Approaches to Leith and Burntisland (1:25,000)
SC 736 Firth of Forth – Granton and Burntisland to Rosyth (1:15,000)
741 Plans in the Firth of Forth and River Forth. Methil (1:10,000)
Tidal Constants
Monifieth: Dover +0340
Crail: Dover +0320
Anstruther Easter: Dover +0320
St Monance: Dover +0330
Lower Largo: HW Dover +0330, LW Dover +0340
Methil: Dover +0340
Dysart: Dover +0340
Burntisland: Dover +0340
Aberdour: HW Dover +0350, LW Dover +0340
Granton: Dover +0340
Sea Area
Forth
Rescue
Inshore lifeboats: Broughty Ferry, Anstruther, Kinghorn, Queensferry
All weather lifeboats: Broughty Ferry, Anstruther
Maritime Rescue Centre
Forth, 01333 450666

39 EAST LOTHIAN

A capital coast for stories

The boat rocks at the pier o' Leith,
Fu' loud the wind blaws frae the Ferry,
The ship rides by the Berwick-law,
And I maun leave my bonnie Mary.

Robert Burns

The main flight path into Edinburgh Airport at Turnhouse crosses the coast between the tower on the shore at Cramond and the turreted tower house of Lauriston Castle, built in 1590 by Sir Archibald Napier, whose son invented logarithms. John Law, the founder of the Bank of France and of the Mississippi Scheme, spent his early years here. The castle houses fine paintings, furniture and Blue John ware. In front of the castle are a golf course and rugby pitch.

The estuary moves out of the control of the Dockyard Port of Rosyth and restrictions ease slightly.

Beyond an aerial and prominent gasworks is Caroline Park, a 17th-century mansion built by Sir George McKenzie, Viscount Tarbat, the chief minister for Scotland. The house was renamed after Queen Caroline in 1740 and is now offices.

Granton Harbour is a small commercial port, partly reclaimed and largely drying. It has 330m of quays, but draws some of its current prestige from the presence of the headquarters of the Royal Forth and Forth Corinthian yacht clubs.

The A901 follows the coast to Newhaven, a fishing harbour which dries but is still used by shellfishing and recreational craft. Amongst its larger neighbours it would hardly be noticed but for the smartly painted disused white lighthouse and the equally smartly painted buildings in a deep plum colour around it. With a name like Newhaven, it isn't, inevitably, having been founded in 1500 by James IV. George IV said the fishwives were the most handsome women he had ever seen. The history of the fishing village is given in the Newhaven Heritage Museum in the former fishmarket.

Leith has become a trendy port town, complete with Crabbie's winery. The dominant harbour here is the Port of Leith at the mouth of the Water of Leith. It contains the royal yacht *Britannia* and is where Queen Mary landed on her return from France in 1561 and there was much trade with the Low Countries, hence the influence on the

Cockenzie power station dominates the shore and the battlefield site

architectural designs by Rennie. 4.8km of quays serve commercial traffic and form an oilfield and pipeline construction base. The deep water approach channel has been dredged northwest from the entrance, across which tidal streams flow east–west at up to 3km/h with an eddy off Leith Breakwater during the flood. There is a ternery on a caisson and a substantial roost of eider ducks, cormorants and blackheaded gulls on the east side of the port entrance where there are stone blocks at first until the coastline deteriorates to broken concrete and twisted reinforcing steel. The base of a Martello tower sits surrounded by stacks of pipes until oil tanks take over. A freight railway passes a sewage works but the end of the industrial area is indicated by a metal framework off the coast. Jellyfish gather in the waters next to the port.

Now come residential areas, a golf course at Craigentinny and views across **Edinburgh**, notably the 251m high Arthur's Seat, Meadowbank stadium, Nelson Monument, Edinburgh Castle and the Pentland Hills beyond. Built on the volcanic rock of Din Eidyn, Edinburgh Castle, including the 12th-century St Margaret's Chapel, is the oldest building in Edinburgh. It includes the Great Hall of James IV, the Old Palace with the Regalia of Scotland, the honours or crown jewels, the Scottish National War Memorial of 1927, Mons Meg (a 500 year old siege cannon) and the Scottish United Services Museum. It is where Queen Mary gave birth to James VI of Scotland and I of England in 1566. The Scottish capital uses an Old English form of a name derived from the Old Welsh, Eidyn Gaer, Eidyn's fort. Edinburgh received its present name when the Angles took Din Eidyn in 638 but it has often been referred to as Auld Reekie, old smokey.

Portobello is a district founded in 1739, the year of capture of Puerto Bello in Panama. The name was given by George Hamilton who fought there with Admiral Vernon. Music Hall's Harry Lauder was born here in 1870 and there is an annual Sir

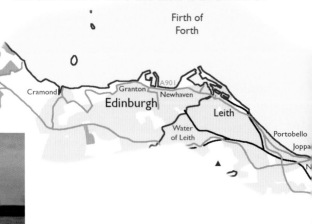

Harry Lauder Festival. A sandy beach with groynes reaches almost to Joppa where there is another daymark.

One of Newhailes' notable buildings is Newhailes House, built in 1686 by architect James Smith for himself.

Fisherrow Harbour dries and is mostly used by yachts. Water skiers have no such needs and cross Fisherrow Sands to operate in Musselburgh Road. The River Esk forms the boundary between Edinburgh and East Lothian. **Musselburgh** was a mussel and herring fishing centre, named in the 11th century, although, sadly, the mussels which form banks off the rivermouth are now too polluted to eat. A third of British wintering scaup gather around the Seafield sewer outfall to feed on grain waste and the area is noted for winter wildfowl and waders. Birds range from oystercatchers and curlews to goldeneyes, eiders and swans. This important Roman seaport became known as the Honest Town in 1332 when the citizens cared for the dying Earl of Moray, the Regent of Scotland, and then declined a reward from his successor, the Earl of Mar. The town has a sporting tradition. In 1504 James IV played on Musselburgh Links, the world's oldest golf course was established in 1672 and there has been a club since 1774. The horse racecourse was established in 1816, the oldest in Scotland, and there has been a shoot on the links in late May by the Royal Company of Archers since the 17th century for the Silver Arrow. There were more serious arrows in 1547 when the Scots were defeated here in battle.

The Tolbooth was built with stones from the Chapel of Loretto of 1590. Loretto School is a public school for boys, part of which is located in Pinkie House with its painted gallery of about 1630 and its plaster ceilings, the seat of the Abbots of Dunfermline.

To the east of the rivermouth are 1.2km^2 of lagoons to take waste pumped 4km as a slurry from Cockenzie power station. The lagoons are intended to take 5,600,000 tonnes of ash during the lifetime of the power station. Coal has been mined here for 800 years, as shown in the Prestongrange Industrial Heritage Museum which has a history of coal mining, a Cornish beam engine installed in 1874 and features on the production of pottery, soap and glycerine together with brewing and weaving.

The B1348 becomes the coast road to Longniddry, passing **Prestonpans**, named after the 12th-century priests' estate pans for salt production. The town has the best Mercat Cross in the country, the Preston Tower (which is a mediaeval fortification with a huge dovecote) and Hamilton House and Northfield, 17th-century lairds' houses. Most importantly, though, is the battlefield where the Jacobites achieved their only significant victory when Prince Charles Edward defeated General Cope in 1745, a monument cairn marking this historic event. For the last forty years power to the Scots has taken a new meaning here as overhead transmission lines run from Cockenzie power station across the battlefield. This power station was built at the same time as Longannet opposite Grangemouth, both to be supplied with coal directly from adjacent coalfields. Cockenzie broke new ground for a power station in that the sandstone bedrock was able to be accurately excavated by motor scrapers.

In days gone by, the fishermen of Prestonpans and Cockenzie would not put to sea if their paths were crossed by pigs, lame men or strangers. A good many fine fishing days must have been lost. **Cockenzie and Port Seton** is now one village with two fishing harbours. Cockenzie Harbour is a small port and Port Seton dries.

Seton House was built in 1790 on the ruins of Seton Palace. Close by is a chapel which was formerly the Collegiate Church, a late 15th-century building with a fine vaulted chancel and apse, buttressed walls of red and grey stone, tracery windows and a stump tower.

Seton Sands are protected by Long Craigs, a line of rocks largely unbroken across the bay. Elsewhere, tank traps are located along the shore. Unsheltered in Cockenzie Road are deep water moorings to Gullane Point.

The golf course in front of **Longniddry** belies the fact that it has been a coal mining village for 500 years until the coal ran out in the 1920s.

From Ferny Ness the A198 generally follows the coast to the A1, initially past bays which drain to

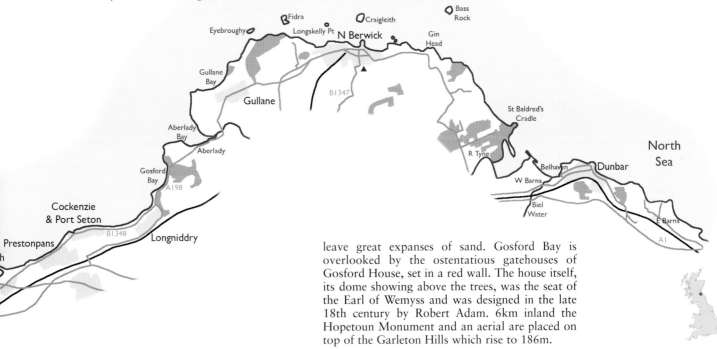

leave great expanses of sand. Gosford Bay is overlooked by the ostentatious gatehouses of Gosford House, set in a red wall. The house itself, its dome showing above the trees, was the seat of the Earl of Wemyss and was designed in the late 18th century by Robert Adam. 6km inland the Hopetoun Monument and an aerial are placed on top of the Garleton Hills which rise to 186m.

Peffer Burn discharges into Aberlady Bay which completely empties at low tide to leave the Gullane Sands, a nature reserve, the burn following the southern edge of the bay to continue past Craigielaw Point and across Gosford Sands. Low dunes separate the nature reserve from Gullane Links with the odd seal keeping watch. There is also saltmarsh at the back of the bay, mussels and winkles which are unsafe to eat and no less than five wrecks.

The roofless church of St Andrew at **Gullane** dates from the 12th century, the last vicar being dismissed by James VI for smoking. At the other end of Gullane Bay are the remains of a chapel and between the two is Muirfield golf course, founded in 1891 by the Honourable Company of Edinburgh Golfers, now with a Heritage of Golf Museum.

As the coast turns east again, a series of isolated islands run parallel with the coast, beginning with the small Eyebroughy, a bird sanctuary.

After caves behind Weaklaw Rocks, the Briggs of Fidra separate the mainland from Fidra, a 30m high island with a 17m white brick towered lighthouse, the remains of a church dedicated to St

Fidra, inspiration for Robert Louis Stevenson's classic adventure book, Treasure Island. Beyond is the Fife shore

North Berwick harbour has 120m of quays used by crab and lobster fishing boats and recreational craft. **North Berwick**, at the end of the B1347, was made a royal burgh by Robert II. In 1590 200 witches were addressed in the church of St Andrew by the Devil in the form of a black goat, possibly the Earl of Bothwell, the heir to the throne, who called for the death of James VI by sorcery. He escaped but many women were condemned to the stake. In the 19th century the town became a fashionable resort. A museum features the local history, fishing, golfing, archaeology, wildlife and the Bass Rock.

Beyond the Sisters rocks off the harbour there is waterskiing in Milsey Bay and a golf course between Rugged Knowes and Leckmoram Ness.

Bass Rock is a 107m high phonolite plug, pyramidal in shape with precipitous sides and a tunnel through which it is possible to paddle, the cliffs white from guano. It is the world's third largest gannetry with 7% of the world population hatched here, hence the scientific name of Sula bassana. As well as 21,000 pairs of gannets there are breeding fulmars, cormorants, razorbills, puffins, guillemots and even the occasional

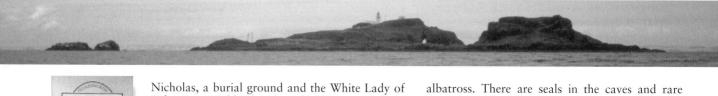

Nicholas, a burial ground and the White Lady of Fidra, a natural bridge shaped like a veiled female figure. This is the island which inspired Robert Louis Stevenson's *Treasure Island* and which he described in *Catriona*. It is a bird sanctuary with puffins and requires RSPB permission to land.

This is considered to be the end of the Firth of Forth. Flows run up to 2km/h along the North Sea coast which is low and sandy to North Berwick. A nature trail follows behind Longskelly Point.

The Lamb is a 24m high cormorantry, again requiring RSPB permission to land, as does Craigleith, which is also known as the Lamb. Craigleith is 51m high with steep sides. Much more conspicuous over most of the estuary, however, is North Berwick Law, a 187m high grassy volcanic pyramid with a Napoleonic watchtower on top and a whale jawbone arch

North Berwick Law behind North Berwick is probably the most distinctive feature on the Forth estuary

albatross. There are seals in the caves and rare plants include Bass mallow. This bird sanctuary needs East Lothian Council permission to land but the birds were not always so well protected. Until the end of the 18th century gannets were harvested for food, peaking at 2,000 per year in 1850, also providing eggs, feathers for bedding and fat for medicine and waterproofing of boots.

St Baldred, a disciple of St Kentigern, sought refuge here in a hermitage in 600. A dry stone chapel was built to the saint's memory in 1400. The island was owned by the Lauders from 1056, always remaining loyal to the Stuarts. A fort was held for James II after his abdication until it surrendered in 1689. Jacobite prisoners seized the island from their guards in 1691 and held it for three years as a garrison for James II against William II. The fort was destroyed in 1701 in case

The striking red clifftop remains of Tantallon Castle

visible from the sea, a second world war lookout and trees planted on its side in 1707 to celebrate the Union.

of another Scottish uprising. Covenanter Richard Blackadder had been a prisoner and mainland people still occasionally hear the chanting of

Bass Rock seen from Seacliff. The tower marks
St Baldred's Boat

psalms by the Sweet Singers, the Covenanter prisoners, on dark nights. There was an addition to the rock's folklore when Robert Louis Stevenson had David Balfour imprisoned here in *Catriona*. The 20m white lighthouse tower and buildings of 1902 were constructed on the old fort site.

After Gin Head the red stone ruin of Tantallon Castle stands on a 30m promontory. A 14th-century Douglas stronghold, it resisted the siege of James V in 1528 and hosted Queen Mary in 1566. It was destroyed in 1651 by General Monk whose siege guns dropped the wall into the moat and allowed it to be taken for Cromwell. It was built with earthwork defences, a 14th-century 15m curtain wall and round corner towers and a four-storey gatehouse across the promontory rock. It contains a display of replica guns.

The Gegan is a surf break at Seacliff. 2km of red sandstone platform running along the coast

Dunbar is from the Gaelic for hilltop fort. Edward II fled from Dunbar after his defeat at Bannockburn. Queen Mary took refuge in the castle three times but after the murder of Darnley and her abdication she was taken there less happily in 1567. The ruin is now the home of kittiwakes. In the 17th century the harbour was Scotland's top fishing centre with 20,000 workers but it declined in the 1920s, apparently as retribution for fishing on Sundays. Notable architecture includes Lauderdale House by Robert Adams while the 17th-century Town House is now a museum featuring local history and archaeology. Dunbar is said to be the sunniest place in Scotland and the leisure pool with its glass roof and sides above the harbour makes good use of the weather. In August the town has a Vintage and Veteran Vehicle Rally.

A conspicuous small tower stands on the low shore beyond a golf course, in contrast with a monument to a battle of 1650 which is well hidden.

White Sands bay has parking and picnic tables surrounded by birdsfoot trefoil, beautifully clear water with codling, mackerel, wrasse, dabs, plaice and flounders and rockpools teeming with wildlife.

reaches out towards the Bass Rock, ending at St Baldred's Boat, marked by a column topped with a cross. A substantial stone wall runs across the fields and ends right at the top of the vertical cliffs.

Once the low sandy coast begins, Ravensheugh Sands produce surf from low to mid-tide and St Baldred's Cradle can produce lefts.

The River Tyne discharges past Tyninghame House with 18th-century walled, secret and terraced gardens, wilderness and church. A substantial beech wood was planted in 1707 by the 6th Earl of Haddington, but it was cut down for the war effort and not replanted until 1945. It is the only place in Scotland where hawfinches breed. The estuary has a heronry and plenty of wildfowl and waders.

The 6.7km² John Muir Country Park is named after the founder of America's national parks and Sierra Club, born in Dunbar in 1838. It includes a natural history trail. Along its southern edge is Biel Water which flows past West Barns and discharges into Belhaven Bay. The bay is a surf break with long rides from mid to high water but strong currents. Belhaven is becoming well known for its brewery although it is the golf course which is prominent.

There are two harbours at Dunbar, the west one, the Victoria Harbour, being approached via a narrow inlet past arches and ruined stonework. It can be difficult to enter when the wind is between west northwest and east. Indeed, it can be difficult even finding the entrance in rough conditions. Victoria Harbour with 180m of quays is used by recreational craft and for landing fish and lobsters. An exit at the far end leads to the Old Cromwell Harbour, partly paid for by him. There was a direct route from the sea, but concrete blocks have been tipped in the Meikle Spiker entrance.

Distance
From Cramond to White Sands is 61km
Campsites
Muirhouse, Liberton, Pinkie Braes, Cockenzie and Port Seton, Aberlady, North Berwick, East Barns
Youth Hostels
Edinburgh Eglinton, Edinburgh Bruntsfield, Coldingham Sands
OS 1:50,000 Sheets
66 Edinburgh
67 Duns, Dunbar and Eyemouth
Imray Charts
C24 Flamborough Head to Fife Ness (1:250,000)
C27 Firth of Forth (1:75,000)
Admiralty Charts
SC 175 Fife Ness to St Abb's Head (1:75,000)
SC 734 Firth of Forth – Isle of May to Inchkeith (1:50,000)
735 Firth of Forth – Approaches to Leith and Burntisland (1:10,000). Approaches to Leith and Burntisland (1:25,000). Leith (1:10,000)
SC 736 Firth of Forth – Granton and Burntisland to Rosyth (1:15,000)
Tidal Constants
Granton: Dover +0340
Leith: Dover +0340
Cockenzie: HW Dover +0330 mins, LW Dover +0340
Fidra: Dover +0340
Dunbar: HW Dover +0340, LW Dover +0400
Sea Area
Forth
Rescue
Inshore lifeboats: Queensferry, Kinghorn, North Berwick, Dunbar
All weather lifeboats: Anstruther, Dunbar
Maritime Rescue Centre
Forth, 01333 450666

Dunbar with the inconspicuous entrance to the Victoria Harbour

40 BORDERS

Crossing the unmarked border

When they had sayled other fifty mile,
    Other fifty mile upon the sea,
They landed low by Barwicke side;
    There Douglas landed Lord Percye.

Perhaps the White Sands get their name from the white dust from the large Blue Circle cement works behind the bay, but it is more likely that the restored limekilns at Catcraig, formerly producing for fertilizer, bleaching agent and iron foundry flux, were relevant. There are fossils in the limestone and there is a geology trail along the shore which is in the vicinity of the Southern Uplands fault here. The hills force the A1 and the East Coast Main Line against the coast as far as Cove.

Barns Ness lighthouse and Torness nuclear power station

A 37m white-towered lighthouse stands on the low Barns Ness, as do a host of caravans. The rock shelf has resulted in a dangerous wreck, but the surf break is appreciated by those in more manœuvrable craft.

A monument on Chapel Point indicates the position of Skateraw Harbour, now unusable. Much more conspicuous is Torness nuclear power station, surrounded by tetrapods which would make landing very difficult in an emergency. More caravans are parked at Thorntonloch and cormorants and gannets are indifferent to the unnatural neighbours.

Cove harbour at low tide

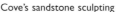

Cove's sandstone sculpting

At the Dunglass Burn, which passes Dunglass church, East Lothian gives way to the Borders region. There are three bridges across the lower end of the burn, one 40m high which was said to have been the highest in the world when built in 1786.

Reed Point with its oystercatchers is a fairly inaccessible surf break and Cove's surf break is hardly more approachable, the latter reached via a 500m track with a locked gate at the top so that it can only be used by approved vehicles. Part of the track is unstable and threatening to disappear down the cliff face. At the bottom a long rock tunnel takes a footpath through to the small drying harbour, used by fishing vessels and formerly used by smugglers who appreciated the caves in the cliffs. A sandstone block by the harbour has been weathered to look like the inside of a human throat. Cove is at the end of the Southern Uplands Way long distance path from Portpatrick. On a quiet day with no surf the cliffs seem to absorb all sounds except those of birds and the occasional sheep.

Further up the hill, Cockburnspath church dates partly from the 14th century and the Mercat Cross has a thistle and a rose of 1502 to celebrate the marriage of James IV to Princess Margaret, the daughter of Henry VI.

Pease Bay has a four-arched viaduct somewhere behind the sea of caravans. If there is surf anywhere it will be found here, but it is frequently blown out and the road down is private. Siccar Point, with its caves, is also a surf break, again without easy access.

For the next few kilometres there are high inaccessible cliffs with small offshore rocks, somewhat reminiscent of the cliffs to the north of Helmsdale. The waters are clear with moon and compass jellyfish amongst the kelp, seals, urchins on the rocks, eider ducks, blackbacked gulls and fulmars. Sometimes there are rock pillars and vertical strata, caves, settlements and forts on the cliff tops and waterfalls, even a measured distance for ship speed gauging although it can be difficult to determine exact landmarks. Fast Castle on

A fisherman checking lobster pots in the mist near St Abb's Head. Note the gulls perched on the gunwale to check the fisherman and his catch

Telegraph Hill was a Home stronghold above the Wheat Stack surf break. One of the caves is said to contain a fortune in 16th-century gold collected to free Mary, Queen of Scots. Contorted grey mudstone cliffs lead to Pettico Wick where the St Abb's Head Fault introduces steeper pink and purple volcanic lavas.

seabirds including guillemots, kittiwakes, razorbills, fulmars, shags, puffins, herring gulls and eiders. Wheatears, meadow pipits, skylarks and stonechats nest on the headland where there is purple milk-vetch and Kirn Hill has rock rose, on which feeds the northern brown argus butterfly. Grey seals, herrings, crabs, lobsters and prawns are found offshore in Scotland's first Marine Nature Reserve, a voluntary designation, relevant because diving is popular here.

At the end of the B6438, St Abbs was named after Aebbe, the daughter of Edilfred, King of Northumbria. She went to sea to avoid the attentions of the King of Mercia and was washed up here where she founded an unusual combined convent and monastery on Kirn Hill, not to be confused with the Nunnery Point ruin which is only mediaeval. St Cuthbert visited in 661 and Aebba ruled as abbess until her death in 683, the buildings being destroyed by raiders, possibly Vikings, in the late 9th century.

Each July a Herring Queen Festival takes place, the Queen being carried from St Abbs along the rugged coast to Eyemouth on the B6355.

Gulls surround a cave near St Abb's Head

St Abb's Head has 90m nearly vertical red sandstone pillars with clefts between them which can be entered in calm conditions. The head appears like an island from the distance. Tidal streams run strongly around the head with turbulence, especially with opposing winds. The southeasterly stream sets towards the head yet there is a surf break for the determined. On top is the St Abb's Head light of 1862, a 9m white tower and buildings. The St Abb's Wildlife Reserve was established in 1983, 78ha including the most important location for cliff nesting birds in southeast Scotland with 50,000

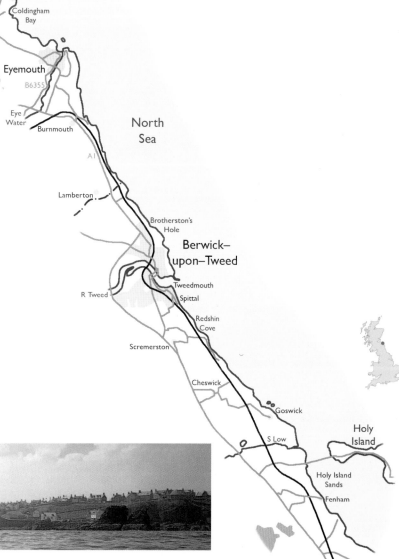

St Abbs comes after the run of cliffs

The inner harbour dries. Beach huts face out into Coldingham Bay where the surf funnels in but a notice bans launching.

An aerial on Hallydown is located above fort sites of 1547 and a more recent caravan site on Hairy Ness.

A new harbour has been built into the golf course at **Eyemouth**, a white fish port which formerly handled herring. The old port had 360m of quays at the mouth of Eye Water. With winds from the north and east the bay is a mass of broken water. The Eyemouth Museum features the Great East Coast Fishing Disaster of October 1881 when 129 men and 23 boats from the port were lost. It also has the wheelhouse of a modern fishing boat, the 4.6m Eyemouth tapestry and displays on the fishing and farming history of east Berwickshire. The Georgian Gunsgreen House to the southeast of the town was a smuggling gang's headquarters and has secret passages.

Brotherston's Hole, last stop before the crowded beaches

decrease towards Berwick-upon-Tweed, once again followed by the A1, the railway and lines of rock teeth. On 199m high Ayton Hill are two aerials.

A notable lack of any distinctive geographical features separates the Scottish Borders region from the English county of Northumberland. The cliffs and the rocky shoreline continue unbroken with not even a stream to mark the national boundary. Caravans on the cliff above Marshall Meadows Bay are the first positive fix on English territory.

The Needles Eye has a large hole through at sea level and is extensively used by nesting kittiwakes, despite the jets streaking across to head for the hills. The holes improve and Brotherston's Hole is a series of caves and passages in the cliffs. Golfers pace about above and waders do the same on occasional pieces of beach. Another caravan site occupies the land between Sharper's Head and Ladies Skerrs but there are also some publicly reachable beaches.

Berwick-upon-Tweed is one of the oldest towns in Britain, having been founded in Saxon times, its name coming from the Old English bere-wic, a corn farm, and was the only crossing place of the Tweed from 1153, being at the height of its prosperity during the reign of Alexander II. As well as having had a long history, it has also had a complex one, changing hands between the Scots and English 14 times from 1482. The Elizabethan town walls and gun emplacements were started in 1558 and the Tudor fortifications are the best preserved of their age in northern Europe. There are also remains of the earlier walls of Edward I including the Black Tower and the Bell Tower to warn of enemy approach. Berwick Barracks of 1717 were amongst the earliest to be purpose built and now give an insight into the life of an 18th-century foot soldier, the history of border warfare, the Kings Own Scottish Borderers Museum and a selection from the Burrell art collection. The ditches and ramparts remain. Holy Trinity Church, near the mediaeval church, rebuilt in 1650, was the only new church constructed during Cromwell's rule. There is a 1750 Guildhall with a 46m spire and a butter market at ground level while there is an 18th-century jail high above the ground.

An unexpected piece of culture is the Lindisfarne Wine and Spirit Museum. Another arose when hotel receptionist Marjorie Ellison finally allowed a regular visitor to paint her portrait in the 1950s after he had pestered her a number of times. She later binned the pictures as amateurish and immature. Fortunately, someone else read the signature, L S Lowry. A further piece of confusion resulted in Berwick's being at war with Russia for many years, having been mentioned specifically in the declaration of war at the start of the Crimean War but not in the subsequent peace treaty.

Another rock sculpture somewhere south of Eyemouth

Needles Eye, home to countless kittiwakes

In another of those coastal anomalies, East Carr lies west of West Carr. Cliffs are up to 93m high to Burnmouth, a small lobster fishing harbour which dries, but thereafter they are only 18m high and

The most notable structure in Berwick is the Royal Border Bridge, of which only the top is visible from the sea 2km downstream. Berwick is a small commercial and fishing port with 460m of quays. The Tweed floods from HW Dover −0250 and ebbs strongly from HW Dover +0330, affected by freshets. It can be dangerous on the ebb,

for the tide to drop while having to portage has the opposite effect.

Holy Island Sands gradually give way to black silty saltmarsh at Fenham where there is a nature reserve around the Mill Burn. There is limited parking allowed in the lane on the neatly mown verges beyond the buildings.

Dunes make their appearance from Scremerston

especially with freshets, and there is a bar. There can also be salmon nets out from mid-February to mid-September. Protecting the northern side of the estuary is a long pier with a 13m white round stone tower lighthouse with red cupola and base.

From late July to September the estuary has one of the largest flocks of swans in the country, together with goldeneyes, red breasted mergansers, pochard and other wildfowl in winter plus a few terns.

On the south side of the estuary Tweedmouth has its own small fishing fleet and the Tweedmouth festival in July. Spittal has a drying sandy spit which is liable to much alteration, especially after westerly gales.

A discoloured stream at Huds Head drains the disused Scremerston coalmines. Cliffs are 30m high at Redshin Cove but they gradually give way to a dune coast, one declining outcrop being topped by a pillbox and some nice lava rolls issuing onto the beach. Cocklawburn Beach has a dangerous undertow on the ebb. 18th-century limekiln remains have lime-loving plants on the spoil and cowslips on the dunes in the spring. A nature reserve is located behind the last of the rock outcrops at Far Skerr and then there are just dunes behind Cheswick Sands, treacherous currents for swimmers, reported unexploded bombs and a golf course. A couple of dunes form high tide islands with views inland to the Cheviots.

Crossing Goswick Sands, with its wrecks, needs to be done within a couple of hours of high tide for there to be sufficient depth. In the vicinity of the causeway to Holy Island the deepest water is in the channel taken by South Low when the tide is out, identified by the more westerly of the two refuges. Paddling across the road irritates motorists waiting

Rich saltmarsh with black silt at low tide at Fenham

One of the refuges for those on foot who get the tide wrong

Distance
From White Sands to Fenham is 57km
Campsites
East Barns, Cockburnspath, Huxton, Coldingham, Lamberton, Spittal, Goswick
Youth Hostels
Coldingham Sands, Wooler
OS 1:50,000 Sheets
67 Duns, Dunbar and Eyemouth
75 Berwick-upon-Tweed
Imray Chart
C24 Flamborough Head to Fife Ness (1:250,000)
Admiralty Charts
111 Berwick to the Farne Islands (1:35,000)
SC 160 St Abb's Head to the Farne Islands (1:75,000)
SC 175 Fife Ness to St Abb's Head (1:75,000)
SC 734 Firth of Forth, Isle of May to Inchkeith (1:50,000)
1612 Harbours and Anchorages on the East Coast of England and Scotland. Eyemouth (1:7,500). Berwick (1:12,500). Holy Island Harbour (1:12,500)
Tidal Constants
Dunbar: HW Dover +0340, LW Dover +0400
Cove Harbour: HW Dover +0330, LW Dover +0350
Eyemouth: HW Dover +0320, LW Dover +0340
Berwick: HW Dover +0340, LW Dover +0320
Holy Island: HW Dover +0350, LW Dover +0320
Sea Areas
Forth, Tyne
Rescue
Inshore lifeboats: Dunbar, St Abbs, Eyemouth, Berwick-upon-Tweed
All weather lifeboats: Dunbar, Berwick-upon-Tweed
Maritime Rescue Centres
Forth, 01333 450666
Humber, 01262 672317

41 NORTHUMBERLAND

Castles and fishing villages

I was but seven year auld
When my mither she did die;
My father married the ae warst woman
The warld did ever see.

For she has made me the laily worm
That lies at the fit o' the tree,
An' my sister Masery she's made
The machrel of the sea.

Bamburgh Castle, one of England's finest

From Fenham, Fenham Flats form a shallow lagoon, muddy at the edges but suitable for lion's mane and moon jellyfish and plenty of birdlife, as indicated by the hide at Lowmoor Point. This is Lindisfarne National Nature Reserve territory. There are streams entirely below the high water mark, including Cathangings Letch and Stinking Goat, between which is the remains of a windpump on the end of White Hill.

Views eastward are dominated by Lindisfarne Castle and by the two leading marks at Guile Point. A break in the dunes at Ross Point may be used by kayaks but there is only 80mm depth of water at the top of spring tides. A notice warns about disturbing nesting shorebirds on the inside of Old Law. This pass is between dunes covered with marram grass, ragwort and rosebay willowherb.

The section of coast to Snook Point at North Sunderland is the most dangerous stretch of coast for shipping north of the Humber, but no problem for craft close inshore except when affected by strong winds. Flows south run to 2km/h.

Budle Bay, the mouth of the Waren Burn, mostly dries. It is a nature reserve, especially for wintering seabirds which seem not to be concerned about waterskiing or the two lots of caravans and the golf course along the south side.

The 9m white tower of Black Rocks Lighthouse overlooks the Harkness Rocks surf break which has tank traps in the dunes at one end.

Bamburgh was the birthplace of Grace Darling, whose father was keeper of the Longstone lighthouse. In September 1838, when she was 23, she and her father rowed out in a coble to rescue 9 survivors of the SS *Forfarshire* who were clinging to Big Harcar rocks, a rescue which caught the public imagination and has helped to attract funds for the RNLI for the subsequent 170 years. The Grace Darling Museum in the village includes the coble. Grace died three years later from tuberculosis and was buried in the churchyard with a monument designed to be seen from ships at sea. Staniland was moved to paint the scene.

The church includes a beam from a wooden church of 635. St Aiden died here in 651. Remains of a 13th-century Dominican friary including part of a church are found in the village, together with the 13 to 15th century church to St Aiden with a fine 13th-century crypt.

A lesser claim for Bamburgh, where the B1342 gives way to the B1340, is that it is home to the Northumbrian sausage.

Bamburgh's most conspicuous asset is the castle, one of the finest in England, standing high on a rock above the beach and surmounted by cannons. There was a wooden fort by 546. King Ida lived here in the 6th century and, after his wife died, married Bethoc the Witch, who was jealous of his daughter, Margaret, turning her into the Laidley Worm, which lived on Spindlestone Haugh and forced villagers to bring food, according to one version of the story. Her brother, Childe Wynde, returned from his travels and went to kill the dragon but recognized her voice, kissing her and breaking the curse. The queen was then changed into a toad which reappears every seven years to seek innocent maidens. The castle was later destroyed by the Vikings. It was rebuilt in the 11th century in the present red stone by Henry I but includes an 8th-century wall. It was used by King Oswald to rule Northumbria and is where Sir Lancelot is said to have eloped with Queen Guinevere. Restoration was again begun in 1704 by Lord Crewe, Bishop of Durham. In 1716 it was the home of Dorothy Forster, who made a daring raid on Newgate Gaol to rescue her brother, Tom. It was once more restored in 1894–1905 by Lord Armstrong with an excellent collection of arms, artwork, china, furniture and Armstrong industrial exhibits including aviation. The castle was used by Roman Polanski for filming *Macbeth* in 1972 and for *Robin of Sherwood* in 1985. It is still the home of Lady Armstrong.

The B1340 follows the coast to Beadnell, passing a pillbox and vandalized lookout point, the last outcrop of the Great Whin Sill. There are between 15 and 28 islands off this stretch of coast depending on the state of the tide, but landing is only permitted on Staple and Inner Farne and there can be fines for disturbing nesting seabirds. The whole area is a nature reserve. It is the only east coast breeding site for Atlantic seals with the largest colony in England, 8,000 of them. The bird sanctuary is one of the most important reserves on the east coast for 20 species of seabird. There are 110,000 breeding birds including 50,000 puffins, 12,000 kittiwakes, 1,500 eiders which have been breeding here since at least the 7th century, 28,000 guillemots, 600 fulmars, 3,000 shags, 150 razorbills, 600 cormorants, 2,000 herring gulls, 2,000 lesser blackbacked gulls, 60 ringed plovers, 400 blackheaded gulls, a tern colony which includes 8,000 sandwiches, 1,000 common, 7,000 Arctic and 40 roseate plus assorted petrels, mallards, shelducks and up to 180 species of migrants with a total of 250 species having been recorded. Plant life is equally varied with 125 species including white flowered scurvy grass, thrift, sea campion, hemlock, sorrel, red goosefoot, sea milkwort, silverweed, bugloss, ragwort, nettle, Yorkshire fog and even a Californian borage, thought to have been imported with chicken feed.

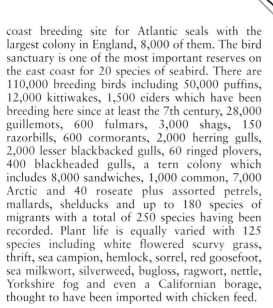

On Inner Farne the Churn is a blowhole which occasionally works at up to 27m. St Cuthbert established a cell on the island in 676 and died here in 687. The Convent of Durham set up a small Benedictine monastery in 1255 and a tiny chapel was built on the cell site in 1370, restored in 1845. Other visitors included the Vikings, who made attacks in the 8th century, and Bartholomew, who was a hermit here about 1150. Sir John Clayton built a light tower in 1669 as a speculative venture, a forerunner of the 13m white round tower which is the 1800 Inner Farne lighthouse. Further out there are towers on Staple Island and Brownsman while the Longstone lighthouse, a 26m red tower with a white band, was built in 1826, damaged in the second world war and repaired in 1952.

Staple Sound flows southeast from Dover HW and northwest from HW Dover +0600 at up to 7km/h, 9km/h near the islands with overfalls, whirlpools and turbulent water. In Inner Sound the flow eases to 6km/h.

Near the lookout a wreck has been left on Greenhill Rocks. St Aidan's Dunes run to the surf break at **Seahouses**, a fishing village which has turned its attention to holidaymakers, their caravans lined behind the beach. Fishing cobles bring in crabs and lobsters. Kippers were first made here in 1843 by smoking herrings, the colour having to come from oak chips, not dyes. Swallow Fish is the last traditional smokehouse. There is a Marine Life Centre and Fishing Museum. At the point where carboniferous limestone gives way to millstone grit, the village was involved in the lime trade. The new harbour was built in 1889 and imposes launching charges. It has an 8m white

Looking out from the coast to the nearer of the Farne Islands

Seahouses, not at its best at low tide

lighthouse tower and a detached breakwater. Away from the holidaymaker front, North Sunderland is less showy and offers better value. The Lodge, in particular, used by divers and anglers, offers five star food at two star prices in a licensed restaurant awash with diving finds. One service no longer available in the village is the North Sunderland Railway which was closed in 1951. It used to take 20 minutes for the 6km journey to Chathill, so slow that passengers were able to jump out, pick flowers and get back in again, but quicker than today.

Curlews search the rocks off Snook Point. Above the 9m cliff is an aerial in front of the golf course although aerials away on the Cheviots are more conspicuous.

Streams are weak to Coquet Island although there may be eddies off points. After Beadnell there are almost no coast roads except in built-up places.

Beadnell was a 19th-century smuggling and fishing village with a three-storey pele tower now used as an inn. 18th-century sandstone limekilns with round towers look like a fortress, the arches now being used to store crab pots. The harbour is well protected from all but southeasterly winds and there is sailing, waterskiing, diving and windsurfing as well as a surf break.

There is a bird sanctuary in the dunes around the mouth of Long Nanny as it discharges into the middle of Beadnell Bay. At the southern end of the bay is another Snook Point before the Football Hole below High Newton-by-the-Sea. St Mary's or Newton Haven is a similar bay, this time with Low Newton-by-the-Sea on the shore, on one side an aerial and on the other the Newton Pool nature reserve with breeding blackheaded gulls, teals, mute swans, dabchicks, sedge warblers and reed buntings plus goldeneyes and pochards in winter. The haven is exposed only to winds from north to east northeast. The rocks forming the southern end to the bay are the Emblestone, a more logical spelling than in Embleton Bay which follows with its gannets, beachbreak, dunes, golf course and Dunstan Steads Park Farm, a working farm with old and modern machinery and a wide range of animals.

The dramatic silhouette of Dunstanburgh Castle

Striking on a section of Whin Sill which slopes down into the sea, with a high rampart facing the land, are the remains of Dunstanburgh Castle on Castle Point. Begun in 1316 by Thomas, Earl of Lancaster, and enlarged by John of Gaunt, who used it to rule England as uncle to the boy king Richard II in the 14th century, it changed hands several times and suffered major gunfire damage during the Wars of the Roses. It has been a ruin since 1538 with an impressive gatehouse tower and immense open bailey surrounded by a long wall with towers. The area once provided protection for Henry VIII's navy and was a harbour when the castle was built although this has since silted up. It was painted by Turner and is now an important wildlife habitat for birds. The reefs at Castle Point can be surfed. One vessel which failed to pull off before the break is a wreck at Cushat Stiel. Along the coast behind are a column of people walking between the castle and Craster.

The village of Craster on lifeboat day

Little Carr, with its white conical concrete beacon, helps protect the entrance to Craster harbour. The harbour was built in 1906 to export the hard whinstone for London kerbstones, but it is now used by leisure craft and cobles landing lobsters and crabs. It was England's kipper smoking capital, smoking 25,000 fish per day, the herrings being gutted by Scottish fishwives who lived in Kip Houses which were only suitable for sleeping, giving rise to the expression 'having a kip'. The herrings are now brought from western Scotland rather than being caught locally. The Craster Tower and a settlement are legacies from earlier years. Wreckage of a steel ship close inshore includes a boiler and pieces of metal which would be uncomfortable if met in surf.

Cullernose Point is a seabird colony, above which is 58m Hips Heugh and then Howick where the gardens have over 600 rhododendrons. Howick Hall was owned by Earl Grey, whose 1832 Reform Act set up our present system of democracy. On a diplomatic mission to China he saved the life of a mandarin who sent him some tea scented with oil of Bergamot in thanks. Earl Grey tea is now the world's most popular blend. The Greys also had a Victorian bathing house.

Boulmer's independently operated lifeboat

Rumbling Kern is a dolerite gully in which heavy seas resonate at low tide. There is a settlement site in a wooded valley and then **Longhoughton** Steel begins 3km of reef with a break in the centre forming Boulmer Haven, a natural harbour with fishing cobles and toilets. A heron standing quietly, watching, is repeating an activity from the days when this was a smuggling village. Boulmer has an independent voluntary lifeboat. This is always the first reporting station on the shipping forecast. The reef ends with Seaton Point where there are caravans, overfalls and reef breaks but Marsden Rocks, in front of the golf course, form another area of reef which has claimed a ship.

England's second oldest golf course is at **Alnmouth**, a resort behind the dunes protected by tank traps. Fishing and recreational craft are faced with the width of the River Aln and the position of the bar changing and there is a surf break. Past changes have been greater and the Saxon cross and Church Hill were cut off when the river moved its course in a storm in 1806.

The millstone grit gives way to coal measures although this is not obvious at first as the dunes sweep on round Alnmouth Bay, only a caravan area above Birling Carrs breaking up the curve. Behind another golf course in a bend in the River Coquet, however, is Warkworth. The early 12th-century church of St Lawrence is on the site of an 8th-century church. It was built by King Coewulf of Northumbria with the longest nave in Northumberland at 27m and a vaulted roof with diagonal ribbing to prevent fire damage during the border troubles, but 300 villagers were massacred in the church by the Earl of Fife in 1174.

Also 12th century with a 15th-century cruciform keep is Warkworth Castle, used by the 1st Earl of

Northumberland, Henry de Percy, and his son, Sir Henry Percy or Harry Hotspur, who was born here, to plot treason and rebellion to put Henry IV on the throne although Hotspur later became the king's enemy. Shakespeare used it as much of the setting for his play. The keep has 8 towers, fine mediaeval masonry, a maze of chambers, passageways and stairways and a keep restored and made habitable again in the 19th century.

The old course of the river has waders and ducks but Warkworth Harbour has been extended with a marina at **Amble**. Use of the fishing port involves negotiating the bar off the entrance with a dangerous short sea over the Pan Bush shoal when a sea is running, although surfers may appreciate small surf in the entrance and north of the breakwater. There is a wreck off the entrance and an RAF boat was lost with many drowned a few years ago. At one time concrete ships were built here. Another unconventional visitor between 1989 and 1994 was Freddie the dolphin, who was very friendly towards swimmers. There is an 8m light tower on each breakwater. A cemetery is located on the front at Amble. The port was built to export coal, there having been 80 mineshafts between Amble and Hauxley, now all closed.

Coquet Island and its lighthouse

Also founded on coal is the 6ha Coquet Island off Amble. Landing is not permitted on this RSPB nature reserve, owned by the Duke of Northumberland, which has 4,000 common, 1,000 Arctic, 1,200 sandwich and 300 roseate terns, 600 eiders in their most southerly breeding colony on the east coast, puffins, oystercatchers, gulls and guillemots. It was occupied in Roman times, jewellery and coins having been found. In the 7th century there was a small Benedictine monastery and chapel where Elfreda, Abbess of Whitby, persuaded St Cuthbert to accept the offer of the bishopric of Lindisfarne from Egfrith, King of Northumbria. A cell was established here by the Dane St Henry the Hermit, who had a vision to become a hermit, so avoiding the arranged marriage his parents were planning. He grew his own food and performed miracles, dying in 1127. Charles I had the island garrisoned in the Civil War but the Scots captured it in 1645. The 22m white and grey tower of Coquet lighthouse dates from 1841, the keepers' cottages being built onto the chapel and hermit's cell.

Coquet Road and then Coquet Channel flow strongly to the south from HW Dover −0040 and north from HW Dover +0520, the flows then becoming weak to Blyth. When Hauxley Point rocks are dry the flow is more in a northwest to southeast direction.

At High Hauxley there is an opencast mine while a lake at Low Hauxley is now a nature reserve with hides and thousands of birds, especially dunlins, curlew sandpipers and other migrants.

Bondi Carrs is a reefbreak. The shoreline is rather unusual, dunes over a thick layer of soft clay at the start of the 9km sweep of tank trap and dune backed Druridge Bay. Much of the land around the bay is restored opencast coal workings, but the power generation looked likely to resurface when it was proposed as a nuclear power station site.

Low Hauxley's unusual formation of dunes over clay

Ladyburn Lake forms the centrepiece of Druridge Bay Country Park at Broomhill with redbreasted mergansers, smew and other diving ducks in winter, scoters, kestrels, lapwings and others.

The restored Radar site workings form Druridge Pools nature reserve with breeding waders and wildfowl, this being on a wildfowl migration route. Behind the pools are a 14th-century chapel and preceptory hostel for passing pilgrims at Low Chibburn, this previously being on a pilgrim migration route. Much of the bay offers a beachbreak.

Cresswell Ponds have good winter wildfowl and little gulls in summer, when the farm trail is also popular and crowds throng the beach. There is parking at Cresswell but care is needed when landing as the tank trap blocks are below the high water line.

Jellyfish beached at Low Hauxley

Distance
From Fenham to Cresswell is 56km
Campsites
Goswick, Waren Mill, Beadnell, Embleton, Craster, Warkworth, Stakeford
Youth Hostels
Wooler, Newcastle-upon-Tyne
OS 1:50,000 Sheets
75 Berwick-upon-Tweed
81 Alnwick and Morpeth
Imray Chart
C24 Flamborough Head to Fife Ness (1:250,000)
Admiralty Charts
111 Berwick to the Farne Islands (1:35,000)
SC 156 Farne Islands to the River Tyne (1:75,000)
SC 160 St Abb's Head to the Farne Islands (1:75,000)
1612 Harbours and Anchorages on the East Coast of England and Scotland. Holy Island Harbour (1:12,500). North Sunderland Harbour (1:7,500)
1627 Harbours on the East Coast of England. Warkworth Harbour (1:15,000)
Tidal Constants
Holy Island: HW Dover +0350, LW Dover +0320
North Sunderland: HW Dover +0340, LW Dover +0330
Craster: HW Dover +0400, LW Dover +0350
Alnmouth: Dover +0400
Amble: Dover +0410
Coquet Road: HW Dover +0420, LW Dover +0410
Sea Area
Tyne
Rescue
Inshore lifeboats: Berwick-upon-Tweed, Seahouses, Craster, Amble, Newbiggin
All weather lifeboats: Berwick-upon-Tweed, Seahouses, Boulmer, Amble
Helicopter: Boulmer
Maritime Rescue Centre
Humber, 01262 672317

42 TYNESIDE

The industrial coast of northeast England

Here's the tender comin', pressin' all the men.
Oh dear, Hinny , what shall we do then?
Here's the tender coming off the Shields bar.
Here's the tender coming full of men o' war.

A marked change comes after Cresswell as industry can no longer be ignored. Cresswell Tower and the caravan site on Snab Point are forgotten as **Lynemouth** comes into sight with its power station and aluminium works and their prominent chimneys. Even the River Lyne is lost in the industrial jungle. The beach is black with coal dust and sea coal is still collected from the shore.

There is a golf course on Beacon Point, beyond which is Woodhorn with the tower of a windmill and St Mary's church, now a museum with Saxon and mediaeval tombstones close to the Woodhorn Colliery Museum and Narrow Gauge Railway.

The power station and aluminium works at Lynemouth indicate a change to a more industrial landscape

Cobles by the beach at Newbiggin. Beyond is Cambois power station

Cresswell
Lynemouth
Beacon Pt
Woodhorn
A197
Newbiggin–
by–the–Sea
A189
N Seaton
R Wansbeck
Cambois
R Blyth
Blyth
B1329
A193
Seaton
Sluice
Hartley
Seaton
Delaval
St Mary's
Island
Whitley
Bay
Cullercoats
Tynemouth
R Tyne
Trow Pt
Marsden
Bay
S Shields
Lizard Pt
Cleadon
Whitburn
A183
Whitburn
Bay
Roker
R Wear
Sunderland
Hendon
Tunstall
North
Sea
A1018
B1287
Seaham
Easington
Beacon Pt
Horden
Blackhall
Rocks

Aerials before and after **Newbiggin-by-the-Sea**, at the end of the A197, mark a measured distance for boats to check their speeds. Newbiggin Point has a church amongst the caravans which is losing its graveyard to the sea so that human bones may be found in the water. There is a coastguard station and an inshore rescue boat in a newly refurbished station, near which cobles are stored. Surprisingly, each seems to have its own tractor for launching and so there are lots of old tractors lined up along the front rather than a few being shared. In the Middle Ages it was a large grain port but now there are only the cobles and leisure craft, the worst of the weather being fielded by a detached stone breakwater although enough waves get in to keep surfers happy. In 1920 the concrete tug *Crete Wheel* was wrecked here. Despite the black coal dust on the beach, Newbiggin remains a resort.

Northumberland fishermen thought it was unlucky to mention pigs except by metaphor. This particularly applies in Newbiggin on Fridays. Another distinctive user of words was John Braine who lived here in the 1950s while writing *Room at the Top*.

Terns and herring gulls live in Newbiggin Bay. More caravans top the low cliffs in front of North Seaton Colliery as the River Wansbeck is crossed by the A189 and discharges over its bar into the bay. Cambois has the trappings of mining superstructure and another large power station.

The River Blyth, named after the Old English blipe or merry, discharges through the harbour at **Blyth**, the biggest town in Northumberland, large enough to have two markets per week and its own dialect, Pitmatic. It was a 19th-century coal exporting and shipping port and still handles coal, together with timber, paper products, general

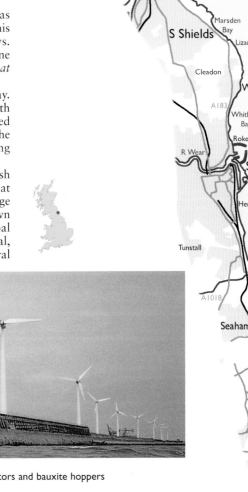

The distinctive harbour wall at Blyth with its aero generators and bauxite hoppers

cargoes and bauxite which is stored in three large red conical hoppers at North Blyth. The rest of the harbour wall is dominated by nine aerogenerators above and kelp below. Each of the piers has a lighthouse on the end. The harbour suffers scend with south southeasterly winds and there are wavetraps inside the east pier. The harbourmouth needs frequent dredging. When the new harbour was constructed in the 1880s the High Light of 1788 was left in the residential streets. Another redundant light is on the wooden lightship in the South Harbour which is now the headquarters of

There is a sheltered beachbreak next to the harbourmouth, overlooked by a nautical school.

Flows are weak to Sunderland and the coast low and sandy to Seaton Sluice, perhaps enhanced by a sprinkling of colliery chimneys inland. The B1329 follows the coast to South Beach and then the A193 takes over to Whitley Bay. Mile Hill is no higher than 18m.

Approaching Seaton Sluice, **Seaton Delaval** Hall was designed in 1718 by Sir John Vanbrugh, his last and most elegant project with antique furniture, pictures and oriental porcelain. One of

The lighthouse on St Mary's Island is now a museum

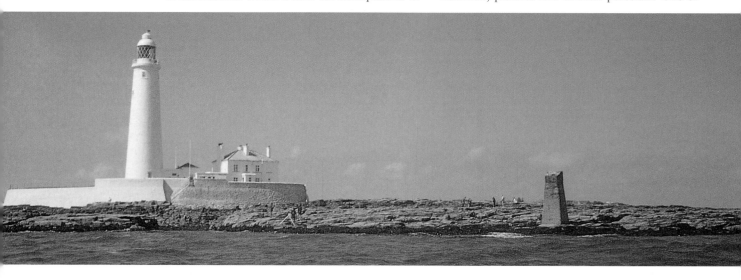

King Edward's Bay with priory remains

the Royal Northumberland Yacht Club. The flood tide starts at HW Dover +0420 but the harbourmaster bans kayaks from the river.

the Delaval family used to buy electors in parliamentary elections by firing golden guineas from a cannon into the crowd. On the bank of

Seaton Burn, Starlight Castle is a folly built overnight in the 1750s. Seaton Sluice was a serious venture, however, built in 1660 by Sir Ralph Delaval as a coal and salt exporting harbour. The sluice was held closed at low tide and horses used to plough the silt before the sluice was opened and then the silt washed away. In the 18th century the village had the largest bottle-making factory in England.

Rocky cliffs with ledges extend to St Mary's Island. At Hartley, right on the Northumberland/North Tyneside boundary, overlooked by a caravan site and half a dozen aerials, there is a reefbreak on the top half of the tide with onshore winds and a northerly swell which can produce waves 600mm higher than at Tynemouth.

A causeway runs from Curry Point to St Mary's, Bait or Bate's Island. Originally it was a monk's place of solitude with a chapel and a cemetery for drowned or plagued sailors, but the chapel light acted as a lighthouse and this function was subsequently taken over by the 37m white tower lighthouse which now stands on the island. This acts as a museum of the history of the island and its wildlife from 1897 to 1984. The island is a SSSI for roosting shorebirds. There is a wreck just south of the island and divers make considerable use of the area.

The shore is sandy to **Whitley Bay** where there is a beachbreak, best on the top half of the tide during storms. The Old English hwit leah or white glade is now a resort with a jazz festival, Childhood Memories Toy Museum with 3,000 toys, Rollercoaster and Spanish City fairground. The latter with its dome is a fine example of an early reinforced concrete building by Hennebique. Most of the buildings along the front are tall and elegant. The former fishing village of Cullercoats with its Smuggler's Cave now merges into one built-up area. In 1749 it was described as the best fishmarket in the north of England. It had smugglers and wreckers but now has interesting geological features in the cliffs, sealife centre with sharks, rays and eels, marine laboratory and the odd wreck. Rocks and ledges to **Tynemouth** are interspersed with sandy beaches. Long Sands have a beachbreak, best at high water near the outdoor pool although the point break can be bigger. King Edward's Bay has a sheltered beachbreak but is plagued by whistle blowing youngsters in lifeguard T-shirts, hardly the Tynemouth Volunteer Life Brigade, set up in 1864, whose timber Watch House contains lifesaving exhibits from 1864 onwards and relics from shipwrecks.

On the headland are the substantial remains of a Benedictine priory founded in 1090 on a 7th-century monastic site within which St Oswin, St Osred and several kings are buried. Two presbytery walls still stand full height and there are splendid roof bosses in the chantry chapel which was fortified and to which a Gate Tower was added by Robert de Mowbray during the border wars at the time of Richard II. After the Dissolution Henry VIII retained it as a castle. Underground chambers beneath the gun battery from the two world wars were mostly dismantled in 1956, but there is a monument to Lord Collingwood with cannons from the *Royal Sovereign*, the ship he commanded at Trafalgar. The area featured in the work of American artist Winslow Homer. It has recently become the end of the Coast to Coast cycle route.

A race can form across the ends of the piers, each topped by a lighthouse. Inside the North Pier the Black Middens break can sometimes be one of the best on the east coast with a left barrel over a boulder reef on the bottom half of the flood. The flood starts at HW Dover +0030 to 2km/h and the ebb runs from HW Dover +0630, the ebb being substantially longer when the River Tyne is in spate.

Spirit of South Shields statue

Having crossed from North Tyneside to South Tyneside, the South Pier is the longer at 1.6km. Built 1855–95, it contains 3,000,000 tonnes of stone and was designed by James Walker. South of the Tyne the geology moves from the coal measures to the post carboniferous.

Near the South Pier at **South Shields** is the Arbeia Roman fort with its reconstructed gateway, used in the building and garrisoning of Hadrian's Wall by the 5th Cohort of Gaul. The foundations of eight granaries remain, one from the Antonine period and the others built under Severus. 1.6ha date from the 2nd-century, in 208 it was enlarged to 22 stone granaries and in 220 it was converted to a normal garrison and may have been used until the 5th century. Weapons, armour, jewellery and coins have been found. The name South Shields comes from the Middle English schele, where shepherds had their summer huts or shielings.

A Catherine Cookson gallery has been added to South Shields Museum and Art Gallery, joining features on local and natural history, paintings, a paddle tug, ship models and photographs and a model of *Original*. This was a self-righting boat designed by William Woodhave and built by Henry Greathead of South Shields in 1789, which formed the basis of the lifeboat, following the loss of the *Adventure* 300m from the shore, watched by thousands. The world's first lifeboat service began here the following year.

The town has a colliery but developed on fishing and shipbuilding, being badly bombed during the second world war. It has a beachbreak which may be better at the cliff end and has urban breeding herring gulls.

The A183 follows the coast to Sunderland and the shore is mostly sandy to Lizard Point. From Trow Point to Lizard Point is a SSSI.

Marsden Bay's cliffs are unstable with frequent collapses of the interesting magnesian limestone formations. In the centre of the bay was a large arch, part of which collapsed in 1996 to give a causeway out to it but it remains a nature reserve with kittiwakes, cormorants, fulmars, guillemots, razorbills, terns, blackheaded

The lifeguard hut at Marsden Bay

Marsden Bay with the lift serving the Grotto, the stack in the bay after the arch collapsed, Souter lighthouse and another arch off Lizard Point

gulls and even gannets. The Grotto, facing it, is a hotel at the foot of the cliff with a lift down to it. It was built into caves as a smugglers' tavern, enlarged in 1782 by ex-miner Jack the Blaster and further enlarged to form an inn with all facilities. On dark and windy nights the groans of Jack the Jibber may be heard, a smuggler who shopped his partners to the customs men but they escaped and left him to die in a bucket suspended halfway down the cliff.

The disused Souter Point lighthouse on Lizard Point takes the form of a 23m white and orange striped tower. Built in 1871, it was the world's first reliable lighthouse, the first with an AC power supply. It only failed twice in 117 years, once mechanically and once when the keeper fell asleep.

Ledges continue to Whitburn Bay, together with some smaller arches around the Whitburn Colliery area, lion's mane jellyfish swimming off the rocks.

Whitburn Rifle Range operates at Souter Point, the extremities marked by light buoys. The range warden will stop the firing to allow passage if given advanced notice.

The Razor Blades are three left reefbreaks which work on the upper half of the tide and there is a sheltered beachbreak at **Whitburn**.

The River Wear discharges into the sea at **Sunderland** between two long curved piers. Outside the northern Roker pier are the sheltered Cats and Dogs break and a memorial to Bede. On the end of the pier is Roker Pier lighthouse, a 23m white tower with three red bands, faced by a disused lighthouse on the southern pier. This early Christian settlement, which takes its name from the Old English sundorland, a satellite part of an estate, became a mediaeval fishing port and then grew on coal exporting and shipbuilding from the 16th century, especially in the 19th century. The docks still handle coal, petroleum products and general cargo and Pallion Yard is the largest totally enclosed shipyard complex in the world but recession has hit Sunderland hard, notwithstanding its elevation to city status. Sunderland Museum and Art Gallery chronicles the city's role in merchant shipping and has equipment from Sunderland lighthouse, the Roker lighthouse of 1903 being moved here from the harbour in 1976. Another noteworthy venue is St Andrew's church of 1906/7 by E S Prior with many fittings by the Arts and Crafts Movement. The latest attraction is the National Glass Centre in a purpose built glass building, covering 1,300

Sunderland seen from Whitburn Bay

The privately run port of Seaham

Lewis Carroll often stayed in Whitburn, gaining inspiration from the locals, and his statue appears in the library. Cleadon is a village located between two windmills.

South Tyneside becomes Sunderland. Beach begins again at South Bents, off which there is a wreck. The local geology is interesting, particularly to boats out of control.

years of the use of glass in the city. This is another place with urban breeding herring gulls.

The river floods from HW Dover −0130 and ebbs from HW Dover +0430. Along the coast, flows are weak to Tees Bay. The A1018 follows the coast briefly.

A railway also follows the coast to Seaton Carew, initially through the tank farms of Hendon

Hawthorn Hive, one of the wooded denes of the Durham coalfield which can serve as emergency exit routes

and then out past the 112m Tunstall Hills or Maiden Paps.

Ryhope Colliery is the first of a number. Close by is the Ryhope Engines Museum in the Victorian Gothic Ryhope Pumping Station with its 49m chimney, designed by Thomas Hawksley. Two beam engines of 1868 are in steam on bank holidays although the 6 Cornish boilers were replaced with Lancashire models in 1908. The engines pumped $3m^3$/min from 43m and 77m deep wells to supply Sunderland, one of them being used for dewatering during construction.

The B1287 emerges from under the railway to pass over a burn and the Sunderland/Durham border, then follows the coast to Seaham. It passes Seaham Hall, where Lord Byron married Anne Isabella Millbank in 1815, and edges past the Vane Tempest Colliery and fine beaches.

Seaham, at a break in the 15–18m limestone cliffs, has harbour breakwaters like a miniature version of Sunderland, built 1828–44 as a commercial coal-exporting port by Lord Londonderry for his mines and still privately run. Coal is tipped 12m down chutes from lorries. There is a 10m white metal light column with black bands. In 1862 the lifeboat capsized and was lost with all hands including four people previously picked up from a fishing boat.

In appearance, the Durham coalfield resembles the coast between Aberdeen and Stonehaven, a plateau with steep cliffs except where ravines are crossed by railway bridges. In fact, the 20–30m cliffs are crumbling coal waste, intercepted by denes which give emergency escape routes on an otherwise inaccessible stretch of coast. At intervals, earthmoving equipment can be seen restoring the landscape above ground, hiding the legacy of collieries which run out under the sea for up to 7km.

At Dawdon Colliery a white arch faces the shore and Liddle Stack is an Eiffel Tower-shaped pillar with an arch at its base.

Kinley Hill is marked with a tower and then comes Beacon Hill, at 85m the highest point on the County Durham coast. A waterfall drops down the cliffs beyond Easington Colliery and black sand on the beaches is further evidence of years of coal working. At **Easington** and **Horden**, colliery villages stand in rows on the cliffs, but Horden also has the largest and least spoiled of the denes and the Castle Eden Denes nature reserve with roe deer and a requirement to keep to approved footpaths.

Approaching the Tees, the beaches become cleaner but the water colour changes to a polluted brown although seals still live here.

After Blackhall Colliery there is a nature reserve on the cliffs at Blackhall Rocks, the rocks themselves being covered in mussels and the site of a wreck. Oystercatchers pick through the delicacies washed up on the beach. Steps lead up to a limited area of parking where a layer of broken windscreen glass suggests the criminal element are frequently active.

The Durham coalfield seen from Blackhall Rocks

Distance
From Creswell to Blackhall Rocks is 59km
Campsites
Stakeford, South Shields, Marsden, Crimdon Park
Youth Hostel
Newcastle-upon-Tyne
OS 1:50,000 Sheets
81 Alnwick and Morpeth
88 Newcastle upon Tyne
93 Middlesbrough
Imray Chart
C24 Flamborough Head to Fife Ness (1:250,000)
Admiralty Charts
SC 152 River Tyne to River Tees (1:75,000)
SC 156 Farne Islands to the River Tyne (1:75,000)
1191 River Tyne to Flamborough Head (1:200,000).
Approaches to the River Tyne (1:75,000)
1626 Blyth (1:6,250)
1627 Harbours on the East Coast of England.
Sunderland (1:10,000). Seaham (1:12,500)
1934 River Tyne (1:12,500)
1935 Approaches to Blyth, the River Tyne and
Sunderland (1:30,000)
2567 Approaches to Tees Bay (1:30,000)
Tidal Constants
Coquet Road: HW Dover +0420, LW Dover +0410
Blyth: Dover +0430
R Tyne Entrance: HW Dover +0440, LW Dover +0420
Sunderland: Dover +0420
Seaham: Dover +0430
Hartlepool: Dover +0440
Sea Area
Tyne
Range
Whitburn
Rescue
Inshore lifeboats: Newbiggin, Blyth, Cullercoats, Tynemouth, Sunderland, Hartlepool
All weather lifeboats: Amble, Blyth, Tynemouth, Sunderland, Hartlepool
Maritime Rescue Centre
Humber, 01262 672317

43 CLEVELAND

From Teesside's modern industry to the clifftop industrial remains on the North York Moors

Blackhall Rocks are the most interesting part of the Durham coalfield coast, a profusion of arches and caves in the limestone, some of complex shapes with multiple exits and various ledges and internal walls, the sort of place where those on foot can easily become cut off by the tide.

This section of coast now comes under Tees and Hartlepool Port Authority control. Beyond Crimdon Park Durham gives way to Hartlepool at the Crimdon Beck. Terns, fulmars, blackbacked gulls, common gulls and guillemots patrol the water.

Beyond the golf course at North Sands is West View, which seems almost to be a snub to the Steetly works with its long pier to the east. The A1049 arrives from behind the works, passes a cemetery and the 1830 Throston Engine House, used for loading coal wagons, and heads for the Headland at Hartlepool.

built by the family of Robert the Bruce on the site of a 7th-century monastery founded by St Aidan. There is also a high water tower. Tidal eddies form off the harbour entrance. Men collecting sacks of coal off the beach and wheeling them away on bikes may seem like something out of the Depression, but the sight has been much more recent.

Hartlepool takes its name from the Old English heorot eg pol, stag island pool. The harbour which once sheltered the Crusader fleet now handles

Waves break onto the beach at Blackhall Rocks

The Headland is a limestone outcrop which forms a migration watchpoint, protected by a Russian cannon captured at Sebastopol in 1854, the 1315 town wall to keep the Scots out, a seawall which produces large clapotis with northeasterly winds and two lighthouses, of which the 1926 Heugh lighthouse is a 13m white metal tower. St Hilda's Early English church of 1189–1293 was

Hartlepool seen from a cave at Blackhall Rocks

West View's pier is a dominant feature on the approach to Hartlepool's Headland

forestry products, coal and fish and constructs North Sea oil platforms and pipes. Hartlepool was an active port, a small fishing village by the start of the 19th century and the third largest port in England and a major shipbuilding centre by the 1890s after the east Durham coalfield opened and the railway arrived. Hartlepool Maritime Museum features the maritime history, fishing, shipbuilding, marine engineering, a rebuilt fisherman's house, a ship's bridge and a gas powered lighthouse lantern. The three masts of the frigate *HMS Trimcomalee* of 1817, the oldest British warship afloat, can be seen in the Historic Ship Centre in the marina

More recent residents have included Compton McKenzie, author of *Whisky Galore*, Ridley Scott, director and producer of *Alien, Blade Runner* and *Thelma and Louise*, Sir Edward Mellenby, who discovered vitamin D deficiency causes rickets, and Reg Smythe, the *Andy Capp* cartoonist.

The A178 follows the bay. The Staincliffe Hotel begins the housing of the resort of **Seaton Carew** with its fire signal basket and clocktower.

Beyond the built-up area, Seaton Sands have a wreck, dunes and a golf course where the Ekofisk oil pipeline lands, destination the Tees Bay industrial complex which looms ahead with a

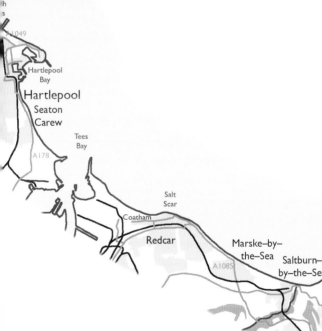

skyline of structures, aerials and columns of various colours of smoke. There is Laing Offshore's rig fabrication basin, nuclear power station, oil terminal, chemical works, refinery, steelworks and the transporter bridge across the Tees, the only one in England. The RSPB said there was a major threat of oil pollution but 22,000 waterfowl enjoy the environment in the winter, including 3,800 knots, 300 sanderlings and flocks of shelducks in one of the most important sites in the north of England, regardless of present pollution.

The North Gare breakwater ends almost due west of the South Gare breakwater, the latter with a 13m white tower lighthouse. Despite the heavy shipping traffic, Tees Mouth is easier to cross than some major estuaries because the fairway is narrow and clearly buoyed, lying close to the South Gare breakwater.

The steelworks at Redcar with other Teesside industry marking the skyline beyond Tees Bay

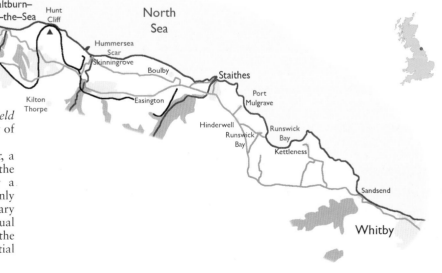

where there is also the paddle steamer *Wingfield Castle*, a coble and displays charting the history of Hartlepool.

In the centre of Hartlepool Bay is Long Scar, a reef formed by a petrified forest. During the Napoleonic Wars in the early 19th century a French privateer was wrecked there, the only survivor being a shivering monkey in a military uniform. Such animal uniforms were not unusual at the time but the local fishermen believed the monkey to be a French spy, held a court martial and hung the poor creature.

Three hundred metres upriver from the lighthouse is a surf break with fast hollow rights onto a boulder dump, excellent but potentially dangerous.

The river divides Hartlepool from Redcar and Cleveland. Cleveland is Viking for cliff land although the cliffs are conspicuously absent from this coast, unlike the neighbouring counties with their high cliffs.

The Tees floods from HW Dover –0040 and ebbs from HW Dover +0300 at up to 6km/h, freshets decreasing the duration and rate of the flood and increasing the duration and rate of the ebb. Off the entrance, flows begin southeast at HW Dover +0140 and begin northwest at HW Dover –0430 at up to 4km/h. Flows then run parallel to the coast at up to 3km/h to Whitby.

Along the front of the steelworks are Coatham Sands with surf during onshore winds. Having the Redcar steelworks and blast furnace as neighbours and the Everest gas pipeline landing might be factors to be ignored by seals and cormorants, even by surfers and golfers, but it would not seem the ideal place for a caravan site.

The 16th-century fishing village of **Redcar**, its name taken from the Old English hreod, reed, and Old Norse kiarr, marsh, has now become a resort. The Tees and Hartlepool Port Authority relinquishes control as reefs break up the shoreline

Refined Saltburn-by-the-Sea with its pier and cliff tramway

Hunt Cliff with Boulby Cliff beyond as the sudden end to the North York Moors

and more. There is a wreck on Salt Scar, the remains of a boiler southwest of High Stone and a wreck on the Flashes. Lion's mane and compass jellyfish float in the shallows. Surf forms on outer and inner scars with an inshore swell. The Zetland

Lifeboat Museum houses the oldest surviving lifeboat which saved 500 lives while in use between 1800 and 1887 and has displays on rescue, local marine life, fishing and an aquarium, all housed in the former lifeboat house of 1877.

Racehorses are exercised on the sands, there being a horse racecourse in the town. More fast footwork can be seen at the Redcar International Folk Music, Dance and Song Festival.

The railway follows the coast to Saltburn-by-the-Sea and the A1085 follows behind the dunes, known as the Stray, to **Marske-by-the-Sea**. All this section of coast can be surfed with onshore winds.

In Marske, the spire remains of St Germain's church, most of which was demolished in 1960. Close by is the 1779 grave of Captain Cook's father, who died unaware that his son had been killed six weeks earlier.

The Cleveland Way footpath now follows the coast to Filey Brigg. A pier was necessary for **Saltburn-by-the-Sea** to become a Victorian resort and the town still has a Victorian festival. The Old English sealt burna, salt stream, suggests the town is much older. The Saltburn Smugglers Heritage Centre in fishermen's cottages covers 18th-century smuggling.

Skelton Beck descends through wooded glens while other water descends more sedately, being used to power a cliff tramway, the oldest of its kind in Britain, dating from 1884 with such features as stained glass windows. There is also a miniature railway in the town.

The surf break is the most popular in northeast England but the waves lose their power on the flat beach. Fast and powerful rights may be taken off Saltburn Scar at Penny Hole although the flat rock platform is the most sheltered part of the beach with the wind from the southeast.

The cliffs of the North York Moors now begin in earnest with marked horizontal strata, rich in fossils, particularly ammonites and belemnites, to Ravenscar. The cliffs run 30–180m high to Sandsend with heavy landslips. The North Yorkshire and Cleveland Heritage Coast stretches from Saltburn to Scarborough. From 1600 to 1870 the cliffs were the site of significant alum workings.

Flows start southeast at HW Dover −0410 and northwards at HW Dover +0200.

Hunt Cliff is the uncompromising start to this section of coast, 110m high, dark red and nearly perpendicular. At the top it continues to rise to Warsett Hill, 166m high, a venue the Romans chose for a signal station.

In 1535 a sea man was caught off Skinningrove and held for several weeks, during which time he would eat only raw fish and communicate in shrieks although he was courteous to visitors, especially maidens. Eventually, he escaped back to the sea.

Skinningrove was chosen as a steelworks site with the village built for iron mines at the head of the valley. Kilton Beck, which discharges near the pier, is stained brown by iron ore waste. The Tom Leonard mining museum explains the industry.

Two shorebreaks work on the lower half of the tide, giving rights off Hummersea Scar, a set of flat rocks with a channel cut through to form a harbour for the alum industry. Disused quarries are located at the top of the cliffs as the coast becomes the edge of the North York Moors National Park to Sandsend. Also on top of the cliffs are a tumulus, a radio aerial and 213m high Rockhole Hill. The cliffs here are 180m high but at Boulby Cliff they increase to 200m. An intrusive feature here is the Boulby Mine, the deepest potash mine in Europe.

Staithes is the jewel of this coast, the fishing village with its drying harbour nestling in a gap in the cliffs. On the east side Easington Beck separates Redcar and Cleveland from North Yorkshire and drains down from Scaling Dam Reservoir and enters the harbour through a channel where a cat's cradle of ropes moor the boats and make it very difficult for boats to enter or leave. Facilities include toilets near the Cod and Lobster. Parking is not permitted except for residents. This village is where Captain Cook worked as a boy in William Sanderson's general store which has since been lost to the sea although some of it has been incorporated into Cook's Cottage. Captain Cook and Staithes Heritage Centre has a 1745 street scene of Sanderson's haberdashery shop, fishermen's warehouse and cottage, chandler's and ale house.

The harbour entrance can be difficult or even too rough to get in. There are three surf breaks on the lower half of the tide, north of the harbour having impressive lefts, south of the harbour also having quite good lefts and the Cove being one of the best breaks in Britain, fast, hollow and powerful.

Black cliffs reach 90m at Old Nab and the serious fossil coast begins at Port Mulgrave which has ruined piers, a drying harbour and a tunnel at the foot of the cliff which carried a narrow gauge railway to take iron ore from Dalehouse to Jarrow.

The sea can break across the entrance to Runswick Bay with onshore winds, but it is more sheltered than the rest of this coast in northerly swells. There are impressive lefts at Cobble Dump and three right reef breaks which work on the lower half of the tide. Outer Reef can have 5m rideable waves, Middle Reef of moderate size and Innermost Reef by the Hob Holes (home to a hobgoblin who could cure whooping cough) sheltered with long rides after easy paddles out. There is also a beachbreak in the middle of the bay. An earlier Runswick slipped into the sea in 1682 but the present one is on firmer ground and is popular with artists.

Staithes where Captain Cook acquired his love of the sea

Above Kettle Ness is the Goldsborough Roman signal station, the best preserved on this coast with a square tower in an 8,000m² fort with 1.2m thick walls, overwhelmed and burned by the Saxons in the 5th century, two skeletons being found in the ruins. Red Cliffs are 90m high and have been excavated for alum, for which a boiling house remains. There were also alum works between 1615 and 1867 at Overdale Wyke, which has a wreck. More recent remains in a field are a Victorian station which was part of the former coastal railway.

A further alum boiling house remains at Sandsend, the start of a significant break in the cliffs to Whitby with a slipway next to a carpark, making a convenient place to land except when the parking becomes overcrowded in the summer.

On the beach it is possible to find small pieces of jet, the fossilized remains of monkey puzzle tree wood which is used for making semiprecious jewellery.

Distance
From Blackhall Rocks to Sandsend is 49km
Campsites
Crimdon Park, West View, Coatham, Guisborough, Margrove Park, Hinderwell, Runswick Bay, Whitby
Youth Hostels
Newcastle-upon-Tyne, Osmotherly, Whitby
OS 1:50,000 Sheets
93 Middlesbrough
94 Whitby and Esk Dale
Imray Chart
C24 Flamborough Head to Fife Ness (1:250,000)
Admiralty Charts
SC 134 River Tees to Scarborough (1:75,000)
SC 152 River Tyne to River Tees (1:75,000)
1612 Harbours and Anchorages on the East Coast of England and Scotland. Runswick Bay (1:25,000)
2566 Tees and Hartlepool Bays. Hartlepool Bay (1:10,000). Tees Bay (1:20,000)
2567 Approaches to Tees Bay (1:30,000)
Tidal Constants
Hartlepool: Dover +0440
Staithes: HW Dover +0500, LW Dover +0450
Whitby: Dover +0500
Sea Area
Tyne
Rescue
Inshore lifeboats: Hartlepool, Redcar, Staithes and Runswick, Whitby
All weather lifeboats: Hartlepool, Teesmouth, Whitby
Maritime Rescue Centres
Humber, 01262 672317

44 NORTH YORKSHIRE

Cliffs and more cliffs

Under the grand old Castle Hill
The town of Scarborough stands,
The Queen of Watering Places she, with bays of golden sands,
And the mussels on her brawny rocks are bait for any man.

O A Deacon

Sandsend, looking towards Whitby

The mouth of the Esk at Whitby with the abbey standing on the cliffs above the town

The Caves break at Sandsend has lefts up to 1.5m at mid-tide with decent northerly swells but is sheltered from the west. There are good beachbreaks along the sandy beach which edges Sandsend Wyke but these close out at the top of the tide.

The A174 also follows the shore to **Whitby**, winding past East Row where there is a coble builder.

Piers protect the mouth of the River Esk, around which there are wrecks. The first Cistercian monastery and abbey, now ruined, were founded by St Hilda in 657 and the dates for Easter were established here by the Synod of Whitby in 664. Also well established was that St Hilda tackled a plague of snakes, driving them over the cliff where they coiled up and petrified to form the snakestones. Regardless of the facts, some local ammonite species have the scientific name Hildoceras. Caedmon, the first English poet, lived here until his death in 680. The name comes from the Old Norse name Hviti, meaning white, and Old Scandinavian by or village. The abbey was destroyed by the Vikings in 867, refounded in 1078 and rebuilt in the 13th century, the work

visible being 12th to 15th century, the three–tiered choir and north transcept. 199 steps lead to part of the 12th-century St Mary's church, restored in the 18th century. It was then that Whitby was a whaling and shipbuilding port, the ships built including the ones in which James Cook circumnavigated the globe, and it was from here that Cook set out to claim Australia for Britain. His ship *HM Bark Endeavour* returned here in 1997, the replica incorporating a small piece of wood from the original vessel which has been to the moon with American astronauts in the intervening period. Cook's statue is on the West Cliff.

Whitby became a herring and kipper port in the 19th century and is now a commercial, fishing and recreational port. In December 1914 the abbey and coastguard station were shelled by two German warships after they had shelled Scarborough. This was a misguided attempt to draw part of the British fleet here as the Germans did not feel able to take on the whole British fleet, but which resulted in anger serving to recruit civilians to fight the Germans.

Whitby's jet industry has been active since Queen Victoria made jet popular by wearing it as mourning jewellery for Prince Albert.

Headless horses are sometimes seen pulling a coach and the town featured in Dracula, this being where Count Dracula was said to have landed in England.

To land involves passing over the bar. The ebb runs at up to 9km/h with freshets and there can also be 9km/h flows across the harbourmouth. Cliffs extend to Scarborough, mostly a rocky ledge backed by a steep bank. Beyond the aerial, swells break heavily over the Scar. The coastline as far as Robin Hood's Bay was used for filming *Carrington* in 1995.

From Saltwick Nab the coast is once again part of the North York Moors National Park as far as Long Nab. Black Nab on the east side of Saltwick Bay has many wild flowers and insects, herring gulls, cormorants, fulmars, another aerial and the

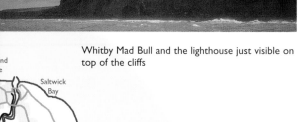

Whitby Mad Bull and the lighthouse just visible on top of the cliffs

Ness Point or North Cheek has a rock platform which uncovers with the tide at the entrance to Robin Hood's Bay at the end of the B1447. The honeycombed cliffs are part of an eroded dome with the centre being 2km out to sea. The cliff is receding at 60mm/year behind sandstone reefs from between which the clay has been washed. In 1975 a 12m seawall was completed after several houses were lost to the sea. The village has narrow precipitous streets in a ravine. The nearest parking is a considerable distance away up a 30% hill. The village was first recorded in 1538. Robin Hood is said to have found refuge disguised as a fisherman or he may have come to Whitby to help the abbot repel the Danes. In the 18th century the village was used for smuggling. King's Beck discharges through a tunnel with interconnecting passages and many houses have interconnecting doors covered by cupboards. It is the end of the Coast to Coast Walk from St Bees Head. Others who have come here are artists, including Leo Walmsley who lived here from 1894 to 1913 and incorporated the village into a number of his books as Bramblewick. In 1986 it was used for filming *David Copperfield*.

Reefs between the Boggle Hole and Old Peak in the distance

remains of an alum boiling house. The 13m white octagonal tower of Whitby High lighthouse stands on the 73m cliffs soon after its fog siren, known as the Whitby Mad Bull or Hawsker Bull, which can be heard 16km away.

Robin Hood's Bay with the latest sea wall at low tide

There is a beach break. Cliffs are particularly rich in 150,000,000–185,000,000 year old fossils to Ravenscar.

Mill Beck enters the sea at the Boggle Hole where there is a youth hostel in the old mill. The next stream runs down past Stoupe Brow where there are the remains of another alum boiling house. Further up the hill are tumuli and Robin Hood's Butts.

At Old Peak or South Cheek there is a turreted tower nestling on the edge of the cliff. Further back is a radio mast and between them a golf course and Raven Hall, built in 1774 on the site of a Roman signal station. In 1890 there were plans to build a resort but the developer went bankrupt. Today the hall is a hotel.

The Peak Alum Works produced a tenth of Yorkshire's output in the 1820's, refined alum being taken from an artificial harbour to Newcastle, Hull and London, extensive remains still existing. The cliffs have the appearance of cliffs that have been subject to heavy slippage. The Ravenscar Coastal Centre features the geology and history of the Yorkshire coast and has a rockpool aquarium. A coastguard lookout hut stands above a wreck site. The 110m cliffs, now of shale and clay laid down in estuarial conditions rather than the marine cliffs further north, have scrub oakwood with wood vetch.

War Dike runs back from the top of Beast Cliff although the only beasts of today are to be found in the Staintondale Shire Horse Farm with everything from Shetland ponies upwards. However, blackbacked gulls can be beastly to other birds. Hayburn Wyke, from the mediaeval wic or dairy farm, is where Thorny Beck's waterfall drops to an area of beach.

Long Nab is followed by Cromer Point with its Sailors' Grave. The last point before Scarborough is Scalby Ness Rocks. The Sea Cut was opened to pass **Scalby** Mills and discharge near the point in 1804, collecting floodwaters from the upper River Derwent to protect land further downstream. Prominent new building draws attention to the Sea Life Centre with its seals and Atlantis, Britain's first outdoor water theme park with two of the world's longest waterslides, river rapids, wave ball and pirates' cove play area. A cable car runs behind North Bay and there is a North Bay Railway while the A165 is to run parallel to the coast to Reighton. In the distance a prominent windmill stands on the skyline.

North Bay also has Peasholm Park where naval battles are fought between large model ships, canoes and other boats are for hire and there are Japanese gardens.

Scarborough hides behind its headland, topped by the castle, a headland which has seen millennia of military activity

One of the most conspicuous landmarks on the coast is the headland topped by **Scarborough** castle, surrounded by a semi-circle of cliff with a road around its base. The headland was used in the Bronze Age. The Romans had a signal station on the site in the 4th century, overcome by the Saxons in the 5th century. The Vikings came in the 10th century and named the town after its founder, Thorgils Skarthi. The castle was begun in the 12th century by William le Gros, Earl of Aumâle. It has a 3-storey rectangular stone keep and buttressed walls. It was seized by Henry II, improved by King John in the 13th century, attacked by the Scots under Robert the Bruce in 1318, attacked by cannons in the Civil War, during which it changed hands several times, and was used for political prisoners including Quaker founder George Fox in 1665/6. In December 1914 it was the first of the ports to be shelled by two German warships, resulting in the recruiting slogan 'Remember Scarborough', and came under fire again in the second world war. The latest controversy is over various issues related to seawall enhancement.

On a quieter note, spa water had been discovered in 1620 and stored in a cistern from 1698. In 1738 the Spa was destroyed by an earthquake, a storm badly damaged its wooden building in 1836, the Grand Hall was destroyed by fire in 1876 and the waters are now unfit to drink. The conspicuous Spa Bridge of 1827 is a rare multi-spanned cast-iron structure with 20m arches on ashlar columns carrying a 6.7m carriageway drive. While Scarborough is the most important resort on Britain's east coast, in 1660 it was probably the first fashionable resort in Britain, developed after Dr Wittie suggested naked sea bathing by both sexes.

The visitors needed somewhere to stay and the Grand Hotel was the biggest brick building in Europe in 1867 when constructed. It has 365 rooms, 52 chimneys, 12 floors and 4 turrets to represent the days, week, months and seasons of the year. It is now a Butlin's holiday centre.

The 12th to 13th-century St Mary's church was restored in the 19th century and has Anne Brontë buried in the churchyard. The town's more recent literary associations relate to Alan Ayckbourn's theatre. Scarborough was used for filming *A Chorus of Disapproval* and *PC Penrose*. Genuine horror filmsets are to be found in Terror Tower. Other historical material is to be found in the Scarborough Millennium which covers the town from 966 to 1966, the Scarborough Lighthouses and Fisheries Museum which covers marine natural history and the Yorkshire fishing industry and the Three Mariners Inn which was a smuggling den but is now a museum with a selection of fishermen's jerseys, all blue but each port with a different stitching which helped with identification of bodies washed up.

The Old and East Harbours are on the south side of the headland with the lighthouse. The harbours are a yachting and angling centre. Speedboats take customers for trips round the North Bay, but they are noisy enough for there to be plenty of warning that they are coming. Surfers find rights off the headland and lefts off the East Pier with a big swell. The northgoing stream is strong off the harbour from HW Dover +0420 to HW Dover –0110 but streams in South Bay are barely perceptible.

Near the bathing pool a semi-circle of rock supports the toe of the cliff where a hotel fell into the sea. Perhaps it was helped by the vibration of the motorcycle events on Oliver's Mount above.

More surf is to be found in Cayton Bay below the A165 where Bunkers is the best beachbreak in the area with lefts and rights. Pump House is usable on the upper half of the flood between the rocks for 1m–1.5m surf although there is a strong rip for anything larger. It gives long rides but can close out. For 1.5m–4.5m surf Point break is one of the longest lefts on the east coast, dangerous but cleaning up even in messy conditions.

Filey Brigg, seen from the north, is extended by low reefs which always offer plenty of interest

Cliffs run out to Filey Brigg, Lebberston Cliff, Gristhorpe Cliff, Newbiggin Cliffs and North Cliff. On top are large areas of caravan park but guillemots and razorbills nest undisturbed on the cliffs and North Cliff Country Park is a bird migration watchpoint.

The cliffs run into what is almost an arête, finishing with an old coral reef which is likely to produce difficult water at all times as it is exposed to wind from any direction. There is a race off the end and the northwesterly flow runs eastwards along the southern side at up to 3km/h. Any misadventures will be watched by the crowds of people drawn to the rocks, whose sightings in the past have included a monster with long neck and several humps. The Romans chose the location for a signal station because of its visibility. Walkers come here because it is the end of the Cleveland Way, Britain's second long distance footpath, opened in 1969, and the start of the Wolds Way and Centenary Way.

Filey Bay provides a contrast with barely perceptible currents and a sweep of sandy beach which is used for everything from sand yachting to donkey rides. The bay can have sheltered surf when Cayton Bay is blown out.

Filey was five glades from the Old English leah. It is a resort with white hotels and refined Victorian terraces, paddling and model boating pools, golf course, miniature golf and Filey Folk Museum featuring the lifeboat, fishing and rural and domestic life in a 1696 farmhouse. This old fishing port with its Coble Landing, lands crabs and lobsters in the summer and cod and haddock in the winter, along with codling and mackerel.

St Oswald's church has Norman pillars and doorways and a 13th-century effigy of a boy bishop. A windmill is another landmark beyond the town.

Holiday villages with large caravan sites follow, Primrose Valley Holiday Village at **Hunmanby** Sands and Reighton Sands Holiday Village at Reighton. Speeton has a church with a funnel-shaped belfry built by the Danes.

The seabird laden chalk cliffs extend to Flamborough Head

The Speeton Hills meet the coast here at the end of the Wolds and there is a change of character as North Yorkshire gives way to the East Riding. High vertical chalk cliffs run unbroken as far as North Landing, Speeton Cliffs, Buckton Cliffs, Bempton Cliffs and North Cliff merging into each other in a line without respite for 8km, although there is chalk shingle when the tide drops. On top is an unusual sloping edge formed by a layer of softer boulder clay. Nothing is seen of the earthwork on Buckton Cliffs, the aerial on Standard Hill or Danes Dyke, an earthwork which cuts right across Flamborough Head, a ditch in which flint arrowheads have been found so it is pre-Iron Age, at least 2,000 years old. A visitor centre on the 120m Bempton Cliffs does not do them justice. They have to be seen from below to appreciate the 200,000 seabirds with 33 species breeding including kittiwakes, fulmars, guillemots, razorbills, puffins and gannets, this being the only gannetry in England and the only one in mainland Britain, part of the largest seabird breeding colony in England. Seals and porpoises join the fishing parties. Northeast of Flamborough Head is a submarine exercise area.

Caves are located around the inlet of Thornwick Bay where the cliffs do an effective job of hiding the holiday centre above. Also well hidden is the entrance to North Landing, used by cobles and small crab and lobster vessels which are winched up onto wooden beams on the steeply sloping face next to the former lifeboat slip, the lifeboat now having been moved to South Landing. The sea can be a luminous turquoise and it is a delightful spot at the end of the B1255, although getting close with a vehicle to load boats can be difficult. There is only a steep single track road down the cliff from the large carpark above, a road used by the local fishermen with no parking area available. Onshore seas can break heavily onto the beach.

Flows start south from Dover HW and north from HW Dover +0600 at up to 6km/h.

Distance
From Sandsend to North Landing is 60km
Campsites
Whitby, Stainsacre, Hawsker Bottoms, Robin Hood's Bay, Ravenscar, Staintondale, Scalby, Scarborough, Cayton, Lebberston, Filey, Hunmanby, Reighton, Flamborough
Youth Hostels
Whitby, Boggle Hole, Scarborough
OS 1:50,000 Sheets
94 Whitby and Esk Dale
101 Scarborough
Imray Chart
C24 Flamborough Head to Fife Ness (1:250,000)
Admiralty Charts
SC 129 Whitby to Flamborough Head
SC 134 River Tees to Scarborough (1:75,000)
1612 Harbours and Anchorages on the East Coast of England and Scotland. Approaches to Whitby (1:25,000). Whitby (1:7,500). Scarborough Bay (1:10,000). Scarborough Harbour (1:5,000)
1882 Bridlington and Filey. Filey Bay (1:20,000)
Tidal Constants
Whitby: Dover +0500
Scarborough: Dover +0520
Filey Bay: Dover +0530
Flamborough Head: Dover +0540
Sea Area
Tyne
Rescue
Inshore lifeboats: Whitby, Scarborough, Filey, Flamborough
All weather lifeboats: Whitby, Scarborough, Filey, Bridlington
Maritime Rescue Centre
Humber, 01262 672317

45 HOLDERNESS

Britain's longest and fastest disappearing beach

First the Dudgeon, then the Spurn:
Flambro' Head comes next in turn.
Flambro' Head as you pass by,
Filey Brigg is drawing nigh.

From North Landing the 46m chalk cliffs continue. There are breeding seabirds, especially gulls, and puffins, guillemots, razorbills and cormorants. On top of the cliffs a golf course, aerials and tower

Cobles up on timbers beside the old lifeboat slipway at North Landing

Caves at Breil Nook, part of Flamborough Head

remain hidden, but there is a fire beacon basket at Selwicks Bay at the end of the B1259 and then the 27m white round tower of Flamborough Head lighthouse. At the head there can be turbulence close inshore with flows strongest close to the cliffs, especially when the tide is on the turn. Along the coast there is no slack and eddies can form on both sides of the head. Flamborough Head is the northeastern extremity of a band of chalk which sweeps round the south of England to Lyme Bay, the cliffs after High Stacks dropping away in height because of the dip of the chalk strata. Flamborough Steel is a rocky ledge extending 400m from the cliffs along the southern side of the head. From here the coastal waters become steadily muddier.

The Flamborough Head Heritage Coast continues past a tumulus. It was off this point in

Selwicks Bay with Flamborough Head lighthouse

Flamborough Head seen from Bridlington

1779 that the American navy had one of their first successes as John Paul Jones captured the *Serapis* and *Countess*. It was not all bad news, however, and Captain Reason of the *Serapis* was knighted for allowing the Baltic convoy to escape in the course of the engagement.

Fishermen used to keep one boat at North Landing and another at South Landing so that there was always one ready for the prevailing

conditions. The inshore lifeboat has recently been moved from the former to the latter.

A nature trail runs below the Mesolithic Beacon Hill site. **Flamborough** has the remains of a 14th-century fortified manor and relics of Constable's family. Just before another golf course is the southern end of Danes Dyke, probably an Iron Age earthwork.

The most notable building in Sewerby is Sewerby Hall, a Georgian mansion on the site of a mediaeval manor. Dating from 1751, it has putting, bowls, croquet, archery, aviaries, zoo, playpark, ponds and 20ha of gardens and parkland, walled gardens, art gallery and displays on archaeology and local aviator Amy Johnson. Sewerby also has the Bondville Miniature Village.

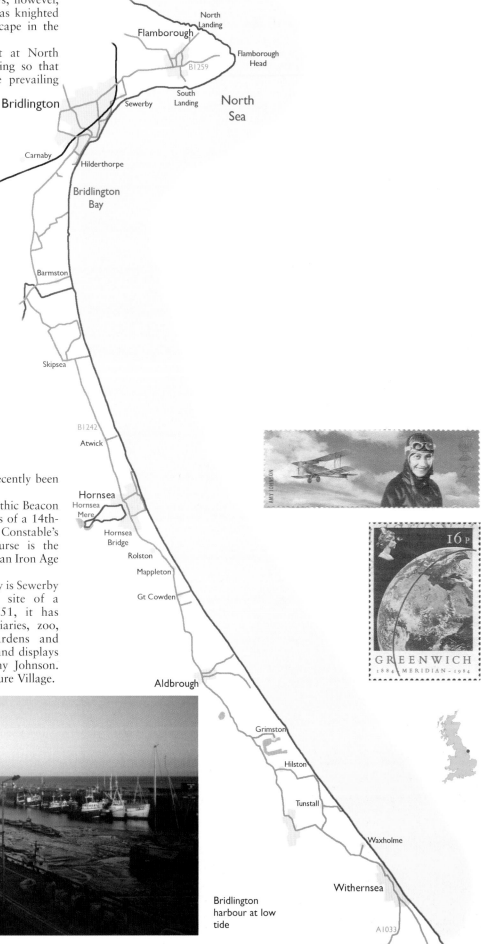

Bridlington harbour at low tide

Holderness was a large bay filled with boulder clay, forming a pre-glacial raised beach at the 30m level from where the chalk ends at Sewerby. Erosion left a line of former cliffs running inland to Hessle.

That line is now broken by the resort of **Bridlington** at what was the site of a mere. Prominent on the front is Leisure World with a fairground, flumes, swimming and surf pools, served by a road train along the esplanade. Bridlington Harbour Aquarium and History Museum features the harbour's history from 1777, the great gale of 1871, Bridlington Bay seabed

Withernsea lighthouse, safe from coastal erosion

finds, the RNLI, air sea rescue, fishing, seabirds and egg climbers. There is a Beside the Seaside exhibition, John Bull's World of Rock, biscuits and chocolate and Park Rose Pottery with 5ha of parkland, an owl sanctuary and other birds of prey. Bridlington Priory was a 14th century priory church.

The harbour has trawlers, cobles and recreational boats but largely drains to mud at low tide although there are plans for a marina. Fish caught include codling, plaice, cod and haddock. A notable 20m Bridlington trawler was the *Pickering* which had experienced many strange events on board and on which a shadowy figure had been seen. The boat was exorcised in 1987 and everything returned to normal. The resort has watersports including windsurfing, scuba diving and yacht racing with a regatta in mid-August. There is an angling week in September. A lifeboat station and a maritime rescue sub-centre keep an eye on things.

At Hilderthorpe the longest beach in Britain begins, backed by dark brown cliffs of clay 9–12m high to Kilnsea. Flows along the coast run to 2km/h with eddies at Bridlington but the velocity increases to 6km/h by Spurn Head, by which point the flow is 1½ hours later. The flows are removing the land faster than at any other point on the British coastline, claiming 12ha/year as the coastline moves inland at 1.7m/year. The site of Hilderthorpe Village is before a golf course and caravan site, then the site of Wilsthorpe Village at the edge of Carnaby Moor and, protected by the first of various sets of tank traps, Auburn Village.

Barmston has a caravan site and East End has three plus a picnic area. Between the two the Barmston Main Drain discharges although not obvious from the sea.

Skipsea with its castle site was another mere, followed by another golf course and more caravans at intervals to Atwick.

The one large mere remaining is **Hornsea** Mere, 3km long and a nature reserve with wigeon, goldeneye, water rail, coot, bearded reedling and cormorant in winter, reed and sedge warbler, reed bunting and bearded tit in summer, mute swan, mallard, pochard, tufted duck, shoveler and gadwall all year and ruff, greenshank, wheatear and whinchat in passage. This is the largest lake in Yorkshire and has boating and large pike despite the angling. The Old English town name refers to the horns or corners on the lake. Hornsea Freeport and Pottery was Britain's first factory outlet and discount shopping centre, set in 11ha of parkland with classic cars, adventure playground, Neptune's Kingdom, model village and butterflies. Hornsea Museum, previously a Small Museum of the Year, shows tools and trades in a former 16th-century farmhouse. There is also bowling. Just along from the Marine Hotel is an Indian takeaway. The promenade is protected by groynes all along the front as far as another caravan site.

Mappleton, with its windmill, is located between Rolston and Great Cowden, both with firing ranges no longer in use although lookout towers remain on the cliffs.

Aldbrough is losing 5m per year of its frontage and steps down to the beach have to be rebuilt each season. Low Farm perches close to the edge, in danger of becoming lower. Notwithstanding, BP are storing North Sea gas in huge caverns beneath the fields, not particularly intrusive and much less visible than conventional gasholders would be.

The only wooded area on this section of coast comes at Grimston, where old moats will soon be having their contents emptied by the sea. Neither Admiral Storr's Tower nor the church are visible at Hilston. Beyond Tunstall the coast forms the most northerly point of solid land in the world on the Greenwich Meridian but with nothing to indicate its position.

Unlike the disused windmill at Waxholme, the white 39m lighthouse of 1893 at Withernsea is clear for all to see, being located at the ends of the B1242 and A1033 some 400m inland, allowing room for the sea to do its worst but now only used as a museum for local history, the coastguard and the RNLI. Yellow castellated brick towers on the front stand at the end of what was the 370m pier of 1875, wrecked by a ship in a storm in 1880 and perhaps encouraging the construction of the lighthouse.

Withernsea is a resort with the Pavilion Leisure Centre, swimming, water flume, sauna, solarium and rifle range while longer shots can be tried on another golf course.

The whole of the front is groyned and can suffer a heavy shore dump at high tide, when cliffs can make it difficult to land elsewhere. Northerly swells bring lefts for surfers. A new inshore lifeboat was inaugurated in 1999. Although not at the best point for rescue conditions, it has easy takeout conditions on land. There is some parking between the lifeboat station and a toilet block, beyond which lives the owner of a taxi fleet, a former Humber lifeboatman.

Distance
From North Landing to Withernsea is 54km
Campsites
Flamborough, Marton, Wilsthorpe, Barmston, Skipsea, Low Skirlington, Hornsea Bridge, Great Cowden, Aldbrough, Tunstall, Withernsea
Youth Hostels
Scarborough, Beverley Friary
OS 1:50,000 Sheets
101 Scarborough
107 Kingston upon Hull
Imray Charts
C24 Flamborough Head to Fife Ness (1:250,000)
C29 Harwich to Whitby (1:285,000)
Admiralty Charts
SC 107 Approaches to the River Humber (1:75,000)
109 River Humber and the Rivers Ouse and Trent (1:50,000)
SC 121 Flamborough Head to Withernsea (1:75,000)
SC 129 Whitby to Flamborough Head (1:75,000)
1882 Bridlington and Filey. Bridlington Bay (1:20,000). Bridlington Harbour (1:5,000)
Tidal Constants
Flamborough Head: Dover +0540
Bridlington: Dover +0540
Bull Sand Fort: Dover –0440
Sea Areas
Tyne, Humber
Rescue
Inshore lifeboats: Flamborough, Bridlington, Withernsea
All weather lifeboats: Bridlington, Humber
Maritime Rescue Centre
Humber, 01262 672317

Entrance to what was once the pier at Withernsea, alas, no longer

46 HUMBER

The estuary draining a quarter of England

'For evil news from Mablethorpe.
Of pyrate galleys warping down;
For shippes ashore beyond the scorpe,
They have not spared to wake the towne:
But while the west bin red to see,
And storms be none, and pyrates flee,
Why ring "The Brides of Enderby"?'

Jean Ingelow

A barn collapsing over the cliff at Holmpton

Modest waves attack the soft brown clay cliffs at Holmpton as the sea eats away relentlessly at the Holderness coast

Easington North Sea gas terminal

From Withensea the coast continues southeast past another caravan site with further soft brown cliffs. At high tide there is a dump at the foot of the cliffs and it does not take much of an onshore wind to throw the broken water higher than the cliffs. At Holmpton a farm perches on the edge of the cliffs, half a red-brick barn having already been lost over the brink.

Beyond Dimlington High Land, 40m high, is the rather better protected Easington gas terminal which was the first destination for North Sea gas and still hosts pipelines from the Amethyst, Ravenspurn, Rough and West Sole gas fields. The water tower and disused windmill are not seen from close inshore, just large blue frameworks around tanks. Experiments continue with storing gas by pumping it back under the North Sea. Aerials around the terminal are conspicuous over a large area.

Easington itself, at the end of the B1445, is a village of sea cobble houses and a 14th or 15th-century thatched red-brick barn. It has pillboxes but these cannot provide protection from the sea. A straight road runs southeast from the village to end abruptly at the clifftop with a line of bollards. 29 villages along this coast have been lost to the sea. So far 4 of them have had their names revived for use by North Sea gas fields. Caravans claim the clifftop.

A road to nowhere at Easington

Coastal waters pass into Humber Port control before Kilnsea, formerly a mere and now primarily a visitor centre for Spurn Head, Yorkshire's final fling. 6km long, Spurn Head is a prime example of a spit. With sand hills 6–10m high, it is sometimes only 50m wide and is moving at 2m per year. About every 250 years the sea succeeds in breaking through, when a new spit forms parallel to it. This has happened four times since 670, the last time in 1608, but groynes now give greater protection. Even so, some heavy staging marks the point where the tarmac road suddenly disappears into the sand and a new road of concrete blocks has been laid on the west side. There is public access to this road

A break in the road which runs out along Spurn Head

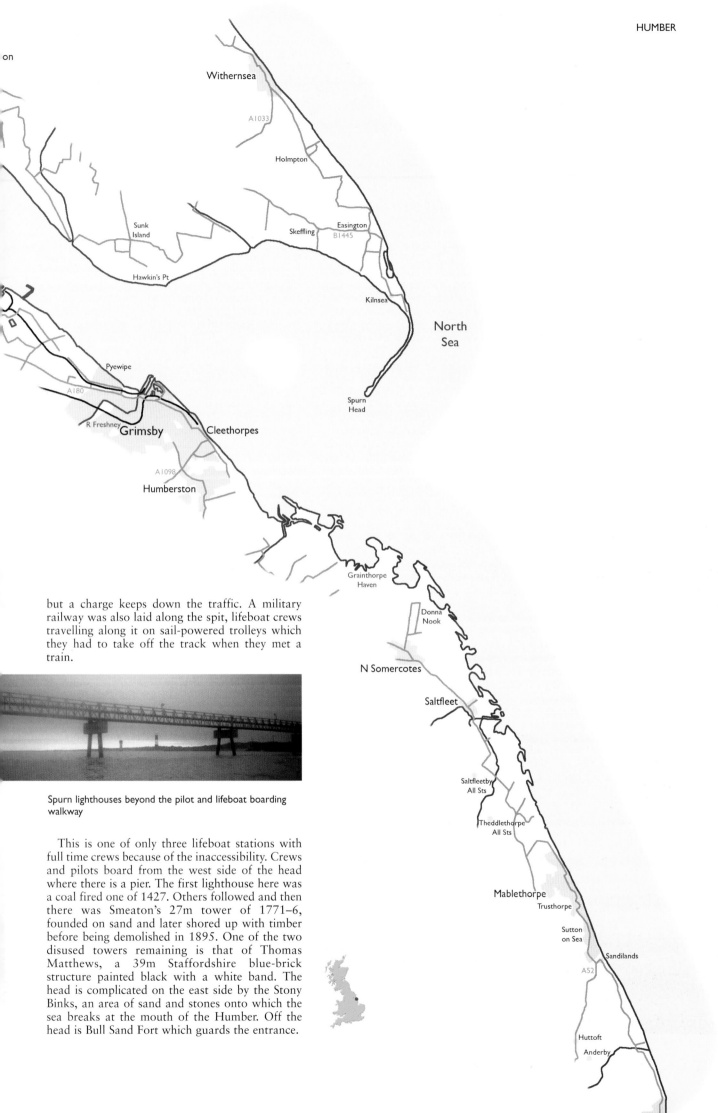

Withernsea

A1033

Holmpton

Sunk
Island

Skeffling

Easington
B1445

Hawkin's Pt

Kilnsea

North
Sea

Pyewipe

A180

Spurn
Head

R Freshney Grimsby   Cleethorpes

A1098

Humberston

Grainthorpe
Haven

but a charge keeps down the traffic. A military
railway was also laid along the spit, lifeboat crews
travelling along it on sail-powered trolleys which
they had to take off the track when they met a
train.

Donna
Nook

N Somercotes

Saltfleet

Spurn lighthouses beyond the pilot and lifeboat boarding
walkway

Saltfleetby
All Sts

Theddlethorpe
All Sts

This is one of only three lifeboat stations with
full time crews because of the inaccessibility. Crews
and pilots board from the west side of the head
where there is a pier. The first lighthouse here was
a coal fired one of 1427. Others followed and then
there was Smeaton's 27m tower of 1771–6,
founded on sand and later shored up with timber
before being demolished in 1895. One of the two
disused towers remaining is that of Thomas
Matthews, a 39m Staffordshire blue-brick
structure painted black with a white band. The
head is complicated on the east side by the Stony
Binks, an area of sand and stones onto which the
sea breaks at the mouth of the Humber. Off the
head is Bull Sand Fort which guards the entrance.

Mablethorpe

Trusthorpe

Sutton
on Sea

Sandilands

A52

Huttoft

Anderby

Sandend light float with Salt End Jetties to its left and the cranes of Hull on the skyline

The spit is a national nature reserve and seabird sanctuary with a bird observatory for migrants plus oystercatchers, blackbacked gulls, terns, cormorants and the wildfowl and waders of the estuary in general. The Humber has 130,000 winter wildfowl including 31,000 knots, 4,000 curlews, 5,200 redshanks, 27,000 golden plovers and 24,000 lapwings. The RSPB said the area was at risk of permanent damage from pollution, port expansion and cockling.

Birds like mud and at any time there is 2,000,000 tonnes of it in suspension in the estuary from five major rivers which drain a quarter of England. The Hawke Channel runs close to the head with strong tidal streams which change suddenly. Tidal streams in the river are rapid and irregular, affected by up to an hour by spates and wind direction. Flows are weaker outside the channels. At high water the tide reaches to Kilnsea and inshore of the Patrington Channel, but at low tide it is mostly dry north of a line from Spurn Head to Hawkin's Point, exposing Kilnsea Clays, Easington Clays, Skeffling Clays, Trinity Sands with their wreck and Sunk Island Sands where shelducks and great crested grebes join the wildfowl. A monument on the shoreline and another behind it on the Winestead Drain are on the Greenwich meridian. 31km^2 of Sunk Island has been reclaimed with dykes and banks.

Sunk Channel is continuously dredged but depths in the Humber are subject to frequent change with moves of buoyage and strong tidal streams. Large vessels use the fairway and must not be obstructed.

At Hawkin's Point there is a measured distance. Gradually the bank of silt builds up until it is a kilometre wide at low tide all the way to Paull through Foulholme Sands. At low tide it is not possible even to see Stone Creek which discharges Keyingham Drain, just the vast expanse of mud used by seals, herring gulls and the odd very noisy hovercraft.

Paull Roads lead up past Paull Holme with the remains of two manor houses. Two lighthouses precede another disused one of 1836 at Paull where there is also a battery and a viewpoint in front of the aerial.

Hedon Haven leads to **Hedon**, now 3km inland but formerly a flourishing port. Earlier, the Humber discharged due east to the sea. Hedonism is not an obvious association at this time. Its place has been taken by Salt End oil jetties which are on the outside of the bend where the East Riding becomes Kingston upon Hull, even without them the most difficult part of the estuary for large vessels to negotiate. Behind the jetties is a large tank farm and works. This is also below the flightpath into Humberside International Airport at Kirmington. The incessant mud gradually reduces in extent but not in value. Coastal defence work would have involved pushing the barrier forward 4m over a kilometre, but bird enthusiasts were not prepared to lose 4,000m^2 of mud or trade it for a corresponding patch of mud elsewhere and threatened European Court action. The alternative design added £1,000,000 to the bill, suggesting this mud might be rather more valuable than prime city centre building land.

Behind the Queen Elizabeth Dock is the King George Dock with vehicle ferries to Rotterdam and Zeebrugge and beyond the A1033 is the company which makes Airfix kits and the Humbrol paint to finish them. Holderness Drain arrives inconspicuously before Alexandra Dock. The River Hull is more obvious because of the lifting tidal surge barrier and a decorative church tower in a waterfront which is primarily of dereliction and silted up entrances along Hull Road. The waterfront is now dominated by the angular nose of the Deep, a £38,000,000 millennium project containing interactive displays for examining ocean sea life from prehistoric times to the 21st century.

Victoria Pier was formerly the cross Humber ferry terminal for New Holland. The docks were widened in 1321, making a defensive channel which produced an island with the River Hull and the Humber. Queen's Dock, built in 1778 by Henry

Hull waterfront with the River Hull tidal surge barrier and the Deep

Berry and John Grundy, was the largest dock in England but has now been infilled. A 15m cast-iron swing bridge of 1846 across the entrance to Humber Dock has now been fixed and the area is a heritage area with Hull Marina and the 1927 Spurn lightship. There is a statue of George Smith, killed in 1904 during the Russian Outrage when the Russian fleet fired on Hull trawlers on the Dogger Bank, mistaking them for gunboats of Japan, with whom they were at war. The Waterfront Hotel was a press-gang venue. Across the A63 Princes Dock is partially filled by a shopping centre.

In the 12th century it was the chief wool exporting port, wine and corn being other important products. The name was King's Town in Edward I's charter of 1299 but, unusually, **Kingston upon Hull** abbreviates itself to Hull, the river on which it sits, rather than the town name. The earliest major building was already in place by then, the 1285 Holy Trinity church, the largest parish church in England with much mediaeval brickwork. Hull Trinity House was set up in the 14th century to look after distressed mariners and their families, expanding into marks, buoys and lighthouses, these latter interests being their current area of activity, Trinity House being one of three such bodies around the British Isles. They also have the oldest kayak in Britain, collected with

with its associated brewery is an old public toilet which must be the best kept in the country, well worth a visit. Also of note is Hull Paragon station with a roof of five spans on cast-iron columns to emulate those of larger stations.

Hull, the city from which Robinson Crusoe began his fictional journey, has produced more tangible travel history by building the *Bounty* and England's first steam packet. It is the UK's foremost deep water fishing port and business includes building materials, vehicles and machinery. The port has a total of 13km of docks including the Albert Dock, lying inside St Andrews Quay which runs along the waterfront for 4km where the tide floods to 9km/h and ebbs to 7km/h.

At Gipsyville aerials mark where the Hull to Doncaster railway joins the shore on the far side of the A63 just before Kingston upon Hull gives way to the East Riding again.

Commercial boats fill the entire channel as they tranship in Hessle Haven, little more than a stream, off which the flow can increase to 11km/h. The *Lincoln Castle*, a paddle steamer which crossed the Humber for 40 years, is now a floating restaurant. There are Georgian houses but a late 13th-century church, Hull being in the chapelry of Hessle until 1661. On the shoreline is a fire signal basket and a viewpoint over the river although a better view is obtained from the bridge.

The Humber Bridge had the world's longest suspension bridge main span when opened in 1981

its occupant on a trip back from Greenland in 1613.

The town was fortified in the 14th century. The Old Grammar School of 1583 is now the Hands on History museum. By the 16th century the port had whaling expertise and Hull remained Britain's main whaling port until the mid-19th-century. Wilberforce House, Jacobean with oak panelled 17th-century rooms, 18th-century staircase with rococo plaster ceilings and Victorian parlour, was the birthplace of William Wilberforce in 1759 and has displays on slavery which he had abolished, Hull silver, dolls, toys and Victorian military costume. Maistre House, rebuilt in 1743 as a typical merchant's house, has a fine plasterwork staircase. Other museums abound. The Ferens Art Gallery has Frans Hals, Ruisdael, Canaletto and 19th-century Humberside marine paintings and contemporary art. There is a Streetlife Museum of Transport and a Maritime Museum with Hull's maritime heritage, models, paintings and the world's oldest planked boat outside Egypt, dating from 1500BC. The Hull and East Riding Museum has fine mosaics, ancient civilization and the Hasholme boat. The University of Hull Art Collection features British prints, paintings, drawings and sculpture of 1890–1940 with the Thompson Collection of Chinese ceramics. In May 1998 a 6m high chalk cylinder sculpture weighting 65 tonnes and entitled Two Sisters was positioned off Minerva Pier by floating crane. It took a month to dissolve, an operation which cost £50,000. Hull is also into trails, the Fish Pavement sculpture trail by Gordon Young leading through the city with fish from A to Z. 35 public houses are included in the Kingston upon Hull Ale Trail. By the Minerva

The Humber Bridge carries the A15 with 30m of clearance. When opened in 1981 its 1.41km main span was the world's longest and it was the world's first major suspension bridge to use hollow concrete piers. The 156m high towers support a total of 44,000km of 5mm diameter high tensile steel in the suspension cables.

The bridge crosses from the East Riding to North Lincolnshire where Barton Waterside is linked by Barton Haven to **Barton-upon-Humber**, a market town. St Peter's church has a 10 to 11th-century tower with some of the finest Anglo-Saxon architecture in England. St Mary's parish church, in turn, has Transitional Norman, Early English and later architecture with a mediaeval wine merchant brass and monuments. Baysgarth House Museum is beyond the windmill. The red brick Georgian houses have left a legacy in the Clay Pits which were dug along the shoreline for several kilometres for brick and tile clay and now form a nature reserve. The Barton-upon-Humber to Habrough railway runs dead straight for 6km to New Holland, then turns sharply and runs almost straight again for a further 11km to Ulceby.

Barrow Haven, fed by the Beck from the direction of **Barrow upon Humber**, passes a windmill or two and the Castles, Norman motte and bailey designs.

New Holland pier is visited by large vessels but in front of an aerial towards Goxhill Haven the only vessels are the craft dumped on the mudflats to rot, snipe now being their main company. Stone groynes protect Skitter Ness as the estuary turns southeast.

Skitter Beck becomes East Halton Beck and discharges at East Halton Skitter or Skitter Haven

Rotting ships near Goxhill Haven

in Halton Marshes, the last respite before the industrial part of this side of the estuary.

The oil terminal with its tank farm at North Killingholme Haven is being brought back into use next to flooded pits occupied by wildfowl at the start of Killingholme Marshes. Lighthouses precede South Killingholme Haven between Whitebooth Road and an oil refinery with its flare stacks.

Bulk carrier moored at Immingham Dock

Passing from North Lincolnshire into North East Lincolnshire brings **Immingham** Dock, a busy port with piers extending out into the estuary. Immingham Gas Terminal, Immingham Bulk Terminal for coal and iron ore, Western Jetty, Eastern Jetty and Immingham Oil Terminal are all part of the complex. The ebb runs up to 13km/h and the flood to 7km/h, in addition to which there can be significant clapotis off ship hulls to add to the interest. Immingham Dock handles dry and liquid bulk cargoes, chemicals, fertilizers and general cargo, the centre of the Humberside chemical and petroleum industries. The dock of 1906–12 was a major Edwardian engineering project by Sir John Wolfe Barry, an 18ha basin with 2.8km of docks and 270km of railway track. Earlier, it was the site from which the Pilgrim Fathers sailed to the Netherlands in 1620.

A factory chimney at Pyewipe looks out over mudflats which have collected various wrecks.

A thousand years ago Grim, a Dane, landed at the mouth of the River Freshney to sell his fish, thus becoming the first fish merchant in the town which bears his name and has the world's largest fish market, dealing in skate, flatfish, scallops and cod, **Grimsby**. The church of St

Grimsby Dock Tower dominates the estuary.

James was originally built in 1110 and the town received its charter in 1201, the first town in England to do so. The docks were begun in 1800, John Rennie designing the lock with hidden brick arches like a viaduct because of the poor ground conditions, a concept repeated by James Rendal in building the Royal Dock in 1846–8. The dominant feature of the lower estuary is the Dock Tower, a 94m folly modelled in 1852 by J W Wild on the Palazzo Publico in Sienna. It contains water tanks for hydraulic operation of dock gate and crane, one of William Armstrong's earliest applications of hydraulic power. The Fish Dock of 1934 and the commercial port cover 55ha and handle Danish dairy products and bacon. Small inshore seine-net trawlers have replaced the larger trawlers of the past. The National Fishing Heritage Centre features 1950s Grimsby when it was the world's largest fishing port, trawlers at war, life on board, an Arctic trip and the *Ross Tiger*. The Welhome Galleries have ship models, paintings by Knell, Tudgay and Carmichael, photographs, folk life and local history and there is a Time Trap exhibition in Grimsby Town Hall cells. Alfred Enderby Traditional Fish Smokers continue one of the older arts of the fish trade.

Cleethorpes pier. The white building on the left houses the inshore lifeboat and coastguard

The railway arrives past a football stadium to run along the shore to its **Cleethorpes** terminus, a shore with a wreck and with fish nets staked out on the sand. Sand at last means that Cleethorpes is a Victorian resort which developed from the village of Clee after the railway arrived but it takes its name from the Old English claeg, clay, and Old Scandinavian thorp, farm. The pier has a disco, bars and restaurant and there is a carnival week in July with model boat display and water gala. The A180 becomes the A1098 which passes sands which flood quickly. Urban foxes cross the road at night to feed on seabirds on the beach. This is a migration route with grey plovers, dunlins and knots plentiful. Entertainment is also plentiful with a Leisure Centre, Discovery Centre with estuary exhibition, aquarium and observatory, Butterfly Gardens, Pleasure Island Theme Park with white knuckle rides, Magic Water Theatre, Kiddies Kingdom, Fantasy World, Jungle World Mini Beast Zoo, Deep Sea Experience, funfair and boating lakes. The promenade has illuminations and the Cleethorpes Coast Light Railway with steam and a 1956 diesel engine. The meridian is marked by a stainless steel bar in the seawall.

In 1956 hundreds of people, including the RAF, watched by telescope and radar a UFO more than 20m in diameter hovering at a height of 16km for an hour until two fighters were sent to investigate.

Haile Sand Fort with its cormorants stands off the **Humberston** Fitties holiday camp as North

Haile Sand Fort with the Spurn visible in the distance to its right

East Lincolnshire becomes Lincolnshire. Landmarks all but disappear for many kilometres if the tide is out, exposing up to 2km of sand with sandhills to Gibraltar Point and the former sea cliffs at the 30m level well inland around the position of Louth.

The Louth Canal emerges onto Tetney High Sands but any discharge reaches the sea at Cleethorpes when the tide is out. Little terns breed in Tetney Marshes and an oil pipeline runs out past several wrecks to serve the Tetney Monobuoy.

There is a disused airfield between Northcoates Point and Horse Shoe Point, the latter used for cockle digging.

Donna Nook is a firing range named after a wrecked ship. It extends 10km seawards and is in use when red flags are flying or red lights show. There is a control tower on the shoreline with orange targets on each side. Grainthorpe Haven to Saltfleet is a nature reserve with 250 species of bird recorded, common and grey seals resting on the sands and moon jellyfish in the water.

Recently a family were cut off by the tide. The father swam with his 5-year old daughter to raise the alarm and the mother was rescued at midnight after being kept afloat by the seals pressing around her to give her support.

Beyond the limit of Humber Port control Sand Haile Flats, Samphire Bed and the saltmarshes are a migration watchpoint.

Saltfleet Haven is one of the few natural harbours in Lincolnshire, fed by South Dike, Mar Dike and Great Eau although difficult to locate from offshore, where there are Saltfleet Overfalls. **Saltfleet** has a disused windmill and notable gardens.

The Saltfleetby–Theddlethorpe Dunes are a nature reserve with sea buckthorne scrub, natterjack toads, reed buntings, sedge warblers and hen harriers. It is also the bombing range for RAF Wittering.

Theddlethorpe St Helen is marked by an aerial.

Mablethorpe is from the Old French name Malbert. Mablethorpe, Trusthorpe and Sutton on Sea run along the A52 by the coast for 6km yet, amazingly, are virtually invisible from the water. Sutton was damaged in the 1953 floods and they don't intend it to happen again. All that can be seen is a high bank topped with beach huts.

First comes a gas terminal which serves the Pickerill and other North Sea fields. Donkeys and a beach train in the summer, together with a fire signal basket, give a clue that a town has been reached although a holiday camp at North End is the only definite sighting. Mablethorpe is a resort with promenade and illuminations, animal and bird gardens, seal and seabird sanctuary, lynx caves, Ice Age display, barn owls, miniature

railway, paddling pool, crazy golf, fairground, seafront theatre, sailing, golf, Olde Curiosity Museum with 4,500 glass lampshades and motor museum. Groynes now provide protection but a white strip offshore is the remains of a village taken in the Middle Ages. Between 1827 and 1843 Tennyson stayed on occasions at Marine Villa, now called Tennyson's Cottage.

Trusthorpe has masts and the Trusthorpe Overfalls further out while the resort of Sutton on Sea also has radio masts. Beyond Sandilands is one positive mark, a tall dolphin about a kilometre out to sea. By this point the Sea Bank has moved inland with a golf course in front of it and then the Moggs Eye picnic area.

At the northern end of some recent houses at Anderby Creek there is a path through to a carpark and toilet where a parking charge needs to be paid at the small shop.

Distance
From Withernsea to Anderby Creek is 146km
Campsites
Withernsea, Easington, Sproatley, Barton Waterside, Goxhill, Humberston, North Somercotes, Theddlethorpe All Saints, Mablethorpe, Trusthorpe, Sutton on Sea, Huttoft
Youth Hostels
Beverley Friary, Woody's Top
OS 1:50,000 Sheets
107 Kingston upon Hull
113 Grimsby
122 Skegness and Horncastle
Imray Chart
C29 Harwich to Whitby (1:285,000)
Admiralty Charts
SC 107 Approaches to the River Humber (1:75,000)
SC 108 Approaches to the Wash (1:75,000)
109 River Humber and the Rivers Ouse and Trent (1:50,000)
SC 121 Flamborough Head to Withernsea (1:75,000)
1188 River Humber – Spurn Head to Immingham (1:25,000). Grimsby (1:10,000)
3497 River Humber – Immingham to Humber Bridge (1:25,000). Hull Docks, Eastern Part, (1:10,000). Hull Docks, Western Part, (1:10,000). Immingham (1:10,000)
Tidal Constants
Bull Sand Fort: Dover –0440
Paull: HW Dover –0450, LW Dover –0440
Kingston upon Hull: HW Dover –0450, LW Dover –0440
Humber Bridge: HW Dover –0440, LW Dover –0420
North Killingholme: HW Dover –0500, LW Dover –0450
Immingham: Dover –0500
Grimsby: Dover –0450
Inner Dowsing Light Tower: HW Dover –0500, LW Dover –0450
Skegness: HW Dover –0450, LW Dover –0440
Sea Area
Humber
Range
Donna Nook
Rescue
Inshore lifeboats: Withernsea, Cleethorpes, Mablethorpe
All weather lifeboats: Humber, Skegness
Helicopter: Leconfield
Maritime Rescue Centres
Humber, 01262 672317
Yarmouth, 01493 851338

47 THE WASH

Eastern England's most technical water

Last summer we decided
(That's the missis, kids and me)
We'd have a week in Skeggy
Where there's sun and sand and sea.

Roger Watson

Anderby Creek is at the end of the Main Drain with Anderby Drainage Museum. It would have been at the end of the Alford Canal which was planned to link Alford with the coast but it was never built. Mudbanks at the mouth can be treacherous. There is a picnic area and dunes continue south to Gibraltar Point, blackbacked gulls striding between the groynes. More picnic areas follow at Wolla Bank and Chapel Six Marshes. **Chapel St Leonards** has Willoughby High Drain discharging to the south of Chapel Point but, like Mablethorpe, the town is seen mostly as a collection of beach huts with the Robin Hood Leisure Park inconspicuous.

Things are different at the resort of **Ingoldmells** with Fantasy Island and Funcoast World including the Funsplash subtropical waterworld, one of Europe's largest, the site of Butlin's first holiday camp in 1936. Inland from Ingoldmells Point is a tower up and down which screaming punters are carried at various speeds, a large pyramid surrounded by the Millennium Roller Coaster, the largest looping rollercoaster in Europe, and a tent structure which would put any other tent to shame. There are donkeys on the beach and jet and water skiers on the sea. At the back of the A52 is Skegness Aerodrome and a windmill while Hardy's Animal Farm is tucked in there somewhere.

Masses of caravans and a golf course fill the gap until amusements announce arrival in **Skegness**. Named as Skeggi's headland after an Old

Scandinavian man, Skegness was a fishing village until Lord Scarborough drew up plans to develop it into a resort in the mid-19th century, one of the first British town plans. The pier was added in 1881 but was badly damaged in 1978. The town's line that 'Skegness is so bracing' is hardly a selling point for today's holidaymaker but it has been around too long to shake off. Indeed, the jolly fisherman of railway advertisements has been employed since 1908 and now has his own statue.

Tennyson stayed in Skegness in later years at Enderby's Hotel, now the Vine. There are the obligatory promenade and illuminations, Natureland Seal Sanctuary, funfair with big wheel and rollercoaster, gardens, theatres, ballrooms, swimming pools, bowling areas, boating lakes, Church Farm Museum with its Victorian interior, Ridgequest Art Foundry and Skegness Model Village. A fire signal basket stands on the shore and starfish abound in the shallows.

Skegness is the last community before Hunstanton, whether going straight across the Wash or round the coast. Initially there is a golf course behind the dunes, giving way to Gibraltar

The pier and assorted white knuckle rides at Skegness

Point Nature Reserve and Visitor Centre, 6km² of sandhills, rough grazing, fresh and saltwater marshes, beach and foreshore with a nature trail, bird observatory, field station, sea buckthorn scrub, little terns, ringed plovers, oystercatchers, dunlins, knots, herons, kingfishers, short-eared owls, cormorants and wildfowl generally plus natterjack toads. A red lorry rigged out as a safari vehicle drives loads of punters noisily along the beach.

Wainfleet Road becomes Wainfleet Swatchway beyond Gibraltar Point where the Steeping River discharges as a mud rapid through Wainfleet Harbour. Beside the Boston Deeps the tide drops to reveal up to 5km of silt. The RSPB/WWF say the Wash is one of the world's most threatened sites for birds because climate change could raise the sea level, doubtless changing surrounding farmland to more mud. The depths are subject to constant change, navigation is difficult as there are few features and it is often misty. Flows can be up to 6km/h inshore, mostly in the channels, possibly with eddies along the sides, and levels, rates and durations are affected by northeasterly and southwesterly winds. The ebbs from the major rivers are usually longer than the floods and may be up to 15km/h with spates.

Some 2km inshore is the Sea Bank which ran for 72km towards King's Lynn, much of it remaining,

probably having been in place by the time of the *Domesday Book*.

Between Wainfleet Sand (mud) and Friskney Flats is the Wainfleet Firing Practice Area which may allow passage if not too busy. Some wrecks on the mud are targets. Seals bask on the banks. The control tower is by the high water line near Friskney.

St Guthlac's church has a window dedicated to the saint holding a whip reputed to have been given to him by St Bartholomew. As long as he held it the village would remain free of rats and mice.

Strong northeasterly winds can give a considerable sea in the Boston Deeps, especially at the northeast end on the top half of the tide.

Wrangle has a coastguard station from where, presumably, they can see the sea from time to time. Wrangle Flats and Butterwick Low are littered with wrecks. Freiston Shore with its windmill is about a kilometre inland from Freiston Low and is good for birdwatching. Freiston itself is about 3km inland but was on the coast when the Freislanders landed and settled there, giving it its name.

More wrecks lie in the mud approaching Tab's Head at the mouth of the River Witham, the line of which is picked out by a few windswept poplar trees. A bird hide watches the entrance, behind which is North Sea Camp, a prison. The Haven is the mouth of the River Witham, flooding from

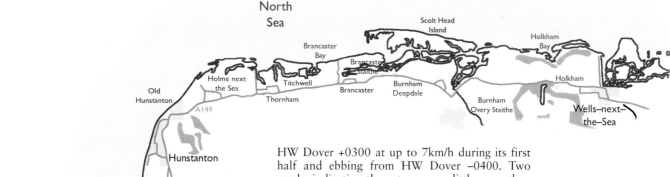

HW Dover +0300 at up to 7km/h during its first half and ebbing from HW Dover −0400. Two marks indicating the entrance are little more than poles and hard to spot. The only clearly visible landmark is the Boston Stump, but it is too far away to give more than a general direction. Large vessels go up to Boston, together with a shoal of fishing vessels.

Beyond the Scalp and Frampton Marsh reserve on the west side and Black Buoy Sand and Herring Hill on the east is the mouth of the River Welland which floods from HW Dover +0320 and ebbs from HW Dover −0400 through Fosdyke Wash.

Progress southeast is dependent on water levels, the water going out typically 4km with fingers of 12km not unknown. High water can bring the surreal view of expanses of ragwort with just their flowers above the water while seals and porpoise hunt amongst them. This is an area where few boats go.

Marshes front Puff and Old Sand which are covered by the Holbeach Firing Practice Area. Boats may transit the area but not linger. Targets include orange barrels on poles and on barges as well as rusty boats with orange and white stripes and plenty of holes. The danger area reaches from Lawyer's Creek to Cox's Creek. Fleet Haven Outfall is in the centre of the range where the control towers are, while Dawsmere Creek is where the Port of Boston Authority hand over to the Port of Wisbech Authority. Gedney Drove End has a reserve and walks by the Wash.

The Nene Outfall Cut or Wisbech Cut floods from HW Dover +0300 and ebbs from HW Dover –0330 with strong flows and times subject to the wind. The cut was made by John Rennie in 1827–30 and completed by Thomas Telford, 60m wide and 8km long with a pair of white daymarks prominent at Guy's Head. Off the entrance is an experimental 10m high freshwater lagoon built of sand. Lincolnshire gives way to Norfolk.

The Peter Scott Walk to King's Lynn runs parallel to Breast Sand where an experimental 8m high bund closer inshore marks where the Port of Wisbech hand control to the King's Lynn Conservancy Board.

The King's Lynn skyline is clearly visible on the River Great Ouse, the exit of which has been straightened as the Lynn Channel, flows being directed by training walls out in the Wash. Flood in the Lynn Channel begins at HW Dover +0300 and the ebb is from HW Dover –0330. Flows are strong and times subject to the wind.

There are more substantial banks up the east side of the Wash. Bull Dog Sand lies on the former line of the Babingley River and this leads to Peter Black Sand off Dersingham, where the emphasis should be placed on Black rather than Sand. Herring gulls and others search for food. Wolferton Creek runs up the coast to clear Ferrier Sand, passing Shepherd's Port where Snettisham Scalp is a bird reserve with access restricted by the RSPB, having common terns in summer and waders and wildfowl in winter.

Heacham can have up to 2km of Stubborn Sand offshore to disperse the scent from Norfolk Lavender, England's only lavender farm, near Heacham Hall. Heacham stands on a former coastal railway line and has attractive almshouses by the ancient church. Native John Rolfe went to America and returned to live here with his bride, the Indian princess Pocahontas, a marriage which brought peace between the Indians and the settlers in America.

East Anglia acts as a groyne, collecting material moving south down the east coast, the coast

building from Hunstanton to Weybourne. Now the water clears, perhaps for the first time since north of the Tees. Edmund landed in 855 to become king of the Angles. He prayed on the beach and a clear spring gushed forth. The location is also marked by the remains of St Edmund's chapel. As the only west facing Victorian resort on the east coast, development of **Hunstanton** was initiated by Henry Styleman Le Strange from 1843. Growth continued, particularly after the arrival of the railway in 1862, although the name is from the Old English man Hunstan. As hereditary Lord High Admirals of the Wash, the Le Stranges could claim anything from the sea as far as a man could ride at low tide and then throw his spear. This still applies to all oysters and mussels from the beach, there being a bank of mussels at St Edmund's Point. Tope, dabs and flounders are also amongst the sea's harvest. The pier was built in 1870 but lost in a storm in the 1970s. Hunstanton's most distinctive feature is its striped cliff, light grey marl on top of brown carrstone, 18m high and packed with fossils. Above is a disused lighthouse and a fire signal beacon. As a resort it has a funfair, a Sea Life Centre with seal rehabilitation, Oasis Leisure Centre with aquaslide, whirlpool spa, bowls, squash, table tennis, racket ball, rollerskating, cafeteria and bar, Jungle Wonderland, deckchairs, pony rides, pitch and putt and crazy golf. On water activities include sailing, powerboat racing, water skiing, windsurfing and jet skis yet there are still jellyfish and fulmars as part of the local environment. Winter birdwatching is popular and there are many nature reserves in the area. *Barnacle Bill* and *Dad Savage* are two films which have been shot in Hunstanton.

There are beach huts at Old Hunstanton as dunes begin. Old Hunstanton Hall is a moated Tudor mansion, owned by the Le Stranges from the Conquest until 1949.

The A149 runs parallel to the coast to Cromer while the Pedders Way and Norfolk Coast Path crosses a golf course and also follows the coast to Cromer. The Peddars Way may be pre-Roman and forms the northern end of a track which includes the Ridgeway and runs right across southern England to Lyme Regis.

In 1999 a 4,000-year old circle of 50 oak trees with a central tree used for religious ritual was exposed at Holme next the Sea, a village surrounded by reserves. Holme Dunes Nature Reserve consists of 2km^2 of dunes and saltmarsh with over 50 species of plant including sea bindweed, sea lavender, bee and pyramid orchids and sea buckthorn. Holme Bird Observatory has recorded over 320 species including wrynecks, hoopoes, ospreys, sooty shearwaters, collared

flycatchers, red rumped swallows and 21 species of warbler. In addition they have recorded 363 species of moth. Permits are needed for entry to both reserves. The coast is an AONB to Mundesley and there are sandhills to Wells.

Gore Point has a wreck. Behind the dunes is Broad Water and then Harbour Channel at Thornham where there is a ruined church tower. The port's last granaries were swept away in the 1953 floods.

Harbours to Cromer have entrances which are masses of broken water with strong winds from the northern half of the compass, worse with a southeastgoing swell after gales.

Marshes on this coast are the best in Britain and contain trees like a petrified forest.

Behind Brancaster Bay is Titchwell with its cross. The 1780 seawall was felled by the 1953 tidal surge but not repaired. Reedbeds, fresh water, brackish marshes, saltmarsh and beach make up the $1.7km^2$ RSPB nature reserve where there are avocets, marsh harriers, terns, ringed plovers, bearded reedlings, Brent geese, shore larks and wildfowl and waders, watched from hides.

There is a golf course at Brancaster, a village where the Romans built their Branodunum fort in about 300 as the northernmost of their forts to defend the Saxon shore. The beach floods quickly

The striped cliffs at Hunstanton mostly stand in shadow

There is plenty of sailing craft activity at the mouth of Brancaster Harbour

so visitors are cleared from Wreck Sands with a siren. Marram grass and barbed wire are features of the shoreline.

Brancaster Harbour's channel is constantly changing, as are the many sailing boats which use it. Tidal flows can be strong, up to 13km/h. Beyond Brancaster Marsh is Brancaster Staithe and the shellfishery begun by the Romans. Whelk sheds and mussel fishermen's huts line the waterside.

Scolt Head Island belongs mostly to the National Trust who bought it from Lord Leicester in 1923 with money raised by local naturalists. The extreme eastern tip was purchased by Norfolk Naturalists' Trust in 1945. During the war it was used as an artillery range. Shells are still found occasionally and should be reported but not touched. In 1953 the Nature Conservancy Council took a 99-year lease on the island and it now acts as an important nature reserve with breeding colonies of common, Sandwich, Arctic and little terns, ringed plovers, oystercatchers, blackheaded

Scolt Head forming a true island for once as Norton Creek reaches maximum depth at the top of a spring tide

gulls and some waders. Redshanks and Arctic skuas have been seen and the island is an ornithologist's paradise. A nature trail has been laid out on the island and a boat takes people out to it during appropriate months. However, there is no access to the west part of the island from May to July and all the terneries are out of bounds from mid-April to mid-August so that breeding birds are not disturbed.

The island is moving westwards and landward, the laterals showing former western ends of the island, in contrast with the Brancaster golf course ridge which has grown eastwards.

An armless windmill stands just outside Burnham Overy Staithe and church towers from a number of villages with the first name Burnham, homestead by the stream, might be seen. Burnham Deepdale has a church with a round flint tower from after the Conquest, a seasonal font from a single block of stone with a monthly farm worker on each face and mediaeval stained glass. In the 1760s they were all under the control of the Reverend Edmund Nelson, whose son Horatio acquired a love of the sea from playing by the sandy harbour. At 12 the lad was a midshipman and was destined to become the greatest seaman in history.

Burnham Overy Staithe has a grade 2 listed watermill 200 years old, last used in 1941, damaged by fire in 1959 and now restored.

Residents of the village included Richard Woodhouse from 1899 to 1926, the master of the *Cutty Sark*. Overy Marshes were drained in the 1630s. The harbour, fed by the River Burn, has sailing and windsurfing with an annual regatta. Gun Hill is growing westwards and the entrance is broken with strong winds, swell or ebb when the bar can be dangerous to small craft.

West Sands in Holkham Bay are a naturist site, behind which is Holkham National Nature Reserve, the largest coastal reserve in England with 40km^2 of sand, mudflats, saltmarsh and sand dunes. Corsican pinewoods were planted in the mid-19th century to stabilize the dunes. Holkham Iron Age fort was built on an island in the marsh, a 2.2ha oval with bank and ditch, perhaps protection for a coastal trading station. The *Shakespeare in Love* shipwreck scene was filmed at Holkham.

A church tower and a monument break the skyline at Holkham Park, now owned by Lord Leicester. The monument of 1845, over 30m high with a wheatsheaf on top and presented by tenants, is to a former owner, the agricultural reformer Coke who began the farming revolution on his own in the first half of the 19th century, changing from rye and wheat and introducing new livestock breeds, increasing crop and livestock yields, and still was able to invent the bowler hat in his spare time.

Holkham Hall is a Palladian mansion of 1734–60, one of Britain's most stately homes, designed by William Kemp with contributions by Rubens, Van Dyck, Glaude, Poussin, Gainsborough, Raphael and Reynolds. It has a Bygones Museum with vintage cars, traction engines, a Victorian kitchen, laundry, pump room, 1900 harness room, brewery tapping room, shoe shop, tools, history of farming, pottery, art gallery, Holkham Nursery Gardens in a 2ha 19th-century walled garden, 12km² deer park designed by Capability Brown, lake and beach.

The Run, the mouth of the harbour at **Wells-next-the-Sea**, is subject to frequent change with a bar which is roughest with northerly winds. Water skiers, sailors and beach huts greet arrival at the lifeboat and coastguard station, behind which is a sheltered inlet near to the carpark. The flood runs from HW Dover +0140 and the ebb from HW Dover –0440. A klaxon warns when the flood starts.

In October 1880 the lifeboat capsized on the bar with the loss of 11 of the 13 crew. The lifeboat station was moved from the town to its present position in 1895, reducing a 4km pull to the sea. The last horsedrawn lifeboat launch took place in 1934. At the end of the second world war German prisoners of war tried to steal the lifeboat but were unable to start the engine.

A steam railway runs alongside the harbour, to complement another one to Little Walsingham. The embankment built to reclaim Holkham Marshes was the work of the Cokes. The harbour gets its odd shape from a dyke built down the middle of the harbour, after which land was reclaimed to its west. Abraham's Bosom is a canoeing and boating lake.

Wells is a commercial and fishing port with whelk and shrimp boats and handles fertilizers, animal feedstuffs, cockles and skate. It has been a port for at least 200 years. The Stone quay was built in the mid-19th century when it imported coal, timber, salt, rape and linseed and exported barley and malt for Guinness. Wells Maritime Museum features fishing, the port, the coastguard, lifeboats, wildfowling and bait digging. The church of St Nicholas of 1879 replaces one of 1640 burnt down after a lightning strike. There is a carnival in August in this village of flint cottages which was used for filming part of *Dad Savage*.

Distance
From Anderby Creek to Wells-next-the-Sea is 113km
Campsites
Huttoft, Ingoldmells, Skegness, Croft, Wainfleet Bank, Old Leake, Fishtoft, Holbeach Hurn, Long Sutton, North Runcton, West Newton, Shepherd's Port, Hunstanton, Holme next the Sea, Wells-next-the-Sea
Youth Hostels
Woody's Top, King's Lynn, Hunstanton, Wells-next-the-Sea
OS 1:50,000 Sheets
122 Skegness and Horncastle
131 Boston and Spalding
132 North West Norfolk
Imray Charts
C28 East Coast – Harwich to Wells-next-the-Sea (1:125,000)
C29 Harwich to Whitby (1:285,000)
Y9 Wash (1:89,740)
Stanfords Allweather Charts
3 East Coast (1:138,000)
Admiralty Charts
SC 108 Approaches to the Wash (1:75,000)
1200 The Wash Ports (1:37,500)
Tidal Constants
Skegness: HW Dover –0450, LW Dover –0440
Clay Hole: HW Dover –0450, LW Dover –0440
Tabs Head: HW Dover –0500, LW Dover –0410
Lawyer's Sluice: Dover –0440
Old Lynn Road: Dover –0440
Wisbech Cut: HW Dover –0440, LW Dover –0340
West Stones: HW Dover –0440, LW Dover –0400
Hunstanton: HW Dover –0440, LW Dover –0420
Brancaster Bar: HW Dover –0430
Burnham (Overy Staithe): Dover –0440
Wells Bar: Dover –0440
Wells: HW Dover –0420, LW Dover –0140
Sea Area
Humber
Ranges
Wainfleet, Holbeach
Rescue
Inshore lifeboats: Mablethorpe, Skegness, Hustanton, Wells
All weather lifeboats: Skegness, Wells
Hovercraft: Hunstanton
Maritime Rescue Centre
Yarmouth, 01493 851338

Gun Hill is in the centre of the picture with the mouth of Burnham Harbour to its left

48 NORFOLK

East Anglia's unspoilt holiday coast

As we were a fishing off Haisboro' Light,
Shooting and hauling and trawling all night.
It was windy old weather, stormy old weather;
When the wind blows, we all pull together.

The tower mill at Cley next the Sea

At low tide 2km of Bob Hall's Sand is exposed beside the Run at Wells-next-the-Sea while at high tide there are various channels through the marshes, particularly East Fleet and Stonemeal Creek which continues as Cabbage Creek when the tide drops, crossing a nature reserve where blackbacked gulls and cormorants are seen. Stewkey blue cockles are gathered from Stiffkey Marshes with their sea lavender.

The River Glaven has been blocked off by shingle and finds its way to the sea through Blakeney Harbour, the entrance of which is difficult with strong onshore winds and which can have a series of races off it. The River Stiffkey also feeds the harbour further west. Blakeney is noted

Cley Eye with more photographers than on a royal holiday

for its flint cottages and windmill. The church acted as a lighthouse and there is a Watch House, recently used by the Guides. The 14th-century guildhall remains have a brick-vaulted undercroft. Sailing is popular and the harbour has the largest fleet of sharpies in England. In the 16th century it had an Icelandic fishing fleet.

Blakeney Point is a 6km spit protecting the harbour and growing thrift, sea lavender and samphire. One of several hides is conspicuous on the point where common, little and Sandwich terns nest and oystercatchers, plovers, redshanks and rare migrants are seen. 500 common and grey seals rest up on the point where they are visited by a flotilla of sightseeing motorboats, the owners of which object to canoeists approaching because the seals take to the water to join the paddlers, not good for business. There is the wreck of the *Hjordis*, sunk for target practice during the war, and a bank of protected mussels off the point.

The bank of shingle and sand does not just form the spit but continues to Weybourne, a 12km wall with a high tide dump. The coast is building and Cley next the Sea is now a good kilometre away from it, although in the Middle Ages it was an important seaport with a custom house and Dutch gables which suggest there was trade with the Netherlands. The landmark is a 15m high 1819 tower mill which was used as a flour mill until

1917 and has been a guesthouse since 1983, complete with sails but no machinery. Other notable buildings in the village include the Made in Cley pottery with jewellery in a Regency shop, Knucklebone House with cornices and panelling made from sheep's vertebrae and a smokehouse for kippers. The George and Dragon has a boules pitch, a stained glass window of the saint and his adversary and a brass lectern in the bar on which birdwatchers can record their sightings. The 2.6km² of Fresh Marshes was the first reserve in the country, set up in 1926, with access by permit. There are rare migrants, bearded tits, bitterns and common terns and in winter shore larks, snow buntings and wildfowl. A 4km bank round Blakeney Marsh and a 3km bank round Cley Marsh were built 3.6–5.4m high, 1.8–3m wide at the top. Begun in 1522 by Sir John Heydon, they were extended in 1630 by van Hasedunch and completed in 1649 by Simon Britliffe, lord of the manor at Cley. They were overwhelmed and breached in 1742, 1897 and 1953, each time being rebuilt and strengthened. A road runs across the marshes beside the river to Cley Eye where there are parking, toilets and a café.

There are yellow-horned poppies at Salthouse where there is a risk of unexploded mines. Approaching Weybourne there is a pillbox and an area with security fencing and aerials. The

Muckleborough Collection is Britain's largest working military collection with sixty armoured vehicles and guns, the home of the Suffolk and Norfolk Yeomanry Museum with its history from 1759 and more recent exhibits from the Falklands and Gulf War plus lifeboats and a Harrier.

Weybourne was garrisoned against the Spanish fleet in 1588 and was defended until 1939. Gold coins found on the beach in 1940 were thought to be from a 1st-century BC tribe. The Romans built a pottery kiln and there is a Saxon church tower, the remains of a priory and a ruined windmill. Dunes are eroding fast. Offshore are flounders, bass, whiting and cod.

Any whistle is likely to come from the North Norfolk Railway as a train approaches, used in filming *Dad's Army* and *Love on a Branch Line*. Also known as the Poppy Line, it has steam and diesel engines and a model railway.

Soft chalky cliffs begin with agate, quartz and cornelian on the sandy beach and extend to Happisburgh. Sandy beaches extend much further. On top is a golf course and, behind that, Upper Sheringham. The church was mentioned in the *Domesday Book* but the more significant church-related building to be constructed there was Sheringham Hall, built in 1812 for Abbot Upcher and his wife, Charlotte, by Humphrey Repton. It is landscaped with rhododendrons, azaleas and woodland, the only man-made structure visible in the 3.1km^2 Sheringham Park being a temple.

Silingham became Siringham then **Sheringham**. Scira's people, the Scirings, were forgotten as it became a resort of flint, Edwardian and Victorian buildings with a promenade and a carnival week in August. There is a Splash Leisure Pool with giant waterslide and wave pool, a lifeboat museum, a railway museum, Sheringham Museum with local history and the lifeboats, the remains of a priory, a cannon in Gun Street and Sheringham Pottery. Deckchairs are hired to the holidaymakers who paddle between the rock groynes. In the late 1800s the Norfolk whelk fishery was developed here for bait and for London shellfish appetites. Fishing vessels still work off the beach, the lobster and crab catch now being sold locally.

Sloping boarding at the high tide mark protects the soft cliffs. On top at Beeston Regis is a church in a field with a 15th-century choir screen. At West Runton is Roman Camp, the highest point in Norfolk at 102m, plus the Shire Horse Centre with native ponies, horsedrawn farm machinery, a children's farm and riding. East Runton's cliffs are topped by a caravan site while crab boats are hauled up on the beach by tractor.

Lobster pots are laid and fishing and crab boats are also launched off **Cromer** beach by tractor. The Rocket House Café and restaurant suggest that lifeboats did the same but the new lifeboat station, with the *Ruby and Arthur Read*, is built at the end of the pier beyond the theatre pavilion. Opened in 1999 and winning the Graham Allen Award for Conservation and Design, it presumably ended what was the last traditional end of pier show in the country. The Gangway approach road has granite setts set with their corners raised to help horses grip. The former lifeboat station has been moved to Southwold as a museum. The Cromer Lifeboat Museum and Lifeboat has Henry Bloggs' 1935–47 lifeboat, *H F Bailey*, which rescued 818 people, together with the medals of Henry, who received more awards than any other coxwain, plus photographs and models. Cromer Museum, in a late Victorian fisherman's cottage, also features lifeboat services with local history, fishing, bathing, archaeology, geology and natural history. Unlike Blakeney, the coast here is eroding. The sea took Shipden, leaving the inland village of Cromer (from the Old English crawe mere, crow's lake) on the coast at the end of the Cromer Ridge. It has another windmill. The 49m knapped flint Perpendicular church tower of St Peter and St Paul is the tallest in Norfolk and served as a daymark before the lighthouse was built. The fishing village became a resort with the coming of the railway. There are a zoo, Funstop children's indoor adventure centre, tennis, putting, squash, cricket, deckchairs and a carnival week in August. The town inspired the Norwich School of Painters including Dixon, Cotman and Bright. *September Song* was filmed here. Black Shuck, a jet black dog as big as a calf, possibly the Devil, is said to haunt the area. Sir Arthur Conan Doyle was believed to have thought of the plot of his *Hound of the Baskervilles* while staying here.

SHERLOCK HOLMES & SIR HENRY
"THE HOUND OF THE BASKERVILLES"

The soft cliffs make their first appearance at Sheringham

The pier at Cromer with its new lifeboat station on the end

The A149 turns south through a series of dangerous chicanes and is replaced by the B1159 which follows the coast to Caister-on-Sea. The eroding chalky cliffs with their fossils have been subject to extensive landslips to Happisburgh because of groundwater in the cliffs, although this does not stop fulmars nesting all along this coast to Yarmouth and herring gulls being resident. An undersea forest is present as far as Winterton. Beyond the groynes Foulness takes its name from the large pieces of chalk lying beneath the surface. Tidal streams follow the coast at up to 5km/h. The 18m white octagonal lighthouse of 1833 replaces the first one built by Sir John Clayton which remained unlit until 1719 because of lack of funds and was then made unsafe by a massive landslip. A searchlight close by gives a narrow vertical beam for 10 minutes per hour to show the cloudbase.

The resort of Overstrand has the Pleasance gardens laid out by Gertrude Jeckyll. The poppies inspired Clement Scott's poem *Garden of Sleep* which led to the Poppyland craze of the late 19th century. There are 30m cliffs but there is no access from the beach as far as Mundesley as the cliffs are dangerous.

Radio masts stand back from the cliffs and the church at Sidestrand was moved in 1880 when the sea got too close.

A water tower behind Cliftonville is a landmark from further out. **Mundesley** appeared in the Domesday Book under its Anglo-Saxon or Norse name of Muleslai. It has become a fishing village with cod, sole, eels and skate, boats being tractor launched off the beach from near a line of beach huts. These days it is a resort with promenade,

Looking back towards Mundesley, the toe of the cliffs protected by a line of boarding in addition to groynes

deckchairs, holiday camp and Mundesley festival week in August with jazz, brass, singers, comedians, jugglers and clowns. Mundesley Boat Day for the RNLI is also in August. The old coastguard lookout point has become a museum on the coastguard and the village's history. Nelson and animal artist Briston Riviere stayed here and William Cowper wrote the hymn *God Moves in a Mysterious Way* after watching a storm over Happisburgh. Golf and horse riding are available.

Mundesley mill has gone although its overshot millwheel remains on the River Mun, believed to be the only one of its kind in Norfolk.

Stowe Mill was built in 1827 by James Gale, whose son, Thomas, was the miller for 45 years. It has sails but no machinery and contains an exhibition of milling.

The long thatched barn at Paston was built by Sir William Paston in 1581. St Margaret's church

Bacton Natural Gas terminal is largely hidden from the sea

has Paston family monuments and 14th-century wall paintings. The *Paston Letters* described life here during the Wars of the Roses.

Much more conspicuous on the cliffs, especially from the east, is the Bacton Natural Gas Terminal with pipelines from the Hewett, North Hewett, Delta, Leman, Camelot and other North Sea gas fields and some high masts.

Groynes, a sloping sea wall and a wreck front the village of Bacton which has the Bacton Gem Museum with amber, gems, minerals and fossils from the Norfolk shore and abroad. At Keswick is the gateway to Broomholm Priory, now a farm as prophesied by Mother Shipton. Founded in 1113, the priory had part of the true cross which could cure leprosy and bring the dead back to life, as referred to by Chaucer in the *Reeve's Tale*.

Walcott reaches to Ostend with holiday camps, a pillbox and another aerial. Happisburgh, named after Haep, has caravans and a fire beacon, also groynes which have recently been supplemented with substantial new sea defences. The church has a 34m tower, possibly as a beacon, and a 15th-century font with the 4 Evangelists, angelic musicians and men carrying clubs. Many shipwrecked sailors have been buried with anchors for gravestones and there is a mound with 119 men from *HMS Invincible*, wrecked in 1801 on her way to join Nelson in Copenhagen. Also buried is Jonathan Balls, an arsenic poisoner who murdered a dozen people, mostly relatives, and then himself by accident, being buried with plum cake, *Bible*, poker and fire-tongs to handle the eternal flames. At Well Corner the ghost of a smuggler murdered in a dispute over booty comes from the sea into the sands. From the 1800s it was seen regularly to empty a sack into the well. The well was excavated to reveal a torso and a sack containing a head and legs.

There were so many wrecks that in the 19th century Trinity House used explosives to clear them. A lighthouse of 1791 has a white 26m tower with three red bands. In the 1860s it was used in experiments to make coal gas during the day to be stored and burnt at night.

Dunes start 9–12m high, gradually declining to Winterton Ness. In 1953 they were breached by the sea at Sea Palling. They now have a concrete seawall which cannot be climbed, only the occasional gap allowing access. The church at Eccles was overwhelmed by dunes which then moved inland, exposing it to the sea, causing the tower to collapse in 1895. The foundations can still be seen on the beach after a scouring tide. From Eccles on Sea to Waxham is a straight line of artificial reefs 1.7m high have been placed 300m offshore. The rock island line's boulders have large wire loops attached and each reef has an Environment Agency notice banning landing.

Curlews fly over the marram grass covered dunes and the beach at Sea Palling is used by naturists and for jet ski hire.

From Waxham to Winterton-on-Sea is an AONB while, less than 2km inland, a line of windmills stand in the rather different landscape of the Broads. The Hall at Waxham is now a farmhouse, accompanied by a magnificent barn which has been supported by the Prince's Trust. It is haunted by the ghosts of six members of the Brograve family who met sudden deaths in major battles over the centuries, all called together by late 18th-century owner Sir Berney Brograve to dine and drink until they vanished at midnight. There is a

derelict church and a Tudor wall with turrets and a gatehouse.

Waxham Farm at Horsey Corner offers a parking field in the summer with a payment box at a caravan site which also has a shop and telephone. Locating it from the sea can be difficult and it may be necessary to do so from the top of the dunes.

The line of artificial reefs to protect the coast at Sea Palling

Marram grass binds the dunes at Horsey Corner. The concrete seawall is hidden from on top

Distance
From Wells-next-the-Sea to Horsey Corner is 61km
Campsites
Wells-next-the-Sea, Stiffkey, Glandford, Weybourne, Sheringham, East Runton, Cromer, Overstrand, Trimingham, Mundesley, Happisburgh, Sea Palling, Horsey Corner
Youth Hostels
Wells-next-theSea, Sheringham, Great Yarmouth
OS 1:50,000 Sheets
132 North West Norfolk
133 North East Norfolk
134 Norwich and the Broads
Imray Charts
C28 East Coast – Harwich to Wells-next-the-Sea (1:125,000)
Y9 Wash (1:89,740)
Stanfords Allweather Charts
3 East Coast (1:138,000)
Admiralty Charts
SC 106 Cromer to Smiths Knoll (1:75,000)
SC 108 Approaches to the Wash (1:75,000)
Tidal Constants
Wells: HW Dover –0420, LW Dover –0140
Wells Bar: Dover –0440
Blakeney Bar: HW Dover –0430, LW Dover –0420
Cromer: HW Dover –0420, LW Dover –0350
Winterton-on-Sea: HW Dover –0400, LW Dover –0320
Sea Area
Humber
Rescue
Inshore lifeboats: Wells, Sheringham, Cromer, Happisburgh
All weather lifeboats: Wells, Cromer, Great Yarmouth and Gorleston
Maritime Rescue Centre
Yarmouth, 01493 851338

49 BROADS

'Twas a fine and a pleasant summer's day.
Out of Yarmouth harbour I was faring
As a cabin boy on a sailing lugger.
We were off to hunt the shoals o' herring.

Ewan McColl/P Seeger

From Warren Farm at Horsey Corner the dunes to 17m high are topped by marram grass and continue almost unbroken to the start of Great Yarmouth. Initially the groynes continue, as does the seawall which was built after the dunes were breached at Horsey in 1938. This used to be an exit from the Broads and the sea may still want to get back to the Hundred Stream.

The dunes run on southwards from Horsey Corner

While there are few landmarks on the coast it hides a totally different landscape beyond the dunes, the Broads. From Warren Farm, with its skylarks to answer the terns on the sea side of the dunes, it is not far to two windmills including the well preserved Horsey Mill. The thatched Saxon

wreck timber. These days there is a little more variety in the building. By the beach is a hotel with separate thatched round houses based on South African rondavels. Behind the village are two rows of wind generators. Today's wrecks have contributed less and the lighthouse with its black banded round white tower is now disused. Wreckage was not just on the shore. The 300-year old Fisherman's Return had its windows permanently boarded up because so many bodies were thrown through them when the fishermen did come back. They have not been the only unwelcome boats, tank traps being seen in the dunes at strategic points, although many submarine cables have been landed in the village.

Flows run to 5km/h from here to Yarmouth with a strong southerly flow at high water and a strong northerly at low water. Along this section of coast the tidal constant changes very rapidly, over 3 hours between here and Southwold. Winterton Overfalls form 6km off the coast beyond the Cockle Gateway.

Hemsby and Newport look over Hemsby Hole, but there is nothing to indicate the whereabouts of the new port itself. Hemsby is a resort and has holiday camps, as does California, part of Scratby named after its public house. This section of coast has unstable sand cliffs with rocks placed at the bottom and bungalows on the brink ready to fall.

Rock protects the crumbling cliff at Scratby

All Saints church in Horsey has a round tower with a 15th-century octagonal belfry. Winterton Ness is just 2km from the head of the River Thurne at West Somerton, a river which flows westward before finally discharging its waters at Great Yarmouth.

The sea probably reached the former cliffs near the Winterton Dunes National Nature Reserve as late as the 18th century. Winterton-on-Sea is a village better known than some, if not by name, as it has been used for some of the BBC's *Dad's Army* sequences and it was the 1930's Cape Cod in the film *Julia*. The church has a 40m tower, a significant landmark, while most of its inside is made from ships' timbers and fittings and there is a Fisherman's Corner. This is not surprising. In 1725 Daniel Defoe wrote that most buildings between Winterton and Yarmouth were built from

It is **Caister-on-Sea**, however, which claims to have invented the holiday camp although the name from castra, a camp, was probably less of a fun place, the town having been founded in the 2nd century, one of the chief towns of the Iceni. Footings of 3rd-century buildings show it was once a Roman commercial port, possibly with a fort, at what was the mouth of the Bure. Fun these days ranges from an ice cream van on the beach to a shopping trolley in the sea. Caister Point is perhaps the most insignificant point in the country on a map, slightly more visible when looking along the shore. 24km of offshore sandbanks act as breakwaters but give a short choppy sea and waves break heavily on Caister Shoal, inside Caister Road. There are also a couple of placed reefs, older than the ones at Sea Palling. The town begins with a radio mast and a water tower and ends with a golf course as the coast turns low and sandy to Great Yarmouth.

Behind the golf course is a helicopter base serving the North Sea platforms, next to Yarmouth dog racing stadium. Beside the golf course is a horse racecourse, formerly a barracks run by Capt Manby who invented lighthouse flash patterns and the line throwing rescue mortar.

Great Yarmouth is primarily a resort with 24km of beaches. The North Beach, backed by the Imperial Hotel and others, is reasonably restrained. The serious fun begins with the Britannia Pier which has slides, a roundabout and a wigwam amongst other items at its seaward end and any amount of amusements thereafter. Further south there are an assortment of eyecatching features, notably the Pleasure Beach and a prominent blue rollercoaster plus log flume, go karts, ghost train and more. The Sea Life Centre is one of the largest with shark tank, rays and Lost City of Atlantis. Treasure World has diving for treasure. There is Louis Tussaud's House of Wax, Merrivale Model Village, Ripley's Believe It or Not and the Living Jungle and Butterfly Centre. There is also a jetty and the Wellington Pier with its pavilion.

Yarmouth takes its name from the River Yare and grew rich in the Middle Ages on herrings, vast

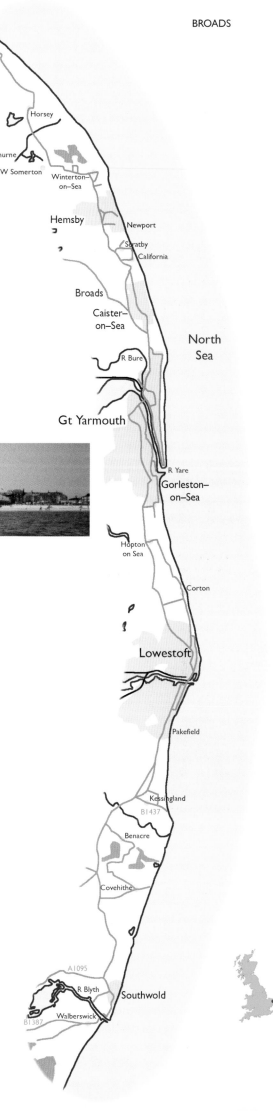

The Britannia Pier packed with amusements at Great Yarmouth

shoals of which gathered off the town each autumn. This led to successive arguments with the Cinque Ports and then the Dutch over herring rights and reached the point where the Cinque Ports attacked the Yarmouth fleet while escorting the king to Flanders in 1297, resulting in the burning of 29 ships and the killing of 200 men. The Yarmouth Free Herring Fair every autumn was one of the greatest mediaeval trade fairs. Thomas Nashe wrote about the Yarmouth fishing in *Lenten Stuff* in 1597. The Yarmouth bloater was invented in 1836 and the herring peaked before the first world war with over 1,100 drifters, but overfishing destroyed the stocks and the last drifter was sold in 1963. The town hall has a golden drifter weathervane. Fish found today include dab, sole, cod, whiting, bass and spined weaver. The town has now become a North Sea gas and oil exploration base. Nelson landed here after the Battle of the Nile in 1798 and sailed to and from the Battle of Copenhagen in 1891. The 43m Norfolk Pillar of 1819 has 217 steps and is topped by Britannia, some think oddly, facing away from the sea. It commemorates Nelson and is located alongside Yarmouth Roads just inside the start of the Yarmouth Port Limit. It was near the monument that Dickens set Peggoty's hut in *David Copperfield*. More drama on the beach in 1900 resulted in Herbert Bennett being hanged for murdering his estranged wife with a bootlace, much evidence pointing to his guilt. Eleven years later another woman was strangled on the beach with a bootlace.

Built 1261–1400, the town walls are one of the most complete sets in England, including the North West Tower. There are some notable old buildings.

The Tolhouse Museum dates from the 13th century, one of the oldest municipal buildings in England, used as a courthouse and jail. The Elizabethan House Museum in a merchant's house of 1596 has contemporary panelling, Lowestoft porcelain, 18/19th-century drinking glasses, Victorian toys, a Tudor bedroom, a Victorian kitchen and displays of 19th-century domestic life. It was said to have been used for plotting against Charles I by owner John Carter, a friend of Cromwell. The daughter of a later owner fell in love with a young man who was sent to sea to get rid of him, where he was drowned. The daughter saw his ghost and drowned herself. The ghosts of the pair were seen floating beside the ship and the guilty crew member confessed, the father dying of a broken heart. The Old Merchant's House is a 17th-century town house with splendid plaster ceilings, local original architectural and domestic

+0540 at up to 4km/h and outgoing from HW Dover −0030 at up to 11km/h although the ebb can be continuous for eighteen hours with heavy rain and wind can also have an effect. There is a slack period at local HW +0130 and at local LW +0200.

Cliffs of sand, gravel and red loam up to 17m high continue to Corton. The whole of the east coast here is popular with holidaymakers during the summer but it is quiet in winter. **Gorleston-on-Sea** has a concrete wall at the back of the beach. It is a resort but was an important seaport and has a disused lighthouse. Still in use is the church built on the site of the small wooden church erected in the 7th century by Felix, Bishop of Dunwich.

A hotel tower is at the port limit inside Gorleston Road. There is a wreck before the golf course starts.

An isolated set of cliffs steps at Hopton with the sea wall rebuilt behind and collapsing again

fittings and 17th and 19th-century ironwork. The customs house dates from 1720 and the Maritime Museum for East Anglia is in a shipwrecked sailors' home of 1861, featuring herring fishing and fishing gear, lifesaving, shipbuilding, sailors' arts and crafts, Nelson, Norfolk wherries, Norfolk's inland waterways, ship models, paintings, photographs, tools and the second world war. St Nicholas' church is the largest parish church in England although not the only one to make the claim. Great Yarmouth Museums Exhibition Galleries have their place and the Anna Sewell House Museum is the birthplace of the author of *Black Beauty*. The filming of *Keeping up Appearances* recorded some of the town more recently and there will be something somewhere on the Norfolk Giant, Robert Hales, who died in 1863 aged 43, 2.34m high and weighing 203kg. Yarmouth was the first place in eastern England to suffer an air raid in 1915.

Just south of Nelson's Monument and an aerial is a power station with a cooling water outfall structure in the sea off the South Beach. The geography of the area has changed significantly over the years. The spit used to reach to Gunton but in Roman times it was an island. The present river mouth was cut in the 16th century and has been maintained since then. Now there are plans to extend the harbour seawards and build a new harbour outside the present entrance. Even without these plans the seabed off Yarmouth is subject to frequent change.

Flows begin south at HW Dover +0600 and north from HW Dover −0020 at up to 5km/h. In addition, the river is ingoing from at HW Dover

Hopton on Sea also has a wreck, overlooked by holiday camps, caravans and a fire beacon on the low crumbling cliffs. The whole length of this section has heavy groynes protecting the coast, but large blocks of concrete with steps formed in them stand well forward of the cliffs in places, showing how far the sea has eaten back behind this former sea wall.

It is an ill wind that blows nobody any good or, in this case, waves. Hopton can have quite decent surfing conditions at times.

Norfolk gives way to Suffolk. Blackheaded gulls are unconcerned by the collapsing seawall below Corton Cliffs where masonry is included in some of the cliff falls, showing that the coastline is still moving inland remorselessly. Naturists enjoy Corton's beach but somebody who didn't was a 17th-century exciseman caught by smugglers, who rammed his head down a rabbit hole and drove a stake between his legs to secure him while they handled a cargo. There are a windmill and the remains of a ruined church but the prime businesses today are holiday camps, caravans and the Pleasurewood Hills American Theme Park with log flume, chairlift, two railways, pirate ship, sealions and waveswinger.

Corton Road becomes Lowestoft North Roads but the wrecks continue. A golf course, Gunton Hall and the mediaeval church of St Peter are the main features of Gunton on the outskirts of Lowestoft.

Progress can be gauged approaching Lowestoft as markers on the shore measure off a nautical mile.

Lowestoft Ness, the most easterly point in the British Isles.

At Lowestoft Denes along the North Beach large mature hotels and guest houses replace the small private houses seen so far. At the Denes the Scores are steep alleyways down the cliff. Much of the Beach Village was lost in the 1953 storm surge. The landmark from Gorleston has been a gas holder, an unromantic structure marking the most easterly point in the British Isles, Lowestoft Ness.

Lowestoft takes its name from the Old Danish man Hlothver and the Old Scandinavian toft, farm. The resort area of Lowestoft was laid out in the second half of the 19th century by Sir Samuel Morton Peto who built the railway so that fish could be delivered fresh to Manchester, a man whose other designs included the Houses of Parliament and Nelson's Column.

The entrance to Lowestoft harbour and Lake Lothing

From here to the harbourmouth at Lowestoft the shoreline is protected with concrete tripods. When approaching from the north, the mouth of the harbour seems so insignificant that the true entrance appears to lie somewhere between the South Pier and the Claremont Pier.

Lowestoft was notorious in 1664 for the case in which Amy Duny and Rose Cullender were hanged as witches with subsequent implications for the Salem witch trials of 1692 in the USA. Mostly, it has been a place of the sea, however. It was the birthplace of Sir Thomas Allen, who struck the

Claremont Pier at Lowestoft, now past its best

However, appearances can be deceptive and that narrow harbour mouth protects a busy harbour. The lighthouse is on the coastal site with the longest continuous use, chosen 400 years ago. The present 18m tower was operational from 1874 with paraffin, then gas, then electricity from 1936. The **Lowestoft** lighthouse now has a range of 45km. The high and low lights of 1609 had lanterns added after the locals complained about flying sparks.

first blow against the Dutch in 1665 and tackled Algerian pirates in 1669. Sir John Ashby, also born here, commanded the Blue Squadron at the victory of La Hogue in 1691. The harbour was opened in 1831 and the town became prosperous after the mid-19th century by exploiting the Dogger Bank. Three thousand drifters came to Great Yarmouth and Lowestoft every autumn and before the first world war there were seven hundred drifters working out of Lowestoft. There are plaice, cod, dab, dogfish and brill, but there are now less than fifty deep sea trawlers as the town's fleet yet it remains a busy fishing port and fishmarket and Birds Eye Walls remain the town's biggest employers.

Lowestoft Maritime Heritage Museum covers the fishing fleets and tools, sailing, lifeboats, shipbuilding, a drifter cabin, commercial models of 1880–1960 and marine paintings by Don and Harry Cox. The Royal Naval Patrol Service Association Museum at Sparrow's Nest, named after landowner Robert Sparrow, based in the depot for crews of minesweepers, drifters and trawlers from 1939 to 1946, features naval documents, uniforms, models and a trawler wheelhouse mockup. In 1916 the town was bombarded by eight German battle cruisers.

Another son of the town was anti-Puritan satirist Thomas Nash while Benjamin Britten was born here in 1913.

A hotelier suggested that the port could operate a hovercraft service across the North Sea to bring in more business.

The East Point Pavilion Visitor Centre in an Edwardian style building at the south side of the entrance to Lake Lothing is themed on a North Sea gas exploration rig.

Flows south begin at HW Dover –0610 and north at HW Dover +0010 at up to 5km/h, flow and levels being affected by the wind.

Claremont Pier was built in 1903 out into Lowestoft South Roads, in all a total length of 204m. Initially the beach is in front of such establishments as the Hotel Hatfield and the Jolly Roger plus the obligatory fire beacon. Low cliffs and beaches follow to Southwold and the Suffolk Coast Path continues to Felixstowe.

There is a water tower as Lowestoft merges into Pakefield and the church of St Margaret and All Saints which, until 1748, was two churches in one with two parishes and two rectors. It was restored after being badly damaged in the second world war. Pakefield also has a holiday camp. On Pakefield Cliffs is a firing range with a conically roofed lookout tower. Pakefield Hall brings a break in the built-up area.

Kessingland has the standard fire beacon and holiday camp so there is probably a procession of people along the B1437 to the Suffolk Wildlife and Country Park to view wildlife from around the world, including wallabies, timber wolves, lynx, leopards, Barbary apes, sacred ibis and black swans, from the safari train. There is an ancient forest on the seabed. Finds of paleolithic and neolithic implements show this has long been a popular resort. In 1745 customs officers watched five cargoes being unloaded by smugglers but made no arrests because of the large numbers present. The *Elizabeth Henrietta* beached in 1810 and the crew got ashore on lines but the captain refused and was lost. A further beaching in 1875 was the landing of a 3.6m shark. The village had a lifeboat until 1936. Sir Henry Rider Haggard was born here, bought the Grange and was visited by Rudyard Kipling.

Offshore banks close with the shore at Benacre Ness, where the Hundred River or Latymere Dam discharges. The coast is eroding so trees may be found in the sea.

From here to Southwold the sea is eating into the ends of several ridges of deep honey-coloured sand separated by low-lying land, some of which contains small broads, a coast joined by the Suffolk Coast and Heaths Path. A number of submarine cables were landed on this easy section of coast. Largest of

Benacre Broad with a small overflow channel leading to the beach

the broads is Benacre Broad where areas of the beach used for nesting by little terns have been fenced off.

Covehithe's 15th-century church became too large to maintain so villagers built a smaller thatched one inside the roofless and windowless shell of its predecessor in 1672.

Covehithe Cliffs lead to Covehithe Broad, a reedy lagoon with much birdlife amongst the dunes. Beyond Easton Broad are 10m high Easton Cliffs, off which jellyfish are found.

Southwold, from the Old English *suth wald*, place in the southern forest, was a prosperous 11th-century fishing port with one of the oldest charters in England, dating from Henry IV and celebrated in late May or early June at the Trinity Fair, opened by the mayor's taking the first ride on the merry go round. The 15th-century Perpendicular church of St Edmunds has a magnificent screen of about 1500 and Southwold Jack, an earlier oak figure of a man at arms with sword and Wars of the Roses equipment, who strikes a bell with his axe when a cord is pulled to signal the start of a service or the entry of a bride at a wedding.

Guncliffe Hill was used to site the six 8kg guns provided by Charles I in the 1630s to protect against Dunkirk privateers. These were replaced in 1745 by George II. The guns were 150 years old at the time so it should be no surprise that a local ghost is a headless gunner after one of the guns exploded. During the first world war they were bombarded by the Germans so the guns were then hidden away during both world wars.

This is Pevsner's most delightful of English seaside towns, with a mixture of Dutch influence, Georgian, Regency and Victorian houses with red brick and flint fishermen's cottages round open greens, the layout the results of a fire in 1659.

At the end of the A1095, Southwold is almost an island, being circled by the Buss Creek which is named after herring busses. Arguments with the Dutch over herrings led to the Battle of Sole Bay in 1672 when 130 Dutch ships under de Ruyter faced 150 English and French ships. Following instructions from Louis XV, who wanted the English and Dutch fleets to destroy each other, the French sailed away before the start. The outcome was as they had hoped, bloody but indecisive. The battle is recalled in Broadside ale brewed in the town by Adnams, the oldest brewery in Suffolk, in business since the 17th century, the largest employer in the town, still pulling some drays with Percheron horses. The British Free Fishery was founded here in 1750. The current catch includes flatfish, sprats and cod.

The lighthouse with its 32km range was built in the 1880s. The pier was destroyed at its seaward end in a storm in 1979. Its landward end is set about with beach huts and in the tarmac are a couple of hoofprints which, it is suggested, represent a relatively recent visit by the Devil.

George Orwell lived here from 1930 to 1933 in his parents' house, writer Neil Bell was born in the town and Southwold was Hardborough in Penelope Fitzgerald's *The Bookshop*. There is a twice yearly Sole Bay Literary Festival. For retired seamen there is the Southwold Sailor's Reading Room along with ship models, local history, archaeology and natural history, the Southwold Railway and a whipping post in the town.

Blackbacked gulls wait on the groynes for food and a ghostly war widow waits at the upstairs window of a restaurant in the town.

Southwold Lifeboat Museum has recently been set up in the former Cromer lifeboat station by the River Blyth which has been re-erected here to house the *Alfred Corry*, one of the oldest lifeboats in existence, a boat which was rowed and sometimes used under sail. The river used to discharge at Dunwich with a long spit, but a new entrance was cut in 1590. It produces fast currents with an ebb of up to 9km/h which can produce a confused sea at the entrance with an onshore wind. The gravel bar changes position off the entrance piers and there can be heavy surf. Slack is at local HW +0030. A protective mole on the north side of the entrance was rejected as it might have further stripped Walberswick's beach.

There is a carpark serving Walberswick beach near the end of the B1387 but it is locked at 7pm over weekends in the summer to deter campers.

The seafront at Southwold with the lighthouse just visible

Distance
From Horsey Corner to Walberswick is 53km
Campsites
Horsey Corner, Hemsby, Newport, California, Great Yarmouth, Gorleston-on-Sea, Corton, Lowestoft, Pakefield, Kessingland, Walberswick
Youth Hostels
Great Yarmouth, Blaxhall
OS 1:50,000 Sheets
134 Norwich and the Broads
156 Saxmundham
Imray Chart
C28 East Coast – Harwich to Wells-next-the-Sea (1:125,000)
Stanfords Allweather Charts
3 East Coast (1:138,000)
Admiralty Charts
SC 106 Cromer to Smiths Knoll (1:75,000)
SC 1536 Approaches to Great Yarmouth and Lowestoft (1:40,000). Great Yarmouth Haven (1:6,250). Approaches to Lowestoft (1:20,000). Lowestoft Harbour (1:6,250)
SC 1543 Winterton Ness to Orford Ness (1:75,000)
SC 2695 Plans on the East Coast of England. Southwold Harbour (1:7,500)
Tidal Constants
Winterton-on-Sea: HW Dover –0400, LW Dover –0320
Caister-on-Sea: HW Dover –0300, LW Dover –0240
Gorleston: HW Dover –0220, LW Dover –0210
Lowestoft: Dover –0140
Southwold: Dover –0040
Sea Areas
Humber, Thames
Rescue
Inshore lifeboats: Happisburgh, Great Yarmouth and Gorleston, South Broads, Southwold
All weather lifeboats: Great Yarmouth and Gorleston, Lowestoft
Maritime Rescue Centres
Yarmouth, 01493 851335
Thames, 01255 675518

50 SUFFOLK

Haunt of authors and ornithologists

When tides were neap, and, in the sultry day,
Through the tall bounding mud-banks made their way
Which on each side rose swelling, and below
The dark warm flood ran silently and slow;
There anchoring, Peter chose from man to hide,
There hang his head and view the lazy tide
In its hot slimy channel slowly glide;
Where the small eels that left the deeper way
For the warm shore, within the shallows play;
Where gaping mussels, left upon the mud
Slope their slow passage to the fallen flood;
Here dull and hopeless he'd lie down and trace
How sidelong crabs had scrawled their crooked race;
Or sadly listen to the tuneless cry
Of fishing gull or clanging golden-eye;
What time the sea-birds to the marsh would come,
And the loud bittern, from the bull-rush home,
Gave from the salt-ditch side the bellowing boom.

Benjamin Britten

Walberswick is sometimes referred to as Hampstead-on-Sea for its superior atmosphere. Holiday homes are located in former quayside sheds of what was a prosperous fishing and shipbuilding village. Its popularity with artists is not new, English impressionist Philip Wilson Steer having lived in Valley Farm. Birdwatchers are another group who flock here and not just for the skylarks by the beach. The village and shore, together with the Suffolk Heritage Coast, are displayed in the Heritage Coast Centre on the Green. Maggie Hemmingway set *The Bridge* in the village.

The tall tower of the ruined mediaeval church of St Andrew has had a new church built inside.

In the mid-1700s black drummer Tobias Gill drank here because he was banned from public houses in Blythburgh where his regiment were quartered as he was badly affected by drink. He was found drunk beside the dead body of local girl Ann Blackmore on the way back to Blythburgh and was hanged for rape and murder. A phantom

Once one of our most important ports, Dunwich is now no more than a small village on the sandy cliffs

coach pulled by headless horses and whipped by a black driver is sometimes seen in the lane.

A windmill stands beyond Corporation and Redland Marshes on the far side of the Dunwich River which joins the River Blyth at Walberswick. Until 1590, when the new exit to the River Blyth was cut, it flowed south to discharge at Dunwich.

A Roman settlement and then an Anglo-Saxon city, Dunwich had 5,000 inhabitants and nine churches in Norman times and was the fifth busiest port in England, the most prosperous town in Suffolk. Beaches used to be protected by piling them with brushwood weighted by stones. In January 1326 the port was inundated, losing 400 houses and three churches. The town lost 400m of coast in 400 years although it is now fairly stable. The Franciscan Grey Friars had their first monastery washed away 12 years after building it in the 14th century, a wall and two gatehouses remaining from a later attempt. The 19th-century church of St James with the remains of the earlier All Saints and the Leper Hospital have just one grave remaining. Shadowy figures of residents of the city are sometimes seen on the clifftops, lights come from the priory, the sound of monks chanting has been heard and the bells from a dozen churches still ring from under the sea on stormy nights. A museum illustrates the city from Roman times and features the local wildlife, the locality having many birds, butterflies and insects amongst the heather and gorse. The sea has produced plaice, dabs, sole, cod and smuggling.

Writers have been attracted here. P D James lived in Dunwich, setting several Adam Dalgleish stories in the vicinity including *The Children of Men* in Southwold. *Unnatural Causes* is set in Minsmere and Dunwich, Dunwich Heath becoming Monksmere Head. Larksoken power station is based on Sizewell and the Black Dog, a phantom which appears at night and causes depression, is well known in the area and has particular associations with Blythburgh and Bungay. Her book *Death in Holy Orders* is set south of

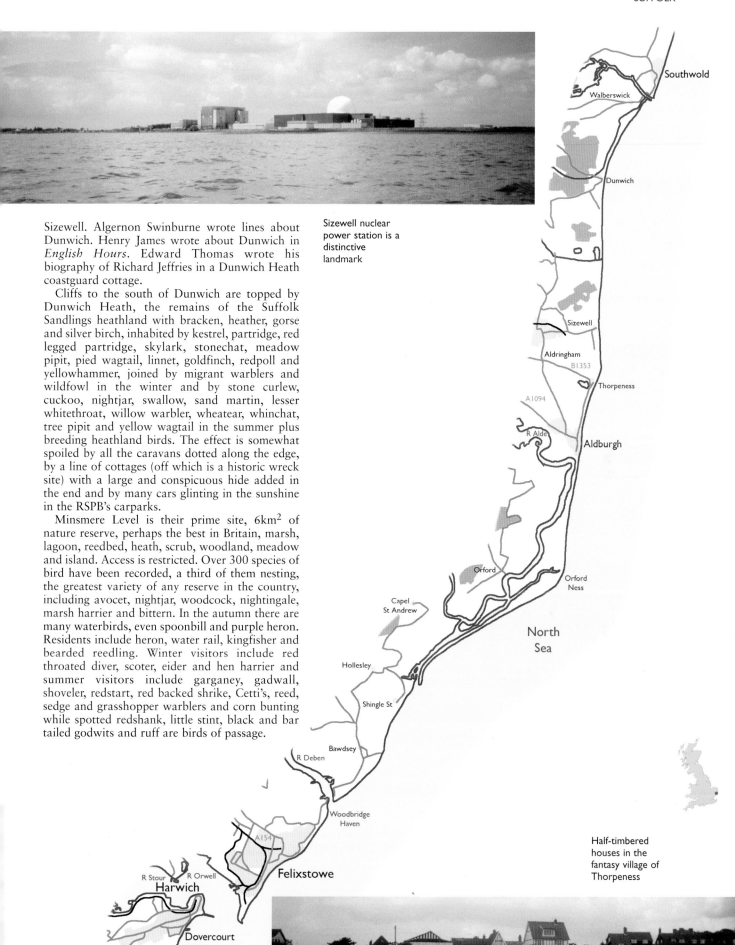

Sizewell. Algernon Swinburne wrote lines about Dunwich. Henry James wrote about Dunwich in *English Hours*. Edward Thomas wrote his biography of Richard Jeffries in a Dunwich Heath coastguard cottage.

Cliffs to the south of Dunwich are topped by Dunwich Heath, the remains of the Suffolk Sandlings heathland with bracken, heather, gorse and silver birch, inhabited by kestrel, partridge, red legged partridge, skylark, stonechat, meadow pipit, pied wagtail, linnet, goldfinch, redpoll and yellowhammer, joined by migrant warblers and wildfowl in the winter and by stone curlew, cuckoo, nightjar, swallow, sand martin, lesser whitethroat, willow warbler, wheatear, whinchat, tree pipit and yellow wagtail in the summer plus breeding heathland birds. The effect is somewhat spoiled by all the caravans dotted along the edge, by a line of cottages (off which is a historic wreck site) with a large and conspicuous hide added in the end and by many cars glinting in the sunshine in the RSPB's carparks.

Minsmere Level is their prime site, 6km² of nature reserve, perhaps the best in Britain, marsh, lagoon, reedbed, heath, scrub, woodland, meadow and island. Access is restricted. Over 300 species of bird have been recorded, a third of them nesting, the greatest variety of any reserve in the country, including avocet, nightjar, woodcock, nightingale, marsh harrier and bittern. In the autumn there are many waterbirds, even spoonbill and purple heron. Residents include heron, water rail, kingfisher and bearded reedling. Winter visitors include red throated diver, scoter, eider and hen harrier and summer visitors include garganey, gadwall, shoveler, redstart, red backed shrike, Cetti's, reed, sedge and grasshopper warblers and corn bunting while spotted redshank, little stint, black and bar tailed godwits and ruff are birds of passage.

Sizewell nuclear power station is a distinctive landmark

Half-timbered houses in the fantasy village of Thorpeness

The cliffs end and the Minsmere River passes a windpump and old chapel site to discharge into Minsmere Haven at the Sluice.

The most conspicuous feature on the coast is Sizewell nuclear power station with its white dome, built in the 1960s and in production from 1966. It uses 120,000m³/h of seawater for cooling, the warm water attracting fish and anglers. Towers off the coast are used as nesting sites by gulls and cormorants, which will not have too far to go for meals, and there are terns in the vicinity.

This smuggling village once handled 36m³ of gin in a single night. Its beacon was last used in 1918 by British warships to get bearings prior to bombarding Zeebrugge.

Sizewell Hall is a grand structure but is to be upstaged. South of Thorpe Ness, where large holes are formed in the shingle by wind and tides, is a pillbox on the sand cliffs and then the unique village of Thorpeness at the end of the B1353, planned before the first world war by dramatist and author Glencairn Stuart Ogilvie as a self catering village for those wanting to experience the Merrie England lifestyle, a project which failed. The houses are mostly of concrete, disguised as Tudor, Elizabethan, 18th-century East Anglian

The magnificent Moot Hall by the beach in Aldburgh

tarred weatherboard and the like. An 1824 post windmill, used to house displays on the village and Suffolk Heritage Coast, was moved from Aldringham in the 1920s to pump water to the House in the Clouds, a water tower disguised as a seven-storey clapboarded house. The Meare is a 26ha boating and wildlife lake.

Aldburgh is from the Anglo-Saxon aldburh, old fort, or the Old English Alda's fort. In the 16th century it was a prosperous fishing port. Lobster pots are laid off the beach and catches are sold straight from the boats drawn up on the beach amongst the sea holly, rest harrow, sea kale, sea pea and horned poppy. Thus, the fish and chips in the village are claimed to be the best in the world.

The village was put on the map by local resident Benjamin Britten who, with singer Peter Pears, started the Aldburgh Festival each June in the Jubilee Hall before moving it to Snape Maltings. The Moot Hall, a magnificent half-timbered

The dof which liked to watch model boats

herringbone brick and stone building of 1520–40, variously used as a market, gaol, ammunition store and council chamber, was the setting for the trial in the opening scene of the opera *Peter Grimes*. This was based on the description of Peter Grimes in *The Borough*, written by poet George Crabbe who was born in the village in 1754 and described the harsh local life of the day. The 16th-century Perpendicular church of Sts Peter and Paul with its 14th-century tower and brasses, used for ship auctions, has a window by John Piper to Britten and a memorial bust of Crabbe. Britten is buried in the churchyard, as is Elizabeth Garrett Anderson, England's first woman doctor and, in 1908, the first lady mayor.

In 1645 the Witchfinder General, Matthew Hopkins, was paid the significant sum of £6 for his gruesome services in clearing the village of witches. It was to become a village with two towers belonging to rival gangs trying to be the first to spot shipwreck cargo. By the early 19th century it had become a respectable resort and many of the remaining houses are 19th century with Flemish gables. Seven of the crew of the lifeboat were drowned in a capsize in 1899 while returning through surf. The beach produces amber and the Amber Shop has been in business for 150 years, the largest and oldest in Britain. Behind the beach is a boating pool watched over by a statue of the terrier of Dr Robin Acheson, the doctor from 1931 to 1959, whose dog liked to watch model boats being sailed. The firebeacon is recent.

Seafront House is where *Billy Budd* was written and E M Forster stayed and was involved in writing the libretto. The village has long been popular with writers. Wilkie Collins set *No Name* in the village in 1862. Ghost and mystery story writer Montague Rhodes James visited regularly, especially from 1922 to 1936, setting *A Warning to the Curious* on the beach. Susan Hill visited in the 1960s and set the ghost story *The Woman in Black* and other novels in the surrounding villages, Barbara Vine, writing as Ruth Rendell, had a house here and set *No Night Too Long* in the village and it was Owlbarrow, Kathleen Hale's holiday home for Orlando the Marmalade Cat.

A number of submarine cables land at Aldburgh, it is at the end of the A1094 and it is at the end of Orford Ness, a 16km spit which is growing at 15m per year, the largest vegetated spit in Europe with shingle, saltmarsh, mudflat, brackish lagoons and grazing marsh, important for breeding and passage birds, and shingle flora with many rare species. Hares are flown over by blackbacked gulls from the sea and shelducks from the river. Aldburgh is almost at the end of the River Alde, later the River Ore, which comes within 100m of the sea here.

Aldburgh is also the end of a line of 102 Martello Towers built in the 1880s to protect the coast against Napoléon. Based on the tower at Cape Mortella (meaning myrtle) in Corsica which had stood up well to a British bombardment, a tower was usually slightly egg-shaped in plan, used 700,000 bricks, had doors high up which were reached by removeable ladders and had an 11kg gun and two 140mm howitzers. The first tower is unusual in being larger and quatrefoil in plan.

Flows begin south–southwest from HW Dover –0550 and north–northeast from HW Dover +0020 at up 6km/h.

Plaice, sole, flounders, bass and cod are found off the 4–5m high gravel ridge of Sudbourne Beach, which anglers are allowed to use but off

which others are kept, initially because of a SSSI with nesting birds including avocets and then because of military interests, being a secret military site from 1913 to the mid-1980s. The numbers and positions of experimental radio masts on Lantern Marshes varied and were used for the USAF's Cobra Mist. From 1967 to 1970 they were used for over the horizon radar for early warning of ballistic missiles. The site was used for experimental testing, including aspects of atomic weapons throughout the Cold War, and some conspicuous structures remain.

Flows are strongest at Orford Ness itself and there are overfalls off the ness on the ebb and a wreck beyond them. There have been lighthouses at the ness since 1627 when 32 ships were lost in one night. The present 30m white lighthouse tower with red bands has a range of 50km and was built in 1792.

In the 16th century the spit ended at Orford but it now extends another 8km along Orford Beach. Orford Haven entrance is dangerous in strong onshore winds, especially with a strong ebb on a spring tide, and is turbulent near the bar. The offshore flow begins southwest at HW Dover –0550 and northeast from HW Dover +0050, the flood into the River Ore beginning at HW Dover –0500 and the outgoing flow from HW Dover +0120 at up to 11km/h.

There is a SSSI around the entrance. A different form of wildlife is associated with Hollesley Young Offenders Institute, the residents of which included

Felixstowe from the heavily slipped cliff at Bawdsey

Brendan Behan, who wrote about Shingle Street in *Borstal Boy*.

The Suffolk Coast and Heaths Path skirts Oxley Marshes and follows the coast to Felixstowe, passing another four Martello Towers before Bawdsey.

Bawdsey Cliff stands 12–15m high with the restricted area of RAF Bawdsey on top. There have been a number of slips and rabbits dig in the exposed material. The beach looks attractive from offshore, but close up it is as dirty as they come with jagged pieces of broken glass everywhere and a thick layer of decaying polystyrene cups along the beach, together with other debris. In the 18th century it was used by smugglers Margaret Catchpole and William Lauder, as recorded in the Rev Richard Cobbald's partly factual novel.

A radio tower stands along from Bawdsey Manor, started in 1886 in a fantasy of Victorian, Gothic, Flemish, Tudor and Oriental styles. It was here that Robert Watson-Watt developed radar before the second world war, to prove of major importance in winning the Battle of Britain.

Cliffs and grassy banks surround Woodbridge Haven, the mouth of the River Deben, dangerous in strong onshore winds, especially with a strong ebb on spring tides, with a further complication that the bar shifts. Flows begin inwards from HW Dover –0620 at up to 7km/h and outwards from HW Dover +0040 at up to 9km/h. There is a passenger ferry across to Felixstowe Ferry, a venue guarded by the Walton Castle Roman fort site and by a pair of Martello Towers now with a golf course between them.

Felixstowe is met with tiers of brightly painted beach huts, a sight to be seen regularly from here southwards. The water comes under the control of Harwich Haven Authority before Cobbald's Point on which a college is sited, surrounded by large and impressive old buildings. Felixstowe, from the Old English for Filicia's meeting place, is an Edwardian resort of gabled houses with gardens and parks, a water clock, waterfall, grotto, arboretum and Italian garden. Alan Jacobson, Mr Suffolk, lived here, as did novelist Robert Greenwood. Stevie Smith used the town in the *Novel on Yellow Paper* and John Betjeman penned lines about the it. Old pier remains cover at low water but there is a much larger affair in the centre of the shallow bay. There are a couple of Martello Towers amongst the buildings, one housing a coastguard station, and the remains of an old fort near low water. The

The first Martello Tower at Aldburgh which begins the line of coastal defences

Orford Ness lighthouse

Brightly painted beach huts at Felixstowe. There are many more to come further south

Landguard Fort on the right, the radar scanner and the cranes of Felixstowe

Fludger Arms are prominent but not so much as a pink construction on the shore. Charles Manning's Amusement Park and a Quasar game are amongst the local entertainments. Dominating the skyline are the cranes of Britain's leading container port which faces onto Harwich Harbour behind the end of the A154, one of the largest container ports in Europe. The harbour was protected by Landguard Fort, first built in the 1540s, attacked unsuccessfully by the Dutch in 1677, the last invasion in England, and rebuilt in 1744. In 1763 the governor caused furore by using the chapel over the gateway for a dance, employing the altar as a bar. The fort was modified in 1875, 1890, 1901 and 1914. The Ravelin block next to the fort houses the Felixstowe Museum which features the fort. A nature reserve with restricted areas for ground nesting birds and overlooked by hides occupies much of the area to Landguard Point, although a large mast bearing a radar scanner is a prominent landmark. St Andrews Spit extends from the point with a wreck on it off the point.

Flows run southwest from HW Dover −0600 at up to 2km/h and northeast from HW Dover +0050 at up to 3km/h. Flows into the harbour, the mouth of the River Orwell and the River Stour, and the ebb flows are up to 2km/h. Occasional isolated waves, the better part of a metre high, can be thrown up by container ships.

In addition to all the container ships there are car ferries from Harwich to Cuxhaven, Turku, Esbjerg, Hamburg, Gothenburg and the Hook of Holland plus many pleasure craft. The Harwich Deep Water Channel is on the east side of the harbourmouth close to Landguard Point, is relatively narrow and is clearly buoyed in an area which sees extensive bed movements.

Crossing the harbourmouth takes the paddler from Suffolk to Essex with the Essex Way running along the front of **Harwich** (from the Old English herewic, army camp) past a line of figures cut in the chalk. Edward III marshalled a fleet here in 1340 to defeat the French at Sluys, the opening major sea battle of the Hundred Years War. It was

a royal naval dockyard from the 17th century when Samuel Pepys was MP. Drake, Frobisher, Hawkins, Cavendish, Nelson and Raleigh sailed from here, it was home to Christopher Jones, master of the *Mayflower*, and Charles II sailed the first pleasure yacht from here.

Dovercourt was a resort from the 1850s with a boating lake and a 3km promenade. Two disused leading lights of 1863 on cast-iron tubular legs are the last surviving pair of iron light towers on the British coast. They were superseded by buoys in 1917.

Landing by the Phœnix Hotel and a café gives access to a limited amount of parking near a boating lake. The beach is of sand and this is where *Hi-de-hi* sequences were filmed by the BBC.

The last surviving cast-iron light towers on the British coast at Harwich

Distance
From Walberswick to Dovercourt is 54km
Campsites
Walberswick, Theberton, Sizewell, Aldeburgh, Sudbourne, Capel St Andrew, Hollesley, Felixstowe
Youth Hostels
Blaxhall, Castle Hedingham
OS 1:50,000 Sheets
156 Saxmundham
169 Ipswich and the Naze
Imray Charts
2000 Suffolk and Essex Coast
C1 Thames Estuary – Tilbury to North Foreland and Orfordness (1:120,000)
C28 East Coast – Harwich to Wells-next-the-Sea (1:125,000)
Y16 Walton Backwaters to Ipswich and Woodbridge (1:35,000)
Stanfords Allweather Charts
3 East Coast (1:138,000)
5 Thames Estuary (1:115,000)
6 Suffolk Rivers
L6 Rivers Orwell and Stour and Harwich Harbour (1:28,500)
L7 Harwich Approaches (1:65,000)
L8 River Deben (1:31,000)
Admiralty Charts
SC 1183 Thames Estuary (1:100,000)
1491 Harwich and Felixstowe (1:10,000)
SC 1543 Winterton Ness to Orford Ness (1:75,000)
SC 2052 Orford Ness to the Naze (1:50,000)
SC 2693 Approaches to Felixstowe, Harwich and Ipswich with the Rivers Stour, Orwell and Deben (1:25,000)
SC 2695 Plans on the East Coast of England. Southwold Harbour (1:7,500). Rivers Ore and Alde (1:25,000). Walton Backwaters (1:12,500)
SC 5607 Thames Estuary, Essex and Suffolk Coast
Tidal Constants
Southwold: Dover –0040
Aldeburgh: HW Dover –0010, LW Dover –0020
Orford Ness: HW Dover, LW Dover –0010
Orford Haven Bar: HW Dover +0020, LW Dover +0010
Bawdsey: HW Dover +0030, LW Dover +0010
Woodbridge Haven: HW Dover +0040, LW Dover +0020
Felixstowe Pier: HW Dover +0040, LW Dover +0020
Harwich: HW Dover +0050, LW Dover +0030
Sea Area
Thames
Rescue
Inshore lifeboats: Southwold, Aldeburgh, Harwich
All weather lifeboats: Lowestoft, Aldeburgh, Harwich
Helicopter: Wattisham
Maritime Rescue Centre
Thames, 01255 675518

The Harwich Deep Water Channel leading into Harwich Harbour is busy but relatively narrow so it can be crossed quite quickly

51 ESSEX

Sunshine holiday beaches amongst remote marshland

We've wallowed in the Wallet,
  awash with sodden deals,
And slipped from Southend jetty,
  the sou'easter at our heels.
Stern winter had his will of us
  on black December days,
Our kedge is on the Buxey
  and our jib is off the Naze.

R E Banyard

Dovercourt to Brightlingsea is called the Sunshine Coast, the driest in England. The town is quickly left behind and the coast soon becomes one of typical Essex saltmarsh, the beach well coated in shells and a heron picking about. Seawalls move in and out past sections of marsh, protected in turn by the occasional pillbox.

Beyond Crabknowe Spit is Pennyhole Bay, at the back of which are the Walton Backwaters with Hamford Water, Walton Channel and a multitude of creeks and hundreds of islands, described by Arthur Ransome as the Secret Waters.

From Stone Point there is a continuous beach, off which is the Medusa Channel, named after Nelson's frigate of 1801 when a local man piloted him out through it after winds prevented him from departing through the usual channel. There is a nature reserve reaching to a sewage works. Harwich Haven Authority is left behind.

The Naze is the start of the greater Thames Estuary. Flows start south at HW Dover −0600

The Naze Tower with the Naze at high water. A slip is taking place with suitcase sized lumps of soil falling in the photograph

Typical Essex marsh shoreline near Dovercourt

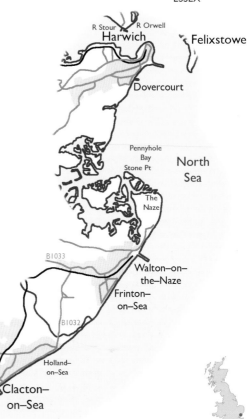

and north from HW Dover +0020 at up to 3km/h although tidal flows may be overridden by tidal surges.

The Naze itself consists of 20m of crumbling red sandstone cliff with many Ice Age fossils of primeval bird skeletons, crabs, shark teeth and reversed whelks, topped by grass and gorse. The brown-brick octagonal Naze Tower on the summit was built in 1720 by Trinity House, the most massive and highest unlit beacon on the British coast. Originally 27m high with 113 steps, it has been reduced to 25m. In transit with Walton Hall it leads through the Goldmer Gat, giving a safe passage to the inside of the Gunfleet Sand bank which dries 7km offshore parallel with the coast. Around the tower is a nature reserve and nature trail with little terns nesting, migrating birds and the Essex skipper and painted lady in summer. There is a picnic site and the point was used for settlement in the Iron Age. The beach produces

black copperas stones, a source of ferrous sulphate which has been used for tanning, dying and ink making. Meanwhile, old pillboxes capsize into the sand.

Ten metre cliffs continue to Frinton but the front seems to be one long line of beach huts. **Walton-on-the-Naze** became a resort in the 1830s, renowned for its candied sea holly which was supposed to be an aphrodisiac.

The coastguard station is the Maritime Rescue Sub-Centre for the whole of the Thames Estuary. The adjacent house now contains a museum on the maritime, seaside, urban and geological aspects of the area.

A Martello Tower was built away from the front where it could watch over the head of the Walton Channel.

The pier is the second longest in the country at 790m and the fourth pleasure pier to be built. When constructed in 1895 it did not reach the sea at low water so it had to be extended. At the shore end it is 46m wide with the remains of an earlier pier underneath, while on top are tenpin bowling,

Another happy holidaymaker with a day old craft at Frinton

giant wheel, Pirate Pete play area and other holiday entertainments. A spur to its construction was the arrival of the railway in 1867.

Brill, cod, dabs, haddock, hake, whiting and sole are found in the sea here.

The beach huts are built on stilts at the foot of the Greensward, an expanse of sloping green bank behind the beach at **Frinton-on-Sea** at the end of the B1033. The name from the Old English frithen tun means protected village or fenced settlement. Developed in the 1890s by Sir Richard Cooker, Frinton is the only British resort of any size without a public house. It retains a quiet, unspoilt 1920s/30s atmosphere with broad treelined esplanade and red-brick houses. Beyond the Copperas Ground is the Wallet where flows southwest run to 3km/h and northeast to 4km/h. Some of the pirate radio stations of the 1960s operated off this section of coast.

Low-lying land occupied by a golf course is fronted by a substantial seawall which winds past Sandy Point and Chevaux de Frise Point to Holland Haven, where the Holland Brook discharges at a country park and nature reserve.

Below a radio mast is a jet ski base. A café beside the water and a fire basket begin 6km of continuous built-up holiday beach or 11km of beach in total, beginning with Holland-on-Sea and the B1032.

small and noisy craft racing round in small and noisy circles. Then it is the naturists and the naturalists with their hides, presumably averting their gaze and their binoculars from their neighbours. Offshore are blackheaded, blackbacked and common gulls, oystercatchers and cormorants. The nature reserve consists of 1.6km² of saltings and shingle with Brent geese, sanderlings, curlews, redshanks and little terns, an area restricted to their own members.

The Colne Bar at the end of the estuary of the River Colne consists of banks of mussel shells. Point Clear is fronted by caravans and chalets. On St Osyth Stone Point at the top of the **Brightlingsea** Reach is a Martello Tower which was used by the Royal Navy as HMS Helder during the second world war. Built in 1810, it now forms the East Essex Aviation Society and Museum with a Mustang recovered from the sea, parts of a Tempest and displays from both world wars. Flows run in to 2km/h and out to 3km/h.

The Mersea Stone marks the corner of Mersea Island, from the Saxon Meres-ig, isle in the mere. A nature reserve leads to a picnic area and Cuckoo Grove Country Park and visitor centre. East Mersea had wildfowling and smuggling. It was important for the defence of Colchester so Henry VIII built a large triangular blockhouse in case the French attacked. It was occupied successively by

Clacton pier has the largest area of any pier in Europe and is packed with amusements for holidaymakers

Clacton-on-Sea is the capital of the Tendring peninsula and the Essex Sunshine Coast. Named after Clacc, an Old English man, Clacton is at the end of the railway and A133 and developed after 1860 with a promenade, seafront gardens and Victorian and Edwardian houses but is unashamedly a holiday town. Its centrepiece is the pier, the largest in Europe at 2ha. Built in 1871, it was extended to 360m in 1893 and carries a sea aquarium, arcades, rides, sealion show, roller skating, dodgems, reptile safari and ice rink. Found around it are a road train, the Magic City play centre, lido and bowling.

The landing strip seems a bit small for Clacton Air Show. Other annual events are Clacton Classic Vehicle Show and Clacton Jazz Festival. It has been used for filming BBC *Eastenders* sequences. More Martello Towers follow including one with a coastguard station and a zoo in a dry moat.

A golf course gives a short break before Jaywick and Seawick and then St Osyth Beach continues to Lee-over-Sands at Colne Point. New rock groynes project at intervals where 100,000 tonnes of rock and 500,000m³ of sand were placed from January to March 1999 dredged from 45km offshore to avoid disturbing holidaymakers and nesting terns. As St Osyth is 3km inland it must be fairly desperate to put its name to a beach. The beach is effectively zoned, firstly jet skis and all manner of

the Royalists and the Roundheads in the Civil War, was refortified against the Dutch and was demolished in the 18th century. Barbed wire and gun emplacements were then prepared in case of a visit by Hitler and there is still the risk of unexploded ordnance.

The village had a priory related to the Priory of Cluny. St Edmund's church is nearly 1,000 years old. Baring-Gould was vicar here for a decade but didn't like the place, the people or the climate, as indicated in his novel *Mehalah*.

Mersea Flats include banks of mussels and there are sprats, cod, herrings and shrimps. The concrete schooner *Molliette* had an interesting career, running through Southend pier then ending up here, first as a scandalous nightclub, then as a second world war army target from which somebody subsequently made a fortune by dredging up the brass shell cases.

Beach huts start **West Mersea** where there are toilets and a café. The village is at the end of the B1025. It has been known for its oysters since Roman times and West Mersea Natives are available on the hard. There is a Roman barrow and the Red Hills are burned soil from Celtic salt workings. The church of Sts Peter and Paul dates partly from 1046 when it served the parish and a small Benedictine priory. By it is the Mersea Island Museum with local and natural history, social and

marine exhibits, the RNLI, oyster production, fishing equipment, wildfowling, fossils and minerals. Duck punts were built here. Now a resort, it is the main sailing centre on the Blackwater with a regatta in August.

Beyond Besom Fleet is Cobmarsh Island with traces of a mediaeval fort. In the complex area of channels Mersea Quarters receives flows from Mersea Fleet, Thorn Fleet, Little Ditch and the Salcott Channel. There are oyster beds here and gulls, cormorants, herons, mute swans, grebes, pewits and, in the winter, greylag geese, blackheaded gulls and widgeon. Beyond Quarters Spit with its pillbox, Virley Channel receives flow from the North and South Channels, divided by

Great Cob Island and contained by Shinglehead Point. The River Blackwater is ingoing to 3km/h and outgoing to 4km/h.

Bradwell nuclear power station, built on a former airfield, is protected by a detached jetty out in the estuary. Commissioned in 1962, these were the first pair of full size Magnox reactors in Britain.

A pillbox on the shore faces its counterpart across the Blackwater and an unplanned defence measure is 12ha of compressed and broken cockle shells which form Bradwell Shell Beach. Leading to Sales Point, a line of 11 sunken barges form a wavebreak which covers at high water.

A black weatherboarded house outside the seawall at Tip Head was occupied by Walter Linnett, the last professional wildfowler, punt gunner and eel spearer until well after the second world war. Haunted by the ghost of an old seaman, it is now used as a bird observatory, local birds including herons, cormorants, terns and herring and blackbacked gulls. Close by is a nature reserve.

The Romans built their Othona fort here, its bricks and stone being reused to build St Peter's on the Wall chapel in 654 by St Cedd, who came from Northumberland as a missionary to the East Anglians. It has been a cathedral and a barn from the 17th century to 1920, now being used by the

Othona Society for nondenominational services, one of the oldest places of worship in England. Looking like a barn, it has served as a navigation mark over the centuries on a section of coast which has had few landmarks.

The St Peter's Way walk goes round the Bradwell Marshes while St Peter's Flat and Dengie Flat offshore offer some shallow conditions. Wrecks lie about the flats and between Sandbeach and Marshhouse Outfalls there is another line of barges, this time 16 of them. Saltings and mudflats ending with a hard clay shelf make up the Dengie Flat SSSI with 24,000 birds including knots, teal,

The detached breakwater in front of the nuclear power station at Bradwell on the River Blackwater.

A line of sunken steel barges act as a breakwater off the Bradwell Marshes

shelducks and, especially, Brent geese. The RSPB said they were threatened by sea level rise and shellfisheries.

active part of the ranges is at this end. Normally, artillery shells bury themselves completely in the sand although it is possible for the sand to be

A large flock of oystercatchers wheel around at the northern end of Foulness Island. Various military towers rise beyond

Crouch Harbour Authority takes control before Grange Outfall, the occasional seal occupying the water in an area generally devoid of people.

It pays to time a run so that Foulness Island is passed at high water. Ray Sand on the north side of the River Crouch is extended along the Whitaker Channel by Buxey Sand for 16km. There is a 700m gap at low water but there is no corresponding gap on the south side of the rivermouth where Foulness Sands run out for 9km. Flows start into the estuary at HW Dover −0430 at up to 5km/h and out from HW Dover +0130 at up to 6km/h

Foulness Island's name derives from the Old English fulga and naess, meaning wild birds promontory, indicating that it has only become an island in recent times.

Foulness is known for its different forms of flight. For some years it was under discussion and public enquiry as one of the proposed sites for London's third airport, although successive governments failed to arrive at a decision on the subject. Direct rail and motorway links to London were proposed for the site which would have covered the island and have involved much reclamation from the Maplin Sands, not unprecedented as much of Foulness itself has been inned from the sea over the years.

The final form of flight is brought about by the Ministry of Defence who purchased the island in 1915. Foulness is the Proof and Experimental Establishment, a military firing range, and the public are not admitted to the island, excepting the couple of hundred civilians who live there and farm the soil which Arthur Young, in 1814, described as being the richest in the county. The 7km of water off the southeast side of the island and running 12km northeast from Foulness Point is a prohibited area for shipping, no great loss for larger vessels because of the shallowness of the water. However, paddlers may go into this area when the ranges are not active.

Crouch Harbour Authority hands over to Port of London Authority at Foulness Point. The most

washed off from time to time. It seems strange that this area should be teeming with birdlife. A third of the world's population of Brent geese winter off Essex, 100,000 of them off Foulness Island. Perhaps they are protected from other predators and do not consider the risk of being hit by shells, but they were enough of a hazard to stop the third London airport being built on the 91km^2 of Maplin Sands. Flocks of oystercatchers wheel noisily but most of the birdlife congregates at the northeast end of the island. Banks of edible cockle shells are met towards this point, indicating the spot from which are taken over 60% of all cockles sold in Britain.

300m out from the high water mark is the Broomway, a public bridleway running parallel to the coast for 9km. It has produced the incident of a sailing barge colliding with a horsedrawn coal cart. It is named after the wooden brooms marking the route. Mackerel leap just off the shoreline, which is embanked marshland to Shoebury Ness, some fine salt marshes. Burial urns, pottery, barrows and red hills show it is an area which has long been occupied.

Although it has some prominent lattice masts and observation cabins, these need to be seen on the charts as the Ordnance Survey do not mark military installations on their maps, simply showing what was there before the military took over.

The observation box at Asplins Head overlooks a set of supports which once carried an overhead pipeline and now rust within a circular protective wall which is submerged at high tide.

Havengore Island is connected to New England Island, in turn linked to Foulness Island. A new bridge crosses Havengore Creek above Haven Point and the Broomway returns to land at **Wakering Stairs**.

Essex gives way to Southend-on-Sea. Beyond Pig's Bay a 2km long obstruction runs out but there are gaps which allow paddlers through. The tide goes out a further kilometre and at low tide firing can take place parallel to the shoreline way out on the sands.

Landing at **Shoeburyness** gives access to parking. There is less clay than there was because the Romans set up a pottery kiln at Shoebury.

Military scrap rusts in Pig's Bay. Beyond is the protective boom

Distance
From Dovercourt to Shoeburyness is 74km

Campsites
Felixstowe, Ramsey, Thorpe-le-Soken, Jaywick, Brightlingsea, East Mersea, West Mersea, St Lawrence, Burnham-on-Crouch, Shoeburyness

Youth Hostels
Castle Hedingham, Medway

OS 1:50,000 Sheets
168 Colchester
169 Ipswich and the Naze
178 Thames Estuary

Imray Charts
2000 Suffolk and Essex Coast
2100 Kent Coast
C1 Thames Estuary – Tilbury to North Foreland and Orfordness (1:120,000)
Y16 Walton Backwaters to Ipswich and Woodbridge (1:35,000)
Y17 River Colne to Blackwater and Crouch (1:49,000)
Y18 River Medway Sheerness to Rochester with River Thames, Sea Reach (1:20,000)

Stanfords Allweather Charts
4 Essex Rivers
5 Thames Estuary (1:115,000)
6 Suffolk Rivers
8 North Kent Coast
L4 River Blackwater (1:35,000)
L5 River Colne and Mersea Flats (1:28,500)
L7 Harwich Approaches (1:65,000)

Admiralty Charts
SC 1183 Thames Estuary (1:100,000)
SC 1185 River Thames Sea Reach (1:25,000)
1491 Harwich and Felixstowe (1:10,000)
SC 1607 Thames Estuary, Southern Part (1:50,000)
1609 Thames Estuary, Black Deep to Sea Reach (1:25,000)
SC 1975 Thames Estuary, Northern Part (1:50,000)
SC 2052 Orford Ness to the Naze (1:50,000)
SC 2693 Approaches to Felixstowe, Harwich and Ipswich with the Rivers Stour, Orwell and Deben (1:25,000)
SC 2695 Plans on the East Coast of England. Walton Backwaters (1:12,500)
SC 3741 Rivers Colne and Blackwater (1:25,000). Brightlingsea (1:12,500). West Mersea (1:12,500)
SC 3750 Rivers Crouch and Roach (1:25,000)
SC 5606 Thames Estuary, Ramsgate to Canvey Island
SC 5607 Thames Estuary, Essex and Suffolk Coast

Tidal Constants
Harwich: HW Dover +0050, LW Dover +0030
Bramble Creek: Dover +0050
Walton-on-the-Naze: Dover +0040
Clacton-on-Sea: Dover +0100
Brightlingsea: Dover +0110
West Mersea: HW Dover +0110, LW Dover +0120
Bradwell-on-Sea: Dover +0110
Holliwell Point: HW Dover +0120, LW Dover +0130
Havengore Creek: Dover +0100
Southend: HW Dover +0120, LW Dover +0130

Sea Area
Thames

Range
Foulness

Rescue
Inshore lifeboats: Harwich, Clacton-on-Sea, West Mersea, Burnham-on-Crouch, Southend-on-Sea
All weather lifeboats: Harwich, Walton and Frinton, Sheerness

Maritime Rescue Centre
Thames, 01255 675518

52 THAMES ESTUARY

The mouth of Britain's best known river

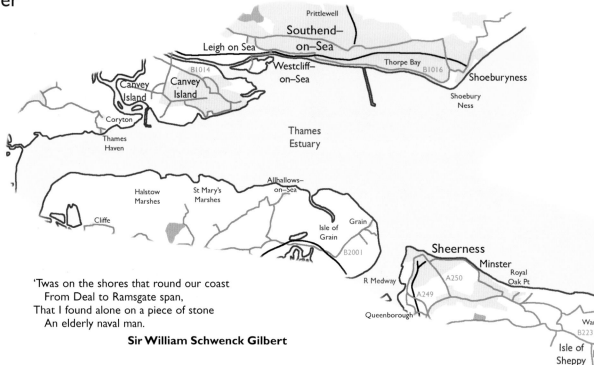

'Twas on the shores that round our coast
  From Deal to Ramsgate span,
That I found alone on a piece of stone
  An elderly naval man.

Sir William Schwenck Gilbert

From Shoeburyness, Shoebury Ness itself is quickly reached, the start of Sea Reach with the Yantlet Dredged Channel and the Southend and Warp Deep Water Anchorage beyond the West Knock daymark. The other side of the 2km of flats, the channels are now used by many large commercial vessels. Pier remains stand around the ness. The artillery barracks of 1858 were used to test Armstrong guns against ironsides. The range has been closed and now forms Gunners Park with a SSSI and trotting track.

Southend-on-Sea, the south end of Prittlewell, is the largest town in Essex, a resort and the nearest seaside town to London. A radio mast as the B1016 comes alongside begins 11km of front. Beyond Shoebury Common and Thorpe Bay is Southend Flat, an extensive mooring for small craft, and beach huts in plenty. There is a marine activities centre and Southend Sea Life Aquarium, fish in the sea including cod, flounders, bass, eels, mullet and tope.

Southend is best known for its pier, the longest pleasure pier in the world at 2.1km. Built in the 1830s for passengers, it was rebuilt in 1889 in iron and extended in 1927. Horsedrawn trains were replaced by 910mm gauge electric trains. Buildings at the seaward end have been burnt out four times, the most recent in 2005, and the pier has been hit by over a score of large vessels, including an 800 tonne coaster which cut through in 1986, marooning two anglers. There are inshore lifeboats stationed at both ends. Southend Pier Museum features the pier, the railway and the disasters. A boating pool has a half-sized model of the *Golden Hinde*, not there when Nelson stayed in Royal Terrace. Peter Pan's Adventure Island has over forty rides including Viking Boats, Raging River Log Flume, Tidal Wave, Vortex, Queen Anne's Revenge pirate galleon, rollercoaster and big wheel. The Kursaal of 1901 has multiple tenpin bowling with roller and ice skating. There is the Victorian Cliffs Bandstand,

Southend Pier, the world's longest pleasure pier despite many attempts to shorten it or burn it down

Never Never Land, Roller City, illuminations from mid-August to early November, fireworks every Saturday from mid-September to October, Europe's largest free airshow over the May bank holiday, Southend Water Festival in September including dragon boat racing, Southend Brass Band Competition, a Spring Festival, London–Southend Classic Car Run, Southend Jazz Festival in August, Southend Cricket Festival and the Thames Sailing Barge Match. 4.5km^2 of parks mostly date from 1900 to 1930. With all this there are still boarded up hotels and increasing numbers coming here to retire, perhaps the very same Mods and Rockers who used to come at bank holidays for running fights along the front. The town has been used for filming *Killing Dad* and for BBC *Eastenders* sequences. There is Mr B's Space Chase Quasar and the Beecroft Art Gallery in an Edwardian building at **Westcliff-on-Sea**, with water colours, oils and prints. Chalkwell Park rose garden faces out onto Chalkwell Oaze. The City or Crow Stone marks the northern limit of the River Thames.

Leigh-on-Sea, settlement in a glade, was a cockle and whelk fishing village using bawleys or boiler boats, collecting cockles from Maplin Sands and also sprats, whitebait and brown shrimps, leading to boatbuilding. Cockles and jellied eels are still on sale near the beach of cockle shells. This is probably where the Essex pilgrims boarded the *Mayflower*. When the Boat Inn was rebuilt in the late 19th century it was found to have many smuggling cellars underneath. Weatherboarded houses front the cobbled high street. Leigh Heritage Centre on Leigh Creek and Leigh Folk Festival add to the folklore.

Ray Gut, separating Southend-on-Sea from Essex, runs between Leigh Sand and Marsh End Sand, an area where waterskiing is permitted and where cormorants, oystercatchers and blackbacked and herring gulls will be found at times.

For the first time since Bridlington there are hills, occupied by Hadleigh Castle. Built for Edward III, curtain walls and two towers remain of the structure immortalized by John Constable.

requisite sea smell. A patch of mist on moonlit nights can transform into a Norse raider looking for a ship to take him home. The island has a substantial concrete seawall with heavy flood doors around it, an item constructed since January 31st 1953 when the floods drowned 58 people. The 12,000 population of those days has now risen to 33,500, living at the eastern end of the island, but the seawall hides most of the buildings. The island has sunk 6m in the last 2,000 years, mostly in the 2nd century. In 1630 Cornelius Vermuyden built the first wall round it and received a third of the island in payment. 200 of his workers settled there and one of their thatched houses faces a prominent road junction in the centre of the island.

Nearby is the Chapman Explosive Anchorage. A degaussing range is situated off Thorney Bay, a popular creek with holidaymakers where deep golden sand is exposed.

A curiosity of the marshes in the area was that men brought up in the area were healthy but wives brought down from higher ground soon deteriorated, so that getting a new wife was an annual occurrence for many men in the 18th century and some outlived dozens of wives.

Beyond Deadman's Point and Scar's Elbow there are gasworks and a Texaco tank farm. In Sea Reach the fairway is on the north side and craft are required to be at least 60m from berthed tankers and jetties. A powerful fixed white light indicates that a large tanker has passed No 6 Sea Reach lightbuoy off Leigh Middle or is less than 15 minutes from leaving its berth. Flows are strongest on the north side of the channel, ingoing to 6km/h and outgoing to 7km/h.

Tucked away at the back of Hole Haven (from holy haven), dividing Essex from Thurrock, is the shiplapped Lobster Smack Inn. The Dutch under Van Gent attacked Hole Haven in 1667, firing buildings and stealing sheep. The attack only lasted three hours, leaving the invaders plenty of

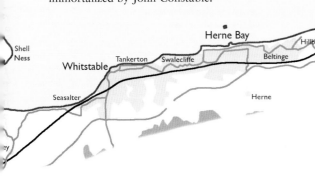

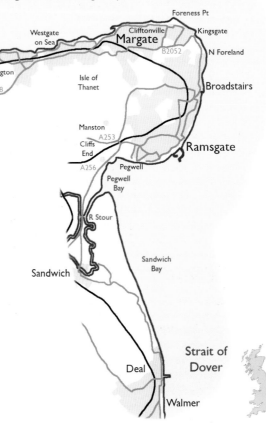

Two Tree Island contains Leigh National Nature Reserve with Brent geese and other winter wildfowl, separated by Hadleigh Ray or Oyster Creek from **Canvey Island**. Smallgains Creek, home for many sailing boats, is where Olympic canoeists Roland and Francis Prout rigged a pair of sprint kayaks with a bamboo frame and sail in the 1950s and then went out to win the local regattas, something that did not go down at all well with the purists although it led to the Shearwater class, of which over two thousand were built.

Canvey, beyond the end of the B1014, is a wildlife sanctuary with waders. The area is one of muddy saltings covered with weed which gives the

One of a number of tankers berthed at Thames Haven alongside one of the refineries

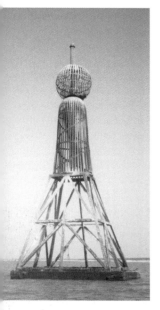

Yantlet Beacon daymark

The London Stone

time to go on and give their attentions to Queenborough the same day.

Twenty tanker berths on the north side of Sea Reach can take the largest supertankers, serving one of the most extensive refinery areas in England. Shell Haven had been named by Henry VIII's time. Shell did not arrive until 1912, by which time the Cory brothers had had a small refinery there for forty years at Coryton. Tanks, flare stacks and large jetties follow the north side of the estuary for 8km and the water smells of organic mud.

As the river turns from the south there is a container terminal behind Mucking Flat. Power station chimneys at Tilbury break the skyline.

Crossing the River Thames from Thurrock to the Medway shore brings very different conditions, the Blythe Sands mud draining for a kilometre from a sloping seawall protecting the Kent marshes, farmland divided up by Cliffe Fleet, Salt Fleet, a peripheral channel and numerous smaller ditches, an area threatened to become suburban sprawl and possibly a new airport. Egypt Bay is particularly good for saltmarsh plants and there are breeding and wintering birds on the Halstow Marshes. St Mary's Bay has a white beach composed entirely of broken shells, contrasting with the adjoining mud below high tide level. Herons find it a quiet environment in which to fish. Offshore, in still conditions, narrowboats make a run for the Medway, strangely small in front of the commercial shipping.

Allhallows Marshes leading across to Yantlet Creek

A water tower stands on the ridge above the pillbox, sea of caravans and dinghy park at Allhallows-on-Sea, the chimneys of Kingsnorth power station on the Medway also showing over the ridge.

The Yantlet Beacon is a daymark indicating the mouth of Yantlet Creek where Thames sailing barges used to serve the wharf. Just beyond the beacon is the London Stone, marking the end of the River Thames and the Medway Approach Area limit.

The Yantlet Demolition Range has to have the least satisfactory management of any range around the British coastline. A contact number for the range is not known by the Port of London Authority, coastguard, police, military national switchboard or Allhallows Yacht Club and they don't reply to letters. A semi-circle of ten orange

buoys is supposed to mark the danger area on the water but most of them are missing. The range is frequently in use and known a week in advance but additional use can arise at an hour's notice. Red flags are claimed to be warnings of the range's being in use, as would be expected. There is one at Cockleshell Beach and another inland at Lees Marshes, where there is a sentry box. Local anglers say these red flags are never taken down and that the range is in use only if there is a sentry in the box. The box cannot be seen from the water, meaning that the sentry cannot see anyone on the water, and it may be too rough to land to check. If anglers are sitting in the danger area there will be no activity. At low tide the mud of Roas Bank extends beyond the danger area. No other range in the country requires walkers and those in small boats to enter a danger area past a flying red flag when the range is not in use.

The Isle of Grain is no longer an island. Grain, at the end of the B2001, takes its name from the Old English greon, sand or mud depending on the size of the grains. The village is insignificant compared with the power station, the chimney of which is visible from much of the Thames Estuary. The Central Electricity Generating Board found themselves held to ransom by the trade unions during its construction, and consequently had to completely rewrite their contract procedures before letting any other large power station contracts go ahead and the lesson has been learned for all major civil engineering contracts. Offshore is the Grain Tower, a Martello Tower but looking more recent. It was at Nore Station in 1732 that the first light vessel was moored.

Here Medway gives way to Kent and Kentish Men give way to the Men of Kent.

Heading southeast involves crossing the narrow and well-buoyed Medway Approach Channel leading out past the Great Nore anchorage. A white light every 7 seconds at Garrison Point warns of a large vessel movement in the Medway or its approaches, but any such movement should be easily visible in plenty of time in good weather conditions. The ebb starts at HW Dover with a strong eddy northeast of Garrison Point during the ebb. Strong southwesterly winds can cause low water to stand for up to an hour and a half and strong northwesterly winds can cause a stand of up to two hours before low water. Heavy rain reduces the rate and duration of the flood and the converse applies for the ebb. A radio mast stands on Garrison Point above the the the car ferry jetty for Flushing.

Situated at the mouths of the Thames and Medway, Sheppey, at the ends of the A249 and A250, has always held an important strategic significance for England and yet has always been the island of sheep, too. Ptolemy mentioned its strategic defensive position in 161. To the Romans it was Insula Ovinium and to the Saxons Scaepige, both meaning island of sheep. The Danes attacked it in 798, 852 and 1004 and the Dutch invaded in

1667. Various kings have lived here. It now houses 32,000 people on the north side and still the marshes on the south side are left to the sheep.

The Blue Town area of **Sheerness** takes its name from the number of houses which were painted in Royal Navy paint. The coast continues low-lying to Minster. At Barton's Point a linear lake has become a coastal park with boat and windsurfer hire, pitch and putt course, model railway and picnic area. The Shingle Bank facing onto the Thames Estuary is the main windsurfing beach and has two sailing clubs.

The shallows were a feature after the Norman conquest. At the time the island had been divided up between four Norman barons. One of these was Robert de Shurland. Lord Robert had a violent temper and, when he came upon a group of mourners arguing with a priest who was refusing to bury a corpse until he had been paid, slew the priest. On reaching home he considered the implications of his act and decided to go to the king before the story reached him. The king's ship was moored conveniently off the coast at the time and Lord Robert rode his horse, Grey Dolphin, a great distance out through the shallow water to reach the king's ship. The king was so impressed with this feat that he granted Lord Robert a pardon. On returning to shore he met the Witch of Scrapsgate to whom he refused alms and who foretold that the horse which had just saved his life would later claim it. To break the curse he butchered his horse on the spot. Some time later he was walking along the beach with a friend when he found the skeleton. He related the tale, giving the skull a kick as he passed. The bone punctured his foot and he died from blood poisoning soon after.

Scrapsgate, with the White House restaurant and Playa public house, is the start of **Minster**, a surprisingly built-up area to see an owl hunting.

At Minster an area of cliff has been battered back and been extensively laid with French drains and a concrete seawall constructed. Minster Abbey, the parish church of St Mary and St Sexburga, was founded in 664 by Sexburga, the widow of a Saxon king. It was attacked by the Danes in 798 and 852, the nuns being killed on the second occasion. It is one of the oldest places of Christian worship in England. The nuns used the northern half and the parishioners the southern. It retains Saxon stonework, the Northwode 13th-century brasses, stone effigies of Sir Robert de

Shurland and Grey Dolphin and the tomb of Sir Thomas Cheyney, Henry VIII's treasurer.

Royal Oak Point is marked by a line of sunken barges, this line being continued with other obstructions for larger ships. The masts of a substantial modern ship break the surface at one point.

A caravan site tops the cliffs at East End. The beach is littered with boulders, some of stone, some of rounded balls of clay. Eocene and Pleistocene fossils are found along this beach.

At Warden Point, Old English for watch hill, one of the few pieces of woodland on the island can be found. Through the woods, on occasions, gallops the ghost of Sir John Sawbridge who lived in Warden Manor in the 17th century and who was said to have led the gang conducting the smuggling which was rife then. He is on his way to supervise the unloading of a cargo. From the manor a lost underground passage is thought to run to Shurland Hall.

Clay cliffs form the northern side of the island. They contain many slips and mud slides and much of Warden, including the church, has already been claimed by the sea. King Cnut lived at Shurland for a time. If it was here that he proved he did not have the authority to command the sea to stop then he is still making his point as the sea steadily advances inland. Pillboxes are amongst the victims as they lie upside down. This is the end of the Medway Approach Area and of Port of London Authority control. The coast now becomes low. Holiday huts, caravans and amusement arcades become thick on the ground at **Leysdown-on-Sea** at the end of the B2231. Metal stakes in the Bay break through the surface at intervals.

Standing behind one group of huts is Muswell Manor. Here, in 1901, J Moore-Brabazon, later Lord Brabazon of Tara, formed a ballooning club. The Short brothers joined it five years later and six Wright biplanes were built at a factory nearby. All the significant aviation pioneers flew from here and it was the start of the Royal Flying Corps, later

The mouth of the River Medway with Garrison Point and Sheerness on the left of the picture and the Grain Tower and Grain power station on the right

The beacon marking the line of obstructions at Royal Oak Point

The Bay fronting Warden and Leysdown-on-Sea. There has been heavy slipping

the Royal Air Force. Moore-Brabazon became the first British pilot to achieve a circular flight of 1.6km.

The final beach before Shell Ness is a naturist beach. The other kind of mussels run out in a bank from the shore.

The bank of brilliant white shells near Shell Ness

Running southeast to Shell Ness is a shanty town of holiday huts. When James II was trying to escape to France his boat ran aground here and was boarded by local fishermen who treated the king in less than royal manner.

At low tide the Columbia Spit can extend 4km northeast from Shell Ness. At the end lies one of the two beds which produce the oysters for which Whitstable is famous. Ships risk having to pay damages if they run aground here. Oyster beds continue to Reculver. A pillbox follows the last building in order to guard the entrance to the Swale. This is a gathering point for waders and is familiar territory to cormorants and oystercatchers.

A Thames sailing barge leaves the Swale

The Harty marshes were once the scene of salt workings, a Roman tile kiln has been found near Shell Ness and Oxford's Ashmolean Museum has a complete Bronze Age foundry from the Isle of Harty. An area of marsh with ground nesting birds such as redshank, lapwing, pochard and shoveler is edged by a bank of brilliant white shells.

Graveney Marshes form the South Swale Nature Reserve with large numbers of wildfowl and waders including Brent geese. From the mussel banks of the Pollard Spit there are shallow flats and sands in front of the coast to North Foreland. The Saxon Shore Way follows the coast round the Oaze and Whitstable Bay and then the coast becomes built-up from Seasalter and buoys marking a 15km/h speed limit are placed 300m offshore all the way to Reculver. A windmill is conspicuous on the top of Duncan Down and a golf course less so on the shore. **Whitstable** was a port for Canterbury. The name is from the Old English Witon stapol, pillar of the council of wise men. The world's first passenger steam railway, the Crab and Winkle line, served this route from 1830 to 1952.

Whitstable Harbour with a relatively large vessel docked

Whitstable harbour manages to squeeze in some large vessels for its small size, just 680m of quays. The town is a yachting centre as well as a resort. It has been known for its oysters since Roman times

and has the largest oyster hatchery in Europe. The Whitstable Oyster Fishing Company may call their best oysters Royal Whitstable Natives. There is a Whitstable oyster festival. A wood-panelled cinema is set in an old oyster warehouse and other attractive buildings include weatherboarded fishermen's cottages and black tarred boat sheds. The world's first diving helmet was invented here and the marine associations continue with the Whitstable Barge Race and waterski championships. Residents have included horror film actor Peter Cushing.

The agreeable waterfront continues with Tankerton Castle surrounded by trees and the Hotel Continental with architecture which would seem appropriate for the Low Countries. A hill is equipped with a ship's mast and cannons. A peculiar local feature is Whitstable Street, a narrow stone causeway which runs out into the sea for 700m at low tide and collects shells.

Beach huts line the shore towards Swalecliff where herring and blackbacked gulls hang about Long Rock. At the end of the seawall at Hampton, used by powerboats, a line of rocks run out to sea, submerging as the tide rises. Beyond the Hampton Inn is the Sea Cadets' TS Triumph.

Herne Bay, from the Old English hyrne, corner, was a fishing village with cod, bass and skate but became a resort in the 1830s. Its central feature was the pier, the second longest in the country at 1.2km until damaged by storms in 1978 and demolished the next year, leaving the ornate pierhead standing well offshore and the root of the pier developed as the Pier Sports Centre with roller skating, squash and a dancehall. The pavilion replaces the grand Pier Pavilion of 1910 which burnt down in 1970. There are original items surviving, notably the ornate 24m clocktower of 1837. The Herne Bay Museum and Gallery feature this Victorian resort, the pier, the archaeology and the fossils and there is a Herne Bay Sculpture Trail. With its high sunshine levels, Heron's Swimming Pool can make maximum use of such items as the flume and beach pool. Seafront gardens and a bandstand complete what a traditional resort should have. The Dolphin Hotel and Divers Arms add further coastal associations.

Much further offshore in the middle of the Thames Estuary are the Maunsell Naval and Army Forts on Shivering Sands and Red Sands, 13 of the original 21 forts remaining like so many balls on posts on the horizon.

30m earth cliffs, initially as a green bank, extend to Reculver from Beltinge where there is a prominent water tower.

Reculver was important because it guarded the northern end of what was formerly the Wantsum Channel, separating the Isle of Thanet from the mainland. The Romans built their Regulbium fort there in the 3rd century to resist the Saxons, some walls remaining. The ghostly crying of children is sometimes heard on stormy nights and babies' skeletons were found beneath the foundations in 1966 so this could be an example of ritual live burial sacrifice. In 669 King Egbert of Kent founded a monastery inside the fort, destroyed by

The twin Reculvers towers act as an important shipping landmark

The River Wantsum, formerly the Wantsum Channel inside the Isle of Thanet

the Vikings in the 9th century. The site of a 7th-century church by St Augustine was used as the site for the 12th-century church of St Mary which was demolished in 1809 and a new one built at Hillborough, after the sea washed away most of the fort and threatened the church. The Reculvers or Two Sisters are twin towers which remain, having been restored without their spires by Trinity House as a shipping landmark. The spires were originally added in the 16th century for Frances St Clare, the Benedictine abbess at Davington, after being shipwrecked with her sister, Isabel, who died from her injuries, as a memorial and landmark. Both are buried under the towers. The site is now part of a country park with a sea of caravans. It is a bird migration watchpoint.

Barnes-Wallis tested his bouncing bomb here. The Copperas Channel, Gore Channel and South Channel lead past the Margate Hook bank, heading on to the larger Margate Sand, both of which dry at low tide.

The embankment across the old Wantsum Channel is reinforced by stone groynes at intervals. On the other side from a mussel bank is the much diminished River Wantsum.

Plumpudding Island is also part of the mainland these days, crossed by the Wantsum Walk which is also a popular cycle route. Minnis Bay faces Margate Hook. The Minnies are drying ledges which continue round to Pegwell Bay. On top of these are chalk cliffs, the first chalk since Flamborough but very different now, low and in manicured blocks with neatly rounded edges, a massive seawall supporting a promenade around the bottom and built up on top. Indeed, virtually the whole of the cliff line of Thanet seems to be built up.

It begins with Birchington, claimed to be the largest village in Kent. The mediaeval church of All Saints has the 1882 grave of Victorian artist Dante Gabriel Rossetti.

Greenham Bay has the risk of rockfalls while in Epple Bay it is more likely to be golf balls. Westgate on Sea is red brick Victorian and Edwardian with landscaped gardens on a promontory, but mostly the buildings seem to be more like low-rise tower blocks. St Mildred's Bay lies between ledges and beyond Westbrook the Nayland Rock ledges occupy most of the bay so that it is almost possible to miss **Margate** harbour. Its 20m stone tower lighthouse on the end of John Rennie's stone pier of 1815 allowed steamboats to bring holidaymakers from London before the railway was built. Margate is from the Old English mere gate, sea gate. Margate Promenade Pier was damaged in storms in 1978 and has now been demolished. The resort was helped when Benjamin Beale invented the bathing machine here in 1753. The 19th-century listed Clock House has become the Maritime Museum covering maritime and navigation exhibits, Goodwin Sands wrecks, the RNLI and the restored dry-dock while the Old Town Hall is the Local History Museum covering the seaside, maritime matters, police and town silver while there is also a lifeboat museum. The Amusement Park was founded in 1920 with log flume, Bounty Ship swingboat, dodgems, miniature train, 43m wheel and more, claimed to be the largest seaside leisure complex in the south of England.

The B2051 climbs away from the A28 past the Ship Inn towards Cliftonville where the jaded air of Southend and the retirement hotels are repeated. The cliff railway has been dismantled and the road train now cuts short its route, yet there are still some interesting finds, like one of the world's smallest theatres, the Tom Thumb, in what was a double garage and a nearby Italian restaurant where the proprietor believes that the meal should be correct and the conversation stimulating. Margate Caves were discovered in 1798 and used as a dungeon, a church and by smugglers, the passages to the sea now having been sealed. The 2,000 year old Shell Grotto, discovered in 1835, was thought to be the only underground temple in the world, covering 190m^2.

Palm Bay with its promenade fronts Cliftonville where T S Eliot had a mild nervous breakdown while staying. Jet Ski World is located alongside for those who want their own.

Long Nose Spit runs out as a ledge in front of Foreness Point. Streams run southeast at HW Dover +0440 to HW Dover −0450, are weak and irregular until HW Dover −0120, run northwest until HW Dover +0040 and then are turbulent for the rest of the cycle.

At the far end of Botany Bay there is an old fort site above an arch at White Ness. The Castle Hotel at the back of Kingsgate Bay occupies an imposing position on top of the cliff at Hackemdown Point.

Herne Bay with the Pier Sports Centre on the remains of the pier, formerly the second longest in the country until damaged by storms in 1978

The Castle Hotel occupies a strategic position overlooking Kingsgate Bay. Beyond Joss Bay is the North Foreland lighthouse

A local resident was Frank Richards, author of *Billy Bunter*. The B2052 is now running along the cliffs. Joss Bay is a surfing venue.

North Foreland, where the Thames Estuary gives way to the Strait of Dover, is marked by the 26m white octagonal tower of 1790, the coal of which was replaced by 18 oil lamps because the glass could not be kept clean. There has been a light here since 1505, the current one with a range of 32km. Beneath it in 1665 was a four-day battle between Dutch and English fleets. The 39 steps down to Stone Bay gave John Buchan the title of his novel, part of which he wrote while his wife was convalescing here in 1914.

Cliffs increase in height to 37m to Ramsgate and flows are southwest from HW Dover +0420 and northeast from HW Dover –0140.

Mark on the entrance to Ramsgate Harbour

Steel added a striking staircase up the cliffs, since called Jacob's Ladder, and a dry-dock followed in 1791. The lighthouse on the West Pier was one of the first to have a revolving light, powered by a

Broadstairs with Bleak House prominent on the cliffs. This is where Charles Dickens wrote David Copperfield, using local characters

A prominent building in **Broadstairs** is the castellated Fort House, summer home of Charles Dickens where he wrote *David Copperfield*, renamed Bleak House in 1853 after he published this book. It is now the Dickens and Maritime Museum featuring the author, Kentish smuggling, Goodwin Sands exhibits from the *Sterling Castle* and Queen Victoria's bed. In *David Copperfield* Mary Strong was the model for Betsy Trotwood and her home now houses the Dickens House Museum. There is a Dickens Festival in June and a folk week in August. Wilkie Collins and Hans Christian Anderson visited.

The broad stairs in the name were stone steps built down the cliff to the shore in 1434. The harbour and pier were once owned by Henry VIII and the York Gate portcullis arch dates from the same time. In the 18th century it was a shipbuilding centre and it was a smuggling centre during the Napoleonic wars. The Crampton House Museum features the work of Victorian railway engineer Thomas Russell Crampton and includes a Broadstairs-Canterbury stagecoach. A weekly firework display takes place over Viking Bay and the Customs House water gala has been running for over 110 years.

The Italianate greenhouse of 1805 in the grounds of the home of Admiral Lord George Keith, in the King George VI Memorial Park at East Cliff, includes a vine imported from Corsica for Queen Caroline who liked grapes.

The Royal Harbour at **Ramsgate**, from the Old English hraefn, raven, was built after a bad storm in 1748 and completed in 1750 by John Smeaton, Samuel Wyatt and John Rennie. In 1754 Jacob

weight dropping within the tower and needing to be rewound each day. The lifeboat was also one of the first, operational from 1802, and holds the record for the number of lives saved because of its proximity to the Goodwin Sands, the graveyard of ships. George IV landed in 1820 and was well treated by the town, resulting in the designation, this being the only royal harbour in the UK. The Royal Harbour is commercial but contains two marinas. Outside is the Western Marine Terminal, Port Ramsgate, which has operated cross Channel services since 1981 to Dunkirk and Ostend and now has 3,300 sailings per year including high speed catamarans. A ferry movement is indicated by an orange flashing light on the East Pier, not the North Breakwater which extends it. Wellington sailed from here to Waterloo and St George's church has a stained glass window to the 82,000 men who landed from Dunkirk, nearly a quarter of them in Ramsgate.

There is a museum of the resort, port and archaeology and the 19th-century clock house houses the Maritime Museum featuring navigation, maritime history and the harbour. West Cliff Hall has historic cars, motorcycles and cycles, a model village houses 6,000m^2 of Tudor houses and there is a local museum in the library. Ramsgate is a town of 19th-century terraces and at Westcliff there is a boating pool. The award-winning A253 approaching the port was built by the innovative technique of using something like a giant chainsaw to cut 200mm slots 5m into the chalk, filled with concrete before further excavation took place, a technique which saved money and the demolition of 11 houses.

Sand builds up in the harbour entrance after northeasterly gales. There is an eddy off the South Breakwater with a northeastgoing stream and strong flows across the entrance, but streams are then weak to Deal, flowing southwest from HW Dover +0600 to the next HW Dover –0100 and northeast from Dover HW to HW Dover +0500.

The cliffs end at Pegwell. Pegwell Bay has a hovercraft slip which served the first international hoverport with a service to Calais from 1968, no longer in use except for maintenance. Beyond is Kent International Airport at Manston beyond the A256.

According to Sellar and Yeatman's spoof history, *1066 and All That*, Thanet was the place where all invaders of note landed, not particularly helpful as it was probably still an island at the time. However, Ebbsfleet probably saw two significant landings. In 449 Jutland chieftains Hengist and Horsa arrived with the Saxons and a banner showing a prancing white horse, now the badge of Kent. In 1949, the 1,500th anniversary, the *Hugin* replica was sailed from Denmark and is now on display at Cliffs End. St Augustine's Well is near where St Augustine landed in 597, celebrating his first mass in the presence of King Ethelbert, the site marked in 1884 by St Augustine's Cross. Two golf courses are fronted by a nature reserve and Pegwell Bay Country Park while the disused Richborough Power Station stands behind, the only obvious source of energy these days being a recent aerogenerator. The estuary of the River Stour has flows inwards from HW Dover –0450 and outwards from HW Dover +0200.

From Shell Ness, where there are fish traps, beacons and a wreck, the shore is followed by the combined Stour Valley Walk, White Cliffs Country Trail and Saxon Shore Way, overlooking the drying mud and sand of Sandwich Flats.

Richborough was a Roman port. Eight centuries ago Sandwich was a coastal port. Now it is 3km inland but the history does not go away. On misty nights a Roman might be seen fighting a Saxon on the shore. During the second world war soldiers on defence watch saw a cohort of Romans march into the sea.

The Battle of Sandwich took place in Sandwich Bay on St Bartholomew's Day in 1217. The French were led by the English traitor Eustace the Monk, who was able to turn his ship invisible by magic. Stephen Crabbe of Sandwich found the ship, perhaps with a little magic of his own, and cut off Eustace's head, making the ship visible again. The English won and the hospital in **Sandwich**, which treated the wounded, was renamed St Bartholomew's after the victory, a name it retains.

Along the back of the bay are the finest dunes in southeast England with a nature reserve and growths of bedstraw broomrape. A bird observatory is surrounded by the Prince's, Royal St George's and Royal Cinque Ports Golf Links. It also has tolls on the road on each side.

A shingle beach at the back of the South Downs is unbroken except for the Sandwich Bay Estate until arrival at the Sandown Castle site, the start of Deal, where there is limited parking, approached up a steep gravel beach and over some large rocks.

A Stour estuary channel mark

Distance
From Shoeburyness to Deal is 123km
Campsites
Shoeburyness, Linford, Sheerness, Minster, Leysdown-on-Sea, Seasalter, Whitstable, Herne Common, Maypole, Reculver, St Nicholas at Wade, Westgate on Sea, Manston, Ramsgate, Sandwich, Walmer
Youth Hostels
Medway, Canterbury, Margate, Broadstairs, Dover
OS 1:50,000 Sheets
178 Thames Estuary
179 Canterbury and East Kent
Imray Charts
2100 Kent Coast
C1 Thames Estuary – Tilbury to North Foreland and Orfordness (1:120,000)
C8 North Foreland to Beachy Head and Boulogne (1:115,000)
Y18 River Medway Sheerness to Rochester with River Thames, Sea Reach (1:20,000)
Stanfords Allweather Charts
4 Essex Rivers
5 Thames Estuary (1:115,000)
8 North Kent Coast
9 North Foreland to Selsey Bill (1:190,000)
20 Dover Strait (1:123,500)
Admiralty Charts
SC 323 Dover Strait, Eastern Part (1:75,000)
SC 1183 Thames Estuary (1:100,000)
SC 1185 River Thames Sea Reach (1:25,000)
1186 River Thames – Canvey Island to Tilbury (1:12,500)
SC 1607 Thames Estuary, Southern Part (1:50,000)
1827 Harbours on the Southeast Coast of England. Margate (1:7,500). Broadstairs (1:5,000). Approaches to Ramsgate (1:12,500). Ramsgate (1:5,000). Pegwell Bay and the River Stour (1:12,500)
SC 1828 Dover to North Foreland (1:37,500). Ramsgate (1:5,000)

SC 1834 River Medway. Garrison Point to Folly Point (1:12,500)
SC 2484 River Thames – Hole Haven to London Bridge (1:25,000)
2571 The Swale – Whitstable to Harty Ferry (1:12,500). Whitstable Harbour (1:5,000)
3683 Sheerness and Approaches (1:12,500) Sheerness (1:6,250)
SC 5605 Chichester to Ramsgate, including Dover Strait
SC 5606 Thames Estuary, Ramsgate to Canvey Island
Tidal Constants
Southend: HW Dover +0120, LW Dover +0130
Benfleet Creek: HW Dover +0140, LW Dover +0130
Thames Haven: HW Dover +0140, LW Dover +0130
Yantlet Creek: Dover +0120
Sheerness: Dover +0120
Hartyferry: Dover +0120
Whitstable Approaches: HW Dover +0130, LW Dover +0140
Herne Bay: Dover +0120
Margate: HW Dover +0050, LW Dover +0100
Broadstairs: HW Dover +0040, LW Dover +0110
Ramsgate: HW Dover +0030, LW Dover +0010
Richborough: HW Dover +00 20, LW Dover +0030
Deal: HW Dover +0020, LW Dover +0010
Sea Areas
Thames, Dover
Range
Yantlet
Rescue
Inshore lifeboats: Southend-on-Sea, Sheerness, Whitstable, Margate, Ramsgate, Walmer
All weather lifeboats: Sheerness, Margate, Ramsgate
Maritime Rescue Centres
Thames, 01255 675518
Dover, 01304 210008

53 STRAIT OF DOVER

Britain's front line and the world's busiest waters

We sailed then by Beachy, by Fairlee and Dung'ness,
Then bore straight away for the South Foreland Light.

The buttresses of Sandown Castle date from the 16th century but little now remains, more a glorified rockery than fortifications. The rocks forming the beach defences are a greater obstruction to getting to and from the water and may be reinforced by a high tide dump and a line of anglers after cod, codling, whiting and flatfish. Larks serenade the dilemma.

Sandown Castle is now little more than a rockery

Fishing boats work off the beach in **Deal** itself and the Deal Rowing Club are also able to get their rowing boats afloat. The 300m pier of 1957 was

Deal has the only post war pleasure pier in Britain

built for larger craft, Britain's only post-war pier of its kind. Buried in the churchyard of St George's church of 1709 by Sir Cloudesley Shovell is Nelson's Captain Parker. Nelson himself stayed in the Royal Hotel to meet Lady Hamilton and Queen Victoria and Winston Churchill often stayed. The nearby Admiral Penn is named after William Penn who sailed from here in 1682 to found Pennsylvania. The time ball tower was used so that boats could set their timepieces to GMT for navigational purposes, the ball dropping at 1pm. One of only four working ones left in the world, it is now controlled electronically from Greenwich. The building contains a museum of

Deal's time ball tower is one of only four working ones left in the world

communications and telegraphy alongside the A258. There was a thriving naval yard from 1703, one of the most important in England, and the centre of the town was used by smugglers in the 18th century. The town hall of 1803 has a museum with Roman pottery, local trading tokens, the robes of the Baron of the Cinque Ports (of which this was a non corporate member) and portraits of William III, William IV and Winston Churchill. The first Royal Marine barracks were built here in 1794 and the Royal Marines School of Music and Barracks contain a Royal Marines History Room. Deal Maritime and Local History Museum contains model and full sized boats, figureheads and compasses. The 18th-century buildings and sea shanty festival on the seafront recall the era, but the stone marking where Julius Caesar landed in 55BC to begin the Roman conquest of Britain takes more imagination. In Daniel Defoe's imagination this is where Gulliver began most of his travels. In Old English times it was a dael or valley.

Beyond the Downs are the Goodwin Sands, the Ship Swallower, 19km x 8km, 6km off, but moving towards the coast. These have claimed innumerable vessels and the lifeboat stationed in Deal since 1865 is one of seven within range of the Goodwins. Nevertheless, the Goodwins did not prove an adequate defence. Deal Castle, built in 1539, was Henry VIII's largest coastal defence and is the largest castle on the south coast. In Tudor rose shape with a circular central keep, six gun bastions, six lower crescent shaped bastions and a dry ditch, it had 119 guns and now features a coastal defences exhibition.

Strong flows begin south at HW Dover +0420 and north at HW Dover −0150.

Walmer was another non-corporate Cinque Port with a Tudor rose castle built by Henry VIII near the shore. It fell to the Parliamentarians in the Civil War in 1642, being recaptured briefly by the Kentish army in 1648. The original Wellington boots are here, Wellington being resident from 1829 until his death here in 1852. It was the residence of the Lord Wardens of the Cinque Ports from 1708 and was visited by the late warden, the Queen Mother. The Beauchamps lived in the castle,

Camber

Hiding behind boats on the beach, Deal Castle was Henry VIII's largest coastal defence

recorded as the Flyte family in Evelyn Waugh's *Brideshead Revisited*. The castle has an 18th-century panelled interior and the most notable garden is the Queen Mother's Garden, laid out for her 95th birthday, but most of the garden is as designed by Pitt the Younger in 1795 with a moat garden, woodland walk, boxed yew hedge and croquet lawn.

A swimming area at Oldstairs Bay and eccentric seaside architecture are aspects of **Kingsdown**. This is where the Downs (land rather than sea) are severed and the white cliffs begin in earnest. Occasionally, a white golf ball may come down off the course on Hope Point. More to the point, it could be a fall of chalk, leaving chalk debris in the sea. Otherwise it is just those uncompromising white cliffs glistening in the sun and the throb of ship engines out in the Strait of Dover. This is the world's busiest shipping lane, complicated by the cross Channel traffic. The Dover Strait Traffic Separation Scheme acts as a dual carriageway for ships, complete with central reserve and Inshore

successive invaders. Pillboxes occur at strategic positions and the granite obelisk of the Dover Patrol Memorial is a reminder of a wartime job which was very exposed.

St Margaret's at Cliffe at St Margaret's Bay has been the normal setting out point for cross Channel

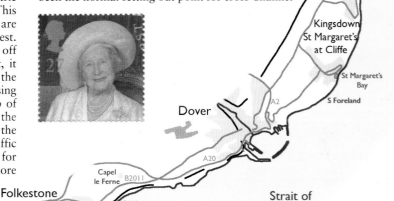

swimmers, not now encouraged, this being just 35km from Cap Griz Nez in France, visible on a clear day, close enough to shell across the Channel in both world wars. The black pebble beach is served by an ice cream seller and toilets, having a holiday camp close by. The church has a window to the memory of the 1987 Zeebrugge ferry capsize victims. Local residents included Noel Coward and also Ian Fleming, who would have used the bus service from Deal to London, the 007. Around the bay are found ivy and carrot broom rapes. The Bay Museum has maritime and Noel Coward exhibits and a Bronze Age skeleton. Above the bay the Pines Garden has 2ha of trees, shrubs, flowers, a lake, a Romany caravan and a bronze Churchill statue of 1972 by Oscar Nemon. Blackbacked gulls, cormorants and jellyfish ignore a hole cut in the chalk cliff face and propped with a brick pillar, suggesting some military purpose in the past.

South Foreland is where the east coast really turns to become the south coast. On top are a white windmill and two disused lighthouses, one a 21m

St Margaret's Bay, starting point for cross Channel swims

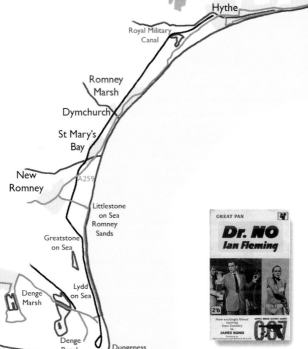

Traffic Zone. The authorities are not keen to see small craft crossing.

Being the nearest point to the Continent has had major military implications over the centuries. This is Britain's front line, the first place to be visited by

The white cliffs at South Foreland with Dover Harbour beyond

Dover Castle, Britain's oldest, strongest and one of the largest, seen over the Western Docks

white castellated tower of 1843 which was used in 1898 by Marconi for the first ship to shore radio transmission.

The Dover Harbour Limit includes Fan Bay and Langdon Bay with wrecks at the bottom of the cliffs, including a historic wreck with a 75m radius exclusion zone. On the cliffs are wild cabbage, a memorial, aerials, the Langdon Battery and the Maritime Rescue Co-ordination Centre.

The current outer harbour at Dover was built from 1892 to 1902 for the Grand Fleet. It is the busiest port in Europe, the principal cross Channel terminal for car ferries and catamarans to Calais, Boulogne, Dunkirk, Ostend and Zeebrugge from the six ferry berths and cargo terminals in Eastern Docks while the Western Docks have hovercraft to Calais, a cruise terminal, a catamaran terminal and, formerly, a Jetfoil terminal. It is the only Head Port of the Cinque Ports which remains a significant harbour.

Port control is on the end of the 900m Eastern Arm so travelling westwards gives the advantage of being able to stop outside the window and be

saved when the Romans demolished it in 270 and left it under the ramparts of a fort extension, the most extensive area of Roman painting to have been found north of the Alps. The 2nd-century Roman pharos is one of two lighthouses they built in Dover. Originally 24m high, 12m of Roman flint rubble in tufa ashlar with mortar and tile reinforcing make it one of the highest remaining Roman structures in Europe. The current top is 15th century, forming the belltower of the Anglo-Saxon church of St Mary Castro with 13th-century two seater sedilia and double piscina in the chancel, greatly restored in the 19th century.

These structures are within the walls of Dover Castle, described as the Key to England. It is England's oldest, strongest and one of its largest fortresses, covering 32ha with a large irregular outer bailey. An 1180s three-storey square keep and curtain with square open-backed wall towers and barbicans by Maurice the Engineer for Henry II, are the finest of their kind. There is a 13th-century outer curtain wall with D-plan wall towers. The castle stands prominently above the town and has been garrisoned continuously since Norman times. It has Queen Elizabeth's Pocket Pistol, a 7m ornamental gun given to her by the Dutch. It was where Churchill watched the Battle of Britain and was the nerve centre for Operation Dynamo, where he planned the successful Dunkirk evacuation of 338,000 members of the British Expeditionary Force and French troops with Vice Admiral Ramsay when 45,000 had been considered a theoretical maximum. The castle has an Iron Age fort and has the only underground barracks in Britain, while 60m below the castle are the warren of secret wartime tunnels which form Hellfire

identified. Making contact with Port Control lets them know what the paddler is planning and gives information on what shipping movements are due. Port Control may allow passage through the harbour and will send the harbour patrol launch as an escort, throwing up an awkward wash if it gets too close. While waiting for clearance the floating current meter should not be touched as it has a 75m radius exclusion zone, but it is a useful guide to what the current is doing as it passes. Each entrance has inward and outward flows in different places at nearly all times, giving turbulence in addition to anything resulting from ferries' manœuvring. The Southern Breakwater is 1.3km long.

Dover takes its name from the River Dour or from the British Celtic dobra, water. Dover Museum has a Bronze Age boat which, at 3,550 years old, is probably the world's oldest seagoing boat, thought capable of carrying a significant load across the Channel. The museum also has a Roman section and a 1940s air-raid street scene. To the Romans Dover was Portus Dubris, the headquarters of the Roman northern fleet, Classis Britannica. A Roman mansion of about 200 is one of the best examples in Britain with painted frescoes and hypocausts and now with an exhibition of Roman Dover. 37m^2 of painted plaster was

Corner, complete with hospital. Exhibitions include a 1216 siege display, Henry VIII's court in the keep, a model of the Battle of Waterloo, armour, cannons, the history of the Princess of Wales' Royal Regiment, spy equipment and a nuclear bunker. The castle has been used for installing the Lord Warden of the Cinque Ports, has been used for filming Zefirelli's *Hamlet* and, not surprisingly, has a ghost. It was also used for filming *Those Magnificent Men in their Flying Machines*. On the cliffs is a memorial to Louis Blériot, where he landed after flying the Channel in 1909, and there is a statue to Stewart Rolls who flew the Channel both ways in a single flight the following year. Another statue celebrates Captain Matthew Webb, in 1875 the first person to swim the Channel.

In 1670 Charles II conducted the secret Treaty of Dover whereby he promised Louis XIV to declare war on the Dutch, convert to Catholicism and to make England Catholic again.

The 12th-century church of St Mary the Virgin, largely rebuilt in the 19th century as the number of burials under the floor was making it unstable, has had major connections with the Lords Warden of the Cinque Ports.

There is a Victorian Old Town Gaol Museum and a White Cliffs Experience.

At the entrance to the Eastern Docks the A2 and A20 meet, a significant traffic terminus. Further along the seafront is a panel taken from the German Battery Todt near Calais by Allied troops in 1944. There is also the Stade, the fishermen's beach, across which not all Dover sole pass. To its west is the Wellington Dock with the restored *Sorceress* in which Edward VII had meetings with Lily Langtree.

On the Western Heights are the foundations of a 12th-century Knights Templar church, extensive 18 to 19th-century fortifications, parts of a moat around a former 19th-century fort, the Citadel and the Grand Shaft, a triple spiral staircase connecting Victorian barracks with the town, plus a current young offender institution.

submarine power cables land so the wreck off the point was probably not appreciated.

Although there are the remains of a Roman villa on East Cliff, **Folkestone**, named after the Old English man Folca, was a fishing village which became a later Cinque Port. Telford's harbour work of 1808–20 was unusual in that slabs up to 2 tonnes each were laid at 45° on broken stone. The town became a resort from the 1840s and the 450m South Pier was added in the late 19th century. Today it has a catamaran link to Boulogne. On display is a Russian hunter killer submarine.

It was unusual for a resort in not having a seafront. Instead there are the Leas, a 1.6km long

Samphire Hoe and the Shakespeare Cliff looking roughly along the line of the Channel Tunnel.

To the west of the harbour is the 110m Shakespeare Cliff which takes its name from a passage in *King Lear*. Running through the cliff in twin high Gothic arch cuts visible from the water is the Shakespeare Cliff Tunnel of 1.3km, 3.7m wide x 8.5m high, separated by a 3m pier because of the poor ground conditions. Passing below is the Channel Tunnel, together with false starts in 1881, 1882 and 1972. If the Samphire Hoe Country Park looks like a slightly landscaped pile of Channel Tunnel spoil retained in vertical sheet piling, there can be no accusations of deception. It is crossed by the Saxon Shore Way and North Downs Way long distance footpaths.

The final major rail tunnel is the 1.8km Abbot's Cliff Tunnel of 1840–4 where the cliff was close to the high water mark. It included a number of shafts driven in from a road at the base of the cliff with the spoil being tipped into the sea. In the process the Lydden Spout gushed forth and was incorporated into the design.

Abbot's Cliff has the best of the listening ear devices. Others were set up at Hythe, Dymchurch, Greatstone and Denge. They were used to detect the sound of approaching enemy aircraft, but climatic conditions made them unreliable and they were replaced by radar. Sculptures of them have been erected. At Capel-le-Ferne on the B2011 above East Wear Bay is a Battle of Britain memorial.

Below this is the Warren, an unstable area of chalk on gault clay which is slipping seawards, slips having been recorded since 1765, ten of them having interrupted railway traffic since 1844. It took its present form in 1915 when a 3km section moved 50m seawards, resulting in closure of the railway for 4 years. The upper part is known as Little Switzerland and there is a caravan site near the shore.

There are more Martello Towers before Copt Point which has a visitor centre and where

Folkestone's cliff railway up to the Leas

clifftop lawn and gardens promenade. To get up and down, a 30m high 40° water-powered cliff railway was installed in 1885, the first on the south coast. The lower terminal has its ticket office, waiting room, pump room and offices listed. A second lift was added in 1890 but was taken out of use in 1960 after an accident, by which time there was already a decline in demand. The other rail related structure just visible from the sea is the yellow brick Foord Viaduct of 1843. 230m long with 19 arches up to 24m high, it was the only major structure on the South Eastern Railway between Dover and London. As at Folkestone Warren, any train other than the Golden Arrow pulled by a rectangular Merchant Navy or Battle of Britain class steam engine crossing this viaduct just does not look right.

St Mary and St Eanswythe's church is part 13th century on the site of a 7th-century Saxon nunnery. Also old, the high street is steep and cobbled. The town has an 1895 bandstand and a statue of William Harvey, who was born here in 1578 and discovered the circulation of blood.

The heavily slipped Folkestone Warren

An event of note is the Shepway Air Festival with fireworks, classic and vintage cars and motorbikes and street entertainment and music. The Sunday market on the front is the largest in the southeast. The Rotunda amusement park has a log flume, bouncy pirate ship and other entertainments.

Flows start southwest at HW Dover +0320 at up to 3km/h and the other way from HW Dover –0200 at up to 4km/h, at which time an eddy forms in the harbourmouth.

There is a picnic site before Mill Point and, after it, the Mermaid for those who prefer to be served.

A 5km parade, esplanade and sea wall run to Hythe, passing a castle built in the 1530s by Henry VIII and a Martello Tower with a Bofors gun inside.

The A259 comes alongside at Sandgate and is to stay fairly close until St Mary's Bay. Fishermen's and coastguard cottages are squeezed in below the cliffs at **Sandgate** and H G Wells built himself a house here. The Royal Military Canal begins, moves away from the coast, leaving room for a golf course, and adds to the defences of the Martello Towers which now become more frequent.

Hythe, Old English for wharf, was a port from Roman times but silted up in the reign of Charles II and is now playing fields. It was a Cinque Port and is now a resort. In 1786 Lionel Lukin converted a Northumberland fishing boat as the first shore based lifeboat. The town received its charter from King Ethelred in 732. St Leonard's church of 1080 has a 13th-century chancel and a crypt containing 2,000 skulls and 8,000 thigh bones from the 13th and 14th centuries plus relics of the Battle of Waterloo, one of two surviving English ossuaries.

Large numbers displayed in the vicinity of two Martello Towers are part of the Hyde Ranges. Range safety craft may allow transit of the area. The ranges are the start of Romney Marsh with sheep grazing, for which the first of the drainage sluices discharges between Dymchurch Redoubt and a holiday centre. For 5.6km Dymchurch Wall follows, a huge embankment which may be Roman. Further work was done on it in Henry VIII's reign. Rennie was consulted in 1803 and it was faced in the 1820s and 1830s with Kentish ragstone from Hythe, in 1892, in the 1930s with Welsh granite and in the 1960s. This does not make it a pleasant place to land in surf but it protects Romney Marsh and Dymchurch, which is 2.3m below high water level. Of the protecting Martello Towers, a 10m one in **Dymchurch** is perhaps the best preserved of all, has an 11kg gun and was used as a lookout point for smugglers in the 19th century and as an observation point for the 1940 Dunkirk evacuation. The Day of Syn is an annual smuggling fête based on the 18th-century fictional smuggler and vicar, Dr Syn. The Norman parish church dates from 1150. A 1574 courtroom with the Law of the Levels was used by the Lords

A section of D Day Mulberry Harbour on Romney Sands. The tower and the power stations are landmarks where others are in short supply

The best preserved of all the Martello Towers at Dymchurch

of the Level of Romney Marsh, who controlled the marsh drainage. These days amusement arcades and funfairs for holidaymakers seem to be more the village's way of life.

St Mary's Bay with its holiday camps is where Edith Nesbit, author of the *Railway Children*, used to live next to the railway. New Sewer, one of the marsh's major drainage channels, discharges through a sluice here. A golf course separates the sluice from Littlestone-on-Sea, marked by a prominent tower. Littlestone and Greatstone were banks of shingle at the mouth of the River Rother until the Great Storm of 1287 switched the estuary to the other side of Romney Marsh and left the port of Romney as an inland village. **New Romney**, the capital of Romney Marsh, was a Cinque Port and the usual meeting place for the Portsmen's Court of Brotherhood and Guestling. St Nicholas' mediaeval church has a 30m tower which was used as a shipping landmark.

The village is also the headquarters of the Romney, Hythe and Dymchurch Railway which runs along the coast for 22km between Hythe and Dungeness. Built for a millionaire racing driver, it is the world's smallest public railway, the 380mm gauge trains being to a third scale. Opened in 1927, it was used during the second world war to move troops and goods. The longest train had 54 coaches. Trains run at 40km/h with steam and diesel engines. Even if not visible from the water, the smoke is seen and the American style horns heard. The railway headquarters also has two model railways and a toy and model museum.

Romney Sands are actually quite silty and a section of 1944 Mulberry Harbour built for the D-Day landings is stranded here. Covered in barnacles and mussels, it has two ladders on the landward side which give access to the top. Weak flows follow the coast.

A continuous line of houses extends through Greatstone-on-Sea to Lydd-on-Sea. Behind a holiday camp is Lydd Airport with light aircraft mostly landing parallel to the coast.

Fishing boats of reasonable size are winched up on the beach which is now of shingle. In the 19th century the locals wore shingle shoes made of wood which acted like snowshoes. Dungeness has the most extensive area of shingle in Britain, growing eastwards with north–south ridges.

The railway turns in a loop near the point and there are some huts made from old railway carriages. Dominating this part of the coast are the nuclear power stations.

The deep water and Inshore Traffic Zone come close to this point which is also susceptible to sudden fogs. The beach is steepest with fastest currents at the corner. The death toll was 1,000 per year here in 1615 when the first of five successive lighthouses was built. The 1862 light was one of the first in England to be electrically powered although it was later changed to oil. The 1904 light was superseded in 1961 when the new power station blocked the sightline. The latest one is a 43m slim black cylinder with white bands.

The change in direction of the coast is such that a change in sea state is likely, with the added complication of significant numbers of anglers with lines out round the point.

Beyond several square kilometres of gravel on what is recorded as Denge Beach, on which Halfway Bush is sufficient of a landmark to be indicated on the OS map, Denge Marsh has gravel pits and a 5km² RSPB nature reserve, from which public access is prohibited. This is a migration point for waders and warblers with 270 species having been recorded including lapwings, herons, swans, little terns, firecrests, stone curlews and various ducks.

The coastline is low to Hastings and the 8km which front **Lydd** Ranges are featureless. There is a range safety craft. Vessels may pass through but should follow instructions. In West Road Kent gives way to East Sussex before cottages and the aerial of the range lookout at Jury's Gap mark the return of the road. There is some parking space next to the lookout's hut.

Distance
From Deal to Jury's Gap is 64km
Campsites
Walmer, Martin Mill, Capel-le-Ferne, Folkestone, Donkey Street, New Romney, Camber
Youth Hostels
Dover, Hastings
OS 1:50,000 Sheets
179 Canterbury and East Kent
189 Ashford and Romney Marsh
Imray Charts
2100 Kent Coast
C8 North Foreland to Beachy Head and Boulogne (1:115,000)
Stanfords Allweather Charts
9 North Foreland to Selsey Bill (1:190,000)
20 Dover Strait (1:123,500)
30 Sussex Coast
Admiralty Charts
SC 323 Dover Strait, Eastern Part (1:75,000)
SC 536 Beachy Head to Dungeness (1:75,000)
1698 Dover (1:6,250)
SC 1828 Dover to North Foreland (1:37,500).
SC 1892 Dover Strait, Western Part (1:75,000)
1991 Harbours on the South Coast of England. Folkestone Harbour (1:5,000)
SC 5605 Chichester to Ramsgate, including Dover Strait
Tidal Constants
Deal: HW Dover +0020, LW Dover +0010
Dover
Folkestone: Dover –0010
Dungeness: HW Dover –0010, LW Dover –0020
Rye Approaches: Dover
Sea Area
Dover
Ranges
Hythe, Lydd
Rescue
Inshore lifeboats: Walmer, Littlestone-on-Sea, Rye Harbour
All weather lifeboats: Ramsgate, Dover, Dungeness
Maritime Rescue Centre
Dover, 01304 210008

Dungeness power stations and lighthouse

The lookout point at Jury's Gap with the bunting out

Fishing boats on the beach at Dungeness

54 EAST SUSSEX

Then a very great warman, called Billy the Norman,
Cried 'Hang it! I never liked my land;
It would be more handy to leave this Normandy,
And live on yon beautiful Island.'

From Jury's Gap at the end of the Jury's Gut Sewer Broomhill Sands lead along the back of Rye Bay to Camber Sands where Pontins have a holiday camp. Dunes are studded with second world war pillboxes, bunkers and gun emplacements which protected the entrance to the River Rother and now give shelter to a golf course.

Seas break heavily onto the bar with southwesterly winds, the river channel being protected by training walls which cover at half tide and militarily by a pillbox. Flows inwards start at HW Dover –0520 at up to 9km/h and outwards less strongly from HW Dover.

Streams in the bay are weak but there is the added complexity of many gill nets. The whole coast from here to Selsey Bill is a scallop fishing ground.

Dolphins also fish while birds hunting food include blackheaded gulls, oystercatchers, cormorants and turnstones. Rye Harbour Nature Reserve forms a major part of a 7km^2 SSSI with shingle ridges, saltmarsh, grazing marsh, arable fields and gravel pits. It has one of the finest examples of shingle vegetation in Britain with rare wild flowers, dragonflies, other insects and frogs with good wildfowl in winter and terns breeding in summer.

An indication of the rate of change of the geography of this area is that Camber Castle, built in Tudor times to defend the mouth of the Rother, is now nearly 2km from both the river and the sea and Rye Harbour, 2km seawards of Rye, is well over a kilometre from the sea. Winchelsea Beach is over a kilometre from the old sea cliffs at **Winchelsea**, at the foot of which is the Royal Military Canal running behind Pett Level and ceasing its military defence duties at Cliff End where there are dragon's teeth second world war concrete blocks. A large white house has been built to look like a castle. On Hog Hill a windmill is conspicuous.

The shoreline is a well-groyned steep beach, the level horizon broken only by the buildings of Winchelsea Beach.

A historic wreck at the approach to Cliff End has a 75m radius exclusion zone round it.

Dolphin off
Winchelsea Beach

Cliff End and the
cliffs return after
Romney Marsh

One source for material being deposited around Rye Bay is Fairlight Cove where erosion is resulting in houses being lost over the cliffs despite a series of reefs providing protection in the centre of the village. Covered with mussels, these are frequented by blackbacked and herring gulls. On the west side of the village is a naturist beach, protected by gorse bushes below a white coastguard lookout tower, a radar scanner and an aerial or two although one of them, like the tower of Fairlight's Victorian St Andrew's church, is hidden by the cliffs. On the shore is Lover's Seat where the girl concerned waited for her sweetheart to be rowed ashore from his ship. This part of the coast is the 2.1km^2 Hastings Country Park with woodpeckers, linnets, greenfinches and redpolls, forming part of the High Weald AONB.

Hastings was named after Haest's tribe. The town was subdued by King Offa of Mercia on his way to Bexhill in 771. In the 9th century the locals rose against the sleeping occupying Danes but they were woken by a cockerel, as a result of which the locals played cock-in-the-pot on Shrove Tuesday until the 19th century, throwing sticks to break a pot, the winner taking the cockerel inside. The town had its own mint in Saxon times, run by the Dunk family who still live here. In 1287 much of the town was washed away in a great storm. It declined from a major port to a fishing town with many attacks by the French between 1337 and 1453 in the Hundred Years War, the remains of the town walls dating from this time. It became a Cinque Port, probably the original one. There was smuggling in the 19th century but it became one of the first resorts.

Hastings has two cliff railways. East Hill Cliff Railway of 1903 is the steepest in Britain. It leads from the Stade where Europe's largest fleet of beach launched fishing boats are got afloat over rollers. Tall black huts were used from 1750 for drying nets because they were charged rent

South
Downs

Seaford

R Cuckmere

Hope Pt

Seven Sisters

Birling
Gap

Beachy
Head

English
Channel

according to their frontage. These huts are unique and some are featured at a fishing museum in a former Victorian fishermen's church with a 1909 lugger, the first horse capstan, model fishing and lifeboats and figureheads. The fishermen's beach has squid, octopus and cuttlefish. The Shipwreck Heritage Centre is Britain's only specialist shipwreck museum and has finds from 3,000 years of wrecks. Undersea World has the live denizens of the deep, seen from an underwater tunnel. Also here is the Stade Family Fun Park including Swan Lake. The Old Town was the original fishing village. The lifeboat station, begun in 1858, is located near a ruined detached harbour arm.

The A259 runs along the front. Despite the appeals of the people of Hastings and of motorists for a bypass, it has been refused. Perhaps the congestion is the reason why adjacent beaches in the centre of town remain largely deserted, even at the height of the holiday season.

The West Hill Cliff Railway of 1891 runs through a brick tunnel and a natural cave. St Clement's Caves contain over 4,000m^2 of sandstone passages and caves, used for presenting Smugglers Adventure. St Clement's church has a 1066 brass-rubbing centre. A Flower Makers' Museum has had the biggest exhibition of flower making tools in Europe since 1910 and further entertainment comes with Treasure Island and its boating lake. The Old Town Hall Museum of Local History in the Georgian building of 1823 has the history of Hastings, the battle and the Cinque Ports, maritime history and John Logie Baird who invented television locally.

A bungalow poised ready to fall over the cliff at Fairlight Cove

The ruined Hastings Castle, begun in 1066, was the first Norman castle in Britain, built by the Count of Eu. It covered 4.5ha and features an 11th-century siege tent and the Battle of Hastings. The circular St Mary in the Castle Regency church hosts jazz breakfasts. One of the most significant churchmen was Thomas a' Becket who was dean here.

Fishing boats drawn up on the beach at Hastings

The 1872 pier is 280m long with a ballroom and hosts pop concerts. Near the end is the Conqueror's Stone where William ate lunch after landing from France. His every move seems to have been documented. The White Rock Theatre has the Hastings Embroidery, 74m long by the Royal School of Needlework, featuring 900 years of history from 1066 including the Cinque Ports, Spanish Armada, Cabot, Raleigh, Nelson, Trafalgar and the *Mayflower*. The Museum and Art Gallery features the round the world voyage of the *Sunbeam* in 1876/7 plus fish, seabirds, maritime paintings, pottery, ironwork and ceramics. There is the world's oldest chess congress at the end of the year and Hastings Week with craft fairs, sports, Norman archery and poetry competitions around October 14th, the anniversary of the battle. An unlikely local resident was Archie Belaney, better known as the Red Indian environmentalist Grey Owl.

in the 1880s by Lord De La Warr. In 1935 the De La Warr Pavilion was built by the B2182 along the front and 3km long promenade and is a grade 1 Modernist building being restored with its theatre, exhibitions, bars and restaurant. The town has a museum, a bandstand and an Edwardian festival in May with 9 days in period costume. Obelisks mark the start and finish of the world's first international motor race in 1902, remembered each year with the Bexhill 100 classic and vintage car rally.

Offshore, Jenny's Stool and My Lord's Rock draw attention to the shortage of self-respecting mineral samples in the area. The coast continues low to Beachy Head. This Jewel of the South Coast was the first place to permit mixed bathing. Now there is naturist use between the beach huts at the end of the town and Norman's Bay.

Waller's Haven drains Hooe Level to Norman's Bay and Pevensey Haven does the same for the Pevensey Levels to Pevensey Bay. On 28th

Marine Court at St Leonards, stacked up like the decks on a cruise liner

St Leonards was built in the 1880s by James Burton as a new town and included the Mercatoria area for a market and Lavatoria Square for washerwomen. There is a promenade and the 1930s Marine Court was built to look like an ocean liner with sun decks. Many members of royalty have stayed in the Royal Victoria Hotel. The parish church replaces one of Adrian and Sir Giles Gilbert Scott destroyed by a flying bomb in 1944. Robert Tressell's *Ragged Trousered Philanthropists* was based on the town. From here the railway runs along the front to Pevensey.

At Bulverhythe there are dinosaur footprints at low tide and there is a 100m radius exclusion zone round the 1748 wreck of the Dutch East Indiaman *Amsterdam* near Bopeep Rocks. The nursery rhyme, written for the daughter of the landlord of the Bo-Peep public house in the 18th century, is not as innocent as it seems. Sheep were smugglers and tails were casks of French brandy.

Bexhill, from the Old English byxe, box, was founded in 772 and burned to the ground by William the Conqueror as a warm up for the Battle of Hastings. The Bexhill Stone in the side of the tower of St Peter's church is evidence of its Saxon origins. A Cinque Port and a garrison town for George III's German Legion, it was developed fully

September 1066 the Normans landed at Pevensey, now over a kilometre inland. The Roman fort of Anderitum was built on a 4ha site on the shoreline in 300 on a peninsula in marshland, with water on three sides, where it commanded the harbour entrance. It was unusual for a Roman fort in being oval. It sheltered the invading French in 1066. It provided defence against the Armada, was besieged by Simon de Montfort in 1264, was given to John of Gaunt in 1372 and was used again in the second world war, over the years having been progressively upgraded.

Meanwhile, the Martello Towers have begun again on the modern shoreline at Norman's Bay, the first of this set being prominent.

Gravel pits in the Crumbles area have been converted to the Sovereign Harbour with berths for 330 boats. Two green buoys off the entrance mark a first world war wreck within sight of the Martello Tower near Langney Point which has been converted to a lighthouse. The harbour name comes from the Royal Sovereign Shoals 8km offshore, guarded by the Royal Sovereign lighthouse which was towed out and sunk on site after construction in Newhaven, the first lighthouse to be designed with an integral helicopter deck from the start.

The Modernist De La Warr Pavilion on the front at Bexhill

Eastbourne was a village until 1877 but was developed by the Duke of Devonshire in a decade to become the Empress of Watering Places, visited by holidaymakers and by politicians for their party

How We Lived Then museum of shops and social history, the Heritage Centre, the Winter Garden, petanque and sailing. The town was used for filming *Waiting for God*.

The pier at Eastbourne.

conferences. First come all kinds of entertainments. The Sovereign Centre has four pools, flume and wave machine, Fort Fun has Formula Fun go-karts, there is miniature golf, a boating lake, a ride on miniature steam and diesel railway for well over a kilometre, the Amazon Jungle Experience, Treasure Island children's play area and galleon, crazy golf and the Redoubt in an 1804 moated Napoleonic tower containing the Sussex Combined Services Museum with the military history of Sussex, the Cinque Ports, Martello Towers, naval events, Sussex sailors, battlements and gun emplacements. The 5km front is followed for much of the way by the promenade, flowerbeds and the Dotto road train. The 300m pier of 1872–88 has the Funtasia entertainment centre and speedboat rides. Military bands give concerts from the bandstand. England's first RNLI museum has the most comprehensive official collection of lifeboats in a building in memory of actor William Terriss, who was murdered outside a London theatre. The Wish Tower, named after the Saxon wisc, marshy place, is a Martello Tower with an exhibition of puppets. A mat is unrolled across the beach, but it is not reachable for six weeks in the summer because a line of orange buoys off the beach marks an exclusion zone for craft. Other delights of Eastbourne include the Musgrave Collection with coins from the Romans onwards and mini sculptures, paintings and Victoriana, the

Tumuli define the end of the town as chalk cliffs begin to rise again, chalk reefs forming the Pound, and the South Downs Way ascends to the Countryside Centre. Between Eastbourne and Seaford is a Heritage Coast.

Beachy Head takes its name from the French beau chef, beautiful headland, and originally extended to Boulogne where the chalk cliffs continue. At 162m these are the highest chalk cliffs in England and are a favourite spot for suicides. They are at the end of the South Downs. Since Margate the sea has been attacking the ends of the strata, but it now goes with the trend. This is also the longest stretch of chalk cliffs in Britain. On top are field systems and evidence of Stone Age cultures between 8500 and 4000BC with earlier human activity going back nearly 250,000 years, before the English Channel cut through. Vegetation includes sea lavender, hoary stock, round-headed rampion, sheep's fescue and quaking grass, carnation sedge and fragrant, common spotted, pyramidal, bee and early spider orchids in some of the best remaining grassland in Sussex. It attracts such butterflies as red admirals, painted ladies, large and small marbled whites, clouded yellows and Adonis and chalkhill blues. It is a migration watchpoint for butterflies and birds. Peregrine falcons, skylarks, meadow and rock pipits, wheatears, spotted flycatchers, nightingales, linnets, stonechats,

Departure from Eastbourne as chalk grassland leads up onto the South Downs

Beachy Head and one of the best known British lighthouses

The Belle Tout lighthouse back from the brink

jackdaws, herring gulls and cormorants are all seen.

The 1899–1903 Beachy Head light, a 43m white round tower with a red band, was built of Cornish granite at the foot of the cliffs where it was more often below cloud level. A race runs off the light. It replaced the 17m Belle Tout lighthouse of 1834 which was built 30m from the cliff edge so that any boat unable to see it was getting dangerously close inshore. During the second world war the disused light became a target for the Canadians to practise against and it was featured in *Dick Barton at Bay*, *The Life and Loves of a She-Devil* and an episode of the BBC *Doomwatch* science fiction series when it was supposed to have attenuated the sound of an aircraft flying over. The Channel is still getting

wider at 500mm/year and when the lighthouse was only 4m from the edge the 850 tonne grey tower was slid 17m back onto a new basement. The difficult task involved cutting a trench round the outside and jacking against this, action which could have equally brought down more of the cliff face instead of moving the tower. Erosion continues and the 60m high Devil's Chimney outcrop fell in 2001. The Iron Age settlement and tumuli nearby were formerly 2–3km inland. Falling Sands beach below is more used to falling chalk.

Cottages are falling over the cliff at the Birling Gap where access to the beach is down a staircase tower. Fishing boats are winched up a nearly vertical slope. On top is a sheep centre.

Went Hill Brow, Baily's Hill, Flat Hill, Flagstaff Point, Brass Point, Rough Brow, Short Brow and Haven Brow are of progressively increasing height and, with English idiosyncrasy, are known as the Seven Sisters. Rabbits play around the obelisk and tumuli.

The Cuckmere is the only Sussex rivermouth with no port. In the 18th century this assisted the smugglers who operated from Cuckmere Haven. Today the river flows through the Seven Sisters Country Park and is followed by the Vanguard Way. A heron might move out onto the sea rocks in search of booty.

The Hope Gap sees autumn migrants after berries, willow warblers, blackcaps, redstarts and even hoopoes and ortolan buntings while fulmars and gannets are seen off the 86m high chalk cliff streaked with rust. There are a settlement and a golf course on top while a waterski lane is accepted on the sea.

Sheet piling protects an outfall pipe running into the sea at **Seaford**, near where it may be possible to land on a steeply shelving gravel beach, behind which there is parking.

Distance
From Jury's Gap to Seaford is 58km
Campsites
Camber, Pett, Ore, Crowhurst, Bexhill, Gotham, Norman's Bay, Pevensey Bay, Seaford
Youth Hostels
Hastings, Eastbourne, Alfriston
OS 1:50,000 Sheets
189 Ashford and Romney Marsh
198 Brighton and Lewes
199 Eastbourne and Hastings
Imray Charts
C8 North Foreland to Beachy Head and Boulogne (1:115,000)
C9 Beachy Head to Isle of Wight (1:110,000)
Stanfords Allweather Charts
9 North Foreland to Selsey Bill (1:190,000)
30 Sussex Coast
Admiralty Charts
SC 536 Beachy Head to Dungeness (1:75,000)
SC 1652 Selsey Bill to Beachy Head (1:75,000)
SC 1892 Dover Strait, Western Part (1:75,000)
1991 Harbours on the South Coast of England. Rye Harbour (1:25,000)
SC 5605 Chichester to Ramsgate, including Dover Strait
Tidal Constants
Rye Approaches: Dover
Hastings: HW Dover, LW Dover –0030
Eastbourne: HW Dover –0010, LW Dover +0020
Newhaven: HW Dover –0010, LW Dover
Sea Areas
Dover, Wight
Rescue
Inshore lifeboats: Rye Harbour, Hastings, Eastbourne
All weather lifeboats: Dungeness, Hastings, Eastbourne, Newhaven
Maritime Rescue Centres
Dover, 01304 210008
Solent, 023 9255 2100

The Seven Sisters stretch away from the Birling Gap towards Seaford Head

55 WEST SUSSEX

A coast for free thinkers

Five and twenty ponies,
Trotting through the dark –
Brandy for the Parson, 'Baccy for the Clerk
Them that ask no questions isn't told a lie –
Watch the wall my darling while the Gentlemen go by!

Rudyard Kipling

on the rest of the south coast. They are trimmed and have a walkway along the bottom. At intervals there are massive sets of steps cut into them. The water is clear and lobster pots are laid to Brighton, somehow too artificial an environment for them or for the blackheaded and herring gulls and oystercatchers.

A shoal of fish disturb the water off the beach at Seaford

Facing Seaford Bay at the Cinque Port of Seaford is the 103rd and last of the Martello Towers, containing a museum of local history. Seaford was at the mouth of the River Ouse until the great storm of 1579 and had tide mills.

In 1915 businessman Charles Neville designed Anzac-on-Sea, named after the Australian and New Zealand troops stationed nearby and renamed **Peacehaven** at the end of the first world war. A monument to George V marks the meridian and

A cross Channel ferry leaves Newhaven

Newhaven was the new port which developed after the river shifted. A pier with a lighthouse and tide gauge is sheltered by an 1878 concrete breakwater, 850m long with a 14m lighthouse tower, the fairway running close to the breakwater. Cross Channel paddle steamers began a service to Dieppe in 1847 and car ferries continue today, including high speed catamarans.

The entrance is guarded by Newhaven Fort, a scheduled Ancient Monument, which was garrisoned until 1956. On display are 1860s Victorian barrack rooms, underground tunnels, cliff ramparts and big guns. Flows run into the river from HW Dover –0450 and out from HW Dover +0100 at up to 4km/h.

From Friars' Bay the chalk cliffs become like those around the Isle of Thanet rather than those

Manicured cliffs topped by the meridian marker at Peacehaven

there is also a fire beacon on the cliffs. The A259 has been edging towards the top of the cliffs, which it reaches after Telscombe Cliffs, and runs parallel with the coast to Bognor. Below the cliffs much of the coast is used by naturists as far as Brighton Marina, Brighton having had the first naturist beach in Britain and Sussex still having more liberated attitudes than most of the country.

East Sussex gives way to Brighton and Hove and Saltdean gives way to the flint houses of Rottingdean after the White Horse and a black windmill. Sir Edward Burne-Jones lived in the village. The Grange, now with antique toys, is an

18th-century vicarage remodelled by Sir Edwin Lutyens. The Gardens are where Rudyard Kipling wrote *Kim*, the poem *Sussex* and many of his *Just So Stories*. A stone head built into the wall grants wishes if the nose is stroked in the correct way. In

the 1890s the village name was brought up market for the top girls' finishing school of Roedean and the yellow brick St Dunstan's Training Centre for the Blind was opened in the 1930s.

Along the shore the groynes of 1907 were the first to be made in reinforced concrete and are now showing their age.

At the foot of the 30m chalk cliffs the 2,000 berth Brighton Marina was built between 1971 and 1979. 1.1km and 600m arms were constructed by having a 1,200 tonne crane placing 110 12m diameter concrete caissons weighing up to 625 tonnes each

medicinal, but it was not until the 18th century when it became one of the world's earliest resorts because of the patronage of the Prince of Wales, later George IV. It has been called London by the Sea, the place Londoners traditionally went for a naughty weekend, and is claimed to be England's loveliest and liveliest seaside city, the city status being bestowed in 2001.

The area near the marina is Kemp Town, named after lord of the manor, Thomas Kemp. Lewis Carroll lived in Sussex Square off Lewes Crescent, the opening chapter in *Alice in Wonderland* being

The end of Brighton Marina's western arm

and partly filled with sand. At 31ha, it is the largest man-made marina in Europe and the inner basin is reached via the largest non-commercial lock in Europe. It acts as the terminal for a passenger catamaran to Fécamp, has holding tanks for locally caught crabs and lobsters and a fish farm with tanks for 3,000,000 oysters and has bowling, a new Walk of Fame and **Brighton**'s largest cinema.

The wall of cylinders produces irregular clapotis with a sea of any size. On the west side divers are required to keep 200m away because of a historic wreck. Some anglers interpret this as meaning this 200m zone is for their own exclusive use.

Running west from the marina is Volks' electric railway of 1883, the world's oldest public electric railway. The 2km 830mm gauge line was designed

inspired by the tunnel between two gardens. Actress Dame Anna Neagle lived in Lewes Crescent itself and Brighton had one of the first film studios. Madeira Drive, along the front, has been the finishing point for the Veteran Car Run which has taken place in November since 1896, the Historic Commercial Vehicle Run in May and the Stock Exchange Walk in June, all of which begin in London. At the end of the drive is the oldest aquarium in Europe in the Victorian architectured Sea Life Centre but it has the largest underwater tunnel in Europe with sharks, stingrays, octopuses and seahorses amongst its exhibits.

The UK's second most visited leisure facility is the grade 2 Victorian Palace Pier of 1899, 536m long with a 58m head and outsides of the pavilions to echo the Royal Pavilion. It has a funfair, mechanical slot machines and music blasting out over the sea. It stands just east of and replaced the 1823 342m chain pier for French steamers, painted by Constable and Turner but destroyed by a storm in 1896.

In 1995 the inshore lifeboat carried out a very difficult rescue from under the pier, when two girls from a beach party were recovered in the middle of the night in gale force conditions, during which the boat ripped its port side on metalwork and lost much of its buoyancy.

Break in the cliffs at Rottingdean. Brighton's tower blocks are visible in the distance

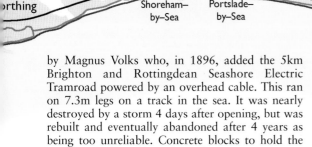

by Magnus Volks who, in 1896, added the 5km Brighton and Rottingdean Seashore Electric Tramroad powered by an overhead cable. This ran on 7.3m legs on a track in the sea. It was nearly destroyed by a storm 4 days after opening, but was rebuilt and eventually abandoned after 4 years as being too unreliable. Concrete blocks to hold the tracks are still visible in the rocks.

The fishing village of Brighthelmstone, named after the Old English man Brihthelm, saw sea bathing from 1641 when it was pronounced to be

Brighton's most striking building is the Royal Pavilion, converted from a farmhouse in 1787 to a neoclassical villa and then, in 1815–22, made into the most exotic palace in Europe, an oriental domed seaside palace with Chinese decoration and Indian exterior. John Nash was the only architect using cast-iron at the time and he also used

laminated timber ribs and prestressed timber beams here. In the grounds is an oak in which Charles II is said to have hidden after the Battle of Worcester, subsequently sailing to France from Shoreham in 1651. The nearby Dome Complex for the performing arts is in a former stable block of 1803 which accommodated 44 horses and their grooms. The mood was summed up by Rex Whistler's painting of *The Prince Regent Awakening the Spirit of Brighton*, a nearly naked prince lifting the veil of a sleeping girl. There is a Prince Regent Swimming Complex with 4 pools and a waterslide, the grade 2 Theatre Royal and Brighton Museum and Art Gallery with important Art Nouveau and Art Deco collections. Not all liberal thinking was appreciated, however. In Meeting House Lane the ghost of a monk disappears through the

ironwork, to which perching cormorants add character.

All of this is the setting for the 3-week Brighton Festival in May, England's largest. There is surf after southwesterly winds with pier legs for added slalom interest.

Moving west, the 1820 terraced grade 1 Regency Townhouse is becoming a heritage centre while the King Alfred Leisure Centre was one of the first on the south coast.

Despite the name derived from hufe, Old English for a hovel, **Hove** sees itself as the more refined extension of Brighton and Constable painted the beach in 1824. The Hove Museum is in a Victorian villa with a film gallery, contemporary craft, childhood room and 18th-century furniture. The beach becomes shingle to Bognor with a 5m raised beach to Worthing.

A fire beacon at **Portslade-by-Sea** locates a large boating pool which has been isolated at the head of the Southwick Canal, a non-tidal eastern basin of Shoreham Harbour. The chimneys of Brighton power station mark the progress from Brighton and Hove to West Sussex and the point where foam is discharged into the sea. The following beach is used by naturists.

The westgoing stream begins at local HW −0200 for six hours at up to 4km/h.

The Eastern Arm and Southwick Canal were part of the River Adur until the new harbour entrance was established in 1817–21, a triangular pier being built opposite the entrance in 1826 at Telford's suggestion to help flows and reduce sedimentation. Even so, the harbour silts rapidly following dredging. A disused lighthouse of 1846 faces the rivermouth at **Southwick**. A Victorian fort was constructed in 1857 when a French invasion was expected.

The harbour entrance is protected by a pair of breakwaters and a bar shifts in the entrance after prolonged westerly winds. There are flows up to 4km/h at the entrance.

Shoreham-by-Sea is on a long peninsula and is named after the Old English scora, a steep hill. Until 500 years ago the River Adur flowed straight out to sea near Lancing church and had the River Arun as a tributary. Shingle pushed the mouth of the Adur eastwards while the Arun broke through to the west in several places.

Shoreham Airport is Britains' oldest licensed airport and has an Art Deco terminal building, D-Day aviation museum, second world war blister hanger, Horsa glider, Spitfire and air sea rescue gallery.

Noisy and extremely popular, Brighton's Palace Pier. Beyond is the West Pier

wall of the Friends' Meeting House, apparently having been bricked in after running away with a local girl.

The Lanes are a maze of 17th-century streets and alleyways with small shops, leading down to the Artists' Quarter studios in the Victorian seafront arches and the new fishing museum. The area has been used for filming *Only Fools and Horses* and for *Brighton Rock* by the Boulting brothers who lived in Hove. It is a Regency seafront with large hotels used by political parties for their conferences. The Grand Hotel was bombed by the IRA during a Conservative Party conference.

Offshore are lanes for powerboats. At midnight on May 17th a ship capsizes on a reef. It was that of Lord Manfred returning after placing St Nicholas' belt on the tomb of the Blessed Virgin at Byzantium in the 14th century to fulfill an initially forgotten vow. St Nicholas' church was subsequently built by his father, the 4th Earl de Warrenne, to remind people to honour their vows. Under a plinth in the church are buried a knight and his horse, both in full armour, the horse

Worthing's Victorian pier is a very respectable structure, even if outclassed by those of Brighton

galloping round the churchyard on moonlit nights.

The grade 2 Middle Street synagogue is one of the finest in Europe with abstract stained glass and ornate brass and ironwork. Churchill Square was declared the Best Designed UK Shopping Centre in 1999. On the beach is the Ellipse with outdoor theatre, concerts, dances, beach volleyball, basketball, paddling pool, sandpit and new works of art. This is next to the West Pier which is disused and dangerous. The country's only grade 1 pier, it was opened in 1866 as Birch's best work. 340m long with a 94m head, it has elegant wrought

Lancing merges into Worthing which continues into Ferring with no break obvious from the sea. **Worthing**, named after the Old English man Weorc, was just a few fishing cottages and a smuggling centre but became the biggest resort in west Sussex from the end of the 18th century, encouraged by Princess Amelia, the delicate younger sister of the Prince Regent. It features Regency housing and inter-war elegance with a horsedrawn bus operating along the long seafront. Oscar Wilde wrote his *Importance of Being Ernest* here and used the name of the town for his main

character. The town also boasts Elisabeth Frink head sculptures while the Museum and Art Gallery covers archaeology, geology, local history and bathing costumes. The major feature on the seafront is the 290m Victorian pier with a pavilion at the end.

Goring-by-Sea's English Martyrs Church has a 1993 replica of the ceiling of the Sistine Chapel.

Beach huts around **Ferring** are all that break up the line of housing behind the beach through Kingston Gorse, East Preston, Rustington and Littlehampton, completing what is effectively a 16km run of housing. There is a windmill on the Downs behind Kingston Gorse at **Angmering**. Birdlife is limited but there are terns, blackbacked and herring gulls and swans. Between Worthing and the River Arun a chalk anticline continued southwards but it has been shortened and the top 240m removed, which does much to reduce its impact on the landscape.

Rustington is a village with a mediaeval church and flint cottages plus a modern sports centre. In this village Sir Hubert Parry wrote the setting to Blake's *Jerusalem*.

Littlehampton was another fishing town which became a resort. The Little was only added in the 15th century to distinguish it from Northampton and Southampton. Along the promenade are bathing huts. What looks like a castle is actually a pumping station feeding a long sea outfall. When the latter was built in the early 1970s four boreholes were put down along its line to sample the seabed. Two hit wartime mines.

Littlehampton's timber breakwater at the mouth of the River Arun

On the east bank of the Arun is a prominent funfair. There is a commercial and yachting port on the river. In the Middle Ages it was used for unloading Caen stone for major Sussex buildings. A white over a red flag on a pilot boat indicates a large vessel movement is due. A training wall running out from the lighthouse covers at half tide. The open structure timber breakwater extends on the west side of the harbourmouth to protect shipping. With a westerly wind blowing, dry sand can be blown through it in a veritable sandstorm. The pierhead has a tide gauge. Overfalls form on the bar with winds from force 5 between southeast and southwest against ebbing spring tides. Flows go in from HW Dover –0400 and out from HW Dover+0100 at up to 11km/h, being affected by heavy rain.

To the west of the river, dunes and a golf course put a stop to housing for a while. North of Climping is the former Ford Aerodrome. Further inland beyond the Arundel to Chichester line there are former raised beaches at the 30m level.

In fact, Atherington did have more building along the front but mediaeval houses and the church were taken by the sea.

The 1849 church in **Middleton-on-Sea**, a first world war seaplane base, replaces another church taken by the sea. Unusually, the houses along the front include some thatched ones and this section of coast is now protected by a line of rock islands. Patches of loose bootlace weed proliferate and with any kind of a swell it is hard to avoid picking up quantities with the bows or even the paddles.

There is an 11km unbroken front of houses through Felpham and Bognor. Felpham has flint walled cottages and was the home of William Blake, about as far as he could get both geographically and in environment from his dark satanic mills. Stopping at SZ950993 allows toilets, a seafront café and some shelter for landing if the wind is from the west but parking is limited.

Recent rock islands protect the coast at Middleton-on-Sea

Distance
From Seaford to Felpham is 54km
Campsites
Seaford, Whitehawk, Woodmancote, Small Dole, Washington, Wick, Ford, Bognor Regis
Youth Hostels
Alfriston, Telscombe, Brighton, Truleigh Hill, Littlehampton
OS 1:50,000 Sheets
197 Chichester and the South Downs
198 Brighton and Lewes
Imray Chart
C9 Beachy Head to Isle of Wight (1:110,000)
Stanfords Allweather Charts
9 North Foreland to Selsey Bill (1:190,000)
11 Solent and Isle of Wight (1:84,000)
30 Sussex Coast
Admiralty Charts
SC 536 Beachy Head to Dungeness (1:75,000)
SC 1652 Selsey Bill to Beachy Head (1:75,000)
1991 Harbours on the South Coast of England.
Brighton Marina (1:5,000). Littlehampton Harbour (1:6,250)
2044 Shoreham Harbour and Approaches.
Approaches to Shoreham (1:15,000)
2154 Newhaven Harbour (1:5,000)
SC 5605 Chichester to Ramsgate, including Dover Strait
Tidal Constants
Newhaven: HW Dover –0010, LW Dover
Brighton: HW Dover –0010, LW Dover
Shoreham: HW Dover
Worthing: HW Dover, LW Dover –0010
Littlehampton Entrance: HW Dover, LW Dover –0010
Bognor Regis: HW Dover, LW Dover –0010
Sea Area
Wight
Rescue
Inshore lifeboats: Eastbourne, Brighton, Shoreham Harbour, Littlehampton
All weather lifeboats: Newhaven, Shoreham Harbour, Selsey
Maritime Rescue Centre
Solent, 023 9255 2100

56 EAST HAMPSHIRE

Passing the south coast's natural harbours

There cam' a lord from Southsea baulks,
  I mean from fair England;
He lichtit at her father's gate,
  And his name's Lord Lamington.

Aldingbourne Rife separates Felpham from **Bognor**, of which the most prominent structure is the tented roof on Butlin's holiday camp, from another building of which colourful slides emerge.

Butlin's distinctive holiday camp at Bognor Regis

The inconspicuous entrance to Pagham Harbour

Late 18th-century architecture was by London hatter Sir Richard Hotham who wanted to call it Hothampton, but Queen Victoria called it 'dear little Bognor' and the royal opinion took precedence. The name derives from the name of the Old English woman Bucge and ora, meaning shore. George V added the Latin Regis for king's while recovering from a lung operation in Aldwick in 1928. It was one of the first seaside resorts to be favoured by royalty. The pier is disused but the 2km seafront including the B2166 has a road train and one of the star attractions has to be the Bognor Birdman competition in August.

The shingle beach continues to Selsey Bill, accompanied by housing to the resort of Pagham. Bognor Rocks and Barn Rocks run southeast in two lines, the former having a wreck at the inshore end at Aldwick. The one break in the beach comes at the exit of Pagham Harbour, a 4km² nature reserve with strong streams in the entrance. There are 200 bird species here including terns, shelducks, curlews, redshanks and oystercatchers. Red admirals and other butterflies and moths are present with plant life including spartina grass, sea purslane and glasswort. The harbour is silted up but Sidlesham was a working port until the mid-19th century.

There is an earthwork at the southern corner of the harbour at Church Norton where St Wilfred's church is named after a 7th-century missionary.

Lines of moorings at Selsey lead to a fire beacon, an RNLI museum and a prominent gantry feeding out to the lifeboat station. It is a coast where lobsters, crabs, whelks and cockles are found. Important in Saxon times, Selsey is a quiet resort today.

Selsey Bill is a low sharp point where the coast has eroded more than any other in Britain in the 20th century. The site of **Selsey** cathedral of 680–1080 is now some 2km offshore. Flows run eastwards from HW Dover +0600. Fast currents come right to the shore with a race close inshore

The catwalk out to the lifeboat station at Selsey

and an eddy on the corner so sharp that a stopper can be formed like that beside a jet into a weirpool. Further out there is a mark on the Mixon, from where it can dry most of the way back to the bill, leaving just a narrow passage through. For larger boats the Outer Owers, further out, are the most dangerous shoals in the English Channel. An interesting half-timbered tower on a house near the bill is a useful mark for shipping. The heavily groyned beach sees oystercatchers picking about between cuttlefish bones and terns are present. Towards the west of Selsey is a windmill. Selsey is old English for seal island and it is still all but an island at the end of the B2145, Broad Rife following the coast of Bracklesham Bay for some 3km, often only 100m away from the sea, before turning northeast to Pagham Harbour.

Off the holiday village of Bracklesham at the end of the B2198 is a historic wreck with a 100m radius exclusion zone around it. 2–3km out is the probable site of a Roman station served by the road, Roman coins having frequently been washed up on the beach. 6km of surf beach, heavily used by windsurfers, stretch past **East Wittering** and West Wittering to the entrance to Chichester Harbour. East Wittering has a windmill and the tower of Cakeham Manor House as a nautical mark. There is a wreck onshore at East Wittering and two cardinal marks out on the East Pole Sands locate wrecks used as targets. West Wittering is

any swell and can break right across the entrance, being dangerous with a southerly wind against a strong ebb. Conditions are quietest from local HW −0300 to local HW +0100. Flows are ingoing for seven and a quarter hours to 5km/h and outgoing for five and a quarter hours to 12km/h. In quieter conditions the world's largest fleet of International Canoes will be seen in action from Hayling Island Sailing Club, otherwise they stay in the harbour.

Crossing to Hayling Island is to move from West Sussex to Hampshire, England's oldest county. Hayling Island takes its name from helige, holy. **South Hayling** faces Hayling Bay with huts, holiday bungalows and the garish accoutrements of the seaside holiday resort, bingo halls, amusement arcades, chip and ice cream shops and the Cutter public house. Near the end of the A3023 is the Funlands Amusement Park with assorted fairground rides. Thereafter, West Town pulls back and there is a golf course on Sinah Common. From Gunner Point the mouth of Langstone Harbour is crossed from Hampshire to Portsmouth, both sides of the harbour have spits, the Winners and Woolsners which are subject to frequent shift, and at low water springs the East Winner can extend 2km out from the high water mark. Again, this corner is a surf venue and is popular with kite surfers, not always with too much control of either kites or boards. Foils come down with significant impacts. To the south of the West Winner off the mouth of the harbour the sea breaks heavily on the Langstone Bar with high

A conspicuous tower on a house at Selsey Bill acts as a landmark

Bracklesham is not keen on dogs anywhere

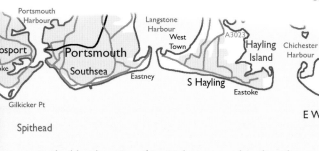

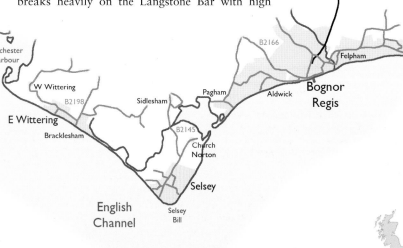

marked by the spire of its 11th-century church and is where the Rolls Royce design team were moved when their leader contracted cancer.

East Pole Sands can dry out for a considerable distance, as can West Pole Sands on the other side of the harbourmouth and over which large standing waves can develop at the inshore end at Eastoke Point near high water. The fairway is on the west side of the entrance but the banks are subject to great change. Waves break heavily with

The Chichester Bar marker with Hayling Island beyond

onshore winds, particularly during a strong ebb. Eastney Point protects this entrance with Fort Cumberland, built in 1746 as a pentagon by the Duke of Cumberland, the most impressive piece of 18th century defensive architecture in England.

The Dockyard Port of Portsmouth takes control beyond a line running southeast from Eastney Point. This is also the Fraser Gunnery Range danger area. A windsock is a noticeable marker.

A chimney, only half its original height, marks Eastney beam engine house of 1887 with its fine Victorian industrial architecture and its pair of James Watt beam engines. These were used to empty the contents of three 20m³ holding tanks into an outfall to the entrance of Langstone Harbour during the middle two hours of the ebb, there having previously been a problem with beach fouling. Now Eastney Pumping Station has been connected to the 7.9km x 2.8m diameter Portsmouth Transfer Tunnel to Havant.

Crossley gas engines 1904 are located next to the barracks where a 3ha site contains the Royal Marines Museum with silver, portraits, the history of the Royal Marines from 1664, badges, bands, 7,000 medals including all 10 Royal Marine Victoria Crosses, landing craft, rigid raider and helicopter at the grade 2 artillery officers' mess with its superb Victorian architecture. Also featured is Operation Frankton, the kayak raid to mine shipping in Bordeaux harbour in 1942.

From near the canoe lake a submerged barrier of concrete blocks runs out to Horse Sand Fort, one of the offshore forts dotted across the Solent, from the former Lumps Fort. There are passages for small craft. A recent proposal has been for a £60,000,000 rail link to Ryde. 1.6km embankments would run out from each coast with a similar length of tunnel connecting them under the main shipping channel.

Southsea is the southern extension of **Portsmouth**, which covers most of Portsea and is Britain's only island city. This is the more refined resort end with 7km of front and the usual holiday resort features such as pitch and putt, model village and Southsea rose gardens. It was Hardy's Solentsea. The Natural History Museum and Butterfly House has geology, an iguanadon, birds, mammals, insects, shore life and an aquarium.

The South Parade Pier hosts concerts, bands and cabaret and is next to the Pyramids Centre with tropical and conventional pools, sidewinder and conventional super flumes, waves, fountains, bubblers and geysers.

At the southern point of the island is Southsea Castle, built in 1545 by Henry VIII to protect Portsmouth against the French and Spanish and used until 1960. It shows the military history of Portsmouth through Tudor, Civil War and Victorian times, artillery and underground tunnels. A lighthouse is located on the point. There is also

The South Parade Pier at Southsea.

the D-Day Museum and Overlord Embroidery by the Royal School of Needlework, 23m x 900mm, and displays from the 1944 Battle of Normandy, landing beaches, landing craft, DUKW and Sherman tank. A Sea Life Centre has giant octopus, rays, eels and sharks and there is a bandstand for those who wish to be entertained outdoors. Southsea Common is one of the finest and broadest seaside gardens around the coast, leading to a naval war memorial, the original anchor from *HMS Victory* and the Clarence Pier with Pirate Pete's Adventure Playground and its Wild River, Golden Horseshoe Arcade, Games Wharf, bowling, bingo and log flume. Life was less fun when H G Wells worked in a draper's shop in Southsea from 1881 to 1883, soul destroying work from which he ran away although he used it as a basis for *Kipps*.

One kilometre off is the nearest of the Spithead forts, Spitbank Fort, built by Lord Palmerstone in the 1850s with 4.6m thick walls, a 120m deep well, a cannon with a 38 tonne barrel and a Victorian kitchen. It was beyond this that the *Mary Rose* capsized. The cod and bass have plenty of interest to see in these waters.

Channel car ferries and other large craft and is subject to the International Regulations for Preventing Collisions at Sea, including no use of whistles, because the narrow channel is clearly defined. The difficulty is the rest of the crossing where smaller craft spread out so that Isle of Wight car ferries, hovercraft, work boats and a mass of yachts race past. There are more pleasure craft in the Solent than there are commercial ships in the whole world so it gets a bit busy at times.

Man-of-War Anchorage is located off the entrance and large vessel movements take place on the first three hours of the flood and first, second and fifth hours of the ebb on spring tides but at all times on neaps. Flows across the entrance are to 1km/h. Off Southsea Castle the flood into the harbour is weak until HW Dover –0340 then it increases to 2km/h while the maximum flow on the ebb is 5km/h at HW Dover +0400. Tides become increasingly complex from here to Southampton Water where there is a double high tide on springs yet neap tides are more conventional and there may be a stand of water on intermediate tides. No doubt it was all simpler when Spithead was part of the valley of the River Frome.

The Spitbank Fort off Southsea Castle. Beyond is the Isle of Wight. The warship is entering Portsmouth Harbour via the fairway

The entrance to Portsmouth Harbour with Portsmouth and Southsea on the right. To the left is the Spinnaker Tower

The mouth of Portsmouth Harbour sees a return from Portsmouth to Hampshire. It is one of the most difficult pieces of inshore water round our coast to cross. The problem is not the fairway, close to the east shore, which carries aircraft carriers, destroyers, frigates, cargo vessels, cross

After the Haslar Royal Naval Hospital razor wire surrounds a prison. The Solent Way footpath leads past Fort Monckton. A stone's throw from this is Fort Gilkicker on Gilkicker Point, later a signal station with excellent visibility. Spithead gives way to the Solent.

Fort Monckton with Gilkicker Point beyond

Gilkicker Point with Fawley power station and refinery on the skyline

Stokes Bay begins with a golf course. It is where Queen Victoria used to embark for Osborne House on the Isle of Wight and there are the remains of an exposed pier which received boat trains from 1863 until the first world war, these days not receiving trains of any sort. Number 2 Battery is prominent by the River Alver before Browndown Point.

Portsmouth control passes to the Port of Southampton. In the 18th century Hillhead Harbour conducted smuggling. There is now a coastal nature reserve with wigeon while there are bass, mullet and cockles in the sea. The soft cliffs also give some protection to naturists in what is quite an effective afternoon suntrap.

Lee-on-the-Solent with the hovercraft slipway just left of centre of the picture and HMS Daedalus behind the houses

The B3333 runs along the front of **Lee-on-the-Solent** until it becomes the B3385 and disappears inland. The village has a new beach, 20m wide over 2km at a cost of £4,000,000 in front of the Old Ship. There are buoyed jet ski and waterski areas with a passage between them for hovercraft to approach their service area at HMS Daedalus, the Fleet Air Arm Training Establishment. The airfield was a seaplane base for the Royal Flying Corps before the first world war. Royal Marines often exercise with helicopters low over the water. Elmore Angling Club made the *Guinness Book of Records* here with the biggest beach angling contest, funds going to the RNLI.

Beyond **Hill Head** the River Meon enters through Titchfield Haven and the Dockyard Port of

Calshot with the coastguard tower, Calshot Castle and the historic hangars now used by Calshot Activities Centre

Beyond Hook Park the River Hamble enters and from it emerge the pride of the British luxury yachting fleet. Southampton Water itself is the River Test valley drowned in the Ice Age and was the birthplace of common cordgrass which has spread right round the British coast in the 20th century. This part of Southampton Water is subject to considerable gusts when wind of any strength is from the northwest. The flood runs for nine hours and the ebb for three and a half, affected in a complex pattern by heavy rain and southwesterly winds in addition to the double high waters north of Calshot.

On the west side are Fawley Refinery with the Esso Marine Terminal and its flares and **Fawley** power station. It is served by tankers up to 360,000

tonnes. This part of the estuary is more simple to cross than the mouth of Portsmouth Harbour in that shipping is all going along the same track with the fairway on the Calshot side. However, notice does need to be taken of the fairways on the chart to the south, the North Channel cutting across in front of Lee-on-the-Solent, but large inbound craft needing to pass close to Cowes before turning northeast into the Thorn Channel in an exaggerated S-movement. A vessel over 150m long, flying a black cylinder and usually preceded by a Southampton Harbour patrol launch, has a rolling prohibited entry zone for 1km ahead and 100m to each side, much of which is a blind spot from the wheel. The sheer size of some of these craft is brought home by seeing one towering above and beyond each end of the main hangar at Calshot. The simple rule is not to start crossing if there is anything big or fast in sight. Tankers, container ships, liners and car ferries all use this water, together with many yachts. The most important craft to spot are the passenger launches between Southampton and Cowes as these are quite small but travel very fast. If plans to develop a new container hub at Dibden Bay are eventually successful this stretch of water will be used by container ships up to 350m long. Most of this traffic will be ship to ship so there will be a corresponding increase in smaller vessels, the number of containers handled at Southampton more than tripling.

The Calshot site has much of interest although there is no longer a Calshot Spit light vessel. One of these, in wood, is now the headquarters of the Royal Northumberland Yacht Club in Blyth harbour. A coastguard lookout point and radar scanner are on top of a tall column. For years a large Princess flying boat was moored off this point. On the other side is Calshot Castle, built in 1540 by Henry VIII and restored as it was before the first world war with bunks and uniforms on display.

The three main buildings on the site are hangars. It was a flying boat base from 1913 to 1961 and by the 1920s carried out nearly all the maritime air training. It is the most complete surviving seaplane/flying boat base in the UK, if not the world, and includes Britain's second oldest seaplane hangar. It has been used by the navy and the RAF in the 20th century and was the site of the first Royal Naval Air Station in the UK as well as being the site of coastal artillery and anti-aircraft guns. Another hangar is the Schneider Trophy hangar. T E Lawrence was based here in 1929–31, the period of the Schneider Trophy races which took place round a triangular course over the Solent and were to lead to Britain's retaining the Schneider Trophy after winning it three times in succession, in the process doing the preparatory work for the Spitfire which was to be of major importance during the second world war.

The site's use for Calshot Activities Centre has also been important in recent years, especially for sea kayak training. There are plenty of other activities, too, the main hangar having an indoor dry ski slope, huge climbing wall and banked cycle track used by the British cycle racing team. The accommodation blocks were used by refugees from Tristan da Cunha when volcanic eruption threatened their island in the south Atlantic.

Calshot Spit is not the piece of land which runs northeast then north, but the underwater feature which is growing and which runs southeast then

southwest from its end, throwing up testing water conditions to the south of the centre. Large vessels are required not to create excessive wash which could endanger those on the beach.

There is parking around the end of the B3053 where beach huts line what an old notice proclaims to be a private beach but which is clearly used by the public. A hut on the beach sells refreshments.

Distance
From Felpham to Calshot is 53km
Campsites
Bognor Regis, Selsey, East Wittering, West Wittering, Eastoke, Eastney, Browndown, Hamble-le-Rice
Youth Hostels
Littlehampton, Portsmouth
OS 1:50,000 Sheets
196 Solent and Isle of Wight
197 Chichester and the South Downs
Imray Charts
2200 Solent
C3 Isle of Wight (1:52,500)
C9 Beachy Head to Isle of Wight (1:110,000)
C15 Solent – Bembridge to Hurst Point and Southampton (1:35,000)
Y33 Langstone and Chichester Harbours (1:21,500)
Stanfords Allweather Charts
9 North Foreland to Selsey Bill (1:190,000)
10 Eastern Solent, Harbours and Approaches
11 Solent and Isle of Wight (1:84,000)
24 Solent and Approaches
25 Solent Harbours
30 Sussex Coast
L1 Portsmouth Harbour (1:21,000)
L2 Langstone Harbour (1:21,000)
L3 Chichester Harbour (1:21,000)
Admiralty Charts
SC 1652 Selsey Bill to Beachy Head (1:75,000)
SC 2022 Harbours and Anchorages in the East Solent Area. Hillhead Harbour (1:3,000)
SC 2036 Solent and Southampton Water (1:25,000)
SC 2037 Eastern Approaches to the Solent (1:25,000)
SC 2045 Outer Approaches to the Solent (1:75,000)
2625 Approaches to Portsmouth (1:7,500)
2629 Portsmouth Harbour – Southern Part (1:5,000)
SC 3418 Langston and Chichester Harbours (1:20,000)
SC 5600 Solent and Approaches
SC 5605 Chichester to Ramsgate, including Dover Strait
Tidal Constants
Bognor Regis: HW Dover, LW Dover –0010
Pagham: HW Dover +0010, LW Dover –0020
Selsey Bill: HW Dover +0020, LW Dover +0100
Chichester Harbour Entrance: HW Dover +0020 , LW Dover +0040
Portsmouth: Dover +0020
Lee-on-the-Solent: HW Dover +0020, LW Dover +0010
Calshot Castle: HW Dover +0010, LW Dover
Sea Area
Wight
Range
Eastney
Rescue
Inshore lifeboats: Littlehampton, Selsey, Hayling Island, Portsmouth, Calshot
All weather lifeboats: Selsey, Bembridge, Calshot
Helicopter: Lee-on-the-Solent
Maritime Rescue Centre
Solent, 023 9255 2100

57 WEST HAMPSHIRE

Up the former River Frome valley

If the wind is in the east,
Old Harry ledge can be a beast.

From Calshot to Cornwall there is a steady regression back in time along the coast from recent sedimentary rocks to some of the oldest granite in the world. After Luttrell Tower (a conical brick structure on a house) Stanswood Bay is edged with rich golden sandy cliffs, topped by pines on the edge of the New Forest which continues until the Lymington River. A boathouse stands above assorted obstructions including a tide gauge while there are oyster beds further offshore.

Between Stansore Point and Stone Point at Lepe is Lepe Country Park, the setting for Nevil Shute's *Requiem for a Wren*, written after being based here while working on a secret rocket launched pilotless plane for D–Day. At the back of Lepe Spit are old coastguard cottages with a search and rescue station and what looks like a small lighthouse and a boathouse.

Smugglers used to meet in the Shipp Inn and also in the Solent Marshes, broad mudflats from here to Hurst Point, intersected by narrow creeks. A dolphin stands at the mouth of the Beaulieu River, the most beautiful of the Solent creeks, an entrance which can be dangerous to two hours either side of

The pine lined sandy cliff behind Stanswood Bay

Port of Southampton control comes to an end at Stansore Point with its mark as a free for all of telephone and high voltage cables and gas pipelines begins, crossing to Egypt Point at **Cowes** on the Isle of Wight. Three Stone Farm is named after the legend that when the island approached the mainland it was possible to leap across three stepping stones with the aid of a pole.

low water. It was an entrance negotiated by the *Agamemnon*, *Swiftshure* and *Euryalus* of the Trafalgar fleet in addition to many others built at Beaulieu. A causeway connects to Gull Island, which is awash at high water. In the 18th century the Bull Lake or Bull Run was cut through the end of the island but it ceased to be used in the 20th century as the island was being eroded. Boats from

Dolphins stand in the Solent at Stansore Point

The mouth of the Beaulieu River at Lepe

the Beaulieu River Sailing Club, the masts of which are seen over Needs Ore Point, now have to go round Beaulieu Spit to reach the open Solent.

Old coastguard cottages overlook a shingle bank to which they no longer have access as 3km of the shoreline has been designated the North Solent National Nature Reserve on which landing is forbidden. The bird sanctuary is home to Britain's largest colony of blackheaded gulls, 14,000 of them, plus an important breeding colony of little terns, oystercatchers and cormorants. The mudflats attract waders but the RSPB said the Solent was at risk from oil exploration.

The westgoing stream is stronger than the eastgoing stream, reaching 6km/h off Lepe Middle. The shore continues low and quiet from Great Marsh past Park Shore, Little Marsh, Thorns Beach, Durns Point and a ruined jetty to a beacon marking where a line of underwater obstructions crosses to the west of the Newtown River on the Isle of Wight.

Tidal marsh gradually widens through Pitts Deep Quay and Pylewell Point until it is 1km wide at Lymington Spit at the end of the Lymington River's Long Reach, which has the narrow fairway well marked from the Jack in the Basket mark so it is easy to keep clear of Wightlink's Yarmouth to **Lymington** car ferries. In 1790 *HMS Pandora* set out from here with the brief of searching the Pacific for the mutineers from the *Bounty*. The Royal Lymington Yacht Club's starting platform ensures that many sailing boats with more short term objectives set out from here and the occupants of Lymington Yacht Haven make certain of plenty of other sailing activity.

Plans for a deep water port got as far as an Act of Parliament but Oxey Marsh, behind Oxey Lake, and the Pennington Marshes with their former saltworks site remain quiet with the Lymington

and Keyhaven Nature Reserve, important for plants, insects and birds with plovers, ducks, swans, egrets, winter visitors including Brent geese, shelducks, teal, dunlins and lapwings, these days disturbed by no more than the Solent Way long distance footpath, as marram grass covers the marshes and saltmarsh nature reserve reaches right along this stretch of coast. It was not always so civilized. Between 1802 and 1853 Colonel Peter Hawker was reported to have killed 29 species of bird including 1,300 Brent geese, 2,200 wigeon and 1,300 dunlins.

Looking back from Hurst Beach over the nature reserve towards the Solent

The Royal Lymington Yacht Club's starting platform

The saltmarsh of Pennington Spit reaches out to Hurst Castle, the narrow low water creek of Keyhaven Lake disguising the fact that Keyhaven was once a working harbour. In 1901 there were plans for a rail tunnel from here to the Isle of Wight.

A 26m white round tower lighthouse stands at Hurst Point and shines over Hurst Castle, on which a former low red light was placed. The castle was constructed from 1541 to 1544 with stones from Beaulieu Abbey after the Dissolution. Built to control the entrance to the Solent, it was one of Henry VIII's most sophisticated, a twelve–sided central tower in a curtain wall with three semi–circular bastions. In

An embankment protects the Pennington Marshes and their lakes

Hurst Castle and lighthouse with the Isle of Wight opposite and the Needles in the distance

HM Coastguard 1822/1972

7½p

Sculpture on the beach at Milford on Sea points towards the Needles

Hengistbury Head with Mudeford to the right and Durlston Head in the far distance

1648 it was the prison for Charles I for 19 days. Despite its sophistication it was quite a small structure, on a par with Calshot Castle, until 1860 when the Victorians added two long wings, making it look huge from the water. They also added two 38 tonne guns which, together with searchlights, were not removed until 1956.

Fort Albert on Cliff End controls the other side of the gap and this is the closest the Isle of Wight gets to the mainland, just over 1km away. The constriction means fast flows and there may be heavy overfalls off Hurst Point reaching right to the shore and over the Trap ridge of sand and gravel, especially with the northeastgoing stream, with the possibility of strong eddies off the point with flows in either direction. Currents round the point can be swift. These difficulties can be avoided by using Mount Lake and portaging over Hurst Beach. Ahead, the Needles and their lighthouse on the end of the Isle of Wight are prominent.

The steep shingle Hurst Beach is 2.4km long, a narrow spit which appears to be very exposed to the weather yet remains stable, albeit with some reinforcement by rubble and building materials when breaches have threatened. In Christchurch and Poole Bays flows start west at HW Dover –0100 and east from HW Dover +0510 at up to 2km/h although speeds can be up to 7km/h at the east end of the North Channel which runs inside the Shingle Bank and North Head.

Where the bank flattens out to give some sandy beach there are slipper limpet shells, whelk egg cases and cuttlefish bones on the beach. Behind is Sturt Pond. There may not be any bones left, but it is fed by the Danes Stream which still runs red from the blood of Danes slaughtered on its banks more than a millennium ago or perhaps from the iron rich soil. The Mineway bank takes its name from a track leading up from the sea, used to bring ironstone concretions up for smelting.

From here to Poole Harbour the water is edged by earth cliffs which are cut by small streams to form steep bunnies and chines, much used by 18th-century smugglers, and there are frequent landslips as the sea encroaches. The groynes at **Milford on Sea** are just the first of many such defences. Likewise, the colourfully painted beach huts are the first of several such clusters.

Road access has been very limited since Calshot but the B3058 now comes close and the coast is largely built up to Poole Harbour.

Christchurch Bay wave research tower is moored offshore while the teak and steel schooner *Lamorna* found out about the waves in about 1950 when she was wrecked here.

golf course, Beckton Bunny was mined during the second world war as it offered an easy landing place.

Groynes protect **Barton on Sea** and prehistoric reptiles are found in fossil bearing strata.

The groynes at Highcliffe are of rock at the end of Chewton Bunny which marks the transition from Hampshire to Dorset. Chewton Glen bridge carries the A337 over on the first reinforced concrete arched bridge in the UK, not planned as such but used to make up for the incorrect setting out of the abutments of a 36° skewed bridge, being designed to take a 20 tonne traction engine.

A yellow buoyed area inshore along this coast in the summer marks a zone where swimmers have priority. The shore is exposed to southerly winds and large swells break a long way out. Steamer Point takes its name from a wreck and the coastguard have their training centre above on the low cliffs at **Highcliffe**.

A resident of Highcliffe was Gerald Gardner, the founder of modern witchcraft. Gothic style was used in the 1830s for Highcliffe Castle for Lord Stuart. It was badly damaged in a fire in the 1960s but the dilapidated structure is grade 1 listed and has been used for TV film settings, despite having a ghost which turns on lights.

The Rivers Avon and Stour enter **Christchurch** Harbour and then discharge into the sea through the Run, a difficult stretch of water with flows inwards to 7km/h and ebb flows to 13km/h with an entrance channel which moves and a bar over which the depth changes frequently. It is a fishing and sailing centre with lobster and whelk pots on the quayside at Mudeford. A major incident on Mudeford Quay in 1784 was a bloody fight between smugglers and revenue men.

Dorset becomes Bournemouth here. Clarendon Rocks run out into the sea much further than the rock groynes along this section of the bay.

Hengistbury Head stands out as a conspicuous block of dark red Bracklesham beds ironstone surrounded by low land. As such, it has attracted attention and was occupied from Stone Age to Roman times. There are six bowl barrows on the head and two on low ground, one of which has yielded valuable finds. There was an Iron Age promontory fort when it guarded one of the country's busiest ports and Iron Age coins, pottery and bronze items have been found. In 1848 a coal merchant began excavating the ironstone and sending it to Lymington for processing, but the sand eroded very fast and the spit extended northwards until the Run was only 30m wide. This was not checked until 1938 when a large groyne was built southwards from the head.

Gordon Selfridge planned to return dwelling to the head with a 250 room castle with turrets, but he

Below Hordle Cliff, Hordle beach has second world war tank traps and a single ochre coloured building was once a light anti-aircraft gun practice range. Pillboxes are collapsing into the sea as the cliffs recede. Cutting in obliquely in front of Barton

blew his retailing fortune on two sisters and was unable to proceed with the project. Today the head is visited by 1,000,000 people per year, many by a land train. Around the head are heath, woodland, meadow, salt and freshwater marshes, dunes, rocky

foreshore and shingle with a nature reserve good for small annual spring plants.

There is a small race at the long groyne and it can also produce surf if the wind is in the right direction. Streams run strongly over Christchurch Ledge which runs southeast nearly halfway across Christchurch Bay, a totally different direction from the growth of the spit, as at Calshot.

Now in Poole Bay, the Hengistbury Head site ends with Double Dykes, 460m long with a 5.5m central entrance gap.

The high earth cliff shoreline is continuously built from Southbourne to Poole Head. There are eight chines in the Bracklesham beds and it was the use of these by smugglers which led to the eventual establishment of the resort which claims the best weather in Britain. Outfalls, groynes and other obstructions keep larger boats out of the inshore area although boating further out includes offshore powerboat racing. The sandy beach at Southbourne occasionally dumps. It has zones for swimming, for kids, no dogs, no bottles, can recycling, in fact, pretty highly regimented. There is a cliff lift, land train and Fisherman's Walk.

Bourne flows down past the Vistarama Balloon through gardens to reach the sea by Bournemouth Pier, a popular and better surf venue than Boscombe but visited by pleasure steamers. By the pier at West Cliff is the Oceanarium and there are donkey rides and Punch and Judy shows on the beach and then another cliff lift.

Durley has the Durley Inn but no dogs, no smoking, can recycling and zones for swimming and for kids.

There can be surf at the sheltered beach at Alum Chine although the beach covers completely at high water. This is where Stevenson wrote *Dr Jeckyll*. As

Bournemouth Pier and environs

Looking west from Alum Chine towards Poole Head on a fine summer's morning

Beyond Stourcliff and Pokesdown is **Boscombe** with its pier, a surf venue which it is hoped to improve by installing two artificial reefs of sand in bags in a V-shape to give waves peeling to both left and right. Valentine tanks on the sea bed were being developed with canvas flotation collars and propellers for second world war amphibious use, but were blown up more recently as they contained live ammunition. For more gentle explosions the BBC have used the area for filming *One Foot in the Grave* and the Hotel Miramar was the set for *Separate Tables*.

East Cliff has a cliff lift. Above Harry Ramsden's are the Imax Waterfront Complex and the refurbished Russell-Cotes Art Gallery and Museum in a Victorian mansion with Renaissance pottery, 17th to 20th-century oil paintings, watercolours, sculptures, miniatures, ceramics, furniture, plate, Japanese art, theatrical effects, early Italian paintings and pottery, armoury, keyboard instruments, Maori items, a Bath chair and a marine collection with models, ships, shells and wreck items, rather a varied set of themes. Behind is the more straightforward Sega Park.

Bournemouth was a Victorian town from 1850, Hardy's Sandbourne where his *Tess of the D'Ubervilles* was filmed and included in his *The Hand of Ethelberta*, *The Well-Beloved* and *Jude the Obscure*. It has 8km² of parks and gardens, including the Upper Pleasure Gardens and the Lower Pleasure Gardens, the latter having been renamed as just the Pleasure Gardens because people were getting the wrong message. The River

well as toilets just behind the beach, the chine has two interesting footbridges. One of 1904 is a 70m steel suspension bridge with tapered steel lattice pillars which were encased in concrete in 1973 to protect them. The other is a 20m reinforced concrete arch of 1912. Bournemouth gives way to Poole.

Branksome Chine, again with no beach at high water, is a narrow gorge cut into an earlier wider valley. There are lion's mane jellyfish despite the jet skiers, waterskiers, windsurfers and surfers. Here and at Canford Cliffs Chine, Flag Head Chine, Poole Head and Sandbanks there are steep waves on southerly to southeasterly force 5/6 winds.

The soft cliffs finally end at Poole Head and the B3369 runs out along the spit to affluent Sandbanks, which overlooks the entrance to Poole Harbour, perhaps the largest natural harbour in the world, used for at least two millennia. Poole returns to Dorset. The combined estuary of the Piddle, Frome and Corfe Rivers is used by car ferries from Poole to Cherbourg, St Malo, Guernsey and Jersey, freight vessels and 5,000 yachts. The rule of thumb is to stay out of the way of large commercial vessels. Beyond the chain ferry across the entrance is Brownsea Island with Branksea Castle in a commanding position. The 2km² island was the location of the world's first Scout camp in 1907 under Robert Baden-Powell.

Approach to the harbour is through the Swash Channel which runs between Hook Sand and a rubble training bank of 1876–1927 which extends out for a kilometre from the southeast end of Shell Bay and which covers at half tide. Flows out of the

The chain ferry crosses the entrance of Poole Harbour towards Sandbanks. Behind are Brownsea Island and Branksea Castle

The partly submerged training bank off Shell Bay. Looking across Studland Bay towards the Foreland

harbour are to 9km/h from HW Dover –0130 and they go in at up to 6km/h from HW Dover +0610. There is a strong rip on the northeast side of the entrance with either flow direction. Strong southerly winds give heavy seas over the bar and strong easterly winds alter the depth of the bar. South Haven peninsula is growing. In Shell and Studland Bays there are short surf waves with easterly winds of force 5.

This is the start of the South West Coast Path, Britain's longest footpath, featured in Mark Wallington's *500 Mile Walkies*, and the start of an AONB which extends to Bowleaze Cove.

In Studland Bay the Milkmaid Bank drying patches keep most craft away from the natural beauties on the naturist beach (designated by the National Trust). Behind are dunes which edge heathland with scrub and spartina grass and the

The 65,000,000 year old Ballard Down was previously connected to the Needles, the chalk dipping nearly vertically and the River Frome continuing along the syncline and through the Solent with tributaries from the north and south, but is now the end of the isolated Isle of Purbeck. In the same way, Studland Bay mirrors Alum Bay on the Isle of Wight.

The magnificent Dorset cliff coast begins abruptly at the 60m Foreland or Handfast Point where vertical chalk cliffs have the Yards, three projections from the cliffs, caves, arches and stacks, notably Old Harry (the Devil) and Old Harry's Wife, the top of whom broke off in a storm in 1896, making her a fallen woman, no doubt. The clear water is popular with shags, shelducks, fulmars, cormorants, kittiwakes, razorbills, oystercatchers, peregrine falcons,

Old Harry and his wife and other chalk features of the Foreland

Swanage Bay with Peveril Point on the left and Swanage itself on the right

Little Sea, a nature reserve adjoining Studland Heath with common and sand lizards, smooth and grass snakes, adders, slow worms and bird hides which overlook Slavonian grebes, teal, wigeon, tufted ducks, pochard, Brent geese, water rails and bar-tailed godwits in winter and nightjars, sedge, reed, Dartford and willow warblers, chiffchaffs, whinchats, stonechats, linnets, redpolls and common Sandwich terns in summer plus sanderlings, shearwaters, gannets and skuas in the autumn.

Crab pots are laid out from here to St Alban's Head. These are some of the warmest seawaters in Britain and Studland is a resort at the end of the B3351. Launching of kayaks is charged. Beyond Redend Point are Redend Rocks and the Seven Sisters show themselves at very low tides. The church of St Nicholas of Myra dates from Norman times. In the 16th century the village was used by pirates. A circular pillbox and gun emplacement are reminders that Churchill, Montgomery and Eisenhower watched practice wartime landings from the Manor House hotel.

The Pinnacles and Ballard Point, looking south towards Swanage

Old Harry Rocks, Studland Bay
South-west England 2nd

guillemots, puffins and blackbacked gulls. There are also many 20mm shell cases from Spitfire and Hurricane wartime live bombing practice raids in targets in the sea and on four tanks on the cliff top, these days with plenty of wild cabbage.

There is a strong race off the point with a southerly flow. All three east-facing bays at the end of the Isle of Purbeck have complex patterns of eddies.

The mainland cliff begins with St Lucas Leap and then has Parson's Barn above the 21m Little Pinnacle, followed by the 37m Pinnacle. The dramatic chalk cliff ends at Ballard Point, off which there is a race on the ebb.

Ballard Cliff, reaching off beyond Pinfold Cove round the northern edge of Swanage Bay, becomes cliff of sand and coloured clay. Streams are weak in the bay, in the middle of which is Potters Shoal which is used for shrimp fishing from February to April. There are also flounders, plaice, sole, bass and mackerel. New Swanage becomes **Swanage** where the Tanville Ledges run out eastwards, Phippards Ledge doing the same just to the south. As further north, there is short surf with force 5 easterly to southeasterly winds.

It was an easterly wind which drove 120 Danish ships ashore at Peveril in 877. They raided frequently in Anglo-Saxon times but this was not one of their successes, a monument on the seafront commemorating King Alfred's naval battle victory. The church of St Mary the Virgin was built in 1859, the fourth on the site since Norman times, the lower half of the tower of 1250 remaining and thought to have been built as a refuge against pirates. The Tithe Barn is now a museum and art centre covering the stone industry, fossils, handicrafts and paintings.

Swanage was Knollsea to Hardy, who lived here in 1875/6 while completing *The Hand of Ethelberta*. In Old English times it was Swana-wic, the herdsmen's workplace.

The Victorian resort developed at the end of the A351 and the railway, which is now the steam Swanage Railway and goes only to Nordham although there are hopes to extend it back to Wareham again. There is a promenade, Punch and Judy, a sandy beach and canoe and pedalo hire, features needed for a self-respecting resort. The Swanage Heritage Centre was established in 2001 and there is a Mowlem theatre, recalling civil engineering contractor John Mowlem. Producing and exporting Purbeck stone and marble was an important industry for the town and a derelict wooden jetty exported the stone to build Salisbury Cathedral, Westminster Abbey and others. There were also some significant imports. The Wellington Clock Tower of 1854 on the shore originally obstructed the southern approach to London Bridge and was moved here in 1867. The town hall of 1883 has a façade which was designed by Edward Jermain, a pupil of Wren, and moved here from Mercer's Hall in London's Cheapside. The police station with its gaol of 1803 at the back is now a shop, presumably more secure than most. Swanage pier is Victorian. Windsurfing and diving are popular in the area.

The bay ends at Peveril Point which is overlooked by a National Coastwatch Institution lookout point and is backed by low cliffs, off which is a strong race with a south southwesterly stream. Taking out is straightforward in various places but it will be necessary to move across to the centre of town to get a vehicle close as the parking areas near the point seem to be privately owned and not welcoming of visitors.

Distance
From Calshot to Peveril Point is 60km
Campsites
Hamble-le-Rice, Gt Thorness, Newbridge, Totland, Downton, Bransgore, Hurn, Hamworthy, Ulwell, Swanage
Youth Hostels
Portsmouth, Totland Bay, Burley and Swanage
OS 1:50,000 Sheets
195 Bournemouth and Purbeck
196 Solent and Isle of Wight
Imray Charts
2200 Solent
C3 Isle of Wight (1:52,500)
C4 Needles Channel to Bill of Portland (1:75,000)
C15 Solent – Bembridge to Hurst Point and Southampton (1:35,000)
Y23 Poole Harbour (1:17,000)
Stanfords Allweather Charts
7 English Channel Central Section (1:156,000)
11 Solent and Isle of Wight (1:84,000)
12 Needles to Start Point (1:175,000)
15 Dorset Harbours and Approaches
24 Solent and Approaches
25 Solent Harbours
L9 Western Solent (1:29,000). Lymington River (1:7,100). Keyhaven (1:9,300)
L10 Western Solent Harbours. Beaulieu River (1:11,000)
L12 Poole Harbour (1:14,500)
Admiralty Charts
SC 2021 Harbours and Anchorages in the West Solent Area. Beaulieu River (1:10,000). Lymington River (1:5,000). Approaches to Keyhaven (1:7,500)
SC 2035 Western Approaches to the Solent (1:25,000)
SC 2036 Solent and Southampton Water (1:25,000)
SC 2045 Outer Approaches to the Solent (1:75,000)
SC 2172 Harbours and Anchorages on the South Coast of England. Christchurch Harbour (1:7,500). Swanage and Studland Bays (1:12,500)
SC 2175 Poole Bay (1:20,000)
SC 2610 Bill of Portland to Anvil Point (1:40,000)
SC 2611 Poole Harbour and Approaches (1:12,500)
SC 2615 Bill of Portland to the Needles (1:75,000)
SC 5600 Solent and Approaches
Tidal Constants
Calshot Castle: HW Dover +0010, LW Dover
Stansore Point: HW Dover –0010, LW Dover +0010
Lymington: HW Dover –0020, LW Dover
Hurst Pt: Dover –0020
Christchurch Entrance: HW Dover –0040, LW Dover –0020
Bournemouth: HW Dover –0030, LW Dover –0020
Poole Harbour Entrance: HW Dover –0020, LW Dover –0010
Swanage: HW Dover –0030, LW Dover –0040
Submarine Area
O1
Sea Areas
Wight, Portland
Rescue
Inshore lifeboats: Calshot, Lymington, Mudeford, Poole, Swanage
All weather lifeboats: Calshot, Yarmouth, Poole, Swanage
Maritime Rescue Centres
Solent, 023 9255 2100
Portland, 01305 760439

58 DORSET

Britain's most fascinating coastal scenery

Had I but lived a hundred years ago
I might have gone, as I have gone this year,
By Warmwell Cross on to a Cove I know,
And Time have placed his finger on me there:

'You see that man?' – I might have looked, and said,
'O yes: I see him. One that boat has brought
Which dropped down Channel round Saint Alban's Head.
So commonplace a youth calls not my thought.'

Thomas Hardy

The 150km of Jurassic Coast from Swanage to Exmouth was declared England's first natural World Heritage Site in 2001 because of its fossils which cover 180,000,000 years, new fossils appearing after rough weather. It also includes some of the most interesting cliff scenery and other coastal geology around Britain.

tonne Portland stone feature. This is also the best place to see the early spider orchid.

There is a race off the head on the southwestgoing stream, which begins at HW Dover –0030 and begins northeastwards at HW Dover +0530 at up to 6km/h.

Puffins, guillemots, razorbills and cormorants like this coast. The dark limestone cliffs with extensive quarries from Anvil Point to St Alban's Head are also very popular with climbers.

A measured distance is marked out above the cliffs, the start of which is near Tilly Whim Caves which were used by smugglers. The quarry owner was George Tilly and his whim or gantry crane was used for lowering stone, but could be equally effective for raising contraband.

A 12m round white lighthouse tower of 1881 and a dwelling are located on Anvil Point on the end of Round Down, the light only 45m above sea level to remain below orographic cloud. It was electrified in 1960 and the optic donated to the Science Museum in London.

At the northern end of Durlston Bay there is surf with a force 4 southerly wind and southwesterly swell. On the other hand, if conditions are settled the water can be clear to 7m as far as Weymouth and lone divers might be met, just wetsuited heads and floating torpedo buoy markers. From Peveril Point to Anvil Point is a Marine Research Area and Voluntary Marine Nature Reserve, including a marine hydrophone to pick up any indiscretions.

Durlston Head slopes up from a low undercut cliff to the 1.2km^2 Durlston Country Park. Durlston Castle began life in 1890 as a restaurant, the reverse of the normal procedure. Three years earlier civil engineering contractor John Mowlem had presented the Great Globe, a 3m diameter 40

Durlston Head with its undercut cliff

Many of the coastal features have intriguing names with sound reasoning. Topmast refers to the loss of the sailing ship *Alexandranova* in 1882 with her 77 crew in a violent storm, following

which a topmast was found on top of the cliffs. Long Hole is 6m deep. Blackers Hole has jackdaws although there used to be breeding peregine falcons. Dancing Ledge is as big as a dance floor and has ruts for stone carts, having supplied much of the rock to build Ramsgate Harbour. After Durnford preparatory school's pool and the Cannon is Pig and Whistle Cave, named after the noise made by waves.

chapel to St Aldhelm with 1.2m thick walls, circular on top to hold a lit beacon.

West of the head is used as a warship exercise area with firing from the sea. Yellow DZ buoys are targets and should not be approached within 1.6km, the nearest being 4km offshore.

It seems a remote coast but there are 26,000 lobster pots from here to Portland Bill, meaning quite a lot of fishing boat inspections. From here to

Seacombe Cliff and St Alban's Head

The horizontal strata have left some large rectangular holes around Seacombe Cliff and there are a mixture of caves and disused quarries. The Romans had a number of quarries around the Isle of Purbeck and stone has been a regular export from the area since then.

Mike's Cove and Willie's Cove are separated by the cylindrical Watch Rock, on which a watch was found after a ship was lost with all her crew. In 1786 the East Indiaman *Halsewell*, on passage from Dover to Bengal, was lost here with 158 of the 240 on board.

Winspit Bottom below Worth Matravers had coastal quarries which provided stone for Allhallows school and is overlooked by the hills of East Man and West Man, each with strip lynchets. Greater horseshoe bats now occupy the quarries. Crab Hole, no doubt, was somebody's favourite fishing spot.

St Aldhelm's or St Alban's Head is unusual in that the point is neither high nor steep, so that landing on the rocks is not too difficult but then high cliffs rise up behind. St Alban's Ledge runs out for some 8km to the southwest. There is a strong

Kimmeridge Bay there are dark cliffs fringed by hard clay ledges.

Chapman's Pool has a long hollow reef break after a force 5 southwesterly. It is overlooked by the 50m Houns-tout Cliff, tout being Old English for lookout, the vertical face attracting birds. On Egmont Point, to the west of Chapman's Pool, is

The weed protected projecting nose in Egmont Bight

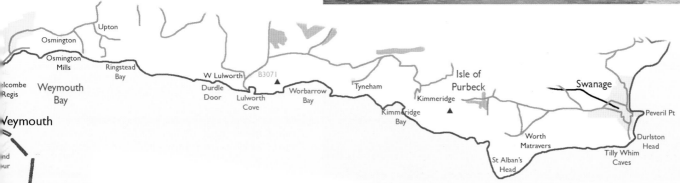

the Powder House, the remains of a gun battery position.

The cliffs are very fragmented blackstone shale to Kimmeridge, producing an unusual situation where a stream enters Egmont Bight. Normally it would have carved a valley, as it has done at higher levels. When it reaches the cliffs, however, the green vegetation growing in the water is more resistant than the rocks alone and so the water trickles down from the top of a nose projecting into the sea while cliffs have been eaten back on each side. Cliff falls are frequent and reveal fossils. There are the remains of the Freshwater Steps and the foundations of a pumphouse to pump water to a large bath at Lord Eldon's Encombe House.

race over it with a calm passage on the inside which may be only 50m wide with a mere half hour free of overfalls at the turn of spring tides. Flows west-northwest begin at HW Dover –0020 and they begin east-southeast at HW Dover +0540 at up to 9km/h. There are eddies on both sides of the head, especially on the west side.

It was visited in about 700 by the Saxon bishop St Aldhelm while waiting for winds to sail to see the Pope. On the top of the head is a Norman

The wreck of the *Treveal* is 800m south, sunk in a gale with the loss of 36 of the 43 on board while on her maiden voyage from Calcutta. The drifter *Abide* tried to salvage the jute on board and was holed on the wreckage. In 1952 the *Glenmore* also sank on the wreckage, all of which has since been flattened. However, a barge with a cargo of stone sank 400m northwest and can dry with some tides.

Swyre Head, at 203m, overlooks Rope Lake Head. There have been many wrecks on the Kimmeridge Ledges from here, popular with divers.

The Clavell Tower at the approach to Kimmeridge Bay

In the 1630s Sir William Clavell of Smedmore House used the oil shale as a fuel to extract salt from sea water, established an alum factory and exported his product by ship although he failed to build a stone jetty to make Kimmeridge a port. Shale mines followed in the 19th century. These days Clavell's Hard has sea cabbages, rock pipits, oystercatchers, mallards and herring gulls but no industry. All that remains overlooking Kimmeridge Bay is the 1820 Clavell Tower folly built with classical motifs and Tuscan columns by the Revd John Clavell for astronomy.

Gad Cliff feels very powerful and threatening

Worbarrow Bay with the forbidden beach of Arish Mell

Beside Kimmeridge Bay is the Fine Foundation Marine Centre which opened in 2001 with displays on the Purbeck Marine Wildlife Reserve which reaches from St Alban's Head to the far side of Worbarrow Bay, even having a live link to a seabed camera. Here are blennies, gobies, prawns, crabs, corkwings, ballan wrasse, pipe fish, 15-spined sticklebacks, bass, pilchard, snakelocks anemones and sargassum seaweed while brittlestars, piddocks, sponges, anemones, sea fans and soft corals live in the deeper water where an underwater nature trail has been laid out for divers. Giant ammonites and other fossils are found around the bay. On the west side of the bay is an oil well with a nodding donkey which draws 1.8m^3/day from the Kimmeridge shales through a 550m well of 1958, making it second only to Wytch Farm as a British onshore well. In the 19th century there were also glass and cement works here.

Kimmeridge is known for its surf with Ledges Bay and Broad Bench giving rides of up to 1.6km under the right conditions. Broad Bench is a reef break which can give 4m waves, more after a southwesterly force 5 or 6, best in a light north to northwesterly breeze. Board surfers and windsurfers are attracted. Approach is down a toll road.

The pillbox and tank traps at the entrance are reminders of wartime concern, as was a German mine taken out of a fishing net in 1951. More relevant today, however, is the 28km^2 Lulworth Gunnery Range which runs from here to Lulworth Cove. It has been used since 1916 with tanks firing from the shore, usually to 10km out but sometimes to 19km. 70,000 high velocity shells are fired per year and anything suspicious on a beach should be reported but not touched. Red flags and lights are shown on St Alban's Head and Bindon Hill when the range is in use. Firing stops for passing vessels but a range control vessel is able to prevent loitering, which is a significant part of the pleasure in such scenery.

Charnel was an old landing site inside Broad Bench. Between Broad Bench and Long Ebb is Hobarrow Bay, a Roman industrial site. There was also a Roman settlement behind Brandy Bay, which was later used by smugglers, as the name suggests. These days goats, adders, peregrines and ravens nesting are the occupants. Tyneham Cap is a reminder of Tyneham village, beyond, which was temporarily evacuated in 1943 when the range was extended, the surviving occupants still waiting for permission to return. There is an exhibition in the church, which may be visited when the range is not in use.

Beyond Gad Cliff and Wagon Rocks, with a conical hill on its summit, is Worbarrow Tout, just before which is an inlet with dragon's teeth tank traps, probably less effective than the rocks.

Behind Worbarrow Bay remains much of the part of Flower's Barrow which has not been eroded by the sea, 2.4km of a unique beach head fortification by Iron Age invaders of about 400BC to control Lulworth Cove. Later, the Romans camped here after conquering the Veniti.

Halfway along the back of the bay is the white sandy beach at Arish Mell where landing is prohibited. There are concrete blocks across the

outfall from the Winfrith Heath nuclear establishment.

Butcher's Rock, Cockpit Head, Black Rock and Mackerel Rock lead to Mupe Bay with Mupe Ledges and Mupe Rocks, used by shags. Outside is the Bacon Hole cave used in the 19th century by smugglers. A fossil forest resulted when trees became submerged in a swamp and covered in algae, to which sediments stuck.

Below Bindon Hill, Southcliff is a fine example of broken beds while Potter's Hole was a dwelling. At Little Bindon the 12th-century Cistercian abbey was converted to a chapel and cottage in 1250, remodelled in 1500 and brick faced in the 18th century. It also has 18th-century sailing ships scratched in the plaster and a ceiling painted with stars and planets.

Lulworth Cove attracts varied watersports as well as many holidaymakers on foot

One of the most popular beauty spots on the south coast is Lulworth Cove at the end of the B3071, the prime jewel in a coast rich with geological jewels. It has attracted authors, poets and painters since the 18th-century. Rupert Brooke stayed with the Neo Pagans, Keats wrote his last sonnet here and perhaps *Bright Star*, to Hardy it was Lulwind Cove where Sgt Troy was drowned in *Far from the Madding Crowd* and it was used for filming *Mansfield Park*. Between 1879 and 1955 the public came from Weymouth by paddle steamer. The heritage centre features paddle steamers, smuggling, oil and local flora, fauna and history. A stone jetty enclosed an oyster pond and the mill pond was used for washing clothes and sheep, not necessarily together, fed by a spring which also provided West Lulworth's water, now lacking its cob and thatched mill which collapsed. The Doll's House began life as a Canadian log cabin brought over on the deck of a ship, to which were added a brick skin, chimney stack and two bedrooms in the roof. The locality has also given its name to the Lulworth skipper butterfly, only found between Swanage and Sidmouth.

South Ledge had low tide impressions of fossil pine trees. More impressive to most visitors is the heavy swell which results from southerly winds, not helping such bodies as the diving school operating within the cove.

Inside Stair Hole, showing the tortured strata

Just west is Stair Hole in which there are several arches where the sea has eaten into the Lulworth crumple rock strata. This coast is very popular for geology field trips because the whole sequence is here. Stair Hole will later widen out like Lulworth Cove, lose its protective Portland stone and excavate the Wealden clays as at Worbarrow and Mupe, further widening like Man o' War, then producing a straight coast as further west, before eroding it completely as in Poole Bay.

Beyond Dungy Head, St Oswald's Bay below Hambury Tout has surf with southwesterly winds but dumps at the west end. Blackbacked gulls frequent the vicinity.

At the west end of Man o' War Cove is the best of all the Dorset coast features, Durdle Door, a 12m natural arch of Purbeck limestone. After the wonderfully named Scratchy Bottom, the protective layer of rock is reduced to a series of bovine bottom scratching subsurface rocks. The Bull, the Blind (hidden) Cow, the Cow and the Calf lead past the precipice of Bat's Head where a wave carved bat cave or mousehole at the bottom passes through from east to west. Like most of these arches and holes, it just asks to be paddled through, easily done at the right state of the tide.

The Warren, with Wardstone Beacon, tumuli and field systems, has guillemots nesting. Once a herd of cattle fell to their deaths here.

Stair Hole with various entrances. Note the climbers on the cliffs

The great chalk
arch of
Durdle Door

The cliffs at White Nothe are 50m high and chalky white. On top, the coastguard cottages are the highest buildings on the Dorset coast. Now the cliffs begin to decline in height and to vary in colour. Hang gliders ridge soar. A smugglers' path passes behind the Bear, which perhaps ought to be the Bare as it is used by naturists.

Upton Fort of 1902 had two 230mm guns and was used until after the second world war.

Osmington Mills was used by the late 18th-century smuggler French Peter. It has thatched stone cottages and a coastguard built slip which had a lifeboat during the second world war and occasional fishing boats since then. It now has an

Bat's Head with its
tunnel

Ringstead Bay has windsurfers and lobster pots but made its name with Burning Cliff above the bay. From 1826 the oil shale burned for 4 years, the oil having a high sulphur content which produced a lot of smoke and a strong smell. With the fire safely out it now has a 46ha nature reserve with kestrels and green woodpeckers. Ringstead Village itself was abandoned in the Middle Ages because of the combined effects of pirates and Black Death.

Ringstead Ledges run out from Bran Point. Wrecks on the rocks include the 1927 loss of the coal barge *Minx*. There is a bad weather anchorage further off.

Oxfordshire field study centre. Above is an 85m x 98m high white horse of 1808 on the hillside, the only English white horse to have a rider, George III.

Black Head correctly gives the change of cliff colour but is slightly concave rather than being a headland. A wreck obviously got it wrong, too, on Black Head Ledges. Beyond, at Osmington, is a Pontin's holiday centre. Rocks behind beaches here have sand ripples and burrows fossilized.

Redcliffe Point is a more accurate description of the next coastal feature and is the limit of Port of Weymouth control. From Bowleaze Cove a modern sea wall runs along the foot of Furzy Cliff, above which are the remains of a Roman temple. Suddenly it gets busy as the A353 arrives on land and buoys funnel in windsurfers, waterskiers and jet skiers from Weymouth Bay over a submerged wall towards a landing with toilets. Within the areas of buoys in summer it is necessary to give way to swimmers. Surf is best at low water with southeasterly winds.

Weymouth Bay is one of the warmest, driest, sunniest areas in the country. Certainly the lion's mane jellyfish like it. The flows are mostly westgoing to 1km/h but may be negligible to the southeast from HW Dover –0510 for two hours.

The 1.4km² Lodmore Country Park has picnic tables and barbecue stands, SR2 flight simulator, Rio Grande Railway, Leisure Ranch with Cresta Run, go-kart circuit, bumper boats, hundreds of models in Model World, 9 hole mini golf, Sea Life Centre and Butterfly Farm with one of the largest marine life displays in Europe at 2.4ha, ocean tank, cliff habitat, sand basin, fish farming, tidepool tank and intertidal deep tank, Tropical Jungle with birds and iguanas and RSPB nature reserve with hides and seamarsh birds, being good for migrating and wintering birds including bearded tits.

Melcombe Regis has a statue of George III from 1810 and an ornate Queen Victoria jubilee clock of 1887. It also has St John's church which was fully restored before being attacked by an arsonist in 2001.

harbour which was at one time a Roman port. Brewers Quay in a former Victorian Devenish brewery shows brewing with a Timewalk through the town's history, looking at the Black Death, a Spanish galleon, a Georgian ballroom and Discovery science. The Museum of Local History features paddle-steamers, cross-Channel ships, shipwrecks, fishing, George III's bathing machine of 1789, an 18th-century fire engine, wartime relics, a Larret mackerel boat, an Armada treasure chest, a Roman pavement, coffin and skeleton and paintings by Hogarth and others. Deep Sea Adventure includes the *Titanic* and underwater exploration.

One of Weymouth harbour's breakwaters was built in 1903 to deflect waves rebounding off the northern breakwater of Portland Harbour. Overlooking it is the Nothe, 15m high with a fort built in 1860–72 to defend Portland Harbour against the threat of Napoleonic invasion. The fort has been restored with the Museum of Coastal Defence and has the only operational coastal defence searchlight in the country, displays of 40mm anti-aircraft and other guns, weapons, Mk VIII torpedo, underground magazines, garrison life of Victorian and second world war soldiers, Ferret Scout Car and other military vehicles and paddle-steamers and a children's assault course. It was used by the BBC for filming *Beau Geste* and *Knockback*. The Nothe has band concerts and the

Paddle-steamer *Waverley* at Weymouth pier

Weymouth with the Nothe prominent, the harbourmouth in the centre and the esplanade and main beach on the right

Weymouth has made two notable introductions to England, firstly Black Death in 1348. In 1789 George III was sent there because of his health, making it the first resort by beginning the practice of nude sea bathing, not at some secluded cove but out of a bathing machine with a small orchestra playing the *National Anthem*. The Gloucester Hotel was the Gloucester Lodge at that time, George III's summer home where Cabinet meetings were held, part of a Georgian seafront. The gently sloping beach is ideal for children and, with the

Nothe Gardens with picnic tables, barbecue facilities, a floodlit waterfall and Newton's Cove, which now has a new promenade and seawall as part of a scheme to stop housing and a DEFRA laboratory slipping into the sea as Nothe Clay slides over Nothe Grits, a scheme which was difficult because the contractor could only reach it from the beach at low tide. The Mixon, an underwater ridge, runs out towards a degaussing range after the Port of Weymouth gives way to Portland Port control.

The North Ship Channel leading into Portland Harbour. Portland Heights rise beyond

esplanade, offers all the facilities of a resort, a land train, Punch and Judy shows, donkey rides, swingboats, merry-go-rounds, helter-skelter, trampolines, pedaloes, sandcastles and sand sculptor in what is called the Naples of England, Budmouth Regis to Hardy, who used it in *The Trumpet-Major* and *Under the Greenwood Tree*. It was used for filming his *Far from the Madding Crowd* in 1967 and also *The French Lieutenant's Woman*. There is a fireworks festival barge. Angling contests also take place with a fleet of boats racing out of Weymouth Road at a set time, usually 9am.

Fishing and recreational vessels are joined in the summer by catamarans to Guernsey, Jersey and St Malo. 3 green lights indicate a vessel arriving and 3 red lights one departing from the 17th-century

Portland Harbour is Britain's largest artificial harbour, the second largest man-made harbour in the world and, in the 19th century, one of the greatest civil engineering projects undertaken in England, being 4km across. It has been naval since the Crimean War until the recent decision to pull out the Royal Navy from HMS Osprey. The west side is protected by land and the east side by breakwaters, on which landing is forbidden without a licence. The harbour was constructed on a Saxon stronghold in 1847 by convicts awaiting transportation to Australia. In 1893 the two northern breakwaters were added to give protection against torpedo attacks. The breakwaters are of Portland stone, up to 7 tonnes per block, tipped from trucks on a temporary railway built along the top. Sections of Mulberry

Harbour, used for D-Day landings, can be seen on the southern side of Portland Harbour.

The entrances have semi-circular walls faced with granite above water level. Notices require craft to keep 30m from these. Flows through the gaps reach 2km/h and there are eddies off the ends of the breakwater but there is negligible flow in the Inner Harbour. Regulations required craft to keep clear of naval squadrons, the arrival of which was indicated for the North Ship Channel by a particular flag flying from the *northern* arm of the flagstaff at the East Ship Channel 1.5km away. A torpedo firing point operates eastwards from the North-eastern Breakwater when orange flags fly but operates in an easterly direction so that entering the North Ship Channel avoids any conflicts.

Above Balaclava Bay the Verne citadel on Portland Heights was a 19th-century battery with 320mm guns with a 6km range, used as a prison since 1950. St Peter's church of 1872 was built entirely by convicts with a fine floor, mosaic borders, a superb mediaeval style timber roof and much creative work. Before a rifle range, the original transportation prison has become a Borstal Institution.

Less conspicuous than the masts and the white radome on the summit is the Nicodemus Knob left as a navigation mark but also showing the ground level before quarrying began, Portland stone starts grey but weathers to white, is easy to carve but is very durable and has been used for many of London's public buildings including St Paul's cathedral and all Wren's churches, Buckingham

The port area in Portland Harbour. The three sea kayaks in front of the building on the left are in the prohibited area

A prison ship has been located at the southern end to supplement overcrowded jails, recalling prison hulks of the 19th century. There is a prohibited area to the west of the approach to the South Ship Channel but direct approach avoids this. The port could be reopened to the navy as it is said that the next generation of aircraft carriers will be too deep for any UK port, something which might have seemed a basic design criterion. The former naval base and dockyard are currently a commercial port.

Palace, the Monument, the Cenotaph, Somerset House, Bush House, the Bank, the Royal Exchange, the Mansion House, the Law Courts and the British Museum.

Off Grove Point, Fiddler's Race runs for seven hours from local high water. A pillbox protects the area. A derrick crane serves Durdle Pier, the first of a number to lift boats onto the rock ledges along this side of the island. Another pillbox or perhaps a hide is built of best Portland stone, well camouflaged in the area, unlike the park of

The South Ship Channel with a power cable suspended across. HMS Hood lies in the gap. The Nicodemus Knob shows the original cliff level

The South Ship Channel can have a nasty sea in the entrance, especially with strong westerly, southwesterly or easterly winds. In 1914 *HMS Hood* was sunk across the entrance as a blockship and is now popular with divers. In addition, an overhead power cable hangs low across the entrance.

Weymouth and Portland were at their busiest during the second world war when they despatched 600,000 men and 140,000 vehicles in a year. In June 1944 they were two of the main departure points for the Normany landings with embarkation for Omaha Beach, the largest invasion fleet ever assembled.

The Isle of Portland consists mostly of Portland stone, so beloved of architects for public buildings. Portland takes its name from Porta, a Saxon pirate who seized the island in 501. To poet and novelist Thomas Hardy it was the Isle of Slingers or the Gibraltar of Wessex. It is a 7km wedge of limestone nearly 150m high at the northern end but sloping nearly to sea level at the southern end.

caravans, and looks over clear water with bootlace weed, blackbacked gulls and cormorants. Broadcraft Quarry was Britain's first butterfly reserve, the silver studded blue not being found anywhere else in Britain, and it also has rare ivy broomrape and ravens. A dismantled railway previously ran close to the shoreline.

Portland Museum covers the navy, maritime history, shipwrecks, smuggling, convicts, Portland stone, fossils, geology, natural history, household items, Portland sheep and Thomas Hardy, being based in a pair of 300-year old cottages which inspired Alice's cottage in *The Well-Beloved*, the island also being featured in *The Trumpet-Major*.

The limit of Portland Port control is reached by Church Ope Cove. Above the water are the ruins of Rufus Castle, captured in 1142 by the Earl of Gloucester. Pennsylvania Castle of 1800 is now a hotel standing amongst the only trees on an island with generally spartan vegetation more reminiscent of Mediterranean limestone landscapes. Slightly older is St George's church of 1776, perhaps the

most impressive 18th-century church in Dorset with an unspoilt original interior and the grave of a local woman shot by a press gang. Almost to the 20th century, land transactions were recorded by church gift, the cutting of notches in reed poles kept in churches, the distances between the notches showing the quantity of land and being legally binding. To the north of Church Ope Cove are Boy's Rocks and to the south Girl's Rocks, 150 steps up from the beach between with the Pirates Grave Yard.

Marguerita lost in a gale in 1946 with a Danish crew, while an engine on the seabed is from the 1949 wreck of the *Reliance*. The area is popular with divers. The Ledge runs eastwards from the southern part of the island with a race or shaffle over it. Hardy referred to it as the Race, off the Beal.

The 140,000,000 year old Bill of Portland is 6m high. Two lighthouses were completed in 1716 in transit to clear the Shambles bank, the higher a 41m tower. The lower was converted in the late

Church Ope Cove with Rufus Castle on the right and Pennsylvania Castle amongst the trees

In calm conditions it is possible to land in Freshwater Bay, popular with climbers although marred by a rubbish tip. A pumping station supplied water from a spring for the naval base. At Southwell, St Andrew's church remains have gravestones marked with skulls and crossbones, indicating Black Death. St Andrew's Avalanche church is in memory of those lost from the clipper *Avalanche* off Portland in 1879 en route to New Zealand and houses artefacts from the ship.

Field systems and the Culverwell mesolithic site on top of the island are outdone for interest by all the caves, derricks, disused quarries and undercut rocks along the edge of the island, where fishing boats were entered by climbing down knotted ropes. The east side of the island is losing 300mm/year as the rocks are undercut and fall into the sea. The Butts have the remains of the

1780s to be the first to have glass lenses and Argand lamps. It is now a bird migration watchpoint observatory. The light also attracted the French so two 8kg cannons were installed. In 1906 a new 41m white round towered lighthouse was built with a red band. The Comber family were lighthouse keepers from 1721 to 1911. There is a nearby 18m white stone beacon. Off the bill is the most difficult piece of water on the south coast of England. Southward eddies on both sides of the head cause violent disturbance where they meet east–west flows over the Portland Ledge, resulting in cathedral-sized holes and noise which can be heard over a considerable distance. There is always smooth water inside the race, up to 1.6km wide, with weaker and shorter eddies off spring tides. Flows southwards on both sides of the island can run for 9 hours in 12 at up to 19km/h, the streams

Freshwater Bay with one of the derrick cranes used for boat launching

The Bill of Portland with the current lighthouse and a daymark on the southern end of the island

weakening around Lyme Bay to 3km/h on the west side. An anticlockwise eddy on the east side begins at HW Dover +0620 to be 18km long after ten hours twenty minutes. A clockwise eddy on the west side begins at HW Dover –0150 to grow to 13km long but affects the coast further west. The best time to pass west is at HW Dover –0140 and the best time eastwards is at HW Dover +0550. To Berry Head all of the water lies within the 37m contour.

The first British battleship to be torpedoed by a German U boat, *HMS Formidable*, went down off Portland Bill in 1915.

also a nature reserve with orchids, rock roses and other rare limestone plants attracting unique butterflies.

Chesil Cove has surf with a southwesterly wind. On the other side of the A354 behind West Bay is a tank farm and what was a naval helicopter base, still used in part for search and rescue helicopters, the rest now a sailing centre which will host the 2012 Olympic sailing. Immediately adjacent and facing into Portland Harbour, which was not there at the time of its construction in 1539, is Portland Castle, one of Henry VIII's finest coastal forts, used to defend against the French and Spanish and then used

Pulpit Rock with a tempting gap inside

Chesil Beach with the head of the Fleet on the right and Lyme Bay on the left

Heading north, the first structure of significance is Pulpit Rock, the gap between it and the main mass of island rock occupied by a wedged rock. The location is associated with smuggling and there are several caves close by. The next 200m are known as Whitehall as it supplied much of the stone for government buildings in London's Whitehall. Near the Old High lighthouse, now a guesthouse, there is a blowhole.

The west side of the island has disused quarries, particularly between Weston and **Fortuneswell**. Tout Quarry has become a sculpture park with over 40 sculptures in the rock face or on loose rocks. It is

to deter piracy. It was one of the last forts to surrender to Cromwell. It was used as the private residence of harbour builder Captain Charles Manning in Victorian times. It was a seaplane station in the first world war, was used in 1944 when US troops were departing for D-Day and has been home to Wrens. It has reproduction Elizabethan armour and impressive cannons.

The sea has risen 60m since the Ice Age, when the coastline was 16km further south. Chesil Beach, Old English cisel, shingle, is a tombolo and is moving slowly northwards. The 13km of graded pebbles of flint, quartzite and limestone, including some chert

and jasper, form part of a 29km sweep of shingle around Lyme Bay and is the most fascinating shingle structure in Britain and possibly the longest in Europe. The beach gets lower (from 13m) and narrower (from 180m) towards its western end, the depth of shingle decreasing from 15m to 11m in this direction and the size of the pebbles being carefully graded from fist size at Chesilton to pea size at Bridport, so precisely that fishermen lost in the fog

and West Bexington there are chalets with caravan sites at Swyre and Cogden Beach. Carparks are easy to spot because these are the sections of beach in use, the rest being largely deserted.

Cogden Beach effectively brings an end to the Chesil Beach although shingle beach continues for some distance. The parking area is up towards the B3157 and just along from the Othona community's centre.

can tell their location from the size of stones on the beach. Below water level the stones are graded in the opposite direction. Some of the stones have been recovered from Maiden Castle where they were used with slings. Blue clay lies below the shingle some 900mm–1.2m above low water springs. Cans or hollows on the inside of the beach are where water has seeped through and washed the bank away.

Occasionally the beach is overtopped by storms after strong southwesterly winds. In 1795 seven ships under Rear Admiral Sir Hugh Christian, on their way to the West Indies, were lost here with 200 men and women. In 1824 the West Indiamen *Carvalho* and *Colville* were lost with all hands in the storm which carried the 95 tonne sloop *Ebenezer* into the Fleet on a wave. A ship was left on top of the beach in 1853. In 1872 a number of looters died of hypothermia after starting on the cargo of schnapps carried by the wrecked *Royal Adelaide*. Even whales and dolphins may be washed up and an 18th-century mermaid turned out to be a dead camel.

The beach is steep and can have heavy breakers, a dump and a strong undertow. Behind Chesil Beach the Fleet occupies what Hardy called the Waddon Vale.

Chesil Beach forms part of the West Dorset Heritage Coast but is closed to walkers for half the year. It has a diverse range of bird and animal life. Three species of tern breed on the shingle bank, being a protected breeding site for the little tern. There are bass, pollock and flatfish in the water and a line of anglers along the beach.

Red flags and lookout points on Chesil Beach, opposite Charlestown at Tidmoor Point, mark the limits of the danger area from the Chickerell firing range which operates from the camp on the north side but is a danger even on the open sea.

The top of the bank is littered with cuttlefish bones and fishing floats.

St Catherine's chapel of 1376–1401 on Chapel Hill has an elaborately vaulted stone roof, rare in England. It may have been built as a landmark for sailors and its survival was perhaps due to its use as a tower for a maritime fire beacon.

Abbotsbury Gardens are subtropical, the shingle absorbing the sun's heat and Chesil Beach providing shelter so that there are enormous exotic trees, shrubs and flowers, azaleas, ancient camellias, rhododendrons, 8ha of woodland and formal gardens, 18th-century walled gardens of the former Abbotsbury Castle, Victorian garden, New Zealand garden, an aviary, peacocks and rare pheasants and there is still room for some cow parsley. Abbotsbury was Hardy's Abbotsea.

Pillboxes guard the coast near Lawrence of Arabia's cottage. Between Labour in Vain Farm

Distance
From Peveril Point to Cogden Beach is 78km
Campsites
Swanage, Langton Matravers, Acton, Harman's Cross, Church Knowle, East Creek, West Lulworth, Osmington Mills, Preston, Lanehouse, Charlestown, Chickerell, Portesham, Burton Bradstock
Youth Hostels
Swanage, Lulworth Cove, Portland, Litton Cheney
OS 1:50,000 Sheets
194 Dorchester and Weymouth
195 Bournemouth and Purbeck
Imray Charts
2200 Solent
C4 Needles Channel to Bill of Portland (1:75,000)
C5 Bill of Portland to Salcombe Harbour (1:100,000)
Stanfords Allweather Charts
7 English Channel Central Section (1:156,000)
12 Needles to Start Point (1:175,000)
15 Dorset Harbours and Approaches
22 South Devon Coast
Admiralty Charts
SC 2172 Harbours and Anchorages on the South Coast of England. Swanage and Studland Bays (1:12,500). Chapman's Pool (1:12,500). Worbarrow Bay (1:12,500). Lulworth Cove (1:5,000). Weymouth Harbour (1:5,000)
2255 Approaches to Portland and Weymouth (1:20,000)
2268 Portland Harbour (1:10,000). Portland Port Berthing Plan (1:5,000)
SC 2610 Bill of Portland to Anvil Point (1:40,000)
SC 2615 Bill of Portland to the Needles (1:75,000)
SC 3315 Berry Head to Bill of Portland (1:75,000)
SC 5600 Solent and Approaches
SC 5601 East Devon and Dorset Coast, Exmouth to Christchurch
Tidal Constants
Swanage: HW Dover –0030, LW Dover –0040
Lulworth Cove: HW Dover –0430, LW Dover –0440
Portland: HW Dover –0500, LW Dover –0540
Chesil Cove: HW Dover –0450, LW Dover –0540
Chesil Beach: HW Dover –0450, LW Dover –0540
Bridport (West Bay): HW Dover –0510, LW Dover –0540
Ranges
Lulworth, Chickerell
Submarine Areas
O1, D031 N1, D026 Lulworth Inner, X 5021B, D014 Chesil Bank, X 5018, D012 Lyme Bay North
Sea Area
Portland
Rescue
Inshore lifeboats: Swanage, Weymouth, Lyme Regis
All weather lifeboats: Swanage, Weymouth
Maritime Rescue Centre
Portland, 01305 760439

Wears Hill rises beyond Abbotsbury

59 LYME BAY

Britain's Jurassic coast

There was an old loony of Lyme,
Whose candour was simply sublime;
  When they asked, 'Are you there?'
  'Yes,' he said, 'but take care,
For I'm never "all there" at a time.'

Brit is too small for **Bridport** to function as a port and West Bay served this purpose, declining after the railway arrived. Quite large vessels can use West Bay to deliver timber and take away sand and gravel. Pea-sized Bridport gravel has been used for surfacing the skid pan of the Transport Research

The golden coloured Burton Cliff with its marked strata

From Cobden Beach the coast passes the Bronze Age Bind Barrow burial mound to arrive at Burton Beach with Burton Cliff, a deep golden colour with stratified sand. The beach has sea kale, wild cabbage, pink bindweed, white sea campion, yellow horned sea poppies and horse mushrooms. The River Bride discharges past Burton Bradstock and a caravan site and East Cliff with its golf course. The resort of Burton Bradstock was a centre for making rope and nets with locally grown flax. These days the ropes are used for water skiing and local nets even for Wimbledon's tennis.

Laboratory at Crowthorne. The harbour was in use in the 13th century and rebuilt in 1740 with many ships in the 19th century, the sluice gates being added in 1823 to hold water to scour the entrance. Entry is dangerous with a swell and the sluice gates open. The sea breaks across the entrance with southerly to southeasterly gales and the bar dries. Schooners and naval vessels were built here until 1897 and it was used for filming *Harbour Lights*. Pier Terrace on the east side of the entrance was designed by Edward Prior, an enthusiast of the Arts and Crafts movement. In 1915 the body of John Lassie from *HMS Formidable*, the first British battleship to be sunk by a German U-boat, was recovered by fishermen, taken to the Pilot Boat Inn and covered with a tarpaulin. The landlord's dog made a great deal of fuss, licking the face of the victim who later

The working harbour at West Bay

Burton has a farm museum, while the Harbour Museum at West Bay is in a converted salt house and covers the history of the harbour and the rope and net-making industry of Bridport. The west pier has been rebuilt, the east one extended, the seawall strengthened and the beach replenished. The River

recovered. Hollywood based a film on the incident and named their dog after the survivor.

The unstable cliffs have started by Eype's Mouth and there is an undertow, not that the mackerel, bass and herrings are worried. Cormorants and blackbacked gulls search for booty. Below Thorncombe Beacon the coast kicks out past Great Ebb to East Ebb Cove and East Ebb and the foot of Doghouse Hill, beyond which is Seatown which can have a heavy dump, it being difficult to land or launch with a swell.

Cromwell at Worcester and was to escape to France with the help of local boatmen, but news of the plan leaked and he had to flee on horseback. St Andrew's church has the 1792 tomb of James Warden, killed in a duel with his neighbour, and the coffin of the Rev Edward Bragge which was made from his kitchen table as he had been so keen on his food. A plaque on Gwyle bridge warns vandals of the penalty of transportation.

In 1825 the Old Lyme Road was built to avoid the Lyme Regis toll road, but it had to be closed in

The rocks of the Corner and Western Patches protect the foot of Golden Cap, at 191m the highest cliff on the south coast, the gorse, broom, bracken, heather and golden sandstone at the top accounting for the name. There is a monument on the summit and the peak was used for filming *The History of Tom Jones: A Foundling* and *Gulliver's Travels*. There is a tremendous range of birdlife to be found, thrushes in the spring, cuckoos, swallows, grasshopper and willow warblers, chiffchaffs, lesser whitethroats and tree pipits in the summer and buzzards, kestrels, partridges, lapwings, skylarks, rooks, stonechats, goldcrests, meadow pipits, pied wagtails, linnets, yellowhammers and reed buntings all year, even mallards as a stream feeds down to St Gabriels Mouth where it runs down from the top of a nose of loose rock. There are many rare insects including bees and beetles in the undercliff. From Seatown to Charmouth was a favourite smuggling area and, while the soft, black, brooding cliffs would not have been the easiest of places to land

1924 after the Black Ven landslip, the largest coastal mudslide in Europe. It was at the Black Ven cliffs in 1811 that 12-year old Mary Anning found a 6.4m ichthyosaurus, beginning the hunting of fossils around Charmouth and Lyme Regis. The Charmouth Heritage Coast Centre features the coast, fossils (especially ammonites), local history and an 1850s cement works, which ground limestone pebbles from the beach with steam powered millstones and burned them in limekilns behind. There is a 65ha nature reserve, disturbed only by the noise of geologists' hammers from behind Canary Ledges.

Broad Ledge has its best surf after a southwesterly gale but can be difficult. It played a central role in the March 1993 accident in which four school pupils out of six, paddling with a teacher and two inexperienced instructors from an outdoor centre in Lyme Regis, died after a

Golden Cap beyond Doghouse Hill with Charmouth in the distance

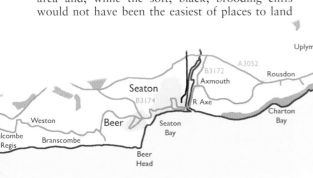

contraband, the slipped hillside above would not have been easy for revenue men to patrol.

Ducks and swans occupy the pools where the River Char enters the sea by the Beach Café. Surf is best at low water with a southwesterly wind, but there may be a launching charge. Charmouth is a resort of honey-coloured stone houses, thatched cottages and Regency houses. A 14th-century new town by the Abbot of Forde, it was a refuge from the feudal system, allowing people to buy property and trade. The Street is part of the Dorchester to Exeter Roman road. The George was a coaching inn on this south coast route and Catherine of Aragon stayed in 1501 in a mediaeval hotel since given a 19th-century façade. Charles II hid in the Queen's Arms Inn in 1651 after his defeat by

catalogue of errors by various people. Britain's worst ever canoeing accident and the only fatalities ever of canoeists under instruction, it resulted in the setting up of the AALA system for outdoor centres.

The unstable cliffs at Cain's Folly

Looking along the front at Lyme Regis

The Cobb at Lyme Regis, one of Britain's oldest artificial harbours

famous. Photographs of the filming, Lyme Bay fish tanks, fishing gear, wreckage and boats are shown in the Lyme Regis Marine Aquarium and Cobb History in the Cobb warehouse. A new danger of late has been the stealing of whelks from fishing boats by gulls and dropping them onto the Cobb to break them, much as thrushes do with snails on concrete paths.

Fishing boats also catch mackerel, prawns and conger eels. In addition, the harbour houses pleasure craft although the sea breaks right across the entrance with southerly or southeasterly gales. Experienced surfers find the best surf in Poker's Pool on the bottom half of the tide with a southwesterly wind.

There is a Dinosaurland Jurassic exhibition while the village museum has not only local history, lace prints and documents, but also fossils

In 774 King Cynewulf gave the monks of **Lyme** permission to produce salt from sea water. Lyme takes its name from the River Lim, British Celtic for the flooding river. The mediaeval port and cloth town was given its charter in 1284 by Edward I who added Regis to the name and used the village as a base for his wars against the French. Set on seabed limestone outcrops, the 180m Cobb was built about 1300, one of the earliest artificial harbours in Britain, William Jessop reporting in 1805 that the cliff had receded 83m since its construction. It was repaired in Portland stone in 1825 and has been rebuilt several times, now having a main southwestern arm 270m long x 12m x 3.7m high with buildings on top and an eastern breakwater 3.7m x 5.8m high, the gap to the shore being closed by blockwork. The first clash between Drake and the Armada occurred in the bay in 1588, assisted by five local boats. In 1644 Prince Maurice arrived with Royalist forces but the smaller Parliamentary army in the town were swelled by townswomen dressed as men and supplied by sea, so the Royalist siege failed. The Duke of Monmouth landed in 1685 on what is now called Monmouth Beach and stayed in the George Inn to raise an army to fight James II. He was defeated at Sedgemoor and a dozen Lyme men were hung in chains on the beach where he landed. Judge Jeffreys dined in the former Great House in Broad Street the night before the hangings and his ghost still haunts the spot, perhaps chewing a bloody bone. To Thomas Hardy, Lyme Bay was Dead-man's Bay. Although on the A3052 today, the village had no wheeled access until 1759.

Now a resort with a promenade and the Cobb Arms, it has Georgian architecture, the 16th-century St Michael's church and a town crier. It was a watering hole which attracted Jane Austen who had a seafront cottage and set Louisa Musgrove's accident here in *Persuasion*, which was filmed here. Local resident John Fowles set *The French Lieutenant's Woman* here and the 1980 film with Meryl Streep waiting on the end of the Cobb is the image of the village which has become

from the blue lias including the ichthyosaurus which started it all.

After Virtle Rock the coast passes from Dorset to Devon, a very remote section to Seaton but with a high sunshine rating and a mild climate. Coastal woodlands are rare in the southwest but are extensive from here to Seaton. Beyond Seven Rock Point is Pinhay Bay, where oystercatchers will be seen on 200,000,000 year old rocks. After Humble Point is Charton Bay to which there is a path down from near Allhallows College. The bay leads to Dowlands Cliffs and Landslips. From Lyme Regis to Axmouth the coast is particularly prone to slipping as the iron-rich red sandstone is overlain by impermeable clays topped with porous chalk and younger mudstones. On Christmas Day 1839

Looking back to Humble Point

Dowlands Cliffs, site of Britain's largest recorded landslide a 1.2km length of coast weighing 8,000,000 tonnes and involving 8ha of earth, chalk and cottages collapsed into the sea, Britain's biggest recorded landslide. Nobody was hurt as warning had been given. Today it is covered with ash woods, bluebells, wild garlic, maple, beech, hazel, hawthorn yew, rhododendrons, privet, brambles, ivy, ferns and a selection of less usual plants and insects. The year after the landslide, farmers managed to get a crop of wheat off what was called Goat Island.

The undercliff has fossils, plants and over a hundred bird species. Crab pots are laid around Seaton Bay, which can be busy with powerboats and waterskiing.

The B3174 winds round the back of Seaton Hole to Beer. Landing is difficult with a swell. Small crab and lobster boats are launched from the steep shingle beach and are pulled back up by capstan. In 1837 Jack Rattenbury, the king of the smugglers, retired after 50 years to become a fisherman and publish his *Memoirs of a Smuggler*.

Culverhouse Point is usually difficult for landing and leads to Sparrowbush Ledge and Haven Cliff with the Axe Cliff Golf Club on top.

In Roman times Axmouth was one of the busiest ports in Britain, but the River Axe silted up and the town is now 1.5km inland. The Roman Fosse Way began from here and ran via the older Ridgeway and Icknield Way to north Norfolk. Fishing vessels and yachts still use the quay but the shifting bar of shingle dries and the mouth is dangerous on the ebb. Surf in the estuary is best on the lower half of the tide with a southerly wind. There can be a dump, the best landing being at the end of the beach.

The B3172 arrived over one of the first bridges in Britain to be built of unreinforced concrete. It has three arches but during construction in 1877 the west one settled 600mm, causing the main arch to crack right across. In 1956 timber planks on steel girders were placed across to take the load off the main span and in 1990 it was made an Ancient Monument and retired to being a pedestrian bridge, a new road bridge being built upstream.

Another transport route here is the Seaton and District Electric Tramway, moved here from Eastbourne in 1970. 838mm gauge, it has the world's only open-top trams in public service. Out of season they are used as mobile hides for birdwatching trips, stopping when anything interesting is spotted.

Seaton has a beach of large round pebbles which were exported for paint blending and rubber processing. Today the village is a resort of Victorian and Edwardian houses with a largely Norman church and a promenade. The seawall dates only from 1980, following flooding in a violent storm. There is an annual arts and drama festival.

Most striking is the colour change where the white chalk gives way to red sandstone, dominated by 130m Beer Head. There was a Stone Age settlement at Beer. In 1665 the village was hit by the plague. Shipwrecked Spanish sailors found it undefended and stayed. Flemish refugees set up the lace industry which supplied the lace for Queen Victoria's wedding dress. The Clifftop Jubilee Gardens date from 1897 and there is the 1.6km long 184mm gauge Beer Heights Light Railway, Peco model railway exhibition and the Peco Pleasure Gardens and Exhibition, floral gardens, aviary, crazy golf and assault course. The town was also used in filming *Harbour Lights*. Herring gulls and a large caravan site look down on Beer Roads.

Beer Quarry Caves have been mined since Roman times and have supplied stone for such prominent buildings as Hampton Court, Windsor Castle, the Tower of London, St Stephen's at Westminster and Salisbury Cathedral. There has been a dramatic slip from South Down Common near Beer Head.

A high mast stands north of Beer and another back on South Down Common. From Sherborne Rocks to Sidmouth the cliffs are unstable, the subsequent lack of easy access making them popular with naturists. At Hooken Cliffs 4ha slipped 76m in 1790.

The sea dumps at Branscombe Mouth, by which is the 14th-century Great Seaside Farm and a selection of more recent static caravans. Flint and stone thatched cottages occupy Branscombe. The 12th-century St Winifred's church has a three-decker pulpit, one of only two in Devon, and the remains of a mural showing the Devil spearing adulterers. The thatched Branscombe Forge of 1580 was begun in Norman times and there is a notable Old Bakery.

Beer Head with its slips and the last of the chalk

Branscombe Mouth, the last accesible break in the cliffs before Sidmouth

The undercliff is a good place for migrant birds and there are buzzards, kestrels, rooks, stonechats, meadow pipits, goldfinches, linnets and yellowhammers plus swallows, house martins, lesser whitethroats and tree pipits in summer and the thistles attract finches in the autumn and winter.

There is a fort site above Branscombe Ebb and Berry Camp above Littlecombe Shoot. At 152m Weston Cliff is the highest cliff on the south Devon coast despite the sandstones having been laid down in the Triassic era on the bed of a vast southwards flowing river. Weston Wild Flower Meadow has almost 100 species of flowers and grasses as well as birds, butterflies and other insects. Weston Mouth has caves which were used by smugglers despite the dump. Hook Ebb Rocks precede Salcombe Mouth, again liable to dump. 172m Salcombe Hill leads to Salcombe Hill Cliff where falls of red sandstone cause the seawater to be deep red. On top of the cliffs are an aerial and an observatory.

The mouth of the River Sid at Sidmouth during a Sidmouth International Folk Arts Festival

Tortoiseshell Rocks with Big Picket Rock at the end

The stacks in Ladram Bay stretching away towards Brandy Head

Dunscombe Cliff and Salcombe Hill Cliff

Sidmouth was a fishing village until the River Sid (Old English for low-lying river) silted up, fishing boats now being winched onto the beach. Surf is best on the bottom half of the tide with winds between southeast and southwest, although there may be a landing charge. With choppy conditions landings are safer at the east end at high water. The town was Hardy's Idmouth.

Sidmouth is a resort of Georgian, Regency and Victorian buildings with an esplanade and a row of seafront hotels, the Royal York and Faulkner, the Elizabeth, the Devoran, the Marine and the Riviera. The Royal Glen Hotel was Woodbrook Cottage when Queen Victoria lived here as a girl while her parents avoided their creditors. A Russian eagle on a roof is a reminder that Grand Duchess Helena of Russia had a house here. Jacob's Ladder leads from the beach to Connaught Gardens where the floral displays are especially good. In the summer there are band concerts but the former International Folk Arts Festival held in early August for the last 50 years, was on a higher plane with folk dancing and music all along the front where the B3176 pays a brief visit. There are tennis, bowls, golf and sailing. The museum has the maritime history of the town. Arthur Conan Doyle played cricket here with the MCC but was put off by howling dogs, later writing his *Hound of the Baskervilles*. The BBC used the town to film the *Sleeping Murder* episode of *Miss Marple*.

There are two offshore rock breakwaters before Chit Rocks. Red cliffs front 156m Peak Hill behind the long enclosed beach past Tortoiseshell Rocks. A sequence of impressive red stacks are met, able to be explored by many small boats, rowing boats and sit on top kayaks on hire from Ladram Bay, a busy

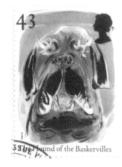

43

Hound of the Baskervilles

sheltered cove with the large Ladram Bay Holiday Centre caravan site.

Crab Ledge, Brandy Head, Black Head and Danger Point are a series of points which are little more than curves in the cliffs, although one has a large circular hole with a flight of steps up to it. Off Otterton Point is Otterton Ledge which can produce surf.

The River Otter was used for the cross Channel wool and salt trades as far as Otterton until the 15th century when it silted up almost overnight with a bank of pebbles, some of which look like muffins. Laid down in sandstones in Brittany 400,000,000 years ago, they were transported north by vast rivers in the Triassic era and deposited in the Budleigh Salterton Pebble Beds, subsequently falling onto the beach and being washed eastwards by the sea. The area was used for smuggling in the 18th century despite the fact that it dumps here again. The Otter Estuary Nature Reserve is on a marsh which was larger until French Napoleonic prisoners of war built an embankment to reclaim some of it. Small lobster fishing boats are winched up the beach.

Budleigh Salterton is a 19th-century resort which takes its name from the 13th-century saltpans in the marshes and from the glade of the Old English man Budda. It has Georgian and Regency houses and the Fairlynch Arts Centre and Museum in an 18th-century thatched house, featuring the local environment and history and with a smugglers' cellar and lookout tower. There are golf, bowls and croquet and the seawall is unchanged from when, in 1870, Sir John Millais painted *The Boyhood of Raleigh*, who was born locally at Hayes Barton near Yettington. It was also used by the BBC for filming the *Sleeping Murder* episode of *Miss Marple*.

The B3178 visits briefly before the beach again becomes inaccessible by vehicle and is used by naturists, blackbacked gulls, cormorants and

razorbills. The water is clear and there are strangely pocked red sandstone cliffs with pine trees on top. Heather and gorse grow on top of the cliffs at Beacon Hill beyond the East Devon Golf Course.

There are the caravans of the Devon Cliffs holiday camp behind Littleham Cove. Otter Cove and a cave are the start of the Royal Marines' rifle ranges on Straight Point, marked by red flags or lights. There is a 7m metal light mast. Oystercatchers are undisturbed.

Earth cliffs to 62m high extend to Orcombe Point from the popular beach at Sandy Bay, where there can be surf with southerly or southwesterly winds. The World of Country Life has a Victorian street, vintage cars, owls, pets, a safari deer train and goat walking.

From Orcombe Point an esplanade leads to Exmouth past 250,000,000 year old Maer Rocks with surf on southerly winds and past Conger Rocks, off which is a jet ski area and where windsurfers also operate. The Maer offers a carpark by various amusements for children and the largest OO gauge model railway complex in the world. The 4ha Maer nature reserve has 400 flowering plant species.

Exmouth is one of the oldest seaside resorts in England. Despite its sandy beach and its safe bathing, it does have a substantial seawall to face winter storms and there is a dangerous area where the water swirls out past Pole Sands, the intertidal part of Dawlish Warren. The Point was the normal landing place for raiders, including the Celts and Romans. It was burned by the Danes under King Swayn in 1001. One of the principal Devon ports by 1199, it sent 10 ships and 190 men to Calais for Edward III. It was Royalist in the Civil War. It was a busy port in the early 16th century and was used as a base by Sir Walter Raleigh. In the 17–19th centuries it was subject to attacks by Algerian and Tunisian pirates. The resort use began in 1720 with large scale development from 1792.

The River Exe floods to 7km/h and ebbs to 8km/h in the channels when banks are uncovered. The sea breaks across the entrance in south or southwesterly gales and sandbanks move. Pole Sand spit reaches nearly to Orcombe Point while the spit of Dawlish Warren reaches nearly to Exmouth and has a 2km^2 nature reserve, a low spit running from Warren Point, now half the width it was in the 18th century. It is noted for 180 bird species including blacktailed godwits, greenshanks, curlews, sandpipers and winter migrants, amongst them Brent geese with up to 20,000 birds at a time present. Plants include the sand crocus, which only opens in April when the sun is shining. There are a wind generator and a golf course.

Flows are west–southwest from Dover HW and northeast and east from HW Dover –0440 at up to 2km/h. There can be surf with easterly winds.

There are a visitor centre and chalets at the root of the spit, used as a sandy resort with go-karts and safe beach for children. There is parking nearby but it is busy in summer.

Budleigh Salterton with Straight Point in the distance

The etched cliff and naturist beach west of Budleigh Salterton

Distance
From Cobden Beach to Dawlish Warren is 59km
Campsites
Burton Bradstock, West Bay, Lower Eype, Seatown, Charmouth, Uplyme, Rousdon, Axmouth, Seaton, Branscombe Cross, Salcombe Regis, Otterton, Littleham, Dawlish Warren
Youth Hostels
Litton Cheney, Beer, Exeter
OS 1:50,000 Sheets
192 Exeter and Sidmouth
193 Taunton and Lyme Regis
194 Dorchester and Weymouth
Imray Charts
2400 West Country
C5 Bill of Portland to Salcombe Harbour (1:100,000)
Stanfords Allweather Charts
12 Needles to Start Point (1:175,000)
22 South Devon Coast
L12 Poole Harbour (1:14,500)
Admiralty Charts
SC 2290 River Exe and Approaches Including Exeter Canal (1:12,500)
SC 3315 Berry Head to Bill of Portland (1:75,000)
SC 5601 East Devon and Dorset Coast, Exmouth to Christchurch
SC 5602 West Country, Falmouth to Teignmouth
Tidal Constants
Bridport (West Bay): HW Dover –0510, LW Dover –0540
Lyme Regis: HW Dover –0450, LW Dover –0540
Exmouth Approaches: HW Dover –0500, LW Dover –0530
Range
Straight Point
Submarine Area
D012 Lyme Bay North
Sea Area
Portland
Rescue
Inshore lifeboats: Lyme Regis, Exmouth
All weather lifeboats: Weymouth, Exmouth
Maritime Rescue Centres
Portland, 01305 760439
Brixham, 01803 882704

60 SOUTHWEST DEVON

Skirting around Dartmoor

Stand each shock
Like Thurlestone Rock.

far as Holcombe a force 4 easterly will give surf at mid-tide, used by board surfers around **Dawlish**. The A379 follows the coast to Broadsands but is only seen briefly at Torbay.

Langstone Rock at the end of Dawlish Warren

The railway runs along the front at Dawlish

Between Dawlish Warren and Teignmouth the Paddington to Penzance railway reaches its best. The most impressive part of the South Devon Railway, it was built after 1844 by Brunel, initially as an atmospheric railway. The railway has already followed the estuary shoreline since the end of the Exeter Canal, but beyond the red block of Langstone Rock with its natural arch it moves out onto the foot of the cliffs and, with a walkway, runs 5m above the beach with a seawall which is concave to throw back

The Regency and Victorian resort of Dawlish developed during the Napoleonic Wars when travel to the Continent was prevented and is built around the Lawn, gardens with Dawlish Water running through the centre, giving the British Celtic dubo glais, black stream, home to black swans, East Indian game ducks, South African shelducks and Chinese swan geese. The museum features a more sinister creature. In the snow and very hard frosts of February 1855 a 160km trail of footprints

Coryton's Cove with a train disappearing into one of the five tunnels on this stretch of line

waves, causing clapotis when conditions are rough. This is probably the most exposed piece of railway line in the country and when conditions get serious trains use only the line furthest from the water. This section of line passes through five tunnels 34–46m long and was used for filming *The Ghost Train*. As

appeared over several nights from Totnes to Littleham, passing through the town. They looked as if they had been cut by hot cloven hooves and went over roofs, under hedges and through pipes, surely the work of the Devil. Dickens set the opening of *Nicholas Nickleby* here.

Coryton's Cove and Horse Cove are sandy. The rocks become increasingly interesting, particularly

The Parson and Clerk with Shag Rock beyond

the red sandstone formation of the Parson and Clerk and the following Shag Rock, a venue which attracts cormorants and blackbacked gulls. The beach tends to collect flotsam and can be difficult

for landing to Sprey Point when conditions are choppy. This area is a spoil bed so there is also jetsam, in addition to which is a historic wreck with a 200m radius restricted area around it near Church Rocks.

Teignmouth with the River Teign estuary beyond the pier

Teignmouth had Saxon origins, was burnt by the Danes in 800, was ravaged by the French in 1340 and in 1690 and became a Victorian and Regency tourist centre and resort before being attacked by the Germans in the second world war. Den Green, once used for horse racing and fish net drying, has floral displays and Keats worked on *Endymion* here in 1818. It has had a port from the first half of the 19th century with a quay from the 1930s, used by yachts. Exports include cereals, potters' clay from the River Teign (the sparkling river) and stone for sea defences, following on from the granite exported in 1831 to build London Bridge, imports including building materials, timber, coal and paper, coasters using the harbour at high water. The Grand Pier has amusements. Powerboats and jet skis offshore contrast with the relative peace of Punch and Judy shows on the sandy beach near the Dive In! Snack Bar.

There is a light beacon on the low sandy Point, off which there are eddies. Surf is best on the bottom half of the tide. Spratt Sand constantly changes, as does the Bar, with the sea breaking across the entrance in southerly and southeasterly gales. The channel moves all the time, there is a small race over the pipeline across Pole Sand on the southern side of the entrance and there are swift outgoing streams to 5km/h from HW Dover +0110, ingoing from HW Dover –0510 to 3km/h. Offshore, the flows south–southwest are from HW Dover –0030 and north–northeast from HW Dover +0510.

There is a daymark off the Ness, the bold red sandstone headland on the south side of the estuary where a wildlife trust have owls, ravens, monkeys and a crocodile. The sandy Ness Cove is reached through a smugglers' tunnel. There is also a limekiln.

The coast continues cliffy with vegetation on top, not to mention a golf course, and many secluded and inaccessible coves to Long Quarry Point. Beyond Bundle Head is Labrador Bay and then Smugglers Cove has a small wreck visible at the southern end at low water.

Babbacombe is sheltered from the prevailing wind

The waters become part of Tor Bay Harbour. Herring Cove offers limited landing in bad weather, as does Mackerel Cove. After Blackaller's

Cove is Maidencombe, a private beach from which launching is not permitted.

Bell Rock, not unlike Thurlestone Rock in shape

The split Bell Rock precedes Watcombe Head and the secluded beaches seem to be used increasingly by naturists, despite the lion's mane jellyfish in the water. Torquay Golf Course is above Tor Point.

Babbacombe Bay, where Devon gives way to Torbay, and Oddicombe Beach have fine pink and white shingle and canoe hire. St Marychurch is said to be the oldest church in Devon, set up by early missionaries. More recent is Babbacombe Model Village, 2ha at 1:12 scale, and a cliff railway makes access more easy than in the past. In the 19th century there was smuggling and wrecking by luring ships onto Oddicombe and Babbacombe beaches with lanterns hung on the horns of grazing cattle. In 1853 excisemen found 153 casks of spirits.

There is a field system on Walls Hill which slopes down to Long Quay Point where there are the remains of a quarry. Agatha Christie used to come here for moonlight picnics and had a romantic encounter with Amyas Boston, whose name she later used in *Five Little Pigs*. The Bishops Walk was built in 1840 for the Bishops of Exeter, who lived in what is now the Palace Hotel.

Beyond the smuggling venue of Anstey's Cove and Black Head is the Kents Cavern Showcave, opened in 2003, two main chambers and a series of galleries which have been inhabited for 100,000 years by people and animals. The bones of a sabretooth tiger and a great cave bear have been found as well as many archaeological items

including implements and tools from all ages, being one of the oldest known habitations in Britain. There are stalactites and stalagmites, now with a sound and light show and candlelit caves. Agatha Christie's father helped fund the 1805 excavations and Hempsley Cavern appears in her *Man in a Brown Suit*.

Hope's Nose and a group of Swedish student's who were studying English here

Hope's Nose has Devon's biggest kittiwake colony and is a nesting place for migratory birds. Further off is another resting place, an anchorage for deep draught vessels. Between the two are the Lead Stone or Flat Rock, the Ore Stone with an 8m long tunnel through it and, further round, the

Christie used to swim from Meadfoot Beach most days, but mixed bathing was not allowed and men had to stay at least 50m from the ladies' bathing machines.

The resort and yachting centre of **Torquay**, named after the Cornish tor, hill, was Hardy's Tor-upon-Sea. It had its inner harbour from 1870 with stone cut from Beacon Hill, which was levelled, the 1.2m square x 3 or 4m blocks being placed by divers. Built on seven hills, the town had its pirates but Tennyson called it the 'loveliest sea village in England' and Ruskin 'the Italy of England'. It accommodated the British fleet for long periods, during the Napoleonic Wars yet it can produce a heavy sea with strong easterly or southeasterly winds. These days Tor Bay can actually be rougher than the open sea at times because of all the washes of the many powered boats, waterskiers and jet skis. The pilot warns shipping to watch out for frequent canoeists but washes travel far and in many directions. Tidal streams are weak and there are 18 beaches in the bay, many with controlled areas for swimmer priority in the summer. There may also be launching charges. Surf is best on the bottom half of the tide with southerly or easterly winds or there are a wave machine and flume in the Riviera Centre pool. A regular cargo service runs to the Channel Islands.

The English Riviera is named for its mild climate, the palm trees planted by the Victorians

Thatcher Rock and freighters moored in Tor Bay

Thatcher Rock, a 40m high seabird nesting sanctuary which is thought to look as if it has a thatched roof and, in the 1930s, had two youths marooned on it for several days. East Shag rock

and the fact that it had to replace the French one in Napoleonic times. It includes Aqualand, the largest aquarium in the West Country with marine and freshwater fish, local marine life, turtles and others

London Bridge with Corbyn's Head and Livermead beyond

separates Meadfoot Beach from Daddyhole Cave, overlooked by a tower, and then the natural arch of London Bridge hides Peaked Tor Cove. Agatha

although bass and pollock might be seen swimming freely in the bay. Torquay Museum has 400,000,000 years of Torbay history, finds from

Torquay, at the heart of the English Riviera

Kents Cavern, geology, archaeology, natural, social and local history, ceramics and Agatha Christie, who was born in the town and set many stories in the area under fictitious place names. Also set here was the John Cleese BBC comedy series *Fawlty Towers*.

Torre has one of three remaining pumping stations for Brunel's atmospheric South Devon Railway from Exeter. Better known is Torre Abbey, founded in 1196 by Premonstratensian canons, the wealthiest abbey in England for four centuries, converted to a manor in 1600 and now housing the town's art gallery with an Agatha Christie room. The land may have been given by William de Brewer, lord of the manor, in thanks for the safe return of his son who went to Austria with other hostages to secure the release of Richard the Lionheart. Its tithe Spanish Barn was used in 1588 to hold 397 prisoners from *Nuestra Señora del Rosario* which foundered in the bay and from which the ghost of a Spanish woman dressed as a boy is sometimes seen in the lane. Also remaining are the 12th-century entrance to the chapter house, the early 14th-century gatehouse, the Palm House and grounds with golf, tennis and bowling plus a model world display including an animated circus.

Roundham Head, has pleasure craft, guided by a red 5m metal light column.

The most conspicuous aspect of Goodrington Sands are the waterslides with Quaywest claimed to be the UK's only outdoor water park. Surf is best on the lower half of the tide with easterly winds. A steam train, complete with observation car, might be seen on the Paignton and Dartmouth Steam Railway as it climbs past **Goodrington** and Saltern Cove with its nature reserve and caravan park. Hercule Poirot used this train in *The ABC Murders* and *Dead Mans Folly*.

There are country walks marked around the red sandy beach at Broadsands, where surf is best on the lower half of tides with northeasterly winds. Elberry Cove, below a golf course, has a pebble beach with a submarine freshwater spring and a waterski approach lane. It was where Sir Carmichael Clark met his death in *The ABC Murders*. Churston station featured in *The ABC Murders* and as Nassecombe Station in *Dead Mans Folly*. Lines of large red and blue buoys stretch out across the southern side of the bay. A wooded hillside extends past Fishcombe Point to Churston Cove.

Brixham Battery was built in 1940, now the Battery Gardens and Brixham Battery Heritage

Fishcombe Point with Brixham beyond

Between the red sandstone cliffs of Corbyn's Head and Livermead Head there is a waterski approach lane. Behind, the railway reappears and the main road becomes the A3022 for a while.

The best surf at Hollicombe is on the lower half of the tide with an easterly wind. The village was used for filming *The French Lieutenant's Woman*.

Beyond Hollicombe Head is the 115 room Oldway Mansion, built by American sewing machine inventor Isaac Singer as his Victorian dream palace. It was extended by his son in the style of the Versailles Hall of Mirrors with marble grand staircase and gallery, vaulted painted ceiling, ballroom with silver mirrors, 7ha of grounds by Duchesne, Italian garden, two lakes, waterfall, rock gardens, lawns and woods. It is now used as offices by the council, the accounts doubtless done with mirrors, and was used for filming *Isadora*.

In red stone, Kirkham House is rather older, 14th century, but not as old as the church which has Saxon foundations on a Bronze Age site.

In this part of Torbay the surf is best on the lower half of the tide with winds from the east and northeast. There may be a launch fee. **Paignton** has an esplanade and a Victorian pier. It was a Bronze Age settlement, then Saxon and a fishing village built on saltmarshes and dunes until the 19th century when it became a resort with a red sandy beach safe for children. It was used by the BBC for filming the *Sleeping Murder* episode of *Miss Marple*. Paignton Harbour, on the north side of

Centre museum. There have been nine centuries of fishing from **Brixham**, named after the Old Englishman Boerhtsige. For three hundred years it was the premier English fishing port as a result of perfecting the Brixham trawler, which reigned supreme until the first world war when steam replaced sail. In the late 18th century it was the centre for the Channel fleet and also one for smugglers. It has yachts in a marina as much as fishing vessels these days, although a 1940s trawler is popular since conversion to a replica of Drake's *Golden Hind*. The British Fisheries Museum is in the old Market House of 1800 while Brixham Museum covers the maritime and fishing history of Brixham, Brixham trawlers, brigs, topsail schooners, sail lofts, ropewalks, costumes, handicrafts and the great gale of 1866. HM Coastguard National Museum is also here. There is a statue of William of Orange who landed in 1688 to claim the throne from James II. Painters are attracted in numbers.

Following a report by James Rendell in 1836, the 910m Victoria Breakwater was built between 1843 and 1916 of limestone blocks from Berry Head, faced with jointed masonry on the outside only and topped with a 6m white light tower. The slipway on the pebble Breakwater Beach near the Oystercatcher Bistro was built by the Americans for the second world war invasion of France.

Shoalstone Beach of shingle has a seawater pool near Shoalstone Point.

There is a lookout point at Berry Head. In 1967 the coastguard here reported a UFO at 500m over Brixham, domed in shape with a door in the side, which climbed rapidly and disappeared but not before it had been seen by many other people.

Berry Head has nearly vertical limestone cliffs. On top have been found arrowheads, scrapers, coins and many remains from the Stone Age, Iron Age and Romans. A fort for 1,000 men was located on the top, begun in the American War of Independence to deter attacks by the Americans and French, and Napoléon dined here, the only time he set foot on English soil. A Royal Observer Corps post was set up during the second world war and in the late 1950s an underground Cold War monitoring station was added.

The white light tower of 1906 is the shortest in Britain at 5m but one of the highest, the light 58m above sea level on the cliff, from which a 45m shaft descends to house the pendulum which turned the light. A mast completes the major structures but Berry Head Country Park has a nature reserve with white rock rose, pelitory of the wall, navelwort, rusty back fern, rock sea lavender, goldilocks aster, honeywort, gentian, small hare's ear, small rest harrow, shags and breeding kittiwakes, razorbills, fulmars and herring gulls with zoom cameras hidden on the cliffs covering them for visitors. There are overfalls off the head and a 30m long cave. Further off is the point where pilots are picked up for the English Channel, North Sea and Skagerrak.

To Inner Froward Point the cliffs are 120m high. There is a tunnel through Durl Head after Cod Rock. Above St Mary's Bay are caravans and the hospital which became the home of the Revd Henry Lyte, where he wrote the hymn *Abide With Me*. A Pontin's holiday village is here plus a landslip. Surf is best on the lower half of the tide with easterly winds.

Tor Bay Harbour authority ends at Sharkham Point just before Mudstone Ledge runs out and Torbay returns to Devon.

Apart from compass jellyfish, the coast now becomes much more lonely and dramatic where

Cave system at Durl Head

huge slabs of rock have delaminated and slid away. Beyond Southdown Cliff, Man Sands also have their best surf on the bottom half of the tide with an easterly wind before Crabrock Point, as do Scabbacombe Sands before Scabbacombe Head. There is an old limekiln on the beach at Man Sands.

Ivy Cove comes before the much larger Pudcombe Cove where, during his circumnavigation, Geoff Hunter twice saw a fish go 3m across the surface of the water while travelling vertically on its tail. The mood of the area is dramatic. Above are the gardens of Coleton Fishacre, designed in 1925 for Rupert and Lady Dorothy D'Oyly Carte in the Arts and Crafts tradition with luxuriant, rare and exotic plants, gazebo and water features.

Eastern Black Rock or East Blackstone stands off the cove, followed after Outer Froward Point by the guano covered Mew Stone. Inner Froward Point and Newfoundland Cove are overlooked by a day beacon which marks the mouth of the River Dart. Castle Ledge runs out from well east of Kingswear Castle. Flows are ingoing from HW Dover +0100 until HW Dover –0520. Off the entrance the flows are southwest from HW Dover –0100 and northeast from HW Dover +0540 at up to 3km/h, but there can be a northwesterly eddy across the entrance from HW Dover +0100 until HW Dover +0540. Cruise liners enter the river. On the far side the estuary tapers out from Blackstone

Contorted rock strata near Berry Head

Rock carving by P Jackson in 1933 near Sharkham Point

Also near Sharkham Point, fine quartz intrusions into the rock

Scabbacombe Head runs out next to Scabbacombe Sands

The Mew Stone off Outer Froward Point

Rock arch near Stoke Fleming

Point to Combe Point where the Dancing Beggars feature an arch and a blowhole.

Above Leonard's Cove is Stoke Fleming where the high church tower forms a significant navigation mark. Blackpool Sands is a resort with pines and rhododendrons, a recently restored subtropical garden with southern hemisphere species, windsurfers, a selection of hire sit-on-top kayaks from the leading manufacturers and what were voted the best beach toilets in England. It is not obviously a submarine cable landing point, nor clear that the Bretons landed here in 1404 in order to attack **Dartmouth** but were defeated.

Matthew's Point at the end of Blackpool Sands beach

From Matthew's Point to Pilchard Cove at Strete is a final length of low cliff studded with caves, the beach in front used by naturists.

Pilchard Cove begins the long beach round Start Bay

Slapton Sands then sweep round the back of Start Bay. A woodland walk at Strete Gate, with its steep flint shingle beach, is where the Gara ceases to have a clear watercourse and subsides into the marsh of the Higher Ley.

In Slapton the 14th and 15th-century church of St James the Great has a mediaeval broached spire on a Norman tower. One of the great in the congregation was the wife of Admiral Sir Richard Hawkins, Lady Judith, who had two Negroes to unroll a red carpet in front of her as she went to church. She died in 1629 and was buried in a tomb with a full length oak screen. There is a field study centre in the village, the major feature of interest

Torcross with its distinctive pale blue hotel

being Slapton Ley, a lagoon cut off by Slapton Sands with the A379 running in front. The lagoon is a nature reserve and has a nature trail at the northern end. It is the 3,000-year old largest natural freshwater lake in the country, covering 1.1km², a reed fringed bird sanctuary with water lilies, yellow irises, herons, terns, mallards, great crested grebes, swans, breeding coots, a winter wildfowl roost, otters, pike and perch as well as being a boating lake. In the 16th century Slapton was reached over a drawbridge. There are two limekilns, 19th-century fish cellars and a carpark in a former shipyard. The cellars were converted to the Royal Sands Hotel but this was destroyed in 1940 when a passing dog set off 6 coastal defence mines. Seven villages in the area were evacuated to allow it to be used as a practice area for the D-Day landings in 1943/4. A Sherman tank monument remembers 639 Americans killed when a force of them on an exercise were intercepted here by a German E-boat.

The road was built in 1856 and has been protected in part by low profile sheet piling defences since 1918. In the winter of 2001 the sea broke through the Slapton Line and locals fought for the road to be adequately protected, fearing that the council approach of soft defences will result in the closure of the road.

The seawall in Torcross was built in 1980 after previous defences were damaged. The whole of the bay suffers a heavy dump with easterly winds. Torcross is very conspicuous from the north, particularly because of the pale blue hotel. Inland from Limpet Rocks is a mast.

Beesands is a fishing village with shellfish processing. The Skerries Bank offshore provides protection with the sea breaking on it, especially at the southwest end in bad weather. There is an inside passage but there can be broken water all the way to the coast to Tinsey Head with strong easterly winds.

When Devonport dockyard was being extended a source of gravel was needed and it was decided to take it from off Beesands and Hallsands. Dredging started in 1897 and 650,000 tonnes was removed before protests by the local fishermen at the effects on the seabed managed to stop the work but the damage had already been done. Hallsands, built on a raised beach, began to be affected immediately but a combination of high spring tides and an easterly storm in January 1917 destroyed 29 of the 30 houses in the village, just a few pieces of wall remaining at the foot of the cliffs. The village has been rebuilt further inland and is used for waterskiing and sub-aqua. A wooden sentry box was used by the mullet spotter for the village. Two radio masts stand on the top of the ridge.

Start Point has five 60m hillocks like a cockscomb, near the end being an 1836 battlemented lighthouse with a 28m white round granite tower with its light 62m above the water, attracting night birds. Many birds, especially migrants, come to the nature reserve. In 1989 the fog signal building collapsed because of coastal erosion.

The remains of Hallsands, once a village of 30 houses by a beach

Start Point, a low but strategic headland

There is a race off the point with strong streams in the area. With a northeasterly flow there is an eddy close to the northern side of the point from HW Dover +0540 to HW Dover −0240. Five ships were claimed by the rocks at Start Point in a single night in 1891.

There are coloured old hard schists to Bolt Tail with dissected rock platform and 6km of raised beach, limpets, anemones, sea pinks and blue spring squill on the cliffs to Prawle Point in April. Sleaden Rocks at the west end of Ravens Cove are a favourite place for seals to haul out.

Sleaden Rocks with a seal basking

Lannacombe Bay has its best surf on the bottom half of the tide with a southerly wind, while Woodcombe Sand offers the best landing in those conditions.

At Langerstone Point, Brimpool Rocks feature a number of large rockpools. East Prawle is not too far away but it is a section of coast where there are not many people.

Prawle Point is a prominent gneiss headland with Arch Rock on the end, a heavy swell and a race off it. Prawle is Old English for lookout and the lookout point is now operated by Coastwatch.

Prawle Point with its Arch Rock and lookout

Local birds include cirl buntings, gannets, great skuas and herring gulls.

There is a passage inside the island at high water and some carelessly parked pieces of a large Russian freighter below Signalhouse Point, being towed to the breakers when deposited here, to be subject to other breakers. Beyond Elender Cove and Gammon Head with its bluebells and ferns the porky analogies continue with the Ham Stone and Pig's Nose, near which is a historic wreck with a 300m radius restricted area. A whitewashed lookout has a conical thatched roof.

Start Point, Start Bay
South-west England
40

Pieces of ship on the rocks west of Prawle Point

Gammon Head with Bolt Head across the Kingsbridge Estuary

The Kingsbridge Estuary is a drowned valley without any significant rivers feeding it. Possibly it was once the estuary of the Avon, which now flows further west. The swell breaks heavily on the Bar at low water or with an easterly to southerly wind against the ebb, thought to be the inspiration for Tennyson's *Crossing the Bar*. This is where 13 of the 15 members of the Salcombe lifeboat were drowned in 1913. The ebb runs to 6km/h between a battery and Splatcove Point towards the castle at **Salcombe** and this should have added to its defensive position, although it is now a yachting centre.

Sharpitor has a warm microclimate so it can sustain 2ha of rare plants and shrubs with magnolias, palms, camphor trees, bananas, figs, flax and other subtropical species. Overbecks Museum in an Edwardian house has local shipbuilding models, shipwrights' tools, photographs, fossils, shells, birds' eggs, butterflies, handcuffs, a 19th-century polyphon, precursor to the jukebox, an electrical rejuvenating machine and drawings by scientist Otto Overbeck. A transmission mast stands back from Splatcove Point.

The Great Eelstone overhangs at Sharp Tor with its rock pinnacle and stare hole. To the west of the Range is Starehole Bay, used by divers and by waterskiers who cut close to other boats in their area. The Mew Stone, Little Mew Stone and a race are found off Bolt Head with its concrete lookout, from where dark cliffs run to Bolt Tail. Off Cove and Steeple Cove are two of the larger indentations at the foot of the Warren. In 1936 the Ham Stone claimed the Finnish barque *Herzogen Cecilie*, one of the last sailing ships to be wrecked off the British coast. In 2002 some of the beaches disappeared, together with pieces of engine lying on them.

Hope Cove, the first bolt hole after the exposed section from Bolt Head to Bolt Tail

Soar Mill Cove can offer a sheltered landing at high water, but its location is hard to spot from the sea and it breaks across the entrance with a southern swell.

120m high Bolberry Down was fortified in the Iron Age. In 1760 770 people died when the *Ramillies* went down, one of many wrecks in this area. There is a cave in the approach to Redrot Cave. Bolt Tail is a prominent headland with another Iron Age fort.

The coast continues mostly high, precipitous and rocky to Thurlestone Rock, but the streams are weak in Bigbury Bay and Hope Cove offers a selection of sheltered landings on protected beaches. In 1588 many Armada sailors came ashore from the wreck of the *San Pedro el Major* but 40 people were drowned at Hope Key in 1620. Spanish coins have been found in recent years.

Distinctive knob near Warren Point with Burgh Island and Bigbury-on-Sea beyond

Popular with surfers is Bantham, one of the best surfing beaches on the south coast and in the southwest, cleaner on the flood. It is used by windsurfers, board surfers, kite surfers and kayaks. It is surrounded by marram covered sand dunes. The bay forms the eastern side of the estuary of the River Avon, the mouth of which can close out.

Much of this is applicable to Bigbury-on-Sea at the end of the B3392 where there is small to medium surf at most times, supported by the Venus Café and toilets.

A covering sand causeway runs out to Burgh Island, with a sea tractor on long legs making the crossing to and from the Pilchard Inn at high water. There tends to be clapotis where the waves meet along the line of the causeway after coming round each side of the island, presumably its cause. Murray's Rock shelters at the eastern end of Burgh Island, which is known to fishermen as St Michael's Rock as there is a small ruined chapel of 1411 to St Michael on the summit. In the 18th century this was converted to a pilchard huer's lookout, the island having an important pilchard fishery. The 1395 Pilchard Inn has a smuggler's ghost and there were 18th and 19th-century smugglers, fireplace carvings showing Tom Crocker, both a smuggler and an excise officer. Wrecking went on and in 1772 the *Chanteloup* from the West Indies was wrecked on the island. The only survivor put on her jewels and swam to the shore where she was killed by the mob who cut off her fingers and ears for the jewels and buried her in the sand.

The thatched village of Outer Hope

Beyond Inner Hope and Outer Hope the Great Ledge begins. Thurlestone Rock, from the Saxon torlestone, pierced stone, has a hole through but

Thurlestone Rock, a natural arch in the centre of the bay

Burgh Island with the Pilchard Inn to the fore and the sea tractor crossing the sand causeway

The island is a herring gull nesting site. In the 1920s Agatha Christie stayed and wrote *And Then There Was None* and *Evil Under the Sun*. In 1946 it was bought by millionaire Archibald Nettlefold of GKN, not his best investment as he built a 40-room luxury Art Deco hotel with a pool and then sold it at a considerable loss. It was visited by Noël Coward, Edward and Mrs Simpson and the Mountbattens. The BBC filmed the *Nemesis* episode of *Miss Marple* here.

can look like a wreck and was painted by Turner. There is also a real wreck. Leas Foot Sand is sheltered and Thurlestone has a beach of coarse sand. Above Loam Castle and Butter Cove is Thurlestone Golf Course. This rocky section of coast is popular with naturists.

On the north side of Warren Point, Challaborough Bay is a sandy cove with the best surf when the wind is between south and northeast. Ayrmer Cove, Westcombe Beach and other smaller inlets are relatively secluded but with persistent people on foot able to reach them. Near vertical slabs of exposed rock look almost like chalk from the distance because they reflect so much light. At sea level there are increasing numbers of reefs, the rocks becoming really vicious with sharp edged strata nearly vertical, especially around Meddrick Rocks where there is a blowhole.

The dead straight channel inside Battisborough Island at the mouth of the Erme

After Beacon Point is the small rock fringed Fernycombe Beach and then the mouth of the River Erme, on the far side of which is Battisborough Island, the channel inside it with angular stacks and sides so straight they appear to have been artificially cut. At Erme Mouth Mothecombe Beach is private and may only be used at weekends and on Wednesdays, there being surf at low water with moderate onshore winds and landing difficult with a heavy swell. There are two historic wrecks in the lower estuary.

Past Gull Cove, Butcher's Cove, St Anchorite's Rock, Blackaterry Point, Wadham Rocks and Ivy Island the shoreline remains rocky and inhospitable. Beacon Hill has a ruined coastguard lookout point on top. There are many caravans behind Stoke Beach, which is sheltered from the west and southwest but exposed to the east, but footpaths to the nearest public parking require climbing a steep hillside, on which is an old church site.

Stoke Point with its disused lookout point begins some 5km of isolated reef fringed coast, the rocks not high but not accessible, either, in any swell, the hillside rising behind. Warren Cottage, overlooking Hilsea and Blackstone Points, is conspicuously isolated.

Gara Point is at the end of the River Yealm, discharging into Wembury Bay, a yachting centre. In strong southwesterly winds the mouth of the bay closes out and the sea also breaks over the irregular ground within the bay. Flows are outgoing from HW Dover −0520 to 5km/h, setting north of the Great Mew Stone, and ingoing from HW Dover +0100 to 3km/h.

Wembury Marine Conservation Area operates inside a line bounded by Gara Point, the Little Mewstone, the Shag Stone and Fort Bovisand while there is a Special Area of Conservation north of the line from Gara Point to Rame Head.

There is surf at all states of the tide with northwesterly to easterly winds, best on the lower half of the tide, particularly for lefts off the slate Blackstone Rocks although surf is smaller than at Bantham.

Wembury has a marine centre, an old water mill and a church which was probably built to guide sailors into the estuary. The village also has toilets and a National Trust carpark which overlooks the beach.

Distance
From Dawlish Warren to Wembury is 91km
Campsites
Dawlish Warren, Ringmore, Daccombe, Marldon, Goodrington, Galmpton, Brixham, Hillhead, Stoke Fleming, Strete, Slapton, Cotmore, Rew, Soar, Bolberry, Modbury, Newton Ferrers
Youth Hostels
Exeter, Dartington, Maypool, Salcombe
OS 1:50,000 Sheets
192 Exeter and Sidmouth
201 Plymouth and Launceston
202 Torbay and South Dartmoor
Imray Charts
2400 West Country
C5 Bill of Portland to Salcombe Harbour (1:100,000)
C6 Salcombe to Lizard Point (1:100,000)
C14 Plymouth Harbour and Rivers (1:20,000)
Stanfords Allweather Charts
12 Needles to Start Point (1:175,000)
22 South Devon Coast
L14 Salcombe Harbour (1:20,800)
L15 Dartmouth Harbour (1:18,000)
Admiralty Charts
SC 26 Harbours on the South Coast of Devon. Teignmouth Harbour (1:7,500). Tor Bay (1:12,500). Brixham Harbour (1:7,500)
SC 28 Salcombe Harbour (1:12,500)
SC 30 Plymouth Sound and Approaches (1:12,500)
SC 1267 Falmouth to Plymouth (1:75,000)
SC 1613 Eddystone Rocks to Berry Head (1:75,000)
SC 1634 Salcombe to Brixham. Start Point to Brixham (1:25,000). Salcombe to Start Point (1:25,000)
1900 Whitsand Bay to Yealm Head Including Plymouth Sound (1:25,000)
SC 2253 Dartmouth Harbour (1:6,250)
SC 2290 River Exe and Approaches Including Exeter Canal (1:12,500)
SC 3315 Berry Head to Bill of Portland (1:75,000)
SC 5601 East Devon and Dorset Coast, Exmouth to Christchurch
SC 5602 West Country, Falmouth to Teignmouth
Tidal Constants
Exmouth Approaches: HW Dover −0500, LW Dover −0530
Teignmouth Bar: HW Dover −0500, LW Dover −0530
Torquay: HW Dover −0500, LW Dover −0540
Brixham: HW Dover −0510, LW Dover −0530
Dartmouth: HW Dover −0520, LW Dover −0540
Start Point: HW Dover −0520, LW Dover −0530
Salcombe: Dover −0540
River Avon Bar: Dover −0540
River Yealm Entrance: HW Dover −0530, LW Dover −0540
Submarine Area
D009
Sea Areas
Portland, Plymouth
Rescue
Inshore lifeboats: Exmouth, Teignmouth, Torbay, Salcombe
All weather lifeboats: Exmouth, Torbay, Salcombe, Plymouth
Maritime Rescue Centre
Brixham, 01803 882704

Sketching Burgh Island from Bantham

Patriotic rocks in red, white and blue near Toby's Point

61 SOUTHEAST CORNWALL

Warships ancient and modern

O the Harbour of Fowey
Is a beautiful spot,
And it's there I enjowey
To sail in a yot;
Or to race in a yacht
Round a mark or a buoy –
Such a beautiful spacht
Is the Harbour of Fuoy!

Sir Arthur Quiller–Couch

At Wembury divers in the clear water see sea fans and wrasse. Above them are cormorants, oystercatchers, blackbacked gulls and herring gulls as well as swallows.

The Great Mew Stone, seen over the beach at Wembury

Off Wembury Point the Great Mew Stone rises 60m to a sharp apex. Landing is best at the northeast end at low water when there is some sand exposed, but there are breaking waves in

Bay leads to Bovisand Bay which has its best surf at half tide with a southwesterly swell. Fort Bovisand was a 19th-century coastal defence and is now a major diving centre, other users of the Sound including compass jellyfish.

Plymouth Breakwater occupies the centre of the Sound but is not connected to the land to avoid trapping silt. Designed in 1811 by Rennie, it was completed in 1841. With a crest 600mm above high water, it has no protective top wall. It defends against gales. Landing requires the permission of the Queen's Harbour Master although there are 4 stone shelters along its 1.6km length. A light beacon at the east end has a ball topmark which doubles as a shipwreck rescue centre, able to hold six people. In the centre is the Breakwater Fort with a landing pier on the north side while a 23m white round granite tower lighthouse is located at the west end.

The Sound, the mouths of the drowned valleys of the Plym and Tamar, is the boundary between Devon and Cornwall. 3km inland is **Plymouth**, its dome and Smeaton's Tower on the Hoe at the waterfront.

Warships and auxiliaries carry out operational training with unusual manœuvres, especially north of the breakwater, using both entrances, 0730–0830 on weekdays being usual except in August. The main channel is west of the breakwater with warships sometimes opening up full throttle once clear of the breakwater. On the other hand, small boats may be towed out of the way to leave a clear path for nuclear submarines. Other users include car ferries from Roscoff and

Fort Bovisand on the right with Plymouth lost in the summer heat haze over the eastern end of Plymouth breakwater

heavy weather and conditions are worst at half ebb with southwesterly winds. Residents lived rent free on the 1.2ha island in the past but had to provide fish and rabbits for the landlord. The most successful was Sam Wakeham who, with his wife and two children, took out tourists by boat and provided them with porter, tea, eggs, ham, biscuits, cabbage and rabbits. One of the visitors in 1837 was an exciseman who exposed the smuggling and found the caves and hiding places. Sam was not replaced on the island.

The HMS Cambridge Gunnery Range has now been closed despite the radar scanner still in place.

At Heybrook Bay a tidal causeway runs out to the quartzite Renney Rocks, on which a heron might be quietly fishing. The Shag Stone is a little further out, located by a striped mark. This is the start of the Dockyard Port of Plymouth. Andurn

Santander and increasing numbers of cruise liners. There can be a scum left on the water.

It was also the route used in 1588 by Drake to defeat the Spanish Armada, having first finished his game of bowls on the Hoe. Had he failed in his mission, Spanish admiral Don Alonso Perez de Guzman, Duke of Medina Sidona, planned to live at Mount Edgcumbe after his conquest. The 3.5km^2 Mount Edgcumbe Country Park was the earliest landscaped garden in Cornwall, the only grade 1 historic garden in the southwest and one of the most beautiful in England with parkland, formal English, French and Italian gardens, the International Camellia Society's collection, bracken, gorse, woodland set above red cliffs, a deer park, temples, coastal walks and 16km of coastline, Plymouth to Whitsand being registered as Heritage Coast. Central to this was a 1547 Tudor mansion, garrisoned for the King in the Civil War and incendiary bombed during the 1941 blitz on Plymouth. It was restored between 1958 and 1960 and is the home of the Earl of Edgcumbe, which he allowed to be used for filming *Twelfth Night*.

A nature reserve is designated above vertical red strata topped by stunted trees. Penlee Point has breaking waves in heavy weather, worst with southwesterly winds at half ebb. Onshore are a grotto and Queen Adelaide's chapel, a 19th-century folly. Offshore is a naval degaussing range. There are two historic wrecks just west of the point, one

Penlee Point with Queen Adelaide's chapel folly on the skyline

Fort Picklecombe at Picklecombe Point has been converted to flats, along from which is the Maker mark on the shore at the start of an area of Cawsand Bay used by waterskiers. Kingsand and Cawsand are red sandstone fishing villages, exposed to the east but sheltered to the southwest. Between them is a stream which was the national boundary between Saxon England and Celtic Cornwall, later becoming the county boundary between Devon and Cornwall until 1844. There are many pilchard cellars, mostly from the 1580s, doubtless useful for subsequent business, Cawsand having had one of the largest smuggling fleets in the West Country with 50 boats said to have been involved in 1804, bladders of brandy being smuggled into Plymouth beneath women's voluminous skirts.

Cawsand Bay has anchorages and was particularly important for this purpose before the breakwater was built. It was used in 1815 by the ship taking Napoléon to exile in St Helena. The locals foiled a rescue attempt by towing his ship out to sea, action which suggests the guarding of the world's most wanted prisoner was not all it might have been.

onshore and *HMS Coronation* about a kilometre out. Cuttlefish bones may also be found washed up.

Above Lillery's Cove is the 13th-century St Germanus church, lit by candles and with a stone spire. A radio mast stands on top of the 12m cliffs of Rame Head, which has breaking waves in heavy weather, worst with southwesterly winds at half

The lighthouse on the western end of the breakwater. Fort Picklecombe is conspicuous below Mount Edgcumbe Country Park

HMS Campbelltown leaves Plymouth Sound at speed

ebb. This added to the impregnability of the Iron Age fort with bulwarks built across the neck of the head. A later structure is the ruined St Michael's chapel of 1397 on the probable site of a Celtic hermitage which had a blazing beacon by 1486 and a watchman to bring news of raiders or returning fleets. A National Coastwatch lookout performs a

Rame Head with its chapel on top

The Napoleonic Tregantle Fort looks down on Long Sands and Tregantle Cliff in Whitsand Bay

green slates. Butterflies go well out to sea while mackerel, shrimps and mussels are found inshore. There is a wreck off Captain Blake's Point, one of many which have met their ends here. Swimming can also be difficult and there is a cross at Tregonhawke for three family members drowned in 1878. Surf is generally best on the bottom half of the tide with a fast break but at Tregantle Cliffs it works at high water.

Tregantle Rifle Ranges are a danger area with black and white beacons at the ends but firing is supposed to stop for passing boats. Tregantle Fort was built by French prisoners during the Napoleonic Wars, after which Tregantle Barracks were built as a national monument. An unusual aerial takes the form of a huge horizontal ring suspended above the cliffs. Long Sands have their best surf on the bottom half of the tide with a fast break when the ranges are not in use.

comparable function today from a lookout at the end of the Dockyard Port of Plymouth.

Important though it was to mark the head, there was always a toll of shipping lost to the Eddystone Rocks out to sea. The history of the Eddystone light is one of drama. The first was built by Winstanley in 1698 and rebuilt by him the following year. He said he would like to spend a night in it in the worst possible weather. How much of his wish he got will never be known because he was in it on a November night in 1703 when it was struck by the worst night of storm ever recorded in Britain. In the morning the lighthouse and Winstanley had gone. It was followed by the Rudyard Tower of 1706 which caught fire in 1755. The 1759 Smeaton Tower was the first of modern shape, based on the trunk of an oak tree, and the first to use dovetailed stones to lock to adjacent stones to the sides, the ends, above and below. Labourers were issued with Eddystone Medals to protect them against press gangs. The lighthouse survived but the foundation became unsafe and it was dismantled and rebuilt on Plymouth Hoe in 1879 as a monument. It had such respect that it appeared on the reverse of the penny coin with Britannia and is the one structure featured on the coat of arms of the Institution of Civil Engineers, the most famous lighthouse in the world. The Douglas Tower of 1832, for which Douglas was knighted, is a 49m grey granite tower with a 27km range, automated in 1982 and now with a helicopter platform on top.

Off Queener Point is a spoil dumping ground, previously used for explosives. The National Maritime Museum have bought the decommissoned warship *HMS Scylla* which has been sunk off Whitsand Bay as Europe's first artificial reef, also to be a diving centre.

Cliffs vary between 30 and 80m in height behind Whitsand Bay, cliffs of pink, purple and

Portwrinkle stands at the end of Whitsand Bay

A golf course leads to Portwrinkle where the Whitsand Bay Hotel was rebuilt, having been moved brick by brick from **Torpoint** in 1909. The fishing harbour was first built in 1600 but destroyed by a storm in 1882. There is a pier with a stone beacon marking the entrance and the walls of pilchard cellars can be seen. The surf works at low water on big swells with wind from the northwest but it is smaller than in Whitsand Bay.

Beyond the Brawn and the Long Stone, the beach below Battern Cliffs is used by naturists. The land

Working the pots near the Brawn off the Long Stone

is also being stripped away and at Downderry the ends of seafront gardens are showing marked scour. On the B3247, Downderry developed from a fishing village, above which is an aerial and where the warm climate allows the growth of palm trees.

The River Seaton enters at Seaton where there is a café by the beach. The surf, which is smaller than in Whitsand Bay, works from low to mid-tide but there can be a vicious dump in bad weather.

There are further slips at Keveral Beach, above which is the Amazon Woolly Monkey Sanctuary founded in 1964, the world's first protected breeding colony. There is also a bat cave, Victorian herbalists' flower garden and wild flower meadows to encourage such butterflies as the pearl bordered fritillary.

Colmer Rocks and Bodigga Cliff lead to Millendreath, after which there are unusual flying butresses and commoner flying blackheaded gulls plus an aquarium.

Holidaymakers pack the beach at Seaton

Millendreath beach gets rather busy at high water

The mouth of the East Looe River

Flying butresses southwest of Millendreath

Looe, Cornish for pool, is formed by East and West Looe, divided by the East Looe River below its confluence with the West Looe River. Until the 14th century it was one of the busiest ports in the southwest and in the 19th century was used for exporting copper ore from north of Liskeard. The earliest major estuary bridge in Devon and Cornwall connected them in 1411, replaced by a Victorian one of seven arches.

The Cornish Museum with the village's maritime past, smuggling, pilchard industry, lifeboat, old port, Cornish life, culture, arts, crafts and local history is housed in a building of 1500. The Ian Cooper Gallery features local scenes, wildlife, marine subjects and steam trains.

The two halves of the village were combined in 1593 but each continued to have two MPs until 1832. In 1852 it was visited by Wilkie Collins, who

Natural rock diving platforms at East Looe

Looe Island stands off Hannafore Point

described it in *Rambles Beyond Railways*. It is a fishing village with pleasure craft and is the headquarters for shark angling. Flows in the rivermouth are to 9km/h in either direction and a red flag is flown when conditions outside the harbour have become unsuitable or the ebb has started. At the entrance is the unique Banjo Pier with a light on a red 6m metal column. The old church tower used to be whitewashed as a sea mark. Looe Bay has surf with strong southwesterlies.

Rocks covered with lichen and thrift face the Hore Stone

Cliffs to Falmouth are cut in killas slate. After Hannafore Point the last house at Hannafore was a Celtic monk's cell with slit windows.

commemorate a visit by Joseph of Arimathea and the young Jesus on their way to Glastonbury with the Holy Grail. The presence of smugglers and treasure caves, reputedly connected by passages, is more likely, even more so the suggestion that there were many rabbits and rats from ships wrecked on the Ranneys, but locals caught most of them in the 19th century for food. Evelyn Atkins described the venue in *We Bought an Island* and *Tales from Our Island*. Today there is a daffodil farm and pottery and folk craft centre but landing requires the owners' permission.

Black and white striped pairs of beacons establish a measured distance for speed trials but

Looking across Talland Bay to Downend Point

Looe Island, also known at St George's, St Michael's or St Nicholas', is the largest island close to the Cornish coast. Rising to 46m and covering 9ha, it was bombed during the second world war by a pilot who mistook it for a British warship. The remains of a chapel on top are said to

on a bearing significantly different from that likely to be followed by a boat inshore, especially if crossing Portnadler Bay and turning round the Hore Stone and across Æsop's Bed into Talland Bay, which has been used by modern smugglers. In the 18th-century Parson Dodge of Talland was a

notable exorcist, including ridding Lanreath of a spectral coach and headless horses. Such was his reputation that people were afraid of meeting him driving evil spirits down to the sea at night, a benefit being that it left the way clear for his associates bringing spirits the other way. The tall church tower by a prominent caravan site is separate from the church but connected by a passage, the church being noted for its fine bench ends and the graveyard for its beautifully engraved slate headstones.

There is parking behind the rocks at Porthallow and this can be important as cars are barred from Polperro and also Polruan with no road access between, making this an unnecessarily committing section.

A granite cross on Downend Point below Brent is a war memorial, while a light on a 3m white concrete pillar on Spy House Point marks the

tunnels behind the entrance. His spirit stills roams the passages, seeking escape, and his cries mingle with the wind on dark nights. Near the Bridges are the remains of fish drying houses.

The cliff at Nealand Point threatens to fall

entrance to Polperro. The fishing village is sheltered by two piers, one with a light on a 3m post. It has yachts as well as crab and lobster boats but southerly or southeasterly winds or a groundswell make the entrance dangerous so it is closed by a storm gate, indicated by a black ball or a red light. The great storm of 1824 destroyed houses, breakwaters and about 50 boats. Saxons and Romans both built bridges here. Buildings include the 16th-century House on Props over the water, Couch's house of 1595 and the Old Watch House. Smuggling resulted in the setting up of the Preventative Service, forerunners of HM Customs and Excise. Polperro Heritage Museum of Smuggling and Fishing past and present is based in a cottage cellar and there is a Land of Legend and Model Village. Polperro was discovered in 1810 by Joseph Farington of the Royal Academy and has recovered from a subsequent typhoid outbreak to become the most photographed harbour in the country.

Beyond Peak Rock there is a TV mast on Hard Head. Below Chapel Cliff is Willie Wilcock's Hole, named after a fisherman who searched a maze of

In quiet conditions there are routes inside the reefs to the larger Larrick Rock off the overhanging cliff at Nealand Point. Some sheltered rockpools in Colors Cove can become pleasantly warm. A white painted patch on Shag Rock lines up with a white daymark above to give a leading line which, taken with Pencarrow Head and another white mark on the other side of Lantic Bay, find Udder Rock, also protected by a cardinal light pillar.

Lansallos means ancient holy place but the mood has sometimes been less respectful. The 14th-century church has a mediaeval bell broken by drunken villagers in the 19th century and the base of the pulpit is part of a pinnacle felled by lightning in 1923. There is a smugglers' cave and waterskiing in Lantivet Bay.

Beyond 80m high Pencarrow Head, Lantic Bay is surrounded by gorse, bracken and blackberries and has moorings despite being exposed to southwesterly winds and being part of a spoil dumping ground to Blackbottle Rock.

Polruan is older than Fowey and is protected on the south and west by high cliffs, on top of which

Polperro, the most photographed harbour in the country

A Dutch sailing vessel slips out of Polruan. Note the blockhouse, one of a pair which held a chain across the harbour at one time

are a National Coastwatch lookout, St Saviour's church tower ruin and Headland Garden where plants withstand gales in a coastal rock garden above Washing Rocks. There is a castle ruin on Polruan Point and blockhouses had a chain across the River Fowey to protect against invaders. The harbour is on the north side of the village and the boatyard, on the site of Slade's Yard, is a reminder

Wreckage in Coombe Haven, Gribbin Head is to the left

Charlestown with the Danish Kaskelot moored and a Cornish racing gig on the trailer

that the village built many wooden ships, the basis of Daphne Du Maurier's *The Loving Spirit*.

Flows run into the River Fowey from HW Dover +0030 to 2km/h and out from HW Dover –0600 to 3km/h.

In the Middle Ages **Fowey** was one of Britain's foremost ports, in 1346 sending 47 ships and 770 Fowey Gallants for Edward III's Siege of Calais and continuing with 15th-century piracy against Channel shipping. It is one of Britain's finest sailing centres with 1,300 moorings, but is also a china and ball clay exporting port with some surprisingly large vessels using the estuary. It was Troy Town to Sir Arthur Quiller-Couch, Q.

St Catherine's Castle, now a ruin, was built for Henry VIII. Near it on St Catherine's Point is a 6m octagonal white lighthouse marking the entrance

which is easy for boats to miss. In Coombe Haven is a wheel and other wreckage of a boat which got it wrong.

Southground Point shelters Polridmouth but it has a heavy swell with the prevailing wind. It was the setting for Du Maurier's *Rebecca* and may have been where part of *The Wind in the Willows* was composed by Kenneth Graham, a friend of Q. Above the inlet are decoy lakes, intended to draw German bombers away from the Fowey munitions port, and beyond them is Menabilly, home of Daphne Du Maurier and Manderley in *Rebecca*.

The 26m daymark of 1832 on top of Gribbin Head takes the form of a red and white striped square tower. To its south is Sandy Cove and the Cannis rock while to its west is the beach of Platt, exposed to southwesterly winds, the sea breaking heavily on the head in bad weather.

Gribbin Head is the start of St Austell Bay and the Cornish Riviera which continues to Dodman Point. Gorse grows around the Little Gribbin. The inner part is Tywardreath Bay, the name translating as the house on the strand, used in its English form as a title by Du Maurier and based on her house at Kilmarth. Nearby are the remains of a chieftain's hall, possibly King Mark of Cornwall, the uncle of Tristan. The pier at Polkerris was built in the 1730s by the Rashleighs of Menabilly with pilchard salting cellars and the largest seine house in Cornwall for processing fish oil. There is a café in the lifeboat station used from 1859 to 1914 and there is a public house in a boatshed after a previous one was swept away by the sea. There is surfing on big swells but there may be a launch fee. The village has not been developed because of the powerful influence of the Rashleighs.

Par Sands, between Little Hell and Par, are brilliant white from china clay, are backed by dunes and have their best surf at mid-tide.

With its 370m breakwater, Par is the busiest small port in the British Isles with up to two dozen

movements on one tide, not helped by Killyvarder Rock in the middle of the bay. The docks were built in the 1820s by J T Treffry on a silting up arm of the sea to serve his clay mining operation, initially with smelting works, brickworks, pilchard fishery, shipbuilding, sail lofts, granite cutting and dressing, candle making, chandlery, limekilns, blacksmith, carpentry and flourmill, from the 1940s concentrating completely on exporting china clay and importing oil and timber. The tall chimneys of the china clay processing works are prominent. In front of the A3082 the Paddington to Penzance railway makes its only appearance between Teignmouth and Penzance, Par being the nearest station to the Cornish Riviera on a line where the Cornish Riviera Express was the flagship train.

From Spit Point to Fishing Point the coast is fronted by rocks with grating fronted caves in the cliffs, then comes Polgaver beach, the only accredited naturist beach in Cornwall although the designation was withdrawn in 2000, perhaps having outlived its need as many beaches are now used for that purpose. Carlyon Bay is backed by a golf course and has Cornwall's largest leisure centre and entertainment complex, a resort with Cornish Leisure World and the Cornwall Coliseum including a 50m Olympic pool. A new housing development on the beach has resulted in a row with the Environment Agency over wave protection.

It is possible to land on the beach on the west side of the harbour entrance at Charlestown, a Georgian village mostly built between 1791 and 1800. The small harbour was constructed by Smeaton for mine owner Charles Rashleigh. Protected by a 4 gun battery, it had lime burning, brick making, net houses, rope making, bark houses with oak for tanning, pilchard curing, a foundry and clay brought by an underground tramway. It exported copper then china clay and imported coal, timber, iron and limestone, a mix of black and white dusts gathering. It has a tidal basin and an inner wet basin. Despite the difficult entry for coasters, the gates being widened in 1976, it imported fertilizer and general cargo and exported grain and clay, used in porcelain, rubber, plastics, paint, ink, dyes and toothpaste. It has the Shipwreck Rescue Heritage Centre museum with the largest exhibition in the UK of diver recovered artefacts plus naval guns and anchors outside. It features village life, shipwrecks, diving from 1740, ocean liners, remote controlled boats, lifeboat equipment, the *Titanic*, Roland Morris' Collection of Nelson artefacts, the Natural Gas Museum collection and Cornish mining.

It is for its sailing ships that Charlestown is best known, though, and it is not unusual to see historical sailing ships and replicas moored out in Polmear Cove. The Danish 3-master *Kaskelot* has been based here for over a decade and the port has been used for filming *Poldark*, *The Onedin Line*, *Voyage of the Beagle*, *The Eagle has Landed*, *The*

Three Musketeers, *Moll Flanders*, *Frenchman's Creek*, *Mansfield Park*, *Rebecca*, *Wives and Daughters*, *A Respectable Trade*, *Pandemonium* and *The Day of the Triffids*. It seems that any self-respecting film including old sailing ships also features Charlestown. Parking is back behind the port after a steep climb up the road.

Distance
From Wembury to Charlestown is 54km
Campsites
Newton Ferrers, Tregonhawke, Downderry, No Man's Land, Great Tree, Portlooe, Talland, Crumplehorn, Polruan, Polkerris, Par, Biscovery, Carlyon Bay
Youth Hostels
Salcombe, Golant
OS 1:50,000 Sheets
200 Newquay and Bodmin
201 Plymouth and Launceston
Imray Charts
2400 West Country
C6 Salcombe to Lizard Point (1:100,000)
C14 Plymouth Harbour and Rivers (1:20,000)
Stanfords Allweather Charts
22 South Devon Coast
23 West Country
L13 Plymouth Harbour (1:22,700)
Admiralty Charts
SC 30 Plymouth Sound and Approaches (1:12,500)
SC 31 Harbours on the South Coast of Cornwall. Fowey Harbour (1:6,250). Par Harbour (1:7,500). Charlestown Harbour, (1:5,000).
SC 147 Plans on the South Coast of Cornwall. Looe (1:5,000)
SC 148 Dodman Point to Looe Bay (1:30,000)
SC 871 Rivers Tamar, Lynher and Tavy (1:12,500)
SC 1267 Falmouth to Plymouth (1:75,000)
SC 1613 Eddystone Rocks to Berry Head (1:75,000)
1900 Whitsand Bay to Yealm Head Including Plymouth Sound (1:25,000)
SC 5602 West Country, Falmouth to Teignmouth
Tidal Constants
River Yealm Entrance: HW Dover –0530, LW Dover –0540
Bovisand: HW Dover –0550, LW Dover –0540
Whitsand Bay: Dover –0540
Looe: HW Dover –0550, LW Dover –0540
Polperro: HW Dover –0550, LW Dover –0540
Fowey: Dover –0550
Par: Dover –0550
Charlestown: HW Dover –0550, LW Dover –0540
Range
Tregantle
Submarine Areas
D009, Whitsand Bay
Sea Area
Plymouth
Rescue
Inshore lifeboats: Salcombe, Looe, Fowey
All weather lifeboats: Plymouth, Fowey
Maritime Rescue Centre
Brixham, 01803 882704

The busy industrial harbour area at Par

62 SOUTH CENTRAL CORNWALL

South to the end of Britain

Hail Mevagissey! With such wonders fraught!
Where boats and men, and stinks, and trade are stirring;
Where pilchards come in myriads to be caught!
Pilchards! A thousand times as good as herring.

Peter Pindar

Sailing ship anchored off Duporth

Semiprecious stones such as agates, citrine, carnelian, chalcedony, amethyst, serpentine and rock crystal are found along this coast.

Outside Charlestown, Duporth with its holiday village reaches to Carrickowel Point, site of the 18th-century Crinnis Cliff Battery. On the hillside above the bay are Porthpean House Gardens, noted for their camellias, primroses and violets.

Black Head seen from Porthtowan

Lower Porthpean, with its sailing club based in old fish cellars, was a pilchard fishing centre, but is now more a place of prawns in rockpools. The best surf is with southeasterly winds but there is a registration charge. Between Phoebe's Point and Gwendra Point is Silvermine Beach, suggesting previous industry, while Ropehaven implies another trade.

Black Head is bold and steep, topped by a fort site and a block of granite in memory of poet A L Rowse. A stream enters the sea as a waterfall.

Laid back sailing off Pentewan beach with Chapel Point beyond

Beyond Gamas Point in Mevagissey Bay is Pentewan. At one time the port used to ship the best church building stone in Cornwall from Polrudden quarry and tin from the Pentewan valley where the works went to 15m below sea level. A new harbour was built in the 1820s but had to be abandoned after it silted up with china clay. The beach is popular with motor boats these days and, for surfing, best with the wind from the north or northwest and a huge swell, hollow at high water although there may be a charge in the summer or a locked gate to be negotiated in the winter.

Mevagissey, at the end of the B3273, takes its name from its two saints, Meva and Issey. St Peter's church is on a Saxon site, mostly 13th century with a Norman font and a 16th-century north aisle of Pentewan stone. The first stone pier was built in 1430 and the village developed on pilchards, curing them in the 18th and 19th centuries for Italy and then for the Royal Navy as Mevagissey Duck. In the 19th century there were experiments in smoking pilchards and large scale curing in brine, the village being the first to can in oil. Although the village pump outside the Ship Inn was used as the village water supply because there was no mains water until 1944, it was the first place to have electric lights, powered by pilchard oil generators, and the South Pierhead light on its 8m white metal tower was the first in the country to be lit by electricity. It

was a smuggling village, contraband mostly collected from Roscoff by cutter, and also had its wrecks. No 1, the Hoss is an 18th-century cottage built from the recovered timbers from *The Horse*. Now it is a busy tourist resort with slate and cob whitewashed houses, shops and restaurants being established in old fish cellars. A folk museum in a

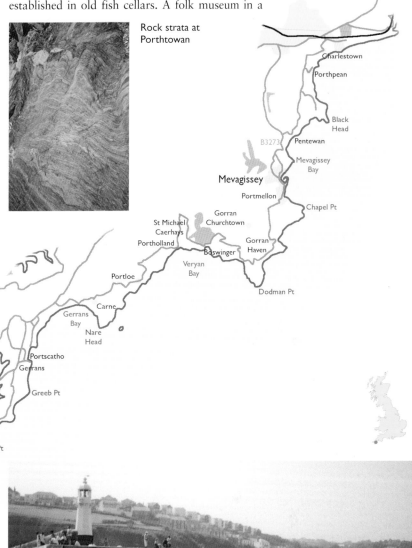

Rock strata at Porthtowan

Mevagissey harbour and the first electric harbour light in the country

1745 boatbuilder's workshop with three ship masts as supports and ship timbers for the walls covers seafaring, boatbuilders' tools and machinery, local crafts, agriculture, mining, fishing and a Cornish kitchen with a 6 tonne granite cider press. There is an aquarium and an extensive World of Model Railways. The inner and outer harbours have shell fishing and pleasure craft but there are harbour fees.

The sandy cove at Portmellon has a slip from the boatyard. Buildings have 900mm thick walls and boards to slot into gateways to keep out the sea.

Protected from the north by Chapel Point, Colona Beach has its best surf from mid to low water with an onshore wind. It is not too accessible by land. Near Turbot Point is Bodrugan's Leap where Sir Henry Treworth of Bodrugan, a supporter of Richard III at Bosworth, rode his horse over a cliff in 1485, pursued by Sir Richard Edgcumbe, to reach a boat to escape to Ireland.

Compass jellyfish are in the sea around the Gwineas or Gwinges. Onshore, an earthwork and a tumulus are above the start of Great Perhaver Beach, which reaches to Gorran Haven, a 13th-century village with a 15th-century 34m church tower used as a shipping mark. After the Reformation the chapel was split into two floors, the Wesleyans upstairs and a fishing tackle store below, only being restored to full church use in the 1860s. The pier is below high sloping cliffs and there were limekilns as well as cellars used by fishermen. Gorran boats were some of the best in the country and their willow crab pots also sold widely.

Vault Beach leads to Dodman Point

Dodman Point seen from below Boswinger

After Pen-a-maen or Maenease Point, divers use the waters off Bow or Vault Beach while naturists use its southern end. Dodman Point has a steep east face and a sloping west one covered in gorse and bracken. An earth bank cuts across the headland and there was an Iron Age fort. A local clergyman installed a large granite cross in 1896 in anticipation of the second coming. There have been many unexplained tragedies in the area, including the loss of the *Darlwin* with 31 people in 1966. Whether these can be attributed to the race

off the head or to the naval training gunfire further off is unknown.

Cliffs around Veryan Bay range between 6 and 60m in height. Porthluney Cove has its best surf on the bottom half of the tide with a southerly wind. Above is Caerhays Castle on the site of a mediaeval manor house which the Trevanion family had owned from the 14th century, although the 1808 conversion by John Nash was to ruin them. It is noted for its 24ha of gardens started by plant hunters to China a century ago, now with oaks, rhododendrons, huge Asian magnolias and the national camellia collection.

A wreck sits at East Portholland while West Portholland has a limekiln on the shore and surf which is best over the bottom half of the tide with the wind from the east to southeast.

The sheltered harbour at Porthloe

An easterly wind also brings the best surf at Portloe, another village with a limekiln, but there is a launching charge and a private slipway. The lifeboat was never used in 17 years as the entrance was always too bad in rough conditions, the lifeboat station eventually being converted to a church and a school. The fishing village with its pilchard cellars and crab pots was used for filming

The Camomile Lawn. The 17th-century Ship Inn is claimed to make the best crab sandwiches in Cornwall.

Gull Rock is a nesting place of cormorants, shags, guillemots and razorbills. It has claimed

Gull Rock stands beyond the Blouth

Clear water and pierced rock at Nare Head

Nare Head seen across Gerrans Bay from Treloan Farm

many sailing ships, including the *Hera* with 19 lives in 1914. It is accompanied by the Middle Stone and the Outer Stone, the Whelps. There are strong currents between these offshore rocks and 79m Nare Head at the start of Gerrans Bay. There is another wreck near Shannick Point where there are also egrets. The Carne Beacon tumulus may be the grave of the 5th-century King Geraint or Gerennius of Cornwall who was reputed to have been rowed across Gerrans Bay in a golden boat with silver oars, buried with him although excavations have not found it. Pendower Beach, backed by bracken and gorse and also with a 19th-century limekiln, has best surf with wind from the east after a persistent onshore wind.

Dingerein Castle site on the A3078 could be associated with the Iron Age King Geraint of the Britons in the 8th century, recorded in the Anglo-Saxon Chronicle, or Sir Geraint of the Round Table, the father of Jestyn or St Just. Porthbean Beach has surf with an easterly wind while Porthcurnick Beach, under the gaze of the National Coastwatch station on Pednvadan and the Rosevine Hotel in its own subtropical gardens, has its best surf on the bottom half of the tide with the wind between east and southeast.

Portscatho means harbour of large boats but the notable large one was the 900 tonne *Carl Hirschberg* which arrived in the Great Blizzard of 1891, which also wrecked houses and quays. After a month the Board of Trade allowed the rocks holding it to be dynamited if a breakwater was built to replace them. There are also smaller boats. In less extreme conditions easterly winds bring the best surf. As well as the jetty this fishing village has a steep slip and 6–12m cliffs, above which rises the spire of Gerrans church. Some of *The Camomile Lawn* was also filmed here.

Roseland takes its name from rosinis, moorland isle. A signpost by the shore points to Treloan Coastal Farm, a site with caravans, camping and the first camping barn in Cornwall. Victor Barry took on the tenancy of the 28ha farm in 1988 and hopes to work it with 1930s/40s methods using heavy horses, acquiring and restoring horse-powered machinery and running NVQ courses with the Cornish Heavy Horse Society.

Off Greeb Point there are overfalls over the Bizzies. Birdlife includes oystercatchers, curlews, herons, fulmars, kittiwakes and blackbacked and herring gulls but red admirals and other butterflies might also be seen flying over the sea. Porthmellin Head divides Towan Beach from Porthbeor Beach which is used by divers. St Anthony faces onto the river side of the peninsula. It has palms and a 13th-century church lit by a brass candelabra, with a modern door and a mediaeval latchet door for dogs, also allowing hens to use the belfry as a roost.

There are seals to Zone Point, off which there can be a race. After centuries of a coal burning light on St Anthony's Head the current 19m white octagonal tower lighthouse was built in 1834, an old world air of elegance not seen on every lighthouse and making it the choice for filming *Fraggle Rock*. A moated fort was built close by in 1895, to which a second world war battery with 150mm guns was added.

The two major fortifications at the mouth of Falmouth Harbour were for Henry VIII. **St Mawes** Castle is Tudor rose in plan, completed in 1543, the best preserved of his castles, unique in having

Shipwreck at Maenporth

Brightly coloured rock at Newporth Head

no internal changes. It fell quickly to the Parliamentarians in 1646 because they attacked from landward while all the guns face seawards. Now with subtropical gardens, it was used for filming *Poldark*. Opposite it is Pendennis Castle of 1545, Cornwall's greatest fortress and one of Henry's finest, built on an Iron Age fort site, the end of his chain of castles to defend against the French, the penultimate garrison to be taken by Cromwell in 1646 after holding out for 5 months. It includes Elizabethan ramparts, a first world war guardhouse with cells and a second world war gun battery which was used. A gun is fired at noon during July and August.

Between the two is Black Rock, on which is a mark. Mr Trefusis of Trefusis rowed his wife out for a picnic then left her to drown but fishermen rescued her. Flows into the harbour run to 3km/h while there is 4km/h outwards with freshets.

A ria, Falmouth Harbour is the world's third largest natural harbour after Sydney and Río. It is the most westerly safe anchorage in the Channel and the first safe port after an Atlantic crossing. The Romans traded from here for tin but its heyday was with the sailing ships, the tea clippers and the windjammers. The Falmouth Packets began regular Post Office services to Spain, Portugal, America, the West Indies, the Mediterranean and Brazil. In 1810 it was the last place in Britain where the Riot Act was read to mutinous crews. It was a second world war convoy assembly point and has become a refuelling and repair port for passenger ships, cargo vessels and tankers. There are also numerous small pleasure craft.

As well as the castle, Pendennis Point has a Maritime Rescue Co-ordination Centre mast and a blockhouse. From here a wooded ridge runs northwest along the northern edge of Falmouth Bay. The angular roof at the other end of the ridge is the main hall of the National Maritime Museum Cornwall, opened in 2002 with 120 small boats, an underwater window which allows the full depth of the murky water to be viewed, the only one in Europe and one of only three such windows in the world, and a 29m tower with extensive views up Carrick Roads and over the rest of the harbour. It was the point from which Sean Morley set off in 2004 to be the first person to circumnavigate all the inhabited islands in Great Britain and Ireland solo by sea kayak and the point to which Ellen MacArthur returned after her record breaking round the world sailing voyage.

Falmouth, at the end of the A39, was formed by the villages of Smithike and Penny-Come-Quick, renamed by Charles II. It has many 18/19th-century buildings and became a fashionable resort after the railway arrived. Its improvement of hundreds of houses by installing double glazing, central heating and other conservation measures won it the first Deputy Prime Minister's Award for Sustainable Communities.

The town has a shark angling centre. There were many sightings in the 1970s, some more recent, of Morgawr, a sea monster like a giant seal with a long neck. This Nessie lookalike has been reported from Pendennis Point, Rosemullion Head and Parson's Beach but has probably been frightened away now by the snarling of jet skis.

Gyllyngvase Beach prides itself on its Queen Mary Gardens while, beyond Swanpool Point, the popular Swanpool Beach has a Swan Pool with both swans and ducks, the best surf being at mid-

tide with easterly winds. A golf course tops the cliffs to Pennance Point, where there is a monument, the cliffs running about 15m high to Rosemullion Head.

There is a wreck between Newporth Head and Maenporth, the most popular surf beach in the area with its best surf at mid-tide on an easterly wind. There are caves in High Cliff.

Looking up the estuary of the Helford River

Beyond Bream Cove, Rosemullion Head is the end of Falmouth Harbour control and also the end of the Helford River's drowned valley. The tower of the 13th-century church at Mawnan served as a navigation landmark and a lookout point for invaders.

Crossing the river, as swallows do, leads to the Lizard peninsula, the name a corruption of the Cornish for rocky height. Plateau heathland, its grows Cornish heath.

St Anthony-in-Meneage has a 12th-century church founded by Normans for being spared after being shipwrecked, built from Normandy stone. To its east is Dennis Head from dynas, a fort, there being an Iron Age fortress which was strengthened by the Royalists in the Civil War and was one of the last three places in Cornwall to fall to the Roundheads. Behind it, Gillan Harbour is a yachting centre.

Nare Point is low but cliffs mostly run to 60m to Lizard Point. Relics from the 4-masted *Bay of Panama*, driven onto the point in 1891, are to be found in the Five Pilchards in the former fishing village of Porthallow, with a beach which is still difficult in an easterly wind.

Porthallow on the Lizard peninsula

After Porthkerris Point the Porthallow Search and Rescue Diving School have a wind-sock and an austere building heavily defended by security fencing. Beyond it is a vineyard.

Porthallow Search and Rescue Diving School at
Porthkerris Point

Porthoustock was the chief fishing village on the
Lizard with pilchard cellars, one net taking over
4,000,000 fish. Another noteworthy landing was
9m³ of contraband brandy in one session. A beach
of spoil from the roadstone quarry means that it
does not appear as attractive as it sounds.

from the *Despatch* and the 18 gun brig *Primrose*
bringing home troops from the Peninsular War in
Spain. In 1855 196 were lost from the emigrant
ship *John* bound from Plymouth to Canada and in
1898 106 were lost from the liner *Mohegan*, the
dead being stripped of their belongings. 400 victims
are buried in St Keverne where the octagonal
church spire has acted as a marker for sailors for
300 years, the spire being rebuilt after a lightning
strike in 1770.

Gantry loads of stone from Dean Quarries are
taken to Dean Point beyond Godrevy Cove for

The Manacles, graveyard of ships and sailors

A lookout is located by the Giant's Quoits
megaliths on Manacle Point. From Cape Wrath to
the Lizard some of our most imaginative names
come from anglicization of names in other
languages. Such is the case with the Manacles, the
Cornish men eglos meaning stone church.
Nevertheless, their fearful reputation has been well
acquired, having claimed hundreds of ships and
thousands of lives as the strong tidal currents sweep
between Maen Chynoweth, the Shark's Fin, the
Gwinges, the Manacles, Carn-du Rocks, Maen
Land and the cliffs. In 1809 200 were lost in hours

loading into bulk carriers. Shipping close inshore is
warned by VHF radio about blasting. Perhaps they
also warn Roskilly's Open Farm behind their
quarry.

Lowland Point has confused water with strong
tidal streams. Small surf is to be found at North
Corner with southeasterly winds. The green and

Cadgwith provides
shelter for small
craft

Jagged rocks
threaten
Carrick Lûz

Coverack is popular with windsurfers

purple cliffs at Coverack at the end of the B3294 are set off by the whitewashed cottages in this fishing and former smuggling village. One smuggler's wife used to peg a bright red shirt on the line when it was safe for her husband to come ashore with contraband. There is a shop in a former pilchard barrel salt store and there is the Paris Hotel, named after the *Paris* which grounded on Lowland Point in 1899, 756 people being saved

Lizard Point and its light seen across Housel Bay

The Lizard lifeboat is now housed in Kilcobben Cove

The rocks of Vellan Drang at Lizard Point

and the ship being refloated six weeks later, again to be refloated at Rame Head after grounding there in 1914. There is a disused slip into a sea with bass and pollock. Dolor Point has a small pier with a restaurant and bakery in a former lifeboat station. In Perprean Cove the smell around the Oxen might be more that of a piggery. Chynhalls Point has an Iron Age fort site on top and a tide race playspot at the end while Black Head has a white coastguard lookout on top. There is another fort site overlooking the angular rocks of Carrick Lûz before Spernic Cove and the gorse and heather

covered Eastern Cliff, Poldowrian Garden having a large pond, woodland, a prehistoric museum and a hut circle not far away.

Kennack Sands are a low point in the cliffs but a popular beach with interesting cliffs for all that, a nature reserve and many flowers. The best surf is with northwesterly or northerly winds against big swells. Divers like the clear waters at other times. Beacons mark the landing point of the main submarine cables from Spain and Portugal but the main communications centre is 5km north, the Goonhilly Earth Station, the world's largest satellite station with 16 dishes aimed at every continent.

A stream flowing into Carleon Cove at Poltesco used to power a wheel for the 19th-century Lizard Serpentine Company which had a hundred workers making everything from ornaments to shop fronts for London and Paris.

A cove beyond Kildown Point has England's only wood of dwarf elms. Cadgwith is windswept and the tall serpentine and whitewashed cottages have their thatched roofs held down with chains. Gig racing is based at an old lighthouse. The boats drawn up on the Stick, the beach, catch crabs, lobsters, mackerel and some red and grey mullet. There are pilchard cellars and a huer's house on the cliff, the best day's catch being 1,300,000 fish, but the last pilchards were in 1910.

Fisherman Buller and postman Hartley led singing sessions in the Cadgwith Cove Inn and later on the beach, on one notable occasion being joined by an Italian lady opera singer on holiday in the village.

Just south of the village is the Devil's Frying Pan, a 60m hole in the cliff caused by the collapse of a large cave. Smaller caves survive near Polbarrow. Gorse backs Whale Rock and then there is a quarry. The Balk Beacon is a red and white mast at Church Cove, one of the leading line beacons to locate Vrogue Rock. Crab and lobster boats are drawn up by pilchard cellars. St Wynwallow church has a chequered tower of granite and serpentine blocks, a Norman doorway, a castellated porch, wood from the wreck of a Portuguese treasure ship and a memorial to 11 crew of the *MV Polperro* sunk in Mount's Bay by an E-boat in 1944. It was from the red serpentine pulpit in 1678 that the last sermon in Cornish was preached. The late 19th-century lifeboat house is unused, as it almost was then, the boat having only been launched once in 14 years. The Lizard lifeboat is now launched from Kilcobben Cove, served by a lift. At Bass Point there are more Vrogue Rock transit beacons, it generally being a difficult area as the ebb runs to 6km/h over shallow ground. Overlooking it is Lloyds Signal Station, a National Coastwatch lookout.

It was from Pen Olver that the Spanish Armada was first sighted in 1588 and from where Guglielmo Marconi made radio contact with the Isle of Wight, 110km away, in 1901. His Lizard Wireless Station has been restored.

At the front of Housel Bay the Lion's Den hole collapsed in 1842. There has been a lighthouse above Bumble Rock since 1619, built by Sir John Killigrew although there was no local help as it would stop the wrecks, of which there have been over 200 here. It was replaced in 1751 with a lighthouse with two coal fires in transit. The current light is on the eastern tower. Designed in 1874 by J N Douglass, it is one of Britain's brightest with a range of 31km at a turning point on one of the world's busiest shipping lanes, usually the first

object seen by inbound transatlantic shipping. It was one of the first to be electrified in 1878 and has the only large engine room surviving from that period.

Above Polbrean Cove a youth hostel was originally built in the 1860s as a villa for artist Thomas Hart.

In calm conditions there is a passage inside the rocks of Vellan Drang, off which there is a race in an area exposed to wind, strong tides and obstacles. A swell makes the trip exciting. Nearby is a meadow with over 200 bodies buried from the 1720 wreck of the *Royal Anne*.

Distance
From Charlestown to Lizard Point is 63km
Campsites
Carlyon Bay, London Apprentice, Pentewan, Gorran Churchtown, Boswinger, Tippetts Shop, Trewince, Falmouth, Pennance, Porthallow, Coverack, Kuggar, Lizard
Youth Hostels
Golant, Boswinger, Coverack, Lizard
OS 1:50,000 Sheets
203 Land's End and Isles of Scilly
204 Truro and Falmouth
Imray Charts
2400 West Country
C6 Salcombe to Lizard Point (1:100,000)
C7 Falmouth to Isles of Scilly and Newquay (1:100,000)
Y58 River Fal Falmouth to Truro ((1:20,000)
Stanfords Allweather Charts
23 West Country
L16 Falmouth Harbour (1:18,000)
Admiralty Charts
SC 31 Harbours on the South Coast of Cornwall. Charlestown Harbour, (1:5,000).
SC 32 Falmouth Harbour (1:12,500)
SC 147 Plans on the South Coast of Cornwall. Helford River (1:12,500). Porthallow and the Manacles (1:15,000). Porthoustock (1:15,000). Coverack (1:15,000)
SC 148 Dodman Point to Looe Bay (1:30,000)
SC 154 Approaches to Falmouth (1:30,000). Nare Head to Dodman Point (1:35,000)
SC 777 Land's End to Falmouth (1:75,000)
SC 1267 Falmouth to Plymouth (1:75,000)
SC 2345 Plans in South – West Cornwall. Lizard Point (1:15,000)
SC 5602 West Country, Falmouth to Teignmouth
SC 5603 Falmouth to Padstow, including the Isles of Scilly
Tidal Constants
Charlestown: HW Dover –0550, LW Dover –0540
Pentewan: HW Dover –0550, LW Dover –0540
Mevagissey: HW Dover –0600, LW Dover –0550
St Mawes: HW Dover –0610, LW Dover –0550
Falmouth: HW Dover –0600
Helford River Entrance: HW Dover –0610, LW Dover –0550
Coverack: HW Dover +0610 mins, LW D –0600
Lizard Point: Dover –0610
Submarine Area
Mounts Bay
Sea Area
Plymouth
Rescue
Inshore lifeboats: Fowey, Falmouth
All weather lifeboats: Fowey, Falmouth, Lizard
Maritime Rescue Centres
Brixham, 01803 882704
Falmouth, 01326 310811

INDEX